SEXUALITY, GENDER, AND THE LAW

ABRIDGED EDITION

by

WILLIAM N. ESKRIDGE, JR.
John A. Garver Professor of Jurisprudence
Yale Law School

NAN D. HUNTER
Professor of Law
Brooklyn Law School

FOUNDATION PRESS

2006

© 2006 By FOUNDATION PRESS
     395 Hudson Street
     New York, NY 10014
     Phone Toll Free 1–877–888–1330
     Fax (212) 367–6799
     foundation-press.com
Printed in the United States of America

ISBN–13: 978– 1–58778-804–8
ISBN–10: 1–58778-804–7

TEXT IS PRINTED ON 10% POST CONSUMER RECYCLED PAPER

To Morgan Young, Daniel Eaton, and Abigail Thornhill
                    — from WNEJr

To Lisa Duggan
                    — from NDH

To the litigators and scholars who created this field
                    — from both of us.

*

INTRODUCTION

A major part of the excitement of writing—and, we hope, using—this book lies in the emerging nature of the field. Sexuality, gender, and the law is an area which has seen an explosion of scholarly writing and academic offerings in the last two decades. This book is one of our contributions, and has multiple goals. We seek to map out this developing field and to introduce students to it in a way that conveys the richness of the issues it encompasses, while also providing conceptual handles for understanding and organizing disparate areas of law and scholarship. We hope that this book will help shape the field itself. Most importantly, we want to make a claim for the centrality of the field.

As an area of study, sexuality, gender, and the law is often thought to be marginal to "core" law. We believe that such a view is wrong today and will become only more wrong in the future. No one disputes that the field has grown to be vast: courts adjudicate hundreds of new cases each year, and legislatures routinely address these issues in the areas of civil rights law, family law, and criminal law. But the field is more than big; it is central. We offer three examples.

First, sexuality-related issues now repeatedly provide the critical defining line for the public-private boundary in law. This is true in privacy doctrine under the due process clause, in distinguishing between protected and unprotected speech under the First Amendment, in questions of whether state action constitutes a subsidy or penalty, and in adjudications of whether certain "private" information can be classified as newsworthy. The co-incidence is not simply coincidental. The state has taken on the function not only of regulating sexuality, but of contributing to its very production, through a multitude of discursive interventions. In turn, these interventions help shape the contours of what Americans believe to be the appropriate role of the state. A mutually constitutive dynamic operates between sexuality and the state, just as one operates between the market and the state. With the Supreme Court's breakthrough decision in *Lawrence v. Texas*, the nuances of this dynamic will become even more complex.

Second, sexuality and gender issues are confounding and shaping equality law. The Supreme Court's 1996 decision in *Romer v. Evans* marked a turning point in how courts analyze classifications based on sexual orientation; the new skepticism toward such classifications can only be heightened by the decision in *Lawrence*. These cases have also provided the opportunity for the Court to suggest how it may apply a newly flexible rational basis test as to other classifications that may be infected with animus, even if they are not formally designated as suspect under traditional equal protection doctrine. Moreover, in the statutory realm, federal courts are struggling with cases, such as those involving same-sex sexual harassment, which raise the core question of what "because of sex" really means. Debates over the extent of the connection between sexuality and gender bubble underneath some of the thorniest equality questions in current law.

Third, issues of sexual speech now permeate First Amendment analysis. Once, political speech and sexual speech were mutually exclusive categories. They are now thoroughly blurred. Speech about the topic of sexuality is now recognized as core political speech, although unevenly so. First Amendment doctrine is also uncertain about sexually explicit speech. The traditional category of obscenity remains in the law, but mostly as a vestige: speech barred from First Amendment protection as obscene appears in practice to constitute almost a nil category. At the same time, however, speech subject to enhanced regulation and effective submersion as "indecent" threatens to include an enormous proportion of contemporary expression that is rebellious, impolite, and provocative—in short, political. New forms of technology such as the Internet give new urgency to the question of which rules will prevail.

Indeed, one way to teach a sexuality and gender course would be to teach an advanced constitutional law course using this field as a focus, so critical have these issues become to the cutting edge of public law. This body of law also makes a natural focus for a feminist theory course. Most teachers will opt for either a broad survey of sexuality, gender, and law or for a course that highlights either sexual orientation or gender. The book is designed so that it can be used in any of those frameworks.

Throughout the book, we draw on non-legal materials, carefully linking them to the law. In addition to notes following the major cases, we include several extended problems in each chapter, which can serve as the focus for class discussions or assignments. These are intended to probe current questions that are particularly difficult and to inspire debate among students. Our six appendices include statutory provisions, a category of legal materials often overlooked or slighted in legal education, and we encourage readers to avail themselves of close analysis of those texts.

Although one can slice the field (or this text) in numerous ways, we view sexuality and gender in intellectual terms as so inextricably linked as to cast doubt on the ability to separate them completely and still attain a thorough understanding of either. As a taxonomic matter, we use "sex" to mean anatomic categories of males and females, "gender" to mean social characteristics associated with (and constituting) maleness and femaleness, and "sexuality" to mean social understandings of erotic desire. Of these three, we focus least on the first. One theme of the book is that debates over gender now lie at the heart of the most serious disputes over sex discrimination doctrine. Thus we concentrate on those aspects of discrimination "because of sex" that most clearly illustrate its linkages to gender—for example, the attempt by Virginia to preserve VMI's training of young men in the ways of masculinity and the lively debates over employment policies related to sexual harassment and pregnancy.

The scope of the book is sexuality in its broadest sense. One enterprise in these pages is the deconstruction and analysis of sexual identity, and we do not limit that to gay, lesbian, bisexual, and transgender identities. We explore how the law constructs homosexuality and heterosexuality in diacritical relationship to each other. We explicate at some length the law's impact on stigmatized sexualities, but we also examine aspects of sexuality—such as pregnancy and rape—that help constitute social and legal understandings of heterosexuality. We use this approach to achieve two goals: to render visible the lives of LGBT people, who are often overlooked or unmentioned, and at the same time to analyze the social meanings of heterosexuality, which is often unquestioned.

WILLIAM N. ESKRIDGE, JR.
WASHINGTON, D.C.

NAN D. HUNTER
NEW YORK, NEW YORK

*

ACKNOWLEDGMENTS

We gratefully acknowledge the help of many colleagues, students and other supporters in producing this and earlier editions of this book. We want first to acknowledge the founders of the field. The practitioners who advocated on behalf of lesbians and gay men before it became respectable carved out protections from disparate strands of law, often before hostile courts. Their work made possible the body of law and theory which forms this book. Building on this effort (and often participating as well), a handful of scholars created the early sexuality and the law courses. We especially thank Rhonda Rivera of Ohio State, Don Knutson of the University of Southern California, Harlon Dalton of Yale, Arthur Leonard of New York Law School, and the late Thomas Stoddard of NYU for their work as pioneers.

Many colleagues and friends have contributed suggestions or comments about earlier versions of these materials or the ideas therein. We are particularly grateful to Mary Becker, Matt Coles, Jane Dolkart, Paula Ettelbrick, Lisa Duggan, Chai Feldblum, James Garland, Jeanne Goldberg, Suzanne Goldberg, Ruth Harlow, Marcia Kuntz, Art Leonard, Shannon Minter, Steve Pershing, Marc Poirier, Nancy Polikoff, Robert Raben, Bill Rubenstein, Jane Schacter, Tim Westmoreland, Wendy Webster Williams, and Michele Zavos.

Numerous students have contributed to these materials, and in a variety of ways. Students in our sexuality, gender, and the law classes at Brooklyn, Georgetown, Harvard, and Yale stimulated our thinking about these issues generally and provided critical as well as supportive feedback for earlier versions of this book. We are especially grateful for the research assistance provided by Kristen Bebelaar (Brooklyn, Class of 1996); Dan Bird (Yale, Class of 2005); Ranmali Bopitiya (Yale, Class of 2006); Anthony Brown (Brooklyn, Class of 2003); Glenn Edwards (Yale, Class of 1997); Eden Fitzgibbons (Brooklyn, Class of 1997); Christopher Fowler (Brooklyn, Class of 2001); Robin Fukuyama (Brooklyn, Class of 2005); Jamal Greene (Yale, Class of 2005); Bonny Harbinger (Georgetown, Class of 1997); Mitsuka Herrera (Georgetown, Class of 1998); Ronnie Ann Himmel (Brooklyn, Class of 1994); Emily Kern (Brooklyn, Class of 2005); Travis Le Blanc (Yale, Class of 2003); Barnett McGowan (Georgetown, Class of 1997); Sharon McGowan (Harvard, Class of 2000); Monica Marquez (Yale, Class of 1997); Margaret McWilliams (Harvard, Class of 1999); Jennifer Nash (Georgetown, Class of 1997); Mara Rosenthal (Georgetown, Class of 1998);

Michael Shumsky (Yale, Class of 2003); Darsana Srinivasan (Yale, Class of 2006); Kristina Wertz (Brooklyn, Class of 2004); Rebecca Elizabeth Wexler (Harvard College, Class of 2004); Elisa Wiygul (Yale, Class of 2007); and Jordan Young (Georgetown, Class of 1998).

We are grateful to our deans—Judy Areen of Georgetown University Law Center, Anthony Kronman and Harold Koh of Yale Law School, and Joan Wexler of Brooklyn Law School—for making available funds that materially supported this project. Professor Eskridge is also grateful to the Simon Guggenheim Foundation for its grant which enabled him to do archival research that contributed to the project. Special thanks to Gene Coakley and the Yale Law School Library staff and to Mabel Shaw and Karen Summerhill of the Georgetown University Law Center Library. And we greatly appreciate the staff support provided by Golda Lawrence of Brooklyn Law School and Mary Ann DeRosa and Karen Neal of the Georgetown University Law Center.

WNE, Jr.
NDH

SUMMARY OF CONTENTS

*

TABLE OF CONTENTS

*

TABLE OF CASES

Principal cases are in bold type. Non-principal cases are in roman type. References are to Pages.

*

SEXUALITY, GENDER, AND THE LAW

*

CHAPTER 1

LAW AND THE LEGAL SYSTEM

Students will come to this book with many different levels of knowledge about the legal system. The purpose of this chapter is to explain certain basic concepts and to clear up questions that might make it difficult to understand the meaning of what you will read in the remainder of the text. The first section of this chapter will provide an overview of the U. S. legal system. The second section will focus on the aspects of constitutional law most relevant to this book: the Due Process Clauses of the Fifth and Fourteenth Amendments; the Equal Protection Clause of the Fourteenth Amendment; and the protection of expression guaranteed by the First Amendment. The last section will briefly map the sources of law most relevant to the final three chapters of the book, each of which addresses a specific realm of life: the military, the workplace, and the family.

SOURCES OF "RIGHTS" ARGUMENTS

The primary sources of law for our purposes are constitutions (both the U.S. Constitution and the constitutions of each state) and statutes (federal and state). In addition, "case law" develops as courts interpret and elaborate the constitution and statutes in judicial decisions.

The U.S. Constitution, of course, is our fundamental charter of government. The most important provisions for this book lie in certain amendments that address the rights of individuals as against the government. The Constitution limits the ways in which the government can encroach upon individual liberty, but it usually does not apply unless there is "state action." This means that the Constitution protects an individual only against the government, not against the actions of private sector organizations or corporations, no matter how large they are, unless they literally take on the functions of government (e.g., privately-run prisons). For example, an employee of a private company has no "constitutional rights" against that company (although she may have numerous statutory rights—see below). Merely accepting federal funds does not turn a private organization into a state actor.

State constitutions are similar but not identical to the U.S. Constitution. The requirement of governmental action also applies to most of the protections offered by a state constitution. But most state constitutions are either broader or more specific (or both) than the federal text. For example, ten state constitutions contain explicit protection for a "right to privacy," words that do not appear in the U.S. Constitution.

Statutes are the laws passed by Congress or a state legislature or a local legislative body. They are usually more detailed and specific than the broad general statements in the Constitution. Also, because Congress has the authority (granted to it by the Constitution, of course) to regulate in areas such as commerce, as well as to implement the broad commands contained in the Constitution, statutes are not restricted to state action. Congress and state legislatures enact innumerable laws that apply to private organizations, employers, landlords, and so forth.

An example of the difference between constitutional and statutory sources of rights are "equality" and "civil rights" claims. A constitutional equality claim, or equal protection claim, arises under the clause in the Fourteenth Amendment which forbids any state from "deny[ing] to any person within its jurisdiction the equal protection of the laws." The term "civil rights law" usually refers to anti-discrimination statutes enacted by a legislature at some level of government—the Congress, a state legislature, or a city or county council.

Judicial decisions are the written opinions issued by judges in cases brought by the party who initiates a lawsuit (the "plaintiff") against another party (the "defendant"). Judicial decisions interpret and apply "the law" as contained in constitutional and statutory provisions and in previous cases. As judicial decisions build up over time, they become part of the law (often called "case law"), and thus are also subject to interpretation in future cases. Decisions by appellate courts control the decisions of trial-level courts within the same jurisdiction, because every judge is bound by the "precedent" of the courts at a higher level. Of course, very often the precedent cited by lawyers in a particular case is not clear or directly on point, and thus new decisions with additional interpretations are generated.

Statutes can be unconstitutional. The U.S. Constitution trumps all other law, state and federal, statutory or case law. The judiciary is vested with the authority and responsibility of applying the Constitution, and the Constitution governs every branch of government. Thus, some court decisions declare statutes to be unconstitutional and therefore unenforceable even if they remain on the books.

If there is a direct conflict between federal and state law, federal law trumps. The U.S. Supreme Court can invalidate a state law when and only when that law directly contradicts federal law, either the U.S. Constitution or a federal statute. This power is based on the "Supremacy Clause" in Article VI of the Constitution, which declares that federal law shall prevail over state law.

When is state law not subject to review by the U.S. Supreme Court? The U.S. Supreme Court will hear a case involving a challenge to a state law only if there is some issue of federal law involved in the case. Thus, the state supreme court is the final and highest authority in cases involving only that state's law.

Legislatures rather than courts can sometimes have the last word. If a court decision has interpreted the meaning of a statute, the legislature can amend the statute to make clear that it wants the provision to be interpreted to mean something else. In that situation, the court decision will be overridden by subsequent legislative action. Of course, if the new statutory language violates the Constitution, the Supreme Court could later declare it invalid on that basis. If there is no constitutional question in the case, however, the legislature gets the last word. If the Court rules that a statute is unconstitutional, the outcome of the case can usually be changed *only* if either the Court reverses itself or the Constitution is amended.

There are two parallel court systems: federal and state. In each, there are trial level and appellate level courts. The federal system has three levels: U.S. District Courts are the trial level courts; almost all cases are tried by a single judge at that level. U.S. Courts of Appeal are the intermediate level; these courts are organized by region of the country (called "circuits," as in "the Sixth Circuit"), and arguments on appeal are heard by a three-judge panel. Sometimes all the judges of a particular circuit will vote to hear an especially important case, which will lead to an "en banc" decision. The highest level, of course, is the U.S. Supreme Court.

There are various configurations of state court systems. Every state system has a trial court level, but they have different names: "Superior Court," or "District Court," or even, in New York, "Supreme Court." Every state system has a final level of appeal, known as the "Supreme Court" in most states, but sometimes called "the Court of Appeals." Many states, but not all, also have an intermediate level of appellate court, again with wide variations in the names.

CONSTITUTIONAL LAW

The Framers of the Constitution of 1789 believed that the main protection for the rights of the individual citizen was to be found in the Constitution's relentless division of powers among the states and federal government, the three branches of the federal government, and even within the legislative branch itself. But in 1791, as one of the deals made to get the Constitution ratified, the Bill of Rights was adopted; most of the amendments in the Bill of Rights protect rights directly against federal intrusion. The Bill of Rights and other pertinent constitutional amendments are reproduced in Appendix 1 to this book. The Due Process Clause of the Fourteenth Amendment has been interpreted to apply most of the individual rights of the first ten amendments to state governments as well.

The states have their own separate constitutions, which create individual rights against the states. This layer-cake arrangement tends to multiply rights. On the one hand, if the U.S. Supreme Court declines to recognize a right under the U.S. Constitution, state high courts might still recognize a right under their state constitutions. On the other hand, if the U.S. Supreme Court does recognize a federal constitutional right, state courts cannot diminish that right, because to do so would violate the Supremacy Clause.

PART A. DUE PROCESS, INCLUDING PRIVACY

The Fifth and Fourteenth Amendments, the former applicable to the federal government and the latter to the states, protect citizens against deprivation of life, liberty, and property without "due process of law." Since the Warren Court (1954–69), the Due Process Clause has been read in light of the general policy it embodies, that individual life, liberty, and property should not be at the mercy of arbitrary state intrusion.

The Right of Privacy. The Supreme Court has held that there is a "substantive" feature to the Due Process Clause that empowers courts to strike down laws that are purely arbitrary or that unduly trench on people's "fundamental" rights. The right of privacy is the most relevant substantive due process right for our purposes. It is the right people have to be free of state interference in the most fundamental decisions of human life and intimacy.

Although there is no such right expressed in the U.S. Constitution, Supreme Court decisions have recognized fundamental rights to decisions about family and child-rearing. A 1961 dissenting opinion by Justice Harlan is still one of the most important substantive due process opinions. Justice Harlan wrote that the Due Process Clause's "principle of liberty" protects the "most intimate details of the marital relation," including contraception. *Poe v. Ullman*, 367 U.S. 497 (1961) (Harlan, J., dissenting) (Chapter 2, Section 1). Four years later, the Supreme Court struck down the law prohibiting contraceptives in *Griswold v. Connecticut*, 381 U.S. 479 (1965) (Chapter 2, Section 1). Speaking of the freedom of married couples to choose the terms of their sexual intimacy, Justice Douglas' majority opinion found a right to privacy in the shadows ("penumbras") of the First, Fourth, Fifth, and Ninth Amendments.

Subsequent moves by the Supreme Court applied *Griswold* in ways that expanded the breadth of the precedent. The Court's decision overturning abortion statutes in *Roe v. Wade* (1972) (Chapter 2, Section 2) confirmed that the right of privacy was not limited to married couples and suggested that this right entailed a freedom for women to control not just their bodies, but to enjoy sexual liberty previously unheard of. *Roe* also authoritatively established the right of privacy in the Due Process Clause and formally abandoned *Griswold*'s experiment in penumbral reasoning. See also *Planned Parenthood v. Casey* (Chapter 2, Section 2) (reaffirming the central holding of *Roe* and adopting the rationale of Harlan's *Poe* dissent).

In *Loving v. Virginia*, 388 U.S. 1 (1967) (Chapter 3, Section 1), the Court recognized a fundamental right to marry as one ground for invalidating Virginia's law criminalizing miscegenation, or different-race marriages. The leading right to marry case is *Zablocki v. Redhail*, 434 U.S. 374 (1978) (Chapter 9, Section 2), which struck down a Wisconsin law preventing remarriage by people in arrears on outstanding child and spouse support obligations. Notwithstanding the worthy state goal, the Court held that there were other ways of meeting it that did not deprive people of a fundamental constitutional right.

The right of privacy has also been a basis for challenging laws criminalizing consensual sodomy. New York struck down its consensual sodomy law in *People v. Onofre*, 415 N.E.2d 936 (N.Y. 1980) (Chapter 2, Section 3). New York's highest court distinguished between public and private morality and held that the right to privacy is "a right of independence in making certain kinds of important decisions, with a concomitant right to conduct oneself in accordance with those decisions, undeterred by governmental restraint." The U.S. Supreme Court reached a different result in *Bowers v. Hardwick*, 478 U.S. 186 (1986) (Chapter 2, Section 3), which held that *Griswold, Roe,* and *Stanley* were limited to situations of sexual intimacy involving marriage and childbearing.

The Court overruled *Hardwick* in *Lawrence v. Texas*, 539 U.S. 558 (2003). Accepting academic criticisms that *Hardwick* rested upon a distorted understanding of both the historical materials and the lives and worth of lesbians, gay men and bisexuals, the Court ruled that a state could not make it a crime for two adults to engage in consensual oral or anal intimacy in a private space.

PART B. EQUAL PROTECTION

The Fourteenth Amendment also provides, "nor shall any State * * * deny to any person within its jurisdiction the equal protection of the laws." The Supreme Court has regularly upheld state policies that rely on classifications such as income, height, emissions levels, public conduct and appearance, and the like upon a showing that the classifications have a *rational basis*: they are plausibly related to a legitimate state goal. The big question in equal protection law is when the Court should demand something more than a rational basis to support statutory classifications. An ancillary question is when does a law not have even a rational basis.

Strict Scrutiny. The modern Court's classic equal protection analysis came in a case involving the constitutionality of a federal law prohibiting the interstate transportation of "filled milk." In *United States v. Carolene Products Co.*, 304 U.S. 144 (1938), the Court deferred to the legislative health rationale for the filled milk classification, but stated in famous footnote 4 that the "presumption of constitutionality" might be rebutted in other kinds of cases, including those where statutes are "directed at particular religious * * * or national * * * or racial minorities" or reflect "prejudice against discrete or insular minorities * * * which tends seriously to curtail the operation of the political processes ordinarily to be relied upon to protect minorities."

Consistent with both the original focus of the Fourteenth Amendment and the *Carolene* formulation, the Supreme Court has insisted on more than a rational basis when evaluating race-based classifications. In *Korematsu v. United States*, 323 U.S. 214 (1944), where the Supreme Court notoriously upheld federal internment of Japanese Americans during World War II, the Court stated that "all legal restrictions which curtail the civil rights of a single racial group are immediately suspect" and "courts must subject them to the most rigid scrutiny."

Brown v. Board of Education, 347 U.S. 483 (1954), held that racial segregation of public schools violates the Equal Protection Clause. In a companion case, *Bolling v. Sharpe*, 347 U.S. 497 (1954), the Court held for the first time that the federal government is also subject to equal protection limits. *Loving v. Virginia*, 388 U.S. 1 (1967) (Chapter 3, Section 1), noted above as the first due process right to marry case, ruled as its primary holding that the Virginia miscegenation law violated the Equal Protection Clause because it deployed an unsupported race-based classification: a black-white couple could not marry, whereas a similarly situated black-black or white-white couple could.

Cases involving race-based classifications have been the most dramatic occasions for judicial application of the Equal Protection Clause to strike down state and federal laws, but *Carolene*'s concern with laws reflecting "prejudice against discrete or insular minorities" has been interpreted to subject other classifications to strict scrutiny. See *Graham v. Richardson*,

403 U.S. 365 (1971), which held that state (but not necessarily federal) rules based on alienage would be subjected to heightened scrutiny for *Carolene* reasons. In *Levy v. Louisiana*, 391 U.S. 68 (1968), the Court held that illegitimacy is also a *suspect classification*. Although the Court has been willing to uphold some illegitimacy classifications, heightened scrutiny and changing social mores have basically eliminated illegitimacy as a legal classification. Children born outside of marriage are now treated the same by the law as those born within marriage.

Intermediate Scrutiny. Because women are not a "discrete and insular minority" but have been objects of legislation based on gender- or sex-based stereotypes, classifications based on sex posed a difficult problem for the *Carolene Products* formulation. The Supreme Court routinely upheld sex-based classifications as rational until *Reed v. Reed*, 404 U.S. 71 (1971). Apparently applying the rational basis test, the Court invalidated an Idaho statute preferring men over women as executors of estates. The next year Congress passed the Equal Rights Amendment, which would have made sex a suspect classification. While the ERA was in the process of state ratification, four Justices on the Court argued for strict scrutiny under the Equal Protection Clause in *Frontiero v. Richardson*, 411 U.S. 677 (1973) (Chapter 3, Section 1).

The ERA was never ratified, but at least seventeen states have added ERAs to their state constitutions,[a] and the U.S. Supreme Court has inched toward making sex a suspect classification. In *Craig v. Boren*, 429 U.S. 190 (1976), the Court struck down a state law allowing 18-year-old girls to buy low-alcohol beer but requiring boys to be 21 years old. Writing for six members of the Court, Justice Brennan's opinion held that "classifications by gender must serve important governmental objectives and must be substantially related to achievement of those objectives." This verbal formulation is not as demanding as that the Court uses to scrutinize race-based classifications, and so it is considered "heightened" or "intermediate" rather than "strict" scrutiny. In *United States v. Virginia*, 518 U.S. 515 (1996) (Chapter 3, Section 1), Justice Ginsburg's opinion for six Justices held that sex-based classifications must be supported by a justification that is "exceedingly persuasive." Also, the "justification must be genuine, not hypothesized or invented post hoc in response to litigation.

a. "Sex" is inserted into a broader equal protection clause in the Alaska Constitution, article I, § 3 ("sex" added 1972); Connecticut Constitution, article I, § 20 (added 1974); Hawaii Constitution, article I, § 5; Illinois Constitution, article I, § 17 (1970 revised constitution); Massachusetts Declaration of Rights, part I, article I (added 1976); Montana Constitution, article II, § 4 (1972 revised constitution); New Hampshire Constitution, part I, article 2 (added 1974); Texas Constitution, article I, § 3a (added 1972); Virginia Constitution, article I, § 11 (added 1970); Wyoming Constitution, article I, § 3 (1889 constitution). Following the ERA, other states have clauses specially protecting against sex discrimination, namely, Colorado Constitution, article II, § 29 (equal rights amendment added 1972); Illinois Constitution, article I, § 8 (1970 revised constitution); Maryland Declaration of Rights, article 46 (added 1972); New Mexico Constitution, article II, § 18 (added 1972); Pennsylvania Constitution, article I, § 28 (added 1971); Utah Constitution, article IV, § 1 (1896 constitution); Washington Constitution, article 31, § 1 (added 1972).

And it must not rely on overbroad generalizations about the different talents, capacities, or preferences of males and females.''

Both strict and intermediate scrutiny doctrines contain an important caveat. Such scrutiny only applies to statutes or regulations that explicitly discriminate on the basis of, e.g., race or sex, *or* that can be shown to be motivated by a discriminatory purpose. Thus, the Supreme Court has not strictly scrutinized facially neutral employment policies that disproportionately hurt women in the workforce. See *Geduldig v. Aiello*, 417 U.S. 484 (1974) (discrimination on the basis of pregnancy); *Personnel Administrator v. Feeney*, 442 U.S. 256 (1979) (discrimination in favor of military veterans) (both in Chapter 8, Section 1). Note that Congress responded to these decisions by enacting statutes that made both kinds of discrimination unlawful under Title VII of the Civil Rights Act (Chapter 8, Section 1).

In the most interesting application of a state ERA, the Hawaii Supreme Court held in *Baehr v. Lewin*, 852 P.2d 44 (Haw. 1993) (Chapter 3, Section 3) that it is sex discrimination for the state to deny a marriage license to two women when a similarly situated man and woman would receive one. The analogy to *Loving* is striking: where *Loving* subjected laws prohibiting different-race marriage to heightened scrutiny because they denied marriage licenses based on the race of one of the partners, *Baehr* subjected laws prohibiting same-sex marriage to heightened scrutiny because they deny marriage licenses based on the sex of one of the partners.

Sexual orientation and the rational basis test. What level of scrutiny should be applied to discrimination based on sexual orientation? State courts in interpreting their own constitutions have sometimes applied a form of heightened scrutiny to sexual orientation classifications. Some states, like Hawaii in *Baehr*, have treated sexual orientation as a subset of sex and thus applied the law governing sex discrimination. However, one might criticize that approach as transvestic, dressing sexual orientation discrimination claims in sex discrimination garb. Other states have found an independent basis in state law for applying heightened scrutiny to sexual orientation. *Commonwealth v. Wasson*, 842 S.W.2d 487 (Ky. 1992); *Tanner v. Oregon Health Sciences University*, 971 P.2d 435 (Or. Ct. App. 1998).

The U.S. Supreme Court has never explicitly used heightened scrutiny when analyzing sexual orientation discrimination. (For an example of what such analysis might look like, see *Watkins v. U.S. Army*, 847 F.2d 1329 (9th Cir. 1988), *vacated*, 875 F.2d 699 (9th Cir.1989) (en banc) (Chapter 3, Section 2).) However, in *Romer v. Evans*, 517 U.S. 620 (1996) (Chapter 3, Section 2), the Court invalidated an anti-gay initiative under the rational basis test. Like *Reed v. Reed*, this might be a harbinger for future Courts to apply heightened scrutiny to sexual orientation classifications.

In general, it is rare that laws subjected to only a rational basis inquiry are struck down. For example, the Court in *Massachusetts Bd. of Retirement v. Murgia*, 427 U.S. 307 (1976), held that age-based classifications such as mandatory retirement ages do not justify heightened scrutiny because old people have not been a discrete and insular minority disadvantaged in the political process. Similarly, the Court has held that neither financial status, *San Antonio Indep. School Dist. v. Rodriguez*, 411 U.S. 1 (1973), nor personal disability, *City of Cleburne v. Cleburne Living Center*, 473 U.S. 432 (1985), is a classification that triggers heightened scrutiny. Justice O'Connor's concurring opinion in *Lawrence v. Texas* (Chapter 4), which she based on equal protection rather than due process principles, argued that what one might call a "heightened rational basis" test applies when the Court finds a law to be motivated by animus toward a group.

Fundamental Rights and Equal Protection. Another aspect of the *Carolene Products* formulation is that courts will apply heightened scrutiny when classifications affect the distribution of "fundamental rights." An example is the early procreation case of *Skinner v. Oklahoma*, 316 U.S. 535 (1942). The state law struck down in *Skinner* required sterilization of habitual criminals committing crimes of "moral turpitude" but not those committing white collar crimes such as embezzlement. The Supreme Court held the legislative classification to a higher standard not because the class of persons affected was entitled to heightened scrutiny, but because of the nature of the deprivation concerned one of "the basic civil rights of man," the right to marry and procreate. Similarly, in *Eisenstadt v. Baird*, 405 U.S. 438 (1972) (Chapter 2, Section 1), the Court struck down a Massachusetts law which criminalized the distribution of contraceptives to unmarried people. Unmarried people as a class have not been accorded heightened scrutiny, but the Court found that deprivation of the right to contraception found in *Griswold* to be fundamental justified applying the more stringent test.

PART C.   FIRST AMENDMENT

The First Amendment on its face protects (1) free speech; (2) freedom of the press; (3) peaceful assembly; (4) the right to petition the government; (5) free exercise of religion; and (6) the right not to have a state-established religion. Although the First Amendment only limits Congress' power, the Supreme Court has held it to be one of the rights "incorporated" in the Fourteenth Amendment's Due Process Clause and therefore applicable to the states as well. The Court has also recognized a right of association as implied in the First Amendment, *NAACP v. Alabama*, 357 U.S. 449 (1958), which has been applied to protect the rights of LGBT persons to congregate in bars, to form clubs at public universities, and to form organizations (Chapter 5, Section 1). Also the Court has extended the First Amendment's protection to "expressive conduct" such as draft card and flag-burning, marches, and erotic dancing.[b]

b. In "expressive conduct" or symbolic speech cases, such as flag-burning or nude dancing, the applicable test is that of *United States v. O'Brien*, 391 U.S. 367 (1968), which allowed state regulation of draft card burning. When pure speech is mixed with nonspeech, "a government regulation is sufficiently justified if it * * * furthers an important or substantial governmental interest; if the governmental interest is unrelated

Generally, it is unconstitutional for the state to censor individual or group expressive communications unless the state can prove that the speech regulation is the "least restrictive means" necessary to advance a compelling governmental interest. Fatal to First Amendment inquiry is the state's regulation of speech because it offends others; the so-called heckler's veto is not allowed as a defense. *Cohen v. California*, 403 U.S. 15 (1971), where the Court disallowed state regulation of a young man whose bomber jacket bore the words "Fuck the draft." "If there is a bedrock principle underlying the First Amendment, it is that the Government may not prohibit the expression of an idea simply because society finds the idea itself offensive or disagreeable." *Texas v. Johnson*, 491 U.S. 397 (1989) (the flagburning case).

Generally, therefore, one would expect that the state would rarely be allowed to censor expression or expressive conduct, either before the fact (through a prior restraint, which is especially disfavored) or after the fact. That generalization is subject to a range of caveats relating to exceptions for certain types of expression, the circumstances of the expression, and some state justifications.

"Low Value" Expression Receiving Less or No First Amendment Protection. Certain kinds of expression are considered to be so low in value that the Court refuses to give them First Amendment protection. Categories include:

- *Obscenity.* Expression that is "obscene" is outside the protection of the First Amendment, the Court held in *Roth v. United States*, 354 U.S. 476 (1957) (Chapter 5, Section 3). As refined by subsequent decisions, expression is obscene only if it (1) appeals mainly to people's prurient interest in sex, (2) is offensive to community standards, and (3) has no redeeming social, artistic, or scientific value. Material presenting minority sexualities in a positive light was once regularly considered obscene (Chapter 5, Section 3).

- *Libel.* Expression that is false and injures other people is not protected, although the First Amendment does require that defamatory speech about "public figures" or private figures engaged in a "public event" is immune from lawsuits unless the victim can show that the publisher acted with "actual malice." *New York Times v. Sullivan* (1964).

- *Fighting Words and Inciteful Speech.* Speech that is directed toward the incitement of imminent lawless action and is likely to have that effect can be suppressed. This is a narrow exception to the First Amendment. *Brandenburg v. Ohio*, 395 U.S. 444 (1969) (*per curiam*) (overturning prosecution of a KKK group where racist and lawless advocacy was generalized and unlikely to produce imminent lawless actions). Possibly broader is the "fighting words" doctrine of *Chap-*

to the suppression of free expression; and if the incidental restriction on alleged First Amendment freedoms is no greater than is essential to the furtherance of that interest."

linsky v. New Hampshire, 315 U.S. 568 (1942), which held outside the First Amendment abusive epithets which are inherently likely to provoke a violent reaction.

Nondiscrimination versus the First Amendment. Free expression values can be sacrificed when the state seeks to advance equality values, which can be "compelling" or "substantial" state interests, so long as the regulation is the "least restrictive means" for meeting the state equality goal. The foundational case is *Roberts v. Jaycees*, 468 U.S. 609 (1984) (Chapter 5, Section 2), where the Supreme Court held that Minneapolis could require a private association to end its longstanding discrimination against women. The District of Columbia Court of Appeals held in *Gay Rights Coalition v. Georgetown University*, 536 A.2d 1 (D.C. 1987) (en banc) (Chapter 5, Section 2), that the District's anti-discrimination law justified a requirement that a Roman Catholic university provide equal access and services to gay student groups.

Two more recent Supreme Court decisions have addressed the equality/expression balance. In *Hurley v. Gay and Lesbian Irish of Boston*, 515 U.S. 557 (1995) (Chapter 5, Section 2), the Court held that Massachusetts could not apply its public accommodations law to require a parade to include a gay, lesbian, and bisexual contingent. Although a government parade could not exclude lesbians and gays, the privately-organized St. Patrick's Day parade could exclude them to further its own expressive rights. Similarly, the Court ruled that the Boy Scouts could exclude openly gay scoutmasters to preserve its own message regarding homosexuality. *Boy Scouts of America v. Dale*, 530 U.S. 640 (2000) (Chapter 5, Section 2).

Another dramatic clash between expression and equality involves pornography. Some feminists maintain that much pornography hurts women not only by perpetuating sexist stereotypes, but also by stimulating physical violence against women. Other feminists have argued that suppression of sexual speech carries more risk than benefit for efforts to empower women. American courts have not accepted this basis for regulation of non-obscene pornography, *American Booksellers Ass'n v. Hudnut*, 771 F.2d 323 (7th Cir. 1985), *aff'd mem.*, 475 U.S. 1001 (1986), but Canada's Supreme Court reached the opposite result (Chapter 5, Section 3).

SPECIAL REALMS—SPECIAL DEFERENCE

Legal issues relating to sexuality and gender are central to America's post-industrial understanding of national military service, the workplace, and the family. The armed forces have traditionally been a microcosm of American citizenship debates and experiences—and the role of women and sexual minorities remains fraught with symbolic as well as real-life consequences. Constitutional law in this area is refracted through the lens of *deference* which judges pay to executive and legislative decisions. Judges accord some deference to disciplinary and even exclusionary rules devised for regulating governmental and private workplaces, and these rules have a deep effect upon the everyday lives of many Americans. The family is both the most private realm for sexuality and gender issues (and therefore a realm where the government defers to private choices, sometimes compelled by constitutional precedent) and the cutting edge for the symbolic politics implicated in surrogate parenting, same-sex marriage, and decisions about child custody and adoption.

PART A.   THE ARMED FORCES

The Supreme Court often defers to decisions made within the military context on the ground that the special circumstances of military life necessitate special rules. It is a truism that some constitutional rights which Americans take for granted do not exist for those in the armed forces. The deference to the military principle is not absolute, however; a military policy that fails even the rational basis test would be vulnerable to judicial invalidation. Nonetheless, courts have routinely invoked deference in response to serious First Amendment as well as to due process and equal protection claims. In *Goldman v. Weinberger*, 475 U.S. 503 (1986), for example, the Court allowed a military dress code to prohibit a rabbinical officer from wearing the yarmulke required by his religion. The Court justified its decision as necessary to protect the level of discipline and chain of command authority in the armed forces. (A state workplace rule barring yarmulkes would probably not have passed First Amendment scrutiny, and a law prohibiting their public display on the street would be flatly unconstitutional.)

Beyond constitutional claims, much of the other relevant statutory and case law is also unique to the military. For example, none of the statutory

13

protections against discrimination, such as Title VII, covers service members. Largely for this reason, much of the changing law on military policy has developed in military-specific legislation, executive orders, and Department of Defense regulations. Chapter 7 traces the legal, political, and cultural developments that have shaped military policy at the intersection of sexuality and gender with race, sex, and sexual orientation.

PART B.   THE WORKPLACE

Chapter 8 covers employment law, and is divided into sections analyzing discrimination based on sex, discrimination based on sexual orientation, and the law related to sexual harassment. Both for sex and sexual orientation, the materials first treat situations in which the government is the employer and thus where constitutional law applies. In these cases, you will see examples of where equal treatment and free expression (coming out) doctrines converge. See, e.g., *Shahar v. Bowers* (Chapter 8, Section 2). A second set of cases illustrates how, for employees in the private sector, courts interpret statutory anti-discrimination protections.

Chapter 8 also addresses two more specific issues, one particular to women, the other of greater concern to lesbian, gay, bisexual, and transgendered (LGBT) people. Pregnancy, the first issue, has been a recurring barrier to equality for women workers, and advocates have sought for decades to normalize it, i.e., to reshape our notion of the typical worker to incorporate not just a traditionally male norm, but also workers who become pregnant. For LGBT people, partner benefits have become a central workplace demand. Should a refusal to provide such benefits be considered sexual orientation discrimination, or is it equal treatment so long as benefits are denied to everyone? As you will see, courts and legislatures have developed many different approaches to this issue.

In the last section of the chapter, we analyze cases concerning sexual harassment, both that directed against women and that targeting LGBT people. The sexual harassment cases have forced courts to identify when harassment occurs "because of sex" (the words of Title VII), even if both the harassers and the victims are of the same sex. No dominant theory has emerged of how to interpret the meaning of that phrase when, for example, men harass men; for multiple theories in one case, see *Rene v. MGM Grand Hotel, Inc.* (Chapter 8, Section 3).

PART C.   THE FAMILY

The book both opens (Chapter 2) and closes (Chapter 9) with the area of law that is most private *and* most fraught with public symbolism—the family. Marriage and the family have changed dramatically in the last century, mainly in response to greater opportunities outside the home for women, and their evolving status within the home. Thematically, the dominant legal change has been *privatization*: the state honors most of the private choices made by spouses and parents. In 1900, marriage carried with it many inescapable rights and duties and was exceedingly hard to exit; theoretically, the state barred non-procreative sexual activities within marriage, and almost any sexual activities outside it. Today, consenting adults can engage in sexual activities under almost any circumstances in most states, couples deciding to marry can waive or reconfigure many of the rights and duties of marriage, and marital exit is much easier under the no-fault divorce laws that swept the country in the 1970s.

Chapter 9 poses the question: How much further, if at all, should privatization go in our country? Should the state offer other off-the-rack regulatory options in addition to marriage? Should civil marriage even continue? Why shouldn't the state get out of the marriage business altogether (leaving it to religious communities to celebrate)?

Another, analytically distinct, issue is whether the state should expand *eligibility* for civil marriage. Different-race couples, people with certain disabilities or illnesses, and same-sex couples were excluded from marriage in 1900 (in most states). The first two exclusions have largely melted away. Should the third one survive? If not, what other eligibility bars should fall: Age? Blood relation? Relationship by affinity? Does a state that marries same-sex couples also have to open its doors to polygamy?

Finally, and perhaps most important, are issues of sexuality and gender that have roiled child custody and adoption law. If the state does not allow lesbian and gay couples to marry, should it allow them to raise children within their households? Should the state recognize parental rights in both partners (not just the biological or adoptive parent)? Are there circumstances where a child might not only have two mommies, but also a daddy (a third parent) as well?

A NOTE ON FINDING FULL TEXTS OF CASES

The decisions in this book are excerpted to highlight the most important portions. For readers who want to read the full texts, the best source for both federal and state court cases is www.law.cornell.edu/index.html. Recent federal court decisions are available at www.supremecourtus.gov and www.uscourts.gov. Most state courts also have web pages.

Citations to cases refer to published decisions; all follow the same format:

Number—Abbreviation—Number (Court, Date)

For example—92 F.3d 446 (7th Cir. 1996). The abbreviation in the middle identifies the court. For example, in the federal system, "U.S." cites are from the Supreme Court, "F.2d" or "F.3d" cites are from courts of appeal, and "F. Supp." or "F. Supp. 2d" cites are from district courts. The first number tells you the volume number of the book of decisions from that court, and the second number tells you the page. References within the parenthesis like "7th Cir." or "3d Dist." tell you the particular division of that level of the court system. The date is the year of decision.

Thus, the citation 92 F.3d 446 (7th Cir. 1996) would send you to the reporters for U.S. Courts of Appeal (third series), volume 92, and page 446.

CHAPTER 2

THE RIGHT TO SEXUAL PRIVACY

The regulation of sex in America is as old as Cotton Mather. From colonial times into the twentieth century, virtually all American state or colonial jurisdictions had laws criminalizing fornication (sex outside of marriage), adultery (sex by a married person with anyone other than her or his spouse), sodomy (anal and, later, oral sex), incest (sex with a close relative), seduction (sex with a minor woman), and rape (forcible vaginal sex). Many jurisdictions added laws criminalizing interracial sex, cohabitation, and marriage.

The middle part of the nineteenth century (about 1840–80) witnessed the emergence of an intense interest in sex regulations targeting women's control of their bodies. Most states and cities adopted statutes not only criminalizing prostitution (a woman's agreement to engage in "promiscuous" sex, often but not necessarily in exchange for money), but also making it a crime to operate a "disorderly house," to solicit for prostitution, or to associate with a disorderly house or purveyors of prostitution. Laws against disorderly conduct and vagrancy were often extended or amended to cover prostitution and other forms of public sex. Shortly after cities and states began developing these anti-prostitution measures (generally, the 1850s through 1870s), they adopted laws prohibiting abortion and the sale or use of contraceptives. The federal Comstock Act of 1873 prohibited the interstate transportation of contraceptives as part of its ban against obscene materials. Municipalities in this period adopted laws prohibiting the wearing of apparel of the opposite sex; such laws were used against women who passed as men in order to gain economic and social advantages.

The turn of the century (1880–1920) yielded yet another twist in American regulation of sex, as cities and states with large cities began to focus regulatory attention on sexual "inverts" and "degenerates," later called "homosexuals." Sodomy laws were broadened in this period to include prohibitions of oral sex, often between two men. Disorderly conduct, lewdness, and cross dressing laws came to be applied to homosexuals with great vigor, and some jurisdictions adopted new laws targeting homosexual cruising, social gatherings, and even literature.

The foregoing constituted the classic regime of sex regulation in the United States as of 1920. Most of these laws reached conduct that was personal, intimate, consenting, and private between two individuals. After World War I and, even more so, World War II, American sexual practices became increasingly discordant with this classic regime. First heterosexual women, and then lesbians and gay men, turned to the Constitution as a basis for challenging this regulatory regime.

The Contraception Cases

The articulation of a right to sexual privacy grew directly out of the birth control movement. Although the American campaign to empower women to avoid unwanted pregnancy originated in the provocative speeches and writings of radicals such as Emma Goldman, it was Margaret Sanger, more than any other individual, who transformed those ideas into a new social movement.

Margaret Higgins Sanger was born to a poor Irish family in Corning, New York in 1879. Convinced that her own mother's ill health and eventual death resulted from bearing eleven children, Sanger developed a fierce belief in a woman's right to sexual and reproductive autonomy. For her, the means to this end were legalized birth control and greater public candor about sexuality. A nurse before she became a reformer, Sanger attacked a social structure that denied information to women about even simple methods of birth control. Lacking the power to control pregnancy led to enormous hardships for women, ranging from the economic strain of large families to possible death or impaired health.

Sanger's first writings about sex education were published in *The Call*, a socialist newspaper. Sanger soon started her own magazine, *The Woman Rebel*, which led to a federal indictment in 1914 for sending indecent material through the mails. Sanger was charged under the Comstock law, a federal obscenity statute. Prosecutions for obscenity under federal or state law were then the primary legal tool used to suppress birth control materials. While under indictment, Sanger wrote and disseminated *Family Limitation*, a pamphlet detailing birth control methods and encouraging women to seek their own gratification in heterosexual relations. At the time, other Socialist Party members were also being prosecuted and jailed under the federal Comstock law and analogous state obscenity statutes. Sanger fled to Europe to avoid prosecution. There she worked with sexologist Havelock Ellis and other reformers, and visited the world's first birth control clinic in the Netherlands. Upon her return the following year, growing public sympathy for the birth control movement led the U.S. Attorney's office to drop charges against her. Sanger made plans to open the first birth control clinic in the United States.

New York v. Sanger

Margaret Sanger decided that birth control reform would come about more quickly by challenging the laws through the judiciary than by seeking legislative change. She saw her chance to test that approach with the New

York obscenity law. Under one section of the statute, physicians could provide contraceptives to prevent or cure disease. The prevailing interpretation at the time was that this exception referred only to venereal disease and the distribution of condoms. "In that case," Sanger wrote, "the intent was to protect the man. * * * I wanted the interpretation to be broadened into the intent to protect women from ill health as the result of excessive childbearing and, equally important, to have the right to control their own destinies."

To test the law, Sanger opened the first birth control clinic in the United States in 1916 in Brooklyn, New York. She notified local press and police, and distributed announcements that read,

> Mothers! Can you afford to have a large family? Do you want any more children? If not, why do you have them? Do not kill, Do not take life, But Prevent. Safe, harmless information can be obtained of trained nurses. * * * All mothers welcome.

After nine days of providing services, during which 464 women came for help, Sanger and her staff were arrested.

Sanger's trial drew enormous public attention, including a rally at Carnegie Hall. The courtroom was packed each day with press, clinic patients, and wealthy society women whom Sanger had adroitly solicited to support birth control. Both the prosecution and the defense relied on former patients as witnesses. The District Attorney elicited testimony that each woman had met with Sanger at the clinic, having gone there to "have her stop the babies." Sanger's attorney asked them to describe the miscarriages, sickness, and poverty they endured.

Sanger was convicted, and served 30 days in a women's prison. The appeals court affirmed, interpreting the statute to permit physicians to treat disease but not to give "promiscuous advice to patients irrespective of their condition." It also ruled, however, that "disease" could be broadly defined as "any alteration in the state of body which caused or threatened pain or sickness." *People v. Sanger*, 118 N.E. 637, 638 (N.Y.1918), *appeal dismissed*, 251 U.S. 537 (1919) (*per curiam*). This interpretation extended "disease" far beyond venereal disease, to include pregnancy, thus achieving one of Sanger's goals. The *Sanger* case produced the first legal victory for the birth control movement, and the approach of using litigation to broaden the doctors' exception shaped legal and political strategy for decades. The decision fell far short, however, of Sanger's desire to make birth control available to women for economic and social reasons.

For this reason, Sanger appealed her conviction to the U.S. Supreme Court. Her brief explicitly celebrated the joy people can find in marriage and parenting but insisted that both be the result of the voluntary choice of the man and the woman—not "compulsory motherhood" forced upon them by state prohibitions and regimes of ignorance. The brief implicitly valorized the sexual relationship between a man and a woman as an end in itself and not as a means toward procreation. Sanger's lawyer tied this human good to the Due Process Clause and to the cases recognizing some kind of privacy right: "Personal 'liberty' includes not only freedom from physical restraint, but also the right 'to be let alone,' to determine one's mode of life ... and is invaded not only by a deprivation of life, but also by a deprivation of those things which are necessary to the enjoyment of life according to the nature, temperament and lawful desires of the individual." The Supreme Court dismissed the appeal in *Sanger v. People*, 251 U.S. 537 (1919) (per curiam).

> *You ought to be ashamed, I said, to look so antique.*
>
> *(And her only thirty-one.)*
>
> *I can't help it, she said, pulling a long face.*
>
> *It's them pills I took, to bring it off, she said.*
>
> *(She's had five already, and nearly died of young George.)*
>
> *The chemist said it would be all right, but I've never been the same.*
>
> *You are a proper fool, I said.*
>
> *Well, if Albert won't leave you alone, there it is, I said.*
>
> *What you get married for if you don't want children?*
>
> T.S. Eliot, *The Waste Land* (1922).

The Early Birth Control Movement

Sanger's experience in Europe had convinced her of the need for a single-minded, single-issue strategy, and she never wavered from that approach. She built the birth control movement from a combination of elements of the Socialist Party, radical unions such as the International Workers of the World (popularly known as the Wobblies), women's suffragists, civil libertarians, eugenicists, and the "free love" movement. She herself drew on the full spectrum of those views, advocating both "the joys of the flesh," and arguing that "more children from the fit, less from the unfit—that is the chief issue of the birth control movement." She fused radical tactics such as civil disobedience with a growing de-radicalization of the substance of her arguments, while building a political organization independent of any other movement.

1.   Sanger's "Doctors Only" Strategy

Sanger believed that the tactical advantages of a "doctors only" strategy outweighed its shortcomings. Under her direction, the birth control movement used the language of "health" and medical authority to associate itself with the respectability of a conservative and male-dominated profession. Her primary coalition partners were physicians, joined by social welfare groups and some religious organizations. Building on the decision in the Brooklyn clinic case, birth controllers argued that any limitation—*e.g.*, to prevent disease—on the use of such devices should be jettisoned, to allow doctors the discretion to prescribe as they saw fit. As this strategy evolved, Sanger's lawyers developed the legal argument that restrictive laws abridged the right of physicians to practice medicine.

The "doctors only" strategy also had negative ramifications. It encouraged the pathologizing of contraception, and downplayed the social and economic needs of women. It reinforced an income barrier because, despite advances in the law, contraception was to be available to women only through the advice of a physician. (The only reliable form of women's contraception then was the diaphragm.) Restricting access through physician intermediaries also reassured those who feared that easier access would promote immorality (although access by men to condoms was commonplace). A third effect of medicalization was to dampen consciousness of birth control as a political issue.

Despite—or because of—its shortcomings, the "doctors only" argument worked as a legal strategy. In 1936, the Second Circuit ruled that Congress had not intended to bar importation of diaphragms by doctors because a physician's goal of promoting health or saving lives was not immoral and therefore not within the intent behind the Comstock law. *United States v. One Package*, 86 F.2d 737 (2d Cir. 1936). At the federal level, *One Package* effectively removed all obstacles limiting private physicians' access to birth control information and supplies. Interpretation of state obscenity laws followed suit. By 1960, Massachusetts and Connecticut were the only states left with statutes that banned contraception without providing for a physician exception. After winning *One Package*, Sanger and her allies shifted the bulk of their activities from opposing restrictive laws to opening clinics and lobbying for the inclusion of birth control in public health programs.

2. The "Free Speech" Strategy

Mary Ware Dennett, a rival birth control advocate, opposed the concept of a doctors only exception because it left birth control information classified as obscene. Dennett attempted, to no avail, to get sponsors for a bill repealing the New York obscenity statute as it applied to contraception. Deciding instead to focus on federal legislation, Dennett formed a federal lobbying organization, the Voluntary Parenthood League. In 1923, Dennett persuaded Senator Cummins of Iowa to introduce her legislation by agreeing to a requirement of five physicians to certify the reliability of any contraceptive product protected by law. The legislation never made it to the floor of either chamber of Congress. Support for repeal eroded, and within a year Dennett's Voluntary Parenthood League closed. Later court decisions held that birth control information did not fall within the scope of obscene speech. In 1930, the Second Circuit reversed Dennett's own obscenity conviction for having mailed copies of a sex education pamphlet she had written for her own two children. *United States v. Dennett*, 39 F.2d 564 (2d Cir. 1930). The *Dennett* decision cleared the way for development of formal sex education curricula.

3. Race–Based Arguments, Pro and Con

Groups on all sides of the birth control issue invoked race-based arguments. Anti-birth controllers asserted that upper-class persons were more likely to use birth control, meaning that the "fit" stock would die off. They argued that birth control amounted to "race suicide," language that left ambiguous whether the reference was to the human race or to certain racial groups. Birth control proponents also capitalized on the fear that native stock was being replaced by immigrants, but argued that providing access to birth control for the poor would help reverse that trend. Opponents on the left asserted that the duty of women, especially in minority racial and ethnic groups, was to bear children.

The African–American community developed its own birth control organizations. In 1918, the Women's Political Association of Harlem included birth control as a topic in its lecture series. In 1919, W.E.B. DuBois published an essay arguing that a woman "must have the right of motherhood at her own discretion." Black community organizations started and supported birth control clinics throughout the United States. Debate about whether birth control was good for the community or destructive of its future was a common feature of the black press.

Official government actions were also divided. In the South, then the region of the United States where the majority of African Americans lived, racist policy manifested itself in divergent ways. Some state agencies offered contraceptive services to whites only. In other states, birth control was funded as a method of limiting African–American population growth.

African–American organizations balanced these pressures by creating new approaches to the issue. In 1941, the National Council of Negro Women became the first national women's organization to endorse birth control. Its resolution argued that birth control should be used to help families have all the children they could afford. Racial betterment, rather than individual freedom, was the predominant theme of birth control advocates within the African–American community.

4. Women's Sexuality

Divergent perspectives on women's sexuality split birth control advocates from feminism in the early twentieth century. The women's movement divided between the suffragist wing, which sought equality in public realms such as voting and employment, and maternalist or welfare feminism, which emphasized the special needs of mothers and young children. For both, sexual propriety was an important characteristic of the respectable woman.

Sanger and her allies deliberately sought to change the terms of the debate, which upset feminists in both camps. Sanger argued that good mothers had a right to heterosexual gratification: "a mutual and satisfied sexual act is of great benefit to the average woman." She began using the phrase "birth control" as a substitute for "voluntary motherhood," an earlier slogan that had been used to advocate the right of married women to abstain from sex.

The very technology of diaphragms (then called pessaries) was controversial: not only did women control their usage, but no one claimed that diaphragms stopped sexually transmitted diseases; their *only* function was to prevent conception. Diaphragms were the first birth control technology to enable women to engage in intercourse for pleasure and intimacy, without the threat of pregnancy as a penalty.

The claim for women's sexual freedom is evident in appellate briefs in the Brooklyn clinic prosecutions. Counsel argued that the law "denied [a woman] her absolute right of enjoyment of sexual relations unless the act be so conducted that pregnancy may be the result." *People v. Byrne*, 163 N.Y.S. 682, 686 (N.Y.Sup.Ct.1917). It was an argument that the court declined to consider.

The concepts of women's rights and of sexual pleasure in early birth control discourse ebbed and flowed with the tide of public opinion. In the late 1930s and 1940s, Planned Parenthood de-emphasized feminism and emphasized social planning, in part through its very name. The tide shifted back again when the second wave of feminism began in the late 1960s.

5.   Birth Control as "Public Health"

In the Depression years of the 1930s, pressure mounted on government agencies to include birth control information in their services for the poor. Gradually and quietly, such policies were developed. As of 1935, for example, the Federal Emergency Relief Administration underwrote the cost of birth control services to the poor, but would not admit it publicly. Sanger formed the Committee for Public Progress to pressure government agencies into full recognition of contraception as an integral part of public health. Two pieces of legislation were instrumental in this effort. Title V of the Social Security Act of 1938 provided funding to state maternal and child health services. The Venereal Disease Control Act in 1939 authorized federal dollars to be used for contraceptives for the purpose of "fighting disease." Despite the legislation, however, implementation did not come easily. Only intervention by Eleanor Roosevelt eventually led officials of the Children's Bureau and the Public Health Service to support birth control programs openly.

During World War II, the executive branch changed its approach from passive approval to active initiation of birth control programs. Defense industries required the labor of women who would not be disabled by unwanted pregnancies. Birth control and women's health became national security interests.

In the 1950s and 1960s, population growth became an international issue. In perhaps the movement's high-water mark of respectability, former Presidents Truman and Eisenhower became honorary co-chairs of the 1965 Planned Parenthood fundraising campaign. In 1970, Congress passed Title X of the Public Health Service Act, which provided federal funds to support family planning clinics.

6.   The Claim to "Privacy"

The assertion that law should recognize a right of privacy originated in an 1890 law review essay by Samuel Warren and Louis Brandeis calling for "a general right to privacy for thoughts, emotions, and sensations," and focusing on tort law. After Brandeis was appointed to the Supreme Court, he advocated a "right to be let alone" from government intrusion in his dissent in *Olmstead v. United States*, 277 U.S. 438, 478 (1928).

In two forerunners to modern privacy jurisprudence, the Court used the Due Process Clause of the Fourteenth Amendment to strike down a law prohibiting the teaching of foreign languages in elementary schools, *Meyer v. Nebraska*, 262 U.S. 390 (1923), and a law requiring that all children attend public schools, *Pierce v. Society of Sisters*, 268 U.S. 510 (1925). Both decisions emphasized the rights of parents to control the education of their children and the limits on state power to indoctrinate, but neither referred to "privacy" as such. In *Meyer*, however, the Court described the "liberty" guaranteed by the Due Process Clause as follows:

> Without doubt it denotes not merely freedom from bodily restraint, but also the right of the individual to contract, to engage in any of the common occupations of life, to acquire useful knowledge, to marry, establish a home and bring up children, to worship God according to the dictates of his own conscience, and, generally, to enjoy those privileges long recognized at common law as essential to the orderly pursuit of happiness by free men. (262 U.S. at 399.)

The procreative aspect of privacy was presaged in *Skinner v. Oklahoma*, 316 U.S. 535 (1942), in which the Court struck down a law that permitted forced sterilization of persons convicted three times of certain crimes, but not of other similar crimes. The defendant had been convicted of robbery; had his offense been embezzlement, he would not have been subject to the sterilization law. The Court held that "[m]arriage and procreation are fundamental to the very existence and survival of the race," *id.* at 541, and thus subjected the classification drawn by the statute to strict scrutiny under the Equal Protection Clause.

As Sanger and her allies grew pessimistic about repealing the hold-out anti-contraception laws in Massachusetts and Connecticut, they invoked decisions like these to challenge the constitutionality of those statutes. Appeals to read broad exceptions into the statutes (*i.e.*, to adopt a *One Package* interpretation of state law) or to overturn them entirely lost by narrow margins in the Massachusetts Supreme Judicial Court in 1938 and the Connecticut Supreme Court in 1940. They turned to federal courts and made arguments combining the rights of doctors with a right of privacy. In 1961, a case reached the Supreme Court which did not resolve the issue, because the majority found that the plaintiffs had not shown sufficient harm. However, this case–*Poe v. Ullman*–did produce an extremely important opinion: the dissent of Justice Harlan, whose analysis of the tension between liberty and morality remains important to this day, even though the law has changed as to some of his examples. Following Justice Harlan's dissent in *Ullman*, you will read the opinions of the Justices in *Griswold v. Connecticut*, where the Court did reach the underlying issues and finally struck down the Connecticut birth control law. The victory in *Griswold* came nearly 50 years after Margaret Sanger served her 30–day prison sentence.

Paul and Pauline Poe et al. v. Abraham Ullman

United States Supreme Court, 1961.
367 U.S. 497, 81 S.Ct. 1752, 6 L.Ed.2d 989.

■ JUSTICE HARLAN, dissenting. [Justice Harlan began his argument by asserting that the Due Process Clause safeguards more than procedural rights.]

* * * Due process has not been reduced to any formula; its content cannot be determined by reference to any code. The best that can be said is that through the course of this Court's decisions it has represented the balance which our Nation, built upon postulates of respect for the liberty of the individual, has struck between that liberty and the demands of organized society. If the supplying of content to this Constitutional concept has of necessity been a rational process, it certainly has not been one where judges have felt free to roam where unguided speculation might take them. The balance of which I speak is the balance struck by this country, having regard to what history teaches are the traditions from which it developed as well as the traditions from which it broke. That tradition is a living thing. A decision of this Court which radically departs from it could not long survive, while a decision which builds on what has survived is likely to be sound. No formula could serve as a substitute, in this area, for judgment and restraint.

It is this outlook which has led the Court continuously to perceive distinctions in the imperative character of Constitutional provisions, since that character must be discerned from a particular provision's larger context. And inasmuch as this context is one not of words, but of history and purposes, the full scope of the liberty guaranteed by the Due Process Clause cannot be found in or limited by the precise terms of the specific guarantees elsewhere provided in the Constitution. This "liberty" is not a series of isolated points pricked out in terms of the taking of property; the freedom of speech, press, and religion; the right to keep and bear arms; the freedom from unreasonable searches and seizures; and so on. It is a rational continuum which, broadly speaking, includes a freedom from all substantial arbitrary impositions and purposeless restraints, and which also recognizes, what a reasonable and sensitive judgment must, that certain interests require particularly careful scrutiny of the state needs asserted to justify their abridgment.

* * * For it is the purposes of those guarantees and not their text, the reasons for their statement by the Framers and not the statement itself, which have led to their present status in the compendious notion of "liberty" embraced in the Fourteenth Amendment.

* * * Yet the very inclusion of the category of morality among state concerns indicates that society is not limited in its objects only to the physical well-being of the community, but has traditionally concerned itself with the moral soundness of its people as well. Indeed to attempt a line between public behavior and that which is purely consensual or solitary would be to withdraw from community concern a range of subjects with

which every society in civilized times has found it necessary to deal. The laws regarding marriage which provide both when the sexual powers may be used and the legal and societal context in which children are born and brought up, as well as laws forbidding adultery, fornication and homosexual practices which express the negative of the proposition, confining sexuality to lawful marriage, form a pattern so deeply pressed into the substance of our social life that any Constitutional doctrine in this area must build upon that basis.

It is in this area of sexual morality, which contains many proscriptions of consensual behavior having little or no direct impact on others, that the State of Connecticut has expressed its moral judgment that all use of contraceptives is improper. Appellants cite an impressive list of authorities who, from a great variety of points of view, commend the considered use of contraceptives by married couples. What they do not emphasize is that not too long ago the current of opinion was very probably quite the opposite, and that even today the issue is not free of controversy. Certainly, Connecticut's judgment is no more demonstrably correct or incorrect than are the varieties of judgment, expressed in law, on marriage and divorce, on adult consensual homosexuality, abortion, and sterilization, or euthanasia and suicide. If we had a case before us which required us to decide simply, and in abstraction, whether the moral judgment implicit in the application of the present statute to married couples was a sound one, the very controversial nature of these questions would, I think, require us to hesitate long before concluding that the Constitution precluded Connecticut from choosing as it has among these various views.

* * * Precisely what is involved here is this: the State is asserting the right to enforce its moral judgment by intruding upon the most intimate details of the marital relation with the full power of the criminal law. Potentially, this could allow the deployment of all the incidental machinery of the criminal law, arrests, searches and seizures; inevitably, it must mean at the very least the lodging of criminal charges, a public trial, and testimony as to the *corpus delicti*. Nor could any imaginable elaboration of presumptions, testimonial privileges, or other safeguards, alleviate the necessity for testimony as to the mode and manner of the married couples' sexual relations, or at least the opportunity for the accused to make denial of the charges. In sum, the statute allows the State to enquire into, prove and punish married people for the private use of their marital intimacy.

This, then, is the precise character of the enactment whose Constitutional measure we must take. The statute must pass a more rigorous Constitutional test than that going merely to the plausibility of its underlying rationale. This enactment involves what, by common understanding throughout the English-speaking world, must be granted to be a most fundamental aspect of "liberty," the privacy of the home in its most basic sense, and it is this which requires that the statute be subjected to "strict scrutiny." *Skinner*, 316 U.S. at 541. * * *

Of course, just as the requirement of a warrant is not inflexible in carrying out searches and seizures, so there are countervailing considerations at this more fundamental aspect of the right involved. "[T]he family * * * is not beyond regulation," *Prince v. Massachusetts*, [321 U.S. 158, 166 (1944)], and it would be an absurdity to suggest either that offenses may not be committed in the bosom of the family or that the home can be made a sanctuary for crime. The right of privacy most manifestly is not an absolute. Thus, I would not suggest that adultery, homosexuality, fornication and incest are immune from criminal enquiry, however privately practiced. So much has been explicitly recognized in acknowledging the State's rightful concern for its people's moral welfare. But not to discriminate between what is involved in this case and either the traditional offenses against good morals or crimes which, though they may be committed anywhere, happen to have been committed or concealed in the home, would entirely misconceive the argument that is being made.

Adultery, homosexuality and the like are sexual intimacies which the State forbids altogether, but the intimacy of husband and wife is necessarily an essential and accepted feature of the institution of marriage, an institution which the State not only must allow, but which always and in every age it has fostered and protected. It is one thing when the State exerts its power either to forbid extra-marital sexuality altogether, or to say who may marry, but it is quite another when, having acknowledged a marriage and the intimacies inherent in it, it undertakes to regulate by means of the criminal law the details of that intimacy.

In sum, even though the State has determined that the use of contraceptives is as iniquitous as any act of extra-marital sexual immorality, the intrusion of the whole machinery of the criminal law into the very heart of marital privacy, requiring husband and wife to render account before a criminal tribunal of their uses of that intimacy, is surely a very different thing indeed from punishing those who establish intimacies which the law has always forbidden and which can have no claim to social protection. * * *

Estelle Griswold et al. v. Connecticut

United States Supreme Court, 1965.
381 U.S. 479, 85 S.Ct. 1678, 14 L.Ed.2d 510.

■ JUSTICE DOUGLAS delivered the opinion of the Court [striking down the 1879 Connecticut law prohibiting the sale or use of contraceptives].

[W]e are met with a wide range of questions that implicate the Due Process Clause of the Fourteenth Amendment. * * * This law * * * operates directly on an intimate relation of husband and wife and their physician's role in one aspect of that relation.

The association of people is not mentioned in the Constitution nor in the Bill of Rights. The right to educate a child in a school of the parents' choice—whether public or private or parochial—is also not mentioned. Nor is the right to study any particular subject or any foreign language. Yet the First Amendment has been construed to include certain of those rights.

[The Court then reviewed *Meyer v. Nebraska* and *Pierce v. Society of Sisters*, as well as First Amendment cases dealing with freedom of association.]

The foregoing cases suggest that specific guarantees in the Bill of Rights have penumbras, formed by emanations from those guarantees that help give them life and substance. Various guarantees create zones of privacy. The right of association contained in the penumbra of the First Amendment is one, as we have seen. The Third Amendment in its prohibition against the quartering of soldiers "in any house" in time of peace without the consent of the owner is another facet of that privacy. The Fourth Amendment explicitly affirms the "right of the people to be secure in their persons, houses, papers, and effects, against unreasonable searches and seizures." The Fifth Amendment in its Self–Incrimination Clause enables the citizen to create a zone of privacy which government may not force him to surrender to his detriment. The Ninth Amendment provides: "The enumeration in the Constitution, of certain rights, shall not be construed to deny or disparage others retained by the people."

The Fourth and Fifth Amendments were described in *Boyd v. United States*, 116 U.S. 616, 630, as protection against all governmental invasions "of the sanctity of a man's home and the privacies of life." We recently referred in *Mapp v. Ohio*, 367 U.S. 643, 656, to the Fourth Amendment as creating a "right to privacy, no less important than any other right carefully and particularly reserved to the people." * * *

The present case, then, concerns a relationship lying within the zone of privacy created by several fundamental constitutional guarantees. And it concerns a law which, in forbidding the use of contraceptives rather than regulating their manufacture or sale, seeks to achieve its goals by means having a maximum destructive impact upon that relationship. Such a law cannot stand in light of the familiar principle, so often applied by this Court, that a "governmental purpose to control or prevent activities constitutionally subject to state regulation may not be achieved by means which sweep unnecessarily broadly and thereby invade the area of protected freedoms." *NAACP v. Alabama*, 377 U.S. 288, 307. Would we allow the police to search the sacred precincts of marital bedrooms for telltale signs of the use of contraceptives? The very idea is repulsive to the notions of privacy surrounding the marriage relationship.

We deal with a right of privacy older than the Bill of Rights—older than our political parties, older than our school system. Marriage is a coming together for better or for worse, hopefully enduring, and intimate to the degree of being sacred. It is an association that promotes a way of life, not causes; a harmony in living, not political faiths; a bilateral loyalty, not commercial or social projects. Yet it is an association for as noble a purpose as any involved in our prior decisions. * * *

■ JUSTICE GOLDBERG, joined by CHIEF JUSTICE WARREN and JUSTICE BRENNAN, concurred.

* * * This Court, in a series of decisions, has held that the Fourteenth Amendment absorbs and applies to the States those specifics of the first eight amendments which express fundamental personal rights. The language and history of the Ninth Amendment reveal that the Framers of the Constitution believed that there are additional fundamental rights, protected from governmental infringement, which exist alongside those fundamental rights specifically mentioned in the first eight constitutional amendments.

The Ninth Amendment simply shows the intent of the Constitution's authors that other fundamental personal rights should not be denied such protections or disparaged in any other way simply because they are not specifically listed in the first eight constitutional amendments. * * *

I [do not] mean to state that the Ninth Amendment constitutes an independent source of rights protected from infringement by either the States or the Federal Government. Rather, the Ninth Amendment shows a belief of the Constitution's authors that fundamental rights exist that are not expressly enumerated in the first eight amendments and an intent that the list of rights included there not be deemed exhaustive. * * *

And, the Ninth Amendment, in indicating that not all such liberties are specifically mentioned in the first eight amendments, is surely relevant in showing the existence of other fundamental personal rights, now protected from state, as well as federal, infringement. In sum, the Ninth Amendment simply lends strong support to the view that the 'liberty' protected by the Fifth and Fourteenth Amendments from infringement by the Federal Government or the States is not restricted to rights specifically mentioned in the first eight amendments. * * *

In determining which rights are fundamental, judges are not left at large to decide cases in light of their personal and private notions. Rather, they must look to the 'traditions and (collective) conscience of our people' to determine whether a principle is 'so rooted (there) * * * as to be ranked as fundamental.' The inquiry is whether a right involved is of such a character that it cannot be denied without violating those 'fundamental principles of liberty and justice which lie at the base of all our civil and political institutions' * * *

* * * Of this whole 'private realm of family life' it is difficult to imagine what is more private or more intimate than a husband and wife's marital relations.

The entire fabric of the Constitution and the purposes that clearly underlie its specific guarantees demonstrate that the rights to marital privacy and to marry and raise a family are of similar order and magnitude as the fundamental rights specifically protected.

* * * The fact that no particular provision of the Constitution explicitly forbids the State from disrupting the traditional relation of the family—a relation as old and as fundamental as our entire civilization—surely does not show that the Government was meant to have the power to do so. Rather, as the Ninth Amendment expressly recognizes, there are funda-

mental personal rights such as this one, which are protected from abridgment by the Government though not specifically mentioned in the Constitution.

■ [JUSTICE HARLAN concurred in the Court's opinion, based upon his dissenting opinion in *Poe v. Ullman*.]

■ JUSTICE WHITE, concurring in the judgment.

* * * [T]he statute is said to serve the State's policy against all forms of promiscuous or illicit sexual relationships, be they premarital or extramarital, concededly a permissible and legitimate legislative goal.

Without taking issue with the premise that the fear of conception operates as a deterrent to such relationships in addition to the criminal proscriptions Connecticut has against such conduct, I wholly fail to see how the ban on the use of contraceptives by married couples in any way reinforces the State's ban on illicit sexual relationships. Connecticut does not bar the importation or possession of contraceptive devices; they are not considered contraband material under state law, and their availability in that State is not seriously disputed. The only way Connecticut seeks to limit or control the availability of such devices is through its general aiding and abetting statute whose operation in this context has been quite obviously ineffective and whose most serious use has been against birth-control clinics rendering advice to married, rather than unmarried, persons. * * *

In these circumstances one is rather hard pressed to explain how the ban on use by married persons in any way prevents use of such devices by persons engaging in illicit sexual relations and thereby contributes to the State's policy against such relationships. Neither the state courts nor the State before the bar of this Court has tendered such an explanation. It is purely fanciful to believe that the broad proscription on use facilitates discovery of use by persons engaging in a prohibited relationship or for some other reason makes such use more unlikely and thus can be supported by any sort of administrative consideration. * * * At most the broad ban is of marginal utility to the declared objective. * * * I find nothing in this record justifying the sweeping scope of this statute, with its telling effect on the freedoms of married persons, and therefore conclude that it deprives such persons of liberty without due process of law.

■ [The dissenting opinions of JUSTICE BLACK and JUSTICE STEWART objected to the Court's creation of a constitutional right to "privacy" that is not moored in a firmer constitutional text. Although Justice Stewart found this an "uncommonly silly law," he and Justice Black found it violative of no provision of the Constitution.]

NOTES ON *GRISWOLD* AND THE RIGHT OF SEXUAL PRIVACY

1. *What Was the Best Constitutional Basis for the Result in* Griswold? In particular, which opinion best states a constitutional basis for a right of privacy? How do the jurisprudential approaches of Justices Douglas,

Goldberg, and Harlan differ? All three approaches create a right that is not clearly instantiated in the Constitution's text. Douglas' penumbral theory is the most creative, for he implies an underlying constitutional right from the emanations of existing provisions. Goldberg's reliance on the Ninth Amendment is only slightly less creative. Although he relies on actual text in the Constitution, the Ninth Amendment seems like a residual "catch-all" provision. Harlan's invocation of the Due Process Clause likewise relies on a specific provision but expands text that on its face refers only to process into a substantive provision with considerable constitutional bite.

Critics have accused the Court of becoming a "super-legislature" with this decision. Which approach (penumbras, Ninth Amendment, due process) best avoids this difficulty by tying the Court's decision to "principled" criteria that have a defensible connection to the Constitution? Does Justice White avoid the problem by focusing on the irrationality of the means? Is a broader opinion necessary?

2.   *The Justices' Reticence About Sex.* Identify where the Justices' opinions describe the contours of the right of privacy: What language is used? Is the Court most interested in the locale (*i.e.*, the home, the bedroom)? Or the relationship (marriage)? Or sexuality? To the extent the Court anchors the decision on marriage, what is the Court's understanding of that institution?

Note that the Court employs numerous euphemisms referring to sexual relations. The opinion stops just short of holding that the right to sexual relations within marriage is a fundamental right. Indeed, explicitness may be part of the problem. Perhaps one reason *Griswold* is so frustratingly vague is that the Court could not bring itself to be sexually explicit. An alternative view is that the Court's conscious goal was to insure social stability and reinforce traditional family structures. *See* Thomas Grey, "Eros, Civilization and the Burger Court," 43 *L. & Contemp. Probs.* 83 (1980). What do you think: Is *Griswold* about marriage? Sex? Procreation?

3.   *How the Lawyers Argued the Case.* The briefs in the case were more direct. The appellants' brief argued that "the inner core of the privacy right" lay in "the sanctity of the home and the intimacies of the sexual relationship in marriage." Counsel for appellants and for amicus Planned Parenthood in *Griswold* apparently drew on the language of the petitioner's brief and the ACLU's amicus brief in *Poe*. These were the first briefs to articulate a right of privacy for "sexual union and the right to bear and raise a family." Appellants' brief, written by Yale Law School Professor Fowler Harper, argued in *Poe* that "sexual pleasure" is an important end in itself, and frustration of one's preferred sexual outlet, by the state or otherwise, is psychologically harmful to the individual as well as the family. The ACLU brief, written by Melvin Wulf and Ruth Emerson, argued that the Connecticut law forced married couples to choose between planning the size of their family and engaging in sexual intercourse, which "is no choice at all." In *Poe*, the Planned Parenthood brief centered on the rights of the doctors and on the potential medical harm caused by the statute.

In *Griswold*, counsel for Planned Parenthood dramatically altered their arguments, beginning their brief with a claim for "privacy," not mentioned in their *Poe* brief, based on Harlan's dissent and the earlier arguments. The *Griswold* brief referred repeatedly to sexual relations and the "sex drive," cited Kinsey's study on sexuality, and argued that restricting sexual intercourse to procreation is not a legitimate state purpose. Like the earlier briefs, it carefully linked sexuality to marriage, however. The brief framed the privacy right as one to engage in marital sexual relations *and* to decide whether to have children. Given the one-way operation of the statute, that phrasing is euphemistic for having sexual relations and *not* having children, but it is framed as the right to decide, a conscience right. What strategic choices are embedded in this shift? Were they wise?

4. *Marriage and Sex: An Implicit Promise?* Are there other contexts in which the state recognizes a right to sexual relations in marriage? And indeed enforces it? "The point is that the state has undertaken to sponsor one institution that has at its core the love-sex relationship. That relationship demands liberty in the practice of the sexual act." Harry Wellington, "Common Law Rules and Constitutional Double Standards: Some Notes on Adjudication," 83 *Yale L.J.* 221, 292 (1973). The practical import of the Connecticut statute would be to force married couples to modify the frequency of intercourse in order to avoid pregnancy, a result which, according to Wellington, "smacks of fraud." *Id.* at 293. *Cf. Barretta v. Barretta*, 46 N.Y.S.2d 261 (Sup. Ct. Queens Cty. 1944) (denying request for separation by wife who had refused sexual relations with her husband unless he used contraceptives, on the ground that her refusal violated the marital contract and was contrary to public policy of the state).

5. *Racial Issues.* During the same 1964 Term in which *Griswold* was argued, the Court also decided *McLaughlin v. Florida*, 379 U.S. 184 (1964). In *McLaughlin*, the Court struck down a Florida law forbidding interracial cohabitation because it violated equal protection. Florida defended the fornication provision as auxiliary to another section of the same statute that prohibited interracial marriage. The Court declined to examine whether the state's purpose of deterring interracial sexual relations was valid, but instead held that a race-neutral fornication law served that purpose as well as a race-specific one. Two terms later, the Court tackled the miscegenation issue head-on and ruled the Virginia law unconstitutional in *Loving v. Virginia*, 388 U.S. 1 (1967) (Chapter 3).

6. *"Safer Sex" for Women? The Forgotten Equality Argument.* In today's terms, we might refer to birth control as "safer sex" for heterosexual women. Is a sex discrimination claim possible on the facts of *Griswold*? If so what would it be? Why was its possibility not mentioned in either *Griswold* or *Poe*? See Chapter 3 for a discussion of sex discrimination law.

7. *The Public–Private Dynamic and the Role of Clinics.* The problem that the plaintiffs in both the Connecticut cases had in formulating a test case was that there had never been a prosecution against private doctors for violating the law, although their activities in prescribing contraceptives were well known. Nor had any but a few been prosecuted for purchasing condoms. What the law did succeed in doing, however, was to prevent the establishment of an openly operating birth control clinic in Connecticut after 1940, when the Connecticut courts upheld the statute and refused to import a *One Package* medical exception into its broad terms.

Note several ironies. The right recognized in *Griswold* purports to protect "private" sphere activities in the spirit of John Stuart Mill and Louis Brandeis. Because the contraceptive gendarmerie did not patrol bedrooms and contraceptives were available in drug stores, the private sphere (the marital bedroom) was essentially unregulated, leaving only the public sphere (birth control clinics) to actual regulation. But look again. The public sphere for men's access to condoms was not policed; only the clinics (which prescribed diaphragms and later pills for women) were. Most women in Connecticut found it hard to practice birth control (private sphere) without access to birth control clinics that could provide information (public sphere). A final look: The Roman Catholic Church, which had spearheaded political opposition to repealing anti-contraception laws, believed that the anti-procreation features of contraception (private sphere) had profound implications for marriage and religious community (public sphere). The availability of contraception, whether private or public, undermined the private as well as public (procreative) goals of marriage.

In short, the concept of "privacy" is easy to deconstruct. Does this ease of deconstruction vitiate the usefulness of the concept?

8. *Foundational Critiques of the Right of Privacy.* Probably the most controversial debate triggered by Griswold has focused on what process the judiciary should use to identify and recognize a substantive due process right, *i.e.*, an intrinsic component of liberty under the Due Process Clause. It is especially difficult to derive guidance from this decision, because not only are there four separate opinions from a seven-person majority, but most of them focus on what Justice Harlan termed "the obnoxiously intrusive means" chosen by the state to effectuate its goals. Before imposing the strictest level of scrutiny on the means, however, a court must find that a "fundamental" due process right is abridged.

After *Griswold*, which focused heavily on marriage, Massachusetts amended its birth control law to forbid the distribution of contraceptives only to unmarried persons. Planned Parenthood challenged that law, and this case confronted the Supreme Court again with the tension between liberty and morality.

Thomas Eisenstadt v. William Baird

United States Supreme Court, 1972.
405 U.S. 438, 92 S.Ct. 1029, 31 L.Ed.2d 349.

■ Justice Brennan delivered the opinion of the Court.

Appellee William Baird was convicted * * * first, for exhibiting contraceptive articles in the course of delivering a lecture on contraception to a group of students at Boston University and, second, for giving a young woman a package of Emko vaginal foam at the close of his address. * * *

Massachusetts General Laws Ann., c. 272, § 21, under which Baird was convicted, provides a maximum five-year term of imprisonment for "whoever ... gives away ... any drug, medicine, instrument or article whatever for the prevention of conception," except as authorized in § 21A. Under § 21A, "(a) registered physician may administer to or prescribe for any married person drugs or articles intended for the prevention of pregnancy or conception. [And a] registered pharmacist actually engaged in the business of pharmacy may furnish such drugs or articles to any married person presenting a prescription from a registered physician." As interpreted by the State Supreme Judicial Court, these provisions make it a felony for anyone, other than a registered physician or pharmacist acting in accordance with the terms of § 21A, to dispense any article with the intention that it be used for the prevention of conception. The statutory scheme distinguishes among three distinct classes of distributees—first, married persons may obtain contraceptives to prevent pregnancy, but only from doctors or druggists on prescription; second, single persons may not obtain contraceptives from anyone to prevent pregnancy; and, third, married or single persons may obtain contraceptives from anyone to prevent, not pregnancy, but the spread of disease. This construction of state law is, of course, binding on us.

The legislative purposes that the statute is meant to serve are not altogether clear. In *Commonwealth v. Baird*, the Supreme Judicial Court [of Massachusetts] noted only the State's interest in protecting the health of its citizens: "[T]he prohibition in § 21," the court declared, "is directly related to" the State's goal of "preventing the distribution of articles designed to prevent conception which may have undesirable, if not dangerous, physical consequences." In a subsequent decision, *Sturgis v. Attorney General*, 260 N.E.2d 687, 690 (1970), the court, however, found "a second and more compelling ground for upholding the statute"—namely, to protect morals through "regulating the private sexual lives of single persons." The Court of Appeals, for reasons that will appear, did not consider the promotion of health or the protection of morals through the deterrence of fornication to be the legislative aim. Instead, the court concluded that the statutory goal was to limit contraception in and of itself—a purpose that the court held conflicted "with fundamental human rights" under *Griswold*, where this Court struck down Connecticut's prohibition against the use of contraceptives as an unconstitutional infringement of the right of marital privacy.

We agree that the goals of deterring premarital sex and regulating the distribution of potentially harmful articles cannot reasonably be regarded as legislative aims of §§ 21 and 21A. And we hold that the statute, viewed as a prohibition on contraception *per se*, violates the rights of single persons under the Equal Protection Clause of the Fourteenth Amendment. * * *

* * * The question for our determination in this case is whether there is some ground of difference that rationally explains the different treatment accorded married and unmarried persons under Massachusetts Gen-

eral Laws Ann., c. 272, §§ 21 and 21A. For the reasons that follow, we conclude that no such ground exists.

First. Section 21 stems from Mass. Stat. 1879, c. 159, § 1, which prohibited without exception, distribution of articles intended to be used as contraceptives. In *Commonwealth v. Allison*, 116 N.E. 265, 266 (1917), the Massachusetts Supreme Judicial Court explained that the law's "plain purpose is to protect purity, to preserve chastity, to encourage continence and self restraint, to defend the sanctity of the home, and thus to engender in the State and nation a virile and virtuous race of men and women." Although the State clearly abandoned that purpose with the enactment of § 21A, at least insofar as the illicit sexual activities of married persons are concerned, the court reiterated in *Sturgis*, that the object of the legislation is to discourage premarital sexual intercourse. Conceding that the State could, consistently with the Equal Protection Clause, regard the problems of extramarital and premarital sexual relations as "[e]vils ... of different dimensions and proportions, requiring different remedies," *Williamson v. Lee Optical*, 348 U.S. 483, 489 (1955), we cannot agree that the deterrence of premarital sex may reasonably be regarded as the purpose of the Massachusetts law.

It would be plainly unreasonable to assume that Massachusetts has prescribed pregnancy and the birth of an unwanted child as punishment for fornication, which is a misdemeanor under Massachusetts General Laws Ann., c. 272, § 18. Aside from the scheme of values that assumption would attribute to the State, it is abundantly clear that the effect of the ban on distribution of contraceptives to unmarried persons has at best a marginal relation to the proffered objective. * * * §§ 21 and 21A do not at all regulate the distribution of contraceptives when they are to be used to prevent, not pregnancy, but the spread of disease. Nor, in making contraceptives available to married persons without regard to their intended use, does Massachusetts attempt to deter married persons from engaging in illicit sexual relations with unmarried persons. Even on the assumption that the fear of pregnancy operates as a deterrent to fornication, the Massachusetts statute is thus so riddled with exceptions that deterrence of premarital sex cannot reasonably be regarded as its aim. * * *

Second. Section 21A was added to the Massachusetts General Laws by Stat. 1966, c. 265, §§ 1. The Supreme Judicial Court in *Baird* held that the purpose of the amendment was to serve the health needs of the community by regulating the distribution of potentially harmful articles. It is plain that Massachusetts had no such purpose in mind before the enactment of § 21A. As the Court of Appeals remarked, "Consistent with the fact that the statute was contained in a chapter dealing with 'Crimes Against Chastity, Morality, Decency and Good Order,' it was cast only in terms of morals. A physician was forbidden to prescribe contraceptives even when needed for the protection of health." Nor did the Court of Appeals "believe that the legislature [in enacting § 21A] suddenly reversed its field and developed an interest in health. Rather, it merely made what it thought to be the precise accommodation necessary to escape the *Griswold* ruling."

Again, we must agree with the Court of Appeals. If health were the rationale of § 21A, the statute would be both discriminatory and overbroad. * * * If there is need to have physician prescribe (and a pharmacist dispense) contraceptives, that need is as great for unmarried persons as for married persons. * * *

Third. If the Massachusetts statute cannot be upheld as a deterrent to fornication or as a health measure, may it, nevertheless, be sustained simply as a prohibition on contraception? The Court of Appeals analysis "led inevitably to the conclusion that, so far as morals are concerned, it is contraceptives *per se* that are considered immoral—to the extent that *Griswold* will permit such a declaration." We need not, however, decide that important question in this case because, whatever the rights of the individual to access to contraceptives may be, the rights must be the same for the unmarried and the married alike.

If under *Griswold* the distribution of contraceptives to married persons cannot be prohibited, a ban on distribution to unmarried persons would be equally impermissible. It is true that in *Griswold* the right of privacy in question inhered in the marital relationship. Yet the marital couple is not an independent entity with a mind and heart of its own, but an association of two individuals each with a separate intellectual and emotional makeup. If the right of privacy means anything, it is the right of the *individual*, married or single, to be free from unwarranted governmental intrusion into matters so fundamentally affecting a person as the decision whether to bear or beget a child.

* * * Mr. Justice Jackson, concurring in *Railway Express Agency v. New York*, 336 U.S. 106, 112–13 (1949), made the point:

> * * * Conversely, nothing opens the door to arbitrary action so effectively as to allow those officials to pick and choose only a few to whom they will apply legislation and thus to escape the political retribution that might be visited upon them if larger numbers were affected. Courts can take no better measure to assure that laws will be just than to require that laws be equal in operation. * * *

[T]he principle * * * has equal application to the legislation here. We hold that by providing dissimilar treatment for married and unmarried persons who are similarly situated, Massachusetts General Laws Ann., c. 272, §§ 21 and 21A, violate the Equal Protection Clause.

■ JUSTICE POWELL and JUSTICE REHNQUIST took no part in the consideration or decision of this case.

■ [JUSTICE DOUGLAS concurred in the result on the ground that Baird's First Amendment rights were violated. Justice Douglas argued that Baird's act of passing around one sample of vaginal foam was protected as ancillary to his speech. JUSTICE WHITE and JUSTICE BLACKMUN concurred in the result, on the grounds that there was no evidence to suggest that medical supervision was necessary to protect health when the contraceptive being distributed was, as here, vaginal foam; nor was there record evidence as to the recipient's marital status. CHIEF JUSTICE BURGER dissented on the grounds that there was "nothing arbitrary in a requirement of medical supervision."]

NOTES ON *EISENSTADT* AND THE EXPANDING PRIVACY RIGHT

1. *What Was the State's Interest Underlying This Statute?* Justice Brennan's opinion refused to accept either a morals or a health concern as the basis for the statute because he found both to be so imperfectly related to the impact of the law. In its brief and in oral argument, the state had claimed both justifications. Does this rationale hold up?

Essentially the same questions regarding the legitimacy of the state's interest in using anti-contraceptive laws to discourage sexual activity arose in the context of a New York statute prohibiting distribution of contraceptives to persons younger than 16, except by a physician. *Carey v. Population Services International*, 431 U.S. 678 (1977). In *Carey*, Justice Brennan again wrote a plurality opinion for four Justices, holding that minors have a privacy right that includes access to contraceptives, and that a state cannot impose restrictions on contraception for the purpose of deterring sexual activity by increasing the hazards of engaging in it. *Id.* at 694–95. Justice Stevens derided as "frivolous" the plurality's argument "that a minor has the constitutional right to put contraceptives to their intended use," but agreed with the plurality's result, because the state could not communicate its policy against teenage sexuality by imposing a risk of physical harm, regardless of whether minors had an underlying constitutional right. *Id.* at 713–16. Also concurring in the result, Justice Powell wrote that the state's interest in deterring such activity was sufficient to withstand review, although the New York statute failed because it infringed the rights of married teenagers and of parents. *Id.* at 703–08. Justice White did not reach the question of the propriety of the state's interest because he found that there was no indication that the statute actually had a deterrent effect. *Id.* at 702–03.

2. *From Sex to Procreation in Three Easy Steps.* Justice Brennan found that the "real" state interest was that the legislature had considered "contraceptives *per se*" to be immoral. In other words, he rejected the notion that the state's interest in morality was the instrumental one of deterring nonmarital sexual activities, but rather was the intrinsic immorality of preventing new life. Apply Brennan's over-and under-inclusiveness analyses to this rationale—how does it fare? This first step eliminated any need to scrutinize the sexual morality justification.

Both the plaintiffs and *amicus* Planned Parenthood had argued that even if the state could criminalize nonmarital sexual conduct, it could not penalize it by the less direct, but harsher, method of forcing individuals to risk pregnancy as a result. Such a means to that end, they argued, was arbitrary and capricious. Brennan sidestepped the question of what means could be utilized toward that end, however, by step two: finding that "whatever the rights of the individual to access contraceptives may be, the rights must be the same for the unmarried and married alike." Thus, equal protection doctrine decides the case.

In step three, the Court returns to privacy. Brennan elaborated the holding with what is the most quoted portion of the opinion, the "[i]f the right of privacy means anything" sentence. At the end of that sentence, we have arrived at "the right to decide whether to bear or beget a child." With marriage absent from the case, Brennan ignored those aspects of *Griswold* that focused on sexuality, and instead grounded this opinion solely in the decision-making aspects of procreation. By step three, the Court had substituted procreation for sexuality or sexual morality. Does that work? Is the conclusion supported by the cases Brennan cites? Is it a euphemistic cop-out or an artful dodge?

Note when you read *Lawrence v. Texas* in the next section, that Justice Kennedy's opinion for the Court not only answers the question of whether consenting adults have a right of privacy outside the context of procreative decision-making, but that in doing so, he cites this language in *Eisenstadt* as support, thus obviating the linguistic minuet from thirty years earlier.

3. *The Role of Doctors.* In an ironic turning of the tables, Chief Justice Burger would have used the fact that a non-physician distributed the contraceptive as grounds for upholding the restrictive statute. Planned Parenthood had argued in its *amicus* brief that the statutory requirement of a doctor's involvement, when the device carried no risk, violated the Equal Protection Clause because as applied, it discriminated against the poor who could not afford physicians. The Planned Parenthood *amicus* brief also contained, for the first time since Margaret Sanger's early, more radical days, an explicit sex discrimination argument.

THE RIGHT TO CHOOSE ABORTION

By the time the last contraception laws were swept off the books, a powerful "pro-choice" social movement had formed around the issue of abortion: If contraception was not available or was unable to prevent pregnancy before the fact, abortion ought to be available after the fact. Doctors (fearful of state liability) joined feminists in pushing for a revision of abortion laws. Many states modernized their laws to allow abortion under specified circumstances, and four states repealed their laws altogether by 1972. As the civil rights and planned parenthood movements had done, the pro-choice movement went to court. The case that reached the Supreme Court and defined the right to choose began with a women's liberation group at the University of Texas in which the members first sought to provide counseling for women who wanted abortions, and then decided to challenge the law itself. The challengers in *Roe v. Wade* maintained that state prohibitions, and even regulation, of abortion violated *Griswold*'s privacy right. Because "a pregnancy to a woman is perhaps one of the most determinative aspects of her life," argued Sarah Weddington for the unmarried pregnant plaintiff, it is of fundamental importance that she have the freedom to terminate it. Texas argued that its interest in human life justified broad regulatory authority. The state's brief contained eight pages of photographs of the human fetus *in utero* to make its point.

At its conference on December 16, 1971, the seven-member Court was unusually fragmented. At least four Justices voted to strike the Texas statute, but the Chief Justice (who voted to uphold) assigned the opinion to a relatively new Justice, Harry Blackmun. Blackmun circulated an opinion striking down the law as unconstitutionally "vague" but other Justices did not want to rely on that reasoning. Given the disagreements, Burger took the opportunity to set the cases for reargument the next Term, when two new Brethren (Powell and Rehnquist) could participate. The vote to strike the statute was even stronger the next time around: six Justices voted to invalidate the law on privacy grounds, with two in dissent and the Chief concurring in the result.

Jane Roe v. Henry Wade

United States Supreme Court, 1973.
410 U.S. 113, 93 S.Ct. 705, 35 L.Ed.2d 147.

■ JUSTICE BLACKMUN delivered the opinion of the Court.

This [appeal presents] constitutional challenges to state criminal abortion legislation. The Texas statutes under attack here [which make procuring an abortion a crime except "by medical advice for the purpose of saving the life of the mother"] are typical of those that have been in effect in many states for approximately a century. * * *

* * * [The] restrictive criminal abortion laws in effect in a majority of States today are of relatively recent vintage. * * * [They] derive from statutory changes effected, for the most part, in the later half of the 19th century.

* * * [Abortion] was practiced in Greek times as well as in the Roman Era. * * * If abortion was prosecuted in some places, it seems to have been based on a concept of a violation of the father's right to his offspring. Ancient religion did not bar abortion. * * *

* * * [At] common law, abortion performed before "quickening"—the first recognizable movement of the fetus *in utero*, appearing usually from the 16th to the 18th week of pregnancy—was not an indictable offense. [Justice Blackmun explored the historiographical debates over the precise common law position and concluded that it was not until the middle and late 19th century that the "quickening" distinction was abandoned and the degree of the offense and the penalties increased, both in England and in the American states.]

It is thus apparent that at common law, at the time of the adoption of our Constitution, and throughout the major portion of the 19th century, abortion was viewed with less disfavor than under most American statutes currently in effect. Phrasing it another way, a woman enjoyed a substantially broader right to terminate a pregnancy than she does in most States today. At least with respect to the early stage of pregnancy, and very possibly without such a limitation, the opportunity to make this choice was present in this country well into the 19th century. * * *

Three reasons have been advanced to explain historically the enactment of criminal abortion laws in the 19th century and to justify their continued existence.

It has been argued occasionally that these laws were the product of a Victorian social concern to discourage illicit sexual conduct. Texas, however, does not advance this justification in the present case, and it appears that no court or commentator has taken the argument seriously. * * *

A second reason is concerned with abortion as a medical procedure. When most criminal abortion laws were first enacted, the procedure was a hazardous one for the woman. Thus, it has been argued that a State's real concern in enacting a criminal abortion law was to protect the pregnant woman, that is, to restrain her from submitting to a procedure that placed her life in serious jeopardy.

Modern medical techniques have altered this situation. * * * Mortality rates for women undergoing early abortions [appear] to be as low as or lower than the rates for normal childbirth. * * * Of course, important state interests in the areas of health and medical standards do remain. The State has a legitimate interest in seeing to it that abortion, like any other medical procedure, is performed under circumstances that insure maximum safety for the patient. * * * Thus, the State retains a definite interest in protecting the woman's own health and safety when an abortion is proposed at a late stage of pregnancy.

The third reason is the State's interest—some phrase it in terms of duty—in protecting prenatal life. Some of the argument for this justification rests on the theory that a new human life is present from the moment of conception. * * * In assessing the State's interest, recognition may [also] be given to the less rigid claim that as long as at least *potential* life is involved, the state may assert interests beyond the protection of the pregnant woman * * *

The Constitution does not explicitly mention any right of privacy. [But] the Court has recognized that a right of personal privacy, or a guarantee of certain areas or zones of privacy, does exist under the Constitution. In varying contexts, the Court or individual Justices have, indeed, found at least the roots of that right in the First Amendment; in the Fourth and Fifth Amendments; in the penumbras of the Bill of Rights; or in the concept of liberty guaranteed by the first section of the Fourteenth Amendment. These decisions make it clear that only personal rights deemed "fundamental" or "implicit in the concept of ordered liberty," *Palko v. Connecticut*, 302 U.S. 319, 325 (1937), are included in this guarantee of personal privacy. * * *

This right of privacy, whether it be founded in the Fourteenth Amendment's concept of personal liberty and restrictions upon state action, as we feel it is, or, as the District Court determined, in the Ninth Amendment's reservation of rights to the people, is broad enough to encompass a woman's decision whether or not to terminate her pregnancy. The detriment that the State would impose upon the pregnant woman by denying this choice altogether is apparent. Specific and direct harm medically diagnosable even in early pregnancy may be involved. Maternity, or additional offspring, may force upon the woman a distressful life and future. Psychological harm may be imminent. Mental and physical health may be taxed by child care. There is also the distress, for all concerned, associated with the unwanted child, and there is the problem of bringing a child into a family already unable, psychologically and otherwise, to care for it. In other cases, [the] additional difficulties and continuing stigma of unwed motherhood may be involved. All these are factors the woman and her responsible physician necessarily will consider in consultation.

On the basis of elements such as these, appellant and some *amici* argue that the woman's right is absolute and that she is entitled to terminate her pregnancy at whatever time, in whatever way, and for whatever reason she alone chooses. With this we do not agree. * * * The Court's decisions recognizing a right of privacy also acknowledge that some state regulation in areas protected by that right is appropriate. As noted above, a State may properly assert important interests in safeguarding

health, in maintaining medical standards, and in protecting potential life.
* * *

[Justice Blackmun set the "compelling" point, where the state can begin regulation, at approximately the end of the first trimester, when the fetus "quickens" in the old common law sense. During the first trimester the state cannot interfere with decisions by "the attending physician, in consultation with his patient." During the second trimester the state can set licensing and other medical regulations to protect the safety of the mother and to recognize the potential life.]

■ [We omit the separate concurring opinions of JUSTICES STEWART and DOUGLAS and of CHIEF JUSTICE BURGER. JUSTICES WHITE and REHNQUIST dissented in separate opinions.]

NOTE ON THE ABORTION RIGHT FROM *ROE* TO *CASEY*

The pro-choice movement and its astounding constitutional victory triggered a "pro-life" counter-movement seeking to preserve traditional ideas about family and the origins of human life. *Roe v. Wade* energized the counter-movement, which persuaded state legislatures to adopt numerous measures to make abortions more difficult for women, including (1) rules against abortions for minors without parental consent or (2) for wives without their husbands' consent; (3) requirements that women be given state-specified information (meant to discourage this choice) and (4) be required to wait for a period of time before they could have abortions; (5) refusal to fund abortions in state Medicaid and employee health insurance programs; and (6) closure of municipal hospitals to abortions.

In the wake of *Roe*, the Court invalidated most of the new restrictions in categories (1)–(4), and none in categories (5)–(6). In the 1980s, the Reagan Administration mounted a constitutional attack on *Roe v. Wade*. Justice Department officials argued that *Roe* created a fundamental right that was not supported by constitutional text, intent, or traditions; denigrated the state's interest in potential human life without any legal or moral basis; and engaged in judicial activism in the teeth of popular demands for regulation of this controversial activity. *Roe's* fate seemed sealed when Justices Brennan and Marshall left the Court and were replaced by Bush I appointees David Souter and Clarence Thomas. The next abortion case to reach the Court, from Pennsylvania, elicited a powerful debate on due process principles.

Planned Parenthood of Southeastern Pennsylvania v. Robert Casey

United States Supreme Court, 1992.
505 U.S. 833, 112 S.Ct. 2791, 120 L.Ed.2d 674.

■ JUSTICE O'CONNOR, JUSTICE KENNEDY, and JUSTICE SOUTER announced the judgment of the Court and delivered the opinion of the Court with respect to Parts I, II, and III. [This is referred to by the other Justices and in our Notes as the "Joint Opinion."]

[Pennsylvania required a woman seeking an abortion to wait 24 hours (except in a medical emergency), so that she could consider information regarding the nature and risks of the procedure and the probable gestational age of the fetus, which the law required the physician to provide. The law required minors to obtain the consent of one parent, with a judicial-bypass option. Married women were required to notify their spouses.]

I.   Liberty finds no refuge in a jurisprudence of doubt. Yet 19 years after our holding that the Constitution protects a woman's right to terminate her pregnancy in its early stages, *Roe v. Wade*, that definition of liberty is still questioned. Joining the respondents as *amicus curiae*, the United States, as it has done in five other cases in the last decade, again asks us to overrule *Roe*. * * *

After considering the fundamental constitutional questions resolved by *Roe*, principles of institutional integrity, and the rule of *stare decisis*, we are led to conclude this: the essential holding of *Roe v. Wade* should be retained and once again reaffirmed.

It must be stated at the outset and with clarity that *Roe*'s essential holding, the holding we reaffirm, has three parts. First is a recognition of the right of the woman to choose to have an abortion before viability and to obtain it without undue interference from the State. Before viability, the State's interests are not strong enough to support a prohibition of abortion or the imposition of a substantial obstacle to the woman's effective right to elect the procedure. Second is a confirmation of the State's power to restrict abortions after fetal viability, if the law contains exceptions for pregnancies which endanger a woman's life or health. And third is the principle that the State has legitimate interests from the outset of the pregnancy in protecting the health of the woman and the life of the fetus that may become a child. These principles do not contradict one another; and we adhere to each.

II.   Constitutional protection of the woman's decision to terminate her pregnancy derives from the Due Process Clause of the Fourteenth Amendment. It declares that no State shall "deprive any person of life, liberty, or property, without due process of law." The controlling word in the case before us is "liberty." Although a literal reading of the Clause might suggest that it governs only the procedures by which a State may deprive persons of liberty, for at least 105 years * * * the Clause has been understood to contain a substantive component as well, one "barring certain government actions regardless of the fairness of the procedures used to implement them." * * * "[T]he guaranties of due process, though having their roots in Magna Carta's *'per legem terrae'* and considered as procedural safeguards 'against executive usurpation and tyranny,' have in this country 'become bulwarks also against arbitrary legislation.' " *Poe v. Ullman* (Harlan, J., dissenting from dismissal on jurisdictional grounds). * * *

It is * * * tempting * * * to suppose that the Due Process Clause protects only those practices, defined at the most specific level, that were protected against government interference by other rules of law when the Fourteenth Amendment was ratified. But such a view would be inconsistent with our law. It is a premise of the Constitution that there is a realm of personal liberty which the government may not enter. We have vindicated this principle before. Marriage is mentioned nowhere in the Bill of Rights and interracial marriage was illegal in most States in the 19th century, but the Court was no doubt correct in finding it to be an aspect of liberty protected against state interference by the substantive component of the Due Process Clause in *Loving*. * * *

Neither the Bill of Rights nor the specific practices of States at the time of the adoption of the Fourteenth Amendment marks the outer limits of the substantive sphere of liberty which the Fourteenth Amendment protects. See U.S. Const., Amend. 9. As the second Justice Harlan recognized in [*Poe v. Ullman*]:

> * * * "[L]iberty" is not a series of isolated points pricked out in terms of the taking of property; the freedom of speech, press, and religion; the right to keep and bear arms; the freedom from unreasonable searches and seizures; and so on. It is a rational continuum which, broadly speaking, includes a freedom from all substantial arbitrary impositions and purposeless restraints[.] * * *

Justice Harlan wrote these words in addressing an issue the full Court did not reach in *Poe v. Ullman*, but the Court adopted his position four Terms later in *Griswold v. Connecticut*. * * * It is settled now, as it was when the Court heard arguments in *Roe v. Wade*, that the Constitution places limits on a State's right to interfere with a person's most basic decisions about family and parenthood, as well as bodily integrity.

The inescapable fact is that adjudication of substantive due process claims may call upon the Court in interpreting the Constitution to exercise that same capacity which by tradition courts always have exercised: reasoned judgment. Its boundaries are not susceptible of expression as a simple rule. That does not mean we are free to invalidate state policy choices with which we disagree; yet neither does it permit us to shrink from the duties of our office. [The Joint Opinion again quoted Justice Harlan's *Poe* dissent.]

Men and women of good conscience can disagree, and we suppose some always shall disagree, about the profound moral and spiritual implications of terminating a pregnancy, even in its earliest stage. Some of us as individuals find abortion offensive to our most basic principles of morality, but that cannot control our decision. Our obligation is to define the liberty of all, not to mandate our own moral code. * * *

Our law affords constitutional protection to personal decisions relating to marriage, procreation, contraception, family relationships, child rearing, and education. Our cases recognize "the right of the *individual*, married or single, to be free from unwarranted governmental intrusion into matters so fundamentally affecting a person as the decision whether to bear or beget a child." *Eisenstadt v. Baird* (emphasis in original). Our precedents "have respected the private realm of family life which the state cannot enter." These matters, involving the most intimate and personal choices a person may make in a lifetime, choices central to personal dignity and autonomy, are central to the liberty protected by the Fourteenth Amendment. At the heart of liberty is the right to define one's own concept of existence, of meaning, of the universe, and of the mystery of human life. Beliefs about these matters could not define the attributes of personhood were they formed under compulsion of the State.

These considerations begin our analysis of the woman's interest in terminating her pregnancy but cannot end it, for this reason: though the abortion decision may originate within the zone of conscience and belief, it is more than a philosophic exercise. Abortion is a unique act. It is an act fraught with consequences for others: for the woman who must live with the implications of her decision; for the persons who perform and assist in the procedure; for the spouse, family, and society which must confront the knowledge that these procedures exist, procedures some deem nothing short of an act of violence against innocent human life; and, depending on one's beliefs, for the life or potential life that is aborted. Though abortion is conduct, it does not follow that the State is entitled to proscribe it in all instances. That is because the liberty of the woman is at stake in a sense unique to the human condition and so unique to the law. The mother who carries a child to full term is subject to anxieties, to physical constraints, to pain that only she must bear. That these sacrifices have from the beginning of the human race been endured by woman with a pride that ennobles her in the eyes of others and gives to the infant a bond of love cannot alone be grounds for the State to insist she make the sacrifice. Her suffering is too intimate and personal for the State to insist, without more, upon its own vision of the woman's role, however dominant that vision has been in the course of our history and our culture. The destiny of the woman must be shaped to a large extent on her own conception of her spiritual imperatives and her place in society.

It should be recognized, moreover, that in some critical respects the abortion decision is of the same character as the decision to use contraception, to which *Griswold v. Connecticut, Eisenstadt v. Baird,* and *Carey v. Population Services International* afford constitutional protection. We have no doubt as to the correctness of those decisions. They support the reasoning in *Roe* relating to the woman's liberty because they involve personal decisions concerning not only the meaning of procreation but also human responsibility and respect for it. * * *

While we appreciate the weight of the arguments made on behalf of the State in the case before us, arguments which in their ultimate formulation conclude that *Roe* should be overruled, the reservations any of us may have in reaffirming the central holding of *Roe* are outweighed by the explication of individual liberty we have given combined with the force of *stare decisis*. We turn now to that doctrine.

III. [The Joint Opinion analyzes whether *stare decisis* should apply and concludes that it should: " * * * The sum of the precedential inquiry * * * shows *Roe*'s underpinnings unweakened in any way affecting its central holding. While it has engendered disapproval, it has not been unworkable."]

* * * The Court's duty in the present case is clear. In 1973, it confronted the already-divisive issue of governmental power to limit personal choice to undergo abortion, for which it provided a new resolution based on the due process guaranteed by the Fourteenth Amendment. Whether or not a new social consensus is developing on that issue, its divisiveness is no less today than in 1973, and pressure to overrule the decision, like pressure to retain it, has grown only more intense. A decision to overrule *Roe*'s essential holding under the existing circumstances would address error, if error there was, at the cost of both profound and unnecessary damage to the Court's legitimacy, and to the Nation's commitment to the rule of law. It is therefore imperative to adhere to the essence of *Roe*'s original decision, and we do so today.

IV. [The Court upheld the viability line as the point before which a pregnant woman has a right to choose abortion, but rejected the trimester framework of *Roe*. Instead the Joint Opinion adopted an "undue burden" standard, under which plaintiffs must show "that a state regulation has the purpose or effect of placing a substantial obstacle in the path of a woman seeking an abortion of a nonviable fetus." Under that test, the Court upheld Pennsylvania's requirements for a waiting period, the reading to the woman of mandated information about what occurs in an abortion, and consent by one parent if a minor was seeking abortion.]

VI. Our Constitution is a covenant running from the first generation of Americans to us and then to future generations. It is a coherent succession. Each generation must learn anew that the Constitution's written terms embody ideas and aspirations that must survive more ages than one. We accept our responsibility not to retreat from interpreting the full meaning of the covenant in light of all of our precedents. We invoke it once again to define the freedom guaranteed by the Constitution's own promise, the promise of liberty.

[**Justices Blackmun** and **Stevens** filed concurring opinions, applauding Parts I through III of the Joint Opinion, but arguing that the *Roe* trimester system should be retained.]

[**Chief Justice Rehnquist**, joined by **Justices White**, **Scalia**, and **Thomas**, concurred in the portions of the judgment upholding most of Pennsylvania's law, but dissented from the reaffirmance of *Roe*. The Chief Justice argued that the right to abortion fails the "implicit in the concept of ordered liberty" test of *Palko*: abortion is *sui generis*—and therefore different from parenting (*Meyer* and *Pierce*), contraception (*Griswold*), and marriage (*Loving*)—because it involves the "purposeful termination of potential life." Additionally, the dissent argued that the numerous anti-abortion laws in existence throughout U. S. history demonstrated that there was "deeply rooted tradition" sufficient to support the classification of the right to abortion as "fundamental" for due process purposes.]

JUSTICE SCALIA, with whom **THE CHIEF JUSTICE**, **JUSTICE WHITE**, and **JUSTICE THOMAS** join, concurring in the judgment in part and dissenting in part.

* * * [T]he issue in this case [is] not whether the power of a woman to abort her unborn child is a "liberty" in the absolute sense; or even whether it is a liberty of great importance to many women. Of course it is both. The issue is whether it is a liberty protected by the Constitution of the United States. I am sure it is not. I reach that conclusion not because of anything so exalted as my views concerning the "concept of existence, of meaning, of the universe, and of the mystery of human life." [Quoting Joint Opinion.] Rather, I reach it for the same reason I reach the conclusion that bigamy is not constitutionally protected—because of two simple facts: (1) the Constitution says absolutely nothing about it, and (2) the longstanding traditions of American society have permitted it to be legally proscribed. * * *

[W]hether it would "subvert the Court's legitimacy" or not, the notion that we would decide a case differently from the way we otherwise would have in order to show that we can stand firm against public disapproval is frightening. * * * [W]hen [this idea] is in the mind of a Court that believes the Constitution has an evolving meaning; that the Ninth Amendment's reference to "othe[r]" rights is not a disclaimer, but a charter for action; and that the function of this Court is to "speak before all others for [the people's] constitutional ideals" unrestrained by meaningful text or tradition—then the notion that the Court must adhere to a decision for as long as the decision faces "great opposition" and the Court is "under fire" acquires a character of almost czarist arrogance. * * * We should get out of this area, where we have no right to be, and where we do neither ourselves nor the country any good by remaining.

NOTES ON *ROE, CASEY* AND THE RIGHT TO ABORTION

1. *Procreation as the Foundation.* With the Court's decision in *Roe*, the privacy line of cases became firmly grounded in the right to decide whether to bear a child. Note that although the *Griswold–Eisenstadt–Roe* line of cases is thought of as *in seriatim* building blocks, they may not have been so distinct in the minds of the Justices. *Eisenstadt* was argued before the Court on November 17 and 18, 1971; *Roe* was first argued less than a month later, on December 13. How might the pendency of *Roe* have affected the way the Court structured its decision in *Eisenstadt*?

2. *Finally a Home for the Right to Privacy.* After roosting in the penumbras of the Bill of Rights (the Douglas opinion in *Griswold*), the Ninth Amendment (the Goldberg concurrence), and even the Equal Protection Clause (the Brennan opinion in *Eisenstadt*), the Court in *Roe* finally gave the right of privacy its constitutional home in the jurisprudential location where Justice Harlan's *Poe v. Ullman* opinion had identified it in the first place: the Due Process Clause's protection of "liberty." The Joint Opinion of Justices O'Connor, Kennedy, and Souter in *Casey* reaffirmed that placement.

3. *The Missing Argument: Sex Discrimination.* Many commentators have opined that the abortion right would have been more strongly grounded in the Constitution and in social reality had it been based on a sex discrimination, rather than a privacy, argument. The point has been made most famously by then-Judge, now Supreme Court Justice, Ruth Bader Ginsburg, in a law review article entitled "Some Thoughts on Autonomy and Equality in Relation to *Roe v. Wade,*" 63 *N.C.L. Rev.* 375 (1985). In fact, a sex discrimination argument was made to the Court in *Roe* in an *amicus* brief filed by Nancy Stearns for the Center for Constitutional Rights. The CCR brief argued that abortion laws were a way to punish unmarried women for being heterosexually active. Another *amicus* brief, filed by Joan Bradford for the California Committee to Legalize Abortion, argued that forced childbearing was a form of involuntary servitude, prohibited under the Thirteenth Amendment. These arguments were made to a Court actively considering how to frame its equal protection analysis of classifications based on sex. A third case pending before the Court in the 1971 Term was *Reed v. Reed,* 404 U.S. 71 (1971), which marked the first time the Court struck down a sex-based classification as unconstitutional. *Reed* was argued on October 19, 1971—before either *Eisenstadt* or *Roe*—and decided quickly, on November 22 of the same year. (See Chapter 3 for an examination of constitutional protections against sex discrimination.)

By the time of *Casey*, the Court's language gave greater emphasis to the impact of reproductive choice on the capacity of women to function as social and economic equals to men. Justice Blackmun's concurring and dissenting opinion in *Casey* went further and briefly suggested an explicit sex discrimination argument. On the other hand, *Casey* weakened the level of scrutiny applied to restrictive regulations (*e.g.*, waiting periods). Previously, the Court had required a state show compelling reasons to uphold such restrictions, but the standard changed in *Casey* to acceptance unless the restrictive regime amounted to an "undue burden."

4. *The Logic of Biological Determinism. Roe* also marked the apex of the medicalization of the law of reproductive decisionmaking, both in its consideration of medical history and in its vesting of the decision-making in "the woman and her responsible physician." In an extensive critique of *Roe*, Reva Siegel argues that this medicalization served as a mask for using "[f]acts about women's bodies * * * to justify regulation enforcing judgments about women's roles."

> *Roe* * * * defines [the state's] regulatory interest in potential life physiologically, without reference to the sorts of constitutional considerations that normally attend the use of state power against a citizen. In the Court's reasoning, facts concerning the physiological development of the unborn provide "logical and biological justifications" both limiting and legitimating state action directed against the pregnant woman. * * * [T]he Court has never described the state's interest in protecting potential life as an interest in forcing women to bear

children. *Roe's* physiological reasoning obscures that simple social fact.
* * *

Abortion-restrictive regulation is state action compelling pregnancy and motherhood, and this simple fact cannot be evaded by invoking nature or a woman's choices to explain the situation in which the pregnant woman subject to abortion restrictions finds herself. A pregnant woman seeking an abortion has the practical capacity to terminate a pregnancy, which she would exercise but for the community's decision to prevent or deter her. If the community successfully effectuates its will, it is the state, and not nature, which is responsible for causing her to continue the pregnancy. * * *

Reva Siegel, "Reasoning From the Body: A Historical Perspective on Abortion Regulation and Questions of Equal Protection," 44 *Stan. L. Rev.* 261, 276–77, 350–51 (1992).

5.   *The Critique of Negative Liberty.* The major critique of privacy, especially in the abortion context, has been its susceptibility to the claim that, under a negative rights analysis, the state is compelled only to refrain from creating obstacles to choosing abortion, but has no duty to assist in the effectuation of that right, by, for example, including abortion within the realm of medical procedures provided to indigent women in the Medicaid program.

In *Harris v. McRae*, 448 U.S. 297 (1980), the Supreme Court upheld the validity of the Hyde Amendment, a provision (named for its author, Rep. Henry Hyde of Illinois) that barred use of Medicaid program funds (which provide health services for the poor) to cover abortions, unless the pregnant woman's life was endangered or the pregnancy resulted from rape or incest. "The Hyde Amendment * * * places no governmental obstacle in the path of a woman who chooses to terminate her pregnancy, but rather, by means of unequal subsidization of abortion and other medical services, encourages alternative activity deemed in the public interest. * * * [I]t simply does not follow that a woman's freedom of choice carries with it a constitutional entitlement to the financial resources to avail herself of the full range of protected choices. The reason [is that] although government may not place obstacles in the path of a woman's exercise of her freedom of choice, it need not remove those not of its own creation. Indigency falls in the latter category. The financial constraints that restrict an indigent woman's ability to enjoy the full range of constitutionally-protected freedom of choice are the product not of governmental restrictions on access to abortions, but rather of her indigency. Although Congress has opted to subsidize medically necessary services generally, but not certain medically necessary abortions, the fact remains that the Hyde Amendment leaves an indigent woman with at least the same range of choice in deciding whether to obtain a medically necessary abortion as she would have had if Congress had chosen to subsidize no health care costs at all."

Justice Brennan, joined in dissent by Justices Marshall and Blackmun, wrote that "the Court fails to appreciate * * * that it is not simply the woman's indigency that interferes with her freedom of choice, but the combination of her own poverty and the government's unequal subsidization of abortion of childbirth."

6. *The Role of Sexuality?* Perhaps the one area in which issues of sexuality (as distinct from procreation) remain closest to the surface in contemporary abortion jurisprudence is the question of whether the state can intervene to regulate abortions for minor women in ways that it cannot for adult women. States continue to impose parental notice and consent requirements on adolescents seeking abortion, and the Supreme Court in *Casey* reaffirmed the state's authority to restrict the privacy right in this way.

SODOMY: "THE UTTERLY CONFUSED CATEGORY"

Of the laws prohibiting consensual sexual activity, the category that generated the most challenges in the period following the invalidation of abortion laws was the regulation of sodomy. Given the intensity of these battles, one might assume that the combatants on both sides would have been clear on exactly what conduct they were fighting about so strenuously. Not true. Sodomy laws came to be seen as prohibitions of "gay sex," and even as "traditional" prohibitions of gay sex, even though historically such statutes targeted acts of non-procreative sex, *i.e.*, oral or anal sex between any two persons, not homosexual sex. Both pro-gay and anti-gay groups often described the laws as being about homosexuality, and, as you will see, the Supreme Court itself misread them as such. But the "crime against nature," as sodomy was often euphemistically called in older statutes, was not a crime against heterosexuality; it was a crime against procreation.

Even if incorrect, however, these misreadings were not without reason: as the stigma for heterosexual sex outside of (especially prior to) marriage virtually evaporated, coupled with a cultural backlash against an increasingly larger and more visible gay rights movement, the *meaning* of sodomy became more indeterminate. This shift in social meaning produced shifts in legal meaning. Starting in the mid–1970s and continuing through the 1980s, a counter trend developed in the United States: some states decriminalized sodomy between opposite sex partners, while enacting for the first time statutes that specified criminalization of same-sex sodomy.

We will examine sodomy law in three chronological segments: the debates and developments that led up to the Supreme Court's upholding of Georgia's sodomy law in *Bowers v. Hardwick*, 478 U.S. 186 (1986); the *Hardwick* era of 1986 to 2003; and in Chapter 4, the Supreme Court's dramatic reversal of *Hardwick* in *Lawrence v. Texas*, 539 U.S. 558 (2003).

1. THE PRE-HISTORY OF *BOWERS V. HARDWICK*

As you will read in Chapter 4, the Supreme Court in *Lawrence* relied extensively on historical research into the derivation and uses of sodomy laws in its decision to reverse *Bowers v. Hardwick*. One of its most significant conclusions was that, traditionally, very few prosecutions were begun under sodomy statutes in cases where both partners were consenting adults. Although this was the social reality, however, formal calls for the repeal of such laws gained ground much more slowly.

The first major cultural breakthrough paving the way for these developments was the publication of two books: Alfred Kinsey, et al., *Sexual Behavior in the Human Male* (1948) and *Report on Sexual Behavior in the Human Female* (1953). Kinsey, an entomologist who made his scientific reputation in a definitive study of the gall wasp, brought an astringent empiricism to the study of human sexuality. Although later studies have produced more scientifically reliable estimates of the percentage of Americans who engage in various sexual acts, Kinsey's studies were shocking as much because of the non-judgmental frame in which they were presented as because of the specific numbers. Among his most dramatic findings were that many more men than was commonly believed had significant homosexual experience, including 10 per cent who had been more or less exclusively homosexual for at least three years; half of the married men and a quarter of the married women had engaged in adulterous sexual relations, and significantly more had engaged in pre-marital sex (which was then a crime in 35 states); and that women, rather than being merely passive, asexual partners, experienced orgasm, often through masturbation and also during sex with other women. The two Kinsey Reports became best sellers; their publication triggered complaints of moral decay, but also allied scientific rationalism with sexual non-judgmentalism in U. S. culture.

In 1952, drafting began on the Model Penal Code. Ten years later, the American Law Institute adopted the proposed MPC, which endorsed the decriminalization of private consensual adultery, fornication, and sodomy. Note that the period of its drafting and early adoption, as well as of debates over *The Wolfenden Report* (see below), coincided with the pendency of *Ullman* and *Griswold* before the Supreme Court. How might these events have influenced the approaches of the Justices? In 1961, the same year that *Ullman* was decided, Illinois became the first state to repeal its sodomy law, by adopting a draft version of the MPC. The next sodomy law repeal did not occur until 1969 (Connecticut), and then a number of states followed suit through the 1970s and 1980s. Most of these repeals occurred when states modernized their entire criminal codes, so that dropping or lightening of penalties for consensual sexual practices was often part of a larger overhaul of the statutory scheme.

During roughly the same period of the 1950s and 1960s, a somewhat similar process occurred in England. Concerned by an increasing number of street arrests for sexual activity, the Office of the British Home Secretary in 1954 commissioned *The Report of the Wolfenden Committee on Homosexual Offences and Prostitution*, published in 1957. *The Wolfenden Report* recommended both the decriminalization of private consensual homosexual conduct and an increase in penalties for prostitution, concluding that "[t]here must remain a realm of private morality and immorality which is, in brief and crude terms, not the law's business." The logic of the Report was that both homosexuality and prostitution were repugnant, but that society's interests could be served by concentrating the prohibitions of law on the public manifestations of these behaviors. Parliament largely followed the *Wolfenden* recommendations, quickly increasing the maximum sentence for open prostitution in the Street Offences Act of 1959, and some years later repealing the prohibition against private consensual sodomy in the Sexual Offences Act of 1967. (Adultery and fornication were not part of the British criminal code.)

The Wolfenden Report triggered a famous debate between Lord Patrick Devlin and Professor H.L.A. Hart over the proper role of the state in regulating sexual conduct. In a 1959 lecture later published as *The Enforcement of Morals,* Lord Devlin argued that the use of law to enforce widely-held moral judgments was essential to society. "[A]n established morality is as necessary as good government to the welfare of society." Therefore, Devlin wrote, "society is justified in taking the same steps to preserve its moral code as it does to preserve its government and other essential institutions." Devlin asserted that a society's moral consensus could be based on the beliefs of the "reasonable man." He argued that "the man in the jury box" could determine whether proper moral principles were violated by certain behaviors; a unanimous vote that certain acts were "beyond the limits of tolerance" by twelve randomly-selected jurors would constitute a sign of moral principles that "every right-minded person would accept as valid." As to homosexuality specifically, Devlin believed that although there was "a general abhorrence of homosexuality," the predominant public feeling was that "if confined, it is tolerable."

In 1963, Professor Hart responded to Devlin with his equally classic text, *Law, Liberty and Morality*. Hart elaborated on principles first articulated by Jeremy Bentham and John Stuart Mill, who had argued that the state had no legitimate right to intrude in individual conduct unless that conduct threatened to harm others. Hart agreed with Devlin that *"some shared morality is essential to the existence of any society"* (emphasis in the original), but argued that the responsibility of government was to secure the safety and liberty necessary for citizens to debate and continuously re-assess what they wished the moral code of their society to be. Such a code was better protected by non-governmental institutions and private actions than by coercion based on enforcement of the law, he argued.

How well do the majority and the dissenting judges in the following opinion frame the proper role of the law?

People v. Ronald Onofre et al.

New York Court of Appeals, 1980.
51 N.Y.2d 476, 434 N.Y.S.2d 947, 415 N.E.2d 936, *cert. denied sub nom.* New York v. Onofre, 451 U.S. 987 (1981).

■ JONES, JUDGE.

[The appeal consolidated several cases involving New York's 1965 law against "consensual sodomy," New York Penal Law § 130.38, which made it a misdemeanor to engage in "deviate sexual intercourse" (defined to include anal and oral but not vaginal sex) with another person. Ronald Onofre was convicted of having sex with his 17–year-old male lover at his home. Conde Peoples, III and Philip Goss were convicted for engaging in oral sex in an automobile parked in downtown Buffalo. Mary Sweat was convicted for having oral sex with a man in a parked truck, also in Buffalo. All these defendants appealed their convictions and argued that the consensual sodomy statute was unconstitutional.]

The People are in no disagreement that a fundamental right of personal decision exists; the divergence of the parties focuses on what subjects fall within its protection, the People contending that it extends to only two aspects of sexual behavior—marital intimacy (by virtue of the Supreme Court's decision in *Griswold*) and procreative choice (by reason of *Eisenstadt* and *Roe v. Wade*). Such a stance fails however adequately to take into account the decision in *Stanley* and the explication of the right of privacy contained in the court's opinion in *Eisenstadt*. In *Stanley* the court found violative of the individual's right to be free from governmental interference in making important, protected decisions a statute which made criminal the possession of obscene matter within the privacy of the defendant's home. Although the material itself was entitled to no protection against government proscription, the defendant's choice to seek sexual gratification by viewing it and the effectuation of that choice within the bastion of his home, removed from the public eye, was held to be blanketed by the constitutional right of privacy. That the right enunciated in *Griswold* to make decisions with respect to the consequence of sexual encounters and, necessarily, to have such encounters, was not limited to married couples was made clear by the language of the court in *Eisenstadt*. * * *

In light of these decisions, protecting under the cloak of the right of privacy individual decisions as to indulgence in acts of sexual intimacy by unmarried persons and as to satisfaction of sexual desires by resort to material condemned as obscene by community standards when done in a cloistered setting, no rational basis appears for excluding from the same protection decisions—such as those made by defendants before us—to seek sexual gratification from what at least once was commonly regarded as "deviant" conduct, so long as the decisions are voluntarily made by adults in a noncommercial, private setting. Nor is any such basis supplied by the claims advanced by the prosecution—that a prohibition against consensual sodomy will prevent physical harm which might otherwise befall the participants, will uphold public morality and will protect the institution of marriage. Commendable though these objectives clearly are, there is nothing on which to base a conclusion that they are achieved by [this statute]. No showing has been made, even in references tendered in the briefs, that physical injury is a common or even occasional consequence of the prohibited conduct, and there has been no demonstration either that this is a danger presently addressed by the statute or was one apprehended at the time the statutory section was enacted contemporaneously with the adoption of the new Penal Law in 1965. Indeed, the proposed comprehensive penal statute submitted to the Legislature by the Temporary Commission on Revision of the Penal Law and Criminal Code dropped all proscription against private acts of consensual sodomy. That the enactment of [this statute] was prompted by something other than fear for the physical safety of participants in consensual sodomy is suggested by the statement contained in the memorandum prepared by the chairman of the Temporary

Commission: "It would appear that the Legislature's decision to restore the consensual sodomy offense was, as with adultery, based largely upon the premises that deletion thereof might ostensibly be construed as legislative approval of deviate conduct." (N.Y. Legis. Ann., 1965, pp. 51–52.)

Any purported justification for the consensual sodomy statute in terms of upholding public morality is belied by the position reflected in the *Eisenstadt* decision in which the court carefully distinguished between public dissemination of what might have been considered inimical to public morality and individual recourse to the same material out of the public arena and in the sanctum of the private home. There is a distinction between public and private morality and the private morality of an individual is not synonymous with nor necessarily will have effect on what is known as public morality. So here, the People have failed to demonstrate how government interference with the practice of personal choice in matters of intimate sexual behavior out of view of the public and with no commercial component will serve to advance the cause of public morality or do anything other than restrict individual conduct and impose a concept of private morality chosen by the State. * * *

In sum, there has been no showing of any threat, either to participants or the public in general, in consequence of the voluntary engagement by adults in private, discreet, sodomous conduct. Absent is the factor of commercialization with the attendant evils commonly attached to the retailing of sexual pleasures; absent the elements of force or of involvement of minors which might constitute compulsion of unwilling participants or of those too young to make an informed choice, and absent too intrusion on the sensibilities of members of the public, many of whom would be offended by being exposed to the intimacies of others. Personal feelings of distaste for the conduct sought to be proscribed by [this statute] and even disapproval by a majority of the populace, if that disapproval were to be assumed, may not substitute for the required demonstration of a valid basis for intrusion by the State in an area of important personal decision protected under the right of privacy drawn from the United States Constitution—areas, the number and definition of which have steadily grown but, as the Supreme Court has observed, the outer limits of which it has not yet marked. * * *

■ [JUDGE JASEN concurred in the result. He rejected the *Griswold* analysis but found that the law had no currently rational basis, much like Justice White's concurring opinion in *Griswold*.]

■ GABRIELLI, JUDGE [joined by COOKE, CHIEF JUDGE], dissenting. * * *

Under the analysis utilized by the majority, *all* private, consensual conduct would necessarily involve the exercise of a constitutionally protected "fundamental right" unless the conduct in question jeopardizes the physical health of the participant. In effect, the majority has held that a State statute regulating private conduct will not pass constitutional muster if it is not designed to prevent physical harm to the individual. Such an analysis, however, can only be based upon an unnecessarily restrictive view of the scope of the State's power to regulate the conduct of its citizens. In my view, the so-called "police powers" of the State must include the right of the State to regulate the moral conduct of its citizens and "to maintain a decent society." Indeed, without mentioning specific provisions, it is apparent that our State's penal code represents, in part, an expression of our society's collective view as to what is or is not morally acceptable conduct. And, although the Legislature may not exercise this power in a manner that would impair a constitutionally protected "fundamental right", it begs the question to suggest, as the majority has, that such a right is necessarily involved whenever the State seeks to regulate conduct pursuant only to its interest in the moral well-being of its citizenry. * * *

The "fundamental" rights recognized in *Griswold, Roe* and their progeny are clearly not a product of a belief on the part of the Supreme Court that modern values and changing standards of morality should be incorporated wholesale into the due process clause of the Fourteenth Amendment. To the contrary, the language of the Supreme Court decisions makes clear that the rights which have so far been recognized as part of our due process guarantee are those rights to make certain familial decisions which have been considered sacrosanct and immune from governmental intrusion throughout the history of western civilization. * * *

* * * [T]he fact remains that western man has never been free to pursue his own choice of sexual gratification without fear of State interference. Consequently, it simply cannot be said that such freedom is an integral part of our concept of ordered liberty as embodied in the due process clauses of the Fifth and Fourteenth Amendments.* * *

2.   THE ERA OF *BOWERS V. HARDWICK*

Michael Bowers v. Michael Hardwick et al.

United States Supreme Court, 1986.
478 U.S. 186, 106 S.Ct. 2841, 92 L.Ed.2d 140.

■ JUSTICE WHITE delivered the opinion of the Court.

In August 1982, respondent [Hardwick] was charged with violating the Georgia statute criminalizing sodomy[1] by committing that act with another adult male in the bedroom of respondent's home.* After a preliminary

---

1. Georgia Code Ann. § 16–6–2 (1984) provides, in pertinent part, as follows:

"(a) A person commits the offense of sodomy when he performs or submits to any sexual act involving the sex organs of one person and the mouth or anus of another....

"(b) A person convicted of the offense of sodomy shall be punished by imprisonment for not less than one nor more than 20 years...."

* [Eds.] Michael Hardwick later told an interviewer that the police had come to his home to serve an expired arrest warrant, issued for drinking in public, by a police officer who saw him leaving a gay bar. Hardwick strongly suspected that this incident, and an unexplained physical assault shortly before his arrest, were engineered by police wanting to harass him for being gay. Peter Irons, "What Are You Doing in My Bedroom?," in *The Courage of Their Convictions* 392 (1988).

hearing, the District Attorney decided not to present the matter to the grand jury unless further evidence developed.

Respondent then brought suit in the Federal District Court, challenging the constitutionality of the statute insofar as it criminalized consensual sodomy.[2] He asserted that he was a practicing homosexual, that the Georgia sodomy statute, as administered by the defendants, placed him in imminent danger of arrest, and that the statute for several reasons violates the Federal Constitution. The District Court granted the defendants' motion to dismiss for failure to state a claim * * *. [The Eleventh Circuit Court of Appeals reversed, and the Supreme Court reversed it in turn and reinstated the District Court judgment.]

This case does not require a judgment on whether laws against sodomy between consenting adults in general, or between homosexuals in particular, are wise or desirable. It raises no question about the right or propriety of state legislative decisions to repeal their laws that criminalize homosexual sodomy, or of state-court decisions invalidating those laws on state constitutional grounds. The issue presented is whether the Federal Constitution confers a fundamental right upon homosexuals to engage in sodomy and hence invalidates the laws of the many States that still make such conduct illegal and have done so for a very long time. The case also calls for some judgment about the limits of the Court's role in carrying out its constitutional mandate.

We first register our disagreement with the Court of Appeals and with respondent that the Court's prior cases have construed the Constitution to confer a right of privacy that extends to homosexual sodomy and for all intents and purposes have decided this case. The reach of this line of cases was sketched in *Carey v. Population Services International. Pierce* and *Meyer* were described as dealing with child rearing and education; *Prince*, with family relationships; *Skinner* with procreation; *Loving* with marriage; *Griswold* and *Eisenstadt* with contraception; and *Roe v. Wade* with abortion. The latter three cases were interpreted as construing the Due Process Clause of the Fourteenth Amendment to confer a fundamental individual right to decide whether or not to beget or bear a child.

Accepting the decisions in these cases and the above description of them, we think it evident that none of the rights announced in those cases bears any resemblance to the claimed constitutional right of homosexuals to engage in acts of sodomy that is asserted in this case. No connection

---

2. John and Mary Doe were also plaintiffs in this action. They alleged that they wished to engage in sexual activity prohibited by § 16–6–2 in the privacy of their home, and that they had been "chilled and deterred" from engaging such activity by both the existence of the statute and Hardwick's arrest. The District Court held, however, that because had neither sustained, nor were in immediate danger of sustaining, any direct injury from the enforcement of the statute, they did not have proper standing to maintain the action. The Court of Appeals affirmed * * * and the Does do not challenge that holding in this Court.

The only claim properly before the Court, therefore, is Hardwick's challenge to the Georgia statute as applied to consensual homosexual sodomy. We express no opinion on the constitutionality of the Georgia statute as applied to other acts of sodomy.

between family, marriage, or procreation on the one hand and homosexual activity on the other has been demonstrated, either by the Court of Appeals or by respondent. Moreover, any claim that these cases nevertheless stand for the proposition that any kind of private sexual conduct between consenting adults is constitutionally insulated from state proscription is unsupportable. Indeed, the Court's opinion in *Carey* twice asserted that the privacy right, which the *Griswold* line of cases found to be one of the protections provided by the Due Process Clause, did not reach so far.

Precedent aside, however, respondent would have us announce, as the Court of Appeals did, a fundamental right to engage in homosexual sodomy. This we are quite unwilling to do. It is true that despite the language of the Due Process Clauses of the Fifth and Fourteenth Amendments, which appears to focus only on the processes by which life, liberty, or property is taken, the cases are legion in which those Clauses have been interpreted to have substantive content, subsuming rights that to a great extent are immune from federal or state regulation or proscription. Among such cases are those recognizing rights that have little or no textual support in the constitutional language. *Meyer*, *Prince*, and *Pierce* fall in this category, as do the privacy cases from *Griswold* to *Carey*.

Striving to assure itself and the public that announcing rights not readily identifiable in the Constitution's text involves much more than the imposition of the Justices' own choice of values on the States and the Federal Government, the Court has sought to identify the nature of the rights qualifying for heightened judicial protection. In *Palko v. Connecticut* it was said that this category includes those fundamental liberties that are "implicit in the concept of ordered liberty," such that "neither liberty nor justice would exist if [they] were sacrificed." A different description of fundamental liberties appeared in *Moore v. East Cleveland*, 431 U.S. 494, 503 (1977) (opinion of Powell, J.) where they are characterized as those liberties that are "deeply rooted in this Nation's history and tradition." *Id.* at 503.

It is obvious to us that neither of these formulations would extend a fundamental right to homosexuals to engage in acts of consensual sodomy. Proscriptions against that conduct have ancient roots. Sodomy was a criminal offense at common law and was forbidden by the laws of the original 13 States when they ratified the Bill of Rights. In 1868, when the Fourteenth Amendment was ratified, all but 5 of the 37 States in the Union had criminal sodomy laws. In fact, until 1961, all 50 States outlawed sodomy, and today, 24 States and the District of Columbia continue to provide criminal penalties for sodomy performed in private and between consenting adults. Against this background, to claim that a right to engage in such conduct is "deeply rooted in this Nation's history and tradition" or "implicit in the concept of ordered liberty" is, at best, facetious.

Nor are we inclined to take a more expansive view of our authority to discover new fundamental rights imbedded in the Due Process Clause. The Court is most vulnerable and comes nearest to illegitimacy when it deals with judge-made constitutional law having little or no cognizable roots in the language or design of the Constitution. That this is so was painfully demonstrated by the face-off between the Executive and the Court in the 1930s, which resulted in the repudiation of much of the substantive gloss that the Court had placed on the Due Process Clauses of the Fifth and Fourteenth Amendments. There should be, therefore, great resistance to expand the substantive reach of those Clauses, particularly if it requires redefining the category of rights deemed to be fundamental. Otherwise, the Judiciary necessarily takes to itself further authority to govern the country without express constitutional authority. The claimed right pressed on us today falls far short of overcoming this resistance.

Respondent, however, asserts that the result should be different where the homosexual conduct occurs in the privacy of the home. He relies on *Stanley*, where the Court held that the First Amendment prevents conviction for possessing and reading obscene material in the privacy of one's home: "If the First Amendment means anything, it means that a State has no business telling a man, sitting alone in his house, what books he may read or what films he may watch."

Stanley did protect conduct that would not have been protected outside the home, and it partially prevented the enforcement of state obscenity laws; but the decision was firmly grounded in the First Amendment. The right pressed upon us here has no similar support in the text of the Constitution, and it does not qualify for recognition under the prevailing principles for construing the Fourteenth Amendment. Its limits are also difficult to discern. Plainly enough, otherwise illegal conduct is not always immunized whenever it occurs in the home. Victimless crimes, such as the possession and use of illegal drugs, do not escape the law where they are committed at home. *Stanley* itself recognized that its holding offered no protection for the possession in the home of drugs, firearms, or stolen goods. And if respondent's submission is limited to the voluntary sexual conduct between consenting adults, it would be difficult, except by fiat, to limit the claimed right to homosexual conduct while leaving exposed to prosecution adultery, incest, and other sexual crimes even though they are committed in the home. We are unwilling to start down that road.

Even if the conduct at issue here is not a fundamental right, respondent asserts that there must be a rational basis for the law and that there is none in this case other than the presumed belief of a majority of the electorate in Georgia that homosexual sodomy is immoral and unacceptable. This is said to be an inadequate rationale to support the law. The law, however, is constantly based on notions of morality, and if all laws representing essentially moral choices are to be invalidated under the Due Process Clause, the courts will be very busy indeed. Even respondent makes no such claim, but insists that majority sentiments about the morality of homosexuality should be declared inadequate. We do not agree, and are unpersuaded that the sodomy laws of some 25 States should be invalidated on this basis.[8] * * *

---

8. Respondent does not defend the judgment below based on the Ninth Amendment, the Equal Protection Clause, or the Eighth Amendment.

◼ CHIEF JUSTICE BURGER, concurring. * * *

As the Court notes, the proscriptions against sodomy have very "ancient roots." Decisions of individuals relating to homosexual conduct have been subject to state intervention throughout the history of Western Civilization. Condemnation of these practices is firmly rooted in Judeo–Christian moral and ethical standards. Homosexual sodomy was a capital crime under Roman law. During the English Reformation when powers of the ecclesiastical courts were transferred to the King's Courts, the first English statute criminalizing sodomy was passed. Blackstone described "the infamous crime against nature" as an offense of "deeper malignity" than rape, an heinous act "the very mention of which is a disgrace to human nature," and "a crime not fit to be named." The common law of England, including its prohibition of sodomy, became the received law of Georgia and the other Colonies. In 1816 the Georgia Legislature passed the statute at issue here, and that statute has been continuously in force in one form or another since that time. To hold that the act of homosexual sodomy is somehow protected as a fundamental right would be to cast aside millennia of moral teaching. * * *

◼ JUSTICE POWELL, concurring.

I join the opinion of the Court. I agree with the Court that there is no fundamental right—i.e., no substantive right under the Due Process Clause—such as that claimed by respondent, and found to exist by the Court of Appeals. This is not to suggest, however, that respondent may not be protected by the Eighth Amendment of the Constitution. The Georgia statute at issue in this case authorizes a court to imprison a person for up to 20 years for a single private, consensual act of sodomy. In my view, a prison sentence for such conduct—certainly a sentence of long duration—would create a serious Eighth Amendment issue. Under the Georgia statute a single act of sodomy, even in the private setting of a home, is a felony comparable in terms of the possible sentence imposed to serious felonies such as aggravated battery, first-degree arson, and robbery.

In this case, however, respondent has not been tried, much less convicted and sentenced. Moreover, respondent has not raised the Eighth Amendment issue below. For these reasons this constitutional argument is not before us.

◼ JUSTICE BLACKMUN, with whom JUSTICE BRENNAN, JUSTICE MARSHALL, and JUSTICE STEVENS join, dissenting.

This case is no more about "a fundamental right to engage in homosexual sodomy," as the Court purports to declare, than *Stanley* was about a fundamental right to watch obscene movies, or *Katz v. United States* was about a fundamental right to place interstate bets from a telephone booth. Rather, this case is about "the most comprehensive of rights and the right most valued by civilized men," namely, "the right to be let alone." *Olmstead* (Brandeis, J., dissenting). * * *

* * * I believe we must analyze respondent's claim in the light of the values that underlie the constitutional right to privacy. If that right means anything, it means that, before Georgia can prosecute its citizens for making choices about the most intimate aspects of their lives, it must do more than assert that the choice they have made is an " 'abominable crime not fit to be named among Christians.' " *Herring v. State*, 46 S.E. 876, 882 (Ga.1904). * * *

[T]he Court's almost obsessive focus on homosexual activity is particularly hard to justify in light of the broad language Georgia has used. Unlike the Court, the Georgia Legislature has not proceeded on the assumption that homosexuals are so different from other citizens that their lives may be controlled in a way that would not be tolerated if it limited the choices of those other citizens. The sex or status of the persons who engage in the act is irrelevant as a matter of state law. * * * I therefore see no basis for the Court's decision to treat this case as an "as applied" challenge to § 16–6–2, or for Georgia's attempt, both in its brief and at oral argument, to defend § 16–6–2 solely on the grounds that it prohibits homosexual activity. * * *

* * * I disagree with the Court's refusal to consider whether § 16–6–2 runs afoul of the Eighth or Ninth Amendments or the Equal Protection Clause of the Fourteenth Amendment. * * * I believe that Hardwick has stated a cognizable claim that § 16–6–2 interferes with constitutionally protected interests in privacy and freedom of intimate association. But neither the Eighth Amendment nor the Equal Protection Clause is so clearly irrelevant that a claim resting on either provision should be peremptorily dismissed. * * *

The Court concludes today that none of our prior cases dealing with various decisions that individuals are entitled to make free of governmental interference "bears any resemblance to the claimed constitutional right of homosexuals to engage in acts of sodomy that it asserted in this case." While it is true that these cases may be characterized by their connection to protection of the family, the Court's conclusion that they extend no further than this boundary ignores the warning in *Moore v. East Cleveland*, against "clos[ing] our eyes to the basic reasons why certain rights associated with the family have been accorded shelter under the Fourteenth Amendment's Due Process Clause." We protect those rights not because they contribute, in some direct and material way, to the general public welfare, but because they form so central a part of an individual's life. "[T]he concept of privacy embodies the 'moral fact that a person belongs to himself and not others nor to society as a whole.' " *Thornburgh v. American College of Obstetricians & Gynecologists* 476 U.S. 747, 777 n. 5 (1986) (Stevens, J., concurring), quoting Fried, "Correspondence," 6 *Phil. & Pub. Affairs* 288–289 (1977). And so we protect the decision whether to marry precisely because marriage "is an association that promotes a way of life, not causes; a harmony in living, not political faiths; a bilateral loyalty, not commercial or social projects." *Griswold*. We protect the decision whether to have a child because parenthood alters so dramatically an individual's self-definition, not because of demographic considerations or the Bible's command to be fruitful and multiply. And we protect the family because it contributes so powerfully to the happiness of individuals, not because of a preference for stereotypical households. The Court recognized in *Roberts* [*v. United States Jaycees*, 468 U.S. 609, 619 (1984)] that the "ability independently to define one's identity that is central to any concept of liberty" cannot truly be exercised in a vacuum; we all depend on the "emotional enrichment from close ties with others."

Only the most willful blindness could obscure the fact that sexual intimacy is "a sensitive, key relationship of human existence, central to family life, community welfare, and the development of human personality," *Paris Adult Theatre I v. Slaton*, 413 U.S. 49, 63 (1973). The fact that individuals define themselves in a significant way through their intimate sexual relationships with others suggests, in a Nation as diverse as ours, that there may be many "right" ways of conducting those relationships, and that much of the richness of a relationship will come from the freedom an individual has to *choose* the form and nature of these intensely personal bonds. See Karst, "The Freedom of Intimate Association," 89 *Yale L.J.* 624, 637 (1980). * * *

The central place that *Stanley* gives Justice Brandeis' dissent in *Olmstead*, a case raising *no* First Amendment claim, shows that *Stanley* rested as much on the Court's understanding of the Fourth Amendment as it did on the First. Indeed, in *Paris Adult Theatre I v. Slaton*, the Court suggested that reliance on the Fourth Amendment not only supported the Court's outcome in *Stanley* but actually was *necessary* to it: "If obscene material unprotected by the First Amendment in itself carried with it a 'penumbra' of constitutionally protected privacy, this Court would not have found it necessary to decide *Stanley* on the narrow basis of the 'privacy of the home,' which was hardly more than a reaffirmation that 'a man's home is his castle.' " *Id.*, 413 U.S. at 66. "The right of the people to be secure in their ... houses," expressly guaranteed by the Fourth Amendment, is perhaps the most "textual" of the various constitutional provisions that inform our understanding of the right to privacy, and thus I cannot agree with the Court's statement that "[t]he right pressed upon us here has no ... support in the text of the Constitution." Indeed, the right of an individual to conduct intimate relationships in the intimacy of his or her own home seems to me to be the heart of the Constitution's protection of privacy.

The Court's failure to comprehend the magnitude of the liberty interests at stake in this case leads it to slight the question whether petitioner, on behalf of the State, has justified Georgia's infringement on these interests. I believe that neither of the two general justifications for § 16–6–2 that petitioner has advanced warrants dismissing respondent's challenge for failure to state a claim.

First, petitioner asserts that the acts made criminal by the statute may have serious adverse consequences for "the general public health and welfare," such as spreading communicable diseases or fostering other criminal activity. Inasmuch as this case was dismissed by the District Court on the pleadings, it is not surprising that the record before us is barren of any evidence to support petitioner's claim. In light of the state of the record, I see no justification for the Court's attempt to equate the private, consensual sexual activity at issue here with the "possession in the home of drugs, firearms, or stolen goods," to which *Stanley* refused to extend its protection. None of the behavior so mentioned in *Stanley* can properly be viewed as "[v]ictimless": drugs and weapons are inherently dangerous, and for property to be "stolen," someone must have been wrongfully deprived of it. Nothing in the record before the Court provides any justification for finding the activity forbidden by § 16–6–2 to be physically dangerous, either to the persons engaged in it or to others.[4]

The core of petitioner's defense of § 16–6–2, however, is that respondent and others who engage in the conduct prohibited by § 16–6–2 interfere with Georgia's exercise of the " 'right of the Nation and of the States to maintain a decent society,' " *Paris Adult Theatre I v. Slaton*, 413 U.S. at 59–60. Essentially, petitioner argues, and the Court agrees, that the fact that the acts described in § 16–6–2 "for hundreds of years, if not thousands, have been uniformly condemned as immoral" is a sufficient reason to permit a State to ban them today.

I cannot agree that either the length of time a majority has held its convictions or the passions with which it defends them can withdraw legislation from this Court's scrutiny. *Roe v. Wade*; *Loving v. Virginia*; *Brown v. Board of Education*.[5] As Justice Jackson wrote so eloquently for the Court in *West Virginia Board of Education v. Barnette*, 319 U.S. 624, 641–42 (1943), "we apply the limitations of the Constitution with no fear

---

4. Although I do not think it necessary to decide today issues that are not even remotely before us, it does seem to me that a court could find simple, analytically sound distinctions between certain private, consensual sexual conduct, on the one hand, and adultery and incest (the only two vaguely specific "sexual crimes" to which the majority points), on the other. * * * [A] State might conclude that adultery is likely to injure third persons, in particular, spouses and children of persons who engage in extramarital affairs. With respect to incest, a court might well agree with respondent that the nature of familial relationships renders true consent to incestuous activity sufficiently problematical that a blanket prohibition of such activity is warranted. Notably, the Court makes no effort to explain why it has chosen to group private, consensual homosexual activity with adultery and incest rather than with private, consensual heterosexual activity by unmarried persons or, indeed, with oral or anal sex within marriage.

5. The parallel between *Loving* and this case is almost uncanny. There, too, the State

relied on a religious justification for its law. Compare 388 U.S., at 3 (quoting trial court's statement that "Almighty God created the races white, black, yellow, malay and red, and he placed them on separate continents. . . . The fact that he separated the races shows that he did not intend for the races to mix"), with Brief for Petitioner 20–21 (relying on the Old and New Testaments and the writings of St. Thomas Aquinas to show that "traditional Judeo–Christian values proscribe such conduct"). There, too, defenders of the challenged statute relied heavily on the fact that when the Fourteenth Amendment was ratified, most of the States had similar prohibitions. There, too, at the time the case came before the Court, many of the States still had criminal statutes concerning the conduct at issue. Yet the Court held, not only that the invidious racism of Virginia's law violated the Equal Protection Clause, but also that the law deprived the Lovings of due process by denying them the "freedom of choice to marry" that had "long been recognized as one of the vital personal rights essential to the orderly pursuit of happiness by free men."

that freedom to be intellectually and spiritually diverse or even contrary will disintegrate the social organization. . . . [F]reedom to differ is not limited to things that do not matter much. That would be a mere shadow of freedom. The test of its substance is the right to differ as to things that touch the heart of the existing order." It is precisely because the issue raised by this case touches the heart of what makes individuals what they are that we should be especially sensitive to the rights of those whose choices upset the majority. * * *

■ JUSTICE STEVENS, with whom JUSTICE BRENNAN and JUSTICE MARSHALL join, dissenting.

* * * Sodomy was condemned as an odious and sinful type of behavior during the formative period of the common law. That condemnation was equally damning for heterosexual and homosexual sodomy. Moreover, it provided no special exemption for married couples. The license to cohabit and to produce legitimate offspring simply did not include any permission to engage in sexual conduct that was considered a "crime against nature." * * * Indeed, at one point in the 20th century, Georgia's law was construed to permit sexual conduct between homosexual women even though such conduct was prohibited between heterosexuals. [citing *Thompson v. Aldredge*] * * *

Our prior cases make two propositions abundantly clear. First, the fact that the governing majority in a State has traditionally viewed a particular practice as immoral is not a sufficient reason for upholding a law prohibiting the practice; neither history nor tradition could save a law prohibiting miscegenation from constitutional attack. Second, individual decisions by married persons, concerning the intimacies of their physical relationship, even when not intended to produce offspring, are a form of "liberty" protected by the Due Process Clause * * *

If the Georgia statute cannot be enforced as it is written—if the conduct it seeks to prohibit is a protected form of liberty for the vast majority of Georgia's citizens—the State must assume the burden of justifying a selective application of its law. Either the persons to whom Georgia seeks to apply its statute do not have the same interest in "liberty" that others have, or there must be a reason why the State may be permitted to apply a generally applicable law to certain persons that it does not apply to others.

The first possibility is plainly unacceptable. Although the meaning of the principle that "all men are created equal" is not always clear, it surely must mean that every free citizen has the same interest in "liberty" that the members of the majority share. From the standpoint of the individual, the homosexual and the heterosexual have the same interest in deciding how he will live his own life, and, more narrowly, how he will conduct himself in his personal and voluntary associations with his companions. State intrusion into the private conduct of either is equally burdensome.

The second possibility is similarly unacceptable. A policy of selective application must be supported by a neutral and legitimate interest—

something more substantial than a habitual dislike for, or ignorance about, the disfavored group. Neither the State nor the Court has identified any such interest in this case. The Court has posited as a justification for the Georgia statute "the presumed belief of a majority of the electorate in Georgia that homosexual sodomy is immoral and unacceptable." But the Georgia electorate has expressed no such belief—instead, its representatives enacted a law that presumably reflects the belief that *all sodomy* is immoral and unacceptable. Unless the Court is prepared to conclude that such a law is constitutional, it may not rely on the work product of the Georgia Legislature to support its holding. For the Georgia statute does not single out homosexuals as a separate class meriting special disfavored treatment. * * *

NOTES ON *BOWERS v. HARDWICK*

1.   *Judicial Discomfort and the Near Miss.* Justice Powell's original vote was reportedly with Justice Blackmun, which would have meant five votes to invalidate the Georgia statute, but Justice Powell changed his mind. John Calvin Jeffries, Jr., Powell's biographer, writes that Powell agonized over his decision in the case and was aware of his ignorance about homosexuality. Jeffries, *Lewis F. Powell, Jr.* 313–30 (1993). At one point he engaged in a discussion of the matter with the "liberal" law clerk in his chambers that term. The clerk tried to explain to the Justice that "homosexuals" are normal human beings who are part of the everyday environment of virtually everyone. Justice Powell apparently found it hard to understand how this could be and confessed to the clerk that he had never met a "homosexual" that he knew of. In truth, however, several of Justice Powell's clerks had been gay, including the law clerk to whom he made this confession, but apparently none had come out to him.

2.   *Supreme Court Hall of Shame. Hardwick* quickly became one of the most criticized opinions in the history of the Court, with virtually no defenders in the academy or established bar. (We are aware of no decision of the Court *upholding* a statute that was the object of such immediate and overwhelming criticism as the decision in *Bowers*.) Doctrinally, it may be read as simply drawing a line beyond which the much-criticized reasoning of *Griswold* and *Roe*, in finding a right of privacy implied in the Constitution, would not venture. Yet the contemptuous tone of its language seems, ironically, to have been its own undoing as a legitimate attempt at interpretation. Compare, for example, the majority in *Hardwick* with the dissent in *Onofre*. The latter comes to exactly the same conclusion, as to a New York statute which was virtually identical to the Georgia law, *i.e.*, it prohibited sodomy for both opposite-sex and same-sex partners. Yet the language of the *Onofre* dissent simply continues the public-private morality debate in measured tones, whereas the *Hardwick* opinion reads as an anti-gay screed. When you read *Lawrence v. Texas* below, consider whether the Court in 2003 might have treated the *Onofre* dissent more kindly than it did the opinions of Justice White and Chief Justice Burger.

3. *State Court Sodomy Law Challenges.* In the aftermath of *Hardwick*, litigators continued to challenge consensual sodomy laws, but under state constitutions. There seemed no point in presenting equal protection or freedom of expression arguments to the Justices who had just rebuffed the privacy claims in such harsh terms. And many state constitutions had textual protections of personal privacy that the U.S. Constitution did not. These litigators had considerable success in invalidating sodomy statutes on state constitutional grounds. Two of the most significant rulings were issued by southern state supreme courts.

Commonwealth of Kentucky v. Wasson, 842 S.W.2d 487 (Ky. 1992). A narrowly divided Kentucky Supreme Court ruled that its same-sex-only sodomy law violated the privacy guarantee of the state constitution, relying on a line of Kentucky constitutional case law establishing protection from surveillance for illegal alcohol. "At the time *Campbell* [a decision striking down a law criminalizing the possession of intoxicating liquor] was decided, the use of alcohol was as much an incendiary moral issue as deviate sexual behavior in private between consenting adults is today. * * * The clear implication is that immorality in private which 'does not operate to the detriment of others' is placed beyond the reach of state action by the guarantees of the Kentucky Constitution."

More remarkably, the court found that the sodomy law violated the equal protection guarantee of the Kentucky Constitution. "To be treated equally by the law is a broader constitutional value than due process of law as discussed in the [*Hardwick*] case. We recognize it as such under the Kentucky Constitution, without regard to whether the United States Supreme Court continues to do so in federal constitutional jurisprudence. 'Equal Justice Under Law' inscribed above the entrance to the United States Supreme Court, expresses the unique goal to which all humanity aspires. In Kentucky it is more than a mere aspiration. It is part of the 'inherent and inalienable' rights protected by our Kentucky Constitution. Our protection against exercise of 'arbitrary power over the ... liberty ... of freemen' by the General Assembly and our guarantee that all persons are entitled to 'equal' treatment forbid a special act punishing the sexual preference of homosexuals. It matters not that the same act committed by persons of the same sex is more offensive to the majority because Section Two states such 'power ... exists nowhere in a republic, not even in the largest majority.'

"The purpose of the present statute is not to protect the marital relationship against sexual activity outside of marriage, but only to punish one aspect of it while other activities similarly destructive of the marital relationship, if not more so, go unpunished. Sexual preference, and not the act committed, determines criminality, and is being punished. Simply because the majority, speaking through the General Assembly, finds one type of extramarital intercourse more offensive than another, does not provide a rational basis for criminalizing the sexual preference of homosexuals."

Powell v. State, 270 Ga. 327, 510 S.E.2d 18 (1998). Citing the fact that "[t]he right of privacy has a long and distinguished history in Georgia," the Georgia Supreme Court struck down the same sodomy statute that the U. S. Supreme Court had upheld. *Powell* arose in the context of a rape case, where the jury acquitted the defendant of using force, but found him guilty of sodomy based on his admission that he had engaged in what he described as consensual cunnilingus with the complainant.

"[I]t is clear that unforced sexual behavior conducted in private between adults * * * is recognized as a private matter by '[a]ny person whose intellect is in a normal condition.' Adults who 'withdraw from the public gaze' to engage in [such] behavior are exercising a right 'embraced within the right of personal liberty.' We cannot think of any other activity that reasonable persons would rank as more private and more deserving of protection from governmental interference * * *

"While many believe that acts of sodomy, even those involving consenting adults, are morally reprehensible, this repugnance alone does not create a compelling justification for state regulation of the activity. * * * [L]egislative enactments setting 'social morality' are not exempt from judicial review testing their constitutional mettle. * * * "

3.   ACADEMIC REFLECTIONS ON *HARDWICK*

***Bowers v. Hardwick* and Historiography**. Several legal scholars assailed the history-based conclusions by Justice White and Chief Justice Burger in *Bowers*. Two big anachronisms were immediately detected by Anne Goldstein, "History, Homosexuality and Public Values: Searching for the Hidden Determinants of *Bowers v. Hardwick*," 97 *Yale L. J.* 1073 (1988). "All of the Justices seem to have assumed that 'homosexuality' has been an invariant reality, outside of history. In fact, however, like most ways of describing aspects of the human condition, 'homosexuality' is a cultural and historical artifact. No attitude toward 'homosexuals' or 'homosexuality' can really be identified before the mid-nineteenth century because the concept did not exist until then. * * * Even the word 'homosexual' is new. It was coined in the nineteenth century to express the new idea that a person's immanent and essential nature is revealed by the gender of his desired sex partner. * * * Thus, by referring to 'homosexual sodomy' in ancient times, in 1791, and even in 1868, White and Burger were inserting their modern understanding of 'homosexuality' anachronistically into systems of values organized on other principles, obscuring the relative novelty of the distinction between 'homosexuality' and 'heterosexuality' with a myth about its antiquity."

Goldstein also demonstrates that the conduct Michael Hardwick was convicted of—oral sex—was not considered "sodomy" until decades after the Fourteenth Amendment was ratified. The leading nineteenth century precedent was *Rex v. Jacobs*, where the English courts held that oral sex was not sodomy under the common law and its statutory complement; only anal sex was sodomy. Parliament created a new crime, "gross indecency" in

1885 to cover oral sex (it was this statute and not the sodomy law for which Oscar Wilde was convicted in 1895). Most American jurisdictions followed suit between 1885 and 1930, usually by new statutory enactments broadening state law beyond "sodomy" to include oral sex and other "perversions." Sometimes state courts expanded state statutes without legislative amendments, but this was exceptional. See generally William Eskridge, Jr., *Gaylaw: Challenging the Apartheid of the Closet* 328–37 (1999) (App. A1) (documenting the state-by-state expansion of sodomy laws to include oral sex, 1879–1998).

The irony of these anachronisms was not lost on Goldstein and other commentators: "Thus, *Hardwick*'s originalist approach to the fourteenth amendment stands in contrast not only to the Court's previous refusal to follow an originalist approach to that amendment (*Griswold* and *Roe*), but also to the Court's nonoriginalist approach to state sodomy laws it charged the framers with knowing and approving. At the level of *specific intent*, there is no evidence that a single framer would have thought sodomy involved consensual oral sex in 1868. At the level of *general intent*, every framer would have thought the purpose of sodomy laws to be insurance that sex occurred only within the context of procreative marriage, an unconstitutional goal under the Court's post–1960 privacy jurisprudence." Eskridge, *Gaylaw* 162.

William Eskridge, Jr., "*Hardwick* and Historiography," 1999 *U. Ill. L. Rev.* 631, further maintained that, after the American Revolution and adoption of its libertarian Constitution, the policy and purpose of vaguely phrased sodomy and crime against nature laws were focused on practices that were either public or predatory (a powerful man attacking someone weaker). Eskridge demonstrates that every reported American sodomy decision in the nineteenth century involved either predatory or public conduct by the defendant, to the extent one can tell from reading the reported cases. Indeed, state criminal codes categorized the crime against nature as either a crime against the person (with rape and other forms of unconsented assault) or a crime against *public* decency (with unlawful cohabitation, indecent exposure in public places, and other public misconduct).

Conversely, sodomy laws in the nineteenth century were never (as a matter of public record) enforced against activities between consenting adults in private. Eskridge further demonstrates that common law rules of evidence rendered such prosecutions virtually impossible: when the crime against nature involved a consenting adult, the state could not rely on the testimony of the legal "accomplice" and had to corroborate it with independent evidence, obviously unobtainable if the acts were committed in the defendant's home or another private place. This pattern of enforcement was consistent with the constitutional tradition of liberty for Americans (1) in their homes, and as regards (2) their bodies and (3) their intimate relationships.

Janet Halley, "Reasoning About Sodomy: Act and Identity in and After *Bowers v. Hardwick*," 79 *Virginia Law Review* 1721, 1739–40, 1746–49, 1768–70, 1772 (1993).* The Court's opinion creates a double bind that exploits the ambiguity of homosexuality and sodomy. "In the first volume of his *History of Sexuality*, Foucault claimed that the late nineteenth century saw 'a new specification of individuals':

"As defined by the ancient civil or canonical codes, sodomy was a category of forbidden acts; their perpetrator was nothing more than the juridical subject of them. The nineteenth-century homosexual became a personage, a past, a case history, and a childhood, in addition to being a type of life, a life form, and a morphology, with an indiscreet anatomy and possibly a mysterious physiology. Nothing that went into his total composition was unaffected by his sexuality. It was everywhere present in him. . . . It was consubstantial with him, less as a habitual sin than as a singular nature[,] . . . [and was] constituted . . . less by a type of sexual relations than by a certain quality of sexual sensibility. . . . The sodomite had been a temporary aberration; the homosexual was now a species."

These celebrated lines do not explain what Foucault thought happened to sodomy after the great nineteenth-century shift from acts to sexualities. One reading, depending on the equation of sodomy with homosexual identity, assumes that sodomy (a regime of acts) was *transformed into* homosexuality (a regime of identities). Wherever this assumption operates, sodomy-the-act is thought to have been subsumed into homosexuality-the-identity; if sodomy nevertheless stubbornly reasserts its importance as a category of acts, the move is to save appearances by absorbing it into the newly invented personage of the homosexual.

"An alternative reading of Foucault's paragraph assumes less, and leaves in place a more complex and more adequate set of analytic categories for understanding the reasoning of sodomy. On this reading, the rhetoric of acts has not been evaporated or transformed; it has merely been displaced, set to one side and made slightly more difficult to discern by the rhetoric of identity. Thus sodomy—even sodomy between two people of the same sex or gender—is not necessarily the equivalent of acts or of identities; it is now unstably available for characterization as a species of act *and/or* as an indicator of sexual-orientation personality. * * *

" * * * As Justice White informed us,

"The issue presented is whether the Federal Constitution confers a fundamental right *upon homosexuals* to engage in *sodomy* and hence invalidates the laws of the many States that still make *such conduct* illegal and have done so for a very long time.

"What does the 'such' of 'such conduct' refer to? To sodomy generally? Or does it refer to sodomy as inflected by the homosexuals who do it? When Justice White invoked a historical argument to justify rejecting the fundamental rights claim framed in this way, he found that '[p]roscriptions against that conduct have ancient roots'—a conclusion that maintains a binocular vision of its object, hanging in delicate equipoise between act and identity."

"Are 'homosexuals' definitive of 'such conduct' or not? These formulations (and others appearing throughout Justice White's opinion for the majority and Chief Justice Burger's concurring opinion) keep the Court in suspense: it remains ready to answer yes or no. Sodomy can receive its definitive characteristic from the 'homosexuals' who do it, or can stand free of persons and be merely a 'bad act.' The majority Justices have enabled themselves to treat sodomy as a metonym [invoking something related to x, to stand in for x] for homosexual personhood—or not, as they wish. The question Justice White sets out to answer is thus apparently single but actually multiple: 'such conduct' represents not a purely act-based categorical system but an unstable hybrid one, in which identity and conduct simultaneously diverge and implicate one another. * * *

"A comparison of the Court's fundamental rights holding with its application of rational basis review reveals the advantages of the majority Justices' labile strategy by exposing the systematic ways in which acts and identities generate incoherence and instability. In his fundamental rights analysis, Justice White (cheered on by Chief Justice Burger) exploited the rhetoric of acts to make plausible his claim that sodomy has been, transhistorically and without surcease, the object of intense social disapprobation. In the rational basis holding, on the other hand, Justice White moved into a rhetoric of identities, holding that Georgia's sodomy statute rationally implements popular condemnation of *homosexuality*. Even within these distinct and opposed arguments, however, the two rhetorics are interlocked: that of acts implies and depends upon, even as it excludes, that of identities—and vice versa. The fundamental rights holding cannot actually constitute a coherent history of sodomy based on acts alone, for the acts that constitute sodomy are too various: Justice White achieves the appearance of coherence here only through persistent, implicit invocations of homosexual identity as the unifying theme of sodomy's prohibition. Conversely, his rational basis claim—that a facially neutral sodomy statute is reasonable because it makes a legitimate popular statement condemning homosexuality—is frontally incoherent. If the rational basis holding and its invocation of identity make sense at all, it is because they confer invisibility and immunity on a certain type of act. Indeed, heterosexual acts of sodomy are so thoroughly detached from the rhetoric of identity that those who do them are not even acknowledged as a class of persons."

Jed Rubenfeld, "The Right of Privacy," 102 *Harvard Law Review* 737, 777–800 passim (1989).* The individualistic concept of privacy embedded in *Griswold* and in the *Hardwick* dissents is an imprisoning strategy. "Let us look carefully at personhood's stance on homosexuality. The personhood position, as we have seen, is that homosexual sex should receive constitutional protection because it is so essential to an individual's self-definition—to his identity. * * *

"There is, however, an ambiguity in the idea that homosexual sex is central to the identity of those who engage in it. Is homosexual sex said to be self-definitive simply because it is sex, or especially because it is homosexual sex? In fact, proponents of personhood appear to argue for the second proposition. One reason for this is that the first version of the argument would be quite difficult to sustain. To begin with, it would * * * be required to claim that prostitution, for example, is an exercise of one's constitutional rights. (Personhood could, of course, choose to defend this position.) Moreover, it simply seems implausible to assert that the act of sex on any given occasion is necessarily fundamental in defining the identity of the person engaging in it.

" * * * Prohibiting homosexual sex, personhood can say, violates the right to privacy because homosexual sex is for homosexuals 'expressive of innermost traits of being.' It 'touches the heart of what makes individuals what they are.' * * *

"Without doubt, personhood's arguments for homosexual rights are intended to show and to seek the highest degree of respect for those on behalf of whom they are made. Nevertheless, in the very concept of a homosexual identity there is something potentially disserving—if not disrespectful—to the cause advocated. There is something not altogether liberating. Those who engage in homosexual sex may or may not perceive themselves as bearing a 'homosexual identity.' Their homosexual relations may be a pleasure they take or an intimacy they value without constituting—at least qua homosexual relations—something definitive of their identity. At the heart of personhood's analysis is the reliance upon a sharply demarcated 'homosexual identity' to which a person is immediately consigned at the moment he seeks to engage in homosexual sex. For personhood, that is, homosexual relations are to be protected to the extent that they fundamentally define a species of person that is, by definition, to be strictly distinguished from the heterosexual. Persons may have homosexual sex only because they have elected to define themselves as 'homosexuals'—because homosexuality lies at 'the heart of . . . what they are.' Thus, even as it argues for homosexual rights, personhood becomes yet another turn of the screw that has pinned those who engage in homosexual sex into a fixed identity specified by their difference from 'heterosexuals.' * * *

"To put it another way, the idea of a 'homosexual identity' has its origin in precisely the kind of invidious classification described earlier. Homosexuality is first understood as a central, definitive element of a person's identity only from the viewpoint of its 'deviancy.' Indeed, there is from the outset an imbalance: within its own self-understanding, heterosexuality is merely normality, and the heterosexual must make some further, more particular decisions—pursuing certain kinds of partners or forms of sexual pleasure—before he will be said to have defined his identity according to sexual criteria. To the extent that heterosexuality does understand itself as definitive per se, it does so only in the face of and in contradistinction to a homosexuality already classified as abnormal and grotesque. By contrast, the mere act of being homosexual is seen as definitive in itself precisely because of its supposed abnormality, and it remains categorically definitive regardless of what sort of partners or sexual encounters the homosexual pursues. In defending homosexuality because of its supposedly self-definitive character, personhood reproduces the heterosexual view of homosexuality as a quality that, like some characterological virus, has invaded and fundamentally altered the nucleus of a person's identity.

" * * * Obviously, differences of sexuality, gender, and race exist among us. These are not, however, differences in *identity* until we make them so. Moreover, it is the desire to count oneself 'superior' to another, or even to count oneself 'normal,' that converts such differences into those specified identities in opposition to which we define ourselves. To protect the rights of 'the homosexual' would of course be a victory; doing so, however, because homosexuality is essential to a person's identity is no liberation, but simply the flip side of the same rigidification of sexual identities by which our society simultaneously inculcates sexual roles, normalizes sexual conduct, and vilifies 'faggots.'

" * * * We must reject the personhood thesis, then, not because the concept of 'self-definition' is analytically incoherent, nor because it is too 'individualistic,' but ultimately because it betrays privacy's—if not personhood's own—political aspirations. By conceiving of the conduct that it purports to protect as 'essential to the individual's identity,' personhood inadvertently reintroduces into privacy analysis the very premise of the invidious uses of state power it seeks to overcome."

Michael Sandel, "Moral Argument and Liberal Toleration: Abortion and Homosexuality," 77 *California Law Review* 521, 535–38 (1989).* Arguments from neutral principles and procedural protections miss the point; homosexual intimacy should be defended as a positively good thing. "Like Blackmun and Stevens, the appeals court [in *Hardwick*] constructed an analogy between privacy in marriage and privacy in homosexual relations. But unlike the Supreme Court dissenters, it did not rest the analogy on voluntarist grounds [the argument that government should be neutral among competing concepts of morality] alone. It argued instead that both practices may realize important human goods.

"The marital relationship is significant, wrote the court of appeals, not only because of its procreative purpose but also 'because of the unsurpassed opportunity for mutual support and self-expression that it provides.' It recalled the Supreme Court's observation in *Griswold* that '[m]arriage is a coming together for better or for worse, hopefully enduring, and intimate to the degree of being sacred.' And it went on to suggest that the qualities the Court so prized in *Griswold* could be present in homosexual unions as well:

'For some, the sexual activity in question here serves the same purpose as the intimacy of marriage.'

"Ironically, this way of extending privacy rights to homosexuals depends on an 'old-fashioned' reading of *Griswold* as protecting the human goods realized in marriage, a reading the Court has long since renounced in favor of an individualist reading. By drawing on the teleological dimension of *Griswold*, the substantive case for homosexual privacy offends the liberalism that insists on neutrality. It grounds the right of privacy on the good of the practice it would protect, and so fails to be neutral among conceptions of the good.

"The more frequently employed precedent for homosexual rights is not *Griswold* but *Stanley v. Georgia*, which upheld the right to possess obscene materials in the privacy of one's home. *Stanley* did not hold that the obscene films found in the defendant's bedroom served a 'noble purpose,' only that he had a right to view them in private. The toleration *Stanley* defended was wholly independent of the value or importance of the thing being tolerated. * * *

"The problem with the neutral case for toleration is the opposite side of its appeal; it leaves wholly unchallenged the adverse views of homosexuality itself. Unless those views can be plausibly addressed, even a Court ruling in their favor is unlikely to win for homosexuals more than a thin and fragile toleration. A fuller respect would require, if not admiration, at least some appreciation of the lives homosexuals live. Such appreciation, however, is unlikely to be cultivated by a legal and political discourse conducted in terms of autonomy rights alone. * * *

"Admittedly, the tendency to bracket substantive moral questions makes it difficult to argue for toleration in the language of the good. Defining privacy rights by defending the practices privacy protects seems either reckless or quaint; reckless because it rests so much on moral argument, quaint because it recalls the traditional view that ties the case for privacy to the merits of the conduct privacy protects. But as the abortion and sodomy cases illustrate, the attempt to bracket moral questions faces difficulties of its own. They suggest the truth in the 'naive' view, that the justice or injustice of laws against abortion and homosexual sodomy may have something to do with the morality or immorality of these practices after all."

CHAPTER 3

Equality Challenges to State Sex and Sexuality Discriminations

In the normal equal protection case, the Supreme Court will uphold any regulatory classification (such as good eyesight for getting a driver's license) so long as there is a "rational basis" for the classification: the legislature's goal (traffic safety) is a valid one, and its means (good sight) is rationally related to the achievement of that goal. The state is given wide latitude to make reasonable regulatory distinctions—or discriminations—under rational basis review. *Bowers v. Hardwick* (Chapter 2, Section 3) is an example of ordinary rational basis review, but only in the context of a substantive due process challenge. Neither *Bowers* nor *Roe v. Wade* (Chapter 2, Section 2) discussed equal protection challenges to classifications of persons based on characteristics related to sexuality. Indeed, claims that the Georgia sodomy law or the Texas abortion law denied gay people or women the equal protection of the laws would have faced some formal obstacles, suggested by the materials below.

That the modern Equal Protection Clause has a great deal of constitutional bite owes much to the success of the civil rights movement, whose legal foundation was laid primarily by the NAACP Legal Defense and Education Fund, Inc. In the 1930s and 1940s, these lawyers successfully challenged the exclusion of African Americans from jury service, voting in all-white primaries, and voting in general elections. The Inc. Fund's greatest success was its challenge to apartheid, namely laws requiring segregation by race in education, transportation, and other public activities. The flagship precedent was *Brown v. Board of Education*, U.S. (1954), which interpreted the Equal Protection Clause to bar the state from segregating children in public schools by race. Chief Justice Warren's opinion for the Court emphasized the importance of public education to American citizenship, but subsequent opinions for the Court extended *Brown* to overturn racial segregation of state parks, swimming pools, and other public spaces.

Some of the Inc. Fund lawyers believed that the emotional as well as legal root of apartheid was fear about "the mixing of the races." Although many blacks as well as whites disliked interracial sexuality, the Inc. Fund in the 1960s mounted a strong challenge to such policies. Its lawyers prevailed in *McLaughlin v. Florida*, 379 U.S. 184 (1964), which struck down a law making it a crime for two people of different races to cohabitate openly with one another. As in *Brown*, the Court clearly applied something more critical than rational basis review, but was unclear as to its rationale. The next case was not only a constitutional jackpot for the Inc. Fund, but also reframed the Equal Protection Clause for the next generation of constitutional litigators—including those who would later object to sex and sexual orientation discriminations harming women, lesbians, gay men, bisexuals, and transgendered people.

Richard and Mildred Loving v. Virginia

United States Supreme Court, 1967.
388 U.S. 1, 87 S.Ct. 1817, 18 L.Ed.2d 1010.

■ CHIEF JUSTICE WARREN delivered the opinion of the Court.

[In 1958, Mildred Jeter, an African–American woman, and Richard Loving, a white man, both residents of Virginia, got married in the District of Columbia. Upon returning to Virginia and making their home there, they were prosecuted for violating the state law making different-race marriage a crime. After they pleaded guilty in 1959, the Virginia trial judge imposed a one-year jail sentence, but suspended it for 25 years on condition that the Lovings leave Virginia and not return together for 25 years. The state courts later denied the Lovings' motion to vacate the conviction and sentence on the ground that the anti-miscegenation law was unconstitutional.]

Virginia is now one of 16 States which prohibit and punish marriages on the basis of racial classifications. Penalties for miscegenation arose as an incident to slavery and have been common in Virginia since the colonial period. The present statutory scheme dates from the adoption of the Racial Integrity Act of 1924, passed during the period of extreme nativism which followed the end of the First World War. * * *

[I]   In upholding the constitutionality of these provisions in the decision below, the Supreme Court of Appeals of Virginia referred to its 1955 decision in *Naim v. Naim*, 197 Va. 80, 87 S.E.2d 749. * * * In *Naim*, the state court concluded that the State's legitimate purposes were "to preserve the racial integrity of its citizens," and to prevent "the corruption of blood," "a mongrel breed of citizens," and "the obliteration of racial pride," obviously an endorsement of the doctrine of White Supremacy. * * *

* * * [T]he State argues that the meaning of the Equal Protection Clause, as illuminated by the statements of the Framers, is only that state penal laws containing an interracial element as part of the definition of the offense must apply equally to whites and Negroes in the sense that members of each race are punished to the same degree. Thus, the State contends that, because its miscegenation statutes punish equally both the white and the Negro participants in an interracial marriage, these statutes, despite their reliance on racial classifications do not constitute an invidious discrimination based upon race. The second argument advanced by the State assumes the validity of its equal application theory. The argument is that, if the Equal Protection Clause does not outlaw miscegenation statutes because of their reliance on racial classifications, the question of constitutionality would thus become whether there was any rational basis for a State to treat interracial marriages differently from other marriages. On this question, the State argues, the scientific evidence is substantially in doubt and, consequently, this Court should defer to the wisdom of the state legislature in adopting its policy of discouraging interracial marriages.

Because we reject the notion that the mere "equal application" of a statute containing racial classifications is enough to remove the classifications from the Fourteenth Amendment's proscription of all invidious racial discriminations, we do not accept the State's contention that these statutes should be upheld if there is any possible basis for concluding that they serve a rational purpose. The mere fact of equal application does not mean that our analysis of these statutes should follow the approach we have taken in cases involving no racial discrimination where the Equal Protection Clause has been arrayed against a statute discriminating between the kinds of advertising which may be displayed on trucks in New York City, *Railway Express Agency, Inc. v. New York*, or an exemption in Ohio's ad valorem tax for merchandise owned by a non-resident in a storage warehouse, *Allied Stores of Ohio, Inc. v. Bowers*, 358 U.S. 522 (1959). In these cases, involving distinctions not drawn according to race, the Court has merely asked whether there is any rational foundation for the discriminations, and has deferred to the wisdom of the state legislatures. In the case at bar, however, we deal with statutes containing racial classifications, and the fact of equal application does not immunize the statute from the very heavy burden of justification which the Fourteenth Amendment has traditionally required of state statutes drawn according to race.

The State argues that statements in the Thirty-ninth Congress about the time of the passage of the Fourteenth Amendment indicate that the Framers did not intend the Amendment to make unconstitutional state miscegenation laws. Many of the statements alluded to by the State concern the debates over the Freedmen's Bureau Bill, which President Johnson vetoed, and the Civil Rights Act of 1866, 14 Stat. 27, enacted over his veto. While these statements have some relevance to the intention of Congress in submitting the Fourteenth Amendment, it must be understood that they pertained to the passage of specific statutes and not to the broader, organic purpose of a constitutional amendment. As for the various statements directly concerning the Fourteenth Amendment, we have said in connection with a related problem, that although these historical sources "cast some light" they are not sufficient to resolve the problem; "[a]t best, they are inconclusive. The most avid proponents of the post-War Amendments undoubtedly intended them to remove all legal distinctions among 'all persons born or naturalized in the United States.' Their opponents, just as certainly, were antagonistic to both the letter and the spirit of the Amendments and wished them to have the most limited effect." *Brown*. We have rejected the proposition that the debates in the Thirty-ninth Congress or in the state legislatures which ratified the Fourteenth Amendment supported the theory advanced by the State, that the requirement of equal protection of the laws is satisfied by penal laws defining offenses based on racial classifications so long as white and Negro participants in the offense were similarly punished. *McLaughlin*.

The State finds support for its "equal application" theory in the decision of the Court in *Pace v. Alabama*, 106 U.S. 583 (1883). In that case, the Court upheld a conviction under an Alabama statute forbidding adultery or fornication between a white person and a Negro which imposed a greater penalty than that of a statute proscribing similar conduct by members of the same race. The Court reasoned that the statute could not be said to discriminate against Negroes because the punishment for each participant in the offense was the same. However, as recently as the 1964 Term, in rejecting the reasoning of that case, we stated "*Pace* represents a limited view of the Equal Protection Clause which has not withstood analysis in the subsequent decisions of this Court." *McLaughlin*. As we there demonstrated, the Equal Protection Clause requires the consideration of whether the classifications drawn by any statute constitute an arbitrary and invidious discrimination. The clear and central purpose of the Fourteenth Amendment was to eliminate all official state sources of invidious racial discrimination in the States.

There can be no question but that Virginia's miscegenation statutes rest solely upon distinctions drawn according to race. The statutes proscribe generally accepted conduct if engaged in by members of different races. Over the years, this Court has consistently repudiated "[d]istinctions between citizens solely because of their ancestry" as being "odious to a free people whose institutions are founded upon the doctrine of equality." *Hirabayashi v. United States*, 320 U.S. 81 (1943). At the very least, the Equal Protection Clause demands that racial classifications, especially suspect in criminal statutes, be subjected to the "most rigid scrutiny," *Korematsu v. United States*, 323 U.S. 214 (1944), and, if they are ever to be upheld, they must be shown to be necessary to the accomplishment of some permissible state objective, independent of the racial discrimination which it was the object of the Fourteenth Amendment to eliminate. * * *

There is patently no legitimate overriding purpose independent of invidious racial discrimination which justifies this classification. The fact that Virginia prohibits only interracial marriages involving white persons demonstrates that the racial classifications must stand on their own justification, as measures designed to maintain White Supremacy.[11] We have consistently denied the constitutionality of measures which restrict the rights of citizens on account of race. There can be no doubt that restricting the freedom to marry solely because of racial classifications violates the central meaning of the Equal Protection Clause.

[II]   These statutes also deprive the Lovings of liberty without due process of law in violation of the Due Process Clause of the Fourteenth Amendment. The freedom to marry has long been recognized as one of the vital personal rights essential to the orderly pursuit of happiness by free men. Marriage is one of the "basic civil rights of man," fundamental to our very existence and survival. *Skinner v. State of Oklahoma*, 316 U.S. 535 (1942). To deny this fundamental freedom on so unsupportable a basis as the racial classifications embodied in these statutes, classifications so directly subversive of the principle of equality at the heart of the Fourteenth Amendment, is surely to deprive all the State's citizens of liberty without due process of law. * * * [Reversed.]

■ [The concurring opinion of JUSTICE STEWART is omitted.]

NOTES ON *LOVING* AND THEORIES OF EQUAL PROTECTION HEIGHTENED SCRUTINY

The Court applied heightened scrutiny under both the Equal Protection Clause (Part I) and the Due Process Clause (Part II). These notes will focus on the former. One can read the Court's opinion to suggest that three different features of the Virginia law rendered it constitutionally suspect and ultimately invalid: the race-based classification, which in turn both reflected a philosophy of "White Supremacy" and represented an effort to entrench a race-based caste system in Virginia. The case was an easy one for the Justices in 1967, because race had been discredited as a state classification, white supremacy had been widely condemned as a divisive state policy, and the idea of a racial caste system had become unacceptable. Where the Justices would take the Equal Protection Clause after *Loving*

---

11. Appellants point out that the State's concern in these statutes, as expressed in the words of the 1924 Act's title, "An Act to Preserve Racial Integrity," extends only to the integrity of the white race. While Virginia prohibits whites from marrying any nonwhite (subject to the exception for the descendants of Pocahontas), Negroes, Orientals, and any other racial class may intermarry without statutory interference. Appellants contend that this distinction renders Virginia's miscegenation statutes arbitrary and unreasonable even assuming the constitutional validity of an official purpose to preserve "racial integrity." We need not reach this contention because we find the racial classifications in these statutes repug-

nant to the Fourteenth Amendment, even assuming an even-handed state purpose to protect the "integrity" of all races. [*Editors' note*: The Virginia statutes stated that "the term 'white person' shall apply only to such person as has no trace whatever of any blood other than Caucasian; but persons who have one-sixteenth or less of the blood of the American Indian and have no other non-Caucasic blood shall be deemed to be white persons." In an earlier footnote, Chief Justice Warren explained this exception by quoting a 1925 publication by a state official, who wrote that it reflected " 'the desire of all to recognize as an integral and honored part of the white race the descendants of John Rolfe and Pocahontas.' "]

was a matter of intense academic speculation. Consider some equal protection theories as applied to *Loving*:

1. *Irrational Classification Theories.* Unlike *Brown*, *Loving* focused on the race-based classification. One way to read *Loving* would be to say, as Gerald Gunther did in "The Supreme Court, 1971 Term—Foreword: In Search of Evolving Doctrine on a Changing Court: A Model for a Newer Equal Protection," 86 Harv. L. Rev. 1 (1972), that the Supreme Court had created a *double standard* of easy-to-pass rational basis review for most state classifications and hard-not-to-flunk strict scrutiny for race-based classifications. One then must ask: What is so constitutionally objectionable about classifications based on race? *Loving* says the Virginia racial classification was "invidious," "irrational," and so forth. What might that mean?

(a) Aristotelian Fairness: Treat Like Things Alike. Aristotle maintained that treating like things alike, and different things differently, is the epitome of reason. Treating like things differently is irrational; equally irrational is treating different things alike. The Warren Court saw different-race couples such as the Lovings as "like" same-race couples. This observation rested upon the civil rights movement's proposition that racial variation is benign and meaningless, from a scientific point of view. Virginia's theory of a "mongrel race" had no scientific support. From an Aristotelian point of view, there was no rational difference between the black-black couple allowed to get married and the black-white couple. It was therefore irrational—and unconstitutional—to treat them differently. (Note that defenders of the Virginia law had an answer to this kind of argument: Blacks and whites were treated the same, *i.e.*, they were both forbidden from marrying a person of the other race.)

One feature of this kind of reasoning is that it does not tell the decisionmaker exactly how the complaining persons are to be treated. The Lovings were asking to be treated as a married couple, and so the Court ruled. But, consistent with equal protection thus understood, the Court could have ruled that Virginia could not recognize same-race marriages so long as it did not recognize different-race ones. (After *Loving*, many states left their anti-miscegenation laws on the books, perhaps for their symbolic effect. There was no urgency to repeal them.) Relatedly, Aristotelian comparisons typically entail the privileging of one of the compared items: By requiring Virginia to elevate black-white unions to the high status it gave white-white unions, the Court was implicitly privileging the latter; white-white marriages are the goal to which different-race couples should aspire.

(b) Max Weber and Administering the Modern State: Bad Policy. Max Weber famously maintained that the core feature distinguishing modern from medieval society is that the former punishes and rewards people based upon what they could do, while the latter did so based upon who they were. Rewards in modern society must be instrumental to social and economic tasks, a system of merit, rather than derivative of social or economic status, a caste system. The modern corporation understands itself as driven by merit rather than by inheritance: the executive who has ideas and drive is

someone the company wants, not the boss's son. (And if the boss has a son, she will require him to "work his way up," learning and proving himself first.)

So the Equal Protection Clause might be read to assure that state policies not reinforce non-merit-based criteria and not contribute to a caste system. When read in context of Virginia's history, its race-based classification was the very opposite of instrumental rationality as understood by Weber: the same conduct was being treated very differently based upon an irrelevant (and legally constructed) status feature; meting out entitlements and punishments based upon disfavored status and not bad conduct is, literally, medieval. Because the Virginia law was a criminal statute (the Lovings could have gone to jail), its violation of the Weberian ideal was particularly significant. Because the state's asserted consequences (a "mongrel race") were so disconnected from respectable science, its Weberian fate was sealed.

(c) Gordon Allport and Prejudice: Bad Motives. Chief Justice Warren called the Virginia law an "invidious" racial discrimination. In this charge, he was probably speaking against the backdrop of learning that "prejudice" was the epitome of human irrationality. Since the 1920s, social scientists had been developing a comprehensive theory of prejudice, and its destructive consequences for society as well as individuals. Gordon Allport and other social scientists had filed a statement in *Brown*, arguing that hatred or disgust based upon someone's race was not only pervasively harmful to black schoolchildren, but also to white schoolchildren and, indeed, to the prejudiced person generally. See generally Allport, *The Nature of Prejudice* (1954). The bigot was an object of social concern, and the state could not admissibly be the forum within which his prejudice could operate. Hence, equal protection might be a constitutional mechanism to purge state policy of the per se irrationality of prejudice, animus, and hatred.

2. *Subordinated Class Theories. Brown* had said nothing about the race-based classification and had, instead, focused on the class of schoolchildren stigmatized by segregated schools While *Loving* focused on the classification, it did so because the Virginia law did not have a sharp class-based harm: the injured class of "miscegenosexuals" (Sam Marcosson's word for people attracted to those of another race) defied the traditional black-white characterization, but race was clearly the classification being deployed. (For more on this, see Section 3 of this Chapter.) But it is easy to see a class-based effect in *Loving*: blacks as a class were harmed insofar as the law's goal was "White Supremacy" (the only time that phrase appears in a Supreme Court opinion). So what is constitutionally wrong with class-based harms?

(a) John Rawls and Fairness. In a series of articles (culminating in his book, *A Theory of Justice*), John Rawls maintained that the liberal state is not entitled to adopt policies which unfairly penalize or subordinate entire groups of people. His famous test for determining which policies meet the test of "justice as fairness" is to imagine ourselves "behind the veil of ignorance": Not knowing what position I shall have in society (including

my wealth, race, sex, etc.), what rules would I adopt for a well-ordered polity? No one in her right mind would propound apartheid policies systematically denying black people opportunities and rights white people have, if there were a chance that the policymaker herself would be a black woman in that apartheid society. (In contrast, one can easily imagine such a policymaker adopting a rule against murder, theft, or rape. Although such rules would constrain her own behavior, they would also be important protections for her whatever her status once the veil had dropped.)

(b) John Harlan and Pluralism: Social Movements and the Law. Dissenting in *Plessy*, Justice Harlan had maintained that a race-based apartheid system subordinating African Americans would intensify racial divisions, a state of affairs deeply harmful to the country's future. America's destiny was intimately linked to the ability of people of both races to cooperate and not fall into acrimonious strife. His intuition was that a state policy openly suppressing one race for the advantage of another was a recipe for long-term political disaster: The subordinated race would harbor hatred against the oppressor race, whose violent intentions toward the former would be heightened thereby. American political theory of the twentieth century strongly supports Harlan's insight. Not only was the United States squandering valuable human capital by subordinating the people of one race, but it was instilling race hatred and internal divisions.

Relatedly, people of color were no longer willing to tolerate their subordination. The NAACP and Dr. King's Southern Christian Leadership Conference represented organized political action by black people and their allies. This was the classic example of an identity-based social movement, engaged in a politics of recognition: We are equal citizens, and state discrimination suggesting our inferiority or second-class citizenship is intolerable. Once such a social movement has persuaded the American mainstream (in this case, America outside the South) that its members are entitled to full participation, the Court will sweep away discriminations against the group.

(c) Carolene Products *and Representation–Reinforcement Theories.* Neither *Brown* nor *Loving* said anything about the delicate issue of which organ of government is best situated to remedy an irrational classification that subordinates a class of human beings. The Supreme Court in *United States v. Carolene Products Co.*, 304 U.S. 144, 152 n.4 (1938), ruled that the legislative process is the most appropriate forum for remedying most unfair state or federal policies and, therefore, that the judiciary should generally refrain from aggressive review. In its famous footnote four, the Court said that the presumption of validity did not apply when state law or policy imposed disadvantages or penalties reflecting prejudice against "discrete and insular minorities." The idea was that, when the state political process was not functioning fairly, the presumption in favor of judicial review should not hold. See John Hart Ely, *Democracy and Distrust: A Theory of Judicial Review* (1980) (defending and articulating the *Carolene* approach).

This idea helped defeat apartheid: Federal judges were particularly willing to strike down discriminations against African Americans in the

South, because they knew that apartheid either excluded people of color from the political process or systematically discriminated against them in the operation of that process. (As to the latter, if most politically active groups of citizens harbor prejudice toward a minority, the minority is likely to be excluded from the normal bargaining process and to be scapegoated.)

3. *Fundamental Interests and Equal Protection Balancing.* Chief Justice Warren's opinion also faulted the Virginia law for infringing the couple's fundamental right to marry. It is odd that Warren deemed this a due process argument; surely, there is not a pre-political right that Americans have for the state to recognize their marriages. It sounds more like an equal protection claim: This one group of citizens is being treated differently as to a matter of fundamental legal (and personal) consequence. After *Loving* and *Harper v. Virginia State Bd. of Elections*, 383 U.S. 663 (1966) (fundamental right to vote), the Supreme Court was willing to apply heightened equal protection scrutiny to state (non-race as well as race) discriminations as to the apportionment of fundamental interests. See *Zablocki v. Redhail*, 434 U.S. 374 (1978) (striking down a law restricting remarriage by parents with outstanding child and spouse support obligations, on equal protection grounds; heightened scrutiny justified by discriminatory treatment of fundamental marriage rights).

"Fundamental" interests have included voting (*Harper*), marriage (*Redhail*), jury service (dozens of race-based exclusion cases). What else? Chief Justice Warren's opinion in *Brown* relied mainly on the fundamental importance of public education in its invalidation of school segregation. This reading of *Brown* was, however, rejected in *San Antonio Independent School District v. Rodriguez*, 411 U.S. 1 (1973). Justice Powell's opinion for the Court not only ruled that discriminatory apportionment of educational benefits did not involve fundamental *rights* triggering strict scrutiny, but reasoned that only those rights "explicitly or implicitly guaranteed by the Constitution" could be understood as fundamental. In dissent, Justice Marshall criticized the majority's rigid approach and maintained that "the degree of care with which the Court will scrutinize particular classifications [depends] on the constitutional and societal importance of the interest adversely affected and the recognized invidiousness of the basis upon which the particular classification is drawn." Note how this *sliding scale* provides a unified equal protection theory, one considering the irrationality of the classification, the importance of the interest, and (in a portion of the dissent not quoted) the ability of the subordinated class to rectify the discrimination in the political process.

PROBLEM 3–1

IN THE WAKE OF THE CIVIL RIGHTS MOVEMENT: WOMEN'S AND GAY PEOPLE'S OBJECTIONS TO STATE EXCLUSIONS, CIRCA 1961[a]

Like people of color, women engaged in a vigorous politics of recognition during the late nineteenth century; unlike the politics of people of

---

a.   This introductory note is based upon Cynthia Harrison, *"On Account of Sex": The* Politics of Women's Issues, 1945–68 *(1988);* William Eskridge, Jr., *"Some Effects of Iden-*

color, theirs won some notable victories early in the twentieth. The Nineteenth Amendment rejected traditionalist arguments that women's role should be limited to the domestic sphere and advanced the norm that women's abilities were on a par with men's. The early birth control movement was part of such a politics (Chapter 2). Potentially important for women's politics of recognition was the proposed Equal Rights Amendment (ERA), first introduced in Congress in 1923. Many feminists opposed the ERA on the grounds that it would preempt labor-protective legislation or wrongfully denied women's genuine difference from men. Women's equality politics picked up speed after World War II. Women who had proved themselves fully equal to men during the war were often unwilling to reassume their subordinate status after the war. In constitutional law, this attitude was displayed most clearly in the cases challenging women's exclusion or exemption from jury service.

Women generally did not serve on juries before World War I. Once women gained the right to vote, some state courts construed their state jury service laws to include women, because the laws tied jury venires to voting lists. Nonetheless, as the nation entered World War II, only 13 states required the same jury service of women that they required of men; 15 states allowed women to opt out of compulsory jury service; 20 states disqualified women as a class. After the war, the situation shifted rapidly, and the Supreme Court gave it a push in 1946. Relying on a federal statute, the Court overturned the conviction of Edna and Donald Ballard for promotion of a fraudulent religious program, because the federal judge excluded women from the jury venire. See *Ballard v. United States*, 329 U.S. 187 (1946). A Court majority declined to constitutionalize that principle in *Fay v. New York*, 332 U.S. 261 (1947), but four dissenters in that case (including Douglas) maintained that a "blue ribbon" jury substantially excluding women and working class people violated the Equal Protection Clause.

After *Fay*, the complete exclusion of women dropped away. By 1961, only three states retained complete exclusions. Of the 47 states where women were eligible, 21 states had no special gender-based rules, 8 states allowed women to be excused if their service would create hardships for their families, 15 states and the District of Columbia allowed women to opt out for any reason, and three states permitted women to serve only if they opted in. Gwendolyn Hoyt killed her husband in Florida, one of the states in the last group. A jury of 12 men found her guilty of murder, and she appealed on the ground that the Equal Protection Clause prohibited the exclusion of women from the jury that convicted her. Dorothy Kenyon persuaded the ACLU to handle Hoyt's appeal to the Supreme Court, arguing that *Ballard*'s federal statutory rule should be extended to the states as a matter of equal protection. The Supreme Court takes the appeal

tity–Based Social Movements on Constitutional Law in the Twentieth Century," 100 Mich. L. Rev. 2062 (2002); Verta Taylor, "Social Movement Continuity: The Women's Movement in Abeyance," 54 Am. Soc. Rev. 761 (1989).

in *Hoyt v. Florida* (1961 Term, No. 31). What arguments should Kenyon emphasize? How should she persuade the Court that the Florida jury law should be subjected to something tougher than rational basis review under the Equal Protection Clause? Would her case have been stronger after *Loving*? For the Court's decision in the case, see *Hoyt v. Florida*, 368 U.S. 57 (1961).

At the same time the ACLU was presenting the Court with equal protection sex discrimination claims on behalf of women, a gay man was presenting the Court with equal protection sexual orientation claims on behalf of "homosexuals." The Civil Service Commission ("CSC") barred Dr. Franklin Kameny, a Harvard Ph.D. astronomer, from any kind of employment in the federal government because of evidence that he was a sexually active "homosexual." Kameny sued the federal government to get his job back. His attorney argued that the government's action was arbitrary and therefore in violation of the the Fifth Amendment. The federal courts summarily dismissed the complaint. Kameny filed a petition for writ of certiorari with the U.S. Supreme Court. Petitioner's Brief, *Kameny v. Brucker* (1960 Term, No. 676).

Kameny made standard due process arguments: the government's decision to fire him and bar him from further employment was not sufficiently supported by the facts of his case, did not follow the proper procedures, and operated under a substantively unsupportable rule barring federal employment of people who commit "immoral conduct." Not only was the "immoral conduct" bar vague, but it imposed an "odious conformity" upon federal employees, inconsistent with the First Amendment. Most of Kameny's brief, however, was an equal protection attack on the CSC's exclusion of "homosexuals" from government employment. (In *Bolling v. Sharpe*, 347 U.S. 497 (1954), a companion case with *Brown*, the Supreme Court had interpreted the Fifth Amendment's Due Process Clause to entail equal protection responsibilities for the federal government.) What kinds of arguments should Kameny have made to warrant heightened scrutiny under the equal protection component of the Fifth Amendment? Would *Loving* improve his chances of success? For the Court's response, see *Kameny v. Brucker*, 365 U.S. 843 (1961).

SEX DISCRIMINATIONS

American history is full of sex-based discriminations. As of 1961, when Dorothy Kenyon challenged Florida's opt-in system for women to serve on juries, the U.S. Supreme Court had never struck down a law on grounds that it discriminated against women or on the basis of sex. Nor was that string of defeats broken in *Hoyt v. Florida*, 368 U.S. 57 (1961): the Warren Court unanimously upheld the sex discrimination. Ironically, *Hoyt* came just as the women's rights movement was gaining mass public support.

Responding to mounting feminist demands, President Kennedy established the President's Commission on the Status of Women, which served as a consciousness-raising and idea-sharing forum for feminist lawyers and thinkers from all around the country. Pauli Murray, a civil rights lawyer working toward her J.S.D. at Yale Law School, drafted a remarkable memorandum for the Commission. The memorandum argued that the Equal Protection Clause could be interpreted to question sex-based discriminations for the same reasons the Court had deployed it against race-based discriminations: sex discriminations (like race discriminations) rested upon a natural law understanding of "inherent differences" that had been deployed to support disadvantages and social inferiority of women; the naturalized view of sex differences rested upon unproven stereotypes or myths about women that were usually an irrational basis for subordinating them; like blacks, women needed to mobilize against pervasive state discrimination through the formation of an organization like the NAACP.[a] Murray's arguments not only persuaded the Commission to endorse the principle that "equality of rights under the law for all persons, male or female, is so basic to democracy and its commitment to the ultimate value of the individual that it must be reflected in the fundamental law of the land," but also helped persuade the ACLU to add sex equality to its civil rights agenda. Moreover, Murray's memorandum served to bridge the concerns of various civil rights activists: her Fourteenth Amendment strategy sought equality for women (desired by liberal ERA feminists), but without sacrificing laws genuinely remedying women's disadvantages in the workplace (desired by labor feminists and ERA opponents). For good measure, Murray, an African American who had been active in the civil

---

a. Pauli Murray, A Proposal to Reexamine the Applicability of the Fourteenth Amendment to State Laws and Practices Which Discriminate on the Basis of Sex Per Se (Dec. 1962), in President's Commission on the Status of Women Papers, Schlesinger Library [Radcliffe Inst.], Box 8, Folder 62, discussed in Cynthia Harrison, *"On Account of Sex": The Politics of Women's Issues, 1945–68*, at 126–34 (1988).

rights movement, sought to unite blacks and women in a common campaign against prejudice and discrimination.

Murray's arguments found their way into the congressional debates over the addition of "sex discrimination" to the jobs title of the civil rights bill. Although the additur was propounded by anti-civil rights Representative Howard Smith of Virginia, Murray and other feminists supported it and ensured that it was preserved in the final statute. The EEOC refused to make sex discrimination a priority in its enforcement of the new law, a stance that drew strong protests. When officials ignored their complaints at a 1966 conference on women's status, Murray, Betty Friedan, and other feminists stormed out in protest and founded the National Organization for Women (NOW). The feminist political energy harnessed by NOW sought a relatively unified political agenda: adoption of an ERA, which would assure constitutional equality; serious enforcement of the Equal Pay Act and Title VII by the EEOC, to assure equality in the workplace; liberalization or repeal of restrictive abortion laws; and adoption of legislation barring sex discrimination in education, accomplished with the enactment of Title IX in 1972.

Like the NAACP had done, NOW established a Legal Defense and Education Fund to litigate issues of women's equality. Most important in the long run, the ACLU in 1971 established its Women's Rights Project, headed by Professor Ruth Bader Ginsburg. Representing a new generation of litigators, Ginsburg followed Kenyon and Murray in pressing the Court to rule that women would have all the same legal rights and duties as men. These lawyers filed constitutional challenges to statutory sex discriminations, and state and federal judges found many of the challenged policies unconstitutional—notwithstanding *Hoyt*. The first case to reach the U.S. Supreme Court was appealed by the ACLU, challenging an Idaho statute which preferred male relatives over female ones for purposes of appointment to administer estates of intestate decedents. Sally Reed's counsel on appeal—Kenyon, Murray, and Ginsburg—urged the Court to renounce the constitutional philosophy of *Hoyt*.

Counsel announced that "a new appreciation of women's place has been generated in the United States." Feminists "of both sexes" had pressed for women's "full membership" in the benefits and duties of constitutional citizenship. "But the distance to equal opportunity for women—in the face of the pervasive social, cultural, and legal roots of sex-based discrimination—remains considerable. In the absence of a firm constitutional foundation for equal treatment of men and women by the law, women seeking to be judged on their individual merits will continue to encounter law-sanctioned obstacles." Accordingly, the ACLU lawyers (and their allies in NOW, which also filed a brief) maintained that sex was a suspect classification for the same reasons race was: Both were natural traits that the dominant culture has treated as a badge of inferiority and stigmatized legally, based upon inaccurate stereotypes about the group defined by the trait.

At the urging of Professor Herma Hill Kay, the California Supreme Court had just accepted such an argument in *Sail'er Inn, Inc. v. Kirby*, 5 Cal.3d 1, 95 Cal.Rptr. 329, 485 P.2d 529 (1971). The U.S. Supreme Court was not prepared to go that far in 1971, nor did the case require it to do so. As Chief Justice Burger said in opening the short conference discussion, the statute was a "carry over from [an] ancient English statute" and "can't stand" because it was an unreasonable discrimination, as the ACLU had also argued. His opinion for a unanimous Court in *Reed v. Reed*, 404 U.S. 71 (1971), rested upon the statute's arbitrariness under the rational basis approach and therefore left the ACLU's other arguments unaddressed. Soon after *Reed*, Congress voted for the proposed ERA and sent it to the states for ratification. This was an important normative moment, for not only did feminists unite behind the proposal, but huge bipartisan majorities in Congress agreed that "Equality of rights under the law shall not be denied or abridged by the United States or any State because of sex."

Sharon Frontiero and Joseph Frontiero v. Elliot Richardson

United States Supreme Court, 1973.
411 U.S. 677, 93 S.Ct. 1764, 36 L.Ed.2d 583.

■ MR. JUSTICE BRENNAN announced the judgment of the Court in an opinion in which MR. JUSTICE DOUGLAS, MR. JUSTICE WHITE, and MR. JUSTICE MARSHALL join.

The question before us concerns the right of a female member of the uniformed services to claim her spouse as a "dependent" for the purposes of obtaining increased quarters allowances and medical and dental benefits under 37 U.S.C. §§ 401, 403, and 10 U.S.C. §§ 1072, 1076, on an equal footing with male members. Under these statutes, a serviceman may claim his wife as a "dependent" without regard to whether she is in fact dependent upon him for any part of her support. A servicewoman, on the other hand, may not claim her husband as a "dependent" under these programs unless he is in fact dependent upon her for over one-half of his support. Thus, the question for decision is whether this difference in treatment constitutes an unconstitutional discrimination against service-women in violation of the [Equal Protection component of the] Due Process Clause of the Fifth Amendment. * * *

[The lower court "surmised that Congress might reasonably have concluded that, since the husband in our society is generally the 'breadwin-ner' in the family—and the wife typically the 'dependent' partner—'it would be more economical to require married female members claiming husbands to prove actual dependency than to extend the presumption of dependency to such members.' " Under the traditional rational basis ap-proach, such an approach was defensible.] But appellants contend that classifications based upon sex, like classifications based upon race, alienage, and national origin, are inherently suspect and must therefore be subjected to close judicial scrutiny. We agree and, indeed, find at least implicit support for such an approach in our unanimous decision only last Term in *Reed.* * * *

There can be no doubt that our Nation has had a long and unfortunate history of sex discrimination. Traditionally, such discrimination was rationalized by an attitude of "romantic paternalism" which, in practical effect, put women, not on a pedestal, but in a cage. * * *

As a result of notions such as these, our statute books gradually became laden with gross, stereotyped distinctions between the sexes and, indeed, throughout much of the 19th century the position of women in our society was, in many respects, comparable to that of blacks under the pre-Civil War slave codes. Neither slaves nor women could hold office, serve on juries, or bring suit in their own names, and married women traditionally were denied the legal capacity to hold or convey property or to serve as legal guardians of their own children. And although blacks were guaranteed the right to vote in 1870, women were denied even that right * * * until adoption of the Nineteenth Amendment half a century later.

It is true, of course, that the position of women in America has improved markedly in recent decades. Nevertheless, it can hardly be doubted that, in part because of the high visibility of the sex characteristic, women still face pervasive, although at times more subtle, discrimination in our educational institutions, in the job market and, perhaps most conspicuously, in the political arena.

Moreover, since sex, like race and national origin, is an immutable characteristic determined solely by the accident of birth, the imposition of special disabilities upon the members of a particular sex because of their sex would seem to violate "the basic concept of our system that legal burdens should bear some relationship to individual responsibility...." *Weber v. Aetna Casualty & Surety Co.*, 406 U.S. 164, 175 (1972). And what differentiates sex from such non-suspect statuses as intelligence or physical disability, and aligns it with the recognized suspect criteria, is that the sex characteristic frequently bears no relation to ability to perform or contribute to society. As a result, statutory distinctions between the sexes often have the effect of invidiously relegating the entire class of females to inferior legal status without regard to the actual capabilities of its individual members.

We might also note that, over the past decade, Congress has itself manifested an increasing sensitivity to sex-based classifications. In Tit. VII of the Civil Rights Act of 1964, for example, Congress expressly declared that no employer, labor union, or other organization subject to the provisions of the Act shall discriminate against any individual on the basis of "race, color, religion, *sex*, or national origin." Similarly, the Equal Pay Act of 1963 provides that no employer covered by the Act "shall discriminate ... between employees on the basis of sex." And '1 of the Equal Rights Amendment, passed by Congress on March 22, 1972, and submitted to the legislatures of the States for ratification, declares that "[e]quality of rights under the law shall not be denied or abridged by the United States or by any State on account of sex." Thus, Congress itself has concluded that classifications based upon sex are inherently invidious, and this conclusion of a coequal branch of Government is not without significance to the question presently under consideration.

With these considerations in mind, we can only conclude that classifications based upon sex, like classifications based upon race, alienage, or national origin, are inherently suspect, and must therefore be subjected to strict judicial scrutiny. Applying the analysis mandated by that stricter standard of review, it is clear that the statutory scheme now before us is constitutionally invalid.

The sole basis of the classification established in the challenged statutes is the sex of the individuals involved. * * * [A] female member of the uniformed services seeking to obtain housing and medical benefits for her spouse must prove his dependency in fact, whereas no such burden is imposed upon male members. In addition, the statutes operate so as to deny benefits to a female member, such as appellant Sharon Frontiero, who provides less than one-half of her spouse's support, while at the same time granting such benefits to a male member who likewise provides less than one-half of his spouse's support. Thus, to this extent at least, it may fairly be said that these statutes command "dissimilar treatment for men and women who are . . . similarly situated." *Reed*.

Moreover, the Government concedes that the differential treatment accorded men and women under these statutes serves no purpose other than mere "administrative convenience." In essence, the Government maintains that, as an empirical matter, wives in our society frequently are dependent upon their husbands, while husbands rarely are dependent upon their wives. Thus, the Government argues that Congress might reasonably have concluded that it would be both cheaper and easier simply conclusively to presume that wives of male members are financially dependent upon their husbands, while burdening female members with the task of establishing dependency in fact.

The Government offers no concrete evidence, however, tending to support its view that such differential treatment in fact saves the Government any money. In order to satisfy the demands of strict judicial scrutiny, the Government must demonstrate, for example, that it is actually cheaper to grant increased benefits with respect to all male members, than it is to determine which male members are in fact entitled to such benefits and to grant increased benefits only to those members whose wives actually meet the dependency requirement. Here, however, there is substantial evidence that, if put to the test, many of the wives of male members would fail to qualify for benefits. And in light of the fact that the dependency determination with respect to the husbands of female members is presently made solely on the basis of affidavits rather than through the more costly hearing process, the Government's explanation of the statutory scheme is, to say the least, questionable.

In any case, our prior decisions make clear that, although efficacious administration of governmental programs is not without some importance, "the Constitution recognizes higher values than speed and efficiency."

Stanley v. Illinois, 405 U.S. 645, 656 (1972). And when we enter the realm of "strict judicial scrutiny," there can be no doubt that "administrative convenience" is not a shibboleth, the mere recitation of which dictates constitutionality. On the contrary, any statutory scheme which draws a sharp line between the sexes, *solely* for the purpose of achieving administrative convenience, necessarily commands "dissimilar treatment for men and women who are . . . similarly situated," and therefore involves the "very kind of arbitrary legislative choice forbidden by the [Constitution]. . . ." *Reed*. We therefore conclude that, by according differential treatment to male and female members of the uniformed services for the sole purpose of achieving administrative convenience, the challenged statutes violate the Due Process Clause of the Fifth Amendment insofar as they require a female member to prove the dependency of her husband.

■ Mr. Justice Stewart concurs in the judgment, agreeing that the statutes before us work an invidious discrimination in violation of the Constitution. *Reed*.

■ [We omit the dissenting opinion of Mr. Justice Rehnquist and the opinion of Mr. Justice Powell (joined by Mr. Chief Justice Burger and Mr. Justice Blackmun) concurring in the judgment. Justice Powell's concurring opinion argued that the statute's sex discrimination was invalid under *Reed* and that it was premature for the Court to decide whether sex is a suspect classification so long as the ERA was pending.]

NOTES ON ARGUMENTS FOR HEIGHTENED SCRUTINY FOR CLASSIFICATIONS BASED ON SEX

1. *Original Intent and the Appropriate Process for Updating the Constitution.* Because only a Court plurality (four out of nine) joined the Brennan opinion, *Frontiero* did not establish strict scrutiny for sex-based classifications, but it did present serious arguments for that proposition. A contrary position is that only race-based classifications should receive strict scrutiny. One could argue that the Framers of the Fourteenth Amendment were only solicitous of protecting the rights of the former slaves and, in fact, rejected the claims of feminists that women be explicitly assured rights during Reconstruction. Section 2 of the Fourteenth Amendment, for example, is an open sex discrimination.

Even proponents of women's rights have conceded that "[b]oldly dynamic interpretation, departing radically from the original understanding, is required to tie to the Fourteenth Amendment's Equal Protection Clause a command that government treat men and women as individuals equal in rights, responsibilities and opportunities." Ruth Bader Ginsburg (who submitted an influential amicus brief in *Frontiero*), "Sexual Equality under the Fourteenth and Equal Rights Amendments," 1979 *Wash. U.L.Q.* 161. What is the normative basis for such "boldly dynamic interpretation"? At the outset, note that most such arguments reason by analogy from race: Sex is just as irrational a basis for state discrimination, and women are analogously harmed by centuries of state discrimination. Reasoning by analogy is an established legal move, and the Equal Protection Clause is nowhere limited to race-based discriminations.

On the other hand, such "boldly dynamic interpretation" would represent a major rearticulation of the Equal Protection Clause way beyond and perhaps also against the expectations of its Framers. The appropriate mechanism for "updating" the Constitution is the amendment process outlined in Article V. Indeed, in 1972 Congress submitted the Equal Rights Amendment to the states. Within months of its submission, the ERA was ratified by half of the 38 states needed for amendment of the Constitution, but then it became stalled by opposition. Justices Powell, Blackmun, and Burger (concurring only in the *Frontiero* result) argued that it was inappropriate for the Court to "amend" the Constitution on its own, while the ERA was pending. Compare Reva Siegel," 'She The People': The Nineteenth Amendment, Sex Equality, Federalism, and the Family," 115 *Harv. L. Rev.* 947 (2002), who argues that the Nineteenth Amendment provides the pertinent textual authority for the interpretation sought by Ginsburg and Brennan in *Frontiero*.

2. *Have Women Been a Subordinated Class the Way African Americans Have Been*? *Frontiero* emphasized the thousands of exclusions and discriminations against women in voting, education, jury service, employment (including public employment), military service, and other important rights and duties. Most of the exclusions and discriminations had precise parallels in America's history of apartheid, and in areas such as voting and military service women were excluded longer than black people were. They could have also pointed to a long history of violence against women that the state has failed to monitor much less prevent. If blacks faced a physical apartheid stigmatizing them and limiting their opportunities, women faced an apartheid of domesticity—the arena to which they were presumptively confined by the web of exclusions and discriminations.

But note how many political successes women had achieved by 1973, including proposal of the ERA by two-thirds majorities in both houses of Congress. Recall the *Carolene Products* idea that special constitutional protection might be extended to "discrete and insular minorities" subjected to systematic discrimination in the political process. Whereas African Americans are discrete and insular minorities, women are neither insular (wherever you find men in our society, you also find women) nor a minority. See Bruce Ackerman, "Beyond *Carolene Products*," 98 *Harv. L. Rev.* 713 (1985). John Hart Ely, *Democracy and Distrust: A Theory of Judicial Review* 164–70 (1980), argues that, although women have long been victims of laws that reflect invidious stereotypes, many of which were enacted in periods when women had no political representation, women are politically salient today. Accordingly, the analogy to race is imperfect: whereas people of color stood no chance of persuading Virginia to repeal its apartheid laws in the *Brown-Loving* era, women could and did persuade state and national legislatures to repeal sex discriminations by the cartload.

3. *Irrationality: Real Differences, Stereotypes, and Immutability. Frontiero* linked race and sex discrimination by demonstrating that they were similarly irrational. Not only were both criteria not reliable bases for public policy, but they reflected base motivations and were singularly unfair. Cutting against these powerful similarities, however, were several complexities. First, social and biological science supported the proposition that race-based differences were trivial, contrary to Virginia's hysterical fears of a "mongrel race." To the extent that race made a difference, it was for social reasons alone. But no respectable scientist in the 1960s maintained that sex-based differences were trivial; many derived from the biological fact that only women can become pregnant and bear children. And respectable policymakers believed that some sex-based categories—especially those relating to pregnancy—were rationally related to good state policy. Are these beliefs in "real differences" still sustainable?

Second, the Court's emphasis on *prejudice* (irrational hatred for a group) in the race cases did not have as much cogency in the sex cases, because there was little social science support for the proposition that men hated women. What the social scientists did believe was that women were held back by cognitive *stereotypes* (men are people in charge like doctors, women are helpers like nurses) even if not by emotional prejudices. In either case, however, the net result was a systemic pattern of male dominance. That state policy might be driven by sex-based stereotypes was potentially just as powerful an idea as the previous idea that state policy in the South was driven by racial prejudice, but it produced a different array of litigants and a different focus for the Equal Protection Clause.

Third, Brennan (following Ginsburg's ACLU amicus brief) argued that strict scrutiny was appropriate because sex, like race, is immutable. Why should immutability make such a difference in an equal protection case? To be sure, some people invoke the notion that because the individual has no control over her race or sex, she should not be penalized for it. That statement can be true, however, only if we believe that race and sex have no legitimate relationship to merit or qualification. There are many characteristics over which an individual may have no control—kleptomania, for example. If it could be shown that most shoplifters act out of an immutable compulsion, could they challenge discrimination against them in the criminal law? Unlikely. Conversely, there are characteristics over which an individual has total control, but which we would all agree should not be the basis for a penalty. Religious affiliation would be one example of that situation. Is sex really immutable? Given the availability of sex-change surgery, one might argue that the only question is the extent to which an individual might elect to change sexes, *i.e.*, by hormone treatment only or by full surgical change. Would race discrimination lose its suspect status if science perfected a method for alteration of skin color? Again, unlikely.

Sequelae to *Frontiero*:—The Disparate Impact Cases. After *Frontiero*, the Supreme Court decided cases on an ad hoc basis for several years. See *Kahn v. Shevin*, 416 U.S. 351 (1974) (upholding a state statute allowing widows, but not widowers, a small property tax exemption; "[w]hether from overt discrimination or from the socialization process," such women faced more difficult barriers in the job market than widowers);

Schlesinger v. Ballard, 419 U.S. 498 (1975) (upholding federal law giving male officers a shorter period in which to attain promotion or be discharged than female officers); *Weinberger v. Wiesenfeld*, 420 U.S. 636 (1975) (striking down a Social Security provision under which a surviving widow and minor children received benefits based on the earnings of the deceased husband and father, but under which only minor children received benefits if the mother died).

An important issue was whether the state could discriminate on the basis of pregnancy. Representing women whose pregnancies were excluded from a state disability program in *Geduldig v. Aiello*, 417 U.S. 484 (1974), Wendy Webster Williams maintained that "the individual who receives a benefit or suffers a detriment because of a physical characteristic unique to one sex benefits or suffers because he or she belongs to one or the other sex"—which surely is sex discrimination, because men are treated differently. Moreover, men are treated more favorably than women, and for exactly the reasons rejected in *Reed* and *Frontiero*: men were privileged and women were denigrated in the public and workplace sphere because of women's unique ability to bear children and a perceived special responsibility for rearing them in the domestic sphere. "Those who would make these unique physical differences a touchstone for unscrutinized differential treatment offer nothing other than the modern version of the historical rationales which were for so long the source of women's second class citizenship under the law." Indeed, "[t]his last prejudice—that women are not serious and permanent members of the workforce and that lurking somewhere in each woman's life is a man fully able to support her—underlies and reinforces discrimination against women in all realms of their lives." Williams' powerful brief was supported by *amicus* briefs from the ACLU and the EEOC. But the nine men on the Court were not persuaded. The discussion in conference revealed little comprehension of Williams' arguments. Most of the Justices agreed with their Chief's complaint that the pregnancy exclusion involves "a different kind of risk than illness covered by [the] Act. [P]rostate problem is covered—as is hysterectomy—different from pregnancy." Based upon this reasoning, the Court upheld the statutory scheme.

Feminists' politics of recognition generally insisted on heightened scrutiny of rules that had an inevitable impact on women. And, generally, the U.S. Supreme Court rejected their stance, just as it had rejected similar arguments for people of color in *Jefferson v. Hackney*, 406 U.S. 535 (1972); *Rodriguez, supra*; and *Washington v. Davis*, 426 U.S. 229 (1976). The leading case was *Personnel Administrator v. Feeney*, 442 U.S. 256 (1979). Helen Feeney found it virtually impossible to advance in the civil service because of the operation of the state's strong preference for veterans. She challenged the preference for its significant adverse impact upon women's opportunities in a state where 98% of the veterans were men. Phyllis Segal's NOW *amicus* brief supporting her claim argued that the preference "inevitably discriminates deeply and pervasively against women as a result of a congeries of laws, regulations and practices which define as overwhelmingly male the class of individuals who qualify as veterans." Invoking

Washington v. Davis, the state responded and the Court agreed that the classification itself (veterans) was benign and there was no evidence whatsoever of any intent to discriminate against women. The Supreme Court agreed with the state and applied a strict understanding of *Davis* to reject the claim.

Craig v. Boren, 429 U.S. 190, 97 S.Ct. 451, 50 L.Ed.2d 397 (1976).
The Court struck down a state law allowing 18–year–old girls to buy low-alcohol beer but requiring boys to be 21 years old. Writing this time for six members of the Court, **Justice Brennan**'s opinion fixed upon a formula for evaluating sex discrimination claims: "To withstand constitutional challenge, previous cases establish that classifications by gender must serve important governmental objectives and must be substantially related to achievement of those objectives. Thus, in *Reed*, the objectives of 'reducing the workload on probate courts' and 'avoiding intrafamily controversy' were deemed of insufficient importance to sustain use of an overt gender criterion in the appointment of administrators of intestate decedents' estates. Decisions following *Reed* similarly have rejected administrative ease and convenience as sufficiently important objectives to justify gender-based classifications. *See, e.g., Stanley v. Illinois*, 405 U.S. 645, 656 (1972); *Frontiero; cf. Schlesinger v. Ballard*. And only two Terms ago, *Stanton v. Stanton*, 421 U.S. 7 (1975), expressly stating that *Reed v. Reed* was 'controlling,' held that *Reed* required invalidation of a Utah differential age-of-majority statute, notwithstanding the statute's coincidence with and furtherance of the State's purpose of fostering 'old notions' of role typing and preparing boys for their expected performance in the economic and political worlds.

"*Reed v. Reed* has also provided the underpinning for decisions that have invalidated statutes employing gender as an inaccurate proxy for other, more germane bases of classification. Hence, 'archaic and overbroad' generalizations, *Ballard*, concerning the financial position of servicewomen, *Frontiero*, and working women, *Weinberger v. Wiesenfeld*, could not justify use of a gender line in determining eligibility for certain governmental entitlements. Similarly, increasingly outdated misconceptions concerning the role of females in the home rather than in the 'marketplace and world of ideas' were rejected as loose-fitting characterizations incapable of supporting state statutory schemes that were premised upon their accuracy. *Stanton*. In light of the weak congruence between gender and the characteristic or trait that gender purported to represent, it was necessary that the legislatures choose either to realign their substantive laws in a gender-neutral fashion, or to adopt procedures for identifying those instances where the sex-centered generalization actually comported with fact. * * * "

The foregoing verbal formulation is not as demanding as the one the Court uses to scrutinize race-based classifications, and so it is considered "intermediate" rather than "strict" scrutiny. Nonetheless, it had considerable bite in *Craig*. The statutory goal, traffic safety, was certainly "important," but the Court held the gender classification not "substantially related" to it. Although young males were more likely to be arrested for traffic offenses while drunk than young females, the Court did not find sex to be the key variable and openly doubted whether sale of 3.2% beer contributed much to drunkenness of either sex. Because Oklahoma's beer-purchase law rested upon the stereotypes of " 'reckless' young men" and responsible young women, it was especially vulnerable to the new, tougher standard of review.

Although six Justices joined the foregoing language in the Brennan opinion for the Court, four Justices wrote concurring opinions. **Justice Stevens**' concurring opinion focused on the classification as it worked in the particular circumstances: "In this case, the classification is not as obnoxious as some the Court has condemned, nor as inoffensive as some the Court has accepted. It is objectionable because it is based on an accident of birth, because it is a mere remnant of the now almost universally rejected tradition of discriminating against males in this age bracket, and because, to the extent it reflects any physical difference between males and females, it is actually perverse."

Justice Rehnquist and **Chief Justice Burger** dissented. They objected that the new test was unsupported by the language and history of the Equal Protection Clause, was inconsistent with all but the most recent precedents of the Court (and unjustifiably expanded *Reed*), and required the judiciary to make policy judgments that are more capably and legitimately made by the political branches.

NOTE ON THE DEFEAT OF THE ERA AND THE COURT'S POST-*CRAIG* SEX DISCRIMINATION JURISPRUDENCE

Handed down in 1976, when it was likely the ERA would not be adopted, *Craig* seemed to satisfy liberal feminists' version of women's politics of recognition; the dissenting Justices certainly thought so. Notwithstanding the ambiguous level of scrutiny, the *Craig* formulation—and its application in a case where there were a plausible safety justification and an arguable Twenty–First Amendment boost for state alcohol regulation—had teeth enough to clear out most sex discriminations from state codes. But the story is not one of unmitigated liberal triumph. In fact, the Supreme Court applied *Craig* through the lens of the ERA's defeat.

The ERA stimulated the formation of an anti-feminist countermovement in the 1970s. Like the feminist movement, the countermovement was normative and expressed its norms in the argot of constitutionalism. Its constitutional tenets included the following: sex-neutral and abortion-protective rules imposed by judges in Washington, D.C. were at war with (1) the values of localism, where the family and the state are the primary situs for rules relating to gender-normative roles in bearing and raising children, without interference from the national government; (2) the separation of powers, whereby the popularly elected legislature is both the most legitimate and the most institutionally competent state organ to handle complex, delicate moral and family issues; and (3) fundamental liberties, particularly the rights articulated on behalf of fetuses and parents. These arguments were prominent in the campaign to defeat the ERA. Phyllis Schlafly and other opponents argued that the ERA was a bad idea because it would undermine the family and deprive states of their ability to legislate morality (including sexual abstinence and compulsory heterosexuality), would empower unaccountable federal judges to impose their own elite views on an unconsenting populace, and would deprive wives and parents of fundamental rights needed for the preservation of families. The power of these arguments and their resonance with many Americans was the main reason Justice Brennan could not garner five votes to make sex a suspect classification in *Frontiero*.

The arguments that sunk the ERA also instructed the Supreme Court regarding the extent to which it could apply the Equal Protection Clause to liberate women from archaic stereotypes. Among Mrs. Schlafly's most popular charges against the ERA were that it would empower the Supreme Court to subject women to the draft and military service, to invalidate gendered statutory rape laws, and to require states to recognize same-sex marriages and other "homosexual rights." Most Americans in the 1970s supported sex segregation in military service, statutory rape laws, and marriage limited to different-sex couples. While the ERA lingered, the Supreme Court reaffirmed or suggested sympathy with all of the foregoing sex discriminations, substantially following the constitutional logic of Mrs. Schlafly and her allies. Between 1972 and 1975, the Court brushed aside sex discrimination (and other) arguments for same-sex marriage and sodomy law nullification without even asking for briefs on the merits. The Court dispatched the other two issues in 1981, just before the period for ERA ratification expired for good (1982).

As *Feeney* and *Frontiero* illustrated, the United States armed forces operated under a cornucopia of sex-discriminatory rules, the centerpiece of which was the exclusion of women from combat roles. Women's second-class role in the military was, from the perspective of most feminists, a textbook example of the way in which sexist public law reinforced women's status as second-class citizens. Traditionalists viewed the sex differentiations as either tolerable or necessary, lest the delicate unit cohesion required for military success be imperiled. When the Carter Administration reactivated registration for the draft in 1980, it bowed to congressional pressure to limit registration to men. A three-judge court ruled that the sex discrimination violated the *Craig* standard, but the Supreme Court reversed and validated the statutory sex discrimination in *Rostker v. Goldberg*, 453 U.S. 57 (1981). Justice Rehnquist's opinion emphasized that the Constitution commits military policy to the political branches, and that Congress had in this case engaged in careful fact-finding and deliberation. The latter established that "the decision to exempt women from registration was not the 'accidental by-product of a traditional way of thinking about females.'" Instead, the decision was a corollary of the proposition that women were barred from combat roles, a bar not challenged by the plaintiffs. Because the goal of registration was to prepare for combat mobilization, it was reasonable to focus administrative energies on men. Writing for three dissenters, Justice Marshall found more at stake in the challenge, because women were being excluded from "a fundamental civic obligation."

Although states in the 1970s redrafted their penal codes to be largely sex-neutral, California continued to make it a felony for a male (of any age) to have sexual intercourse with a female under the age of 18. In *Michael M. v. Superior Court*, 450 U.S. 464 (1981), plaintiffs and their *amici* challenged the statute as a classic sex discrimination based upon traditional gender stereotypes, where the vulnerable girl needs to be protected against predatory boys and men, but boys can take care of themselves. California and the United States (which entered the case as an *amicus*) defended the statute as appropriately focusing regulatory attention on the main problem, the need to protect girls against predation and unwanted pregnancies. The statutory rape law was a prophylactic measure to protect minor women who were in fact vulnerable to sexual assault. Its sex discrimination was permissible, because women rarely assaulted boys; it was necessary to the operation of this policy, because girls would be reluctant to report violations if they themselves could be prosecuted. Five Justices accepted this justification. Justice Rehnquist's opinion for a plurality of the Court emphasized the necessity of this sex classification to protect the rights of minor women and strongly deferred to the state's judgment that a sex-neutral statute would not be effective. Dissenting Justices and feminist critics of the decision disputed both elements of the Court's logic: The historical policy of the gendered statute was rooted in archaic stereotypes of vulnerable girls and predatory boys, and a humane anti-predation policy that recognizes girls' as well as boys' sexual agency can criminalize sex between adults and underage persons of either sex.

Although the Supreme Court proved receptive to traditionalist arguments in the areas of greatest social anxiety about sex equality—same-sex marriage, women in combat, and statutory rape—it did not retreat from *Craig*'s baseline, even after the Court shifted toward the right after President Reagan's election in 1980. Indeed, Reagan's first Supreme Court appointee was Sandra Day O'Connor, the first woman to serve on the Court. In *Mississippi University for Women v. Hogan*, 458 U.S. 718 (1982), Justice O'Connor wrote the opinion for a 5–4 Court striking down a state law allowing only women to enroll at the state nursing college. When a law adopts a sex-based classification, she reasoned, the state has a burden of showing an " 'exceedingly persuasive justification for the classification,' " a burden that cannot be met by post-hoc rationalizations by counsel or policies that ultimately rest upon gender stereotypes. This has proven to be a potent restatement of *Craig*. See, *e.g.*, *J.E.B. v. Alabama ex rel. T.B.*, 511 U.S. 127 (1994) (invalidating state's use of sex-based peremptory challenges in jury selection).

United States v. Virginia, 518 U.S. 515, 116 S.Ct. 2264, 135 L.Ed.2d 735 (1996). Virginia Military Institute (VMI) was the sole single-sex school among Virginia's public institutions of higher learning. VMI's distinctive mission was to produce "citizen-soldiers," men prepared for leadership in civilian life and in military service. Using an "adversative," or constantly challenging and doubting, method of training not available elsewhere in Virginia,[b] VMI endeavored to instill physical and mental discipline in its cadets and to impart to them a strong moral code. The adversative method has yielded a large number of civilian and military leaders in Virginia; VMI alumni have been unusually bonded to one another and to the school. Their school loyalty is legendary, and as a consequence VMI has had one of the largest per-student endowments of all undergraduate institutions in the Nation.

The United States sued Virginia and VMI, alleging that VMI's exclusively male admission policy violated the Equal Protection Clause. The District Court ruled in VMI's favor. The Fourth Circuit reversed and ordered Virginia to remedy the constitutional violation. In response, Virginia proposed a parallel program for women: Virginia Women's Institute for Leadership (VWIL), located at Mary Baldwin College, a private liberal arts school for women. In lieu of VMI's adversative method, the VWIL Task Force favored "a cooperative method which reinforces self-esteem." In addition to the standard bachelor of arts program offered at Mary Baldwin, VWIL students would take courses in leadership, complete an off-campus leadership externship, participate in community service projects, and assist in arranging a speaker series.

The District Court found that Virginia's proposal satisfied the Constitution's equal protection requirement, and the Fourth Circuit affirmed. The appeals court deferentially reviewed Virginia's plan and determined that provision of single-sex educational options was a legitimate objective. Maintenance of single-sex programs, the court concluded, was essential to that objective. The court recognized, however, that its analysis risked bypassing equal protection scrutiny, so it fashioned an additional test, asking whether VMI and VWIL students would receive "substantively comparable" benefits. Although the Court of Appeals acknowledged that the VWIL degree lacked the historical benefit and prestige of a VMI degree, the court nevertheless found the educational opportunities at the two schools sufficiently comparable.

The Supreme Court reversed, in an opinion by **Justice Ginsburg**. "To summarize the Court's current directions for cases of official classification based on gender: Focusing on the differential treatment or denial of opportunity for which relief is sought, the reviewing court must determine

---

b. According to the record in the case, the adversative model of education features "[p]hysical rigor, mental stress, absolute equality of treatment, absence of privacy, minute regulation of behavior, and indoctrination in desirable values." The cadets live in spartan barracks where surveillance is constant and privacy nonexistent; they wear uniforms, eat together in the mess hall, and regularly participate in drills. Freshmen students are exposed to the rat line, "an extreme form of the adversative model," comparable in intensity to Marine Corps boot camp. The punishing rat line bonds new cadets to their fellow sufferers and, when they have completed the 7–month experience, to their former tormentors. VMI also employs a hierarchical "class system" of privileges and responsibilities, a "dyke system" for assigning a senior class mentor to each entering class "rat," and a stringently enforced "honor code," which prescribes that a cadet "does not lie, cheat, steal nor tolerate those who do."

whether the proffered justification is 'exceedingly persuasive.' The burden of justification is demanding and it rests entirely on the State. See *Mississippi Univ. for Women v. Hogan.* The State must show 'at least that the [challenged] classification serves "important governmental objectives and that the discriminatory means employed" are "substantially related to the achievement of those objectives." ' *Id.* The justification must be genuine, not hypothesized or invented *post hoc* in response to litigation. And it must not rely on overbroad generalizations about the different talents, capacities, or preferences of males and females.

"The heightened review standard our precedent establishes does not make sex a proscribed classification. Supposed 'inherent differences' are no longer accepted as a ground for race or national origin classifications. Physical differences between men and women, however, are enduring: '[T]he two sexes are not fungible; a community made up exclusively of one [sex] is different from a community composed of both.' *Ballard v. United States.*

" 'Inherent differences' between men and women, we have come to appreciate, remain cause for celebration, but not for denigration of the members of either sex or for artificial constraints on an individual's opportunity. Sex classifications may be used to compensate women 'for particular economic disabilities [they have] suffered,' *Califano v. Webster*, 430 U.S. 313, 320 (1977) (*per curiam*), to 'promot[e] equal employment opportunity,' see *California Federal Sav. & Loan Assn. v. Guerra*, 479 U.S. 272, 289 (1987), to advance full development of the talent and capacities of our Nation's people. But such classifications may not be used, as they once were, to create or perpetuate the legal, social, and economic inferiority of women."

Justice Ginsburg ruled that Virginia had shown no "exceedingly persuasive justification" for excluding all women from the citizen-soldier training afforded by VMI; therefore there was a violation of the Equal Protection Clause. Virginia justified its sex discrimination on several grounds: "single-sex education provides important educational benefits," and the option of single-sex education contributes to "diversity in educational approaches"; "the unique VMI method of character development and leadership training," the school's adversative approach, would have to be modified were VMI to admit women.

"But Virginia has not shown that VMI was established, or has been maintained, with a view to diversifying, by its categorical exclusion of women, educational opportunities within the State. In cases of this genre, our precedent instructs that 'benign' justifications proffered in defense of categorical exclusions will not be accepted automatically; a tenable justification must describe actual state purposes, not rationalizations for actions in fact differently grounded." Justice Ginsburg's review of the record of single-sex education in Virginia revealed that it originated in the state's belief that only men would benefit from higher education. Virginia persisted in that belief much longer than other states; its public university, the University of Virginia, did not admit female students until 1970. VMI's reexamination of its policy after *Mississippi University for Women* offered "no persuasive evidence" that diversity was the state's goal in maintaining VMI as a single-sex college.

Justice Ginsburg also rejected the state's second justification: preserving the adversative method of education. The District Court had made findings of fact that "[m]ales tend to need an atmosphere of adversativeness," while "[f]emales tend to thrive in a cooperative atmosphere." But gender-based averages, the Court ruled, did not justify complete gender-based exclusions. "The notion that admission of women would downgrade VMI's stature, destroy the adversative system and, with it, even the school, is a judgment hardly proved, a prediction hardly different from other 'self-fulfilling prophec[ies],' see *Mississippi Univ. for Women*, routinely used to deny rights or opportunities. When women first sought admission to the bar and access to legal education, concerns of the same order were expressed."

"Women's successful entry into the federal military academies, and their participation in the Nation's military forces, indicate that Virginia's fears for the future of VMI may not be solidly grounded. The State's justification for excluding all women from 'citizen-soldier' training for which some are qualified, in any event, cannot rank as 'exceedingly persuasive,' as we have explained and applied that standard."

Justice Ginsburg then turned to the remedial plan, whose constitutionality had been upheld in the lower courts. The Supreme Court's race discrimination precedents establish that the remedial decree must closely fit the constitutional violation; it must be shaped to place persons unconstitutionally denied an opportunity or advantage in "the position they would have occupied in the absence of [discrimination]." See *Milliken v. Bradley*, 433 U.S. 267, 280 (1977). Justice Ginsburg found that the establishment of the VWIL did not practically remedy the discrimination, in large part because the women's program was qualitatively different and quantitatively inferior to that retained for males at VMI. Tangible differences included fewer courses for VWIL students, less qualified faculty members, lower admissions standards for students, no comparable athletic facilities, a much smaller educational endowment, and incomplete access to VMI's impressive alumni network. Intangible differences included loss of the adversative method and the bonding it seems to achieve.

"Virginia's VWIL solution is reminiscent of the remedy Texas proposed 50 years ago, in response to a state trial court's 1946 ruling that, given the equal protection guarantee, African Americans could not be denied a legal education at a state facility. See *Sweatt v. Painter*, 339 U.S. 629 (1950). Reluctant to admit African Americans to its flagship University of Texas Law School, the State set up a separate school for Herman [sic] Sweatt and other black law students. As originally opened, the new school had no independent faculty or library, and it lacked accreditation. Nevertheless, the state trial and appellate courts were satisfied that the new school offered Sweatt opportunities for the study of law 'substantially equivalent to those offered by the State to white students at the University of Texas.' "

The Supreme Court struck down the remedy on the ground that the tangible facilities and faculty of the new law school were distinctly inferior and that there was an even greater disparity in "those qualities which are incapable of objective measurement but which make for greatness" in a school, including "reputation of the faculty, experience of the administration, position and influence of the alumni, standing in the community, traditions and prestige." "In line with *Sweatt*," Justice Ginsburg ruled "that Virginia has not shown substantial equality in the separate educational opportunities the State supports at VWIL and VMI."

Six Justices joined the Ginsburg opinion. **Justice Thomas** did not participate. **Chief Justice Rehnquist** concurred in the judgment. He maintained that the six-Justice Court had departed from the traditional test for evaluating sex-based classifications. The approach taken in earlier cases requires the state to offer only an "important government objective" that is "substantially related" to the sex-based classification. The Chief Justice believed that the Court's requirement of an "exceedingly persuasive justification" subtly alters the analysis. Chief Justice Rehnquist also objected to the Court's examination of Virginia's long history of excluding women from higher education on the basis of stereotypes about women's abilities and role. He maintained that the Court should only examine Virginia's justifications since *Mississippi University for Women*, decided in 1982, as it was only with that decision that states could have been on notice that single-sex institutions required any justification beyond tradition. Nonetheless, the Chief Justice found that Virginia had not offered a substantial justification borne out by the evidence in the case and agreed with the Court's judgment.

Justice Scalia, alone, dissented. "Much of the Court's opinion is devoted to deprecating the closed-mindedness of our forebears with regard to women's education, and even with regard to the treatment of women in areas that have nothing to do with education. Closed-minded they were—as every age is, including our own, with regard to matters it cannot guess, because it simply does not consider them debatable. The virtue of a democratic system with a First Amendment is that it readily enables the people, over time, to be persuaded that what they took for granted is not so, and to change their laws accordingly. That system is destroyed if the smug assurances of each age are removed from the democratic process and written into the Constitution. So to counterbalance the Court's criticism of our ancestors, let me say a word in their praise: They left us free to change. The same cannot be said of this most illiberal Court, which has embarked on a course of inscribing one after another of the current preferences of the society (and in some cases only the counter-majoritarian preferences of the society's law-trained elite) into our Basic Law. Today it enshrines the notion that no substantial educational value is to be served by an all-men's military academy—so that the decision by the people of Virginia to maintain such an institution denies equal protection to women who cannot attend that institution but can attend others. Since it is entirely clear that the Constitution of the United States—the old one—takes no sides in this educational debate, I dissent.

" * * * [I]n my view the function of this Court is to *preserve* our society's values regarding (among other things) equal protection, not to *revise* them; to prevent backsliding from the degree of restriction the Constitution imposed upon democratic government, not to prescribe, on our own authority, progressively higher degrees. For that reason it is my view that, whatever abstract tests we may choose to devise, they cannot supersede—and indeed ought to be crafted so as to reflect—those constant and unbroken national traditions that embody the people's understanding of ambiguous constitutional texts. More specifically, it is my view that 'when a practice not expressly prohibited by the text of the Bill of Rights bears the endorsement of a long tradition of open, widespread, and unchallenged use that dates back to the beginning of the Republic, we have no proper basis for striking it down.' *Rutan v. Republican Party of Ill.*, 497 U.S. 62, 95 (1990) (Scalia, J., dissenting). The same applies, *mutatis mutandis*, to a practice asserted to be in violation of the post-Civil War Fourteenth Amendment."

Justice Scalia launched into a litany of criticisms: The Court was silently replacing the intermediate scrutiny standard traditionally applied in sex-discrimination cases with a strict scrutiny standard akin to that in race-discrimination cases; the Court's requirement that VMI must open its adversative method to women so long as there are any women who would benefit from it imported a least-restrictive-means requirement characteristic only of strict scrutiny and not of intermediate scrutiny as articulated in precedents such as *Mississippi University for Women* and, even more prominently, *Rostker v. Goldberg*; and the Court's approach destabilized equal protection law, and without any firm theoretical basis. With respect to his last criticism, Justice Scalia adverted to *Carolene Products*' justification for judicial review when "prejudice against discrete and insular minorities may be a special condition, which tends seriously to curtail the operation of those political processes ordinarily to be relied upon to protect minorities, and which may call for a correspondingly more searching judicial inquiry." Women were not a "discrete and insular minority" and, indeed, were far from politically powerless, so why should they fall under the Court's special protection?

In closing, Justice Scalia delivered an ode to educational diversity. Why shouldn't the state be able to offer single-sex education—especially the education offered by VMI, with its adversative method. According to the District Court, if women were admitted, VMI "would eventually find it necessary to drop the adversative system altogether." Thus, Virginia's options were an adversative method that excludes women or no adversative method at all. In a moment of antic antiquarianism, Justice Scalia quoted VMI's "Code of a Gentleman" and lamented the demise of its philosophy of chivalrous conduct.

NOTES ON THE VMI CASE AND "THE CENTRAL MISTAKE OF SEX DISCRIMINATION LAW"

1. *The Relationship Between Sex and Gender in the Court's Understanding of Equal Protection.* Professor Katharine Franke argued in 1995 that sex discrimination jurisprudence made this assumption:

> Sex is regarded as a product of nature, while gender is understood as a function of culture. This disaggregation of sex from gender represents a central mistake of equality jurisprudence. Antidiscrimination law is founded upon the idea that sex, conceived as biological difference, is prior to, less normative than, and more real than gender. Yet in every way that matters, sex bears an epiphenomenal relationship to gender; that is, under close examination, almost every claim with regard to sexual identity or sex discrimination can be shown to be grounded in normative gender rules and roles. Herein lies the mistake. In the name of avoiding "the grossest discrimination," that is, "treating things that are different as though they were exactly alike," sexual equality jurisprudence has uncritically accepted the validity of biological sexual differences. By accepting these biological differences, equality jurisprudence reifies as foundational *fact* that which is really an *effect* of normative gender ideology.

"The Central Mistake of Sex Discrimination Law: The Disaggregation of Sex from Gender," 144 *U. Pa. L. Rev.* 1–2 (1995). Notice how Justice Ginsburg's opinion in the VMI Case follows this script, as in her celebration of "inherent differences" between men and women.

Franke's prescription is this: "The targets of antidiscrimination law, therefore, should not be limited to the 'gross, stereotyped distinctions between the sexes'," the object of the Court's scrutiny in the VMI Case, "but should also include the social processes that construct and make coherent the categories male and female. In many cases, biology operates as the excuse or cover for social practices that hierarchize individual members of the social category 'man' over individual members of the social category 'woman.' " *Id.* at 3. One can hardly imagine a more dramatic example of the "social processes that construct and make coherent the categor[y] male" than the adversative method at VMI. The Department of Justice (the complainant in this case) and the Court follow Franke in their insistence that the adversative method's superficially masculine features do not render it inappropriate for female participation. But both the Justice Department and the Court also opine that admitting women would not change the operation or the goals of the adversative method.

Neither the Justice Department nor the Court engaged in the more radical critique that Franke advocates: While the VMI Case questions the necessary correlation between toughness/aggression and the male sex, it does not question the correlation of these traits with traditional masculinity and the link between masculinity and honor/citizenship/leadership. (Justice Scalia's defense of VMI's sex discrimination is not only gendered, but seems to accept the traditional linkage among the male sex, masculine gender traits, and honor/leadership/citizenship.) There is no interrogation of the state's valorization of traditionally masculine traits as ones useful for leadership, nor any suggestion that a state where women are equal citizens is one where state policy ought not be gendered in any traditional sense. Is it unfair to characterize the VMI Case as standing for the constitutional proposition that women have the right to become social males? Is this a feature of liberal feminism that ought to be troubling?[c]

2. *Is Public or Private Discrimination Against Transsexuals and Cross–Dressers Illegal "Sex" Discrimination?* Assume that VMI will not admit "transsexuals," people who believe their gender does not match their sex ("a female gender trapped in a man's body"). As Franke points out, transsexuals in the last generation have generally maintained that it is their gender that is fixed; given advances in sex-reassignment surgery, their sex is malleable. Many transgendered people seek such surgery, to bring their sex in line with their gender. Would VMI's exclusion of cross-dressers or transsexuals be "sex discrimination" triggering heightened equal protection scrutiny? What justifications could VMI have for excluding transgendered people that it did not have for excluding women? Consider these questions now, and then read the next case.

Note that most analyses of the relationship between sex and gender in the law occur in the context of statutory civil rights laws, especially Title VII, which prohibits discrimination "because of * * * sex" in the work-place. Early Title VII decisions by appellate courts uniformly ruled that it is not sex discrimination for a company to penalize or fire an employee who undergoes sex reassignment. *E.g.*, *Ulane v. Eastern Airlines, Inc.*, 742 F.2d 1081 (7th Cir. 1984), where the judges found it inconceivable that Congress would have wanted Title VII to protect transgendered people. But isn't it, literally, discrimination "because of sex" to penalize a person because her gender presentation does not match her (alleged) biological sex? The European Court of Justice so held in *P. v. S. and Cornwall County Council*, Case C–13/94 (Eur. Ct. Just. 1996).

American courts might need to rethink these early decisions in light of *Hopkins v. Price Waterhouse* (Chapter 5, Section 3), where the Supreme Court ruled that a woman penalized by her employer because she was not "feminine" enough had a valid Title VII claim. Price Waterhouse argued in *Hopkins*: It was happy to hire and promote women, just not socially "deviant" women; it discriminated against Hopkins because of her gender nonconformity and not because of her sex; Congress did not have gender

c. Consider the aftermath of the VMI decision. After VMI admitted women for the 1997–98 school year, "the Rat Line got harsher and eventually was as intense as in past years. * * * The Rat Line was more physical than 90 percent of the Rat Lines I've observed," said the commandant of cadets. "The rat mass is more militarily prepared and better-trained than others I've seen." Said senior Jon Spitzer, "After a while, you're not thinking female rat, you're just thinking rat." Peter Finn, "Women Reach Rat Finish Line," *Wash. Post*, Mar. 17, 1998; accord, Laura Fairchild Brodie, *Breaking Out: VMI and the Coming of Women* (2000). At the end of the 1999–2000 academic year, one of the first 23 women cadets was selected to be a battalion commander. In television interviews, she defended the Rat Line and VMI's adversarial method.

nonconformists like Ann Hopkins "in mind" when it adopted the sex discrimination provision in Title VII. Yet the Court rejected all these arguments and remanded the case for a factual determination whether Hopkins' gender nonconformity was the primary reason for her failure to make partner. Does this ruling necessarily entail acceptance of the Franke reading of sex discrimination—or can it be limited to cases where a person does not press her gender nonconformity "too far"? Should *Hopkins* be limited in this or some other way?

3. *The Assumption of Sex Binariness.* Judges, including Justice Ginsburg in the VMI case, assume that there are two sexes (male and female), each paired up with specific biological features: chromosomes (women XX, men XY), genitalia (women vaginas, men penises), internal organs (women ovaries, men testes), and hormones (women estrogen, men androgen). As a matter of science, these assumptions are wrong.

Not everyone has XX or XY chromosomal patterns. See John Money, *Venuses Penuses: Sexology, Sexosophy and Exigency Theory* ch. 6 (1986). People with Turner's syndrome have only 45 chromosomes rather than 46, with only one X chromosome. Such people are usually raised as women but do not have ovaries. People with Klinefelter's syndrome have XXY chromosomes. Such people are usually raised as men but have very small testicles and eunuchoid body types; they are usually reproductively sterile. People with XYY chromosomal patterns are usually raised as boys; the primary symptoms are psychological nervousness.

Moreover, many people with XX or XY chromosomes do not unambiguously display female or male sex characteristics, respectively. Anne Fausto–Sterling, "The Five Sexes: Why Male and Female Are Not Enough," *The Sciences*, March/April 1993, at 20–24, calls these people "intersexual" and divides them into the following groups. "True hermaphrodites" possess both a testis and an ovary and usually have ambiguous external genitalia, often a small penis as well as a vagina. "Male pseudohermaphrodites" have testes and some manifestations of female genitalia but no ovaries. "Female pseudohermaphrodites" have ovaries and some manifestations of male genitalia but no testes. She thinks that as many as 4% of human births are intersexual.

As Dr. Fausto–Sterling points out, none of this is new. Intersexuals have been known throughout human history. Perhaps surprisingly, research in this area is hardly new either. An early landmark piece was John Money, Joan Hampson & John Hampson, "An Examination of Some Basic Sexual Concepts: The Evidence of Human Hermaphroditism," 97 *Bulletin of the Johns Hopkins Hospital* 301 (1955). The authors, researchers at Johns Hopkins, examined 76 persons who had "mismatched" markers (such as chromosomes of one sex but external genitalia and/or internal organs of another). They not only found the subjects functional in modern society but, further, found that the subjects had happily assumed the gender roles that had been assigned them by their parents. Dr. Money, in particular, parlayed this kind of research into celebrated claims that sex and gender are wholly constructed by a social rather than a biological process.

Intersexuals themselves object that the social process has not traditionally considered their interests. (The Intersex Society of North America operates a website, <www.isna.org>.) Concerned parents and physicians like Dr. Money have mutilated them, by some of their accounts. By reconstructing their bodies to suit medical and parental assumptions, many intersexuals believe they have been misunderstood, deceived, and brutalized. See, e.g., John Colapinto, *As Nature Made Him: The Boy Who Was Raised as a Girl* (2000); Angela Moreno, as told to Jan Goodwin, "Am I a Woman or a Man?," *Mademoiselle*, Mar. 1998, at 178–81, 208.

Does the Supreme Court's jurisprudence, summarized in the VMI Case, provide relief for intersexuals who are subject to state discrimination? Can the state deny intersexuals the right to marry, on the ground that they cannot firmly be categorized as male or female, in violation of strong state policies recognizing only marriages of "one man and one woman." (Recall *Loving v. Virginia* as you ponder this quandary.)

PROBLEM 3–2

WHICH OF THE FOLLOWING STATE SEX–BASED CLASSIFICATIONS ARE UNCONSTITUTIONAL?

(a) State buildings and workplaces maintain separate restrooms for men and women. Cf. *Ulane*.

(b) The armed forces do not allow women to serve in most combat units. Cf. *Rostker*.

(c) The state runs experimental same-sex charter schools.

(d) Seeking to integrate traditionally sex-segregated jobs, the state gives a big "plus" to female applicants for those jobs. See *Johnson v. Transportation Agency*, 480 U.S. 616 (1987).

(e) State employers do not allow women of childbearing age to engage in certain jobs that would pose risks to pregnant women. See *Auto Workers v. Johnson Controls*, 499 U.S. 187 (1991).

(f) The state issues marriage licenses to adult different-sex couples but refuses to issue such licenses to adult same-sex couples. See Chapter 9.

Would any of these discriminations be constitutional if they were on the basis of race?

SECTION 2

SEXUAL ORIENTATION DISCRIMINATIONS

Local, state, and federal governments in the United States pervasively discriminated against people based on their sexual or gender orientation during the twentieth century. For most of the century, lesbians, gay men, bisexuals, and transgendered people were the objects of special criminal laws against cross-dressing and homosexual solicitation, as well as generic sodomy laws (Chapter 2); saw books, movies, radio programs, and even art depicting their point of view censored or denigrated by the state (Chapter 4); were excluded from service in the United States armed forces; were barred from federal or state government employment (Chapter 6); suffered under the stigma of laws or policies barring schools from depicting sexual or gender minorities positively or requiring them to denigrate such minorities; could not obtain state recognition of their intimate relationships and could not adopt children or even retain custody of their own biological children (Chapter 9); were excluded from entering the United States or becoming American citizens. Although many of these discriminations have been repealed or nullified, new ones have been introduced. Are the thousands of antigay discriminations constitutionally problematic under the Equal Protection Clause?[a]

PART A.   EARLY CHALLENGES TO STATE DISCRIMINATION BASED ON SEXUAL ORIENTATION

Recall Frank Kameny's petition to the Supreme Court to review his discharge from federal employment (Problem 3–1). His brief in *Kameny v. Brucker* (1960 Term, No. 676), was the first brief before the Supreme Court to argue that homosexuality was a benign variation, that "homosexuals" were a minority group like Jews and African Americans, that anti-homosexual discrimination was fundamentally based on prejudice rather than a neutral policy, and that constitutional equality principles barred discrimination on the basis of sexual variation.

Lawyers in a few other cases picked up on some of Kameny's ideas. In *Manual Enterprises v. Day*, 370 U.S. 478 (1962), Stanley Dietz's brief for

---

a. On America's numerous antigay laws and policies, see William Eskridge, Jr., *Gaylaw: Challenging the Apartheid of the Closet* 362–71 (app. B3) (1999) (listing such policies, state by state); *id.* at 139–48, 205–38 (analysis).

Manual Enterprises successfully challenged the Post Office's censorship of male physique magazines as inconsistent with the First Amendment. But he also objected to the government's view that gay erotica should be treated differently from straight: "Our Constitution does not state that only heterosexuals may receive and read the literature of their choice and homosexuals must read the same literature or be denied the right to view a magazine which interests them. To interpret our Constitution ... in the manner that the Post Office Department has done, reduces a large segment of our society to second class citizenship." To the Solicitor General's suggestion that "homosexuals" are sick, Dietz maintained that, according to modern science, homosexuality is neither a disease nor a mental defect, "nor is homosexuality as such intrinsically evil." (Although overturning the censorship under the First Amendment, the Supreme Court ignored this argument.)

The same kind of arguments were made by the attorneys for gay and bisexual men whom the federal government sought to deport as statutory psychopaths. Based on newer and more reliable medical research, counsel maintained that homosexuals were no more mentally defective than hetero-sexuals. The Ninth Circuit's opinion in *Fleuti v. Rosenberg*, 302 F.2d 652 (9th Cir. 1962), *aff'd on other grounds*, 374 U.S. 449 (1963), was the rare decision that recognized some part of this new rhetoric of recognition. The Supreme Court abrogated the Ninth Circuit's interpretation in *Boutilier v. INS*, 387 U.S. 118 (1967). The Court ruled that a Canadian who had sex with men (as well as with women) was a "homosexual" and, therefore, was "afflicted with psychopathic personality," which was the statutory ground for exclusion and deportation.

NOTES ON GAY PEOPLE'S UPHILL STRUGGLE FOR EQUAL CITIZENSHIP, 1961–1986

1. *Judicial Skepticism Regarding Homo Equality Claims.* Although some gay people were making constitutional equality claims against anti-homo-sexual state discrimination, judges of all persuasions were unreceptive. An irony of *Boutilier* is that the Warren Court went out of its way to interpret the spongiest statutory term in the most broadly anti-homosexual way. Chief Justice Earl Warren and Justice Hugo Black voted with the majority, and future Justice Thurgood Marshall was the Solicitor General who defended the position taken by the administration of President Lyndon Johnson. All of these officials were strongly pro-civil rights—but not for "homosexuals and sex perverts." Why might that be? *Boutilier* and *Manual Enterprises* suggest some reasons:

(a) "Unnatural" Conduct Attributed to "Homosexuals." As the Court's opinion emphasized, Boutilier's "homosexual conduct" was key to his deportation. In 1967, consensual sodomy was a crime (almost always a felony) in every state except Illinois. Federal immigration law considered sodomy a "crime of moral turpitude" that could be an independent basis for excluding or deporting a non-citizen or for denying applications for

citizenship. As we saw in Chapter 2, sodomy had long been a crime in Anglo–American law, and the "crime against nature" was officially considered immoral and disgusting—in part for religious reasons. Some Justices openly expressed disgust with sexual activities between two men. See, *e.g.*, *Manual Enterprises*, *supra* (Clark, J., dissenting from First Amendment protection of tame physique magazines, and evidencing near-hysterical reaction to the fact that the magazines were "sex stimulants for homosexuals").

(b) *"Homosexuality" as a Sickness or Mental Defect.* American medical thought in the early twentieth century considered sexual minorities— female sex workers, "fairies," masculine women—physically "degenerate." The INS' early exclusion of sexual minorities was for this reason: they were considered incapable of supporting themselves and so were excluded as "public charges." After World War I, they were excluded on grounds of "constitutional psychopathic inferiority," a term that gave way to "psychopathic personality" in the 1952 Act, as Justice Clark's *Boutilier* opinion carefully recounts. The doctors who considered "homosexuals" to be "psychopaths" were part of a larger public hysteria about sexual minorities after World War II. Not only were they disgusting, but they were dangerous and predatory, especially toward children.

Justice Douglas's relatively "enlightened" dissenting opinion in *Boutilier* considered "homosexuals" to be "freaks" and "narcissistic," the product of some kind of "dysfunction." His main dispute with the majority was that he considered homosexuals generally, and Boutillier in particular, to be potentially productive members of society. Similarly, Justice Harlan's plurality opinion in *Manual Enterprises* condescendingly referred to the physique magazines as "dismally unpleasant, uncouth, and tawdry" and to their readers as "unfortunate persons."

(c) *Republican Fears of Social Turmoil—No Promo Homo.* A new form of anti-homosexual discourse became popular once gay people or their allies were objecting to laws penalizing them. See William Eskridge, Jr., "No Promo Homo: The Sedimentation of Antigay Discourse and the Channeling Effect of Judicial Review," 75 *NYU L. Rev.* 1327 (2000). This new discourse considered the social effects of easing up on anti-homosexual persecution. If states repealed their consensual sodomy laws or the INS ceased excluding "homosexuals and sex perverts," the government would be sending a signal to an undesirable class of people that they and their conduct were tolerable to respectable Americans. Although much of the rhetoric focused on disgusting acts and predatory people, some of the fears were that the public sphere would be polluted. Clive Michael Boutilier was an "alien" in more than one sense—we as Americans can be proud that people like him are not allowed here.

This was also a point raised in Justice Clark's *Manual Enterprises* dissent: Not only was it horrible that the Court was tolerating the dissemination of magazines that were nothing more than "sex stimulants for homosexuals," but it was even more objectionable that the Court was requiring the Post Office to be "the world's largest disseminator of smut."

This language is remarkable in the context of the magazines under surveillance: the pictures were of clean-cut young men striking poses in bathing suits. The presence in the public sphere of stuff eroticized by gay men seemed to have been alarming to him—but why? One theory is that Justice Clark was worried about undermining the rationality of the public sphere by the introduction of sexuality itself. In *Manual Enterprises*, Justice Clark was expressing a fear that public discourse would be (homo)sexualized; in *Boutilier*, his fear was that the "body politic" would be (homo)sexualized if Boutilier were not expunged from it.

2. *It All Changes with Stonewall (1969): "Homosexuals" Insist They Are Not Alien Psychopaths.* When the Supreme Court decided *Boutilier* in 1967 only a small number of people in the United States were openly gay, lesbian, or bisexual. Gay people resided in their respective closets and retained a collective anonymity. Very few people openly challenged the views, held by most Americans (and many medical professionals), that "homosexuals" were unnatural, degenerate, mentally ill, and predatory. This changed, literally overnight—the night of June 26–27, 1969. On that date, New York City police raiding the Stonewall Inn in Greenwich Village triggered physical, indeed violent, resistance by drag queens, fags, and dykes. The following two evenings of rioting, breathlessly reported in *The Village Voice*, touched the spirits of gay people elsewhere. In the next several months, thousands of people "came out" of their closets, formed scores of gay liberation groups, and proclaimed their own civil rights movement. Permanent organizations took shape over the next year, and the gay rights movement developed an agenda.

One item on the agenda was decriminalization of affection and intimacy between consenting adults of the same sex. Supported by professional organizations of lawyers and doctors, gay rights activists and civil libertarians lobbied state legislatures to repeal consensual sodomy laws; pressured police forces to cease or at least ease their enforcement of consensual sexuality rules; and brought constitutional challenges to consensual sodomy, cross-dressing, and private solicitation laws. Consistent with the sexual revolution of the 1960s, lesbian and gay activists maintained that sex between consenting adults in private places was not a matter for criminal law or police enforcement. Their larger normative campaign was to persuade Americans that sexual intimacy between consenting adults was at least a tolerable variation from the procreative norm—and perhaps even a benign variation.

A further item on the gay rights agenda was to persuade professionals and others that homosexuality is not a disease. See generally Ronald Bayer, *Homosexuality and American Psychiatry: The Politics of Diagnosis* (1987). At the 1970 and 1971 conventions of the American Psychiatric Association (APA), protesters challenged the psychiatrists to "delist" homosexuality as a psychiatric disorder in its *Diagnostic and Statistical Manual* (DSM). On December 15, 1973, the APA's Nomenclature Committee voted to drop homosexuality's classification as a disease in *DSM-II*. The Committee's decision survived an unprecedented "referendum" (a vote among APA members) instigated by adherents to the traditional medical view. As a result of an emerging consensus among medical professionals that homosexuality is not per se a mental disease, the Public Health Service (PHS), which jointly administered the medical bases for excluding immigrants with the INS, announced in 1979 that it would not longer cooperate in the exclusion of lesbians, gay men, and bisexuals as people afflicted with "psychopathic personality" or "sexual deviation" (a term added by Congress in 1965). Although the INS continued to follow *Boutilier*, it did little to enforce the exclusion after 1981, and the exclusion was repealed in 1990.

3. *Arguments for Abolishing Antigay Exclusions and Discriminations from State and Federal Policies, 1969–1984.* Recall the kinds of arguments made by civil rights and feminist lawyers against state and federal discriminations based on race and sex, respectively. Although respectable law professors and famous civil rights attorneys ignored the parallels between race and sex discrimination, on the one hand, and sexual orientation discrimination on the other, a small number of gay rights attorneys (many of them affiliated with the ACLU) and a few judges noted these parallels in the 1970s and 1980s.

(a) *Sexual Orientation as an Irrational Classification.* Responding to a challenge to the federal civil service exclusion of gay people brought by lawyers for the Mattachine Society of Washington, Chief Judge David Bazelon ruled in *Norton v. Macy* (Chapter 8, Section 2), that homosexuality alone was not a sufficient basis for exclusion. In the Weberian tradition, Bazelon ruled that the civil service was not the place for the government to follow morality-based dicta and insisted that the civil service exclude sexual minorities only if it could demonstrate a "nexus" between the disapproved characteristic or conduct and the requirements of the government job. Authored by the federal judiciary's leading expert on law and psychiatry, *Norton* was handed down the same week as Stonewall.

Gay rights litigation in the 1970s and 1980s advanced three challenges to the wide deployment of homosexuality as an exclusionary criterion: (1) the Kameny idea that there is no material difference between gays and straights (alleged differences were based on unfounded stereotypes), so that state discriminations were treating similar people unfairly; (2) the Kameny idea that state discriminations grounded in prejudice against gay people are no more acceptable than state discriminations grounded on prejudice against people of color; and (3) the Bazelon idea that the instrumental needs of the modern state are inconsistent with traditional morals-based discriminations. This thinking was the basis for challenges to federal and state discriminations in the United States armed forces, civil service employment, and child custody and adoption rules. As subsequent chapters will trace in detail, these classification-based arguments usually did not prevail in the 1970s but increasingly did in the 1980s.

(b) *Lesbians, Gay Men, and Bisexuals as a Disadvantaged Class.* Kameny had argued in 1961 that gay people as a class were the objects of unfair state oppression, and a major theme of gay rights organizations (which grew exponentially after 1969) was the state's subordination of gay people as second-class citizens. It is telling that the class-based theories of equal protection being developed in the 1970s did not analyze gay people as an oppressed class. A few judges had their say, though.

In *Gay Law Students Association v. Pacific Telephone & Telegraph Co.* (Chapter 6, Section 1), the court ruled that harassment or discharge of openly gay employees violated the state bar to discrimination on the basis of "political activities or affiliations." Because "the struggle of the homosexual community for equal rights, particularly in the field of employment, must be recognized as a political activity," and because "coming out of the closet" and "acknowledg[ing] their sexual preferences" were essential to that politics as understood by gay people, efforts to discourage or penalize such employees and press them back into their closets was within the bar to political activity discrimination. This remarkable decision was the starting point for judges and other officials to think about gay people as an oppressed group who needed constitutional and other legal protection against efforts to suppress them.

An equally remarkable opinion was written by Justice Brennan, dissenting from the Court's denial of certiorari in *Rowland v. Mad River Local School District*, 470 U.S. 1009 (1985), denying cert. to 730 F.2d 444 (6th Cir. 1984) (the lower court opinion is excerpted in Chapter 4, Section 3B). The lower court had upheld the discharge of a bisexual high school guidance counselor. Justice Brennan, joined by Justice Marshall, believed that Rowland's dismissal violated the Equal Protection Clause. Their dissent made three kinds of arguments: (1) like sex, illegitimacy, and race, sexual orientation usually has no connection to the instrumental rationality of modern governance; (2) like people of color, the group stigmatized by the classification has been the object of hostile state action reflecting prejudice and hatred; (3) as a discrete and insular minority that has been the object of prejudice, gay people have been relatively powerless in the political process and need the judicially-enforced protection of the representation-reinforcing Constitution.

(c) Denying Gay People Fundamental Rights. Unlike people of color and women, gay people had never been systematically excluded from voting and jury service. (Although sodomy was a basis for exclusion in many states, most gay people were never convicted of that crime, and so this bar had little practical effect.) Like people of color before the Civil War and miscegenosexuals before *Loving*, lesbians, gay men, and some bisexuals were denied access to the fundamental right to marry the partners of their choice. The most sensational gay rights cases have been the same-sex marriage ones, and the first of those was *Baker v. Nelson*, 191 N.W.2d 185 (Minn. 1971), *appeal dismissed*, 409 U.S. 810 (1972). The *Baker* litigation demonstrates how, as early as 1972, gay rights attorneys were combining all the equality tropes developed in civil rights litigation and on display in *Loving v. Virginia*.

PART B.   SHOULD SEXUAL ORIENTATION BE A SUSPECT CLASSIFICATION?

Building on the arguments articulated over an entire generation by gay rights advocates and on the analytical structure for equal protection law that he and his allies had developed in *Loving*, *Frontiero*, and *Craig*, Justice Brennan's *Rowland* dissent laid out the case for subjecting sexual orientation classifications to strict (*Loving*) or intermediate (*Craig*) scrutiny when they perpetuate harms to gay people. The case for some kind of heightened scrutiny faced several complications by the mid–1980s, however.

One complication was institutional. *Loving* had opened the Court to numerous claims by disadvantaged groups that their defining trait (age, disability, etc.) should be a suspect classification like race or a quasi-suspect one like sex. The Burger Court felt that an expansive approach to suspect classifications risked overextending the judiciary and embroiling it in political turmoil as it evaluated a wider range of discriminatory state policies. Thus, the Court announced in *San Antonio Independent School District v. Rodriguez*, 411 U.S. 1 (1973), that not only was poverty or income level not a suspect classification, but also that the Court was not inclined to expand the list beyond race and ethnicity. Justice Powell's opinion for the Court justified this caution on grounds of institutional competence and democratic legitimacy: An elastic list of suspect classifications was not desirable because it would turn the courts into "super legislatures." Although sex joined the list as a quasi-suspect classification in 1976, the Court rebuffed efforts to treat age and disability as suspect classifications in *Massachusetts Board of Retirement v. Murgia*, 427 U.S. 307 (1976) (per curiam) and *Cleburne v. Cleburne Living Center*, 473 U.S. 432 (1985), respectively.

To distinguish between sexual orientation (proposed suspect classification) and mental disability (found to be not suspect), gay rights lawyers faced a second complication: The conduct (sodomy) deemed to be characteristic of their class (homosexuality) remained a crime in about half of America. Judge Robert Bork argued in *Dronenburg v. Zech*, 741 F.2d 1388 (D.C.Cir. 1984), that there are no constitutional problems with making consensual sodomy a crime (anticipating *Bowers* two years later) and that homosexuals' presumed criminality justified virtually any state discrimination against that class. If the state can put "practicing homosexuals" in jail for long periods of time, surely it can refuse them employment. His opinion remains the leading judicial articulation of the view that "homosexuals" are a class defined by their (criminal) conduct.

A third complication was political. Like the civil rights and women's movements, the gay rights movement had triggered a powerful traditional family values (TFV) countermovement.[d] Some TFV groups maintained that homosexuality was unnatural, diseased, and predatory—the anti-homosexual tropes popular earlier in the century. TFV scientists devoted to reparative therapy revived the medical understanding of homosexuality as a corrigible mental defect and claimed to have "cured" thousands of gay

d. On the TFV countermovement, see Christopher Bull & John Gallagher, *Perfect Enemies: The Religious Right, the Gay Movement, and the Politics of the 1990s* (1996); Didi Herman, *The Antigay Agenda: Orthodox Vision and the Christian Right* (1997); Jane Schacter, "The Gay Civil Rights Debate in the States: Decoding the Discourse of Equivalents," 29 *Harv. C.R.-C.L. L. Rev.* 283 (1994).

people. The Reverend Jerry Falwell and others seized upon the AIDS epidemic of the 1980s to demonize homosexuals as polluted people being judged by God.

The combination of a powerful TFV countermovement and the sanction *Hardwick* gave to laws making "homosexual conduct" a felony would seem fatal to Justice Brennan's argument that sexual orientation should be a suspect classification. Yet the argument was adopted in the least likely setting—a challenge by a black drag queen to the military's antigay exclusion.

Perry Watkins v. United States Army

United States Court of Appeals for the Ninth Circuit, 1988.
847 F.2d 1329, *vacated en banc*, 875 F.2d 699 (9th Cir.1989).

■ NORRIS, CIRCUIT JUDGE.

In August 1967, at the age of 19, Perry Watkins enlisted in the United States Army. In filling out the Army's pre-induction medical form, he candidly marked "yes" in response to a question whether he had homosexual tendencies. The Army nonetheless considered Watkins "qualified for admission" and inducted him into its ranks. Watkins served fourteen years in the Army, and became, in the words of his commanding officer, "one of our most respected and trusted soldiers."

Even though Watkins' homosexuality was always common knowledge, the Army has never claimed that his sexual orientation or behavior interfered in any way with military functions. To the contrary, an Army review board found "there is no evidence suggesting that his behavior has had either a degrading effect upon unit performance, morale or discipline, or upon his own job performance."

In 1981 the Army promulgated new regulations which mandated the disqualification of all homosexuals from the Army without regard to the length or quality of their military service. Pursuant to these new regulations, the Army notified Watkins that he would be discharged and denied reenlistment because of his homosexuality. In this federal court action, Watkins challenges the Army's actions and new regulations on various statutory and constitutional grounds. * * *

We conclude that these regulations, on their face, discriminate against homosexuals on the basis of their sexual orientation. Under the regulations any homosexual act or statement of homosexuality gives rise to a presumption of homosexual orientation, and anyone who fails to rebut that presumption is conclusively barred from Army service. In other words, the regulations target homosexual orientation itself. The homosexual acts and statements are merely relevant, and rebuttable, indicators of that orientation. * * *

The Army * * * argues that it would be "incongruous" to hold that its regulations deprive gays of equal protection of the laws when *Bowers v. Hardwick* holds that there is no constitutionally protected privacy right to engage in homosexual sodomy. We disagree. First, while *Hardwick* does indeed hold that the due process clause provides no substantive privacy protection for acts of private homosexual sodomy, nothing in *Hardwick* suggests that the state may penalize gays for their sexual orientation. *Cf. Robinson v. California*, 370 U.S. 660 (1962) (holding that state violated due process by criminalizing the status of narcotics addiction, even though the state could criminalize the use of the narcotics—conduct in which narcotics addicts by definition are prone to engage).

Second, although *Hardwick* held that the due process clause does not prevent states from criminalizing acts of homosexual sodomy, nothing in *Hardwick* actually holds that the state may make invidious distinctions when regulating sexual conduct. Unlike the Army's regulations, the Georgia sodomy statute at issue in *Hardwick* was neutral on its face, making anal and oral intercourse a criminal offense whether engaged in by partners of the same or opposite sex. In deciding a due process challenge to the Georgia statute as applied to homosexual sodomy, the *Hardwick* Court simply did not address either the question whether heterosexual sodomy also falls outside the scope of the right to privacy or the separate question whether homosexual but not heterosexual sodomy may be criminalized without violating the equal protection clause. We cannot read *Hardwick* as standing for the proposition that government may outlaw sodomy only when committed by a disfavored class of persons. Surely, for example, *Hardwick* cannot be read as a license for the government to outlaw sodomy only when committed by blacks. If government insists on regulating private sexual conduct between consenting adults, it must, at a minimum, do so evenhandedly—prohibiting all persons from engaging in the proscribed sexual acts rather than placing the burden of sexual restraint solely on a disfavored minority. * * *

We now address the merits of Watkins' claim that we must subject the Army's regulations to strict scrutiny because homosexuals constitute a suspect class under equal protection jurisprudence. The Supreme Court has identified several factors that guide our suspect class inquiry. [The first two factors are (A) whether the group at issue has suffered a history of purposeful discrimination, and (B) whether the discrimination embodies a gross unfairness that is sufficiently inconsistent with the ideals of equal protection to term it invidious. The Army conceded the first factor and contested only the second, which Judge Norris broke down into three considerations: (1) whether the disadvantaged class is defined by a trait that "frequently bears no relation to ability to perform or contribute to society;" (2) whether the class has been saddled with unique disabilities because of prejudice or inaccurate stereotypes; and (3) whether the trait defining the class is immutable.]

[B1]   Sexual orientation plainly has no relevance to a person's "ability to perform or contribute to society." Indeed, the Army makes no claim that homosexuality impairs a person's ability to perform military duties. Sergeant Watkins' exemplary record of military service stands as a testament to quite the opposite. Moreover, as the Army itself concluded, there is not a scintilla of evidence that Watkins' avowed homosexuality "had either a degrading effect upon unit performance, morale or discipline, or upon his own job performance."

[B2] This irrelevance of sexual orientation to the quality of a person's contribution to society also suggests that classifications based on sexual orientation reflect prejudice and inaccurate stereotypes—the second indicia of a classification's gross unfairness. We agree with Justice Brennan that "discrimination against homosexuals is 'likely ... to reflect deep-seated prejudice rather than ... rationality.' " *Rowland* (Brennan, J., dissenting from the denial of certiorari). The Army does not dispute the hard fact that homosexuals face enormous prejudice. Nor could it, for the Army justifies its regulations in part by asserting that straight soldiers despise and lack respect for homosexuals and that popular prejudice against homosexuals is so pervasive that their presence in the Army will discourage enlistment and tarnish the Army's public image. Instead, the Army suggests that the public opprobrium directed towards gays does not constitute prejudice in the pejorative sense of the word, but rather represents appropriate public disapproval of persons who engage in immoral behavior. The Army equates homosexuals with sodomists and justifies its regulations as simply reflecting a rational bias against a class of persons who engage in criminal acts of sodomy. In essence, the Army argues that homosexuals, like burglars, cannot form a suspect class because they are criminals.

The Army's argument, essentially adopted by the dissent, rests on two false premises. First, the class burdened by the regulations is defined by the sexual *orientation* of its members, not by their sexual conduct. To our knowledge, homosexual orientation itself has never been criminalized in this country. * * *

Second, little of the homosexual *conduct* covered by the regulations is criminal. The regulations reach many forms of homosexual conduct other than sodomy such as kissing, hand-holding, caressing, and hand-genital contact. Yet, sodomy is the only consensual adult sexual conduct that Congress has criminalized. * * *

[B3] Finally, we turn to immutability as an indicator of gross unfairness. The Supreme Court has never held that only classes with immutable traits can be deemed suspect. We nonetheless consider immutability because the Supreme Court has often focused on immutability, and has sometimes described the recognized suspect classes as having immutable traits, see, *e.g., Parham v. Hughes*, 441 U.S. 347 (1979) (describing race, national origin, alienage, illegitimacy, and gender as immutable).

Although the Supreme Court considers immutability relevant, it is clear that by "immutability" the Court has never meant strict immutability in the sense that members of the class must be physically unable to change or mask the trait defining their class. People can have operations to change their sex. Aliens can ordinarily become naturalized citizens. The status of illegitimate children can be changed. People can frequently hide their national origin by changing their customs, their names, or their associations. Lighter skinned blacks can sometimes "pass" for white, as can

Latinos for Anglos, and some people can even change their racial appearance with pigment injections. At a minimum, then, the Supreme Court is willing to treat a trait as effectively immutable if changing it would involve great difficulty, such as requiring a major physical change or a traumatic change of identity. Reading the case law in a more capacious manner, "immutability" may describe those traits that are so central to a person's identity that it would be abhorrent for government to penalize a person for refusing to change them, regardless of how easy that change might be physically. Racial discrimination, for example, would not suddenly become constitutional if medical science developed an easy, cheap, and painless method of changing one's skin pigment.

Under either formulation, we have no trouble concluding that sexual orientation is immutable for the purposes of equal protection doctrine. Although the causes of homosexuality are not fully understood, scientific research indicates that we have little control over our sexual orientation and that, once acquired, our sexual orientation is largely impervious to change. Scientific proof aside, it seems appropriate to ask whether heterosexuals feel capable of changing *their* sexual orientation. Would heterosexuals living in a city that passed an ordinance banning those who engaged in or desired to engage in sex with persons of the *opposite* sex find it easy not only to abstain from heterosexual activity but also to shift the object of their sexual desires to persons of the same sex? It may be that some heterosexuals and homosexuals can change their sexual orientation through extensive therapy, neurosurgery or shock treatment. But the possibility of such a difficult and traumatic change does not make sexual orientation "mutable" for equal protection purposes. To express the same idea under the alternative formulation, we conclude that allowing the government to penalize the failure to change such a central aspect of individual and group identity would be abhorrent to the values animating the constitutional ideal of equal protection of the laws.

[C]   The final factor the Supreme Court considers in suspect class analysis is whether the group burdened by official discrimination lacks the political power necessary to obtain redress from the political branches of government. Courts understandably have been more reluctant to extend heightened protection under equal protection doctrine to groups fully capable of securing their rights through the political process. In evaluating whether a class is politically underrepresented, the Supreme Court has focused on whether the class is a "discrete and insular minority."

The Court has held, for example, that old age does not define a discrete and insular group because "it marks a stage that each of us will reach if we live out our normal span." *Murgia*. By contrast, most of us are not likely to identify ourselves as homosexual at any time in our lives. Thus, many of us, including many elected officials, are likely to have difficulty understanding or empathizing with homosexuals. Most people have little exposure to gays, both because they rarely encounter gays and because the gays they do encounter may feel compelled to conceal their sexual orientation. In fact, the social, economic, and political pressures to conceal one's homosexuality commonly deter many gays from openly advocating pro-homosexual legislation, thus intensifying their inability to make effective use of the political process. * * *

Even when gays overcome this prejudice enough to participate openly in politics, the general animus towards homosexuality may render this participation wholly ineffective. Elected officials sensitive to public prejudice may refuse to support legislation that even appears to condone homosexuality. Indeed, the Army itself argues that its regulations are justified by the need to "maintain the public acceptability of military service," because "toleration of homosexual conduct ... might be understood as tacit approval" and "the existence of homosexual units might well be a source of ridicule and notoriety." These barriers to political power are underscored by the underrepresentation of avowed homosexuals in the decisionmaking bodies of government and the inability of homosexuals to prevent legislation hostile to their group interests. * * *

In sum, our analysis of the relevant factors in determining whether a given group should be considered a suspect class for the purposes of equal protection doctrine ineluctably leads us to the conclusion that homosexuals constitute such a suspect class. * * *

* * * [E]ven granting special deference to the policy choices of the military, we must reject many of the Army's asserted justifications [for the policy] because they illegitimately cater to private biases. For example, the Army argues that it has a valid interest in maintaining morale and discipline by avoiding hostilities and " 'tensions between known homosexuals and other members [of the armed services] who despise/detest homosexuality.' " The Army also expresses its " 'doubts concerning a homosexual officer's ability to command the respect and trust of the personnel he or she commands' " because many lower-ranked heterosexual soldiers despise and detest homosexuality. Finally, the Army argues that the presence of gays in its ranks "might well be a source of ridicule and notoriety, harmful to the Army's recruitment efforts" and to its public image.

These concerns strike a familiar chord. For much of our history, the military's fear of racial tension kept black soldiers separated from whites. As recently as World War II both the Army chief of staff and the Secretary of the Navy justified racial segregation in the ranks as necessary to maintain efficiency, discipline, and morale. Today, it is unthinkable that the judiciary would defer to the Army's prior "professional" judgment that black and white soldiers had to be segregated to avoid interracial tensions. Indeed, the Supreme Court has decisively rejected the notion that private prejudice against minorities can ever justify official discrimination, even when those private prejudices create real and legitimate problems. * * *

■ REINHARDT, J., dissenting.

["With great reluctance," Judge Reinhardt accepted the Bork argument that the constitutionality of criminal sodomy laws stood in the way of heightened equal protection scrutiny. He read *Bowers* as allowing the state to decriminalize heterosexual sodomy even as it continued to make homosexual sodomy a crime.] Indeed, it is hard to find any basis in the Court's opinion for interpreting it the way the [Ninth Circuit] majority chooses: the Court says explicitly that the statute is justified by "majority sentiments about homosexuality", not by "majority sentiments about sodomy". * * *

* * * The majority opinion concludes that under the criteria established by equal protection case law, homosexuals must be treated as a suspect class. Were it not for *Hardwick*, I would agree, for in my opinion the group meets all the applicable criteria. However, after *Hardwick*, we are no longer free to reach that conclusion.

The majority opinion treats as a suspect class a group of persons whose defining characteristic is their desire, predisposition, or propensity to engage in conduct that the Supreme Court has held to be constitutionally unprotected, an act that the states can—and approximately half the states have—criminalized. Homosexuals are different from groups previously afforded protection under the equal protection clause in that homosexuals are defined by their conduct—or, at the least, by their desire to engage in certain conduct. With other groups, such as blacks or women, there is no connection between particular conduct and the definition of the group. When conduct that plays a central role in defining a group may be prohibited by the state, it cannot be asserted with any legitimacy that the group is specially protected by the Constitution.

NOTES ON *WATKINS* AND THE LEVEL OF CONSTITUTIONAL SCRUTINY FOR SEXUAL ORIENTATION CLASSIFICATIONS

1. *The Relationship Among Classification, Class, and Conduct.* Like Judge Bork before them, Judges Norris and Reinhardt are interested in the relationship among a proposed suspect classification, the class traditionally stigmatized by it, and the conduct of the members of that class. For Bork and Reinhardt (usually not judicial bedfellows), illegal conduct drives the analysis, because it not only defines the class but also creates a perpetually rational basis for the classification. Sexual orientation discrimination becomes a second-best way of enforcing the morally stigmatizing dimensions of sodomy laws. Thus, Aristotle could approve: Different treatment is justified because people are doing different things—straight people are procreating, while "homosexuals" are sodomizing. Max Weber might also agree: The discrimination is not status-based (medieval), but conduct-based (modern). Most judges in the 1980s probably agreed with Bork and Reinhardt.

For Norris and Canby (who joined his opinion), class identity drives the analysis, because they interrogate claims of both classification and conduct in light of the damaged identity that the law is reinforcing or helping create. They would also claim that the Bork–Reinhardt equality analysis is thin. A law that discriminates against gay people is not saved by the fact that most gay people engage in sodomy, because most straight people do, too, and indeed most sodomy in our society occurs between people of different sexes. Under this lens, neither Aristotle nor Weber would be happy: We're all sodomites, but only some sodomites are singled out for stigma. And the trait that distinguishes "bad" sodomites from "good" ones is the sex of their partner, a fishy classification. The ideology that justifies the discrimination is that of compulsory gender role, questionable under one reading the Court's sex discrimination jurisprudence. (Can *Craig* or the VMI Case best be explained by the Court's rejection of compulsory gender role?) Most constitutional law professors of the 1980s agreed with Norris and Canby; many would have felt that the Court's race and sex discrimination jurisprudence required a closer look at antigay laws and policies. Accord, Nan D. Hunter, "Life After *Hardwick*," 27 *Harv. C.R.-C.L. L. Rev.* 531 (1992).

Finally, think about the relationship of class, classification, and the purpose(s) of the Equal Protection Clause. Recall *Carolene Products* and Professor Ely's representation-reinforcing theory of judicial review. In the 1980s, lesbians, gay men, and bisexuals would seem to have been a much better example of a "discrete and insular minority" excluded from or scapegoated by the legislative process than women, and therefore more in need of a judicial helping hand. That the Burger Court gave sexual and gender minorities the back of its hand was attributable not only to the Justices' antigay attitudes, but also to their limited commitment to representation-reinforcing judicial review. *E.g.*, Lewis Powell, Jr., "*Carolene Products* Revisited," 82 *Colum. L. Rev.* 1087 (1982). The Rehnquist Court has been even less influenced by *Carolene Products*, but its centrists have been open to a broader pluralist-influenced theory of equal protection review: The Court's promise of equality will induce minority groups to believe believing that their grievances can be handled through the legal process, but it is a legal process that will pay attention to identity-based groups only after they have shown their political salience, and even then it will require signals of conformity before it will provide them with relief.

2. *Doctrine: Does the Equal Protection Clause* (Watkins) *Play a Different Constitutional Role Than the Due Process Clause* (Bowers)? Cass Sunstein, "Sexual Orientation and the Constitution: A Note on the Relationship Between Due Process and Equal Protection," 55 *U. Chi. L. Rev.* 1161, 1163 (1988), defended the panel opinion in *Watkins* on the ground that *Bowers* should not foreclose applying heightened scrutiny review to sexual orientation classifications because of the intrinsic differences between the Due Process and Equal Protection Clauses:

> The Due Process Clause often looks backward; it is highly relevant to the Due Process issue whether an existing or time-honored convention, described at the appropriate level of generality, is violated by the practice under attack. By contrast, the Equal Protection Clause looks forward, serving to invalidate practices that were widespread at the time of its ratification and that were expected to endure. The two clauses therefore operate along different tracks.

Consider the doctrinal plausibility of this thesis in light of the cases in Chapter 2. Were *Griswold, Roe v. Wade, Casey,* and other due process decisions "backward-looking"? Are the cases in this chapter more "forward-looking"? Recall that the forward-looking opinion for the Court in *Loving v. Virginia* relied on both the Due Process and Equal Protection Clauses. The VMI Case seems no more forward-looking than *Roe v. Wade*. *Nguyen* seems just as backward-looking as *Bowers*.

William Eskridge, Jr., "Destabilizing Due Process and Evolutive Equal Protection,"47 *UCLA L. Rev.* 1183 (2001), disputes Sunstein's distinction. In fact, Supreme Court decisions under both clauses have looked forward, while others under both clauses have looked backward; there is no case law support for the notion that one clause is more forward-looking than the other. Innovation has occurred under each provision (and often, as in *Loving*, under both), and both provisions have been construed non-innovatively when the pull of history has been stronger than presentist needs (as perceived by the Justices). What is distinctive about the Equal Protection Clause may be the way it has become the normative and rhetorical rallying place in the Constitution for identity groups to stake out their claims for equal citizenship, see Kenneth Karst, *Belonging to America: Equal Citizenship and the Constitution* (1989), namely, their "politics of recognition." The equality guarantee has been so powerfully symbolic that the Court imported it into the Fifth Amendment's Due Process Clause in *Bolling v. Sharpe*, 347 U.S. 497 (1954) (the companion case to *Brown*, which involved school segregation in the District of Columbia). Consider other ways that the Due Process and Equal Protection Clauses might serve different constitutional roles.

3. *Sequelae. Was* Watkins *a Pyrrhic Victory?* As the case caption reveals, this decision by a panel of Ninth Circuit judges was vacated *en banc*. The full Ninth Circuit reached the same result as the panel, but on a narrower theory. The full court ruled that Watkins was entitled to reinstatement based on an estoppel theory because the Army had repeatedly re-enlisted him throughout his career, while knowing that he was gay. Judges Norris and Canby concurred in the result on the grounds articulated in their panel opinion. Judge Reinhardt wrote a concurring opinion, expressing relief that justice could be done for Sergeant Watkins notwithstanding his earlier constitutional reservations.

As of 2005, when this edition goes to press, no federal circuit court has followed Judge Norris's analysis in *Watkins* to hold that sexual orientation is a suspect classification subject to strict or heightened scrutiny under the Equal Protection Clause. The Kentucky Supreme Court used the equal protection provision of the Kentucky constitution as an alternative ground for invalidating the same-sex only sodomy law in *Commonwealth v. Wasson*, 842 S.W.2d 487 (Ky. 1992). The court found that there was no rational basis for making the same acts criminal when performed by same-sex sexual partners that were legal when done by opposite-sex partners. In a footnote dismissing its celebrated same-sex marriage case, the Hawaii Supreme Court noted that it considered sexual orientation a suspect classification requiring heightened scrutiny. See *Baehr v. Miike*, 994 P.2d 566 (Haw.1999) (summary disposition). See also *Tanner v. Oregon Health*

Sciences Univ., 971 P.2d 435 (Or. App. 1998), applying strict scrutiny under the Oregon Constitution.

At the same time American courts were recoiling from Judge Norris's analysis, the Supreme Court of Canada was embracing it. In *Vriend v. Alberta*, [1998] 1 S.C.R. 493 (Supreme Court of Canada), the Court (in tandem opinions by Justices Iacobucci and Cory) ruled that sexual orientation discriminations were "analogous" to the race and sex classifications rendered suspect by Article 15 of the Canadian Charter of Rights. Like Judge Norris, they emphasized the irrationality of sexual orientation for most state purposes and the history of prejudice and discrimination afflicting gay people. See also *M. v. H.*, 171 D.L.R. (4th) 577 (Supreme Court of Canada, 1999) (evaluating discrimination against lesbian and gay couples).

NOTE ON THE IMMUTABILITY "REQUIREMENT" FOR SUSPECT CLASSIFICATIONS AND ITS RELEVANCE TO SEXUAL ORIENTATION

Note Judge Norris's assumption (taken from *Frontiero*) that suspect classifications should be immutable. The immutability argument is inspired by Max Weber's idea: The modern regulatory state ought only regulate on the basis of merit and conduct, and presumptively not on the basis of immutable trait and status. In *Weber v. Aetna Cas. & Sur. Co.*, 406 U.S. 164 (1972), the Court relied on this idea to rule that the state cannot penalize nonmarital children for a trait that they could not change. Relying on this idea, the traditional family values countermovement has strongly maintained that sexual orientation ought not be a suspect classification, because it is not immutable in the way race and sex are. Homosexuality is a Weberian *choice* that can be fully regulated by the state, not an immutable *trait*. (Another form of the argument is that the "homosexual conduct" presumptively engaged in by the "avowed homosexual" is a choice, and not a trait, that can be the basis for state regulation.)

One might object that traits we consider protected against state discrimination—sex, religion, and alienage—are mutable; therefore, suspect classifications cannot turn on immutability. It cannot be a *necessary* condition. Nor can it be a *sufficient* condition, as many traits that are immutable—intelligence, mental disability, old age—are not ones considered suspect. Judge Norris took a different tack. Rather than concluding that immutability is irrelevant, he viewed it through the prism of identity: He would treat a trait as "effectively immutable if changing it would involve great difficulty, such as requiring a major physical change or a traumatic change of identity." This is a social understanding of immutability inspired by the race cases. One's race in the South was mainly a legal construct (which of course could be changed by passing a law)—Homer Plessy was "colored" because Louisiana considered anyone "colored" who had one drop of black blood. Immutability should not, Norris maintains, be dispositive in the way that fairness to the group and rationality of the criterion should be.

On the other hand, immutability (as understood by Norris) may be relevant to suspect classification analysis, for several reasons. One is that it will often be unfair to stigmatized individuals to penalize them for a trait they cannot easily change (the idea suggested by the nonmarital children cases). Another reason goes to efficacy of state policy: If the state's goal is to press everyone into the same mold, then it is doomed to failure if the victims of its policy cannot change to fit the mold. A third reason is suggested by social movements theory: A state that stigmatizes a whole group of citizens for morally arbitrary reasons is risking major social turmoil once that group mobilizes to protest its stigma. Immutability is relevant not only to the moral arbitrariness of the stigma, but also to the perseverance of the social group notwithstanding stigma. If gay people will remain part of society notwithstanding legal efforts to extinguish or expel them (the *Boutilier* policy), then it is pluralist suicide for the state to conduct a *Kulturkampf* against them.

There are various theories supporting the proposition that homosexuality is hard-wired (immutable). See Edward Stein, *The Mismeasure of Desire: The Science, Theory, and Ethics of Sexual Orientation* (1999) (critical of the theories). The most famous hypothesis is that there is a genetic cause contributing directly or indirectly toward homosexuality. See Dean Hamer et al., "A Linkage Between DNA Markers on the X Chromosome and Male Sexual Orientation," 261 *Science* 321–27 (1993), elaborated in Dean Hamer & Peter Copeland, *The Science of Desire: The Search for the Gay Gene and the Biology of Behavior* (1994). The authors, researchers at the National Cancer Institute of the National Institutes of Health (NIH), claimed to have found a location on the X chromosome (Xq28, to be precise) where a "gay gene" would likely be found. The study concentrated on pairs of brothers in which both were gay, reasoning that if being gay were genetic, then families with pairs of gay brothers would be more "loaded" with the gay gene than others and would be the best place to look. The NIH group first found that among these families, the maternal uncles and male cousins were more likely to be gay than the general population or the paternal relatives; this pattern suggests a trait linked to the X chromosome, which men get from their mother but not their father. They then examined 40 pairs of gay brothers, and found that 33 of them shared the same markers in the Xq28 region of the X chromosome, a result significantly higher than the 50% one would expect from random distribution. Based on this data, the NIH group concluded (cautiously) that "at least one subtype of male sexual orientation is genetically influenced." This NIH study has been criticized on a number of fronts, and its results have not been satisfactorily replicated.

While *determinist theories* of sexual orientation (such as the gay gene) remain unproven, *voluntarist theories* (such as those of reparative therapists, who say that homosexuality is a "choice" that can be reversed) have found virtually no support among scientists. The professional organizations in psychiatry and psychology have disavowed reparative therapy as sectarian rather than scientific and as unethical in its asserted manipulation of patients. Other theories are *quasi-determinist*. The most famous is Freud's theory that homosexuality is the result of family psychodynamics (the Oedipus Complex). Some scientists maintain that childhood gender deviation (sissy boys and tomboys) correlates with adult sexual deviation. These theories enjoy the greatest empirical support but are subject to the chicken-and-the-egg problem: Does the gender deviation cause or contribute to the sexual deviation? Or do they both derive from the same biological or developmental roots?

PART C. WHEN IS ANTIGAY DISCRIMINATION NOT RATIONAL?

Roy Romer v. Richard Evans et al.

United States Supreme Court, 1996.
517 U.S. 620, 116 S.Ct. 1620, 134 L.Ed.2d 855.

■ JUSTICE KENNEDY delivered the opinion of the Court.

One century ago, the first Justice Harlan admonished this Court that the Constitution "neither knows nor tolerates classes among citizens." *Plessy v. Ferguson*, 163 U.S. 537, 559 (1896) (dissenting opinion). Unheeded then, those words now are understood to state a commitment to the law's neutrality where the rights of persons are at stake. The Equal Protection Clause enforces this principle and today requires us to hold invalid a provision of Colorado's Constitution.

The enactment challenged in this case is an amendment to the Constitution of the State of Colorado, adopted in a 1992 statewide referendum. The parties and the state courts refer to it as "Amendment 2," its designation when submitted to the voters. The impetus for the amendment and the contentious campaign that preceded its adoption came in large part from ordinances that had been passed in various Colorado municipalities. For example, the cities of Aspen and Boulder and the City and County of Denver each had enacted ordinances which banned discrimination in many transactions and activities, including housing, employment, education, public accommodations, and health and welfare services. Denver Rev. Municipal Code, Art. IV §§ 28–91 to 28–116 (1991); Aspen Municipal Code § 13–98 (1977); Boulder Rev. Code §§ 12–1–1 to 12–1–11 (1987). What gave rise to the statewide controversy was the protection the ordinances afforded to persons discriminated against by reason of their sexual orientation. Amendment 2 repeals these ordinances to the extent they prohibit discrimination on the basis of "homosexual, lesbian or bisexual orientation, conduct, practices or relationships." Colo. Const., Art. II, § 30b.

Yet Amendment 2, in explicit terms, does more than repeal or rescind these provisions. It prohibits all legislative, executive or judicial action at any level of state or local government designed to protect the named class, a class we shall refer to as homosexual persons or gays and lesbians. [Justice Kennedy quoted Amendment 2:

Neither the State of Colorado, through any of its branches or departments, nor any of its agencies, political subdivisions, municipalities or school districts, shall enact, adopt or enforce any statute, regulation, ordinance or policy whereby homosexual, lesbian or bisexual orientation, conduct, practices or relationships shall constitute or otherwise be the basis of or entitle any person or class of persons to have or claim any minority status, quota preferences, protected status or claim of discrimination.]

The State's principal argument in defense of Amendment 2 is that it puts gays and lesbians in the same position as all other persons. So, the State says, the measure does no more than deny homosexuals special rights. This reading of the amendment's language is implausible. * * * Homosexuals, by state decree, are put in a solitary class with respect to transactions and relations in both the private and governmental spheres. The amendment withdraws from homosexuals, but no others, specific legal protection from the injuries caused by discrimination, and it forbids reinstatement of these laws and policies.

The change that Amendment 2 works in the legal status of gays and lesbians in the private sphere is far-reaching, both on its own terms and when considered in light of the structure and operation of modern anti-discrimination laws. That structure is well illustrated by contemporary statutes and ordinances prohibiting discrimination by providers of public accommodations. "At common law, innkeepers, smiths, and others who 'made profession of a public employment,' were prohibited from refusing, without good reason, to serve a customer." *Hurley v. Irish–American Gay, Lesbian and Bisexual Group of Boston, Inc.*, 115 S. Ct. 2338, 2346 (1995). The duty was a general one and did not specify protection for particular groups. The common law rules, however, proved insufficient in many instances, and it was settled early that the Fourteenth Amendment did not give Congress a general power to prohibit discrimination in public accommodations, *Civil Rights Cases*, 109 U.S. 3, 25 (1883). In consequence, most States have chosen to counter discrimination by enacting detailed statutory schemes.

Colorado's state and municipal laws typify this emerging tradition of statutory protection and follow a consistent pattern. The laws first enumerate the persons or entities subject to a duty not to discriminate. The list goes well beyond the entities covered by the common law. The Boulder ordinance, for example, has a comprehensive definition of entities deemed places of "public accommodation." They include "any place of business engaged in any sales to the general public and any place that offers services, facilities, privileges, or advantages to the general public or that receives financial support through solicitation of the general public or through governmental subsidy of any kind." * * *

Amendment 2 bars homosexuals from securing protection against the injuries that these public-accommodations laws address. That in itself is a severe consequence, but there is more. Amendment 2, in addition, nullifies specific legal protections for this targeted class in all transactions in housing, sale of real estate, insurance, health and welfare services, private education, and employment. * * *

Amendment 2's reach may not be limited to specific laws passed for the benefit of gays and lesbians. It is a fair, if not necessary, inference from the broad language of the amendment that it deprives gays and lesbians even of the protection of general laws and policies that prohibit arbitrary discrimination in governmental and private settings. At some point in the systematic administration of these laws, an official must determine whether homosexuality is an arbitrary and, thus, forbidden basis for decision. Yet a decision to that effect would itself amount to a policy prohibiting discrimination on the basis of homosexuality, and so would appear to be no more valid under Amendment 2 than the specific prohibitions against discrimination the state court held invalid.

If this consequence follows from Amendment 2, as its broad language suggests, it would compound the constitutional difficulties the law creates. The state court did not decide whether the amendment has this effect, however, and neither need we. In the course of rejecting the argument that Amendment 2 is intended to conserve resources to fight discrimination against suspect classes, the Colorado Supreme Court made the limited observation that the amendment is not intended to affect many anti-discrimination laws protecting non-suspect classes. In our view that does not resolve the issue. In any event, even if, as we doubt, homosexuals could find some safe harbor in laws of general application, we cannot accept the view that Amendment 2's prohibition on specific legal protections does no more than deprive homosexuals of special rights. To the contrary, the amendment imposes a special disability upon those persons alone. Homosexuals are forbidden the safeguards that others enjoy or may seek without constraint. They can obtain specific protection against discrimination only by enlisting the citizenry of Colorado to amend the State Constitution or perhaps, on the State's view, by trying to pass helpful laws of general applicability. This is so no matter how local or discrete the harm, no matter how public and widespread the injury. We find nothing special in the protections Amendment 2 withholds. These are protections taken for granted by most people either because they already have them or do not need them; these are protections against exclusion from an almost limitless number of transactions and endeavors that constitute ordinary civic life in a free society.

The Fourteenth Amendment's promise that no person shall be denied the equal protection of the laws must co-exist with the practical necessity that most legislation classifies for one purpose or another, with resulting disadvantage to various groups or persons. We have attempted to reconcile the principle with the reality by stating that, if a law neither burdens a fundamental right nor targets a suspect class, we will uphold the legislative classification so long as it bears a rational relation to some legitimate end. See, *e.g.*, *Heller v. Doe*, 509 U.S. 312, 319–320 (1993).

Amendment 2 fails, indeed defies, even this conventional inquiry. First, the amendment has the peculiar property of imposing a broad and undifferentiated disability on a single named group, an exceptional and, as we shall explain, invalid form of legislation. Second, its sheer breadth is so discontinuous with the reasons offered for it that the amendment seems inexplicable by anything but animus toward the class that it affects; it lacks a rational relationship to legitimate state interests.

Taking the first point, even in the ordinary equal protection case calling for the most deferential of standards, we insist on knowing the relation between the classification adopted and the object to be attained. The search for the link between classification and objective gives substance to the Equal Protection Clause; it provides guidance and discipline for the legislature, which is entitled to know what sorts of laws it can pass; and it marks the limits of our own authority. In the ordinary case, a law will be sustained if it can be said to advance a legitimate government interest, even if the law seems unwise or works to the disadvantage of a particular group, or if the rationale for it seems tenuous. * * * By requiring that the classification bear a rational relationship to an independent and legitimate legislative end, we ensure that classifications are not drawn for the purpose of disadvantaging the group burdened by the law.* * *

Amendment 2 confounds this normal process of judicial review. It is at once too narrow and too broad. It identifies persons by a single trait and then denies them protection across the board. The resulting disqualification of a class of persons from the right to seek specific protection from the law is unprecedented in our jurisprudence. The absence of precedent for Amendment 2 is itself instructive; "[d]iscriminations of an unusual character especially suggest careful consideration to determine whether they are obnoxious to the constitutional provision." *Louisville Gas & Elec. Co. v. Coleman*, 277 U.S. 32, 37–38 (1928).

It is not within our constitutional tradition to enact laws of this sort. Central both to the idea of the rule of law and to our own Constitution's guarantee of equal protection is the principle that government and each of its parts remain open on impartial terms to all who seek its assistance. " 'Equal protection of the laws is not achieved through indiscriminate imposition of inequalities.' " *Sweatt v. Painter*, 339 U.S. 629, 635 (1950) (quoting *Shelley v. Kraemer*, 334 U.S. 1, 22 (1948)). Respect for this principle explains why laws singling out a certain class of citizens for disfavored legal status or general hardships are rare. A law declaring that in general it shall be more difficult for one group of citizens than for all others to seek aid from the government is itself a denial of equal protection of the laws in the most literal sense. "The guaranty of 'equal protection of the laws is a pledge of the protection of equal laws.' " *Skinner v. Oklahoma ex rel. Williamson*, 316 U.S. 535, 541 (1942) (quoting *Yick Wo v. Hopkins*, 118 U.S. 356, 369 (1886)). * * *

A second and related point is that laws of the kind now before us raise the inevitable inference that the disadvantage imposed is born of animosity toward the class of persons affected. "[I]f the constitutional conception of 'equal protection of the laws' means anything, it must at the very least mean that a bare ... desire to harm a politically unpopular group cannot constitute a *legitimate* governmental interest." *Department of Agriculture v. Moreno*, 413 U.S. 528, 534 (1973). Even laws enacted for broad and ambitious purposes often can be explained by reference to legitimate public policies which justify the incidental disadvantages they impose on certain persons. Amendment 2, however, in making a general announcement that gays and lesbians shall not have any particular protections from the law, inflicts on them immediate, continuing, and real injuries that outrun and belie any legitimate justifications that may be claimed for it. We conclude that, in addition to the far-reaching deficiencies of Amendment 2 that we have noted, the principles it offends, in another sense, are conventional and venerable; a law must bear a rational relationship to a legitimate governmental purpose, and Amendment 2 does not.

The primary rationale the State offers for Amendment 2 is respect for other citizens' freedom of association, and in particular the liberties of landlords or employers who have personal or religious objections to homosexuality. Colorado also cites its interest in conserving resources to fight discrimination against other groups. The breadth of the Amendment is so far removed from these particular justifications that we find it impossible to credit them. We cannot say that Amendment 2 is directed to any identifiable legitimate purpose or discrete objective. It is a status-based enactment divorced from any factual context from which we could discern a relationship to legitimate state interests; it is a classification of persons undertaken for its own sake, something the Equal Protection Clause does not permit. "[C]lass legislation . . . [is] obnoxious to the prohibitions of the Fourteenth Amendment. . . ." *Civil Rights Cases*, 109 U.S., at 24.

We must conclude that Amendment 2 classifies homosexuals not to further a proper legislative end but to make them unequal to everyone else. This Colorado cannot do. A State cannot so deem a class of persons a stranger to its laws. Amendment 2 violates the Equal Protection Clause, and the judgment of the Supreme Court of Colorado is affirmed.

■ Justice Scalia, with whom The Chief Justice [Rehnquist] and Justice Thomas join, dissenting.

The Court has mistaken a Kulturkampf for a fit of spite. The constitutional amendment before us here is not the manifestation of a " 'bare . . . desire to harm' " homosexuals, but is rather a modest attempt by seemingly tolerant Coloradans to preserve traditional sexual mores against the efforts of a politically powerful minority to revise those mores through use of the laws. That objective, and the means chosen to achieve it, are not only unimpeachable under any constitutional doctrine hitherto pronounced (hence the opinion's heavy reliance upon principles of righteousness rather than judicial holdings); they have been specifically approved by the Congress of the United States and by this Court.

In holding that homosexuality cannot be singled out for disfavorable treatment, the Court contradicts a decision, unchallenged here, pronounced only 10 years ago, see *Hardwick*, and places the prestige of this institution behind the proposition that opposition to homosexuality is as reprehensible as racial or religious bias. Whether it is or not is *precisely* the cultural debate that gave rise to the Colorado constitutional amendment (and to the preferential laws against which the amendment was directed). Since the Constitution of the United States says nothing about this subject, it is left to be resolved by normal democratic means, including the democratic adoption of provisions in state constitutions. This Court has no business imposing upon all Americans the resolution favored by the elite class from which the Members of this institution are selected, pronouncing that "animosity" toward homosexuality, is evil. I vigorously dissent.

Let me first discuss [the Court's rejection of] the State's arguments that Amendment 2 "puts gays and lesbians in the same position as all other persons," and "does no more than deny homosexuals special rights." The Court concludes that this reading of Amendment 2's language is "implausible" under the "authoritative construction" given Amendment 2 by the Supreme Court of Colorado.

[Justice Scalia quoted the decision of the Colorado Supreme Court, which construed Amendment 2 as follows: "[It] seeks only to prevent the adoption of antidiscrimination laws intended to protect gays, lesbians, and bisexuals."] The clear import of the Colorado court's conclusion that it is not affected is that "general laws and policies that prohibit arbitrary discrimination" would continue to prohibit discrimination on the basis of homosexual conduct as well. This analysis, which is fully in accord with (indeed, follows inescapably from) the text of the constitutional provision, lays to rest such horribles, raised in the course of oral argument, as the prospect that assaults upon homosexuals could not be prosecuted. The amendment prohibits *special treatment* of homosexuals, and nothing more. It would not affect, for example, a requirement of state law that pensions be paid to all retiring state employees with a certain length of service; homosexual employees, as well as others, would be entitled to that benefit. But it would prevent the State or any municipality from making death-benefit payments to the "life partner" of a homosexual when it does not make such payments to the long-time roommate of a nonhomosexual employee. Or again, it does not affect the requirement of the State's general insurance laws that customers be afforded coverage without discrimination unrelated to anticipated risk. Thus, homosexuals could not be denied coverage, or charged a greater premium, with respect to auto collision insurance; but neither the State nor any municipality could require that distinctive health insurance risks associated with homosexuality (if there are any) be ignored.

Despite all of its hand-wringing about the potential effect of Amendment 2 on general antidiscrimination laws, the Court's opinion ultimately does not dispute all this, but assumes it to be true. The only denial of equal treatment it contends homosexuals have suffered is this: They may not obtain *preferential* treatment without amending the State Constitution. That is to say, the principle underlying the Court's opinion is that one who is accorded equal treatment under the laws, but cannot as readily as others obtain *preferential* treatment under the laws, has been denied equal protection of the laws. If merely stating this alleged "equal protection" violation does not suffice to refute it, our constitutional jurisprudence has achieved terminal silliness.

The central thesis of the Court's reasoning is that any group is denied equal protection when, to obtain advantage (or, presumably, to avoid disadvantage), it must have recourse to a more general and hence more difficult level of political decisionmaking than others. The world has never heard of such a principle, which is why the Court's opinion is so long on emotive utterance and so short on relevant legal citation. And it seems to me most unlikely that any multilevel democracy can function under such a principle. For *whenever* a disadvantage is imposed, or conferral of a benefit is prohibited, at one of the higher levels of democratic decisionmaking (*i.e.*, by the state legislature rather than local government, or by the people at large in the state constitution rather than the legislature), the affected group has (under this theory) been denied equal protection. * * *

I turn next to whether there was a legitimate rational basis for the substance of the constitutional amendment—for the prohibition of special protection for homosexuals. It is unsurprising that the Court avoids discussion of this question, since the answer is so obviously yes. The case most relevant to the issue before us today is not even mentioned in the Court's opinion: In *Bowers v. Hardwick*, we held that the Constitution does not prohibit what virtually all States had done from the founding of the Republic until very recent years—making homosexual conduct a crime. That holding is unassailable, except by those who think that the Constitution changes to suit current fashions. But in any event it is a given in the present case: Respondents' briefs did not urge overruling *Bowers*, and at oral argument respondents' counsel expressly disavowed any intent to seek such overruling. If it is constitutionally permissible for a State to make homosexual conduct criminal, surely it is constitutionally permissible for a State to enact other laws merely *disfavoring* homosexual conduct. * * * And *a fortiori* it is constitutionally permissible for a State to adopt a provision *not even* disfavoring homosexual conduct, but merely prohibiting all levels of state government from bestowing *special protections* upon homosexual conduct. Respondents (who, unlike the Court, cannot afford the luxury of ignoring inconvenient precedent) counter *Bowers* with the argument that a greater-includes-the-lesser rationale cannot justify Amendment 2's application to individuals who do not engage in homosexual acts, but are merely of homosexual "orientation." * * *

But assuming that, in Amendment 2, a person of homosexual "orientation" is someone who does not engage in homosexual conduct but merely has a tendency or desire to do so, *Bowers* still suffices to establish a rational basis for the provision. If it is rational to criminalize the conduct, surely it is rational to deny special favor and protection to those with a self-avowed tendency or desire to engage in the conduct. Indeed, where criminal sanctions are not involved, homosexual "orientation" is an acceptable stand-in for homosexual conduct. A State "does not violate the Equal Protection Clause merely because the classifications made by its laws are imperfect," *Dandridge v. Williams*, 397 U.S. 471, 485 (1970). Just as a policy barring the hiring of methadone users as transit employees does not violate equal protection simply because *some* methadone users pose no threat to passenger safety, see *New York City Transit Authority v. Beazer*, 440 U.S. 568 (1979), and just as a mandatory retirement age of 50 for police officers does not violate equal protection even though it prematurely ends the careers of many policemen over 50 who still have the capacity to do the job, see *Massachusetts Bd. of Retirement v. Murgia*, 427 U.S. 307 (1976) (per curiam), Amendment 2 is not constitutionally invalid simply because it could have been drawn more precisely so as to withdraw special antidiscrimination protections only from those of homosexual "orientation" who actually engage in homosexual conduct. * * *

The foregoing suffices to establish what the Court's failure to cite any case remotely in point would lead one to suspect: No principle set forth in the Constitution, nor even any imagined by this Court in the past 200 years, prohibits what Colorado has done here. But the case for Colorado is much stronger than that. What it has done is not only unprohibited, but eminently reasonable, with close, congressionally approved precedent in earlier constitutional practice.

First, as to its eminent reasonableness. The Court's opinion contains grim, disapproving hints that Coloradans have been guilty of "animus" or "animosity" toward homosexuality, as though that has been established as un-American. Of course it is our moral heritage that one should not hate any human being or class of human beings. But I had thought that one could consider certain conduct reprehensible—murder, for example, or polygamy, or cruelty to animals—and could exhibit even "animus" toward such conduct. Surely that is the only sort of "animus" at issue here: moral disapproval of homosexual conduct, the same sort of moral disapproval that produced the centuries-old criminal laws that we held constitutional in *Bowers*. The Colorado amendment does not, to speak entirely precisely, prohibit giving favored status to people who are *homosexuals*; they can be favored for many reasons—for example, because they are senior citizens or members of racial minorities. But it prohibits giving them favored status *because of their homosexual conduct*—that is, it prohibits favored status *for homosexuality*.

But though Coloradans are, as I say, *entitled* to be hostile toward homosexual conduct, the fact is that the degree of hostility reflected by Amendment 2 is the smallest conceivable. The Court's portrayal of Coloradans as a society fallen victim to pointless, hate-filled "gay-bashing" is so false as to be comical. Colorado not only is one of the 25 States that have repealed their antisodomy laws, but was among the first to do so. See 1971 Colo. Sess. Laws, ch. 121, § 1. But the society that eliminates criminal punishment for homosexual acts does not necessarily abandon the view that homosexuality is morally wrong and socially harmful; often, abolition simply reflects the view that enforcement of such criminal laws involves unseemly intrusion into the intimate lives of citizens. * * *

There is a problem, however, which arises when criminal sanction of homosexuality is eliminated but moral and social disapprobation of homosexuality is meant to be retained. The Court cannot be unaware of that problem; it is evident in many cities of the country, and occasionally bubbles to the surface of the news, in heated political disputes over such matters as the introduction into local schools of books teaching that homosexuality is an optional and fully acceptable "alternate life style." The problem (a problem, that is, for those who wish to retain social disapprobation of homosexuality) is that, because those who engage in homosexual conduct tend to reside in disproportionate numbers in certain communities, see Record, Exh. MMM, have high disposable income, see *ibid.*; App. 254 (affidavit of Prof. James Hunter), and, of course, care about homosexual-rights issues much more ardently than the public at large, they possess political power much greater than their numbers, both locally and state-wide. Quite understandably, they devote this political power to achieving not merely a grudging social toleration, but full social acceptance, of homosexuality. * * *

By the time Coloradans were asked to vote on Amendment 2, their exposure to homosexuals' quest for social endorsement was not limited to newspaper accounts of happenings in places such as New York, Los Angeles, San Francisco, and Key West. Three Colorado cities—Aspen, Boulder, and Denver—had enacted ordinances that listed "sexual orientation" as an impermissible ground for discrimination, equating the moral disapproval of homosexual conduct with racial and religious bigotry. The phenomenon had even appeared statewide: the Governor of Colorado had signed an executive order pronouncing that "in the State of Colorado we recognize the diversity in our pluralistic society and strive to bring an end to discrimination in any form," and directing state agency-heads to "ensure non-discrimination" in hiring and promotion based on, among other things, "sexual orientation." Executive Order No. D0035 (Dec. 10, 1990). I do not mean to be critical of these legislative successes; homosexuals are as entitled to use the legal system for reinforcement of their moral sentiments as are the rest of society. But they are subject to being countered by lawful, democratic countermeasures as well.

That is where Amendment 2 came in. It sought to counter both the geographic concentration and the disproportionate political power of homosexuals by (1) resolving the controversy at the statewide level, and (2) making the election a single-issue contest for both sides. It put directly, to all the citizens of the State, the question: Should homosexuality be given special protection? They answered no. The Court today asserts that this most democratic of procedures is unconstitutional. Lacking any cases to establish that facially absurd proposition, it simply asserts that it *must* be unconstitutional, because it has never happened before. * * * As I have noted above, this is proved false every time a state law prohibiting or disfavoring certain conduct is passed, because such a law prevents the adversely affected group—whether drug addicts, or smokers, or gun owners, or motorcyclists—from changing the policy thus established in "each of [the] parts" of the State. What the Court says is even demonstrably false at the constitutional level. The Eighteenth Amendment to the Federal Constitution, for example, deprived those who drank alcohol not only of the power to alter the policy of prohibition *locally* or through *state legislation*, but even of the power to alter it through *state constitutional amendment* or *federal legislation*. The Establishment Clause of the First Amendment prevents theocrats from having their way by converting their fellow citizens at the local, state, or federal statutory level; as does the Republican Form of Government Clause prevent monarchists. * * *

When the Court takes sides in the culture wars, it tends to be with the knights rather than the villeins—and more specifically with the Templars, reflecting the views and values of the lawyer class from which the Court's Members are drawn. How that class feels about homosexuality will be evident to anyone who wishes to interview job applicants at virtually any of the Nation's law schools. The interviewer may refuse to offer a job because the applicant is a Republican; because he is an adulterer; because he went to the wrong prep school or belongs to the wrong country club; because he eats snails; because he is a womanizer; because she wears real-animal fur; or even because he hates the Chicago Cubs. But if the interviewer should wish not to be an associate or partner of an applicant because he disapproves of the applicant's homosexuality, *then* he will have violated the pledge which the Association of American Law Schools requires all its member schools to exact from job interviewers: "assurance of the employer's willingness" to hire homosexuals. This law-school view of what "prejudices" must be stamped out may be contrasted with the more plebeian attitudes that apparently still prevail in the United States Congress, which has been unresponsive to repeated attempts to extend to homosexuals the protections of federal civil rights laws, see, e.g., Employment Non–Discrimination Act of 1994, S. 2238, 103d Cong., 2d Sess. (1994); Civil Rights Amendments of 1975, H.R. 5452, 94th Cong., 1st Sess. (1975), and which took the pains to exclude them specifically from the Americans with Disabilities Act of 1990, see 42 U.S.C. § 12211(a) (1988 ed., Supp. V).

Today's opinion has no foundation in American constitutional law, and barely pretends to. The people of Colorado have adopted an entirely reasonable provision which does not even disfavor homosexuals in any substantive sense, but merely denies them preferential treatment. Amendment 2 is designed to prevent piecemeal deterioration of the sexual morality favored by a majority of Coloradans, and is not only an appropriate means to that legitimate end, but a means that Americans have employed before. Striking it down is an act, not of judicial judgment, but of political will. I dissent.

NOTES ON *ROMER v. EVANS* AND THE FUTURE OF HOMO EQUALITY

1. *What Is the Holding of* Romer v. Evans? What exactly was wrong with Amendment 2? Some possibilities:

(a) it deprived gay people of the right to participate equally in the political process (the theory advanced by the Colorado Supreme Court for striking down Amendment 2);

(b) the law was a denial of the "equal protection of the laws" in the most literal sense, as it closed off state process to one vulnerable group, see Brief by Laurence Tribe et al., in *Romer*, the so-called "Scholars' Brief" filed in the case;

(c) the law may not draw moral distinctions based upon sexual practices between consenting adults (therefore overruling *Hardwick*), e.g., Robert Bork, *Slouching Towards Gomorrah* 112–14 (1996) (disapproving); William Eskridge, Jr., *Gaylaw: Challenging the Apartheid of the Closet* 150–51, 209–11 (1999) (approving); Thomas Grey, "*Bowers v. Hardwick* Diminished," 68 *U. Colo. L. Rev.* 373 (1997) (approving);

(d) the state cannot, without justification, single out one social group for "pariah" status by creating a constitutional right to discriminate against that group, Daniel Farber & Suzanna Sherry, "The Pariah Principle," 13 *Const. Comm.* 257 (1996), or the state has an obligation to remedy pervasive discrimination against a vulnerable group similar to those the state does protect, see Louis Michael Seidman, "*Romer*'s Radicalism: The Unexpected Revival of Warren Court Activism," 1996 *Sup. Ct. Rev.* 67;

(e) the law's goal—state action reflecting widespread animus against gay people—was impermissible, e.g., Andrew Koppelman, "*Romer v. Evans* and Invidious Intent," 6 *Wm. & Mary Bill of Rights J.* 89 (1997);

(f) the measure, unprecedented in its sweep, was way overbroad, e.g., Richard Duncan, "The Narrow and Shallow Bite of *Romer* and the Eminent Rationality of Dual–Gender Marriage: A (Partial) Response to Professor Koppelman," 6 *Wm. & Mary Bill of Rights J.* 147 (1997).

Which basis is the *best* (most persuasive) basis for *Romer v. Evans*? And consider this: Amendment 2 left anti-discrimination laws on the books but prevented them from being used to protect gay people. As a formal matter, a straight man in Aspen could still invoke the city's anti-discrimination ordinance if a gay bookstore refused to hire him—but a bisexual man could not invoke the ordinance if a homophobic bookstore refused to hire him. Does this technicality, which was emphasized in the amicus brief filed by the American Bar Association, help explain the result—while at the same time providing a basis for reading the case narrowly?

2. *Identity and Conduct; Animus und Kulturkampf.* Echoing Judge Norris, Justice Kennedy in *Romer* reads Amendment 2 through the lens of identity and a history of persecution. Unlike Norris, Kennedy places some emphasis on motive: Amendment 2 was a product of "animus," not rationality. The role that animus plays in the opinion is ambiguous. Colorado had presented itself as a "tolerant" state, because it had long ago shed its consensual sodomy law, and the amendment was a mild "no promo homo" measure—rather than putting gay men, bisexuals, and the occasional lesbian in jail (like neighboring Utah would do), Colorado tolerates them but signals its preference for "heterosexuality." Why did the Court not accept this presentation? (Important: Review the ballot materials in Appendix 3. Do they suggest antigay "animus"?) How does the Court distinguish between morals regulations and laws motivated by animus? From the perspective of the stigmatized person, morality typically seems like animus.

Echoing Judge Reinhardt, Justice Scalia in *Romer* reads Amendment 2 through the lens of conduct and a history of morals regulation. Not only does Scalia accept Colorado's self-presentation as tolerant, but he scorns the Court's finding of "animus," though he does so in an odd way. Consider his rhetoric. *Kulturkampf* is "culture *war*" conducted by the state to erase an unpopular minority. The original *Kulturkampf* was Chancellor Bismarck's effort to domesticate the Roman Catholic Church in Germany. One can read the dissent as a rhetorical invitation for states to accommodate "cultural wars" against gay people, and the majority opinion to be an insistence that the courts should not permit *Kulturkampf*. Does Scalia consign gay people to a state of nature, the essence of *Kulturkampf* if you are a minority and there is a history of opprobrium against you by the majority?

3. *Equal Protection Review After* Romer: *Channeling Antigay Discourse.* Because it involved an oddly drafted and sweeping state initiative, *Romer* can be read as narrowly or as broadly as the Court chooses. One may view it as an experiment on the part of a Court burned by acid criticisms of its performance in *Bowers*: Announce that gay people are indeed within the protection of the Constitution, but don't commit yourselves to "too much" protection—and see how the political process and the lower courts respond.

Accordingly, *Romer* can be interpreted narrowly, and has been. *E.g.,* *Equality Foundation of Greater Cincinnati v. City of Cincinnati*, 128 F.3d 289 (6th Cir. 1997) (upholding municipal charter amendment similar to Amendment 2).

Romer can also be read broadly, and has been. *E.g., Stemler v. City of Florence*, 126 F.3d 856 (6th Cir. 1997) (invalidating discriminatory police enforcement of drunk driving laws to arrest a lesbian seeking to rescue a woman from her drunk and abusive boyfriend, whose own drunk driving killed her).

One reason the case is complex is that Justice Kennedy's text performs multiple functions simultaneously. Most dramatically, it reverses what lower federal courts had interpreted as a rule of categorical inequality in *Bowers*, *i.e.,* despite the absence of an equal protection ruling in that case, many followed Judges Bork (*Dronenburg*) and Reinhardt (*Watkins*) to conclude that it permitted a virtual blank check for adverse treatment. Instead, it substituted the requirement of some reasonable nexus between classification and legitimate legislative purpose, and it held that, at least some of the time for some purposes, laws enacted to foster disapproval of homosexuality were fatally flawed. Nan D. Hunter, "Proportional Equality: Readings of *Romer*," 89 *Ky. L. J.* 885 (2000–2001).

Whatever the correct reading of *Romer*, one effect will be to transform public discourse about homosexuality. Proponents of laws and initiatives that discriminate against gay people will have to focus on neutral policies;

if they want to minimize the chance of a successful equal protection challenge, they will abstain from arguments which demonize gay people or which make wild claims about them. *Romer* and equal protection law will *channel* antigay discourse into more tolerant tropes. Rather than hurting gay people, antigay policies will be justified to avoid hurting third parties. Sometimes, antigay policies are justified under the rationale that the state should *tolerate* "homosexuals" but should *not promote* "homosexuality" or "homosexual conduct." Does *Romer* shed any light on these so-called "no promo homo" arguments?

PROBLEM 3–3

WHICH OF THE FOLLOWING STATE SEXUAL ORIENTATION–BASED CLASSIFICATIONS ARE NOW UNCONSTITUTIONAL?

Consider the following government discriminations against lesbians, gay men, bisexuals, and transgendered persons. Which of these is most vulnerable after *Romer*? Array these discriminations from easiest-to-sustain to most-likely-to-fall:

(A) the exclusion of lesbians, gay men, and bisexuals from the armed forces (*Watkins*, and Chapter 7);

(B) laws making only "homosexual sodomy" a crime, but not "heterosexual sodomy," a crime (see Chapter 4);

(C) laws making it a crime to solicit another person to engage in homosexual (but not heterosexual) activities;

(D) laws barring gay men and lesbians from adopting children (see Chapter 4);

(E) municipal policies against hiring lesbians or gay men to serve in police and fire departments (see Chapter 8);

(F) state laws limiting civil marriage, as well as its legal benefits and duties, to different-sex couples (see Chapter 9, Section 2, as well as the next section).

Make your list now, then revisit the list after you cover Chapter 4. Consider the list a third time at the end of the course.

Sex Discriminations Harming Sexual Minorities

Many discriminations disadvantaging lesbians, gay men, bisexuals, and transgendered people are laws that (as a formal matter) make distinctions on the basis of *sex*, not *sexual or gender orientation*. Thus, gay people can marry in all states, so long as they marry someone of the "opposite" sex; people of the same sex generally cannot marry. In the early 1970s, a challenge to these sex discriminations took shape from arguments posed by lesbian feminists and male anti-feminists, otherwise working at cross-purposes. Feminists argued that patriarchy is the common enemy of both liberated women and gays, because heterosexuality is a practice that instantiates women's dependence upon men.

At the same time, opponents of the proposed equal rights amendment (ERA) were articulating a "miscegenation analogy" for same-sex marriage. In congressional testimony, Professor Paul Freund said that "if the law must be as undiscriminating toward sex as it is toward race, it would follow that laws outlawing wedlock between members of the same sex would be as invalid as laws forbidding miscegenation." 118 Cong. Rec. 9315 (Mar. 20, 1972). Freund's position was based upon *Loving*'s holding that denying a black/white couple a marriage license is race discrimination, because the classification, the regulatory variable, is the race of one partner. Analogously, denying a female/female couple a marriage license is sex discrimination, because the classification, the regulatory variable, is the sex of one partner. Echoing Freund, ERA opponents in Congress and in state ratification debates argued that the ERA would invalidate state sodomy laws and require states to recognize "homosexual marriages," a charge disputed by ERA sponsor, Senator Birch Bayh. Compare 118 Cong. Rec. 9315 (Sen. Ervin, invoking Freund to oppose ERA), with *id.* at 9320–21 (Sen. Bayh, disputing Freund's analysis). See Note, "The Legality of Homosexual Marriage," 82 *Yale L.J.* 573 (1973).

Freund's prediction and feminist hopes did not materialize. Although a third of the states adopted equal rights amendments in the 1970s, no judge in that era accepted Freund's argument; the leading case is *Singer v. Hara*, 522 P.2d 1187 (Wash. App.), *review denied*, 84 Wash.2d 1008 (Wash. 1974). The court ruled that the exclusion of same-sex couples from state marriage and its legal benefits and duties did not violate Washington state's ERA. Distinguishing *Loving*, which involved an arbitrary discrimination on the basis of race, the court ruled that the gay male couple "are not being denied entry into the marriage relationship because of their sex; rather, they are being denied entry into the marriage relationship because of the recognized definition of that relationship as one which may be entered into only by two persons who are members of the opposite sex."

Singer remained virtually undisputed on this issue until 1988, when Professor Sylvia Law and law student Andrew Koppelman revived this line of argument. Drawing on feminist theory, Law linked homosexuality's social stigma to rigid gender roles which maintain women in traditional roles as wife, mother, and man's helper. Law, "Homosexuality and the Social Meaning of Gender," 1988 *Wis. L. Rev.* 187. Koppelman revived Freund's miscegenation analogy, but in support of gay rights rather than in opposition to women's rights. Note, "The Miscegenation Analogy: Sodomy Law as Sex Discrimination," 98 *Yale L.J.* 145 (1988). Would judges be bold enough to accept such daring analysis?

Ninia Baehr and Genora Dancel et al. v. John Lewin

Hawaii Supreme Court, 1993.
74 Haw. 530, 852 P.2d 44.

■ Opinion by LEVINSON, J., in which MOON, C.J., joins.

[In 1991, the plaintiff couples—Ninia Baehr and Genora Dancel; Tammy Rodriguez and Antoinette Pregil; Pat Lagon and Joseph Melilio—filed a lawsuit for declaratory judgment that Hawaii's Marriage Law, Hawaii Revised Statutes § 572–1, unconstitutionally denied same-sex couples the same marriage rights as different-sex couples. Plaintiffs' claims were based on the privacy and equal protection clauses of the Hawaii Constitution. Justice Levinson rejected the privacy claim; that part of his opinion is excerpted in Chapter 8, Section 2A of this Casebook.]

The applicant couples correctly contend that the DOH's refusal to allow them to marry on the basis that they are members of the same sex deprives them of access to a multiplicity of rights and benefits that are contingent upon that status. * * * [Those rights] include: (1) a variety of state income tax advantages, including deductions, credits, rates, exemptions, and estimates; (2) public assistance from and exemptions relating to the Department of Human Services; (3) control, division, acquisition, and disposition of community property; (4) rights relating to dower, curtesy, and inheritance; (5) rights to notice, protection, benefits, and inheritance under the Uniform Probate Code; (6) award of child custody and support payments in divorce proceedings; (7) the right to spousal support; (8) the right to enter into premarital agreements; (9) the right to change of name; (10) the right to file a nonsupport action; (11) post-divorce rights relating to support and property division; (12) the benefit of the spousal privilege and confidential marital communications; (13) the benefit of the exemption of real property from attachment or execution; and (14) the right to bring a wrongful death action. For present purposes, it is not disputed that the applicant would be entitled to all of these marital rights and benefits, but for the fact that they are denied access to the state-conferred legal status of marriage. * * *

* * * Article I, section 5 of the Hawaii Constitution provides in relevant part that "[n]o person shall . . . be denied the equal protection of the laws, *nor be denied the enjoyment of the person's civil rights or be discriminated against in the exercise thereof because of* race, religion, *sex*, or ancestry." (Emphasis added.) Thus, by its plain language, the Hawaii Constitution prohibits state-sanctioned discrimination against any person in the exercise of his or her civil rights on the basis of sex.

"The freedom to marry has long been recognized as one of the vital personal rights essential to the orderly pursuit of happiness by free [people]." *Loving.* So "fundamental" does the United States Supreme Court consider the institution of marriage that it has deemed marriage to be "one of the 'basic civil rights of [men and women].'" *Id.* (quoting *Skinner*).

[Justice Levinson found that the Hawaii Marriage Law, and Lewin acting under it, discriminated against the plaintiff couples in the exercise of this important "civil right" because of their "sex," one of the classifications in the state equal protection clause that triggers "strict" or (at the very least) "intermediate" scrutiny as opposed to "rational basis" analysis.] It therefore follows, and we so hold, that (1) [the Hawaii Marriage Law] is presumed to be unconstitutional (2) unless Lewin . . . can show that (a) the statute's sex-based classification is justified by compelling state interests and (b) the statute is narrowly drawn to avoid unnecessary abridgements of the applicant couples' constitutional rights.

[Justice Levinson then directed a remand to the circuit court for a hearing to determine whether Lewin and the State could overcome the presumption that the Marriage Law is unconstitutional, by showing that its sex discrimination furthers a compelling state interest and is narrowly drawn. He concluded his opinion with some responses to dissenting Justice Heen.]

[W]e have *not* held * * * that [the Hawaii Marriage Law] "unconstitutionally discriminates against [the applicant couples] who seek a license to enter into a same-sex marriage[.]" Dissenting opinion. Such a holding would * * * be premature at this time. What we *have* held is that, on its face and as applied, [the Law] denies same-sex couples access to the marital status and its concomitant rights and benefits, thus implicating the equal protection clause of article I, section 5.

We understand that Judge Heen disagrees with our view in this regard based on his belief that "[the Law] treats everyone alike and applies equally to both sexes[,]" with the result that "neither sex is being *granted* a right or benefit the other does not have, and neither sex is being *denied* a right or benefit that the other has." Dissenting opinion (emphasis in original). The rationale underlying Judge Heen's belief, however, was expressly considered and rejected in *Loving*:

> Thus, the State contends that, because its miscegenation statutes punish equally both the white and the Negro participants in an interracial marriage, these statutes, despite their reliance on racial classifications do not constitute an invidious discrimination based upon

race. . . . [W]e reject the notion that the mere "equal application" of a statute containing racial classifications is enough to remove the classifications from the Fourteenth Amendment's proscriptions of all invidious discriminations. . . . In the case at bar, . . . we deal with statutes containing racial classifications, and the fact of equal application does not immunize the statute from the very heavy burden of justification which the Fourteenth Amendment has traditionally required of state statutes drawn according to race.

Substitution of "sex" for "race" and article I, section 5 [of the Hawaii Constitution] for the fourteenth amendment yields the precise case before us together with the conclusion we have reached.

■ Concurring opinion of BURNS, J.

* * * In my view, the Hawaii Constitution's reference to "sex" includes all aspects of each person's "sex" that are "biologically fated." The decision whether a person when born will be a male or female is "biologically fated." Thus, the word "sex" includes the male-female difference. Is there another aspect of a person's "sex" that is "biologically fated"?

[Justice Burns then quoted from three accounts in the popular press as to the basis for a person's sexual orientation. Two of the accounts suggested the hormonal and genetic basis for a homosexual orientation. A third account, by columnist Charles Krauthammer, disputed that claim.]

If heterosexuality, homosexuality, bisexuality, and asexuality are "biologically fated[,]" then the word "sex" also includes these differences. Therefore, the questions whether heterosexuality, homosexuality, bisexuality, and asexuality are "biologically fated" are relevant questions of fact which must be determined before the issue presented in this case can be answered. If the answers are yes, then each person's "sex" includes both the "biologically fated" male-female difference and the "biologically fated" sexual orientation difference, and the Hawaii Constitution probably bars the State from discriminating against the sexual orientation difference by permitting opposite-sex Hawaii Civil Law Marriages and not permitting same-sex Hawaii Civil Law Marriages. If the answers are no, then each person's "sex" does not include the sexual orientation difference, and the Hawaii Constitution may permit the State to encourage heterosexuality and discourage homosexuality, bisexuality, and asexuality by permitting opposite-sex Hawaii Civil Law Marriages and not permitting same-sex Hawaii Civil Law Marriages.

■ Dissenting Opinion by HEEN, J.

[The Hawaii Marriage Law] treats everyone alike and applied equally to both sexes. The effect of the statute is to prohibit same sex marriages on the part of professed or non-professed heterosexuals, homosexuals, bisexuals, or asexuals, and does not effect an invidious discrimination.

* * * [A]ll males and females are treated alike. A male cannot obtain a license to marry another male, and a female cannot obtain a license to marry another female. Neither sex is being *granted* a right or benefit the

other does not have, and neither sex is being *denied* a right or benefit that the other has. * * *

In my view, the statute's classification is clearly designed to promote the legislative purpose of fostering and protecting the propagation of the human race through heterosexual marriage and bears a reasonable relationship to that purpose. I find nothing unconstitutional in that.

Andrew Koppelman, "Why Discrimination Against Lesbians and Gay Men Is Sex Discrimination"

69 *New York University Law Review* 197, 202, 218 (1994).*

* * * I argue that the taboo against homosexuality is not entirely irrational, but serves a function, and that that function is similar to the function served by the taboo against miscegenation. Both taboos police the boundary that separates the dominant from the dominated in a social hierarchy that rests on a condition of birth. In the same way that the prohibition of miscegenation preserved the polarities of race on which white supremacy rested, the prohibition of homosexuality preserves the polarities of gender on which rests the subordination of women.

* * * Sex-based classifications therefore have been upheld only when the Court has found that they reflected accurate empirical generalizations. Since it began subjecting sex-based classifications to heightened scrutiny, the Court has *never* upheld a sex-based classification resting on *normative* stereotypes about the proper roles of the sexes. Nor has the Court announced any exception to the prohibition of normative stereotyping in cases where the desire for role-typing takes the form of deep moral conviction. It could hardly do so without vitiating the principle altogether, since *all* sexual role-typing has traditionally been thought to possess such moral force.

Laws that discriminate against gays rest upon a normative stereotype: the bald conviction that certain behavior—for example, sex with women—is appropriate for members of one sex, but not for members of the other sex. Such laws therefore flatly violate the constitutional prohibition on sex discrimination as it has been interpreted by the Supreme Court. Since intermediate scrutiny of gender-based classifications is appropriate, and laws that discriminate against gays cannot withstand intermediate scrutiny, our legal argument is concluded. A court applying received doctrine should invalidate any statute that singles out gays for unequal treatment.

* * * Much of the connection between sexism and the homosexuality taboo lies in social meanings that are accessible to everyone. It should be clear from ordinary experience that the stigmatization of the homosexual has *something* to do with the homosexual's supposed deviance from traditional sex roles. "Our society," Joseph Pleck observes, "uses the male heterosexual-homosexual dichotomy as a central symbol for *all* the rank-

ings of masculinity, for the division on *any* grounds between males who are 'real men' and have power and males who are not. Any kind of powerlessness or refusal to compete becomes imbued with the imagery of homosexuality." Similarly, the denunciation of feminism as tantamount to lesbianism is depressingly familiar. The connection between sexism and the homosexuality taboo has been extensively documented by psychologists and historians, and I shall shortly survey their work, but it should be obvious even without scholarly support.

Most Americans learn no later than high school that one of the nastier sanctions that one will suffer if one deviates from the behavior traditionally deemed appropriate for one's sex is the imputation of homosexuality. The two stigmas, sex-inappropriateness and homosexuality, are virtually interchangeable, and each is readily used as a metaphor for the other. There is nothing esoteric or sociologically abstract in the claim that the homosexuality taboo enforces traditional sex roles. Everyone knows that it is so. The recognition that in our society homosexuality is generally understood as a metaphor for failure to live up to the norms of one's gender resembles the recognition that segregation stigmatizes blacks, in that both are "matters of common notoriety, matters not so much for judicial notice as for the background knowledge of educated men who live in the world."

* * * Just as the hierarchy of whites over blacks is greatly strengthened by extreme differentiation of the races, so the hierarchy of males over females is greatly strengthened by extreme differentiation of the sexes. The element of both differentiations that promotes hierarchy is the idea that certain anatomical features *necessarily* entail certain social roles: one's status in society is obviously and unproblematically determined by the color of one's skin or the shape of one's reproductive organs. Blacks are supposed to defer to whites and obey whites' wishes because that is what blacks do. Women are supposed to defer to men and obey men's wishes because that is what women do.

The reification of socially constructed reality is always useful for the maintenance of that reality. But such reification takes on added urgency in modern Western civilization, with its radically egalitarian philosophy that manifests itself in, among other things, the fourteenth amendment of the U.S. Constitution. Thus the miscegenation taboo ultimately could not be justified in terms of its real purpose, and ended its days rationalized as a eugenic measure, on the basis of the shabbiest kind of pseudo-science. Where hierarchies based on birth are illegitimate, their survival is greatly enhanced by invisibility. Overt homosexuality is thus a greater danger to gender hierarchy in our society than it has been in other, more stable cultures. It threatens the hierarchy of the sexes because its existence suggests that even in a realm where a person's sex has been regarded as absolutely determinative, anatomy has less to do with destiny than one might have supposed. It is therefore unsurprising that, as we shall shortly see, the courts, which have enforced both of these putatively "natural" prohibitions, have struggled to conceal their socially constructed character.

The point of emphasizing this socially constructed character is not to argue that since social contexts—taken for granted meanings and habitual practices—can be revealed to be social constructions that restrict human possibilities, they ought to be smashed. Rather, the point is that *certain* meanings and practices operate in furtherance of morally indefensible ends. Where this is true, exposure of those meanings and practices as socially constructed deprives them of the invisibility provided by the appearance of "naturalness" and makes them subject to criticism. In order to survive, these systems of social construction have to lie.

NOTES ON THE SEX DISCRIMINATION ARGUMENT FOR SAME–SEX MARRIAGE

1. *Formalism: Some Technical Objections.* Much of the power of the miscegenation analogy is that it is a technical, formalist argument seeking rights for an unpopular minority. But, at the outset, there are a number of formal or technical objections.[a]

(A) Is Discrimination Because of the Sex of One Partner Really "Sex Discrimination"? As Professor Koppelman puts it, "If Lucy can marry Fred, but Ricky cannot marry Fred, then Ricky is suffering a legal disadvantage because of his sex." Koppelman, *Gay Rights Question* 53. The Supreme Court has repeatedly held that it is race discrimination to treat someone differently because of the race of his or her sexual partner. *E.g.*, *McLaughlin v. Florida*, 379 U.S. 184 (1964); *Bob Jones Univ. v. United States*, 461 U.S. 574 (1983). Is there any reason to treat sex different from race in this regard? See *Baker v. State*, 744 A.2d 864 (Vt. 1999) (Johnson, J., concurring in part) (emphatically not, says Justice Denise Johnson).

Nor does it make a difference that (gay) men and (lesbian) women are treated the same. This argument was made by Florida in *McLaughlin* (white people and people of color were treated the same by laws criminalizing different-race cohabitation), and the Supreme Court unanimously rejected it. This argument was the holding of *Pace v. Alabama*, 106 U.S. 583 (1883), which the Supreme Court said in *Loving* had been overruled by *McLaughlin*. Unless sex discrimination jurisprudence has a reason for departing from the race discrimination cases on this matter, this argument goes nowhere.

(B) Is the Limitation of Marriage to One Man and One Woman So Inherent That It Does Not Really Amount to a "Discrimination"? It is as old as Aristotle that it is not "discrimination" if two dissimilar things are treated differently; indeed, it would be questionable to treat dissimilar things the same! So judges who insist that *marriage* by essential definition

a. Technical arguments against the miscegenation analogy for same-sex marriage are made in Lynn Wardle, "A Critical Analysis of Constitutional Claims for Same–Sex Marriage," 1996 *BYU L. Rev.* 1, and Edward Stein, "Evaluating the Sex Discrimination Argument for Lesbian and Gay Rights," 49 *UCLA L. Rev.* 471 (2001). Andrew Koppelman, *The Gay Rights Question in Contemporary American Law* 53–71 (2002), responds to these arguments.

entails one man and one woman would say that it is no discrimination to deny licenses to woman-woman or man-man couples. Although this was the same kind of argument made by Virginia to defend its miscegenation law in *Loving,* one might distinguish *Loving* on the ground that racial homogeneity, while long a requirement of Virginia marriages, was not a universal requirement of marriage that sex difference has been. This claim is almost always overstated, however, as there is an extensive history of state-or culture-recognized marriages or unions between same-sex couples. See William Eskridge, Jr., *The Case for Same–Sex Marriage* ch. 2 (1996). Even with caveats, though, this is a plausible factual claim. Is it a persuasive basis for denying discrimination, or is the historical evidence more relevant to possible state justifications for the sex discrimination?

(C) Is the Miscegenation Analogy Sufficiently Well–Connected to the Purposes of the Equal Protection Clause or the State ERA? In addition to the foregoing arguments, *Singer* held that discrimination against male couples was not a problem the state ERA was designed to solve. The ERA's goal was only to redress longstanding state discriminations against women. Consider the purposes of constitutional (ERA or Equal Protection Clause) sex discrimination jurisprudence. Among the purposes might be to question laws and policies (1) denying women the same freedoms and rights men have had (VMI Case), and vice-versa (*Hogan*); (2) reflecting archaic stereotypes about women's and men's abilities and roles (*Reed v. Reed*; *Frontiero*; *Craig v. Boren*); or (3) confining women and men to separate domestic and public spheres, respectively (*Reed v. Reed*; VMI Case). Are these purposes advanced or fulfilled by requiring the state to recognize same-sex marriages? Are there other ways of stating the principle or policy underlying the sex discrimination jurisprudence?

2. *Functionalism: Does the Miscegenation Analogy Fit the Purposes of Sex Discrimination Jurisprudence?*

(A) The Transvestic Quality of the Miscegenation Analogy. Many people respond to the miscegenation analogy as though it were legal trickery. "This may be logical, but it cannot be right!" Indeed, as these skeptics suspect, there is a transvestic quality to the miscegenation analogy, as it dresses gay rights up in feminist garb. Consider the following table, adapted from William Eskridge, Jr., *Gaylaw: Challenging the Apartheid of the Closet* 220 (1999):

	Classification	**Disadvantaged Class**	**Ideological Motive**
Loving	Race	Racial Minorities	Racism
Craig/ERA	Sex	Women	Sexism
Baehr	Sex	Sexual and Gender Minorities	Compulsory Heterosexuality

An underlying resistance to the miscegenation analogy might be that the ERA project is to purge law of irrational *sex-based classifications* and thereby to relieve *women as a class* from the stigmatizing or subordinating *ideology of sexism or patriarchy*. For federal equal protection purposes, this project is considered similar to the anti-apartheid project epitomized in

Loving—to purge law of irrational race-based classifications and thereby to relieve people of color from the stigmatizing and subordinating ideology of racism or apartheid. As Section 2 explored, it is plausible to argue that law should also be purged of irrational sexual orientation-based classifications, thereby relieving sexual minorities of the stigmatizing or subordinating ideology of compulsory heterosexuality. But perhaps the argument should be conducted along those lines—without smuggling homo equality into the Constitution under the cover of women's rights precedents.

But does the table accurately characterize the three cases? Rethink the table in light of Professor Koppelman's argument that homophobia is an instrument of sexism and a mechanism for enforcing traditional gender roles (women must be feminine/wifely and men must be masculine/husband-like). Does Koppelman's argument provide a way of redoing the table in a way that supports the miscegenation analogy? Compare Stein, "Evaluating the Sex Discrimination Argument," 496–505 (still skeptical), with *Baker v. State*, 744 A.2d 864 (Vt. 1999) (Johnson, J., concurring in part) (another same-sex marriage case, where Justice Denise Johnson makes this functional defense of the miscegenation analogy).

(B) Intermixing Sexuality and Gender? Another kind of objection to the sex discrimination argument for gay rights is that it either overlooks or marginalizes the driving force in antigay discrimination—Americans' anxiety about sexuality and their hysteria about nonconforming sexuality. Professor Sylvia Law documented the extensive interrelationship of gender and sexual orientation, but cautioned:

> While the desire to privilege and reward gender-differentiated family structures provides the primary impetus and justification for heterosexism, the perceived need to constrain sexuality is also important. In our culture sexual pleasure is both pervasively invoked in the service of materialistic values and pervasively distrusted. Economic and political models built on assumptions of scarcity have difficulty dealing with valued experiences that are, in their nature, not scarce. A culture that rewards hard work and self-sacrifice has difficulty accommodating experiences of self-indulgence and fulfillment. A rationalist tradition has trouble with ecstasy and play.

Law, "Homosexuality and the Social Meaning of Gender," 235.

The history of state persecution and discrimination against sexual minorities demonstrates the "multiple anxieties" animating such policies: (1) transgression of traditional gender roles; (2) disgust with the "unnatural practices" attributable to gay people; and (3) fear of predation by alien types and outsiders to the culture. Eskridge, *Gaylaw* 223–27. Thus, Americans are not willing to give the gay male a marriage license only in part (1) because of sexist views (man must marry woman), but also because of (2) a sex negativity triggered by the awareness that the state would be sanctioning a union whose consummation would be sex that is non-procreative and therefore deviant or sinful and (3) fears of contagion, lest one's own adolescent son's potential for homosexuality somehow be galvanized by the public spectacle of a state-licensed gay wedding. Does this defeat the sex discrimination argument for gay rights? Accordingly, state and social discrimination against lesbian and bisexual women is more strongly driven by sexism and less driven by sex negativity and obsessive fears than is state and social discrimination against gay and bisexual men. See *id.* at 227–28. If this is true, how should that affect the Freund/Law/Koppelman sex discrimination argument for gay rights?

(C) Could the Miscegenation Analogy Dilute the Court's Sex Discrimination Jurisprudence? Ed Stein worries that, if accepted, the sex discrimination argument would threaten to sweep away all (or almost all) laws discriminating against sexual or gender minorities—which is too much for most Americans to swallow. See Stein, "Evaluating the Sex Discrimination Argument," 49 *UCLA L. Rev.* at 507–09, 513–14. Although a growing minority of people believe the state should recognize same-sex marriages, most Americans are still appalled by the possibility, and so there would be tremendous pressure on federal or most state judges to uphold at least some discriminations (like the same-sex marriage bar) notwithstanding their clear sex discriminations. And the Supreme Court's sex discrimination jurisprudence provides a few avenues for such allowance.

Even the VMI Case "celebrated" the differences between the sexes. A state can concede that its same-sex marriage bar is sex discrimination yet still argue that the discrimination is justified by "real differences" between the sexes. This is the famous *complementarity hypothesis* discussed in Justice Johnson's concurring opinion. Is there a danger that an increasingly conservative Court would dilute sex discrimination jurisprudence by allowing states to valorize the "real differences" between men and women—or their complementarity—as a basis for recognizing only different-sex marriages?

Or is there a danger that the miscegenation analogy would invite the Supreme Court or state high courts to reintroduce "original intent" as a limitation on their sex discrimination jurisprudence? Because the Equal Protection Clause and the state ERAs were adopted before it was easily conceivable for gay people to be considered equal citizens by the political mainstream, original intent arguments will almost never help gay rights claims and will often hurt them badly, as in *Singer*. But once original intent has sneaked into sex discrimination law, especially at the federal level (where the constitutional text is almost 150 years old), it could slow down or reverse the development of that jurisprudence and its protection of women.

3. *International Experience with the Sex Discrimination Argument for Gay Rights.* Recall that the European Court of Justice, in *P. v. S.*, ruled that discrimination against transsexuals is sex discrimination, an analytical move few American judges are willing to take. In *Grant v. South–West Trains, Ltd.*, Case C–249/96, ECR 1–621 (Feb. 17, 1998), however, the Court rejected the *Baehr* argument. Cynthia Grant was denied employment benefits for her female partner and claimed this was sex discrimination, contrary to European Union employment law. The Court rejected this claim, on the ground that the discrimination was because of "marital status" and not "sex." The miscegenation analogy has not been a notably successful argument in Europe and Canada. See Koppelman, *Gay Rights Question,* 170 n.8.

Perhaps the reason for the greater popularity of the sex discrimination argument in the United States is that of convenience—as a short cut to heightened scrutiny. But judges who are skeptical of recognizing constitutional protections for sexual orientation discrimination are least likely to accept the miscegenation analogy; indeed, most such judges are literally unable to comprehend it! Is this lack of comparative law support fatal to the miscegenation analogy? Or does it suggest that when the normative climate changes, as is already occurring in Europe toward gay unions, the sex discrimination argument might be available to complement arguments based directly on sexual orientation?

Joining most other countries in the United Nations, the United States has signed and ratified the ICCPR, General Assembly Resolution 2200 A(XXI), 1966, 21 U.N. GAOR Supp. (No. 16), 999 U.N.T.S. 171, U.N. Doc. A/6316. Article 2(1) of the Convention commits the member states to the following proposition:

> Each State Party to the present Covenant undertakes to respect and to ensure to all individuals within its territory and subject to its jurisdiction the rights recognized in the present Covenant, without distinction of any kind, such as race, colour, sex, language, religion, political or other opinion, national or social origin, property, birth or other status.

In *Toonen v. Australia,* U.N. Doc. CCPR/C/50/D/488 (1992), reprinted in 1 *Int'l Hum. Rts. Rep.* 97 (1994), the United Nations Human Rights Committee declared Tasmania's law criminalizing unnatural practices between men to be a violation of article 2(1). Tasmania conceded that its law was drawing a distinction as to the "sex" of the participants, and the panel further concluded that "sex" in article 2(1) included distinctions based on "sexual orientation." As suggested in the previous note, arguments that antigay laws discriminate because of "sex" as well as sexual orientation ("other status" under the ICCPR) might be complementary arguments. Although the legal force of *Toonen* under U.S. law is weak, American courts might look to *Toonen* as a persuasive precedent at the very least.

CHAPTER 4

LAWRENCE V. TEXAS: WATERSHED IN THE LAW

As our materials in Chapter 2 suggest, *Bowers v. Hardwick* was subjected to the most immediate and overwhelming criticism a Supreme Court decision *upholding* a statute has ever suffered. Justice Scalia pronounced *Hardwick* inconsistent with the Court's 1996 decision in *Romer v. Evans* (Chapter 3, Section 2). But the Court's post-*Bowers* privacy precedents hardly augured for an overruling.

In the 17 years between *Hardwick* and *Lawrence*, the two most significant privacy cases decided by the Supreme Court were *Planned Parenthood v. Casey* (Chapter 2), which rested upon and urged respect for *stare decisis* in constitutional cases, and *Washington v. Harold Glucksberg*, 521 U.S. 702 (1997). In the latter case, the Supreme Court unanimously rejected a substantive due process challenge to laws prohibiting assisted suicide by doctors and other potential aiders of euthanasia. Chief Justice Rehnquist's opinion for the Court included this summation of prior cases:

"Our established method of substantive-due-process analysis has two primary features: First, we have regularly observed that the Due Process Clause specially protects those fundamental rights and liberties which are, objectively, 'deeply rooted in this Nation's history and tradition,' and 'implicit in the concept of ordered liberty,' such that 'neither liberty nor justice would exist if they were sacrificed.' Second, we have required in substantive-due-process cases a 'careful description' of the asserted fundamental liberty interest. Our Nation's history, legal traditions, and practices thus provide the crucial 'guideposts for responsible decisionmaking' and direct and restrain our exposition of the Due Process Clause." The Chief Justice noted that the law had long regulated both suicide and assisting suicide.

Four other Justices (Stevens, Souter, Ginsburg, Breyer) disagreed with this rationale but concurred in the result. Justice O'Connor concurred in the Chief Justice's opinion but also wrote separately in support of a more evolutive approach to substantive due process. No single opinion or rationale emerged in opposition to Chief Justice Rehnquist's formulation of substantive due process law.

LAWRENCE: THE SUPREME COURT OVERRULES BOWERS V. HARDWICK

If you were a gay rights lawyer at the turn of the millennium, what strategy would you adopt to undermine or even challenge *Bowers*? Jot down some thoughts now, and then read the following note and revise your thoughts. Then read the Supreme Court's decision in *Lawrence*.

THE STATUS OF CONSENSUAL SODOMY LAWS, JUNE 2003

The following list summarizes the status immediately pre-*Lawrence* of sodomy laws that were in effect in 1986, when *Hardwick* was decided.

Alabama—Sodomy law in effect; applied to both opposite-sex and same-sex acts.

Arizona—Sodomy law repealed in 2001.

Arkansas—Sodomy law declared unconstitutional by the state supreme court in *Jegley v. Picado*, 349 Ark. 600, 80 S.W.3d 332 (2002). Statute criminalized only same-sex acts.

District of Columbia—Sodomy law repealed in 1993.

Florida—Sodomy law in effect; applied to both opposite-sex and same-sex acts.

Georgia—Sodomy law declared unconstitutional by the state supreme court. *Powell v. State*, 270 Ga. 327, 510 S.E.2d 18 (1998) (Chapter 2).

Idaho—Sodomy law in effect; applied to both opposite-sex and same-sex acts.

Kansas—Sodomy law upheld by Kansas Court of Appeals, ruling that the right of privacy under the state constitution is coterminous with the federal right of privacy, as interpreted in *Bowers v. Hardwick*. *City of Topeka v. Movsovitz*, 960 P.2d 267 (Kan.Ct.App.1998) (unpublished). The statute criminalized only same-sex acts.

Kentucky—Sodomy law declared unconstitutional by state supreme court. *Commonwealth v. Wasson*, 842 S.W.2d 487 (Ky. 1992) (Chapter 2).

Louisiana—Sodomy law upheld by state supreme court in *State v. Smith*, 766 So.2d 501 (La.2000). The statute applied to both opposite-sex and same-sex acts.

Maryland—A state trial court ruled that the sodomy law could not be enforced as to consensual, noncommercial sexual activity between same-sex

151

partners in a private space. *Williams v. State*, 1998 WL 965992 (Balt. City Cir. Ct. Oct. 15, 1998) (unpublished). The Maryland Attorney General elected not to appeal. The ruling extended to lesbians and gay men the principle adopted by the state's highest court for heterosexual couples in *Schochet v. State*, 320 Md. 714, 580 A.2d 176 (1990).

Massachusetts—State supreme court "clarified" prior decisions to specify that private consensual sodomy was protected by state constitutional right of privacy. *Gay & Lesbian Advocates & Defenders v. Attorney General*, 436 Mass. 132, 763 N.E.2d 38 (2002). The statute had applied to both opposite-sex and same-sex acts, but prohibited only anal intercourse. A statute criminalizing oral sex was declared unconstitutional as applied to consenting adults in *Commonwealth v. Balthazar*, 366 Mass. 298, 318 N.E.2d 478 (1974). [The Court in *Hardwick* treated Massachusetts as already a state without a sodomy law.]

Michigan—Sodomy law declared unconstitutional by state trial court judge. *Michigan Org. for Human Rights v. Kelley*, No.88–815820 CZ (Wayne County Cir. Ct. 1990) (unpublished). The court declared the sodomy and gross indecency statutes unconstitutional as to "activities between consenting adults taking place in the privacy of one's home." *Id.* at 12. The attorney general did not appeal.

Minnesota—Sodomy law declared unconstitutional by state trial court judge. *Doe v. Ventura*, No. MC 01–249, 2001 WL 543734 (Hennepin County. Dist. Ct. May 15, 2001) (unpublished). State did not appeal.

Mississippi—Sodomy law in effect; applied to both opposite-sex and same-sex acts.

Missouri—In a ruling that had the effect of decriminalization, the Missouri Court of Appeals held that the sodomy law could not be used to prosecute consensual sexual relations. *State v. Cogshell*, 997 S.W.2d 534 (Mo. Ct. App. 1999). The state did not appeal. The Missouri Supreme Court had rejected a state constitutional privacy challenge to the same statute in *State v. Walsh*, 713 S.W.2d 508 (Mo. 1986).

Montana—Sodomy law declared unconstitutional by state supreme court as a violation of state constitution's right to privacy. *Gryczan v. State*, 283 Mont. 433, 942 P.2d 112 (1997).

Nevada—Sodomy law repealed in 1993.

North Carolina—Sodomy law in effect; applied to both opposite-sex and same-sex acts.

Oklahoma—Sodomy law in effect as to same-sex acts. The statute had been found unconstitutional as to opposite-sex acts based on the federal constitutional right to privacy shortly before *Bowers v. Hardwick*. The Supreme Court denied review in the case, thus leaving the statute partially invalidated. *Post v. State*, 715 P.2d 1105 (Ok. Crim. App.), *reh'g denied*, 717 P.2d 1151, *cert. denied*, 479 U.S. 890 (1986).

Puerto Rico—Sodomy law in effect; applied to both opposite-sex and same-sex acts.

Rhode Island—Sodomy law repealed in 1998.

South Carolina—Sodomy law in effect; applied to both opposite-sex and same-sex acts.

Tennessee—Sodomy law declared unconstitutional on state constitutional privacy grounds in *Campbell v. Sundquist*, 926 S.W.2d 250 (Tenn. Ct. App. 1996).

Texas—Sodomy law upheld in *Lawrence v. State*, 41 S.W.3d 349 (Tex. App. 2001) (*en banc*), the ruling that was appealed to the U. S. Supreme Court. Texas's law applied only to "homosexual conduct."

Utah—Sodomy law in effect; applied to both opposite-sex and same-sex acts.

Virginia—Sodomy law in effect; applied to both opposite-sex and same-sex acts.

John Geddes Lawrence and Tyron Garner v. Texas

United States Supreme Court, 2003.
539 U.S. 558, 123 S.Ct. 2472, 156 L.Ed.2d 508.

■ JUSTICE KENNEDY delivered the opinion of the Court.

Liberty protects the person from unwarranted government intrusions into a dwelling or other private places. In our tradition the State is not omnipresent in the home. And there are other spheres of our lives and existence, outside the home, where the State should not be a dominant presence. Freedom extends beyond spatial bounds. Liberty presumes an autonomy of self that includes freedom of thought, belief, expression, and certain intimate conduct. The instant case involves liberty of the person both in its spatial and more transcendent dimensions.

[Acting on a report of a possible burglary, the Harris County Police entered the apartment of John Lawrence and found him engaging in anal sex with another adult man, Tyron Garner. The police arrested and detained the men overnight for violating Texas's "Homosexual Conduct law." Tex. Penal Code Ann. § 21.06(a) (2003). The law provides: "A person commits an offense if he engages in deviate sexual intercourse with another individual of the same sex." The statute defines deviate sexual intercourse to include oral and anal sex. The defendants pleaded *nolo contendere*, were fined $200 apiece (plus court costs of $141.25), and appealed their convictions, on the ground that the Homosexual Conduct law was unconstitutional. The Texas courts rejected their federal constitutional claims, largely on the authority of *Bowers v. Hardwick*.]

[II.] We conclude the case should be resolved by determining whether the petitioners were free as adults to engage in the private conduct in the exercise of their liberty under the Due Process Clause of the Fourteenth Amendment to the Constitution. For this inquiry, we deem it necessary to reconsider the Court's holding in *Bowers*.

* * * [T]he most pertinent beginning point is our decision in *Griswold v. Connecticut*. In *Griswold* * * * [t]he Court described the protected interest as a right to privacy and placed emphasis on the marriage relation and the protected space of the marital bedroom.

After *Griswold*, it was established that the right to make certain decisions regarding sexual conduct extends beyond the marital relationship. *Eisenstadt v. Baird*. * * * The opinions in *Griswold* and *Eisenstadt* were part of the background for the decision in *Roe v. Wade*. * * * *Roe* recognized the right of a woman to make certain fundamental decisions affecting her destiny * * *

The Court began its substantive discussion in *Bowers* as follows: "The issue presented is whether the Federal Constitution confers a fundamental right upon homosexuals to engage in sodomy and hence invalidates the laws of the many States that still make such conduct illegal and have done so for a very long time." That statement, we now conclude, discloses the Court's own failure to appreciate the extent of the liberty at stake. To say that the issue in *Bowers* was simply the right to engage in certain sexual conduct demeans the claim the individual put forward, just as it would demean a married couple were it to be said marriage is simply about the right to have sexual intercourse. The laws involved in *Bowers* and here are, to be sure, statutes that purport to do no more than prohibit a particular sexual act. Their penalties and purposes, though, have more far-reaching consequences, touching upon the most private human conduct, sexual behavior, and in the most private of places, the home. The statutes do seek to control a personal relationship that, whether or not entitled to formal recognition in the law, is within the liberty of persons to choose without being punished as criminals.

This, as a general rule, should counsel against attempts by the State, or a court, to define the meaning of the relationship or to set its boundaries absent injury to a person or abuse of an institution the law protects. It suffices for us to acknowledge that adults may choose to enter upon this relationship in the confines of their homes and their own private lives and still retain their dignity as free persons. When sexuality finds overt expression in intimate conduct with another person, the conduct can be but one element in a personal bond that is more enduring. The liberty protected by the Constitution allows homosexual persons the right to make this choice.

Having misapprehended the claim of liberty there presented to it, and thus stating the claim to be whether there is a fundamental right to engage in consensual sodomy, the *Bowers* Court said: "Proscriptions against that conduct have ancient roots." In academic writings, and in many of the scholarly *amicus* briefs filed to assist the Court in this case, there are fundamental criticisms of the historical premises relied upon by the majority and concurring opinions in *Bowers*. Brief for Cato Institute as *Amicus Curiae* 16–17; Brief for American Civil Liberties Union et al. as *Amici Curiae* 15–21; Brief for Professors of History et al. as *Amici Curiae* 3–10. We need not enter this debate in the attempt to reach a definitive historical judgment, but the following considerations counsel against adopting the definitive conclusions upon which *Bowers* placed such reliance.

At the outset it should be noted that there is no longstanding history in this country of laws directed at homosexual conduct as a distinct matter. [Both English and early American crime against nature laws regulated relations between men and women as well as between men and men.] The absence of legal prohibitions focusing on homosexual conduct may be explained in part by noting that according to some scholars the concept of the homosexual as a distinct category of person did not emerge until the late 19th century. See, *e.g.*, J. Katz, The Invention of Heterosexuality 10 (1995); J. D'Emilio & E. Freedman, *Intimate Matters: A History of Sexuality in America* 121 (2d ed. 1997) ("The modern terms *homosexuality* and *heterosexuality* do not apply to an era that had not yet articulated these distinctions"). Thus early American sodomy laws were not directed at homosexuals as such but instead sought to prohibit nonprocreative sexual activity more generally. This does not suggest approval of homosexual conduct. It does tend to show that this particular form of conduct was not thought of as a separate category from like conduct between heterosexual persons.

Laws prohibiting sodomy do not seem to have been enforced against consenting adults acting in private. A substantial number of sodomy prosecutions and convictions for which there are surviving records were for predatory acts against those who could not or did not consent, as in the case of a minor or the victim of an assault. As to these, one purpose for the prohibitions was to ensure there would be no lack of coverage if a predator committed a sexual assault that did not constitute rape as defined by the criminal law. Thus the model sodomy indictments presented in a 19th-century treatise, see 2 Chitty, *supra,* at 49, addressed the predatory acts of an adult man against a minor girl or minor boy. Instead of targeting relations between consenting adults in private, 19th-century sodomy prosecutions typically involved relations between men and minor girls or minor boys, relations between adults involving force, relations between adults implicating disparity in status, or relations between men and animals.

To the extent that there were any prosecutions for the acts in question, 19th-century evidence rules imposed a burden that would make a conviction more difficult to obtain even taking into account the problems always inherent in prosecuting consensual acts committed in private. Under then-prevailing standards, a man could not be convicted of sodomy based upon testimony of a consenting partner, because the partner was considered an accomplice. A partner's testimony, however, was admissible if he or she had not consented to the act or was a minor, and therefore incapable of consent. See, *e.g.,* F. Wharton, Criminal Law 443 (2d ed. 1852); 1 F. Wharton, Criminal Law 512 (8th ed. 1880). The rule may explain in part the infrequency of these prosecutions. In all events that infrequency makes it difficult to say that society approved of a rigorous and systematic punishment of the consensual acts committed in private and by adults. The longstanding criminal prohibition of homosexual sodomy upon which the

Bowers decision placed such reliance is as consistent with a general condemnation of nonprocreative sex as it is with an established tradition of prosecuting acts because of their homosexual character.

The policy of punishing consenting adults for private acts was not much discussed in the early legal literature. We can infer that one reason for this was the very private nature of the conduct. Despite the absence of prosecutions, there may have been periods in which there was public criticism of homosexuals as such and an insistence that the criminal laws be enforced to discourage their practices. But far from possessing "ancient roots," *Bowers*, American laws targeting same-sex couples did not develop until the last third of the 20th century. The reported decisions concerning the prosecution of consensual, homosexual sodomy between adults for the years 1880–1995 are not always clear in the details, but a significant number involved conduct in a public place. See Brief for American Civil Liberties Union et al. as *Amici Curiae* 14–15, and n. 18.

It was not until the 1970's that any State singled out same-sex relations for criminal prosecution, and only nine States have done so. See 1977 Ark. Gen. Acts no. 828; 1983 Kan. Sess. Laws p. 652; 1974 Ky. Acts p. 847; 1977 Mo. Laws p. 687; 1973 Mont. Laws p. 1339; 1977 Nev. Stats. p. 1632; 1989 Tenn. Pub. Acts ch. 591; 1973 Tex. Gen. Laws ch. 399; see also *Post* v. *State*, 715 P. 2d 1105 (Okla. Crim. App. 1986) (sodomy law invalidated as applied to different-sex couples). Post-*Bowers* even some of these States did not adhere to the policy of suppressing homosexual conduct. Over the course of the last decades, States with same-sex prohibitions have moved toward abolishing them.

In summary, the historical grounds relied upon in *Bowers* are more complex than the majority opinion and the concurring opinion by Chief Justice Burger indicate. Their historical premises are not without doubt and, at the very least, are overstated.

It must be acknowledged, of course, that the Court in *Bowers* was making the broader point that for centuries there have been powerful voices to condemn homosexual conduct as immoral. The condemnation has been shaped by religious beliefs, conceptions of right and acceptable behavior, and respect for the traditional family. For many persons these are not trivial concerns but profound and deep convictions accepted as ethical and moral principles to which they aspire and which thus determine the course of their lives. These considerations do not answer the question before us, however. The issue is whether the majority may use the power of the State to enforce these views on the whole society through operation of the criminal law. "Our obligation is to define the liberty of all, not to mandate our own moral code." *Casey*.

Chief Justice Burger joined the opinion for the Court in *Bowers* and further explained his views as follows: "Decisions of individuals relating to homosexual conduct have been subject to state intervention throughout the history of Western civilization. Condemnation of those practices is firmly rooted in Judeao–Christian moral and ethical standards." As with Justice White's assumptions about history, scholarship casts some doubt on the sweeping nature of the statement by Chief Justice Burger as it pertains to private homosexual conduct between consenting adults. See, *e.g.*, Eskridge, Hardwick and Historiography, 1999 U. Ill. L. Rev. 631, 656. In all events we think that our laws and traditions in the past half century are of most relevance here. These references show an emerging awareness that liberty gives substantial protection to adult persons in deciding how to conduct their private lives in matters pertaining to sex. "[H]istory and tradition are the starting point but not in all cases the ending point of the substantive due process inquiry." *County of Sacramento* v. *Lewis* (Kennedy, J., concurring).

This emerging recognition should have been apparent when *Bowers* was decided. In 1955 the American Law Institute promulgated the Model Penal Code and made clear that it did not recommend or provide for "criminal penalties for consensual sexual relations conducted in private." ALI, Model Penal Code § 213.2, Comment 2, p. 372 (1980). It justified its decision on three grounds: (1) The prohibitions undermined respect for the law by penalizing conduct many people engaged in; (2) the statutes regulated private conduct not harmful to others; and (3) the laws were arbitrarily enforced and thus invited the danger of blackmail. ALI, Model Penal Code, Commentary 277–280 (Tent. Draft No. 4, 1955). In 1961 Illinois changed its laws to conform to the Model Penal Code. Other States soon followed. Brief for Cato Institute as *Amicus Curiae* 15–16.

In *Bowers* the Court referred to the fact that before 1961 all 50 States had outlawed sodomy, and that at the time of the Court's decision 24 States and the District of Columbia had sodomy laws. Justice Powell pointed out that these prohibitions often were being ignored, however. Georgia, for instance, had not sought to enforce its law for decades.

The sweeping references by Chief Justice Burger to the history of Western civilization and to Judeo–Christian moral and ethical standards did not take account of other authorities pointing in an opposite direction. A committee advising the British Parliament recommended in 1957 repeal of laws punishing homosexual conduct. The Wolfenden Report: Report of the Committee on Homosexual Offenses and Prostitution (1963). Parliament enacted the substance of those recommendations 10 years later. Sexual Offences Act 1967, § 1.

Of even more importance, almost five years before *Bowers* was decided the European Court of Human Rights considered a case with parallels to *Bowers* and to today's case. An adult male resident in Northern Ireland alleged he was a practicing homosexual who desired to engage in consensual homosexual conduct. The laws of Northern Ireland forbade him that right. He alleged that he had been questioned, his home had been searched, and he feared criminal prosecution. The court held that the laws proscribing the conduct were invalid under the European Convention on Human Rights. *Dudgeon* v. *United Kingdom*, 45 Eur. Ct. H. R. (1981) ¶ 52. Authoritative in all countries that are members of the Council of Europe (21 nations then, 45 nations now), the decision is at odds with the premise in *Bowers* that the claim put forward was insubstantial in our Western civilization.

In our own constitutional system the deficiencies in *Bowers* became even more apparent in the years following its announcement. The 25 States with laws prohibiting the relevant conduct referenced in the *Bowers* decision are reduced now to 13, of which 4 enforce their laws only against homosexual conduct. In those States where sodomy is still proscribed, whether for same-sex or heterosexual conduct, there is a pattern of nonenforcement with respect to consenting adults acting in private. The State of Texas admitted in 1994 that as of that date it had not prosecuted anyone under those circumstances. *State* v. *Morales*, 869 S. W. 2d 941, 943.

Two principal cases decided after *Bowers* cast its holding into even more doubt. In *Casey*, the Court reaffirmed the substantive force of the liberty protected by the Due Process Clause. The *Casey* decision again confirmed that our laws and tradition afford constitutional protection to personal decisions relating to marriage, procreation, contraception, family relationships, child rearing, and education. In explaining the respect the Constitution demands for the autonomy of the person in making these choices, we stated as follows:

> "These matters, involving the most intimate and personal choices a person may make in a lifetime, choices central to personal dignity and autonomy, are central to the liberty protected by the Fourteenth Amendment. At the heart of liberty is the right to define one's own concept of existence, of meaning, of the universe, and of the mystery of human life. Beliefs about these matters could not define the attributes of personhood were they formed under compulsion of the State."

Persons in a homosexual relationship may seek autonomy for these purposes, just as heterosexual persons do. The decision in *Bowers* would deny them this right.

The second post-*Bowers* case of principal relevance is *Romer v. Evans* (Chapter 3). There the Court struck down class-based legislation directed at homosexuals as a violation of the Equal Protection Clause. *Romer* invalidated an amendment to Colorado's constitution which named as a solitary class persons who were homosexuals, lesbians, or bisexual either by "orientation, conduct, practices or relationships," and deprived them of protection under state antidiscrimination laws. We concluded that the provision was "born of animosity toward the class of persons affected" and further that it had no rational relation to a legitimate governmental purpose.

As an alternative argument in this case, counsel for the petitioners and some *amici* contend that *Romer* provides the basis for declaring the Texas statute invalid under the Equal Protection Clause. That is a tenable argument, but we conclude the instant case requires us to address whether *Bowers* itself has continuing validity. Were we to hold the statute invalid under the Equal Protection Clause some might question whether a prohibition would be valid if drawn differently, say, to prohibit the conduct both between same-sex and different-sex participants.

Equality of treatment and the due process right to demand respect for conduct protected by the substantive guarantee of liberty are linked in important respects, and a decision on the latter point advances both interests. If protected conduct is made criminal and the law which does so remains unexamined for its substantive validity, its stigma might remain even if it were not enforceable as drawn for equal protection reasons. When homosexual conduct is made criminal by the law of the State, that declaration in and of itself is an invitation to subject homosexual persons to discrimination both in the public and in the private spheres. The central holding of *Bowers* has been brought in question by this case, and it should be addressed. Its continuance as precedent demeans the lives of homosexual persons.

The stigma this criminal statute imposes, moreover, is not trivial. The offense, to be sure, is but a class C misdemeanor, a minor offense in the Texas legal system. Still, it remains a criminal offense with all that imports for the dignity of the persons charged. The petitioners will bear on their record the history of their criminal convictions. * * * We are advised that if Texas convicted an adult for private, consensual homosexual conduct under the statute here in question the convicted person would come within the [sex offender] registration laws of a least four States were he or she to be subject to their jurisdiction. This underscores the consequential nature of the punishment and the state-sponsored condemnation attendant to the criminal prohibition. Furthermore, the Texas criminal conviction carries with it the other collateral consequences always following a conviction, such as notations on job application forms, to mention but one example.

The foundations of *Bowers* have sustained serious erosion from our recent decisions in *Casey* and *Romer*. When our precedent has been thus weakened, criticism from other sources is of greater significance. In the United States criticism of *Bowers* has been substantial and continuing, disapproving of its reasoning in all respects, not just as to its historical assumptions. See, *e.g.,* C. Fried, Order and Law: Arguing the Reagan Revolution—A Firsthand Account 81–84 (1991); R. Posner, Sex and Reason 341–350 (1992). The courts of five different States have declined to follow it in interpreting provisions in their own state constitutions parallel to the Due Process Clause of the Fourteenth Amendment, see *Jegley* v. *Picado*, 349 Ark. 600, 80 S.W.3d 332 (2002); *Powell* v. *State*, 270 Ga. 327, 510 S.E.2d 18, 24 (1998); *Gryczan* v. *State*, 283 Mont. 433, 942 P.2d 112 (1997); *Campbell* v. *Sundquist*, 926 S. W. 2d 250 (Tenn. App. 1996); *Commonwealth* v. *Wasson*, 842 S.W.2d 487 (Ky. 1992).

To the extent *Bowers* relied on values we share with a wider civilization, it should be noted that the reasoning and holding in *Bowers* have been rejected elsewhere. The European Court of Human Rights has followed not *Bowers* but its own decision in *Dudgeon* v. *United Kingdom*. See *P. G. & J. H.* v. *United Kingdom*, App. No. 00044787/98, ¶ 56 (Eur. Ct. H. R., Sept. 25, 2001); *Modinos* v. *Cyprus*, 259 Eur. Ct. H. R. (1993); *Norris* v. *Ireland*, 142 Eur. Ct. H. R. (1988). Other nations, too, have taken action consistent with an affirmation of the protected right of homosexual adults to engage in intimate, consensual conduct. See Brief for Mary Robinson et al. as *Amici Curiae* 11–12. The right the petitioners seek in this case has been accepted as an integral part of human freedom in many other countries. There has been no showing that in this country the governmental interest in circumscribing personal choice is somehow more legitimate or urgent.

The doctrine of *stare decisis* is essential to the respect accorded to the judgments of the Court and to the stability of the law. It is not, however, an inexorable command. In *Casey* we noted that when a Court is asked to overrule a precedent recognizing a constitutional liberty interest, individual or societal reliance on the existence of that liberty cautions with particular strength against reversing course. The holding in *Bowers*, however, has not induced detrimental reliance comparable to some instances where recognized individual rights are involved. Indeed, there has been no individual or societal reliance on *Bowers* of the sort that could counsel against overturning its holding once there are compelling reasons to do so. *Bowers* itself causes uncertainty, for the precedents before and after its issuance contradict its central holding.

The rationale of *Bowers* does not withstand careful analysis. In his dissenting opinion in *Bowers* Justice Stevens came to these conclusions:

> "Our prior cases make two propositions abundantly clear. First, the fact that the governing majority in a State has traditionally viewed a particular practice as immoral is not a sufficient reason for upholding a law prohibiting the practice; neither history nor tradition could save a law prohibiting miscegenation from constitutional attack. Second, individual decisions by married persons, concerning the intimacies of their physical relationship, even when not intended to produce offspring, are a form of 'liberty' protected by the Due Process Clause of the Fourteenth Amendment. Moreover, this protection extends to intimate choices by unmarried as well as married persons."

Justice Stevens' analysis, in our view, should have been controlling in *Bowers* and should control here.

Bowers was not correct when it was decided, and it is not correct today. It ought not to remain binding precedent. *Bowers* v. *Hardwick* should be and now is overruled.

The present case does not involve minors. It does not involve persons who might be injured or coerced or who are situated in relationships where consent might not easily be refused. It does not involve public conduct or prostitution. It does not involve whether the government must give formal recognition to any relationship that homosexual persons seek to enter. The case does involve two adults who, with full and mutual consent from each other, engaged in sexual practices common to a homosexual lifestyle. The petitioners are entitled to respect for their private lives. The State cannot demean their existence or control their destiny by making their private sexual conduct a crime. Their right to liberty under the Due Process Clause gives them the full right to engage in their conduct without intervention of the government. "It is a promise of the Constitution that there is a realm of personal liberty which the government may not enter." *Casey.* The Texas statute furthers no legitimate state interest which can justify its intrusion into the personal and private life of the individual.

Had those who drew and ratified the Due Process Clauses of the Fifth Amendment or the Fourteenth Amendment known the components of liberty in its manifold possibilities, they might have been more specific. They did not presume to have this insight. They knew times can blind us to certain truths and later generations can see that laws once thought necessary and proper in fact serve only to oppress. As the Constitution endures, persons in every generation can invoke its principles in their own search for greater freedom. * * *

■ JUSTICE O'CONNOR, concurring in the judgment.

[Justice O'Connor, who had joined the Court's opinion in *Bowers,* was not willing to join the Court's opinion overruling that precedent. But, she concluded, the Texas Homosexual Conduct Law did violate the Equal Protection Clause.]

* * * When a law exhibits such a desire to harm a politically unpopular group, we have applied a more searching form of rational basis review to strike down such laws under the Equal Protection Clause.

We have been most likely to apply rational basis review to hold a law unconstitutional under the Equal Protection Clause where, as here, the challenged legislation inhibits personal relationships. In *Department of Agriculture* v. *Moreno,* for example, we held that a law preventing those households containing an individual unrelated to any other member of the household from receiving food stamps violated equal protection because the purpose of the law was to " 'discriminate against hippies.' " The asserted governmental interest in preventing food stamp fraud was not deemed sufficient to satisfy rational basis review. In *Eisenstadt v. Baird,* we refused to sanction a law that discriminated between married and unmarried persons by prohibiting the distribution of contraceptives to single persons. Likewise, in *Cleburne,* we held that it was irrational for a State to require a home for the mentally disabled to obtain a special use permit when other residences—like fraternity houses and apartment buildings—did not have to obtain such a permit. And in *Romer* v. *Evans,* we disallowed a state statute that "impos[ed] a broad and undifferentiated disability on a single named group"—specifically, homosexuals. The dissent apparently agrees that if these cases have *stare decisis* effect, Texas' sodomy law would not pass scrutiny under the Equal Protection Clause, regardless of the type of rational basis review that we apply.

The statute at issue here makes sodomy a crime only if a person "engages in deviate sexual intercourse with another individual of the same sex." Tex. Penal Code Ann. § 21.06(a) (2003). Sodomy between opposite-sex partners, however, is not a crime in Texas. That is, Texas treats the same conduct differently based solely on the participants. Those harmed by this law are people who have a same-sex sexual orientation and thus are more likely to engage in behavior prohibited by § 21.06.

The Texas statute makes homosexuals unequal in the eyes of the law by making particular conduct—and only that conduct—subject to criminal sanction. It appears that prosecutions under Texas' sodomy law are rare. This case shows, however, that prosecutions under § 21.06 *do* occur. And while the penalty imposed on petitioners in this case was relatively minor, the consequences of conviction are not. As the Court notes, petitioners' convictions, if upheld, would disqualify them from or restrict their ability to engage in a variety of professions, including medicine, athletic training, and interior design. See, *e.g.,* Tex. Occ. Code Ann. § 164.051(a)(2)(B) (2003 Pamphlet) (physician); § 451.251 (a)(1) (athletic trainer); § 1053.252(2) (interior designer). Indeed, were petitioners to move to one of four States, their convictions would require them to register as sex offenders to local law enforcement. See, *e.g.,* Idaho Code § 18–8304 (Cum. Supp. 2002); La. Stat. Ann. § 15:542 (West Cum. Supp. 2003); Miss. Code Ann. § 45–33–25 (West 2003); S. C. Code Ann. § 23–3–430 (West Cum. Supp. 2002).

And the effect of Texas' sodomy law is not just limited to the threat of prosecution or consequence of conviction. Texas' sodomy law brands all homosexuals as criminals, thereby making it more difficult for homosexuals to be treated in the same manner as everyone else. Indeed, Texas itself has previously acknowledged the collateral effects of the law, stipulating in a prior challenge to this action that the law "legally sanctions discrimination against [homosexuals] in a variety of ways unrelated to the criminal law," including in the areas of "employment, family issues, and housing." *State v. Morales*, 826 S. W. 2d 201, 203 (Tex. App. 1992).

Texas attempts to justify its law, and the effects of the law, by arguing that the statute satisfies rational basis review because it furthers the legitimate governmental interest of the promotion of morality. In *Bowers*, we held that a state law criminalizing sodomy as applied to homosexual couples did not violate substantive due process. We rejected the argument that no rational basis existed to justify the law, pointing to the government's interest in promoting morality. The only question in front of the Court in *Bowers* was whether the substantive component of the Due Process Clause protected a right to engage in homosexual sodomy. *Bowers* did not hold that moral disapproval of a group is a rational basis under the Equal Protection Clause to criminalize homosexual sodomy when heterosexual sodomy is not punished.

This case raises a different issue than *Bowers:* whether, under the Equal Protection Clause, moral disapproval is a legitimate state interest to justify by itself a statute that bans homosexual sodomy, but not heterosexual sodomy. It is not. Moral disapproval of this group, like a bare desire to harm the group, is an interest that is insufficient to satisfy rational basis review under the Equal Protection Clause. See, *e.g., Moreno*; *Romer*. Indeed, we have never held that moral disapproval, without any other asserted state interest, is a sufficient rationale under the Equal Protection Clause to justify a law that discriminates among groups of persons.

Moral disapproval of a group cannot be a legitimate governmental interest under the Equal Protection Clause because legal classifications must not be "drawn for the purpose of disadvantaging the group burdened by the law." [*Romer.*] Texas' invocation of moral disapproval as a legitimate state interest proves nothing more than Texas' desire to criminalize homosexual sodomy. But the Equal Protection Clause prevents a State from creating "a classification of persons undertaken for its own sake." And because Texas so rarely enforces its sodomy law as applied to private, consensual acts, the law serves more as a statement of dislike and disapproval against homosexuals than as a tool to stop criminal behavior. The Texas sodomy law "raise[s] the inevitable inference that the disadvantage imposed is born of animosity toward the class of persons affected." [*Romer.*] * * *

A State can of course assign certain consequences to a violation of its criminal law. But the State cannot single out one identifiable class of citizens for punishment that does not apply to everyone else, with moral disapproval as the only asserted state interest for the law. The Texas sodomy statute subjects homosexuals to "a lifelong penalty and stigma. A legislative classification that threatens the creation of an underclass . . . cannot be reconciled with" the Equal Protection Clause. *Plyler* v. *Doe* (Powell, J., concurring).

Whether a sodomy law that is neutral both in effect and application, see *Yick Wo* v. *Hopkins,* 118 U. S. 356 (1886), would violate the substantive component of the Due Process Clause is an issue that need not be decided today. I am confident, however, that so long as the Equal Protection Clause requires a sodomy law to apply equally to the private consensual conduct of homosexuals and heterosexuals alike, such a law would not long stand in our democratic society. In the words of Justice Jackson:

> "The framers of the Constitution knew, and we should not forget today, that there is no more effective practical guaranty against arbitrary and unreasonable government than to require that the principles of law which officials would impose upon a minority be imposed generally. Conversely, nothing opens the door to arbitrary action so effectively as to allow those officials to pick and choose only a few to whom they will apply legislation and thus to escape the political retribution that might be visited upon them if larger numbers were affected." *Railway Express Agency, Inc.* v. *New York,* 336 U. S. 106, 112–113 (1949) (concurring opinion).

That this law as applied to private, consensual conduct is unconstitutional under the Equal Protection Clause does not mean that other laws distinguishing between heterosexuals and homosexuals would similarly fail under rational basis review. Texas cannot assert any legitimate state interest here, such as national security or preserving the traditional institution of marriage. Unlike the moral disapproval of same-sex relations—the asserted state interest in this case—other reasons exist to promote the institution of marriage beyond mere moral disapproval of an excluded group. * * *

■ JUSTICE SCALIA, with whom THE CHIEF JUSTICE [REHNQUIST] and JUSTICE THOMAS join, dissenting.

"Liberty finds no refuge in a jurisprudence of doubt." *Casey*. That was the Court's sententious response, barely more than a decade ago, to those seeking to overrule *Roe v. Wade*. The Court's response today, to those who have engaged in a 17–year crusade to overrule *Bowers* v. *Hardwick* is very different. The need for stability and certainty presents no barrier.

Most of the rest of today's opinion has no relevance to its actual holding—that the Texas statute "furthers no legitimate state interest which can justify" its application to petitioners under rational-basis review. Though there is discussion of "fundamental proposition[s]," and "fundamental decisions," nowhere does the Court's opinion declare that homosexual sodomy is a "fundamental right" under the Due Process Clause; nor does it subject the Texas law to the standard of review that would be appropriate (strict scrutiny) if homosexual sodomy *were* a "fundamental right." Thus, while overruling the *outcome* of *Bowers*, the Court leaves strangely untouched its central legal conclusion: "[R]espondent would have us announce ... a fundamental right to engage in homosexual sodomy. This we are quite unwilling to do." Instead the Court simply describes petitioners' conduct as "an exercise of their liberty"—which it undoubtedly is—and proceeds to apply an unheard-of form of rational-basis review that will have far-reaching implications beyond this case.

[I.]   * * * Today's approach to *stare decisis* invites us to overrule an erroneously decided precedent (including an "intensely divisive" decision) *if:* (1) its foundations have been "eroded" by subsequent decisions; (2) it has been subject to "substantial and continuing" criticism; and (3) it has not induced "individual or societal reliance" that counsels against overturning. The problem is that *Roe* itself—which today's majority surely has no disposition to overrule—satisfies these conditions to at least the same degree as Bowers.

[Justice Scalia maintained that, like *Bowers*, *Roe* has been (1) "eroded" by the Court's decision in *Washington v. Glucksburg* and, indeed, by *Casey* itself, which jettisoned large chunks of *Roe*'s approach; (2) subjected to unrelenting criticism, including acid critique from Professor Fried and Judge Posner, whose books the Court cited as examples of academic critique of *Bowers*; and (3) the object of no less reliance than *Bowers*, which has been the foundation for much of the nation's public policy, including its ban of gay people in the armed forces, as well as state laws against bigamy, same-sex marriage, adult incest, prostitution, masturbation, adultery, fornication, bestiality, and obscenity.]

What a massive disruption of the current social order, therefore, the overruling of *Bowers* entails. Not so the overruling of *Roe*, which would simply have restored the regime that existed for centuries before 1973, in which the permissibility of and restrictions upon abortion were determined legislatively State-by-State. *Casey*, however, chose to base its *stare decisis* determination on a different "sort" of reliance. "[P]eople," it said, "have organized intimate relationships and made choices that define their views of themselves and their places in society, in reliance on the availability of abortion in the event that contraception should fail." This falsely assumes that the consequence of overruling *Roe* would have been to make abortion unlawful. It would not; it would merely have *permitted* the States to do so. Many States would unquestionably have declined to prohibit abortion, and others would not have prohibited it within six months (after which the most significant reliance interests would have expired). Even for persons in States other than these, the choice would not have been between abortion and childbirth, but between abortion nearby and abortion in a neighboring State.

To tell the truth, it does not surprise me, and should surprise no one, that the Court has chosen today to revise the standards of *stare decisis* set forth in *Casey*. It has thereby exposed *Casey*'s extraordinary deference to precedent for the result-oriented expedient that it is. * * *

[III.   Justice Scalia defended the correctness of *Bowers*' holdings that only interests traditionally recognized in American law can be "fundamental" and that the right to engage in consensual sodomy (homosexual or otherwise) is not one of those traditional rights.] Whether homosexual sodomy was prohibited by a law targeted at same-sex sexual relations or by a more general law prohibiting both homosexual and heterosexual sodomy, the only relevant point is that it *was* criminalized—which suffices to establish that homosexual sodomy is not a right "deeply rooted in our Nation's history and tradition." * * *

Next, the Court makes the claim, again unsupported by any citations, that "[l]aws prohibiting sodomy do not seem to have been enforced against consenting adults acting in private." The key qualifier here is "acting in private"—since the Court admits that sodomy laws *were* enforced against consenting adults (although the Court contends that prosecutions were "infrequent"). I do not know what "acting in private" means; surely consensual sodomy, like heterosexual intercourse, is rarely performed on stage. If all the Court means by "acting in private" is "on private premises, with the doors closed and windows covered," it is entirely unsurprising that evidence of enforcement would be hard to come by. (Imagine the circumstances that would enable a search warrant to be obtained for a residence on the ground that there was probable cause to believe that consensual sodomy was then and there occurring.) Surely that lack of evidence would not sustain the proposition that consensual sodomy on private premises with the doors closed and windows covered was regarded as a "fundamental right," even though all other consensual sodomy was criminalized. There are 203 prosecutions for consensual, adult homosexual sodomy reported in the West Reporting system and official state reporters from the years 1880–1995. See W. Eskridge, Gaylaw: Challenging the Apartheid of the Closet 375 (1999) (hereinafter Gaylaw). There are also records of 20 sodomy prosecutions and 4 executions during the colonial period. J. Katz, Gay/Lesbian Almanac 29, 58, 663 (1983). *Bowers*' conclusion that homosexual sodomy is not a fundamental right "deeply rooted in this Nation's history and tradition" is utterly unassailable.

Realizing that fact, the Court instead says: "[W]e think that our laws and traditions in the past half century are of most relevance here. These references show *an emerging awareness* that liberty gives substantial protection to adult persons in deciding how to conduct their private lives *in matters pertaining to sex.*" (Emphasis added.) Apart from the fact that such an "emerging awareness" does not establish a "fundamental right," the statement is factually false. States continue to prosecute all sorts of crimes by adults "in matters pertaining to sex": prostitution, adult incest, adultery, obscenity, and child pornography. Sodomy laws, too, have been enforced "in the past half century," in which there have been 134 reported cases involving prosecutions for consensual, adult, homosexual sodomy. Gaylaw 375. In relying, for evidence of an "emerging recognition," upon the American Law Institute's 1955 recommendation not to criminalize " 'consensual sexual relations conducted in private,' "the Court ignores the fact that this recommendation was "a point of resistance in most of the states that considered adopting the Model Penal Code." Gaylaw 159.

In any event, an "emerging awareness" is by definition not "deeply rooted in this Nation's history and tradition[s]," as we have said "fundamental right" status requires. Constitutional entitlements do not spring into existence because some States choose to lessen or eliminate criminal sanctions on certain behavior. Much less do they spring into existence, as the Court seems to believe, because *foreign nations* decriminalize conduct. The *Bowers* majority opinion *never* relied on "values we share with a wider civilization," but rather rejected the claimed right to sodomy on the ground that such a right was not " 'deeply rooted in *this Nation's* history and tradition' "(emphasis added). *Bowers'* rational-basis holding is likewise devoid of any reliance on the views of a "wider civilization." The Court's discussion of these foreign views (ignoring, of course, the many countries that have retained criminal prohibitions on sodomy) is therefore meaningless dicta. Dangerous dicta, however, since "this Court ... should not impose foreign moods, fads, or fashions on Americans." *Foster v. Florida*, 537 U.S. 990, 991 (2002) (Thomas, J., concurring in denial of certiorari).

[IV.] I turn now to the ground on which the Court squarely rests its holding: the contention that there is no rational basis for the law here under attack. This proposition is so out of accord with our jurisprudence— indeed, with the jurisprudence of *any* society we know—that it requires little discussion.

The Texas statute undeniably seeks to further the belief of its citizens that certain forms of sexual behavior are "immoral and unacceptable," *Bowers*—the same interest furthered by criminal laws against fornication, bigamy, adultery, adult incest, bestiality, and obscenity. *Bowers* held that this was a legitimate state interest. The Court today reaches the opposite conclusion. The Texas statute, it says, "furthers no legitimate state interest which can justify its intrusion into the personal and private life of the individual" (emphasis added). The Court embraces instead Justice Stevens' declaration in his Bowers dissent, that "the fact that the governing majority in a State has traditionally viewed a particular practice as immoral is not a sufficient reason for upholding a law prohibiting the practice." This effectively decrees the end of all morals legislation. If, as the Court asserts, the promotion of majoritarian sexual morality is not even a *legitimate* state interest, none of the above-mentioned laws can survive rational-basis review.

[V.]   Finally, I turn to petitioners' equal-protection challenge, which no Member of the Court save Justice O'Connor embraces: On its face § 21.06(a) applies equally to all persons. Men and women, heterosexuals and homosexuals, are all subject to its prohibition of deviate sexual intercourse with someone of the same sex. To be sure, § 21.06 does distinguish between the sexes insofar as concerns the partner with whom the sexual acts are performed: men can violate the law only with other men, and women only with other women. But this cannot itself be a denial of equal protection, since it is precisely the same distinction regarding partner that is drawn in state laws prohibiting marriage with someone of the same sex while permitting marriage with someone of the opposite sex.

The objection is made, however, that the antimiscegenation laws invalidated in *Loving* v. *Virginia* similarly were applicable to whites and blacks alike, and only distinguished between the races insofar as the *partner* was concerned. In *Loving*, however, we correctly applied heightened scrutiny, rather than the usual rational-basis review, because the Virginia statute was "designed to maintain White Supremacy." A racially discriminatory purpose is always sufficient to subject a law to strict scrutiny, even a facially neutral law that makes no mention of race. No purpose to discriminate against men or women as a class can be gleaned from the Texas law, so rational-basis review applies. That review is readily satisfied here by the same rational basis that satisfied it in *Bowers*—society's belief that certain forms of sexual behavior are "immoral and unacceptable." This is the same justification that supports many other laws regulating sexual behavior that make a distinction based upon the identity of the partner—for example, laws against adultery, fornication, and adult incest, and laws refusing to recognize homosexual marriage.

Justice O'Connor argues that the discrimination in this law which must be justified is not its discrimination with regard to the sex of the partner but its discrimination with regard to the sexual proclivity of the principal actor. * * * Of course the same could be said of any law. A law against public nudity targets "the conduct that is closely correlated with being a nudist," and hence "is targeted at more than conduct"; it is "directed toward nudists as a class." But be that as it may. Even if the Texas law *does* deny equal protection to "homosexuals as a class," that denial *still* does not need to be justified by anything more than a rational basis, which our cases show is satisfied by the enforcement of traditional notions of sexual morality.

Justice O'Connor simply decrees application of "a more searching form of rational basis review" to the Texas statute. The cases she cites do not recognize such a standard, and reach their conclusions only after finding, as required by conventional rational-basis analysis, that no conceivable legitimate state interest supports the classification at issue. Nor does Justice O'Connor explain precisely what her "more searching form" of rational-basis review consists of. It must at least mean, however, that laws exhibiting " 'a ... desire to harm a politically unpopular group,' "are invalid *even though* there may be a conceivable rational basis to support them.

This reasoning leaves on pretty shaky grounds state laws limiting marriage to opposite-sex couples. Justice O'Connor seeks to preserve them by the conclusory statement that "preserving the traditional institution of marriage" is a legitimate state interest. But "preserving the traditional institution of marriage" is just a kinder way of describing the State's *moral disapproval* of same-sex couples. Texas's interest in § 21.06 could be recast in similarly euphemistic terms: "preserving the traditional sexual mores of our society." In the jurisprudence Justice O'Connor has seemingly created, judges can validate laws by characterizing them as "preserving the traditions of society" (good); or invalidate them by characterizing them as "expressing moral disapproval" (bad).

Today's opinion is the product of a Court, which is the product of a law-profession culture, that has largely signed on to the so-called homosexual agenda, by which I mean the agenda promoted by some homosexual activists directed at eliminating the moral opprobrium that has traditionally attached to homosexual conduct. I noted in an earlier opinion the fact that the American Association of Law Schools (to which any reputable law school *must* seek to belong) excludes from membership any school that refuses to ban from its job-interview facilities a law firm (no matter how small) that does not wish to hire as a prospective partner a person who openly engages in homosexual conduct. See *Romer* [dissenting opinion].

One of the most revealing statements in today's opinion is the Court's grim warning that the criminalization of homosexual conduct is "an invitation to subject homosexual persons to discrimination both in the public and in the private spheres." It is clear from this that the Court has taken sides in the culture war, departing from its role of assuring, as neutral observer, that the democratic rules of engagement are observed. Many Americans do not want persons who openly engage in homosexual conduct as partners in their business, as scoutmasters for their children, as teachers in their children's schools, or as boarders in their home. They view this as protecting themselves and their families from a lifestyle that they believe to be immoral and destructive. The Court views it as "discrimination" which it is the function of our judgments to deter. So imbued is the Court with the law profession's anti-anti-homosexual culture, that it is seemingly unaware that the attitudes of that culture are not obviously "mainstream"; that in most States what the Court calls "discrimination" against those who engage in homosexual acts is perfectly legal; that proposals to ban such "discrimination" under Title VII have repeatedly been rejected by Congress, see Employment Non–Discrimination Act of 1994, S. 2238, 103d Cong., 2d Sess. (1994); Civil Rights Amendments, H. R. 5452, 94th Cong., 1st Sess. (1975); that in some cases such "discrimination" is *mandated* by federal statute, see 10 U. S. C. § 654(b)(1) (mandating discharge from the armed forces of any service member who engages in or intends to engage in homosexual acts); and that in some cases such "discrimination" is a constitutional right, see *Boy Scouts of America* v. *Dale* [Chapter 5].

Let me be clear that I have nothing against homosexuals, or any other group, promoting their agenda through normal democratic means. Social perceptions of sexual and other morality change over time, and every group has the right to persuade its fellow citizens that its view of such matters is the best. That homosexuals have achieved some success in that enterprise is attested to by the fact that Texas is one of the few remaining States that criminalize private, consensual homosexual acts. But persuading one's fellow citizens is one thing, and imposing one's views in absence of democratic majority will is something else. I would no more *require* a State to criminalize homosexual acts—or, for that matter, display *any* moral disapprobation of them—than I would *forbid* it to do so. What Texas has chosen to do is well within the range of traditional democratic action, and its hand should not be stayed through the invention of a brand-new "constitutional right" by a Court that is impatient of democratic change. It is indeed true that "later generations can see that laws once thought necessary and proper in fact serve only to oppress;" and when that happens, later generations can repeal those laws. But it is the premise of our system that those judgments are to be made by the people, and not imposed by a governing caste that knows best.

One of the benefits of leaving regulation of this matter to the people rather than to the courts is that the people, unlike judges, need not carry things to their logical conclusion. The people may feel that their disapprobation of homosexual conduct is strong enough to disallow homosexual marriage, but not strong enough to criminalize private homosexual acts—and may legislate accordingly. The Court today pretends that it possesses a similar freedom of action, so that we need not fear judicial imposition of homosexual marriage, as has recently occurred in Canada (in a decision that the Canadian Government has chosen not to appeal). See *Halpern* v. *Toronto*, 2003 WL 34950 (Ontario Ct. App.); Cohen, Dozens in Canada Follow Gay Couple's Lead, Washington Post, June 12, 2003, p. A25. At the end of its opinion—after having laid waste the foundations of our rational-basis jurisprudence—the Court says that the present case "does not involve whether the government must give formal recognition to any relationship that homosexual persons seek to enter." Do not believe it. More illuminating than this bald, unreasoned disclaimer is the progression of thought displayed by an earlier passage in the Court's opinion, which notes the constitutional protections afforded to "personal decisions relating to *marriage*, procreation, contraception, family relationships, child rearing, and education," and then declares that "[p]ersons in a homosexual relationship may seek autonomy for these purposes, just as heterosexual persons do" (emphasis added). Today's opinion dismantles the structure of constitutional law that has permitted a distinction to be made between heterosexual and homosexual unions, insofar as formal recognition in marriage is concerned. If moral disapprobation of homosexual conduct is "no legitimate state interest" for purposes of proscribing that conduct; and if, as the Court coos (casting aside all pretense of neutrality), "[w]hen sexuality finds overt expression in intimate conduct with another person, the conduct can be but one element in a personal bond that is more enduring;" what justification could there possibly be for denying the benefits of marriage to homosexual couples exercising "[t]he liberty protected by the Constitution?" Surely not the encouragement of procreation, since the sterile and the elderly are allowed to marry. This case "does not involve" the issue of homosexual marriage only if one entertains the belief that principle and logic have nothing to do with the decisions of this Court. Many will hope that, as the Court comfortingly assures us, this is so.

The matters appropriate for this Court's resolution are only three: Texas's prohibition of sodomy neither infringes a "fundamental right" (which the Court does not dispute), nor is unsupported by a rational relation to what the Constitution considers a legitimate state interest, nor denies the equal protection of the laws. I dissent.

■ JUSTICE THOMAS, dissenting.

* * * I write separately to note that the law before the Court today "is ... uncommonly silly." *Griswold* v. *Connecticut* (Stewart, J., dissenting). If I were a member of the Texas Legislature, I would vote to repeal it. Punishing someone for expressing his sexual preference through noncommercial consensual conduct with another adult does not appear to be a worthy way to expend valuable law enforcement resources.

Notwithstanding this, I recognize that as a member of this Court I am not empowered to help petitioners and others similarly situated. My duty, rather, is to "decide cases 'agreeably to the Constitution and laws of the United States.' "[*Id.*] And, just like Justice Stewart, I "can find [neither in the Bill of Rights nor any other part of the Constitution a] general right of privacy," [*id.*], or as the Court terms it today, the "liberty of the person both in its spatial and more transcendent dimensions."

NOTES ON *LAWRENCE*

1. *Stare Decisis: Was Bowers Wrong Enough to Be Overruled?* Justice Scalia considers stare decisis no big obstacle to overruling wrongly decided constitutional precedents—but in *Lawrence* he chided the majority Justices for giving nothing more than lip service to the principle that, they said, saved the abortion right from being overruled in *Casey* (Chapter 2). The majority didn't say much in response, but consider some possible defenses. As you read these defenses, jot down responses that Justice Scalia would have to them.

(a) *The Libertarian Presumption and History.* The Constitution is a highly libertarian document, and its structural protection of people's freedom to act in their own interests without state interference was buttressed in the Bill of Rights and then in the Fourteenth Amendment. Under a libertarian constitutional presumption, *Roe v. Wade*, a precedent protecting a liberty interest, gets more stare decisis support than *Bowers v. Hardwick*, a precedent declining to protect a liberty interest. Moreover, it cannot be ignored that the invasions of liberty were in criminal statutes, which have long been subjected to different, and more stringent, liberty-protective limitations than civil statutes. Under this defense, the baseline should be liberty from state intrusion, and the state has the burden of showing that its regulation has been justified by tradition.

(b) *Flipping Act and Identity When the Audience Changes.* As Janet Halley suggests (Chapter 2), there is an unstable relationship between act and identity in *Bowers v. Hardwick*—which rendered the opinion's cogency unstable as well. So long as the audience for Supreme Court opinions can be presumed to be heterosexual, and homo-fearful, Justice White's mobile focus on bad acts (sodomy) to deny a fundamental right and despised identity (homosexuality) to constitute a rational basis, *Bowers* is plausible. But once the audience changes, and the Justices realize that millions of lesbians, gay men, and bisexuals are not only "out" in the United States but are out as lawyers and parents, then *Bowers'* rhetorical mobility becomes evidence of the Justices' antigay bias. Notice how Justice Kennedy's opinion starts with the notion that *Bowers* did not state the issue to be decided in a neutral—judicious—way.

So the *Lawrence* majority insists on a connection between acts and identity, and once that connection is made, *Bowers* loses the presumptive legitimacy that goes with its status as a precedent of the Court. As a soiled precedent, at best, *Bowers* is left stranded. If its bad history undermined *Bowers'* cogency, the fact that *Lawrence* involved an openly discriminatory sodomy law sealed *Bowers'* fate. Texas' exquisite conflation of act ("deviate sexual intercourse," the Model Penal Code's creepy term, copied by Texas) and identity (the statute is entitled "Homosexual Conduct") expose the law as resting on antigay bias.

(c) *Social Movements and Social Norms. Lawrence* and *Casey* can be reconciled on the ground that in both cases the Court majority was following public opinion. By 1992, the pro-choice movement had been successful in persuading substantial majorities of Americans that women have a right to abortion—but not an unlimited right. This was a script *Casey* followed carefully: the *Roe* right was reaffirmed, but state regulatory authority was expanded. By 2003, the gay rights movement had been successful in persuading substantial majorities of Americans that lesbians, gay men, and bisexuals were an acceptable minority whose so-called "life-styles" should be "tolerated" by the state—and that it was ridiculous for the state to criminalize their private intimate activities. This was a script *Lawrence* followed carefully: criminal sodomy laws were invalidated, but the majority disclaimed any endorsement of same-sex marriage or gays in the military, for example.

2. *Soaring Rhetoric, Weak Doctrine.* Justice Kennedy's opinion for the Court draws two essential conclusions: that Americans have a liberty interest in private sexual conduct and that Texas has no rational basis for criminalizing such conduct. The power of the rhetoric in *Lawrence* makes it easy to lose sight of the fact that, unlike in the contraception or abortion cases from the 1960s and 1970s, the Court does not speak of any "fundamental right." Accordingly, the Court does not analyze whether the state demonstrated a "compelling interest" supporting its law. This is similar to the Joint Opinion of Justices Kennedy, O'Connor and Souter in *Casey*, which declared that *Roe v. Wade* would not be overruled at the same time that it weakened the standard of review to be used in scrutinizing restrictions on abortion. The most important point is that the Court treated the liberty right in *Lawrence* as *equivalent* to the abortion right.

Not declaring a fundamental right makes the Court's conclusion even more powerful in certain respects: the interests proffered by Texas are found to be not even rational, much less compelling. It also lowers the stakes for describing the individual's right: the Court's text makes clear that it is somehow a core right, but never crosses the line into denominating it as fundamental. At the same time, however, using this murky test makes a strong decision potentially easy to distinguish in future cases: the Court can always return to an approach that gives much greater deference to state laws, as the typical rational basis test does, without stepping outside of precedent.

At a political level, the Court makes clear that at least some anti-gay laws fail even the lowest constitutional test of rationality, an enormous step forward past the bigotry embodied in the language of *Bowers v. Hardwick*. The Court has committed itself to establishing a floor of fairness below which anti-gay policies cannot sink. But it is also committed (in this field among many others) to deciding only what it must in each case, and foreclosing the fewest possible options for future decisions. This approach will give lower future federal courts great range in calibrating the extent to which the state can, in myriad ways short of criminal prohibition, prefer or discourage forms of sexual orientation.

3. *"Liberty," Not "Privacy."* There are many references to "private" sexual conduct in the decision, but nowhere does the Court describe the right at issue here as "privacy." Ironically, *Lawrence* may mark the end of a "right of privacy" in formal constitutional taxonomy. The negative liberty resonances are at least as strong, if not stronger, as in the privacy decisions of the Court in *Griswold, Eisenstadt*, and *Roe*. But the *only* use of the word "privacy" in this decision, outside of a quotation, is where the Court acknowledges that *Griswold* used that word to describe the relevant liberty interest. Perhaps the Court, while sounding like it is writing to praise "privacy," has come to bury it, by shifting in a subtle way to a word ("liberty") which—unlike "privacy"—does have an unambiguous mooring in constitutional text.

It is difficult to know how much to make of this shift, or whether "privacy" as such will reappear in future decisions. (The word has such widespread popular appeal that it may be impossible for the Court to put this cat back into the constitutional bag, even if the majority wants to.) But it is noteworthy that the Court resuscitates from *Hardwick* not the classic defense of privacy in Justice Blackmun's dissent, but the liberty analysis of Justice Stevens. The Court in *Lawrence* also invokes the contraception-abortion line of cases as protection for choice, control of one's "destiny," and the principle of "autonomy." The individual's right of "choice" and to "choose"—words used three times in five sentences—connects this decision to that earlier line of cases.

4. *Major and Minor Chords.* In some respects, recognition of the individual liberty of adults to engage in consensual sexual acts in private seems merely like the long overdue culmination of principles from the Model Penal Code and *The Wolfenden Report*, both documents from the 1950s. The Court has settled a very old and narrow debate; the same outcome could have occurred in the Eisenhower era. And while this might aptly summarize the Court's holding, it would not capture the full social meaning of the case, because the *Lawrence* decision combines a highly utilitarian holding with the strong rhythms of dignitarian reasoning.

"Liberty" is the Court's major chord. As the opening paragraph states, this case is about "unwarranted government intrusions," about both private *and* public realms where government should not go. Correlatively, where government does not intrude or impede, the substantive components of due process are not threatened. Certainly nothing in this decision undermines the logic of *Harris v. McRae* or *Maher v. Roe*, two decisions which held that the government is not obligated to include abortion among the services covered by the Medicaid program. This is classic libertarian philosophy.

But the civil rights-style rhetoric which forms the Court's minor chord suggests that this is libertarianism with a new inflection, where the desire to erect a buffer against government may be the primary, but is not the sole, driving force. Certainly it sounds nothing like the language of those 1950s texts, which assumed that homosexuality was repugnant and sought only to argue that criminal law was not the method of choice for deterring it. In *Lawrence*, we have a Court opposed to the existence of sodomy laws because they "demean" gay people and create "stigma" for a group that deserves "respect" for the "choices" made in their "private lives."

The combination of these two discursive chords yields a complementarity of individualist liberty and equality, a cultural and political zone where the new libertarians and the neo-egalitarians of the early twenty-first century can meet. The invocation of both strains—liberty as doctrine, equality as rhetoric—also produces an opinion that seems more holistic and connected to life experience and social practice than might have been the case if the Court had separated its analyses of substantive due process and equal protection into distinct segments. Although the opinion of the Court says nothing per se about equal protection, the concept of equality is woven into the text.

5. *History and Political Theory: The Constitution as a Mechanism for Moderating Culture Wars.* Even though they essentially rely on the same secondary sources, the majority and dissent read the history very differently. Without defending the simplistic history in Justice White's opinion, Justice Scalia seeks to rehabilitate *Bowers*: Forget about the details of sodomy law evolution and the fact that "homosexual sodomy" was not the focus of such laws before the nineteenth century; according to Scalia, the thing to emphasize is that sodomy has been a prohibited activity for all of American history, and that alone precludes its being protected by the right to privacy. Recall that Justice Scalia demands a long and unbroken history of affirmative protection before he will acknowledge some kind of fundamental right protection—but that view of the relationship between history and substantive due process was rejected in *Griswold*, *Roe* and *Casey*, and *Loving v. Virginia*.

The relationship between history and constitutional protection that a majority of the Court has followed since *Casey* is that articulated by Justice Harlan's dissenting opinion in *Poe v. Ullman*. The standard objection—originating with Justice Black in *Griswold* and now carried forward by Justice Scalia—is that an "evolving tradition" gives judges and the citizenry insufficient guidance in understanding what are the limits of government. Note how in *Lawrence* this argument is turned around: Justice Kennedy demonstrates that "unevolving tradition" was just as malleable in *Bowers* as Justice Black feared that "evolving tradition" would be. Moreover, Justice Kennedy demonstrates that there can be objective benchmarks for evolving tradition—the ALI's Model Penal Code, the adoption of its deregulatory principle in the next generation of state legislative and judicial deliberation, the experience of other Western countries. All point in the same direction: consensual sodomy laws unnecessarily intrude into people's private lives.

There is another way to understand the Court's deployment of tradition. The level of generality is key. Justice Kennedy emphasizes a higher level of generality than Justice Scalia does. Scalia can hardly question that American constitutionalism has traditionally valued the integrity of the home, one's freedom to control one's own body, and (perhaps) our liberty to form relationships with one another. Kennedy starts with those principles and then announces that "homosexuals" are not exempt from their protection—a point Scalia disputes on the ground that "homosexuals" and their activities have not been *specifically protected* by any American tradition and, indeed, have been *specifically targeted* by the state throughout the twentieth century. Just as people of color (*Loving*) and women (*Roe*) have benefitted from application of traditional principles to their particular situations in ways the Framers of the Fourteenth Amendment never would have imagined, so too lesbians, gay men, and bisexuals now benefit from the same move.

Justice Scalia seems to understand this. His dissent can be read as an invitation for a reinvigorated Traditional Family Values (TFV) counter-movement against both *Roe* and *Lawrence*, especially the latter, which he links to same-sex marriage and other items on the "homosexual agenda." Scalia's idea is that the Court is taking moral issues away from the democratic process; We the People rather than We the Court should be deciding the great moral issues of the day. Kennedy's response, subtly articulated in the opinion, is that consensual sodomy is no longer a great moral issue—it has been decided by consensus, and the Court is engaged in a mop-up operation. The great moral issues Scalia heralds, like same-sex marriage, are in no way resolved by *Lawrence* and will be left to the states to work out in the coming generation.

Underlying Kennedy's approach is *not* the idea that the Court decides great moral issues, but that the Court and its constitutional discourse contribute to a well-managed pluralism. America is a nation of social groups who constantly come into conflict. The political process is the arena where their conflicts are worked out, most of the time. But constitutionalism can serve a useful purpose of managing and channeling intergroup conflict. On the one hand, constitutionalism can prevent the state from being deployed as a means whereby a minority is turned into an outlaw group. That is not only an unfair deployment of the state, but creates resentments and the risk that the pariah groups will go outside normal politics to fight. On the other hand, constitutionalism can protect groups against excessive state intrusion into their own bonding needs. Freedom of religion, of association, the sanctity of the home, and the right of privacy are examples.

6.   *Interrogating Rationality.* The debate between Justices O'Connor and Scalia is a debate about rationality itself. Scalia argues that protection or expression of public morality is a rational state interest. O'Connor argues that expression of public dislike of a class of people (homosexuals) is not a rational state interest. This is the tension between *Bowers v. Hardwick*, which held that moral disapproval could be a rational basis, and *Romer v. Evans*, which held that animus against gay people could not be. O'Connor joined both opinions and seems to reaffirm both in *Lawrence*—but can they be reconciled?

Justice O'Connor's concurring opinion seems to say that it is Texas's focus on "homosexual conduct" alone that transforms its law from a moral disapproval law to a class animus law. But she would not overrule *Bowers v. Hardwick*, which emphasized that it was only evaluating the application of Georgia's law to "homosexual sodomy." Perhaps O'Connor is only reaffirming the holding of *Bowers* and would narrow its reasoning, but then she must confront the fact that Texas may have had a neutral reason for drafting its law to focus on "homosexual conduct."

7.   *Arguments Based Upon Morality Cannot Be Deployed to Create an Underclass.* Justice O'Connor's concurring opinion repeats the proportionality principle of *Romer v. Evans*, that the law cannot target a group of persons for a broad range of disfavored treatment based on a single characteristic bearing little or no relationship to the particular policies at issue. Her opinion takes *Romer* one logical step further, by finding that "moral disapproval of a group cannot be a legitimate governmental interest." In *Romer*, Colorado (which had long ago repealed its sodomy law) did not claim morality as a state interest in support of Amendment 2, so the Court had no occasion to declare whether morality could comprise a proper basis for such a law. In *Lawrence*, Texas did claim morality as the interest behind its sodomy law. It seemed clear even at the time of *Romer*—and is obvious now—that the six-Justice majority in that case would have rejected a claim of morality alone as insufficient, so O'Connor's reasoning is not a surprise. But Justice O'Connor's opinion completes the logic of the *Romer* analysis.

Justice O'Connor's concurring opinion also complements *Romer* by its focus on the argument that the law creates an "underclass." Whatever the motivations of the Texas legislature, the Court ought not tolerate a law that marks a class as presumptive criminals and has so many discriminatory ramifications that it effectively creates an underclass of people outside the protections of the rule of law. The American Bar Association filed an *amicus* brief in *Lawrence* which argued that the Texas law was deeply inconsistent with the neutral rule of law as it must apply to gay people.

THE IMPACT OF LAWRENCE ON LGBT EQUALITY

The most significant ruling on the rights of lesbians and gay men under the U. S. Constitution in the first two years after *Lawrence* did not come out as one might imagine, given the Supreme Court's egalitarian language:

Steven Lofton et al. v. Secretary of the Department of Children and Social Services Et Al.

United States Court of Appeals for the Eleventh Circuit.
358 F.3d 804 (2004).

■ BIRCH, J.

Since 1977, Florida's adoption law has contained a codified prohibition on adoption by any "homosexual" person. 1977 Fla. Laws, ch. 77–140, § 1, Fla. Stat. § 63.042(3) (2002). For purposes of this statute, Florida courts have defined the term "homosexual" as being "limited to applicants who are known to engage in current, voluntary homosexual activity," thus drawing "a distinction between homosexual orientation and homosexual activity." *Fla. Dep't of Health & Rehab. Servs.*, 627 So.2d 1210, 1215 (Fla. Dist. Ct. App. 1993), aff'd in relevant part, 656 So. 2d 902, 903 (Fla. 1995). During the past twelve years, several legislative bills have attempted to repeal the statute, and three separate legal challenges to it have been filed in the Florida courts. To date, no attempt to overturn the provision has succeeded. We now consider the most recent challenge to the statute.

[Steven Lofton and his life partner Roger Croteau, both pediatric nurses, have adopted six HIV-positive children in the last 20 years. One of them, identified by the Court as "John Doe," was born in 1991,and sero-converted after about a year in Lofton and Croteau's care. In September of 1994, Lofton filed an application to adopt Doe but refused to answer the application's inquiry about his sexual preference and also failed to disclose Croteau as a member of his household. After Lofton refused requests from the Department of Children and Families ("DCF") to supply the missing information, his application was rejected pursuant to the homosexual adoption provision.]

[Judge Birch analyzed Florida's adoption law scheme, which trains closely on the "best interests of the child."] Because of the primacy of the welfare of the child, the state can make classifications for adoption pur-

177

poses that would be constitutionally suspect in many other arenas. For example, Florida law requires that, in order to adopt any child other than a special needs child, an individual's primary residence and place of employment must be located in Florida. In screening adoption applicants, Florida considers such factors as physical and mental health, income and financial status, duration of marriage, housing, and neighborhood, among others. Similarly, Florida gives preference to candidates who demonstrate a commitment to "value, respect, appreciate, and educate the child regarding his or her racial and ethnic heritage." Moreover, prospective adoptive parents are required to sign an affidavit of good moral character. Many of these preferences and requirements, if employed outside the adoption arena, would be unlikely to withstand constitutional scrutiny. * * *

[*Burden on Fundamental Right to Private Sexual Intimacy*] Laws that burden the exercise of a fundamental right require strict scrutiny and are sustained only if narrowly tailored to further a compelling government interest. Appellants argue that the Supreme Court's recent decision in *Lawrence v. Texas*, which struck down Texas's sodomy statute, identified a hitherto unarticulated fundamental right to private sexual intimacy. They contend that the Florida statute, by disallowing adoption to any individual who chooses to engage in homosexual conduct, impermissibly burdens the exercise of this right.

We begin with the threshold question of whether *Lawrence* identified a new fundamental right to private sexual intimacy. *Lawrence*'s holding was that substantive due process does not permit a state to impose a criminal prohibition on private consensual homosexual conduct. The effect of this holding was to establish a greater respect than previously existed in the law for the right of consenting adults to engage in private sexual conduct. Nowhere, however, did the Court characterize this right as "fundamental." Cf. [*Lawrence*] (Scalia, J., dissenting) (observing that "nowhere does the Court's opinion declare that homosexual sodomy is a 'fundamental right' under the *Due Process Clause*"). Nor did the Court locate this right directly in the Constitution, but instead treated it as the by-product of several different constitutional principles and liberty interests.

[Judge Birch then distinguished *Lawrence*, quoting language at the end of Justice Kennedy's opinion, that the Texas case did not involve minors.] Here, the involved actors are not only consenting adults, but minors as well. The relevant state action is not criminal prohibition, but grant of a statutory privilege. And the asserted liberty interest is not the negative right to engage in private conduct without facing criminal sanctions, but the affirmative right to receive official and public recognition. Hence, we conclude that the *Lawrence* decision cannot be extrapolated to create a right to adopt for homosexual persons.

[*Equal Protection*] * * * Florida contends that the statute is only one aspect of its broader adoption policy, which is designed to create adoptive homes that resemble the nuclear family as closely as possible. Florida argues that the statute is rationally related to Florida's interest in furthering the best interests of adopted children by placing them in families with married mothers and fathers. Such homes, Florida asserts, provide the stability that marriage affords and the presence of both male and female authority figures, which it considers critical to optimal childhood development and socialization. In particular, Florida emphasizes a vital role that dual-gender parenting plays in shaping sexual and gender identity and in providing heterosexual role modeling. Florida argues that disallowing adoption into homosexual households, which are necessarily motherless or fatherless and lack the stability that comes with marriage, is a rational means of furthering Florida's interest in promoting adoption by marital families. * * *

[T]he state has a legitimate interest in encouraging this optimal family structure by seeking to place adoptive children in homes that have both a mother and father. Florida argues that its preference for adoptive marital families is based on the premise that the marital family structure is more stable than other household arrangements and that children benefit from the presence of both a father and mother in the home. Given that appellants have offered no competent evidence to the contrary, we find this premise to be one of those "unprovable assumptions" that nevertheless can provide a legitimate basis for legislative action. *Paris Adult Theatre I v. Slaton,* 413 U.S. 49, 62–63 (1973). Although social theorists from Plato to Simone de Beauvoir have proposed alternative child-rearing arrangements, none has proven as enduring as the marital family structure, nor has the accumulated wisdom of several millennia of human experience discovered a superior model. See, e.g., Plato, The Republic, Bk. V, 459d–461e; Simone de Beauvoir, The Second Sex (H. M. Parshley trans., Vintage Books 1989) (1949). Against this "sum of experience," it is rational for Florida to conclude that it is in the best interests of adoptive children, many of whom come from troubled and unstable backgrounds, to be placed in a home anchored by both a father and a mother.

[The challengers claimed that the sexual orientation classification was not reasonably related to this goal.] Appellants note that Florida law permits adoption by unmarried individuals and that, among children coming out the Florida foster care system, 25% of adoptions are to parents who are currently single. Their argument is that homosexual persons are similarly situated to unmarried persons with regard to Florida's asserted interest in promoting married-couple adoption. According to appellants, this disparate treatment lacks a rational basis and, therefore, disproves any rational connection between the statute and Florida's asserted interest in promoting adoption into married homes. Citing *City of Cleburne v. Cleburne Living Ctr. Inc.,* 473 U.S. 432 (1985), appellants argue that the state has not satisfied *Cleburne*'s threshold requirement that it demonstrate that homosexuals pose a unique threat to children that others similarly situated in relevant respects do not. * * *

This case is distinguishable from *Cleburne.* The Florida legislature could rationally conclude that homosexuals and heterosexual singles are not "similarly situated in relevant respects." It is not irrational to think that heterosexual singles have a markedly greater probability of eventually establishing a married household and, thus, providing their adopted children with a stable, dual-gender parenting environment. Moreover, as the state noted, the legislature could rationally act on the theory that heterosexual singles, even if they never marry, are better positioned than homosexual individuals to provide adopted children with education and guidance relative to their sexual development throughout pubescence and adolescence. In a previous challenge to Florida's statute, a Florida appellate court observed:

> Whatever causes a person to become a homosexual, it is clear that the state cannot know the sexual preferences that a child will exhibit as an adult. Statistically, the state does know that a very high percentage of children available for adoption will develop heterosexual preferences. As a result, those children will need education and guidance after puberty concerning relationships with the opposite sex. In our society, we expect that parents will provide this education to teenagers in the home. These subjects are often very embarrassing for teenagers and some aspects of the education are accomplished by the parents telling stories about their own adolescence and explaining their own experiences with the opposite sex. It is in the best interests of a child if his or her parents can personally relate to the child's problems and assist the child in the difficult transition to heterosexual adulthood. Given that adopted children tend to have some developmental problems arising from adoption or from their experiences prior to adoption, it is perhaps more important for adopted children than other children to have a stable heterosexual household during puberty and the teenage years.

Cox, 627 So. 2d at 1220. * * *

Appellants cite recent social science research and the opinion of mental health professionals and child welfare organizations as evidence that there is no child welfare basis for excluding homosexuals from adopting. They argue that the cited studies show that the parenting skills of homosexual parents are at least equivalent to those of heterosexual parents and that children raised by homosexual parents suffer no adverse outcomes. Appellants also point to the policies and practices of numerous adoption agencies that permit homosexual persons to adopt.

In considering appellants' argument, we must ask not whether the latest in social science research and professional opinion *support* the decision of the Florida legislature, but whether that evidence is so well established and so far beyond dispute that it would be irrational for the Florida legislature to believe that the interests of its children are best served by not permitting homosexual adoption. Also, we must credit any conceivable rational reason that the legislature might have for choosing not to alter its statutory scheme in response to this recent social science research. * * * Or the legislature might consider, and even credit, the research cited by appellants, but find it premature to rely on a very recent and still developing body of research, particularly in light of the absence of longitudinal studies following child subjects into adulthood and of studies of adopted, rather than natural, children of homosexual parents.

[The Court distinguished *Romer v. Evans*, Chapter 2, Section 2C.] Unlike Colorado's Amendment 2 [struck down in *Romer*], Florida's statute is not so "sweeping and comprehensive" as to render Florida's rationales for the statute "inexplicable by anything but animus" toward its homosexual residents. Amendment 2 deprived homosexual persons of "protections against exclusion from an almost limitless number of transactions and endeavors that constitute ordinary civic life in a free society." *Id.* at 631. In contrast to this "broad and undifferentiated disability," the Florida classification is limited to the narrow and discrete context of access to the statutory privilege of adoption and, more importantly, has a plausible connection with the state's asserted interest. Moreover, not only is the effect of Florida's classification dramatically smaller, but the classification itself is narrower. Whereas Amendment 2's classification encompassed both conduct *and* status, Florida's adoption prohibition is limited to conduct. Thus, we conclude that *Romer's* unique factual situation and narrow holding are inapposite to this case.

On Petition for Rehearing en banc

United States Court of Appeals for the Eleventh Circuit, 2004.
377 F.3d 1275.

[Upon petition for rehearing en banc, six judges of the full Eleventh Circuit voted to rehear the case en banc and six did not. Because there was no majority, the rehearing was denied. Judge Barkett, who voted to rehear the case, critiqued the panel opinion; Judge Birch responded.]

■ BARKETT, J., dissenting from the denial of rehearing en banc

[*Equal Protection*] [T]he classification at issue in this case burdens personal relationships and exudes animus against a politically unpopular group. Under these circumstances, statutes have consistently failed rational basis review. Summarizing these cases, Justice O'Connor observed in her concurrence in *Lawrence* that

> laws such as economic or tax legislation that are scrutinized under rational basis review normally pass constitutional muster, since the Constitution presumes that even improvident decisions will eventually be rectified by the democratic processes. We have consistently held, however, that some objectives, such as a bare ... desire to harm a politically unpopular group, are not legitimate state interests. When a law exhibits such a desire to harm a politically unpopular group, we have applied a more searching form of rational basis review to strike down such laws under the Equal Protection Clause.

Lawrence, 123 S.Ct. at 2484–85 (O'Connor, J., concurring). Justice O'Connor went on to explain how this principle has been applied by the Court in prior equal protection cases. [Justice O'Connor gave as examples of more searching review *Moreno*, *Cleburne*, *Eisenstadt v. Baird*, and *Romer v. Evans*.]

All four of these precedents involved legislation targeting politically unpopular groups to varying degrees: "hippies" (*Moreno*), unmarried users of birth control (*Eisenstadt*), the mentally disabled (*Cleburne*), and homosexuals (*Romer*). Moreover, in each case, the Court invalidated a law that had the effect of inhibiting personal relationships of one sort or another: among mentally disabled or unrelated persons who wished to share a common living space (*Cleburne* and *Moreno*); among unmarried individuals who wished to engage in intimate relations (*Eisenstadt*); and among individuals who wished to live without fear of state-sanctioned discrimination prompted solely by their attachment to persons of the same sex (*Romer*).

* * *

* * * Florida prohibits homosexuals from being considered as adoptive parents because it wishes to place children with married couples. It wishes to do so for two alleged reasons: (1) to provide "stability" in the home, which the panel apparently believes can only be provided by married couples representing the "nuclear" family model; and (2) to properly shape heterosexual "sexual and gender identity," which the panel asserts should be accomplished by married couples.

Like the proffered reasons in *Eisenstadt*, which were "so riddled with exceptions" that the state's asserted goal could not "reasonably be regarded as its aim," the state's proffered rational basis for the statute here (providing adopted children with married couples as parents) cannot be legitimately credited because it fails the equal protection requirement that "all persons similarly situated should be treated alike." *Cleburne*. As noted at the beginning of this dissent, it is plainly false that Florida has established a preference for "married mothers and fathers" as adoptive parents. The 1977 statute prohibiting homosexual adoption expresses no preference whatsoever for married couples, expressly permitting an "unmarried adult" to adopt. Moreover, the DCF administrative regulations that are inextricably tied to Florida's adoption statutes do not prefer married over single candidates for adoption. In short, the Florida legislature never did, and the Florida executive no longer does, express a preference for married over unmarried couples or singles in the area of adoption. The fact that Florida places children for adoption with single parents directly and explicitly contradicts Florida's post hoc assertion that the ban is justified by the state's wish to place children for adoption only with "families with married mothers and fathers." This contradiction alone is enough to prove that the state's alleged reasons are "illogical to the point of irrationality." *Eisenstadt*.

However, instead of acknowledging this glaring gap between the ban on homosexual adoption and the state's purported justification, as did the Supreme Court in invalidating the statutes in *Eisenstadt*, *Moreno*, *Cleburne*, and *Romer*, the *Lofton* panel stretches mightily to construct a hypothetical to bridge this gap. "It is not irrational," the panel opines, "to think that heterosexual singles have a markedly greater probability of eventually establishing a married household and, thus, providing their adopted children with a stable, dual-gender parenting environment." The panel's contrived hypothetical offering blatantly ignores not only the absence of any preference in Florida's statute for married couples but also the realities of the adoption process. Evaluations of prospective parents are based on present, not "eventual," status and conditions.

In addition to its failure to meaningfully distinguish homosexuals from single heterosexuals, the panel never explains why it is rational to believe that homosexuals, as a class, are unable to provide stable homes and appropriate role models for children. With respect to the first of these arguments, there is absolutely no record evidence to show that homosexuals are incapable of providing the permanent family life sought by Florida. To the contrary, as the facts in this case suggest, many children throughout the country are lovingly and successfully cared for by homosexuals in their capacity as biological parents, foster parents, or legal guardians. Furthermore, it is not marriage that guarantees a stable, caring environment for children but the character of the individual caregiver. Indeed, given the reality of foster care in Florida, the statute actually operates to impede, rather than promote, the placement of a child into a permanent family. Florida's statute expresses a clear intent "to protect and promote the well-being of persons being adopted ... and to provide to all children who can benefit by it a permanent family life." Yet, Florida's foster care system has a backlog of more than 3,400 children in it, far more than the number of married couples eligible to adopt. Given this backlog, the state's ban on gay adoption does nothing to increase the number of children being adopted, whether by married couples or anyone else. The state is evidently willing to allow children to live with the potential uncertainties of several foster-care placements rather than enjoy the security and certainty of an adoptive home with one or two caring parents who are also homosexual. * * *

Nor does the panel offer a reason for why it is rational to credit the state's second argument: that homosexuals are incapable of providing good role models. The panel claims that "[heterosexual] children will need education and guidance after puberty concerning relationships with the opposite sex.... It is in the best interests of a child if his or her parents can personally relate to the child's problems and assist the child in the difficult transition to heterosexual adulthood." Is the panel suggesting that heterosexual parents are necessary in order to tell children about their own dating experiences after puberty? For anyone who has been a parent, this will no doubt seem a very strange, even faintly comical, claim. There is certainly no evidence that the ability to share one's adolescent dating experiences (or lack thereof) is an important, much less essential, facet of parenting. The difficult transition to adulthood is a common human experience, not an experience unique to human beings of a particular race, gender, or sexual orientation. It is downright silly to argue that parents must have experienced everything that a child will experience in order to guide them. Indeed, that will generally not be the case. For example, immigrant parents help their children adjust to a world and culture they have not known. It cannot be suggested that such individuals are unfit to parent any more than it could be suggested that a mother is unfit to parent a son or that a white person is unfit to parent an African–American child.

Furthermore, the panel's argument completely neglects to consider the situation of gay children of heterosexual parents. Children simply need parents who will love and support them. * * *

* * * Here, irrational prejudice can be inferred as the basis for this classification because there is no difference in relevant respects between single heterosexual persons and single homosexual persons with reference to the state's purported justification for the ban in the statute. Moreover, when all the proffered rationales for a law are clearly and manifestly implausible, a reviewing court may infer that animus is the only explicable basis. *Romer*. Since Florida's rationale is not plausible given that single persons may adopt, the inference is obvious that Florida's decision to single out homosexuals is based solely on anti-gay animus. Unsurprisingly, animus is just what the legislative history of Florida's ban confirms.

The Florida statute was enacted after an organized and relentless anti-homosexual campaign led by Anita Bryant, a pop singer who sought to repeal a January 1977 ordinance of the Dade County Metropolitan Commission prohibiting discrimination against homosexuals in the areas of housing, public accommodations, and employment. Bryant organized a drive that collected the 10,000 signatures needed to force a public referendum on the ordinance. In the course of her campaign, which the Miami Herald described as creating a "witch-hunting hysteria more appropriate to the 17th century than the 20th," Bryant referred to homosexuals as "human garbage." * * *

In response to Bryant's efforts, Senator Curtis Peterson introduced legislation in the Florida Senate banning both adoptions by and marriage between homosexuals. The legislative history reveals the very close and utterly transparent connection between Bryant's campaign and the Peterson bills. At the May 3, 1977 hearings of the Senate Judiciary Civil Committee, for example, Senator Peterson observed that "it is a possible problem, constantly in the news." Senator George Firestone commented that "this [gay rights controversy] has totally polarized [my] community unnecessarily." And Senator Don Chamberlin explicitly tied the Bryant campaign to the proposed ban on homosexual adoption, arguing that the latter would never have arisen without the ruckus over the Dade County anti-discrimination ordinance. The impetus for Florida's adoption ban exactly parallels the impetus for the state constitutional amendment struck down in *Romer*. * * *

As the House and Senate gave their final approval to the Peterson bills on May 31, Senator Peterson stated that his bills were a message to homosexuals that "we're really tired of you. We wish you would go back into the closet." On June 8, 1977, exactly one day after Dade County voters repealed the anti-discrimination ordinance, the Governor of Florida signed the Peterson bills into law, in what can only be seen as a deliberate acknowledgment of the orchestration between Bryant's campaign and the legislature's actions. In short, the legislative history shows that anti-gay animus was the major factor–indeed the sole factor–behind the law's promulgation, thereby confirming that the standard of review in this case is controlled by *Eisenstadt*, *Cleburne*, *Romer*, and *Moreno*. * * *

Whereas the Texas sodomy statute struck down in *Lawrence* treated homosexuals as criminals, Florida's ban on gay adoption treats criminals with more dignity than homosexuals. Nothing more clearly raises the "inevitable inference that the disadvantage imposed is born of animosity toward the class of persons affected," *Romer*, than this disparity of treatment.

[*Burden on Due Process Right of Sexual Intimacy*] *Lawrence* held that consenting adults have a right under the Due Process Clause to engage in private sexual conduct, including homosexual conduct. Because Florida's law punishes the exercise of this right by denying all active homosexuals the ability to be considered as adoptive parents, we are required to subject Florida's law to heightened scrutiny—not the cursory, attempted rational-basis analysis the panel employs. In addition to its failure to apply heightened scrutiny, the panel makes further errors of law in attempting to evade the application of *Lawrence*. It makes erroneous statements about the proper use of history and tradition in a substantive due process analysis, and mistakenly claims that *Lawrence* does not apply here because adoption is a privilege and not a right, and because Florida's statute is a civil rather than criminal law. These reasons are not only unsupported by, but are directly contrary to, Supreme Court precedent.

[Judge Barkett argued that, by overruling *Bowers* and extending *Griswold*'s privacy right to consensual sodomy, *Lawrence* necessarily recognized a fundamental right to engage in private homosexual intimacy. Florida is penalizing Lofton and Croteau for exercising their fundamental right, a burden which must be justified by a compelling state interest, and not just the rational basis found by the panel.]

■ BIRCH, J., specially concurring in the denial of rehearing en banc

* * * The real point of disagreement between the *Lofton* panel and the dissent is whether rational-basis review should always uphold a law as long as there exists some "conceivable" rational basis—or whether there are certain instances that call for a "more searching" form of rational-basis review that examines the actual motivations underlying the law. Accordingly, I offer the counter-argument to the dissent's "heightened rational-basis review" theory.

Aside from Justice O'Connor's *Lawrence* concurrence, I have found in the Supreme Court's language no explicit support for the theory that rational-basis review should examine the actual motivation behind legislation (assuming that such a thing can be divined with any accuracy). I also note the Supreme Court's own observation that "it is entirely irrelevant for constitutional purposes whether the conceived reason for the challenged distinction actually motivated the legislature." *F.C.C. v. Beach Communications, Inc.*, 508 U.S. 307, 315 (1993). * * *

The *Romer* Court found Colorado's Amendment 2—a "sweeping and comprehensive" measure that imposed a "broad and undifferentiated disability'' on the state's homosexual residents—to be ''inexplicable by any-thing but animus'' because the breadth of the Amendment so exceeded its proffered rationales. As I understand it, the fatal defect in Amendment 2 was not that the Court determined that *actual* animus motivated passage of the Amendment. Indeed, in contrast to the dissent's scrutiny of the legislative history of the Florida statute, the *Romer* Court never examined the actual history of the plebiscite vote that led to passage of Amendment 2, nor the accompanying campaign rhetoric or the ''intent'' of the elector-ate. Instead, the Court found the proffered rationales so implausible that the Court *inferred* that animus was the only conceivable (as opposed to actual) rationale. * * *

[Judge Birch noted that the Supreme Court itself read *Cleburne* more narrowly than Judge Barkett did. In *Board of Trustees of the Univ. of Alabama v. Garrett*, 531 U.S. 356, 367 (2001),

> Justice Breyer [in dissent] suggests that *Cleburne* stands for the broad proposition that state decisionmaking reflecting ''negative attitudes'' or ''fear'' necessarily runs afoul of the Fourteenth Amendment. Al-though such biases may often accompany irrational (and therefore unconstitutional) discrimination, their presence alone does not a con-stitutional violation make. As we noted in *Cleburne*: ''Mere negative attitudes, or fear, *unsubstantiated by factors which are properly cogni-zable* in a zoning proceeding, are not permissible bases for treating a home for the mentally retarded differently....'']

[Likewise, Judge Birch maintained that the Supreme Court itself announced no fundamental right in *Lawrence*.] An important point bears noting here. To say that *Lawrence* overruled *Bowers* is not to say that every question *Bowers* answered in the negative should now be answered in the affirmative (or vice versa). For example, although the *Lawrence* Court specifically noted that *Bowers* misframed the issue as one of whether there is a right to engage in sodomy, the Court never identified how *Bowers* should in fact have framed the inquiry—much less what the precise answer to that inquiry should have been. We see this pattern throughout the *Lawrence* opinion. * * *

The dissent translates [*Lawrence*'s] general references to ''liberty'' under the Due Process Clause into a specific due process right to engage in private sexual conduct. The dissent appears to be: (multiple references to Due Process liberty) + (decision finding Texas sodomy statute unconstitu-tional) = (holding that there is a substantive due process right to sexual intimacy). But even if I were persuaded that *Lawrence* announced, or ''reaffirmed,'' a substantive due process right to sexual intimacy, I still am not convinced that burdens on this right necessarily would require strict scrutiny. First, as the *Lofton* panel observed, the *Lawrence* Court itself never applied, nor used any of the language of, strict scrutiny. Second, with all due respect, as cryptic as some of the Supreme Court's substantive due process precedents are, my recent review of them convinces me of this much: the mere presence of a substantive liberty interest does not automat-ically trigger strict scrutiny, as the dissent seems to suggest. [E.g., *City of Chicago v. Morales*, 527 U.S. 41 (1999).] * * *

I will conclude on a purely personal note. If I were a legislator, rather than a judge, I would vote in favor of considering otherwise eligible homosexuals for adoptive parenthood. In reviewing the record in this case one can only be impressed by the courage, tenacity and devotion of Messrs. Lofton [et al.] for the children placed in their care. For these children, these men are the only parents they have ever known. Thus, I consider the policy decision of the Florida legislature to be misguided and trust that over time attitudes will change and it will see the best interest of these children in a different light. Nevertheless, as compelling as this perspective is to me, I will not allow my personal views to conflict with my judicial duty— conduct that apparently fewer and fewer citizens, commentators and Senators seem to understand or appreciate. And, I hasten to add, the vast majority of federal judges, including each and every judge of the Eleventh Circuit, are similarly sensitive to separate their personal preferences from their duty to follow precedent as they understand it.

NOTE ON THE FLORIDA ADOPTION CASE

Lofton requires the judge (and the student) to figure out how the holdings of *Romer* (on the equal protection issue) and *Lawrence* (on the substantive due process issue) should apply to a statutory policy excluding all practicing lesbians, gay men, and bisexuals from adopting children in Florida. Because both Supreme Court decisions can be read narrowly (as Birch does) or broadly (as Barkett does), the key inquiry becomes: How broadly *should* we read *Romer* or *Lawrence*?

Arguments for Reading the Precedents Broadly include: (1) The Florida statute has the same outlier look as the Colorado initiative. No other state (as of 2005) has such a broad exclusion. (2) The Bryant "Save Our Children" campaign demonized homosexuals as disgusting and subhuman, and it was the backdrop of the statute. Can that be entirely ignored? Isn't this the kind of prejudice-based discourse the Court ought to be discouraging? (3) *Romer/Lawrence* end the regime where homosexuals were second-class citizens. The Florida statute is a result of the old regime's ideology. Jettison it for the same reasons important race-and sex-discriminations were swept away after *Brown* and *Craig*.

Arguments for Reading the Precedents Narrowly include: (1) The new norm to replace *Bowers* might be, tolerate homosexuality and don't make sodomy a crime, but the state still has a lot of room to promote and encourage heterosexuality. The adoption law is an example. (2) Adoption is a special creature of the state, and not some fundamental right, so the state ought to have leeway in defining its nature and terms. (3) A lower court should not make the move Barkett advocates; the Supreme Court is better situated to accomplish such a norm shift, but should not do so immediately. Let the issue percolate for a while. If other states do not follow Florida, then perhaps the Court should settle the issue for challenges like *Lofton*.

After the opinions that you have just read, the plaintiffs sought further review in the Supreme Court, but it denied certiorari. 125 S.Ct. 869 (2005). (Denial of certiorari is not considered to be precedent as to the merits of a case.)

PRIVACY AFTER LAWRENCE: A LIBERTY INTEREST IN ALL PRIVATE CONSENSUAL SEX?

Justice Scalia predicted that *Lawrence* is the end of morals regulation. *Lawrence* does not purport to decide the constitutionality of other laws regulating morals, but lower courts will now have to adjudicate such challenges, if only because the dissenting opinion will inspire lawyers to bring them. The most obvious criterion for evaluating morals laws is the Mill–Hart-*Wolfenden Report* inquiry: Does this private conduct harm third parties? (Does *Lawrence* essentially leave us with Mill's criterion?) We now consider three issues which the Supreme Court in *Lawrence* explicitly declared that it was not deciding: sex between underage minors; adultery; and prostitution.

PART A.   ADOLESCENT SEXUALITY

Kansas v. Matthew Limon, 83 P.3d 229 (Kan. App. 2004), reversed, ___ P.3d ___ (Kan. 2005). Kansas' sodomy law forbids anyone from having oral or anal sex with a minor who is 14 to 16 years old, but it also has a "Romeo and Juliet" exception that covers punishment. The exception applies if the defendant is less than 19 years old, the age difference is less than four years, and the teenagers are of the "opposite sex." Matthew Limon (18 years old) performed oral sex on M.A.R. (15 year-old male) in a residential school for developmentally disabled youth. The state stipulated that the oral sex was consensual, but refused Limon the benefit of the "Romeo and Juliet" penalties, because the partners were of the same sex. Limon was sentenced to 206 months (over 17 years) in prison; had the other participant been female instead of male, he would have been sentenced to approximately 17 *months* imprisonment.

On appeal, the Supreme Court vacated this decision and remanded the case for the court to reconsider after *Lawrence*. See *Limon v. Kansas*, 539 U.S. 955 (2003). On remand from the Supreme Court, the Kansas Court of Appeals reaffirmed the limitation of the Romeo and Juliet exception to different-sex couples, and therefore reaffirmed Limon's seventeen-year sentence. Each of the three judges wrote an opinion.

The opinion of the Court was delivered by **Judge Green**, who found *Lawrence* easily distinguishable on the grounds that it neither involved sex involving minors nor ruled on the equal protection grounds required in the Limon appeal. Judge Green found a number of plausible reasons why the Kansas Legislature would have crafted the Romeo and Juliet exception to apply only to different-sex teenage couples.

One justification was "to encourage and preserve the traditional sexual mores of society. [T]raditional sexual mores have played a significant role in the sexual development of children. During early adolescence, children are in the process of trying to figure out who they are. A part of that process is learning and developing their sexual identity. As a result, the legislature could well have concluded that homosexual sodomy between children and young adults deviates from the traditional sexual mores of society and the historical sexual development of children."

A second justification was the following: "When a child is born from a relationship between a minor and a young adult, the minor is often unable to financially support the newborn child. In many cases, the minor is still a dependent. As a result, the financial burden to support the newborn child properly falls to the young adult. Obviously, the young adult cannot furnish adequate financial support for the newborn child while he or she is incarcerated. The legislature could well have concluded that incarcerating the young adult parent for a long period would be counterproductive to the requirement that a parent has a duty to provide support to his or her minor child. On the other hand, same-sex relationships do not generally lead to unwanted pregnancies. As a result, the need to release the same-sex offender from incarceration is absent. Equal protection is satisfied because [the discriminatory classification] is rationally related to the State's legitimate interest in getting a young adult parent involved in providing financial support for the newborn child."

Judge Green's third justification was the only one that seemed to command a majority of the Court, however. Concurring (essentially) in the judgment, **Judge Malone** agreed that *Lawrence* did not resolve the case but disagreed with the foregoing justifications for the different treatment. He did agree with a third justification suggested by Judge Green. In Judge Malone's words: "As the majority opinion suggests, at this age a child's sexual orientation is more than likely not fully developed. Adolescents are at a higher risk for acquiring sexually transmitted diseases than adults. All sexual activity imposes health risks. However, as the majority opinion points out, there are certain health risks more generally associated with homosexual activity than with heterosexual activity, especially among males. This does not mean that all homosexual activity between males results in sexually transmitted disease, but the risk appears to be increased. Admittedly female-with-female sex has a lower potential for spreading sexually transmitted disease. However, a legislative classification not involving fundamental rights is not required to be drawn with precision. Furthermore, excluding from [the exception] only same sex activity between males *would* involve gender discrimination which presumably the legislature should try to avoid."

Presiding Judge Pierron, the author of the original panel opinion, changed his mind on remand. Judge Pierron dismissed the state justifications that the discrimination is inspired by state policy promoting marriage and procreation and trained on the justification accepted by Judge Malone (as well as Judge Green). "One must first note the obvious fact that there is no difference in the penalties imposed under the Kansas law based on whether the defendant actually does or does not have a venereal disease. This is a very important omission if the law was truly concerned about venereal disease. Perhaps even more unusual is that under the law a female infected with every venereal disease yet identified, and engaging in acts quite likely to infect or actually infecting a male minor, will receive a much lighter sentence. A disease-free male engaging in sex with another male in a manner not likely to spread disease if it was present will receive a much heavier sentence. Perversely, under the law, a male with a venereal disease who infects and impregnates an underage female will also receive a much lighter sentence. We must also recognize the inapplicability of much of this rationale as it applies to female-with-female sex, which usually has an extremely low potential for spreading venereal disease but receives the higher penalty.

"The State and the majority attempt to draw a nexus by pointing to the higher incidence of AIDS among homosexuals than the population in general. However, no attempt is made to draw a connection between punishing any particular individual and the likelihood of that person spreading a disease. Group guilt is not a favored concept in American law. What is the rationality of a law that would punish persons 15 times longer because they may belong to a group that has a higher incidence of AIDS, notwithstanding the fact that there is no evidence the defendant had AIDS or any other disease? This is especially puzzling when, as noted above, a person who actually has AIDS and engages in sex with a minor will receive a much lighter sentence if the defendant is of the opposite sex from the minor."

Judge Pierron concluded his dissent: "Carved in stone above the pillars in front of the United States Supreme Court building are the words 'Equal Justice Under Law.' In bronze letters on the north interior wall of the Kansas Judicial Center we read 'Within These Walls The Balance Of Justice Weighs Equal.' There are reasons why we remind ourselves so graphically of the importance of equal justice. Persons in power and authority have historically been tempted to discriminate against people they do not like or understand. If these personal and political dislikes become law and exceed the bounds of constitutionality, the courts have been given the duty to be the final protectors of our ideal of equality under the law. This blatantly discriminatory sentencing provision does not live up to American standards of equal justice."

NOTES ON THE "ROMEO AND ROMEO" CASE

Neither *Lawrence* nor even *Romer* seemed to play a meaningful role in the analysis of the Kansas Court of Appeals judges. What formal or legal bearing does *Lawrence* in fact have? The *Limon* appeal was premised upon an equal protection, not a privacy, argument. And the case involved minors, which decidedly made it different from *Lawrence*. How should the case be decided under the Supreme Court's precedents? (As this book went to final pages, the Kansas Supreme Court reversed. What reasons *should* have been pervasive?)

The *Limon* case illustrates the particular difficulties that LGBT teenagers face. How does the law treat sexual conduct between heterosexual teenagers? What kinds of direct and indirect penalties can you think of? Are they constitutionally suspect?

PART B.   ADULTERY

At the time *Lawrence* was decided, private acts of sexual intercourse between unmarried persons (fornication) were criminal in seven states; in seven other states, such acts were criminal when "open and notorious" or where the parties were cohabiting. In *In re J.M.*, 575 S.E.2d 441 (Ga. 2003), the Georgia Supreme Court found such conduct to be protected by the state constitution's right to privacy. As the Supreme Court found with regard to sodomy laws, there is a history of non-enforcement of fornication laws as to private, consensual conduct, at least in the last century. Most legal scholars believe that fornication laws are unconstitutional after *Lawrence*. Accord, *Martin v. Ziherl*, 607 S.E.2d 367 (Va. 2005).

But what about adultery laws, prohibiting private consensual sexual acts when one (or both) of the parties is married to someone else? The attorneys who argued for Lawrence and Garner before the Supreme Court carefully distinguished adultery, saying that the Court did not have to reach that question, and Justice Kennedy's reference to "abuse of an institution the law protects" may signal an willingness to permit anti-adultery laws. Are the considerations sufficiently different than what was before the Court in *Lawrence* to justify a different result? Consider whether the following case, decided before *Lawrence*, would come out differently today.

Lewell Marcum v. James McWhorter

U.S. Court of Appeals, Sixth Circuit, 2002.
308 F.3d 635.

■ SILER, CIRCUIT JUDGE.

Plaintiff Lewell Marcum filed this 42 U.S.C. § 1983 action against the * * * Sheriff of Pulaski County, Kentucky, alleging that he was fired as a result of his intimate relationship and cohabitation with a married woman in violation of his right of association as guaranteed by the First and Fourteenth Amendments. * * *

The parties agree that the basic facts in this case concerning the relationship between Lewell Marcum and Rena Abbott are not in dispute. Marcum was hired as a Pulaski County deputy sheriff in February 1986. He separated from his wife on May 8, 1997. Prior to the separation, Marcum lived with his wife and their two children in the martial residence, except for two brief periods in 1996. His divorce was not final until March 11, 1999.

During the course of his work as a deputy sheriff, Marcum met Rena Abbott in 1994 or 1995. When the two met, Abbott was married and living with her husband and their children. From the initial meeting until their cohabitation, Marcum and Abbott were just "good friends" whose respective spouses and families were social acquaintances whose association was marked by family outings and get-togethers.

As an informant, Abbott frequently met with Marcum to discuss cases. At some point, at least by June 1996, their relationship had progressed sufficiently to attract the attention of Chief Deputy Swartz, who counseled Marcum about Abbott's visits to his office and the courthouse. The relationship had become the subject of rumors in and around both the sheriff's department and the courthouse. Additionally, Sheriff Catron received numerous complaints concerning Marcum's association with Abbott from employees within his department, as well as persons working at the courthouse and various citizens within the community.

The relationship reached a turning point in September 1997. While on duty on September 4, Marcum informed Abbott that her husband was making passes at her best friend. Abbott asked Marcum to go with her to confront the woman, which he agreed to do. After receiving confirmation of Marcum's information, Abbott moved out of the marital residence * * * The two then rented a townhouse and began living together on September 9 or 10. * * *

Regardless of their relationship prior to their cohabitation, it is undisputed that Marcum and Abbott were romantically involved during the time they lived together and certainly at the time of Marcum's dismissal. After learning of this living arrangement, Sheriff Catron told Marcum that either he or Abbott would have to move out. Marcum was discharged on September 19, 1997, upon his perceived failure to comply with Catron's directive. * * *

Marcum maintains that his exclusive, romantic and sexually intimate relationship and cohabitation with a married woman is entitled to protection under the constitutional right of association and, as a result, the Sheriff could not legally fire him for such behavior. He argues that the district court erroneously dismissed his claim by categorically denying constitutional protection based on its labeling his relationship "adulterous," offending the spirit of the Constitution and ignoring the factors and analysis set forth by the United States Supreme Court.

* * * [In *Roberts v. United States Jaycees,* 468 U.S. 609 (1984),] the Court has recognized a certain right of intimate association reasoning that

* * * it "must afford the formation and preservation of certain kinds of highly personal relationships a substantial measure of sanctuary from unjustified interference by the State." Without precisely defining every consideration underlying this type of constitutional protection, the Court noted that "certain kinds of personal bonds have played a critical role in the culture and traditions of the Nation by cultivating and transmitting shared ideals and beliefs." The personal affiliations that exemplify the considerations that warrant constitutional protection and suggest limitations on the relationships that might be entitled to constitutional shelter "are those that attend the creation and sustenance of a family," which "are distinguished by such attributes as relative smallness, a high degree of selectivity in decisions to begin and maintain the affiliation, and seclusion from others in critical aspects of the relationship."

To determine the limits of state authority over an individual's freedom to enter into a particular association, it is the task of the court to engage in "a careful assessment of where that relationship's objective characteristics locate it on a spectrum from the most intimate to the most attenuated of personal attachments," taking into consideration factors that may include "size, purpose, policies, selectivity, congeniality, and other characteristics" that may be pertinent. [*Board of Directors of Rotary Int'l v. Rotary Club of Duarte*, 481 U.S. 537 (1987)] added that while the exact boundaries of this type of constitutional protection were not marked, it is not restricted to relationships among family members. The Court emphasized that protection is afforded to those relationships that "presuppose deep attachments and commitments to the necessarily few other individuals with whom one shares not only a special community of thoughts, experiences, and beliefs but also distinctively personal aspects of one's life."

Marcum argues that the district court failed to assess the attributes and qualities of the relationship between him and Abbott. Instead, he contends that the court ignored the factors and analysis set forth in *Roberts* and *Rotary,* and focused exclusively on whether the relationship attends the creation or sustenance of a family. Marcum correctly points out that * * * constitutional protection is not limited to family relationships. The district court, however, noted that relationships afforded this type of constitutional protection are not restricted to those between family members. Moreover, the district court acknowledged the appropriate analysis set forth in *Roberts* and *Rotary* and examined the objective characteristics of the relationship between Marcum and Abbott. While there are relationships other than those between family members that may be afforded constitutional protection, it does not follow that *any* relationship that could be objectively qualified as "intimate" should be protected.

Looking at the factors enunciated in *Roberts,* and *Rotary,* Marcum contends that the court failed to recognize that the association was relatively small—just the two of them; highly selective in the decision to begin and maintain the affiliation; and others were secluded from the relationship. Based on these objective characteristics and the fact that he and Abbott shared thoughts, experiences and personal aspects of their lives, Marcum argues that the relationship is constitutionally protected under the right of intimate association. Although these factors may weigh in favor of a finding of a protected relationship, we find that the adulterous nature of the relationship does not portray a relationship of the most intimate variety afforded protection under the Constitution.

Marcum claims that the district court erred in finding that the adulterous nature of the relationship in question automatically barred constitutional protection. We disagree. * * * The Supreme Court has set forth factors which may be used in determining whether a particular relationship is constitutionally protected. These factors include: "size, purpose, policies, selectivity, congeniality, and other characteristics that in a particular case may be pertinent." The adulterous nature of the relationship between Marcum and Abbott is an objective characteristic that is pertinent to this case and we find that the district court correctly considered it in determining whether the relationship was constitutionally protected. * * *

Bowers [*v. Hardwick*] is factually analogous to this case in that it evaluates a consensual sexual relationship between two adults and it provides an expansion on the analysis set forth in *Roberts* and *Rotary* for cases dealing with private, sexual relationships. Much like sodomy, proscriptions against adultery have ancient roots. Adultery, though not a crime at English common law, was punishable under the canon law, which was administered by the ecclesiastical courts of England. *See United States v. Clapox*, 35 F. 575, 578 (D.Or.1888); 2 Charles E. Torcia, Wharton's Criminal Law § 210 (15th ed.1994). The common law, brought to this country by the American colonists, did not punish adultery unless the conduct was "open and notorious" as to amount to a "public nuisance," as defined by the English canon law. *See Cole v. State,* 126 Md. 239, 94 A. 913, 914 (1915); Torcia, *supra.* The Puritans, however, made adultery with a married woman a capital offense and from this Puritan legacy sprung state laws criminalizing adultery. *See* Jeremy D. Weinstein, Note, *Adultery, Law, and the State: A History,* 38 Hastings L.J. 195, 225–26 (1986). Even today, there are jurisdictions which continue to outlaw extramarital acts. * * * Based on the historical treatment of adultery, a right to engage in an intimate sexual relationship with the spouse of another cannot be said to be either deeply rooted in this Nation's history and tradition or implicit in the concept of ordered liberty. Thus, following the Supreme Court's decision in *Bowers,* we decline to accord Marcum's adulterous relationship the constitutional protection afforded those intimate associations which receive protection as a fundamental element of personal liberty.

Relying on both the language and spirit of *Bowers,* the court in *Mercure v. Van Buren Township,* 81 F.Supp.2d 814 (E.D.Mich.2000), held that the constitutional protections of the First and Fourteenth Amendments, embodied in the right of intimate association, did not extend to a police officer's adulterous relationship with the wife of a fellow officer; thus, there was no liability under 42 U.S.C. § 1983 for his discharge. The district court found *Mercure* to be "both informative and persuasive albeit not binding precedent." Marcum argues that in *Mercure* the officer's relationship with the wife of a fellow officer distinguishes it from the present case. Additionally, he seeks to distinguish *Mercure* based on the fact that the court discussed that Michigan law makes adultery a felony, whereas it is no longer illegal in Kentucky.

As discussed by the district court, Marcum's efforts to distinguish *Mercure* do not succeed. The fact that the plaintiff's relationship in *Mercure* was with the wife of a fellow officer is insufficient to render the court's reasoning inapplicable here; the *Mercure* court did not base its decision on the identity of the parties. Furthermore, * * * the fact that adultery is legal in Kentucky does not automatically create constitutional protection, nor does it change the fact that historically adultery has been considered a crime in many states, including Kentucky. We agree with the *Mercure* court's conclusion that "adulterous conduct is the very antithesis of marriage and family," and that such behavior cannot be compared to any of the "fundamental matters of personal choice that lie at the core of traditional notions of individual liberty."

Marcum has failed to suggest how his decision to enter into an intimate, sexual relationship and cohabitation with a married woman is a fundamental right deeply rooted in the Nation's history and tradition or implicit in the concept of ordered liberty. Though perhaps unfair, his dismissal did not infringe his right of association as guaranteed by the First and Fourteenth Amendments. * * *

■ CLAY, CIRCUIT JUDGE, concurring.

* * * Broadly construed, [the majority opinion's] holding appears to indicate that regardless of any other factors that might be considered in assessing whether a relationship should be afforded constitutional protection, the only relevant factor in determining whether a relationship should be afforded constitutional protection, in a case like the present, is whether the relationship can be deemed adulterous. I believe that while relevant in making such a determination, the adulterous nature of the relationship alone should not be dispositive. Indeed, precedent from this circuit demonstrates as much.

In *Briggs v. N. Muskegon Police Dep't,* 563 F.Supp. 585 (W.D.Mich. 1983), *aff'd mem.,* 746 F.2d 1475 (6th Cir.1984), *cert denied,* 473 U.S. 909 (1985), the district court, after a bench trial, found that defendants violated a plaintiff's constitutional right to privacy by terminating and refusing to reinstate him as a police officer for his cohabitation with a woman while they were both married to other people. The plaintiff contended that the defendants' acts had intruded on his constitutionally guaranteed rights of privacy and association, and the district court agreed.

Although *Briggs* has no precedential value because this Court issued no published opinion, we nevertheless affirmed the judgment of the district court, which found that the adulterous relationship involved in that case warranted constitutional protection. In the dissent from the denial of *certiorari* in *Briggs,* Justice White noted that the circuits were divided over whether extra-marital sexual activity, including adulterous activity, is constitutionally protected in a way that forbids public employers from disciplining employees who engage in such activity. *Briggs,* 473 U.S. at 910. (White, J. dissenting). Justice White would have granted *certiorari* inasmuch as the case would have given the Court an opportunity to consider "the contours of the right of privacy afforded individuals for sexual matters."

The majority opinion correctly notes that the Supreme Court has not restricted the constitutional right of intimate association to relationships among family members. Further, the Supreme Court has rejected the argument that although public employment may be denied altogether, such employment may be subject to any condition at all no matter how unreasonable. *See, e.g., Pickering v. Bd. of Educ. of Township High School Dist.,* 391 U.S. 563, 568 (1968). For a state to dismiss an individual solely because the relationship in which he or she is involved might be labeled adulterous, may be unreasonable under some circumstances. For instance, under the majority opinion's approach, even a long-term relationship in which the participants have resided together, raised children, and lived essentially as a married couple could be beyond the pale of constitutional protection where one or both individuals, for whatever reason, has never legally terminated a prior marriage, and hence could not remarry. This would hold true under the majority's reasoning despite the fact that such a relationship might certainly "presuppose deep attachments and commitments" in which the individuals "share[ ] not only a special community of thoughts, experiences, and beliefs but also distinctively personal aspects of [their lives]." *Roberts.* * * *

In any event, I agree with the majority opinion that Plaintiff fails to show that an assessment of the objective factors of his relationship places it at the end of the spectrum with those relationships that the Supreme Court has found warrant constitutional protection under the First Amendment's right of intimate association. Although Plaintiff's relationship with Rena Abbott involved only two individuals and was sexual in nature, the record does not support the finding that this relationship was entered into and maintained to form deep personal commitments and attachments. Rather, in assessing the relationship's purpose, not only were both Plaintiff and Abbott married to other people, but Abbott testified that the purpose of their moving in together was merely intended to be a "roommate type of arrangement." Further, Plaintiff cannot claim that others truly were excluded from the critical aspects of the relationship inasmuch as Abbott left the relationship and the residence she shared with Plaintiff within approximately one month so that she could reconcile with her own husband. Unlike the majority opinion, I believe that the short duration of the relationship factors into whether it should be afforded constitutional protection.

Plaintiff's relationship also differs markedly from the type of relationship at issue in *Briggs,* where this Court summarily affirmed the district court's finding that the plaintiff's discharge violated his rights to privacy and intimate association. Plaintiff cannot deny on this record that his relationship with Abbott became a public matter and was intertwined with and affected his job performance. Indeed, we have noted that "[t]he significance of *Briggs* lies in the fact that the officer in that case was dismissed solely because of his living status, without any reference as to how that status could have affected his performance as an officer." *Hughes [v. City of N. Olmsted,* 93 F.3d 238, 242 (6th Cir. 1996)]. Plaintiff met Abbott on the job, where she served as a confidential informant; he was reprimanded for the time he spent with her while on duty; and on at least one occasion shortly before his discharge had a public altercation with his adult daughter over the relationship at his workplace. * * *

The Supreme Court has held that there are limits on the types of relationships that might warrant constitutional protection. *Roberts*. Although such protection is extended beyond familial relationships, thus far the Court has nevertheless indicated that the relationships most likely to warrant such protection are those that involve *"deep attachments and commitments"* in which one shares, among other things, those "personal aspects of one's life." *Id*. Because I find that the objective factors that the Supreme Court has instructed courts to employ in determining whether relationships should be afforded constitutional protection weigh against finding Plaintiff's relationship warrants such protection in the instant case, I concur in the judgment of the Court.

NOTES ON THE LAW OF ADULTERY: FORMS OF INDIRECT REGULATION

1. *Employment Law*. Like consensual sodomy and fornication, there have been few if any prosecutions for private consensual adultery in the last fifty years (except where both rape and one of the consensual crimes were both alleged, with the latter being a lesser included offense of the former). However, a series of courts have rejected privacy-based challenges to the firing of employees who engaged in private, off-duty, consensual sexual relations with the spouse of another employee. In addition to the cases cited in *Marcum v. McWhorter*, see, *e.g.*, *Oliverson v. West Valley City*, 875 F.Supp. 1465 (D. Utah 1995); *City of Sherman v. Henry*, 928 S.W.2d 464 (Tex. 1996). In many respects, these decisions parallel the treatment of adultery by the military, where courts have upheld the power of the armed services to discharge an officer for committing adultery, based on the provision of the Uniform Code of Military Justice that prohibits "conduct unbecoming an officer." See, *e.g.*, *United States v. Kroop,* 38 M.J.470 (C.M.A. 1993); *United States v. Frazier,* 34 M.J.194 (C.M.A. 1992). Do you agree that adultery should constitute grounds for firing? Should the distinction rejected by the Sixth Circuit in *Marcum*–whether the other person was the spouse of a co-worker–matter? Can *Marcum* survive *Lawrence*?

2. *Personal Injury Law*. The two common law torts of alienation of affection and criminal conversation form tort law analogs to the crime of adultery. What is the difference between the two? In *Norton*, the court draws a careful distinction between the two, abolishing one but not the other (although Justice Howe wanted to keep both and Justice Durham would have discarded both). Most states which have invalidated one have also invalidated the other, *e.g.*, *Helsel v. Noellsch*, 107 S.W.3d 231 (Mo. 2003). Do these torts work to achieve their purpose, *i.e.*, providing economic incentives for behavior that the society wants to encourage? Even if the incentives work, *should* law be used to incentivize either certain behavior during marriage or marriage preservation?

3. *Family Law.* One court, in a decision abolishing the tort of criminal conversation, noted that "[t]o the extent that laws can discourage adultery, there are other disincentives. Adultery * * * is a ground for dissolution [divorce]. * * * [A]dultery may result in a smaller split of property after a dissolution. Finally, adultery can bar a spouse from certain inheritance rights." *Thomas v. Siddiqui*, 869 S.W.2d 740, 742 (Mo. 1994) (*en banc*). The modern trend, together with no-fault divorce grounds, is to diminish the use of adultery in the determination of matters related to property division or child custody and visitation. See, *e.g.*, *Warner v. Warner*, 807 A.2d 607 (Me. 2002); *Kenneth L.W. v. Tamyra S.W.*, 408 S.E.2d 625 (W.Va. 1991). In a number of states, however, divorce courts have the discretion to take adulterous behavior into account in deciding custody or equitable distribution of property. See, *e.g.*, *Mabus v. Mabus*, 890 So.2d 806 (Miss. 2003); *Shackelford v. Shackelford*, 571 S.E.2d 917 (Va. Ct. App. 2002). What policy concerns are raised by the use of family law to indirectly regulate sexual conduct? How would you compare use of the law in this area to the use of employment, tort or criminal law?

Part C.   Prostitution

In *Lawrence v. Texas*, the Supreme Court made clear that certain categories of sexual conduct remained subject to state intervention, among them "public conduct or prostitution." One of the complexities of this seemingly simple categorization is that it requires determining the criteria for the boundary between "private" and "public." For example, several of the defendants in the cases consolidated in *New York v. Onofre* (Chapter 2) were having sex in a car or truck parked in downtown Buffalo. Private or public?

How would you classify the following situations?

(a) *Soliciting in public for private sex.* Can states criminalize verbal solicitations, in public spaces, to engage in consensual, lawful sexual activity in private? See *Wasson* (Chapter 2, Section 2C) (solicitation from an automobile to an undercover police officer).

(b) *Consensual sex in a private location involving more than two persons.* Could the state have arrested Lawrence and Garner if a third party had joined them for sexual purposes? Cf. *Lovisi v. Slayton*, 539 F.2d 349 (4th Cir.) (en banc), *cert. denied sub nom. Lovisi v. Zahradnick*, 429 U.S. 977 (1976) (ruling that a married couple's right of privacy had been waived by their invitation to a third party to join them in a *ménage à trois*).

(c) *Sexual acts in a commercial space open to the public, but sequestered except for those who knowingly enter*. Can the state prohibit sex clubs? Membership-only sex clubs? Clubs or venues where sex is implicitly encouraged or tolerated? See *Commonwealth v. Bonadio*, 415 A.2d 47 (Pa. 1980) (prosecution of erotic dancers who performed sexual acts was unconstitutional as a morals regulation–a highly unusual decision). Are hotel rooms "private"? Does the kind of hotel matter? ("Any 'personal bonds' that are formed from the use of a motel room for fewer than 10 hours" are not entitled to constitutional protection. *FW/PBS, Inc. v. City of Dallas*, 493 U.S. 215 (1990)).

The authors of *The Wolfenden Report* (Chapter 2) called for longer sentences for public prostitution at the same time that they were recommending de-criminalization of sodomy by consenting adults in private. The public/private boundary reflected in *The Wolfenden Report* spoke to what many persons saw as the problem of prostitution. "[P]rostitution, like obscenity and like other sexual offenses, should be viewed as a nuisance offense whose gravamen is not the act itself, or even the accompanying commercial transaction, but rather its status as a public indecency." Herbert Packer, *The Limits of the Criminal Sanction* 330 (1968). Social conservatives rejected this view as inadequate, refusing to accept that the state cannot reach beyond the public sphere to enforce morality. Progressive Era reformers wanted to eliminate prostitution as they would a naturally-occurring disease, considering it a disease in the body politic. And feminists have been deeply split over how the state and the world of commercial sex should interact, arguing primarily over what would be best for the women involved.

Currently, one shift in the underlying social reality lies in its gender dynamics. Sex work is no longer performed exclusively by women selling sex to men. Increasingly, men also earn their living by engaging in some form of sex work. The term "prostitute" can no longer be assumed to describe only a woman. How should that affect the ways that we think about prostitution? Nonetheless, there are still very few women as purchasers, and almost no instances of women selling sex to other women. What does this unchanging aspect of prostitution signify? Lastly, it is unclear what the impact will be of technological innovations like the Internet, which has become a market where sexual acts are bought and sold. Will the same individual become both buyer and seller?

NOTE ON AMERICAN ANTI–PROSTITUTION CAMPAIGNS

Anti-prostitution campaigns were a staple of American politics from 1870 through World War I, at the municipal, state and federal levels.[a] One

a. Excellent histories of the regulation of prostitution include Vern Bullough, *The History of Prostitution* (1964); John Decker, *Prostitution: Regulation and Control* (1979); Richard Symanski, *The Immoral Landscape:* *Female Prostitution in Western Societies* (1981); Ruth Rosen, *The Lost Sisterhood: Prostitution in America, 1900–1918* (1982); Thomas Mackey, *Red Lights Out: A Legal History of Prostitution, Disorderly Houses,*

initial focal point was St. Louis, where the city adopted a regulatory rather than a criminal approach to prostitution in 1870, legalizing commercial sex by ordinance, licensing brothels for specified red light districts, and requiring periodic medical inspections of sex workers. The reaction was overwhelmingly hostile. A "purity movement" urged that prostitution be suppressed rather than regulated. Purity reformers, especially women, rejected the double standard by which men could sow "wild oats" and women were supposed to remain chaste; the existence of prostitution was a threat to wives, not a safety valve as some claimed. And, most important, some of the purity reformers felt that the prostitute herself was a threat to traditional gender values, for she was a woman not only sexualized but entrepreneurial and public about a matter that the American Victorians were fervently private.

Around the same time that the Comstock Act of 1873 was being adopted to censor sexual obscenity and contraception, American law rejected the St. Louis approach and turned on prostitutes with a vengeance. In cities as diverse as Richmond and San Francisco, Baltimore and New York, and even St. Louis (which abandoned its experiment), the police arrested hundreds of prostitutes a year, pursuant to municipal ordinances and state statutes banning disorderly houses, houses of ill fame, and immoral or lewd solicitation. Ordinances and statutes were adopted in the 1880s and 1890s that added new enforcement weapons under the aegis of "lewd vagrancy" (*e.g.*, California) and "disorderly conduct" (*e.g.*, New York City). Private groups, most prominently Anthony Comstock's Society for the Suppression of Vice, aggressively aided the police in the enforcement of anti-prostitution laws.

One major forum for prohibiting prostitution was immigration policy.[b] Initially, states containing ports of entry controlled immigration policy, which typically provided authority to exclude women on morality grounds. See *Chy Lung v. Freeman*, 92 U.S. 275 (1875) (striking down California's law requiring payment of bonds by immigrant Chinese women identified as "lewd and debauched" by a local official, as violating the Equal Protection Clause and inviting extortion). The Act of March 3, 1875, § 3, 18 Stat. 477, federalized immigration law and forbade the "importation into the United States of women for the purposes of prostitution." Immigration policy in general during this period was based on establishing and enforcing "quality" standards for persons seeking to enter the U.S., and immigration lawmaking became a venue for discourses of sexualized and racialized concepts of citizenship. The Supreme Court, in construing the federal statute, described prostitutes as living lives hostile to "the idea of the family, as

and Vice Districts, 1870–1917 (1987); David Pivar, *Purity Crusade: Sexual Morality and Social Control, 1868–1900* (1973); Leslie Fishbein, "Harlot or Heroine? Changing Views of Prostitution, 1870–1920," 43 *Historian* 28 (Nov. 1980).

b. For histories of prostitution and immigration, see Eithne Luibheid, *Entry De-* *nied: Controlling Sexuality at the Border* (2002); George Peffer, *If They Don't Bring Their Women Here: Chinese Female Immigration Before Exclusion* (1999); Ann Lucas, "Race, Class, Gender, and Deviancy: The Criminalization of Prostitution," 10 *Berkeley Women's L. J.* 47 (1995).

consisting in and springing from the union for life of one man and one woman in the holy estate of matrimony; the sure foundation of all that is stable and noble in our civilization, the best guaranty of that reverent morality which is the source of all beneficent progress in social and political improvement." *United States v. Bitty*, 208 U.S. 393, 401 (1908) (quoting *Murphy v. Ramsey*, 114 U.S. 15, 45 (1885)).

Another important part of the anti-prostitution campaign in law grew out of reaction to "white slavery," the term given to what was believed to be a widespread practice by which (white) women and girls were involuntarily or unknowingly impressed into a life of prostitution. A series of muckraking news reports of international conspiracies to lure young women into "white slavery" yielded a feverish campaign for new statutes starting in 1907.[c] Federal officials commissioned an investigation, which found that "[t]he vilest practices are brought here from continental Europe, and beyond doubt there has come from imported women and their men the most bestial refinements of depravity. The inclination of the continental races to look with toleration upon these evils is spreading in this country an influence perhaps even more far-reaching in its degradation than the physical effects which inevitably follow it." U. S. Senate, Committee on Immigration, *Importing Women for Immoral Purposes* 32 (1909).[d]

What emerged from Congress was the White Slave Traffic Act of 1910, 36 Stat. 825, codified at 18 U.S.C. § 2421, introduced by Representative James Mann. In response to charges that matters of morality should be left to the states, Rep. Mann asserted that "the white-slave traffic, while not so extensive, is much more horrible than any black-slave traffic ever was in the history of the world." 45 *Cong. Rec.* 548 (1910). Other speakers emphasized the same point. At least one, Representative Gordon Russell of Texas, went further, contrasting the supporters of the bill as "men who reverence womanhood and who set a priceless value upon female purity," with opponents, "who hate God and scoff at innocence and laugh at female virtue." *Id.* at 821.

President Taft signed the Mann Act into law June 25, 1910. Section 2 made it a federal crime to transport a woman or girl in interstate or foreign commerce "for the purpose of prostitution or debauchery, or for any other immoral purpose, or with the intent and purpose to induce, entice, or compel such woman or girl to become a prostitute or to give herself up to debauchery, or to engage in any other immoral practice." Section 3 prohib-

c. See generally, David Langum, *Crossing Over the Line: Legislating Morality and the Mann Act* (1994); James Morone, *Hellfire Nation: The Politics of Sin in American History* (2003).

d. Although the language is euphemistic, the phrase "vilest practices" most likely denotes sodomy, *i.e.*, oral and anal sex. The Commission repeatedly linked depraved conduct to "continental races". See comparison of French women and "Hebrews" as to their likelihood of becoming prostitutes before or after they arrived in the United States (64–65), and reference to "a typical Jew pimp" (73). Similar themes appeared in the popular press. A *McClure's* magazine article diagnosed the problem as young women who came to the United States from countries in eastern Europe, "the racial slum of Europe" (Morone 260).

ited any person from persuading or forcing, or assisting in either, a woman to travel in interstate or foreign commerce for the same prohibited purposes ("prostitution, debauchery or any other immoral purpose").

The question soon arose of whether the statute applied to interstate transportation of women for noncommercial but nonetheless "immoral" purposes. The decisive case involved two young Sacramento men from prominent families (Drew Caminetti, whose uncle had been Commissioner of Immigration, and Maury Diggs). Both were married when they became involved with Lola Norris (age 19) and Marsha Warrington (age 20), respectively. The affairs became public knowledge, and the men worried that they could be prosecuted for adultery, then a crime in California. The four slipped out of the city on the early morning train of March 10, 1913. The train arrived in Reno, Nevada later that morning, where the couples disembarked and set up housekeeping. Sacramento was ablaze with the scandal, and the men were indicted, and later convicted, for violating the Mann Act. The charge against them was transporting women for "immoral purposes," namely, adultery and fornication. Did their actions violate the Mann Act?

Drew Caminetti and Maury Diggs v. United States

United States Supreme Court, 1917.
242 U.S. 470, 37 S.Ct. 192, 61 L.Ed. 442.

■ Mr. Justice Day delivered the opinion of the Court. * * *

* * * There is no ambiguity in the terms of this act. It is specifically made an offense to knowingly transport or cause to be transported, etc., in interstate commerce, any woman or girl for the purpose of prostitution or debauchery, or for "any other immoral purpose," or with the intent and purpose to induce any such woman or girl to become a prostitute or to give herself up to debauchery, or to engage in any other immoral practice.

Statutory words are uniformly presumed, unless the contrary appears, to be used in their ordinary and usual sense, and with the meaning commonly attributed to them. To cause a woman or girl to be transported for the purposes of debauchery, and for an immoral purpose, to wit, becoming a concubine or mistress, * * * would seem by the very statement of the facts to embrace transportation for purposes denounced by the act, and therefore fairly within its meaning. * * *

In *United States v. Bitty*, 208 U. S. 393 [1908], it was held that the act of Congress against the importation of alien women and girls for the purpose of prostitution "and any other immoral purpose" included the importation of an alien woman to live in concubinage with the person importing her. In that case this court said:

> * * * [T]he addition [in the immigration statute] of the words, 'or for any other immoral purpose,' * * * show beyond question that Congress had in view the protection of society against another class of alien women other than those who might be brought here merely for

purposes of 'prostitution.' In forbidding the importation of alien women 'for any other immoral purpose,' * * * the immoral purpose charged in the indictment is of the same general class or kind as the one that controls in the importation of an alien woman for the purpose strictly of prostitution. The prostitute may, in the popular sense, be more degraded in character than the concubine, but the latter none the less must be held to lead an immoral life, if any regard whatever be had to the views that are almost universally held in this country as to the relations which may rightfully, from the standpoint of morality, exist between man and woman in the matter of sexual intercourse.

This definition of an immoral purpose was given prior to the enactment of the [Mann Act], and must be presumed to have been known to Congress when it enacted the law here involved. * * *

■ MR. JUSTICE MCKENNA, with whom concurred the CHIEF JUSTICE [WHITE] and MR. JUSTICE CLARKE, dissenting. * * *

* * * "Immoral" is a very comprehensive word. It means a dereliction of morals. In such sense it covers every form of vice, every form of conduct that is contrary to good order. It will hardly be contended that in this sweeping sense it is used in the statute. But, if not used in such sense, to what is it limited and by what limited? If it be admitted that it is limited at all, that ends the imperative effect assigned to it in the opinion of the court. But not insisting quite on that, we ask again, By what is it limited? By its context, necessarily, and the purpose of the statute.

For the context I must refer to the statute; of the purpose of the statute Congress itself has given us illumination. It devotes a section to the declaration that the "Act shall be known and referred to as the 'White-slave traffic Act.'" * * * [T]here is no uncertainty as to the conduct it describes. It is commercialized vice, immoralities having a mercenary purpose, and this is confirmed by other circumstances.

The author of the bill was Mr. Mann, and in reporting it from the House Committee on Interstate and Foreign Commerce he declared for the Committee that it was not the purpose of the bill to interfere with or usurp in any way the police power of the States, and further, that it was not the intention of the bill to regulate prostitution or the places where prostitution or immorality was practised, which were said to be matters wholly within the power of the States, and over which the federal government had no jurisdiction. And further explaining the bill, it was said that the sections of the act had been "so drawn that they are limited to the cases in which there is an act of transportation in interstate commerce of women for the purposes of prostitution." And again:

" * * * The legislation is needed to put a stop to a villainous interstate and international traffic in women and girls. The legislation is not needed or intended as an aid to the states in the exercise of their police powers in the suppression or regulation of immorality in general. It does not attempt to regulate the practice of voluntary prostitution, but aims solely to prevent panderers and procurers from compelling thousands of women and girls against their will and desire to enter and continue in a life of prostitution." House Report No. 47, 61st Cong., 2d sess., pp. 9, 10. * * *

This being the purpose, the words of the statute should be construed to execute it, and they may be so construed even if their literal meaning be otherwise.

NOTES ON THE EVOLUTION OF THE WHITE SLAVE TRAFFIC ACT

1. *The Broader Meaning of "Prostitution."* The dissent seeks to substitute a consent paradigm for a morality paradigm, arguing in part that it offers some limiting principle to "other immoral purposes" and that the for-commercial-reasons principle seems most consistent with the legislative history. The majority believe that their limiting principle, sexual looseness, is defensible. The point of Justice Day's opinion may have been that the Mann Act was aimed at precisely what occurred here: young women (minors) were being induced into a life of extramarital promiscuity. Do you suppose Representative Mann was surprised by the Court's decision? Dismayed? See Langum, *Crossing Over the Line* 119 (quoting letter where Mann professed to be delighted by the decision). See also *Cleveland v. United States*, 329 U.S. 14 (1946) (reaffirming *Caminetti*).

2. *Enforcement Practices Under the Mann Act.* Professor Langum's study of the Mann Act found that most of the Mann Act prosecutions between 1917 and 1928 were noncommercial fornication cases; lots of people, including many women, went to jail for consensual adult intercourse. After 1928, juries stopped convicting defendants for simple intercourse, and prosecutors stopped bringing noncommercial cases unless there was an aggravating factor (*e.g.*, the woman was a minor or was tricked) or the defendant was someone the feds wanted to "get" for other reasons. Among the celebrity defendants the Department of Justice went after was African–American boxing champion Jack Johnson, who was prosecuted for his relationship with a white woman.

3. *Today's Mann Act.* Congress revised the Mann Act, in minor ways in 1978 and more dramatically in 1986. It now criminalizes interstate transportation of "any individual * * * with intent that such individual engage in prostitution, or in any sexual activity for which any person can be charged with a criminal offense." Public Law No. 99–628, § 5(b)(1), 100 Stat. 3511 (1986), amending 18 U.S.C. § 2421. See, *e.g.*, *United States v. Rashkovski*, 301 F.3d 1133 (9th Cir. 2002). Who besides those involved in prostitution could be prosecuted today?

Although the conduct itself was criminalized in every state until Nevada instituted a licensing system in 1971, prostitution itself was not always a crime. State law regulated people we would consider prostitutes in the early and mid-nineteenth century pursuant to vagrancy, disorderly conduct, and public lewdness statutes; in the late nineteenth century, cities and states added laws against lewd solicitation and inhabiting a disorderly house or house of ill fame. Few of the newer laws required commercial consideration, and a 1919 model statute defined prostitution "to include the offering or receiving of the body for sexual intercourse for hire, and shall also be construed to include the offering or receiving of the body for indiscriminate sexual intercourse without hire." Most judges considered a woman a prostitute if she "invites or solicits by word or act. * * * Her avocation may be known from the manner in which she plys it, and not from pecuniary charges and compensation gained in any other manner." *State v. Clark*, 43 N.W. 273, 273 (Iowa 1889) (discussed in Langum 123). The Supreme Court's opinion in *Bitty* explicitly read "prostitution" in this broad way.

NOTE ON THE EVOLUTION OF ANTI–PROSTITUTION LAWS

The scope of prostitution law has both shrunk and expanded since the first half of the twentieth century. Certainly, cases such as Caminetti's would not be prosecuted today. Commerce has replaced morality as the *sine qua non* of what we mean by the term "prostitution." At the same time, other regulatory regimes have occupied the field. For example, because certain forms of prostitution result in a substantial amount of sexually-transmitted disease, police often use both public health laws and criminal laws as bases for prosecution. Surveillance has increased.

Constitutional challenges to prostitution laws have rarely been successful. Claims that such laws violate an individual's right to sexual privacy have all failed on the ground that commercialization of sexual activity was a legitimate subject for state intervention. See, e.g., *Roe v. Butterworth*, 958 F.Supp. 1569 (S.D.Fla.), *aff'd* 129 F.3d 1221 (11th Cir. 1997); *State v. Gray*, 413 N.W.2d 107 (Minn. 1987); *United States v. Moses*, 339 A.2d 46 (D.C. 1975). Also generally unsuccessful have been sex discrimination challenges based on the policies of police agencies to enforce laws only against the (women) prostitutes, never against the (male) johns. See, e.g., *Butterworth*, *supra*; *People v. Superior Court of Alameda County*, 19 Cal.3d 338, 138 Cal.Rptr. 66, 562 P.2d 1315 (1977). Plaintiffs in sex discrimination challenges could not meet the requirement in constitutional law that they prove that a statute had a discriminatory purpose. There have been more mixed results in challenges based on vagueness grounds. Convictions under vaguely-worded loitering laws were overturned in *Wyche v. State*, 619 So.2d 231 (Fla. 1993) and *Virginia v. Moran*, 26 Va. Cir. 287 (Cir. Ct. City of Richmond 1992); a Phoenix city code provision that prohibited manifesting the intent to solicit prostitution by listing suspicious behaviors was upheld in *State v. Savio*, 924 P.2d 491 (Ariz. Ct. App. 1996).

Since the nineteenth century, feminism has had its own debate over the politics of prostitution. For most of that period, there have been two primary positions: those who have argued that sex work should be decriminalized and treated as legitimate work, and those who have campaigned for the eradication of prostitution, viewing it as intrinsically an experience of subjugation. Gail Pheterson, a sociologist and organizer in the prostitutes' rights movement, summarized this debate as "the tension between feminist struggle against male violence and feminist struggle for female self-determination." *A Vindication of the Rights of Whores* 19 (1989).

One legal proposal comes from Margaret Jane Radin, "Market–Inalienability," 100 *Harv. L. Rev.* 1849 (1987): "The issue thus becomes how to structure an incomplete commodification that takes account of our nonideal world, yet does not foreclose progress to a better world of more equal power (and less susceptibility to the domino effect of market rhetoric). I think we should now decriminalize the sale of sexual services in order to protect poor women from the degradation and danger either of the black market or of other occupations that seem to them less desirable. At the same time, in order to check the domino effect, we should prohibit the capitalist entrepreneurship that would operate to create an organized market in sexual services even though this step would pose enforcement difficulties. It would include, for example, banning brokerage (pimping) and recruitment. It might also include banning advertising. Trying to keep commodification of sexuality out of our discourse by banning advertising does have the double bind effect of failing to legitimate the sales we allow, and hence it may fail to alleviate significantly the social disapproval suffered by those who sell sexual services. It also adds 'information costs' to their 'product,' and thus fails to yield them as great a 'return' as would the full-blown market. But these nonideal effects must be borne if we really accept that extensive permeation of our discourse by commodification-talk would alter sexuality in a way that we are unwilling to countenance."

CHAPTER 5

THEORIES OF SEXUALITY, GENDER, AND THE LAW

One reason that our society finds it so difficult to resolve issues related to sexuality is that we disagree so fundamentally about even what it is we are talking about. Three substantially irreconcilable models form the bases for most contemporary thinking about sexuality:

- Sexuality as a *natural force* grounded in universals, which society has the moral and ethical obligation to encourage in its healthy manifestations and discourage in its "distorted" forms.

- Sexuality as a *biological force* grounded in the individual body or psyche, usually described as a "sex drive," which society, usually with great futility, seeks to constrain.

- Sexuality as a *social force*, the product of the complex interaction of the particularities of the cultural and historical eras in which we live and the patterns of socialization that we experience.

Most debate in the legal arena still is limited to the first and second of these models; this Chapter will open with theories of these sorts. It is the third model, however, which is producing most of the current scholarship on theories of sexuality, and it is on variants of this approach that we focus much of this Chapter.

Section 1 examines natural law theories. The best known natural law theories are rooted in philosophy and religion; because they proceed from axioms or religious beliefs, they are arguably premodern forms of thinking. As articulated by current writers such as John Finnis, Robert George, and Gerard Bradley, the *new natural law* offers a nonreligious model premised upon the idea that procreative marital sex is the only valid form of sexual intercourse. Theirs is a sophisticated but difficult theory for modern intellectuals, in part because it is noninstrumental and in part because it rests upon premises that are widely shared but hard to demonstrate to someone who does not already believe them (or the conclusions that derive from them).

Section 2 explores modern theories, by which we mean theories that are interested in causes and consequences; these theories are instrumentalist. Materialist or economic theories of sexuality, for example, take a psychologically or socially instrumental view of sexuality and gender; these theories posit that sexual and gender understandings and practices serve adaptive functions. Richard Posner and Gary Becker, for example, have developed interesting and controversial theories of sexual practices and gender role based upon elementary rational actor models. These kinds of thinkers have no monopoly of materialist theories, however. Equally profound insights have come from social historians.

Also in Section 2, we examine the important feminist theories of gender and sexuality, namely, those which view issues of sexuality and gender from the perspective or interests of women. Catharine MacKinnon was the first law professor to propound an ambitious theory linking an ideology of sexuality to gender role; her argument that women's social inferiority is most deeply rooted in a male-dominated "man fucks woman" understanding of sexuality has generated reform proposals, heated theoretical and policy disagreement, and competing theories. Gayle Rubin, for example, rejects MacKinnon's close association of sexuality and gender role and supports a prosex understanding of feminism.

Section 2 closes with critical race theories of sexuality, gender, and the law. Race theorists fault liberal and even many radical feminists and queer theorists for viewing gender and sexuality exclusively through white eyes. According to the *intersectionality* idea propounded by Kim Crenshaw and other race theorists, one cannot understand sexuality in American legal history without understanding how women and gender-benders of different races have been regulated very differently. The black woman is socially denigrated not just because she is black and is a woman, but because she is a product of cross-cutting stereotypes which yield a unique ideology of subordination. Her distinctive sexualization since the slavery era has created social expectations that socially marginalize and politically isolate her more deeply than either black men or white women.

Section 3 introduces what we have grouped together as postmodern theories, those that view sexuality and gender as social constructions related to complex discursive systems. For example, medicine and law generate specific discourses, or systems of understanding, that in turn profoundly shape broader social meanings. Postmodern scholars pay special attention to how discourse (a system consisting of texts, beliefs, and/or actions) functions both to organize social practices and to constitute our individual understandings and experiences of, for example, gender and sexuality. Note that there is some overlap with the writers in Section 2 as well, since Rubin, for example, can be characterized as a social constructionist. In general, though, the materials in Section 3 tend to differ from those in Section 2 in that they describe sexuality and gender as driven by forces more diverse and dispersed than either patriarchy (feminism) or the market or capitalism (economic theory). Michel Foucault is often viewed as the primary expositor of this school of thought. Judith Butler's work builds on Foucault's, adding a more explicitly feminist approach.

PROBLEM 5–1

APPLICATION OF THEORY TO CONSTITUTIONAL ISSUES OF SEXUALITY AND GENDER

Chapters 2 through 4—presenting the rights of sexual privacy and equal protection—are largely doctrinal; the chapters contained legal and constitutional theory produced by law professors drawing from the overall purposes of the Due Process and Equal Protection Clauses, and other legal materials. In this chapter, we shall present more conceptual theories of sexuality and gender; for the most part, these theories have been generated by intellectuals outside of law schools. But all of them have potential relevance for issues of public law, and we now challenge you to consider the implications of different theories for the cutting edge issues of privacy and equality law surveyed in the previous chapters.

Assume a super-appeals court consisting of natural law scholar John Finnis; economic theorist (and actual federal judge) Richard Posner; feminist thinkers Catharine MacKinnon and Gayle Rubin; critical race theorist Kimberlé Crenshaw; and post-modern theorist Judith Butler. In constitutional cases, this Court is weakly constrained by stare decisis; its judges can rethink precedents contrary to their theoretical commitments and can construe precedents narrowly or broadly. How would each of these judges analyze the following cutting-edge issues:

   (a) Should the privacy right in *Griswold*, *Eisenstadt*, and *Lawrence* (Chapters 2 and 4) be extended to invalidate statutes making adultery a crime? Can the state make it a crime for adult first cousins to engage in consensual intercourse?

   (b) Was the VMI Case (Chapter 3, Section 1) correctly decided? Was it unconstitutional for VMI to have excluded women? If so, what remedy was appropriate?

   (c) Should the state be required to extend the institution of civil marriage to same-sex couples (see Chapter 9, Section 2)? Should the state have to recognize polygamous unions (*i.e.*, one wife and two husbands or one husband and two wives)?

NATURAL LAW THEORIES OF SEXUALITY, GENDER, AND THE LAW

We start with a theory of sex as old as Plato and Aristotle—natural law. Such theory posits humans' *natural* or *universal* needs or constitution and argues for certain *basic goods* that best meet those needs or best fit that constitution. A natural law argument proceeds in this way: (1) The order of nature (human nature however conceptualized) entails a certain basic good. (2) The practice in question is inconsistent with or undermines that basic good. (3) That practice is therefore morally wrong ("unnatural"). For example, (1) human life is a basic good; (2) abortion (and, for most natural law adherents, contraception) destroys human life; therefore, (3) abortion (contraception) is morally wrong. Other basic (or fundamental or natural) goods are *integrity of self*, the harmony of all the parts of a person which can be engaged in freely chosen action, and *marriage*, the procreative union of a husband and a wife committed to one another and to their children.

Roman Catholic theology is the best known form of natural law theory and finds expression in many accomplished works. We shall close this Section with the Roman Catholic Church's pronouncement on same-sex marriage. The views expressed in these works are by no means unique to Catholic theologians, however; they are shared by religious thinkers of many denominations and by thinkers who do not begin with a religious perspective. Oxford philosopher John Finnis maintains that the key precepts held by Roman Catholic natural law thinkers on issues of sexuality are consistent with those advanced by ancient philosophers Plato, Aristotle, Plutarch, and others. Finnis's work, such as the excerpt below, is representative of *new natural law* theory.[a] One of the features of this kind of philosophy is its *nonconsequentialism*. Whereas most modern moralists rely on utilitarian balancing or some hierarchy of values, natural law thinkers maintain that natural basic goods are incommensurable and can never validly be sacrificed; they also maintain that the primary principle of morality is to choose those actions which are consistent with "integral

---

a. Russell Hittinger, *A Critique of the New Natural Law Theory* (1987). Among the exemplars of new natural law theory are John Finnis, *Natural Law and Natural Rights* (1980), and "The Good of Marriage and the Morality of Sexual Relations: Some Philosophical and Historical Observations," 42 *Am. J. Juris.* 97 (1997); Robert George, *In Defense of Natural Law* (1999); Roger Scruton, *Sexual Desire* (1986); "The Homosexual Movement: A Response by the Ramsey Colloquium," *First Things*, Mar. 1994, p.16.

human fulfillment." Accordingly, a decision is judged not by its consequences, but by its consistency with integral human fulfillment.

John Finnis, "Law, Morality, and 'Sexual Orientation' "

69 *Notre Dame Law Review* 1049, 1063–69 (1994).*

Plato's mature concern, in the *Laws*, for familiarity, affection and love between spouses in a chastely exclusive marriage, Aristotle's representation [in *Nichomachean Ethics*] of marriage as an intrinsically desirable friendship between quasi-equals, and as a state of life even more natural to human beings than political life, and Musonius Rufus's conception [in *Discourses*] of the inseparable bonds of marriage, all find expression in Plutarch's celebration of marriage—as a union not of mere instinct but of reasonable love, and not merely for procreation but for mutual help, goodwill and cooperation for their own sake [*Life of Solon* and *Erotikos*]. * * * Genital intercourse between spouses enables them to actualize and experience (and in that sense express) their marriage itself, as a single reality with two blessings (children and mutual affection). Non-marital intercourse, especially but not only homosexual, has no such point and therefore is unacceptable.

The core of this argument can be clarified by comparing it with Saint Augustine's treatment of marriage in his *De Bono Coniugali*. The good of marital communion is here an instrumental good, in the service of the procreation and education of children so that the intrinsic, noninstrumental good of friendship will be promoted and realized by the propagation of the human race, and the intrinsic good of inner integration be promoted and realized by the "remedying" of the disordered desires of concupiscence. Now, when considering sterile marriages, Augustine had identified a further good of marriage, the natural *societas* (companionship) of the two sexes. Had he truly integrated this into his synthesis, he would have recognized that in sterile and fertile marriages alike, the communion, companionship, *societas* and *amicitia* of the spouses—their being married— *is* the very good of marriage, and is an intrinsic, basic human good, not merely instrumental to any other good. And this communion of married life, this integral amalgamation of the lives of the two persons (as Plutarch put it before John Paul II), has as its intrinsic elements, as essential *parts* of one and the same good, the goods and ends to which the theological tradition, following Augustine, for a long time subordinated that communion. It took a long and gradual process of development of doctrine, through the Catechism of the Council of Trent, the teachings of Pius XI and Pius XII, and eventually those of Vatican II—a process brilliantly illuminated by Germain Grisez—to bring the tradition to the position that procreation and children are neither the *end* (whether primary or secondary) to which marriage is instrumental (as Augustine taught), nor instrumental to the good of the spouses (as much secular and "liberal Christian" thought supposes), but rather: Parenthood and children and family are the intrinsic fulfillment of a communion which, because it is not merely instrumental, can exist and fulfill the spouses even if procreation happens to be impossible for them.

Now if, as the recent encyclical on the foundations of morality, *Veritatis Splendor*, teaches, "the communion of persons in marriage" which is violated by every act of adultery is itself a "fundamental human good," there fall into place not only the elements of the classic philosophical judgments on non-marital sexual conduct but also the similar judgments reached about such conduct by decent people who cannot articulate explanatory premises for those judgments, which they reach rather by an insight into what is and is not *consistent with* realities whose goodness they experience and understand at least sufficiently to will and choose. In particular, there fall into place the elements of an answer to the question: Why cannot nonmarital friendship be promoted and expressed by sexual acts? Why is the attempt to express affection by orgasmic nonmarital sex the pursuit of an illusion? Why did Plato and Socrates, Xenophon, Aristotle, Musonius Rufus, and Plutarch, right at the heart of their reflections on the homoerotic culture around them, make the very deliberate and careful judgment that homosexual *conduct* (and indeed all extra-marital sexual gratification) is radically incapable of participating in, actualizing, the common good of friendship?

Implicit in the philosophical and commonsense rejection of extramarital sex is the answer: The union of the reproductive organs of husband and wife really unites them biologically (and their biological reality is part of, not merely an instrument of, their *personal* reality); reproduction is one function and so, in respect of that function, the spouses are indeed one reality, and their sexual union therefore can *actualize* and allow them to *experience* their *real common good—their marriage* with the two goods, parenthood and friendship, which (leaving aside the order of grace) are the parts of its wholeness as an intelligible common good even if, independent of what the spouses will, their capacity for biological parenthood will not be fulfilled by that act of genital union. But the common good of friends who are not and cannot be married (for example, man and man, man and boy, woman and woman) has nothing to do with their having children by each other, and their reproductive organs cannot make them a biological (and therefore personal) unit. So their sexual acts together cannot do what they may hope and imagine. Because their activation of one or even each of their reproductive organs cannot be an actualizing and experiencing of the *marital* good—as marital intercourse (intercourse between spouses in a marital way) can, even between spouses who *happen* to be sterile—it can do no more than provide each partner with an individual gratification. For want of a *common good* that could be actualized and experienced *by and in this bodily union*, that conduct involves the partners in treating their bodies as instruments to be used in the service of their consciously experiencing selves; their choice to engage in such conduct thus disintegrates each of them precisely as acting persons.

Reality is known in judgment, not in emotion, and *in reality*, whatever the generous hopes and dreams and thoughts of *giving* with which some same-sex partners may surround their sexual acts, those acts cannot express or do more than is expressed or done if two strangers engage in such activity to give each other pleasure, or a prostitute pleasures a client to give him pleasure in return for money, or (say) a man masturbates to give himself pleasure and a fantasy of more human relationships after a gruelling day on the assembly line. This is, I believe, the substance of Plato's judgment—at that moment in the *Gorgias* which is also decisive for the moral and political philosophical critique of hedonism—that there is no important distinction in essential moral worthlessness between solitary masturbation, being sodomized as a prostitute, and being sodomized for the pleasure of it. Sexual acts cannot *in reality* be self-giving unless they are acts by which a man and a woman actualize and experience sexually the real giving of themselves to each other—in biological, affective and volitional union in mutual commitment, both open-ended and exclusive—which like Plato and Aristotle and most peoples we call marriage.

In short, sexual acts are not unitive in their significance unless they are marital (actualizing the all-level unity of marriage) and (since the common good of marriage has two aspects) they are not marital unless they have not only the generosity of acts of friendship but also the procreative significance, not necessarily of being intended to generate or capable in the circumstances of generating but at least of being, as human conduct, acts of the reproductive kind—actualizations, so far as the spouses then and there can, of the reproductive function in which they are biologically and thus personally one. * * *

Does this account seek to "make moral judgments based on natural facts"? Yes and no. No, in the sense that it does not seek to infer normative conclusions or theses from non-normative (natural-fact) premises. Nor does it appeal to any norm of the form "Respect natural facts or natural functions." But yes, it does apply the relevant practical reasons (especially that marriage and inner integrity are basic human goods) and moral principles (especially that one may never *intend* to destroy, damage, impede, or violate any basic human good, or prefer an illusory instantiation of a basic human good to a real instantiation of that or some other human good) to facts about the human personal organism.

NOTES ON NATURAL LAW'S THEORY OF SEXUALITY AND GENDER ROLE

1. *Implications of Natural Law for Sexual Morality.* Natural law theory valorizes procreative sex within a companionate male-female marriage. For these theorists, it is immoral to treat sexual pleasure as an end in itself or as instrumental to other ends, such as friendship. These deployments of sexuality are morally wrong because they violate a basic good, *integrity of self*. They do that by treating the body as an instrument for achieving pleasure or friendship, and this instrumental deployment radically alienates the body from the human agent, and in pursuit of an illusory experience. Sex is morally acceptable only when the partners are participating in a basic good, which Finnis and the other thinkers emphasize is marriage. They define marriage as "the community formed by a man and a woman who publicly consent to share their whole lives, in a relationship oriented toward begetting, nurturing and educating children together. This openness to procreation, as the community's natural fulfillment, distinguishes this community from other types." (George, *In Defense* 168.) Natural law thinkers also maintain that penile-vaginal (procreative) intercourse is the only kind that enables the participants to unite "organically"—to join their bodies in a "one-flesh union." (Unlike other forms of intercourse, therefore, it is also consistent with integrity of self.) That such a joint human project can result in procreation unites it with the larger human community.

Accordingly, sex that is not procreative (masturbation, fornication, sodomy, bestiality, contraceptive intercourse, sex with prepubescent children) or that is outside marriage (fornication, adultery, bigamy) is not morally acceptable. The only sex that is not self-alienating and not illusory is penile-vaginal intercourse within marriage. The new natural law on the whole advances a clear and transparent moral code for sexuality. Indeed, one virtue of the new natural law may be that it provides a coherent justification for barring sex with children, animals, multiple partners, etc. that other theories do not provide (George, *In Defense* 179–81).

Other features cause concern in some quarters. Gay people are unenthusiastic, because the new natural law thinkers condemn "homosexual sodomy" as deeply and always immoral because inconsistent with two basic goods, the integrity of self and marriage. Most feminists are also skeptical, noting that the only sexual activity natural law valorizes, penile-vaginal sex, is one where the man is assured an orgasm and the woman typically not. See Mary Becker, "Women, Morality, and Sexual Orientation," 8 *UCLA Women's L.J.* 165 (1998). For wives who cannot come to orgasm from coitus, is it immoral for the husband to assist her orgasm through oral stimulation? If so, is the natural law understanding of marriage not "naturally" gendered? If not, how is the husband's oral sex different in kind from that between two lesbians?

2.   *What Is Wrong with Nonprocreative Sex?* Michael Perry, "The Morality of Homosexual Conduct: A Response to John Finnis," 1 *Notre Dame J.L. Ethics & Pub. Pol'y* 41 (1995), criticizes Finnis's distinction between procreative sex (good) versus non-procreative sex (bad). St. Augustine believed that sterile couples (incapable of procreation) ought to be able to marry, because marriage involves a *unitive* as well as *procreative* good. Finnis does not disagree with St. Augustine's conclusion, but argues that the sterile couple can have moral penile-vaginal sex, a form of intercourse where the unitive goal is consistent, at least generally (even if not in their case), with the procreative goal. For the couple engaged in sodomy or contraceptive intercourse, the unitive and procreative goals can never be consistent, and so their sex is always immoral.

Stephen Macedo, "Homosexuality and the Conservative Mind," 84 *Geo. L.J.* 261, 278 (1995), replies: "What [then] is the point of sex in an infertile marriage? Not procreation * * *. If they have sex, it is for pleasure and to express their love, or friendship, or some other shared good," which seems indistinguishable from the sexual intercourse of unmarried or lesbian or gay couples. Robert George and Gerard Bradley, "Marriage and the Liberal Imagination," 84 *Geo. L.J.* 301 (1995), respond to Macedo: The justifying point of sexual relations between spouses (fertile or not) is the "intrinsic good of marriage," its one-flesh communion of persons consummated by acts "of the reproductive type" which unite the spouses biologically and interpersonally. The spouses are biologically united because their bodies are joined in the one *kind* of act (coitus) that can reproduce the species; the spouses are interpersonally united because their union in one flesh renews their marital commitment.

Is this a sufficient answer to Macedo and Perry? George and Bradley's answer sounds tautological, for it responds to the objection by reiterating their definitional exposition of marriage as an intrinsic human good. A central problem for the new natural law is to persuade neutral observers that only marriage (as they define it) is an intrinsic human good, and lesbian and gay unions (for example) cannot be. Say George and Bradley:

> Intrinsic value cannot, strictly speaking, be demonstrated. * * * Hence, if the intrinsic value of marriage, knowledge or any other basic human good is to be affirmed, it must be grasped in non-inferential acts of understanding. Such acts require imaginative reflection on data provided by inclination and experience, as well as knowledge of empirical patterns, which underlie possibilities of action and achievement. The practical insight that marriage * * * as a one-flesh communion of persons is consummated and actualized in the reproductive-type acts of spouses, cannot be attained by someone who has no idea of what these terms mean; nor can it be attained, except with strenuous efforts of imagination, by people who, due to personal or cultural circumstances, have little acquaintance with actual marriages thus understood. For this reason, we believe that whatever undermines the sound understanding and practice of marriage in a culture—including ideologies that are hostile to that understanding and practice—makes it difficult to grasp the intrinsic value of marriage and marital intercourse.

For a critical view and a suggestion of an alternative understanding of marriage that can include same-sex couples, see Andrew Koppelman, *The Gay Rights Question in Contemporary American Law* 86–93 (2002).

3. *Natural Law and Gender Role.* Natural law valorizes the male-female relationship in a special way, as the foundational relationship for bearing and raising children, and the *old* natural law emphasized the husband as the ruler of the household. It is not clear how *new* natural law thinkers would conceptualize the matter; its most closely allied religions have taken subtly different approaches. The Catholic Church treats marriage as a *companionate* relationship, where the husband and the wife owe *mutual obligations* to one another. In 1994, the Catholic Bishops in the United

States issued a pastoral letter on family life which urged "mutual submission" of husband and wife to one another, and joint submission to their children and the family unit.

In contrast, the Southern Baptist Convention in 1998 amended its statement of beliefs, the Baptist Faith and Message, to include this declaration:

> The husband and wife are of equal worth before God. Both bear God's image but each in differing ways. The marriage relationship models the way God relates to His people. A husband is to love his wife as Christ loved the church [see Ephesians 5:22–33]. He has the God-given responsibility to provide for, to protect and to lead his family. A wife is to submit graciously to the servant leadership of her husband even as the church willingly submits to the headship of Christ [see *id.*]. She, being "in the image of God" as is her husband and thus equal to him, has the God-given responsibility to respect her husband and to serve as his "helper" in managing the household and nurturing the next generation.

Gustav Niebuhr, "Southern Baptists Declare Wife Should 'Submit' to Her Husband," *New York Times*, June 10, 1998, pp. A1, A24. The Faith and Message, originally written in 1925 and rarely amended since, is not binding on Baptists, but does reflect consensus among the Convention delegates and is supposed to guide seminarians.

Which approach—the Roman Catholic or the Southern Baptist—is more consistent with Professor Finnis's articulation of natural law thinking?

Congregation for the Doctrine of the Faith, "Considerations Regarding Proposals to Give Legal Recognition to Unions Between Homosexual Persons"

Rome, from the Offices of the Congregation for the Doctrine of the Faith, June 3, 2003. (Joseph Cardinal Ratzinger, Prefect, and Angelo Amato, S.D.B., Titular Archbishop of Sila, Secretary.)

* * * 3. The natural truth about marriage was confirmed by the Revelation contained in the biblical accounts of creation, an expression also of the original human wisdom, in which the voice of nature itself is heard. There are three fundamental elements of the Creator's plan for marriage, as narrated in the Book of Genesis.

In the first place, man, the image of God, was created "male and female" (*Gen.* 1:27). Men and women are equal as persons and complementary as male and female. Sexuality is something that pertains to the physical-biological realm and has also been raised to a new level—the personal level—where nature and spirit are united.

Marriage is instituted by the Creator as a form of life in which a communion of persons is realized involving the use of the sexual faculty.

"That is why a man leaves his father and mother and clings to his wife and they become one flesh" (*Gen.* 2:24).

Third, God has willed to give the union of man and woman a special participation in his work of creation. Thus, he blessed the man and the woman with the words "Be fruitful and multiply" (*Gen.* 1:28). Therefore, in the Creator's plan, sexual complementarity and fruitfulness belong to the very nature of marriage. * * *

4. There are absolutely no grounds for considering homosexual unions to be in any way similar or even remotely analogous to God's plan for marriage and family. Marriage is holy, while homosexual acts go against the natural moral law. Homosexual acts "close the sexual act to the gift of life. They do not proceed from a genuine affective and sexual complementarity. Under no circumstances can they be approved".

Sacred Scripture condemns homosexual acts "as a serious depravity . . . (cf. *Rom.* 1:24–27; *1 Cor.* 6:10; *1 Tim.* 1:10). This judgment of Scripture does not of course permit us to conclude that all those who suffer from this anomaly are personally responsible for it, but it does attest to the fact that homosexual acts are intrinsically disordered". This same moral judgment is found in many Christian writers of the first centuries and is unanimously accepted by Catholic Tradition.

Nonetheless, according to the teaching of the Church, men and women with homosexual tendencies "must be accepted with respect, compassion and sensitivity. Every sign of unjust discrimination in their regard should be avoided". They are called, like other Christians, to live the virtue of chastity. The homosexual inclination is however "objectively disordered" and homosexual practices are "sins gravely contrary to chastity".

5. Faced with the fact of homosexual unions, civil authorities adopt different positions. At times they simply tolerate the phenomenon; at other times they advocate legal recognition of such unions, under the pretext of avoiding, with regard to certain rights, discrimination against persons who live with someone of the same sex. In other cases, they favour giving homosexual unions legal equivalence to marriage properly so-called, along with the legal possibility of adopting children. Where the government's policy is *de facto* tolerance and there is no explicit legal recognition of homosexual unions, it is necessary to distinguish carefully the various aspects of the problem. Moral conscience requires that, in every occasion, Christians give witness to the whole moral truth, which is contradicted both by approval of homosexual acts and unjust discrimination against homosexual persons. Therefore, discreet and prudent actions can be effective; these might involve: unmasking the way in which such tolerance might be exploited or used in the service of ideology; stating clearly the immoral nature of these unions; reminding the government of the need to contain the phenomenon within certain limits so as to safeguard public morality and, above all, to avoid exposing young people to erroneous ideas about sexuality and marriage that would deprive them of their necessary defences and contribute to the spread of the phenomenon. Those who would move from tolerance to the legitimization of specific rights for cohabiting homosexual persons need to be reminded that the approval or legalization of evil is something far different from the toleration of evil.

In those situations where homosexual unions have been legally recognized or have been given the legal status and rights belonging to marriage, clear and emphatic opposition is a duty. One must refrain from any kind of formal cooperation in the enactment or application of such gravely unjust laws and, as far as possible, from material cooperation on the level of their application. In this area, everyone can exercise the right to conscientious objection.

6. To understand why it is necessary to oppose legal recognition of homosexual unions, ethical considerations of different orders need to be taken into consideration.

From the order of right reason

* * * [O]ne needs first to reflect on the difference between homosexual behaviour as a private phenomenon and the same behaviour as a relationship in society, foreseen and approved by the law, to the point where it becomes one of the institutions in the legal structure. This second phenomenon is not only more serious, but also assumes a more wide-reaching and profound influence, and would result in changes to the entire organization of society, contrary to the common good. Civil laws are structuring principles of man's life in society, for good or for ill. They "play a very important and sometimes decisive role in influencing patterns of thought and behaviour". Lifestyles and the underlying presuppositions these express not only externally shape the life of society, but also tend to modify the younger generation's perception and evaluation of forms of behaviour. Legal recognition of homosexual unions would obscure certain basic moral values and cause a devaluation of the institution of marriage.

From the biological and anthropological order

7. Homosexual unions are totally lacking in the biological and anthropological elements of marriage and family which would be the basis, on the level of reason, for granting them legal recognition. Such unions are not able to contribute in a proper way to the procreation and survival of the human race. The possibility of using recently discovered methods of artificial reproduction, beyond involving a grave lack of respect for human dignity, does nothing to alter this inadequacy. * * *

As experience has shown, the absence of sexual complementarity in these unions creates obstacles in the normal development of children who would be placed in the care of such persons. They would be deprived of the experience of either fatherhood or motherhood. Allowing children to be adopted by persons living in such unions would actually mean doing violence to these children, in the sense that their condition of dependency would be used to place them in an environment that is not conducive to their full human development. This is gravely immoral and in open contradiction to the principle, recognized also in the United Nations Convention on the Rights of the Child, that the best interests of the child, as the weaker and more vulnerable party, are to be the paramount consideration in every case.

From the social order

8.   Society owes its continued survival to the family, founded on marriage. The inevitable consequence of legal recognition of homosexual unions would be the redefinition of marriage, which would become, in its legal status, an institution devoid of essential reference to factors linked to heterosexuality; for example, procreation and raising children. If, from the legal standpoint, marriage between a man and a woman were to be considered just one possible form of marriage, the concept of marriage would undergo a radical transformation, with grave detriment to the common good. By putting homosexual unions on a legal plane analogous to that of marriage and the family, the State acts arbitrarily and in contradiction with its duties. * * *

From the legal order

9.   Because married couples ensure the succession of generations and are therefore eminently within the public interest, civil law grants them institutional recognition. Homosexual unions, on the other hand, do not need specific attention from the legal standpoint since they do not exercise this function for the common good. * * *

10.   If it is true that all Catholics are obliged to oppose the legal recognition of homosexual unions, Catholic politicians are obliged to do so in a particular way, in keeping with their responsibility as politicians. Faced with legislative proposals in favour of homosexual unions, Catholic politicians are to take account of the following ethical indications.

When legislation in favour of the recognition of homosexual unions is proposed for the first time in a legislative assembly, the Catholic law-maker has a moral duty to express his opposition clearly and publicly and to vote against it. To vote in favour of a law so harmful to the common good is gravely immoral.

When legislation in favour of the recognition of homosexual unions is already in force, the Catholic politician must oppose it in the ways that are possible for him and make his opposition known; it is his duty to witness to the truth. If it is not possible to repeal such a law completely, the Catholic politician, recalling the indications contained in the Encyclical Letter *Evangelium vitae,* "could licitly support proposals aimed at limiting the harm done by such a law and at lessening its negative consequences at the level of general opinion and public morality", on condition that his "absolute personal opposition" to such laws was clear and well known and that the danger of scandal was avoided. This does not mean that a more restrictive law in this area could be considered just or even acceptable; rather, it is a question of the legitimate and dutiful attempt to obtain at least the partial repeal of an unjust law when its total abrogation is not possible at the moment. * * *

NOTES ON NATURAL LAW, THE STATE, AND THE CONSTITUTION

As you can see from this Vatican pronouncement on "Unions Between Homosexual Persons," religious as well as new natural law includes a theory of the state, including the rights of citizenship, the common good of society, and the duty of legislators. Because this document speaks for itself, we have made few edits beyond cutting the introduction and the conclusion. Contemplate the ways the ideas about humanity, society, and the state figure into American constitutional discourse.

1. *Implications of Natural Law for the Right to Privacy: Skeptical.* One consequence of natural law thinking is a measured skepticism about the right to privacy. A male-female couple that deliberately thwarts the possibility of procreation by using contraception during coital intercourse would under natural law premises be engaging in immoral activity—yet *Griswold* (married couples) and *Eisenstadt* (unmarried couples) ruled that the state cannot criminalize this activity. The abortion right is, if anything, more strongly inconsistent with natural law premises, which maintain that the fetus is a human life. Natural law, therefore, would not be receptive to *Griswold* or to *Roe v. Wade* and its reaffirmation in *Casey*. Overall, new natural law thinkers would be deeply alarmed that the philosophy of *Griswold* and *Roe v. Wade* contributes to a social culture where it is harder than ever before to appreciate the intrinsic value of marriage and marital intercourse.

As revealed in the foregoing Vatican document and in Professor Finnis's article, the natural law stance as to criminal sodomy is not quite so clear cut. Sodomy is immoral under that philosophy, but there is serious ambivalence as to whether the state should make it a public crime. (The case for making abortion or, theoretically, contraception a crime might be stronger, as natural law considers it the taking of human life.) The natural law position favored by the Roman Catholic Church and Finnis is that of a tolerant pedagogy rather than a criminal prosecution: The state has an obligation to teach the immorality of sodomy, but not to make it a crime. There is room in their natural law for pragmatic concern that criminalization of consensual sodomy is ineffective, creates opportunities for blackmail, and visits unnecessary hardships onto sexual minorities. (In a portion of his article that we deleted, Finnis expresses openness to pragmatic opposition to criminalizing sodomy.) On the other hand, the natural law philosophy would be critical of the Court's willingness in *Lawrence* to say that sodomy laws do not even have a rational basis sufficient to satisfy the Due Process Clause.

2. *Implications of the Right to Privacy for Natural Law Theory: Irrelevance?* In our urban society, sex for procreation is now the exception. Modern Americans engage in sex primarily for pleasure (hedonic utility) and for closeness to another person (unity or friendship). *Griswold* is a reflection of how America's normative culture has decisively rejected natural law premises, that sex is only for procreation or potential procreation. In a constitutional and social world where *Griswold* holds sway, is there any relevance for natural law thinking?

One possibility is that these decisions are constitutionally as well as morally wrong, and thoughtful Americans ought to resist them for the same reasons the abolitionists resisted *Dred Scott* (for natural law reasons, by the way). Like many Catholics, fundamentalist Protestants accept natural law precepts as a matter of faith. What the Vatican and other spiritual authorities have to say is potentially relevant for those faithful. (And many non-Catholics and non-fundamentalist Protestants agree with natural law's critique of abortion and sodomy.) Pope Benedict XVI (the former Cardinal Ratzinger, who authored the Vatican document) can maintain: We might temporarily think that *Griswold* and *Roe* are the final word, but history will teach us better over the longer term; meanwhile, we should resist those decisions. "Unions of Homosexual Persons" demands that Catholic politicians resist this policy innovation.

The reader might object that officials should keep their religious beliefs separate from their constitutional stances. Natural law theorists might respond that unelected judges ought not invalidate laws regulating public morality when such laws rest upon a respectable moral tradition—which is precisely the way natural law theorists would characterize abortion and, perhaps, sodomy laws, as well as laws against bestiality, incest, polygamy, rape, cockfighting, and so forth. Recall Justice Scalia's outraged dissenting opinions in *Casey* (Chapter 2, Section 2) and *Romer/Lawrence* (Chapter 3, Section 2C; Chapter 4), for they reflect the relevance of natural law thinking within the Court itself. And anyone interested in the original intent of constitutional Framers ought to be interested in natural law, which formed the assumptions for many Framers. As Justice Clarence Thomas argued in "The Higher Law Background of the Privileges or Immunities Clause of the Fourteenth Amendment," 12 *Harv. J.L. & Pub. Pol'y* 63 (1989), natural law thinking links the Declaration of Independence, the Constitution of 1787 and its Ninth Amendment, and the Fourteenth and other Reconstruction Amendments.

Another response to the relevance question is that natural law enables even non-adherents to think creatively about some of the privacy precedents. Indeed, the new natural law could provide support for the controversial compromise the U.S. Supreme Court has reached in this arena: The state cannot put people in jail for engaging in contraceptive coitus or sodomy, but the state does not have to pay for their contraceptives, cf. *Maher v. Roe*, 432 U.S. 464 (1977) (state welfare program not required to fund abortions even if it funds childbirth services), or recognize (*i.e.,* "promote") so-called "immoral" relationships the same way it recognizes and promotes marriages. See *Baker v. Nelson*, 409 U.S. 810 (1972), dismissing appeal for lack of a substantial federal question, 191 N.W.2d 185 (Minn. 1971) (no right to same-sex marriage).

3. *Natural Law and Equal Protection for Gay People: No Promo Homo.* The big constitutional punch line of the Vatican's pronouncement on "Unions of Homosexual Persons" is that the state ought not discriminate against or persecute sexual minorities but ought to promote and encourage all citizens to engage themselves in heterosexual marriage as the only institution where their sexuality can be natural and good. This stance is exemplary of what we call "no promo homo" discourse: The state should be *tolerant* of homosexuals but should *not promote homosexuality*. See William Eskridge, Jr., "No Promo Homo: The Sedimentation of Antigay Discourse and the Channeling Effect of Judicial Review," 75 *NYU L. Rev.* 1327 (2000). Accordingly, the natural law position would reject policies that persecuted gay people based upon antigay stereotypes and prejudices— precisely the policy followed by federal and state governments for most of the twentieth century. But a responsible morality, says the Church, is one that recognizes the "homosexual lifestyle" as greatly inferior to one man/ one woman heterosexual marriage—and state policy ought to promote the latter and not the former.

Professor Finnis gave evidence for the state of Colorado in the *Romer v. Evans* litigation (Chapter 2, Section 2C). The State asserted as one of the justifications for Amendment 2 that it expressed the moral judgment of the people of the state. The plaintiffs argued that this expression of morality amounted to no more than prejudice, and the defendants responded with Finnis's affidavit, which asserted that anti-homosexual discourse had been part of western philosophy since the ancient Greeks. Finnis's affidavit read in part:[b]

> A political community that judges that the stability and educative generosity of family life is of fundamental importance to the community's present and future can rightly judge that it has a compelling interest in denying that homosexual conduct is a valid, humanly acceptable choice and form of life, and in doing whatever it properly can, as a community with uniquely wide but still subsidiary functions, to discourage such conduct.

The state sought to link this philosophical tradition with contemporary Colorado by citing polling data which showed that the state's residents did not view homosexuality as morally equivalent to heterosexuality. They were *tolerant* of "homosexuals" but disapproving of "homosexuality" and the "homosexual lifestyle." Amendment 2, the state argued, represented the voters' expression of those views. The new natural law, therefore, provides both a backdrop helping explain the outrage Justice Scalia expressed in dissent, and intellectual support for his dissent.

---

b. Excerpts from Finnis's testimony were published in "Is Homosexual Conduct Wrong? A Philosophical Exchange," *The New Republic*, Nov. 15, 1993, p. 12. See also Daniel Mendelsohn, "The Stand: Expert Witnesses and Ancient Mysteries in a Colorado Courtroom," *Lingua Franca*, September/October 1996, pp. 34 ff; Timothy Tymkovich, "A Tale of Three Theories: Reason and Prejudice in the Battle over Amendment 2," 68 *U. Colo. L. Rev.* 287, 310 (1997) (defense of Amendment 2 by counsel on appeal).

MODERN THEORIES OF SEXUALITY, GENDER, AND THE LAW

By "modern" theories of sexuality, we mean theories that are interested in propounding and testing ideas about causes and consequences. Scientific theories of sexuality developed by Sigmund Freud, Havelock Ellis, and Alfred Kinsey are *positive* or *descriptive* theories; they aspire to tell us what sexuality is, and how it works. The economic theories in Part A of this Section tend to present themselves as positive theories but also have a *normative* or *prescriptive* component, as they typically suggest how sexuality ought to be treated. More explicitly normative theories are the feminist (Part B) and critical race (Part C) theories that follow. Notice that similar starting premises, whether they be principles of economics or of feminism, do not dictate similar conclusions. Catherine MacKinnon and Gayle Rubin disagree as sharply as Richard Posner and MacKinnon.

PART A. MATERIALIST OR RATIONAL CHOICE THEORIES

Materialist or rational choice theories assume that human beings are rational actors; as such, they seek to satisfy their personal needs and preferences through appropriate strategies. They respond to economic, social, and environmental stimuli; patterns of economic and social change decisively contribute to the evolution of understandings about sex, gender, and sexuality. Such theories are classically modernist, for authors advance falsifiable hypotheses that are independently tested, criticized, and elaborated or amended by other authors. These *inductive* theories can be contrasted with *deductive* natural law theories like that of Finnis and his allies. As you read these essays, consider how each author would explain phenomena noted in Chapters 1 and 2, such as the birth control movement and later the abortion movement in the twentieth century, and the women's liberation and gay liberation movements after World War II.

1. *SOCIOBIOLOGY (EVOLUTIONARY PSYCHOLOGY)*

Although we do not treat it in detail, one kind of instrumental theory is rooted in Darwin's idea of natural selection.[a] Evolutionary psychology

a. For application of Darwin's theory to human sexuality and gender role, see Jerome Barkow, Leda Cosmides & John Tooby, *The* *Adapted Mind: Evolutionary Psychology and the Generation of Culture* (1992); Richard Dawkins, *The Selfish Gene* (1976); Edward O.

(EP) starts with the proposition that the human sex drive has been molded by the same kind of evolutionary process that has yielded adaptive, survival-oriented physical features such as our ability to walk upright. The procreative sex drive, where an eager male inserts his penis into the vagina of a woman who will responsibly bear and nurture the resulting child, is not only fundamental to the survival of the species but is also the root of individual incentives. That is, traits that contribute to biological prosperity, *i.e.*, reproduction, will proliferate in human beings; traits not so contributing ought to die out or become rare. This insight is derived from the basic theory of evolution through natural selection.

More strikingly, EP argues that different traits will be biologically selected for women, who bear the offspring, than for men, the inseminators. The male (unconsciously) desires to spread his genes by inseminating as many fertile females as possible; this activity is costless to the male, but he is concerned that offspring be capably reared. Women, who do all the work of childbearing and naturally assume main responsibility for childrearing as well, have incentives to be more discriminating about who inseminates them; they will want a male who will help with the childrearing and who will support the children.

This theory of sex carries with it a theory of gender: Different reproductive strategies have over the eons of natural selection endowed the typical man and the typical woman with different secondary traits. Thus, the female's primary role in child care may result in a selection in favor of females who are nurturant and loyal, while the male's primary role in hunting and fighting may result in a selection in favor of males who are bold and aggressive. EP suggests that at least some stereotypes about aggressive men and cooperative women have deep roots in natural selection and, more provocatively, are hard-wired into the species. That is, because men who are aggressive and not entirely faithful will tend to reproduce more prolifically than less aggressive but more trustworthy men, genes for the former traits will win against genes for the latter traits. Women who are not nurturing will have less reproductive success than nurturing women because fewer of their children will live to maturity, and so nurturant genes ought to win for women over time.

2. *RATIONAL CHOICE THEORY*

Economists and allied law professors have applied the methodology of economics to the operation of domestic and sexual interactions. Economists tend to be skeptical regarding state regulation of markets, and even as to matters of sexual conduct they tend to follow the libertarian philosophy defended in Jeremy Bentham, "On Paederasty" (written 1785) and John Stuart Mill, *On Liberty* (1859). In their search for "efficient" markets and

Wilson, *Sociobiology: The New Synthesis* (1975); as well as Robert Wright, *The Moral Animal: Why We Are the Way We Are: The New Science of Evolutionary Psychology* (1994) (journalistic account). A leading legal account is Richard Posner, *Sex and Reason* (1992), reviewed by Gillian Hadfield, "Flirting with Science: Richard Posner on the Bioeconomics of Sexual Man," 106 *Harv. L. Rev.* 479 (1992).

other human interactions, rational choice models such as those which follow make some interesting observations.

Gary Becker, *A Treatise on the Family* (enlarged edition 1991). Professor Becker maintains that family formation follows the economic model. Individuals form family units because families increase their personal utilities. (Utility can include children and emotional gains, as well as economic gains.) Thus, person A and person B will often enjoy greater utility if they are married and living together than if they are just dating and living apart. Becker assumes a male-female marriage as the foundation of family.

Each partner in a marriage seeks to maximize the goods produced by the union. Thus, each will devote himself or herself to tasks in which he or she enjoys a *comparative advantage*. Even though person A might be absolutely better at both housework and income generation than person B, the couple will be better off if A specializes in income generation and B specializes in housework. Becker explicitly posits the comparative advantage point in gendered terms: Husbands tend to work in the market, while wives tend to specialize in household functions (pp. 14–39). To begin with, men have a comparative advantage in outside-the-home work, because longstanding workplace discrimination assures that women will receive a lower wage for the same work and skills (pp. 14–26). If a wife can make only 60% of the husband's income in the workplace and can do as good a job as he can in housekeeping, she has a comparative advantage in the latter. (The advantage is an absolute one if she is 120% as good as the husband in household tasks.)

Becker also justifies this gendered division of labor by reference to "intrinsic differences between the sexes" (p. 21), which might reveal some EP-based assumptions in his theory. "Women not only have a heavy biological commitment to the production and feeding of children, but they also are biologically committed to the care of children in other, more subtle ways." (*Id.*) Women, according to Becker, are also more willing to spend time on childcare. These biological differences suggest that when the couple has children, it is relatively more productive for the wife to devote her energies to nonmarket production and the husband to devote his to market activities generating income. Because specialization is per se useful for the joint production of the household, even small differences in preference or capacity would support large differences in activity. B, the woman who slightly prefers housework, will often end up doing all of it, while the man with greater career options will often be the sole breadwinner.

Becker does not insist that families seeking advantages of specialization will—or ought to—follow the traditional gendered pattern, but he does maintain that will be the norm, even as patterns of employment change. Becker's arguments have been important ones, earning him among other honors the Nobel Prize for Economics. Normatively, Becker's model of the family might be read to support specialization within the household and, therefore, the traditional gendered family. Like much Chicago School work,

Becker's thesis can be an apologia for the status quo or, less dramatically, a caution that legal or other efforts to reform or change the status quo—to make the family more egalitarian and less specialized—will be hard or impossible to accomplish. The behavior of many individuals behaving rationally (the market) will swallow up or negate efforts to change efficient outcomes.

Becker's thesis has other more exciting possible applications, at least one of them quite radical. That is, it might be deployed as a defense of polygamy. The husband-wife-wife family or the husband-husband-wife-wife family allows more specialization (especially in our era, when families believe they need two incomes) than the husband-wife family: the husband and one wife can work outside the home and build lucrative careers, and the second wife can maintain the home. For an example of such a family, see Elizabeth Joseph, "My Husband's Nine Wives," *N.Y. Times*, May 23, 1991, at A31. Becker's model might also be deployed to oppose same-sex marriages, if one believes that a woman-woman household would not generate as much specialization as a man-woman household. "Complementarity implies that households with men and women are more efficient than households with only one sex," he says (p. 23). If that is right (there is reason to doubt that it is), then Becker's thesis might be deployed to support a gay man-gay man-lesbian-lesbian family, where the women bear the men's children through artificial insemination and the men earn great incomes for the family by specializing in careers. (The obvious problem is whether a four-person family involves too many enforcement and relationship-maintaining costs to justify the advantages.)

CRITIQUES OF THE BECKER THESIS OF THE FAMILY AS A GENDERED SITUS OF SPECIALIZATION[b]

Becker's thesis might be criticized empirically: Do its predictions hold up? It retroactively "predicts" the 1950s family, but does it predict post–1991 developments? Although Becker won the Nobel Prize in Economics for this work, critics have questioned key assumptions or conclusions, including the following:

1. *The New Double–Income Family Model.* In more than half of all marital households, including those with young children, wives work outside the home. This seems inconsistent with the Becker thesis, but some features of this phenomenon might be consistent with it. Women in the workplace are often part-timers; most do not work full 40–hour weeks; they are paid much less than men, because they are in lower-ranked fields and receive lower pay for the same work. Consistent with the Becker thesis, as women have entered the workforce for economic reasons, men have not picked up the slack in housework. Finally, sociologists have found that attitudes

---

b. These critical notes are adapted from Courtney Smith, "Beyond Clean Sheets, Cooked Meals, and Children: The Modern 'Efficient' Division of Labor in Households" (Yale Law School SAW May 2001). Most of the criticisms of the Becker thesis are developed in Ms. Smith's useful paper.

toward male and female roles within the family have been relatively stable, even as many women enter the marketplace.

2. *Do Women Have a Comparative Advantage in Housework?* Sociologists have been unable to substantiate the Becker assumptions that women are better at housework than men *or* that women have more of a taste for housework. Moreover, if housework-loving or -hating attitudes are themselves the result of childhood socialization or gender stereotypes, then one might question Becker's assumption that the preferences are intrinsic to sex differentiation. See George Akerlof & Rachel Kranton, "Economics and Identity," 115 *Q.J. Econ.* 715, 745–48 (2000); Vicki Schultz, "Life's Work," 100 *Colum. L. Rev.* 1881 (2000).

3. *Is Women's Comparative Disadvantage in the Workplace Supportable?* No one disputes Becker's claim that women as a rule do not do as well in the workplace as men—but most people object that men's "comparative advantage" is the result of illegal discrimination, including job segregation. *E.g.*, Vicki Schultz, "Reconceptualizing Sexual Harassment," 107 *Yale L.J.* 1683 (1998); Akerlof & Kranton, "Economics and Identity," 735–37.

4. *Is Specialization Always Efficient?* According to Sarah Fenstermaker Berk, *The Gender Factory: The Apportionment of Work in American Households* 163–64 (1985), specialization of family tasks is not presumptively efficient. The rule of diminishing marginal returns suggests that specialization becomes inefficient at some point: the wife's 50th hour devoted to housework and baby care will not be as effective as the husband's 1st or 10th hour.

5. *Same–Sex Households?* The Becker thesis suggests that lesbian and gay households will engage in less specialization, a notion supported by preliminary studies. Are they less efficient? Consider Lawrence Kurdek in "Relationship Outcomes and Their Predictors: Longitudinal Evidence from Heterosexual Married, Gay Cohabiting, and Lesbian Cohabiting Couples," 60 *J. Marr. & Fam.* 553 (1998), a study of 239 straight couples, 79 gay couples, and 51 lesbian couples. Kurdek found that the lesbian couples— presumably, those with the most egalitarian structure for their relationship—reported the highest level of satisfaction, and by a significant margin. This may call into question the criteria Becker uses for figuring efficiency of a household: If one partner (the wife) is left disempowered, frustrated, and perhaps ultimately pauperized by an unequal but specialized division of labor, is there any meaningful way to call that "efficient"?

6. *Does the Altruism Assumption Hold?* Becker—a Chicago economist who assumes that men act selfishly in the market—assumes that husbands act altruistically in the home. There is virtually no empirical evidence that this is a valid assumption, substantial empirical evidence to the contrary, and strong theoretical models suggesting precisely how the gendered division of labor within the household disempowers and impoverishes women. Consider the next excerpt.

Carol Rose, "Women and Property: Gaining and Losing Ground," 78 *Va. L. Rev.* 421 (1992). Professor Rose assumes that women are, on average, more cooperative than men. Under this assumption, "we can predict that it will be easier for Sam and Louise to arrive at a cooperative use of the grazing field than it would have been for, say, Sam and Tom. This means that Louise's taste for cooperation aids in the creation of the agreement that produces collective gains. We also can predict that Louise will be better off than she was before she and Sam decided to cooperate. But, alas, we also can predict that she will not be *as much* better off as Sam. She will wind up with the smaller share of the proceeds. * * *

"At the outset, Louise has to offer Sam more to induce him to cooperate. He may not even notice so readily that cooperative arrangements are beneficial. In any event, he puts his own interests before a cooperative deal and certainly will not take any risky first steps to get things started. Because a cooperative deal does not rank as high in Sam's priorities as in Louise's, he can insist that he take a disproportionate amount of the proceeds, so that, in the now-familiar example, he gets to run more cows than Louise.

"Louise, of course, is just the reverse. She is quick to see the mutual benefits of cooperation, she likes such cooperative relationships, and she is willing to take responsibility for getting such arrangements off the ground. All those traits mean, however, that she may be willing to accept a deal even though she pays a higher price for it. Sam thus has an advantage in bargaining with Louise, just as he would with anyone who is more anxious than he for the deal, or who has a 'higher discount rate' about it. When Sam knows that Louise is the more eager player, he can offer her less favorable terms right from the start. In other words, when the two of them successfully play the larger positive-sum game, Sam has an advantage in the smaller zero-sum game of splitting the proceeds. * * * *"

Rose then applies the same kind of analysis to male-female relationships. She starts with the Beckerian assumption that Sam and Louise are both better off being married than living separately. "But from Sam and Louise's bargaining pattern, we can predict that Louise is going to have to do more to keep the household together. In particular, she (like wives generally) will be stuck doing the bulk of the housework. She is the one with the taste for commonality, whereas he can bide his time until he gets a favorable offer on the household work front. Moreover, he can make a more credible threat of withdrawing from the household unless she cooks the meals and keeps his shirts ironed. We may think he is a lout for doing so—indeed, he probably is a lout—but that is not the point. The point is that, because her desire or sense of responsibility for cooperative arrangements is stronger than his, he can cut a deal in which he gets the lion's share of their joint gains." For some of the same reasons that wives usually end up with less of the marital surplus than husbands, Professor Rose argues that female employees will tend to bargain for smaller portions of the employment surplus with their bosses than male employees, on average.

"It is important to notice that Louise's taste for cooperation is not a *bad* taste, from the point of view of the world at large. In fact, we are much better off if at least some people have such a taste; otherwise, it would be much harder to start and to sustain cooperative arrangements. Indeed, the taste for cooperation is not a bad taste even for those individuals who have it, so long as they are dealing with other individuals who share the taste. Nor, finally, is a taste for cooperation entirely a bad thing for those who have it even if they have to deal with others who do not share it equally. Even in this circumstance the cooperators do get something out of the deals they make. They just do not get as much as their bargaining partners, who are less eager to work collectively."

NOTE ON THE CONSEQUENCES OF WOMEN'S "TASTE FOR COOPERATION"

In this article and a subsequent book, *Property and Persuasion* (1996), Rose pursues the "men are louts/women are cooperative" point to argue that women would benefit from the legalization of polygamy, where men could marry more than one woman. Under such a regime, the good Sams could attract most of the good women, and the loutish Sams would be left without wives. This would not only increase the satisfaction of women, but could provide really strong incentives for future Sams to clean up their acts. We would applaud Rose's analytic but are inclined to resist the case for polygamy. Instead, Rose's analytic might better support the legal approval of samesex marriage. This twist on Rose has a normative appeal (Why not just lose the louts?), but not if you are one of the louts being left out in the sexuality and gender cold. At best, these louts would be left lonely and perhaps devastated; their pitiable condition would provide incentives for the next generation of heterosexual males to clean up their acts. At worst, however, lonely and devastated louts might become disaffected outlaws and rapists, which would be socially terrible. One might worry that the more women are siphoned off from heterosexual marriages with male louts, the greater the danger of social unrest. Is there any gametheoretic answer to this Rose Nightmare?

Richard Posner, *Sex and Reason* (1992). Judge Posner propounds an eclectic but generally economic theory of sexual practices. In this calculus, people's general sexual appetites are treated as exogenous variables, but their actual sexual practices are driven by their personal "cost-benefit" calculation. Specifically, one's sexual behavior is a function of the benefits and costs of different forms of sexual activity and the possibility of substituting one sexual practice for another.

According to Posner, there are three potential benefits of sex: procreative, hedonistic (pleasure), and sociable (pp.111–12). One's various sexual activities will be determined in part by one's purposes and one's non-volitional preferences. For example, penile-vaginal intercourse between a man and a woman is the primary sexual activity meeting the goal of procreation, but it is not the only activity that can meet the goal of sociability (and indeed may be disfavored unless reliable means of contraception are available), and it may be inferior to masturbation as a means of gratification, especially if one is not predominantly heterosexual. Posner assumes that humans have different sexual preferences, generally heterosexual or weakly bisexual, with a tiny minority (2–5% men, 1% women) "real homosexual[s]" (pp. 294–95).

The costs of sex also fall into three categories: various personal risks or "taxes" associated with different kinds of sex (*e.g.*, children with non-contraceptive vaginal sex, disease with promiscuous sex), social or legal disapproval, and search costs (pp. 115–26). One reason that solitary masturbation is such a popular sexual activity is that it meets one widely shared purpose of sex (pleasure), and does so with nominal search costs, no risk of unwanted children or disease, and ease of concealment (thereby avoiding social disapproval).

In Posner's calculus, the balance of benefits and costs will determine the relative frequency of different sexual practices (p. 116). His concept of substitution of one practice for another renders his analysis particularly dynamic: When the cost of a particular sexual activity increases, humans will tend to reduce their level of that activity but will also tend to substitute previously less desirable activities (pp. 114–19). This is a reason that homosexual behavior is common in prisons. Even strongly heterosexual men will be likely to have intercourse with other men, because the search costs for a female partner are quite high (infinite in some prisons) and for gratification inmates will tend to substitute sex with other inmates.

NOTE ON POSNER'S COST–BENEFIT THEORY: IMPLICATIONS FOR AIDS POLICY

Like most economic analysis, Posner's calculus of sexuality is reductionist, but its idea of substitution may be useful in thinking about human sexual practices and their regulation. For instance, consider the argument (advanced by an *amicus* brief in *Bowers v. Hardwick*, Chapter 2, Section 3) that the spread of AIDS through unprotected anal intercourse is a modern justification for sodomy laws. A hard-headed cost-benefit analysis undercuts such an argument: Sodomy laws are way over-inclusive for this purpose, because oral sex poses little risk of HIV transmission and anal sex little risk if condoms are used; such laws are also way under-inclusive, because they focus on the type of sexual interaction rather than on the taking of precautions (condoms). And because regulation tends to drive criminal activities underground, a modern Benthamite like Posner would fear that criminal sodomy laws contribute to HIV transmission by deterring educational campaigns. Not surprisingly, therefore, *Sex and Reason* is highly skeptical of state sodomy laws—and indeed was cited by the Supreme Court in *Lawrence*.

Tomas Philipson & Richard Posner, *Private Choices and Public Health: The AIDS Epidemic in an Economic Perspective* (1993), represents a more elaborate cost-benefit model and set of policy prescriptions. Philipson and

Posner posit that the decision to engage in HIV-risky sex can be modeled as a two-partner transaction. In their model, partners 1 and 2 will engage in HIV-risky sex only if the "expected utilities" (EU) of risky sex are positive values for both partners:

$$EU_1 = B - C (1-P_1)(P_2)(t)$$
$$\text{and}$$
$$EU_2 = B - C (1-P_2)(P_1)(t)$$

In the first equation, the expected utility of HIV-risky sex for partner 1 (EU_1) is equal to the benefits to partner 1 (B) minus the costs to partner 1 (C), multiplied by the probability of becoming infected (P). The probability of becoming infected, in turn, is the product of the probability that partner 2 is already infected (P_2) multiplied by the probability that partner 1 is not already infected ($1-P_1$) multiplied by the probability that the risky sex will transmit HIV (t). In both cases the probability that one's partner or oneself is infected is based upon a subjective valuation and not an objective criteria (such as actual incidence). A similar analysis applies to the second equation, where the variable EU_2 stands for the expected utility for partner 2.

Philipson and Posner maintain that their model corrects the tendency of some medical models to over-predict the spread of AIDS. Unlike some epidemiological models of infectious diseases, a rational choice model posits that many people will alter their behavior, thereby reducing their risk or avoiding risk altogether. Armed with knowledge that risky sexual practices, such as unprotected anal sex, pose significant costs (even discounted), partners 1 and 2 will be much less likely to engage in such activities and will substitute "safer sex" practices or even abstinence. As a result of these behavior changes, HIV infection rates will decline dramatically. One lesson for public policy is that, rather than criminalizing all anal as well as oral sex (which does not contribute to HIV transmission unless performed unsafely), the state should be educating its citizens about the risks of HIV transmission and ways to minimize or avoid it.

Other people will not change their behavior—an observation which leads the authors to their second, and more striking, assertion. Assuming that the expected utilities of both partners for risky sex are positive, it will be utility-maximizing, ex ante, for the partners to engage in risky sex, even if one of the partners is thereby infected with HIV. Thus, argue Philipson and Posner, most if not all transmissions of HIV are in transactions that are privately utility-maximizing. And, they argue further, there is an efficient level of HIV infection in the United States. This claim was met with disbelief in the medical and health policy community and has been criticized as inconsistent with the premises of rational choice theory and the significant literature on sexual activity. For example, much HIV transmission in the 1990s was from bisexual or drug-using males to their little-suspecting girlfriends; given the fraud and deceit underlying these "transactions," they are not meaningfully consensual, nor are they utility-maximizing. There are many other examples of HIV-transmitting "transactions" that are not properly understood as utility-maximizing. E.g., William Eskridge, Jr. & Brian Weimer, "The Economics Epidemic in an AIDS Perspective," 61 *U. Chi. L. Rev.* 733 (1994). Other critics have argued that predictions about behavior change are baseless without an understanding of the values that individuals assign to social and psychological variables. *E.g.*, David Charny, "Economics of Death," 107 *Harv. L. Rev.* 2056 (1994).

The authors' third observation, flowing from the first two, is that the United States in the 1990s was approaching this efficient level of HIV infection. As a normative consequence of this descriptive hypothesis, Philipson and Posner contended that state intervention to fight AIDS is presumptively unwarranted. They evaluated various policy responses under this presumption, arguing that mandatory testing for HIV is not worth the privacy and other costs and could be counterproductive; that the state is very probably spending far too much money on research for vaccines, cures, and treatment; and that a little money might be spent on targeted education programs that facilitate the operation of peoples' rational calculations. Since AIDS is often, and increasingly, spread by intravenous drug users' sharing of contaminated needles and then by heterosexual intercourse to the drug users' sexual partners, the authors appeared receptive to strategies such as the distribution of latex condoms to the general population and of clean needles to those addicted to intravenous drugs. Ever alert to inexpensive public policies, Philipson and Posner tentatively endorsed samesex marriage as a possibly useful response, because it limits the number of sexual partners and encourages altruism as regards one's spouse.

3. *SOCIAL HISTORY*

John D'Emilio, "Capitalism and Gay Identity," in *Powers of Desire: The Politics of Sexuality* 102–06, 108–09 (Ann Snitow et al. eds. 1983). Social historian John D'Emilio argues that modern gay culture is a product of the expansion of capital and the spread of wage labor. So long as America was a largely agrarian society, procreative marriage and the large families it produced were essential for economic survival. Capitalism and the rise of cities drew more Americans away from "self-sufficient household economy of the colonial era into a capitalist system of free labor. For women in the nineteenth century, working for wages rarely lasted beyond marriage; for men, it became a permanent condition. The family was thus no longer an independent unit of production. But although no longer independent, the family was still interdependent."

"As wage labor spread and production became socialized, then, it became possible to release sexuality from the 'imperative' to procreate. Ideologically, heterosexual expression came to be a means of establishing intimacy, promoting happiness, and experiencing pleasure. In divesting the household of its economic independence and fostering the separation of sexuality from procreation, capitalism has created conditions that allow some men and women to organize a personal life around their erotic/emotional attraction to their own sex. It has made possible the formation of urban communities of lesbians and gay men and, more recently, of a politics based on a sexual identity."

"By the second half of the nineteenth century, this situation was noticeably changing as the capitalist system of free labor took hold. Only when *individuals* began to make their living through wage labor, instead of as parts of an interdependent family unit, was it possible for homosexual desire to coalesce into a personal identity—an identity based on the ability to remain outside the heterosexual family and to construct a personal life based on attraction to one's own sex. By the end of the century, a class of men and women existed who recognized their erotic interest in their own sex, saw it as a trait that set them apart from the majority, and sought others like themselves."

As a consequence of these economics-driven changes, communities of gay people formed in major cities; bathhouses, bars, parks became meeting places for women and, especially, men attracted to those of the same sex. Medical theories of "homosexuality" were, according to D'Emilio, "an ideological response to a new way of organizing one's personal life." He argues that economic circumstances, rather than any innate biological reason, have generated the social reality that gay men became more prominent in cities than lesbians. The reason was that "capitalism had drawn far more men than women into the labor force, and at higher wages. Men could more easily construct a personal life independent of attachments to the opposite sex, whereas women were more likely to remain economically dependent on men." In the same period, lesbian activity correlated strongly with higher education. "College-educated white women, far more able than their working-class sisters to support themselves, could survive more easily without intimate relationships with men."

The material foundation for an organized "gay community" was actualized by World War II and by the McCarthy era persecutions. The war "disrupted traditional patterns of gender relations and sexuality, and temporarily created a new erotic situation conducive to homosexual expression" for the millions of men and women it placed in intense homosocial settings. Many formed intimate relationships with one another and carried over those patterns into civilian life. The postwar witch hunts placed their feelings under siege and solidified a core of resistance that broke into the open in the 1960s; the Stonewall riots of June 1969 were the signal event for "gay liberation." Nonetheless, a "pro-family" backlash against gay liberation developed in the 1970s.

" * * * How is it that capitalism, whose structure made possible the emergence of a gay identity and the creation of urban gay communities, appears unable to accept gay men and lesbians in its midst? Why do heterosexism and homophobia appear so resistant to assault?

"The answers, I think, can be found in the contradictory relationship of capitalism to the family. On the one hand, as I argued earlier, capitalism has gradually undermined the material basis of the nuclear family by taking away the economic functions that cemented the ties between family members. As more adults have been drawn into the free labor system, and as capital has expanded its sphere until it produces as commodities most goods and services we need for our survival, the forces that propelled men and women into families and kept them there have weakened. On the other hand, the ideology of capitalist society has enshrined the family as the source of love, affection, and emotional security, the place where our need for stable, intimate human relationships is satisfied.

"This elevation of the nuclear family to preeminence in the sphere of personal life is not accidental. Every society needs structures for reproduction and childrearing, but the possibilities are not limited to the nuclear family. Yet the privatized family fits well with capitalist relations of production. Capitalism has socialized production while maintaining that the products of socialized labor belong to the owners of private property. In many ways, childrearing has also been progressively socialized over the last two centuries, with schools, the media, peer groups, and employers taking over functions that once belonged to parents. Nevertheless, capitalist society maintains that reproduction and childrearing are private tasks, that children 'belong' to parents, who exercise the rights of ownership. Ideologically, capitalism drives people into heterosexual families: each generation comes of age having internalized a heterosexist model of intimacy and personal relationships. Materially, capitalism weakens the bonds that once kept families together so that their members experience a growing instability in the place they come to expect happiness and emotional security. Thus, while capitalism has knocked the material foundation away from family life, lesbians, gay men, and heterosexual feminists have become the scapegoats for the social instability of the system."

Carroll Smith–Rosenberg, *Disorderly Conduct: Visions of Gender in Victorian America* 176, 180–81 (1985). This book articulates a now-classic historical framework for thinking about issues of sex, gender, and sexuality once American women started to become economically and socially independent of men. At first, during the 1860s and 1870s, women assuming public roles did so in the spirit of "The Cult of True Womanhood" espoused in the earlier nineteenth century: Woman is the nurturing conscience of man, the source of virtue and moderation in a world of selfish aggressive men. Women's clubs, temperance societies, soup kitchens, the Red Cross, and the like were examples of women's activism under the umbrella of traditional male-female relations. At the same time, however, these women were also insisting upon political, social, and economic equality for themselves and their daughters.

"If the urban bourgeois matron of the 1860s and 1870s alarmed, her daughter frightened. The 1880s and 1890s saw the emergence of a novel social and political phenomenon—the New Woman. * * * I use the term [devised by Henry James] to refer to a specific sociological and educational cohort of women born between the late 1850s and 1900. They represented the new demographic trends of later marriages for bourgeois women. Benefiting from bourgeois affluence, which endowed colleges for women, they were college-educated and professionally trained at a time when few men were. Few New Women married." Jane Addams and Willa Cather were examples of New Women's first generation; Gertrude Stein, Virginia

Woolf, and Edna St. Vincent Millay represented the more aggressive and independent second generation of New Women.

Smith–Rosenberg examines the reactions, at first bemused but soon alarmed, of male culture to the New Woman. The main response was an effort to reassert control, not under the agency of traditional ideas, but through a transformation of expressive medical metaphors into agencies for social control—a process Smith–Rosenberg calls "the politicization of the body." Beginning in the Civil War period and intensifying after the war, the medical establishment was enlisted to support laws prohibiting abortion and contraception, as ways to renormalize women around their traditional roles as mother and wife, but within the new scientific vocabulary of the era.

"Whereas the troubled men of Jacksonian America chose a variety of sexual images to express their social concerns, mid-nineteenth century men turned increasingly to the sexually autonomous and gender-deviant woman. At first bourgeois men focused upon the bourgeois matron's declining birthrate. They molded the twin themes of birth control and abortion (always defining them as women's decisions) into condensed symbols of national danger and decay. Whether they appeared in race-suicide jeremiads or in anti-abortion propaganda, the women who practiced birth control and the aborting mother became metaphors for all that appeared 'unnatural' in small-town America. * * *

" * * * The medico-political campaign against abortion [1850s through 1880s] constituted the first effort at an alliance between the male medical leadership and bourgeois politicians. Having defeated and regulated their own women, bourgeois men then sought to control working-class women through state campaigns against the female prostitute [1870s through 1910s]. Only after both campaigns had succeeded did bourgeois men seek to control the bodies and the sexuality of other men." This corollary of Smith–Rosenberg's theory is explored by Anthony Rotundo, *American Manhood* (1982), and Lillian Faderman, *Surpassing the Love of Men: Romantic Friendship and Love Between Women from the Sixteenth Century to the Present* (1981): Medical articulation of a new species of humanity, the "homosexual" (both female and male), found an interested audience in middle-class Europeans and Americans already nervous about the erosion of traditional gender roles. Society sought to suppress communities of sexual and gender "inverts" (fairies, crossdressing women, and male as well as female prostitutes) in order to reaffirm rigid gender and sexual boundaries.

NOTE ON "MODERNIZATION OF JUSTIFICATION" AND IDENTITY–BASED SOCIAL MOVEMENTS (AND COUNTERMOVEMENTS)

There are several ways to contrast the accounts of D'Emilio and Smith–Rosenberg. The former focuses more on changing sexual practices and social stigmatization of homosexuality, the latter focuses more on changing gender role and social stigmatization of independent women. The main difference is that D'Emilio's account is Marxist, while Smith–Rosenberg's is feminist social history. Both, however, emphasize the ways in which traditional mores about sexuality and gender role came under siege in the nineteenth century, essentially because of external economic and demographic changes. And both trace the ideological reaction of mainstream society. Although the nature of that response is different for the two historians, they might be read as complementary accounts with an interesting punch line. True to his Marxist approach, D'Emilio emphasizes the contradictions created by capitalism, facilitating both the formation and persecution of subcultures organized around sexual and gender variation. Smith–Rosenberg provides a conceptual vocabulary for understanding how this dialectic relationship plays out rhetorically.

Smith–Rosenberg shows how traditionalists reacted dynamically to New Women. In the 1850s, they relied on premodern *natural law* tropes to keep women in their places: According to the Bible and other natural law sources, a woman's destiny is to bear and raise children with her husband. The New Women challenged this understanding, and the first wave of feminism won some legal reforms, including the end of coverture (whereby the wife had no separate legal status from her husband). They maintained that women were individuals with similar capacities as men. By the end of the nineteenth century, natural law was no longer so automatically authoritative that it could stand in the way of women's progress. Hence, traditionalists turned to—or created—a new *medical* discourse for keeping women in their places. The sexologists of the late nineteenth and early twentieth centuries created a new anti-feminist discourse: A psychologically healthy woman was one who yearned for a husband's embrace and for children reared with him; women who renounced those goals were hurting themselves, emotionally sick, and deviant. Doctors replaced ministers as policemen enforcing compulsory marriage and motherhood upon women. Women who wanted their own careers were persecuted as "degenerate" (this was the era of the great campaigns against prostitution, a primary avenue of upward mobility for working class women); women who refused to marry men were stigmatized as "inverts" and "lesbians"; men-loving women who sought contraception or abortion to prevent conception were thwarted in the name of their own "protection."

The Smith–Rosenberg idea of an evolving defense of traditionalist status alignments is the basis for what Reva Siegel calls the *modernization of justification*. Siegel, " 'The Rule of Love': Wife Beating as Prerogative and Privacy," 105 *Yale L.J.* 2117 (1996). Focusing on legal reform, Siegel argues that even when reform has been accomplished for women, oppressive practices and attitudes have been reaffirmed through a modernization of justification. By defending practices in terms that are more persuasive to a new generation, modernized justifications, Siegel argues, can actually strengthen oppressive practices (like wife-beating) and status subordination (of wives to husbands).

One of us has deployed the Smith–Rosenberg idea to explain the evolution of antigay discourse, starting with *natural law* theories ("sodomites" are "unnatural") then moving to *medical* theories ("sexual inverts" are "degenerate" and predatory) and later to *republican* tropes ("homosexuals and sex perverts" pollute the public culture and make decent people uncomfortable). William Eskridge, Jr., "No Promo Homo: The Sedimentation of Antigay Discourse and the Channeling Effect of Judicial Review," 75 *NYU L. Rev.* 1327 (2000). As the title suggests, we view the modernization of justification as *sedimented*: each new justification layers over the old ones, which retain at least some of their power, especially at the local level, long after they have passed out of fashion in public discourse. Unlike Siegel, we do not believe that modernized justifications strengthen traditional modes of subordination so much as change them. Indeed, the evolving discourse alters the "objects" of social concern—from the "sodomite" (someone defined solely by his acts) to the "homosexual" (defined by her orientation, her "propensity" to act) to the "openly gay person" (defined by her speech and public presentation as much as anything else).

Moreover, there is the possibility of "progress" under modernized justifications. Nineteenth century natural law regimes considered interracial sex and sodomy abominations and justified potentially harsh criminal penalties for highly *malignant* variations from acceptable behavior. Medical regimes could be just as harsh, but the professionalization of discourse (with doctors and medical scientists) opened the way for society to understand new racial and sexual identities as *tolerable* variations from a preferred norm (whiteness and heterosexuality). Sodomy laws refocused on non-consensual behaviors, and many states repealed or ceased enforcing their miscegenation laws. Once people of color and gay people became politically salient groups, some members of society have shifted their views, to consider race and sex of partner *benign* variations and to deny there is one central norm. Once a state that punished interracial couples and imprisoned (and medically tortured) homosexuals, California is today a jurisdiction where people of color and gay people flourish.

PART B.   FEMINIST THEORIES

Law and philosophy have traditionally been written only by men, and one would expect law and philosophy to reflect men's perspectives and interests. In a society where women are equal citizens, at least formally, and should be equal citizens normatively, this state of affairs seems slanted. Feminist theories start from the perspective and interests of women. One of the earliest, and still among the most prominent, feminist theoreticians of an integrated understanding of sexuality, gender, and the law has been Catharine MacKinnon. MacKinnon's *Sexual Harassment of Working Women* (1979), was instrumental in helping to win recognition of sexual harassment as a form of sex discrimination prohibited by Title VII. Writing in the early 1980s (at roughly the same time that D'Emilio wrote the essay excerpted above and that Gayle Rubin wrote the article that follows), MacKinnon articulated a claim that sexuality is central, not just to women's lives, but to the feminist campaign against patriarchy and the subordination of women.

Catharine MacKinnon, "Feminism, Marxism, Method, and the State: An Agenda for Theory"

7 *Signs* 515, 516–17, 529, 530, 533–35, 541 (1982).*

Sexuality is to feminism what work is to marxism: that which is most one's own, yet most taken away. Marxist theory argues that society is fundamentally constructed of the relations people form as they do and make things needed to survive humanly. Work is the social process of shaping and transforming the material and social worlds, creating people as social beings as they create value. It is that activity by which people become who they are. Class is its structure, production its consequence, capital its congealed form, and control its issue.

[MacKinnon argues that women's sexuality has been systematically expropriated by men in the same way that capital systematically expropriates the labor of workers.] Sexuality is that social process which creates, organizes, expresses, and directs desire, creating the social beings we know as women and men, as their relations create society. As work is to marxism, sexuality to feminism is socially constructed yet constructing, universal as activity yet historically specific, jointly comprised of matter and mind. As the organized expropriation of the work of some for the benefit of others defines a class—workers—the organized expropriation of the sexuality of some for the use of others defines the sex, woman. Heterosexuality is its structure, gender and family its congealed forms, sex roles its qualities generalized to social persona, reproduction a consequence, and control its issue.

Marxism and feminism are theories of power and its distribution: inequality. They provide accounts of how social arrangements of patterned disparity can be internally rational yet unjust. But their specificity is not incidental. In marxism to be deprived of one's work, in feminism of one's sexuality, defines each one's conception of lack of power per se. They do not mean to exist side by side to insure that two separate spheres of social life are not overlooked, the interests of two groups are not obscured, or the contributions of two sets of variables are not ignored. They exist to argue, respectively, that the relations in which many work and few gain, in which some fuck and others get fucked, are the prime moment of politics. * * *

* * * [C]onceiving nature, law, the family, and roles as consequences, not foundations, I think that feminism fundamentally identifies sexuality as the primary social sphere of male power. The centrality of sexuality emerges not from Freudian conceptions but from feminist practice on diverse issues, including abortion, birth control, sterilization abuse, domestic battery, rape, incest, lesbianism, sexual harassment, prostitution, female sexual slavery, and pornography. In all these areas, feminist efforts con-

front and change women's lives concretely and experientially. Taken together, they are producing a feminist political theory centering upon sexuality: its social determination, daily construction, birth to death expression, and ultimately male control.

Feminist inquiry into these specific issues began with a broad unmasking of the attitudes that legitimize and hide women's status, the ideational envelope that contains women's body: notions that women desire and provoke rape, that girls' experiences of incest are fantasies, that career women plot and advance by sexual parlays, that prostitutes are lustful, that wife beating expresses the intensity of love. Beneath each of these ideas was revealed bare coercion and broad connections to woman's social definition as a sex. Research on sex roles, pursuing Simone de Beauvoir's insight that "one is not born, one rather becomes a woman," disclosed an elaborate process: how and what one learns to become one. Gender, crossculturally, was found to be a learned quality, an acquired characteristic, an assigned status, with qualities that vary independent of biology and an ideology that attributes them to nature. * * *

If the literature on sex roles and the investigations of particular issues are read in light of each other, each element of the female *gender* stereotype is revealed as, in fact, *sexual*. Vulnerability means the appearance/reality of easy sexual access; passivity means receptivity and disabled resistance, enforced by trained physical weakness; softness means pregnability by something hard. Incompetence seeks help as vulnerability seeks shelter, inviting the embrace that becomes the invasion, trading exclusive access for protection ... from the same access. Domesticity nurtures the consequent progeny, proof of potency, and ideally waits at home dressed in saran wrap. Woman's infantilization evokes pedophilia * * *.

Socially, femaleness means femininity, which means attractiveness to men, which means sexual attractiveness, which means sexual authority on male terms. What defines woman as such is what turns men on. Good girls are "attractive," bad girls "provocative." Gender socialization is the process through which women come to identify themselves as sexual beings, as beings that exist for men. It is that process through which women internalize (make their own) a male image of their sexuality *as* their identity as women. * * * Sex as gender and sex as sexuality are thus defined in terms of each other, but it is sexuality that determines gender, not the other way around. * * *

Many issues that appear sexual from this standpoint have not been seen as such, nor have they been seen as defining a politics. Incest, for example, is commonly seen as a question of distinguishing the real evil, a crime against the family, from girlish seductiveness or fantasy. Contraception and abortion have been framed as matters of reproduction and fought out as proper or improper social constraints on nature. Or they are seen as private, minimizing state intervention into intimate relations. Sexual harassment was a nonissue, then became a problem of distinguishing personal relationships or affectionate flirtation from abuse of position.

Lesbianism, when visible, has been either a perversion or not, to be tolerated or not. Pornography has been considered a question of freedom to speak and depict the erotic, as against the obscene or violent. Prostitution has been understood either as mutual lust and degradation or an equal exchange of sexual need for economic need. The issue in rape has been whether the intercourse was provoked/mutually desired, or whether it was forced: Was it sex or violence? Across and beneath these issues, sexuality itself has been divided into parallel provinces: traditionally, religion or biology; in modern transformation, morality or psychology. Almost never politics.

In a feminist perspective, the formulation of each issue, in the terms just described, expresses ideologically the same interest that the problem it formulates expresses concretely: the interest from the male point of view. Women experience the sexual events these issues codify as a cohesive whole within which each resonates. The defining theme of that whole is the male pursuit of control over women's sexuality—men not as individuals nor as biological beings, but as a gender group characterized by maleness as socially constructed, of which this pursuit is definitive. For example, * * * women notice that sexual harassment looks a great deal like ordinary heterosexual initiation under conditions of gender inequality. Few women are in a position to refuse unwanted sexual initiatives. That consent rather than non-mutuality is the line between rape and intercourse further exposes the inequality in normal social expectations. * * * Pornography becomes difficult to distinguish from art and ads once it is clear that what is degrading to women is compelling to the consumer. Prostitutes sell the unilaterality that pornography advertises. That most of these issues codify behavior that is neither counter-systematic nor exceptional is supported by women's experience as victims: these behaviors are either not illegal or are effectively permitted on a large scale. As women's experience blurs the lines between deviance and normalcy, it obliterates the distinction between abuses *of* women and the social definition of what a woman *is*. * * *

Sexuality, then, is a form of power. Gender, as socially constructed, embodies it, not the reverse. Women and men are divided by gender, made into the sexes as we know them, by the social requirements of heterosexuality, which institutionalizes male sexual dominance and female sexual submission. If this is true, sexuality is the linchpin of gender inequality. * * *

The substantive principle governing the authentic politics of women's personal lives is pervasive powerlessness to men, express and reconstituted daily *as* sexuality. To say that the personal is political means that gender as a division of power is discoverable and verifiable through women's intimate experience of sexual objectification, which is definitive of and synonymous with women's lives as gender female. * * *

* * * Sexual objectification is the primary process of the subjection of women. It unites act with word, construction with expression, perception

with enforcement, myth with reality. Man fucks woman; subject verb object.

NOTE ON THE RELATIONSHIP BETWEEN COMPULSORY HETEROSEXUALITY AND PATRIARCHY

Although Professor MacKinnon first brought together (hetero)sexuality, gender subordination, and the law under one powerful theoretical umbrella, her contribution critically built upon the foundations laid by earlier feminists, including lesbian feminists. In the 1960s and 1970s, feminism was ambivalent about the important role played by lesbians in their movement; some leading feminists openly sought to distance the movement from lesbianism. Other feminists, including lesbian feminists, responded theoretically as well as personally.

An important synthesis of this literature was Adrienne Rich, "Compulsory Heterosexuality and Lesbian Existence," 5 *Signs* (1980), reprinted in *Blood, Bread, and Poetry: Selected Prose, 1979–1985*, at 23–75 (1986). Just as Margaret Sanger had argued that "compulsory motherhood" (her language) was a political institution which contributed to women's subordination, so Rich argued that "compulsory heterosexuality" was a political institution which contributed to women's subordination. Male culture, she argued, systematically coerced women into frequently unsatisfying marriages to men, by denying women access to means of production and income by which they could maintain female households, by suppressing any mention of lesbian relationships and smothering such mentions as escaped censorship with lies and deceits, by idealizing (heterosexual) romantic marriage and empowering husbands to physically and emotionally dominate their wives under shrouds of privacy and privilege.

In conclusion, Rich professed herself agnostic as to whether more women viewed themselves as lesbians or as women-identified women. What she insisted on was *choice* and *truth*. "[T]he absence of choice remains the great unacknowledged reality, and in the absence of choice women will remain dependent upon the chance or luck of particular relationships and will have no collective power to determine the meaning and place of sexuality in their lives." Other lesbian feminists of the 1970s and 1980s were even more specific than Rich, arguing that homophobia is an instrument of sexism, lesbian-bashing a mechanism of misogyny.

In the context of the feminist movement's ambivalence about its lesbian leaders, MacKinnon's essay was brave as well as path-breaking. It goes well beyond Rich in interrogating heterosexuality as the situs of women's subordination and oppression. She continued this hard-hitting indictment in *Feminism Unmodified: Discourses on Life and Law* 6 (1987): "[O]ur rapists * * *, serial murderers * * * and child molesters * * * enjoy their acts sexually and as men, to be redundant. It is sex *for them*. * * * When acts of dominance and submission, up to and including acts of violence, are experienced as sexually arousing, as sex itself, that is what they are." Gender is "the congealed form of the sexualization of inequality between men and women."

Gayle Rubin "Thinking Sex: Note for a Radical Theory of the Politics of Sexuality"

In *Pleasure and Danger: Exploring Female Sexuality* 11–16, 31–34.
Carole Vance, Editor, 1984.*

The new scholarship on sex has brought a welcome insistence that sexual terms be restricted to their proper historical and social contexts, and a cautionary scepticism towards sweeping generalizations. But it is important to be able to indicate groupings of erotic behavior and general trends within erotic discourse. In addition to sexual essentialism, there are at least five other ideological formations whose grip on sexual thought is so strong that to fail to discuss them is to remain enmeshed within them. These are sex negativity, the fallacy of misplaced scale, the hierarchical valuation of sex acts, the domino theory of sexual peril, and the lack of a concept of benign sexual variation.

Of these five, the most important is sex negativity. Western cultures generally consider sex to be a dangerous, destructive, negative force. Most Christian tradition, following Paul, holds that sex is inherently sinful. It may be redeemed if performed within marriage for procreative purposes and if the pleasurable aspects are not enjoyed too much. In turn, this idea rests on the assumption that the genitalia are an intrinsically inferior part of the body, much lower and less holy than the mind, the "soul," the "heart," or even the upper part of the digestive system (the status of the excretory organs is close to that of the genitalia). Such notions have by now acquired a life of their own and no longer depend solely on religion for their perseverance.

This culture always treats sex with suspicion. It construes and judges almost any sexual practice in terms of its worst possible expression. Sex is presumed guilty until proven innocent. Virtually all erotic behavior is considered bad unless a specific reason to exempt it has been established. The most acceptable excuses are marriage, reproduction, and love. Sometimes scientific curiosity, aesthetic experience, or a long-term intimate relationship may serve. But the exercise of erotic capacity, intelligence, curiosity, or creativity all require pretexts that are unnecessary for other pleasures, such as the enjoyment of food, fiction, or astronomy.

What I call the fallacy of misplaced scale is a corollary of sex negativity. Susan Sontag once commented that since Christianity focused "on sexual behavior as the root of virtue, everything pertaining to sex has been a 'special case' in our culture." Sex law has incorporated the religious attitude that heretical sex is an especially heinous sin that deserves the harshest punishments. Throughout much of European and American history, a single act of consensual anal penetration was grounds for execution. In some states, sodomy still carries twenty-year prison sentences. Outside the law, sex is also a marked category. Small differences in value or behavior are often experienced as cosmic threats. Although people can be intolerant, silly, or pushy about what constitutes proper diet, differences in menu rarely provoke the kinds of rage, anxiety, and sheer terror that routinely accompany differences in erotic taste. Sexual acts are burdened with an excess of significance.

Modern Western societies appraise sex acts according to a hierarchical system of sexual value. Marital, reproductive heterosexuals are alone at the top of the erotic pyramid. Clamoring below are unmarried monogamous heterosexuals in couples, followed by most other heterosexuals. Solitary sex floats ambiguously. The powerful nineteenth-century stigma on masturbation lingers in less potent, modified forms, such as the idea that masturbation is an inferior substitute for partnered encounters. Stable, long-term lesbian and gay male couples are verging on respectability, but bar dykes and promiscuous gay men are hovering just above the groups at the very bottom of the pyramid. The most despised sexual castes currently include transsexuals, transvestites, fetishists, sadomasochists, sex workers such as

The charmed circle:
Good, Normal, Natural, Blessed Sexuality

Heterosexual
Married
Monogamous
Procreative
Non-commercial
In pairs
In a relationship
Same generation
In private
No pornography
Bodies only
Vanilla

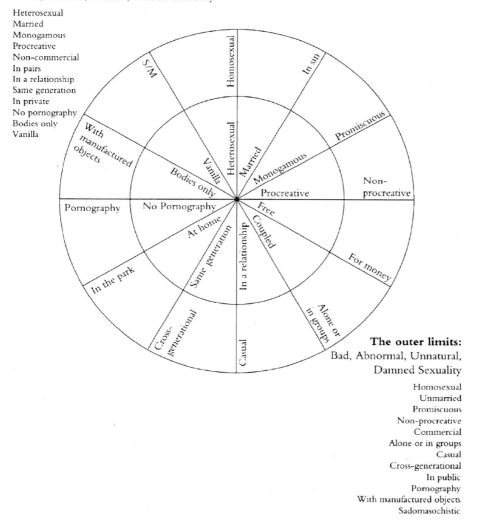

The outer limits:
Bad, Abnormal, Unnatural,
Damned Sexuality

Homosexual
Unmarried
Promiscuous
Non-procreative
Commercial
Alone or in groups
Casual
Cross-generational
In public
Pornography
With manufactured objects
Sadomasochistic

prostitutes and porn models, and the lowliest of all, those whose eroticism transgresses generational boundaries.

Individuals whose behavior stands high in this hierarchy are rewarded with certified mental health, respectability, legality, social and physical mobility, institutional support, and material benefits. As sexual behaviors or occupations fall lower on the scale, the individuals who practice them are subjected to a presumption of mental illness, disreputability, criminality, restricted social and physical mobility, loss of institutional support, and economic sanctions. * * *

Figure 1 diagrams a general version of the sexual value system. According to this system, sexuality that is "good," "normal," and "natural" should ideally be heterosexual, marital, monogamous, reproductive, and noncommercial. It should be coupled, relational, within the same generation, and occur at home. It should not involve pornography, fetish objects, sex toys of any sort, or roles other than male and female. Any sex that violates these rules is "bad," "abnormal," or "unnatural." Bad sex may be homosexual, unmarried, promiscuous, non-procreative, or commercial. It may be masturbatory or take place at orgies, may be casual, may cross generational lines, and may take place in "public," or at least in the bushes or the baths. It may involve the use of pornography, fetish objects, sex toys, or unusual roles (see Figure 1).

Figure 2 diagrams another aspect of the sexual hierarchy: the need to draw and maintain an imaginary line between good and bad sex. Most of the discourses on sex, be they religious, psychiatric, popular, or political, delimit a very small portion of human sexual capacity as sanctifiable, safe, healthy, mature, legal, or politically correct. The "line" distinguishes these from all other erotic behaviors, which are understood to be the work of the devil, dangerous, psychopathological, infantile, or politically reprehensible. Arguments are then conducted over "where to draw the line," and to determine what other activities, if any, may be permitted to cross over into acceptability.

All these models assume a domino theory of sexual peril. The line appears to stand between sexual order and chaos. It expresses the fear that if anything is permitted to cross this erotic DMZ, the barrier against scary sex will crumble and something unspeakable will skitter across.

Most systems of sexual judgment—religious, psychological, feminist, or socialist—attempt to determine on which side of the line a particular act falls. Only sex acts on the good side of the line are accorded moral complexity. For instance, heterosexual encounters may be sublime or disgusting, free or forced, healing or destructive, romantic or mercenary. As long as it does not violate other rules, heterosexuality is acknowledged to exhibit the full range of human experience. In contrast, all sex acts on the bad side of the line are considered utterly repulsive and devoid of all emotional nuance. The further from the line a sex act is, the more it is depicted as a uniformly bad experience.

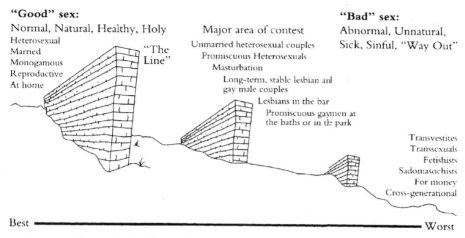

"Good" sex:
Normal, Natural, Healthy, Holy

Heterosexual
Married
Monogamous
Reproductive
At home

"The Line"

Major area of contest
Unmarried heterosexual couples
Promiscuous Heterosexuals
Masturbation
Long-term, stable lesbian and gay male couples
Lesbians in the bar
Promiscuous gay men at the baths or in the park

"Bad" sex:
Abnormal, Unnatural, Sick, Sinful, "Way Out"

Transvestites
Transsexuals
Fetishists
Sadomasochists
For money
Cross-generational

Best ——————————————— Worst

FIGURE 2.   The sex hierarchy: the struggle over where to draw the line

As a result of the sex conflicts of the last decade, some behavior near the border is inching across it. Unmarried couples living together, masturbation, and some forms of homosexuality are moving in the direction of respectability (see Figure 2). Most homosexuality is still on the bad side of the line. But if it is coupled and monogamous, the society is beginning to recognize that it includes the full range of human interaction. Promiscuous homosexuality, sadomasochism, fetishism, transsexuality, and cross-generational encounters are still viewed as unmodulated horrors incapable of involving affection, love, free choice, kindness, or transcendence.

This kind of sexual morality has more in common with ideologies of racism than with true ethics. It grants virtue to the dominant groups, and relegates vice to the underprivileged. A democratic morality should judge sexual acts by the way partners treat one another, the level of mutual consideration, the presence or absence of coercion, and the quantity and quality of the pleasures they provide. Whether sex acts are gay or straight, coupled or in groups, naked or in underwear, commercial or free, with or without video, should not be ethical concerns.

It is difficult to develop a pluralistic sexual ethics without a concept of benign sexual variation. Variation is a fundamental property of all life, from the simplest biological organisms to the most complex human social formations. Yet sexuality is supposed to conform to a single standard. One of the most tenacious ideas about sex is that there is one best way to do it, and that everyone should do it that way.

Most people find it difficult to grasp that whatever they like to do sexually will be thoroughly repulsive to someone else, and that whatever repels them sexually will be the most treasured delight of someone, somewhere. One need not like or perform a particular sex act in order to recognize that someone else will, and that this difference does not indicate a lack of good taste, mental health, or intelligence in either party. Most people mistake their sexual preferences for a universal system that will or should work for everyone.

This notion of a single ideal sexuality characterizes most systems of thought about sex. For religion, the ideal is procreative marriage. For psychology, it is mature heterosexuality. Although its content varies, the format of a single sexual standard is continually reconstituted within other rhetorical frameworks, including feminism and socialism. It is just as objectionable to insist that everyone should be lesbian, nonmonogamous, or kinky, as to believe that everyone should be heterosexual, married, or vanilla—though the latter set of opinions are backed by considerably more coercive power than the former.

Progressives who would be ashamed to display cultural chauvinism in other areas routinely exhibit it towards sexual differences. We have learned to cherish different cultures as unique expressions of human inventiveness rather than as the inferior or disgusting habits of savages. We need a similarly anthropological understanding of different sexual cultures. * * *

* * * [T]he feminist movement will always be a source of interesting thought about sex. Nevertheless, I want to challenge the assumption that feminism is or should be the privileged site of a theory of sexuality. Feminism is the theory of gender oppression. To assume automatically that this makes it the theory of sexual oppression is to fail to distinguish between gender, on the one hand, and erotic desire, on the other.

In the English language, the word "sex" has two very different meanings. It means gender and gender identity, as in "the female sex" or "the male sex." But sex also refers to sexual activity, lust, intercourse, and arousal, as in "to have sex." This semantic merging reflects a cultural assumption that sexuality is reducible to sexual intercourse and that it is a function of the relations between women and men. The cultural fusion of gender with sexuality has given rise to the idea that a theory of sexuality may be derived directly out of a theory of gender. * * *

Catherine MacKinnon has made the most explicit theoretical attempt to subsume sexuality under feminist thought. According to MacKinnon, "Sexuality is to feminism what work is to marxism . . . the molding, direction, and expression of sexuality organizes society into two sexes, women and men." This analytic strategy in turn rests on a decision to "use sex and gender relatively interchangeably." It is this definitional fusion that I want to challenge.

There is an instructive analogy in the history of the differentiation of contemporary feminist thought from Marxism. Marxism is probably the most supple and powerful conceptual system extant for analyzing social inequality. But attempts to make Marxism the sole explanatory system for all social inequalities have been dismal exercises. Marxism is most successful in the areas of social life for which it was originally developed—class relations under capitalism.

In the early days of the contemporary women's movement, a theoretical conflict took place over the applicability of Marxism to gender stratification. Since Marxist theory is relatively powerful, it does in fact detect important and interesting aspects of gender oppression. It works best for those issues of gender most closely related to issues of class and the organization of labor. The issues more specific to the social structure of gender were not amenable to Marxist analysis.

The relationship between feminism and a radical theory of sexual oppression is similar. Feminist conceptual tools were developed to detect and analyze gender-based hierarchies. To the extent that these overlap with erotic stratifications, feminist theory has some explanatory power. But as issues become less those of gender and more those of sexuality, feminist analysis becomes misleading and often irrelevant. Feminist thought simply lacks angles of vision which can fully encompass the social organization of sexuality. The criteria of relevance in feminist thought do not allow it to see or assess critical power relations in the area of sexuality.

In the long run, feminism's critique of gender hierarchy must be incorporated into a radical theory of sex, and the critique of sexual oppression should enrich feminism. But an autonomous theory and politics specific to sexuality must be developed.

It is a mistake to substitute feminism for Marxism as the last word in social theory. Feminism is no more capable than Marxism of being the ultimate and complete account of all social inequality. Nor is feminism the residual theory which can take care of everything to which Marx did not attend. These critical tools were fashioned to handle very specific areas of social activity. Other areas of social life, their forms of power, and their characteristic modes of oppression, need their own conceptual implements. In this essay, I have argued for theoretical as well as sexual pluralism.

NOTE ON THE CLASH BETWEEN TWO FEMINIST VISIONS: SEXUALITY–AS–ENGINE–OF–SEXISM (MACKINNON) AND SEXUALITY–AS–DIFFERENT–FROM–GENDER FEMINISM (RUBIN)

1. *Sex Radical Feminism versus Anti–Dominance Feminism.* The major theoretical point in dispute between MacKinnon and Rubin is the nature of the relationship between sexuality and gender. In MacKinnon's view, the two are seemingly inseparable: The sexual dominance of (most) women by (most) men constitutes the meaning of gender. Gender inequality has a sexual dynamic which sustains it more powerfully than do economic institutions, for example. Rubin, on the other hand, argues that sexuality is analytically independent of gender. She asserts the need for developing theories specifically of sexuality, comparable to our theories of the marketplace or of the state. Specifically, Rubin maintains that a modern theory would view sexuality as a positive, joyful force rather than as a presumptively negative, disdained force and that a non-materialist women's sexuality should be celebrated. See also Katherine Franke, "Theorizing Yes: An Essay on Feminism, Law and Desire," 101 *Colum. L. Rev.* 181 (2001).

2. *Feminism and Gaylaw.* Both MacKinnon and Rubin are theoretically gay-friendly, but of course from different angles. MacKinnon emphasizes the ways in which homophobia is linked to sexism; recall her debt to Rich's critique of compulsory heterosexuality. Rubin emphasizes the ways in which homophobia is linked to sex negativity. Notice how MacKinnon's thinking supports the sex discrimination argument for gay rights (Chapter 3, Section 3), while Rubin's thinking would be more skeptical. See also Francisco Valdes, "Queers, Sissies, Dykes and Tomboys: Deconstructing the Conflation of 'Sex,' 'Gender,' and 'Sexual Orientation' in Euro–American Law and Society," 83 *Cal. L. Rev.* 1 (1995).

3. *The Role of the State.* The MacKinnon–Rubin debate has profound consequences in thinking about the role of the state in regulating sexuality, a topic explored in greater detail in Chapters 6 (pornography) and 8 (workplace). Anti-dominance feminism views private sexuality-based violence as the primary threat to women, and so the state is a natural ally. (This can yield unusual alliances. As to strong regulation of rape, sexual harassment, and pornography, the principled natural law thinker ought to be, and often is, politically allied with the anti-dominance feminist.) Sex radical feminism views sex negativity as a threat to women's sexual agency, and so the state is a frequent adversary. Even when the state is adopting valid rules protecting women against sexual harassment, for example, sex radical feminists are concerned about the way the implementation of those rules will often be sex negative.

An increasing number of commentators are arguing that the state is a potential and needed ally, but only if it structures its rules in ways that are both feminist and efficacious. Vicki Schultz, "The Sanitized Workplace,"112 *Yale L.J.* 2061 (2003), supports state rules against sexual harassment in the workplace but argues that Title VII is being implemented in ways that suppress and distort healthy sexual feelings and interactions in the workplace. The Supreme Court has ruled that employers can escape liability for supervisor harassment of employees if they have in place and enforce anti-harassment rules. See *Farragher v. City of Boca Raton*, 524 U.S. 775 (1998). Encouraged by that interpretation, employers have increasingly monitored workplace sexual interactions—way beyond the requirements of Title VII and, argues Professor Schultz, beyond what is good for female as well as male workers. Under cover of *Farragher* and sexual harassment law, employers are seeking to instantiate a sterile Taylorist conception of the workplace that is bad for female as well as male workers.

Professor Schultz argues for a structural solution to the dilemma of sexual harassment law. Sociologists have found that workplace structure makes a difference. When women hold subordinate positions, workplace sexuality tends to be oppressive—but not when there are a number of women in the office and they hold positions of authority and responsibility. Under conditions of gender integration, workplace sexuality, for all its complex pluses and minuses, does not tend to disadvantage or oppress women. So the best doctrinal solution is not to reward employers for having a disciplinary policy in place, but for actually integrating their workforces. (So a gender-integrated workforce would create some kind of presumption against employer liability for hostile work environments.) How would MacKinnon respond to this kind of thinking?

PART C.   CRITICAL RACE THEORY AND INTERSECTIONALITY

Critical theory in the 1970s and early 1980s questioned the determinacy or objectivity of formalist and legal process theories of law. Critical theory took a big turn in the 1980s, rethinking law from the perspectives of women and people of color. Catharine MacKinnon, Martha Fineman, Sylvia Law, Robin West and others wrote leading articles and books powerfully critiquing law from feminist points of view. At the same time they were writing, other authors were criticizing American law from race-based perspectives. Exemplars of this school of critical scholarship are articles and books by Derrick Bell, Jr., Leon Higginbottham, Charles Lawrence, Mari Matsuda, Alan Freeman, Richard Delgado, Kimberlé Crenshaw, and Ian Haney–López, among others.[c]

Radical or cultural feminists shared much with critical race theorists. Both groups maintained not only that women and people of color need to be represented in American public law, but that American public law needs to be analytically reconceived from the vantage point of women and people of color. A Constitution drafted by white men has little legitimacy for women and people of color without a positive reformulation. Consider some key precepts of such a radical reconceiving of American constitutional law:

1. *An Anti–Subordination Understanding of the Constitution.* An important critical theme is that the Fourteenth Amendment embodies an *anti-subordination* norm, and that this norm must inform the entire constitutional enterprise. The anti-subordination norm posits that the central goal of the Reconstruction Amendments was to overturn laws and practices that unfairly subordinated social groups and to assure all persons the same protection of law that white males have traditionally enjoyed. Although the Supreme Court has occasionally paid lip-service to this goal, its analytical approach, especially after 1968, has been dominated by a *rationality* goal that the Justices have attributed to the Reconstruction Amendments. Critical race theorists as well as many feminists argue that

c. For some of the leading works, see, e.g., Derrick Bell, Jr., *Race, Racism, and American Law* (3d ed. 1992); Ian Haney–López, *White by Law* (1996); Derrick Bell, Jr., "*Brown v. Board of Education* and the Interest–Convergence Dilemma," 93 *Harv. L. Rev.* 518 (1980); Kimberlé Crenshaw, "Race, Reform, and Retrenchment: Transformation and Legitimation in Antidiscrimination Law," 101 *Harv. L. Rev.* 1331 (1988); Richard Delgado, "Storytelling for Oppositionists and Others: A Plea for Narrative," 87 *Mich. L.* *Rev.* 2411 (1989); Alan Freeman, "Legitimizing Racial Discrimination Through Antidiscrimination Law: A Critical Review of Supreme Court Doctrine," 62 *Minn. L. Rev.* 1049 (1978); Charles Lawrence, III, "The Id, the Ego, and Equal Protection: Reckoning with Unconscious Racism," 39 *Stan. L. Rev.* 317 (1987); Mari Matsuda, "Public Response to Racist Speech: Considering the Victim's Story," 87 *Mich. L. Rev.* 2320 (1989); Gary Peller, "Race Consciousness," 1990 *Duke L.J.* 758.

the strong emphasis on rationality over anti-subordination has deprived the Equal Protection Clause of its intended critical bite.

Catharine MacKinnon, "Reflections on Sex Equality under the Law," 100 *Yale L.J.* 1281 (1991), suggests how the judiciary's approach to the Equal Protection Clause has operated doctrinally. "[C]ourts in racial equality cases have largely confined themselves to the Aristotelian framework [where equality means treating like things alike]: qualification for admission into liberal humanity implicitly meant being like the white man. In *Plessy v. Ferguson*, for example, where segregation with equal facilities was held to be equality, the reason given was that Blacks were different from whites, so could be treated differently. When *Brown v. Board of Education* repudiated *Plessy* and held that educational segregation with equal facilities was inherently unequal, what changed was that *Brown* implicitly considered Blacks to be the same as whites. At least, Black school children were potentially so. This was a substantive shift in the political and ideological ground beneath the case law, not a pure doctrinal development. What was different was now the same. Difference could still justify differentiation, presumably including exclusion and subordination as well as segregation (maybe even affirmative action). Being the same as the dominant group remained the equality test." So *Brown*, the great liberal constitutional decision, operated under the same intellectual structure as *Plessy*.

Several consequences of this doctrinal structure have been of specific concern to critical theorists. This kind of thinking allows—and perhaps invites—the modernization of anti-minority norms (Crenshaw, "Race, Reform, and Retrenchment"). For example, the Court's *Brown* jurisprudence disallows arguments that people of color should be excluded because of white prejudice and stereotypes about racial minorities, but it allows continued exclusion based on modern standards of performance and cultural familiarity that many minorities do not meet, in part because of the effects of prior discrimination. This analytic not only permits continued subordination of minorities, but also cloaks it in an aura of enhanced legitimacy. The structure of equal protection analysis also has an assimilative effect. To win an equal protection case, minorities and women must show (à la Aristotle) that they are similar to the unspoken white male norm. This means that women and minorities who are already most like the norm will have the greatest success in equal protection cases; their success in court may translate into status within their cohort, a phenomenon which might press toward indirect suppression of distinctive minority cultures.

Mari Matsuda and other critical race theorists pose another kind of problem with the Court's neglect of the anti-subordination reading of the Equal Protection Clause: equal protection jurisprudence is too reactive, emphasizing limits rather than obligations of government. Both literally and in light of its abolitionist roots, the Equal Protection Clause imposes upon the state an obligation to *protect* women and minorities to the same extent that it protects white men (Matsuda, "Racist Speech"; Robin West,

Progressive Constitutionalism (1994)). Just as the Fourteenth Amendment *required* the state to reconstruct segregated public education systems after *Brown*, so it should now be construed to *require* the state to combat violence against women and prejudice-inspired hate crimes.

2. *The Sexualization of Minorities as an Instrument of Subordination.* The foundational insight of critical race theory is the state's pervasive role in the subordination of minorities and of women, and its responsibility for correcting that historic subordination. An increasing number of critical theorists are now tracing the ways in which the subordination of racial minorities has long involved—and continues to involve—their sexualization as both a cause and a feature of their oppression.[d]

For African Americans, the white majority sexualized them in ways that depicted them as subhuman and facilitated white terror against them. Accordingly, black women were constructed as sexually receptive to the attention of white men, including slaveholders, while black men were considered sexually voracious animals prone to attack the virtue of white women. All kinds of sexual perversions—from rape to sodomy to cross-dressing—were attributed to people of African descent. Rape law was overwhelmingly raced in American history: black women were almost completely unprotected against sexual assault by either white or black men; white women were substantially unprotected against sexual assault by white men but were overprotected against sexual assault by black men; thousands of black men accused of having sex with white women were executed by the state or by private lynch mobs because it was unthinkable that a white woman would consent to sex with a black man. Most of these patterns persist, albeit in attenuated form. See, *e.g.*, Tanya Kateri Hernandez, "Sexual Harassment and Racial Harassment: The Mutual Construction of Gender and Race," 4 *J. Gender Race & Just.* 183 (2001).

Sexuality was also the foundation for apartheid (Hovenkamp, "Segregation Before *Brown*"). The root fear of southern whites was *miscegenation*, sex between people of different races. If people of color were a degraded, even subhuman race, then no good would come of interracial sexuality, especially if it produced children. Recall in *Loving v. Virginia* (Chapter 3) that the state defended its criminalization of different-race marriage as a means to prevent the creation of a "mongrel race." The hysterical desire to prevent cohabitation or sexual interaction among the races was perhaps the most important driving force behind apartheid, and

---

d. Important works include Hazel Carby, " 'On the Threshold of Woman's Era': Lynching, Empire, and Sexuality in Black Feminist Theory," 12 *Crit. Inquiry* 262 (1985); Jacqueline Dowd Hall, " 'The Mind That Burns In Each Body,' "in *Powers of Desire* 328 (Ann Snitow et al. eds. 1983); A. Leon Higginbotham & Barbara Kopytoff, "Racial Purity and Interracial Sex in the Law of Colonial and Antebellum Virginia," 77 *Geo. L.J.* 1967 (1989); Herbert Hovenkamp, "Social Science and Segregation Before *Brown*," 1985 *Duke L.J.* 624; Jennifer Wriggins, "Rape, Racism, and the Law," 6 *Harv. Women's L.J.* 103 (1983). See generally John D'Emilio & Estelle Freedman, *Intimate Matters* (1988); *Critical Race Feminism: A Reader* 165–286 (Adrien Katherine Wing ed. 1997) (essays on the many ways in which sexual harassment and criminalization operate in relation to race, sex, and sexuality).

this helps us understand why it was so important to racists that public schools—potential hotbeds of adolescent sexuality—remain racially segregated.

Other scholars have focused on racial subordination of non-black people of color, especially women. Beginning with the earliest uses of immigration law, U.S. borders have been policed to exclude unmarried women of color, who were often assumed to be prostitutes. Sucheng Chan "The Exclusion of Chinese Women, 1870–1943," in *Entry Denied: Exclusion and the Chinese Community in America, 1882–1943* (Sucheng Chan ed. 1991). In an ironic twist on exclusion, the mail-order bride industry now imports young women to be respectably married, by feeding on racial and sexual stereotyping of Asian Pacific women as subservient, and providing women expected to be compliant to men who seek escape from too-liberated American women. *E.g.*, Christine S. Y. Chun, "The Mail–Order Bride Industry: The Perpetuation of Transnational Economic Inequalities and Stereotypes," 17 *U. Pa. J. Int'l Econ. L.* 1155 (1996). Sexualized stereotypes of the madonna-whore dichotomy have also targeted Latinas. Elizabeth Iglesias, "Rape, Race and Representation: The Power of Discourse, Discourses of Power, and the Reconstruction of Heterosexuality," 49 *Vand. L. Rev.* 869 (1996).

3. *Anti–Essentialism and Intersectionality.* Women of color have challenged the predominant whiteness of the women's movement.[e] Critical race feminist legal scholars also began to question the extent to which the early theories were built on the assumption that the experiences of white women (as sexually subordinated, for example) captured the ways in which patriarchy operated in the lives of women of color. Angela Harris, in "Race and Essentialism in Feminist Legal Theory," 42 *Stan. L. Rev.* 581 (1990), critiqued the writings of both MacKinnon and West as examples of "gender essentialism"—"the notion that there is a monolithic 'women's experience' that can be described independent of other facets of experience like race, class and sexual orientation." *Id.* at 585.

From the anti-essentialist critique grew another important contribution of race theory: the idea that social norms and the law operate not only differently upon black women than upon black men or white women, for example, but that the operation of intersecting prejudices and stereotypes is synergistic. The black woman is not just more subordinated than the white woman or the black man, but subordinated in a different range of ways.

Kimberlé Crenshaw, "Mapping the Margins: Intersectionality, Identity Politics, and Violence Against Women of Color," 43 *Stan. L. Rev.* 1241 (1991).[*] Like Professor MacKinnon, Professor Crenshaw

---

e. Early classics include Angela Davis, *Women, Race and Class* (1981); Paula Giddings, *When and Where I Enter: The Impact of Black Women on Race and Sex in America* (1984); *This Bridge Called My Back: Writings by Radical Women of Color* (Cherie Moraga & Gloria Anzaldua, eds. 1983).

starts with the "almost routine violence" that shapes the lives of women in the United States. Identity politics, whereby women have organized to resist and remedy this violence, has been an empowering development for women.

"The problem with identity politics is not that it fails to transcend difference, as some critics charge, but rather the opposite—that it frequently conflates or ignores intragroup differences. In the context of violence against women, this elision of difference in identity politics is problematic, fundamentally because the violence that many women experience is often shaped by other dimensions of their identities, such as race and class. Moreover, ignoring difference *within* groups contributes to tension *among* groups, another problem of identity politics that bears on efforts to politicize violence against women. Feminist efforts to politicize experiences of women and anti-racist efforts to politicize experiences of people of color have frequently proceeded as though the issues and experiences they each detail occur on mutually exclusive terrains. Although racism and sexism readily intersect in the lives of real people, they seldom do in feminist and anti-racist practices. And so, when the practices expound identity as woman or person of color as an either/or proposition, they relegate the identity of women of color to a location that resists telling."

Crenshaw's article explores the ways in which violence against women of color is captured in neither the feminist nor the anti-racist literature. Crenshaw addresses three dimensions of *intersectionality*: (1) structural intersectionality, the ways in which the experience of women of color with violence is qualitatively different from the experience of white women, often because the substance and process of law pose unique obstacles to certain minority women; (2) political intersectionality, how the separate politics of racism and sexism have operated to marginalize the particular challenges faced by women of color; and (3) representational intersectionality, or the cultural construction of women of color in ways that disempower them.

1.   *Structural Intersectionality*. Black women, Latinas, and other women of color who have been battered or raped by their spouses or partners face obstacles to reporting their battering that middle-class white women do not. Such distinctive obstacles include language barriers for women for whom English is not their first language; concerns that white bureaucrats will not find their claims credible; and fears that the police and other state officials will not only be unsympathetic but (especially in the case of immigrants) will actually punish the complainant. If they do report their injuries, women of color, especially those who are in poverty or immigrants, face remedial obstacles not faced by middle-class white women who are citizens. For example, rape counselors say that they spend much of their time handling problems (housing, childcare, etc.) not involving rapes themselves. Funding agencies typically do not allow for such assistance, says Crenshaw, so that many women of color who have been assaulted are not given the state assistance they need.

2. *Political Intersectionality.* Anti-racist and feminist domestic violence politics often work at cross purposes. For example, civil rights groups in Los Angeles (where Crenshaw gathered most of her examples) lobbied the Police Department to suppress data concerning domestic violence in minority communities, because these groups feared that such data would reinforce white perceptions of black men as violent. By actions like this, violence against women of color becomes officially invisible, and such women become more reluctant to report violence against them. That black men have been the historical objects of rape law has left black women more reluctant to report and the black community supportive of nonreporting.

"Not only do race-based priorities function to obscure the problem of violence suffered by women of color; feminist concerns often suppress minority experiences as well." Well-meaning domestic violence activists often go overboard in dispelling the myth that rape and battering are only problems of poor and minority communities—so much that they minimize or erase the concern society should have about violence against minority women. Domestic violence services are often so focused on their white middle-class constituencies that they do not provide interpreters for women who do not speak English well and frequently locate their centers in areas inaccessible or intimidating to poorer women.

"Although the rhetoric of both [anti-racist and feminist] agendas formally includes Black women, racism is generally not problematized by feminism, and sexism [is] not problematized in anti-racist discourses. Consequently, the plight of Black women is relegated to secondary importance: The primary beneficiaries of policies supported by feminists and others concerned about rape tend to be white women; the primary beneficiaries of the Black community's concern over racism and rape, Black men. Ultimately, the reformist and rhetorical strategies that have grown out of anti-racist and feminist rape reform movements have been ineffective in politicizing the treatment of Black women."

As an example of that politics, Crenshaw draws from and critiques Gary LeFree, *Rape and Criminal Justice: The Social Construction of Sexual Assault* (1989). Analyzing rape prosecutions in Minneapolis, LaFree demonstrated that black defendants were punished most severely by the system when they were charged with raping white women, and that rape victims were often left without redress when they had engaged in nontraditional behavior. The race part of his analysis, Crenshaw maintains, drew attention to the plight of black male defendants, while slighting the ways in which black women are devalued by the differential punishment and ignoring the great problem of intraracial rape of black women by black men. The gender part of his analysis, Crenshaw maintains, made an elementary statistical error. LeFree argued that the criminal justice system is much less responsive in rape cases when female complainants have engaged in nontraditional behavior. That strikes Crenshaw as an incomplete analysis, for LeFree's data support his conclusion only as to black (and not white) female rape victims. "Rape law, that is, serves not only to penalize actual examples of nontraditional behavior but also to diminish and devalue women who belong to groups in which nontraditional behavior is perceived as common. For the Black rape victim, the disposition of her case may often turn less on her behavior than on her identity."

3.   *Representational Intersectionality.* Crenshaw examines the cultural role assigned to women of color through an interrogation of the prosecution of 2 Live Crew, a rap music group charged with obscenity because of the lyrics of *Nasty As They Wanna Be*. In *Nasty*, the group sings of "cunts" being "fucked until backbones are cracked," "asses" being "busted," and "dicks" being rammed down throats. Crenshaw's point is that white discourse assailing 2 Live Crew deployed metaphors pitting whites and black women against black men.

The most famous display of the representational as well as political features of black women's erasure was the Anita Hill/Clarence Thomas confrontation in 1991 Senate Judiciary Committee hearings. As bewildered white male senators looked on uncomprehendingly, a black woman charged the nation's most prominent black male judge with sexual harassment, and he responded with charges that she was a dupe for white liberals intent on executing a "high-tech lynching." Supporters of Judge Thomas, many of them black as well as white men, claimed that he was a victim of whites' racist assumptions about black male sexuality. Supporters of Professor Hill, mainly feminists and male liberals, claimed that she was a victim of inappropriate male behavior. The popular press, and most academics, missed the ways in which black women are situated differently in sexual harassment cases than white women: their reluctance to come forward is a product not only of he said/she said difficulties of proof, but also of stereotypes—fears that their complaints will reinforce stereotypes of black men as rapists and will not be believed because of stereotypes about sexually inviting black women. The humiliating public hectoring of Professor Hill by several of the Senators suggests that these fears were hardly misguided.

Crenshaw concludes with observations on identity politics. She urges that "we first recognize that the organized identity groups in which we find ourselves are in fact coalitions, or at least potential coalitions waiting to be formed." Intersectionality does not, therefore, require that blacks cease organizing as a community of color. "Rather, intersectionality provides a basis for reconceptualizing race as a coalition between men and women of color. For example, in the area of rape, intersectionality provides a way of explaining why women of color have to abandon the general argument that the interests of the community require the suppression of any confrontation around intraracial rape. Intersectionality may provide the means for dealing with other marginalizations as well. For example, race can also be a coalition of straight and gay people of color, and thus serve as a basis for critique of churches and other cultural institutions that reproduce heterosexism."

NOTES ON INTERSECTIONALITY AND ITS IMPLICATIONS FOR THE CONSTITUTIONAL POLITICS OF SEXUALITY AND GENDER

1.   *Intersectionality and Privacy.* Review the materials in Chapter 2. Note how the big privacy cases involved white women and mostly white gay men and were litigated by white lawyers. The big exception is that *Lawrence* (Chapter 4) involved a male couple of different races. According to the Harris County brief defending the law, its police were called to John Lawrence's apartment building upon the report of an alarmed neighbor that a black man [Tyron Garner, Lawrence's sexual partner] had been seen in the building and was thought to be a burglar. Professor Crenshaw's different articulations of intersectionality can be seen in the litigation campaigns and judicial privacy opinions.

Structural Intersectionality: Counsel for the complainants in the privacy cases emphasized American libertarian traditions, which preserve valuable private spaces for those Americans who have the financial resources and social position to enjoy them. The right to an abortion is meaningless to a poor woman of color who cannot afford an abortion, and the same Justices who decided *Roe* later ruled that the state did not have to fund abortions for the indigent, see *Maher v. Roe*, 432 U.S. 464 (1977), nor did the state even have to open its hospitals to abortions. *Poelker v. Doe*, 432 U.S. 519 (1977) (per curiam). Women who can afford abortions have a valuable right; those who cannot, disproportionately people of color, have no meaningful right. Even contraceptives cost money that many women do not have, and state policies against meaningful pro-contraception sex education deprive women of access to information that would be valuable to them. Women who do not speak English are particularly vulnerable to information deficits.

Political Intersectionality: Some birth control advocates maintained that birth control was useful for eugenic reasons—it would encourage poor women of color not to reproduce. A few states in the South offered birth control information mainly to people of color. Obviously, this kind of argument deployed racist stereotypes of black women who could not control their sexuality. Contrariwise, some black males opposed birth control because they feared race suicide. While understandable, this was unfair to black women, who bore most of the burdens of pregnancy and raising children.

Representational Intersectionality: A consequence of the political discourse of privacy was often to depict black women as sexually loose or even promiscuous. Emphasizing the eugenics argument, supporters of birth control warned middle-class whites that immigrants and people of color could overrun the country if their birth rates were not checked. Opponents of birth control warned middle-class whites that their use of contraceptives posed the same risk. Note, however, that black women also spoke for themselves. In 1941, the National Council of Negro Women endorsed the idea of birth control by arguing for racial betterment, rather than individual freedom.

2. *The Relevance of Class and Language as Well as Race for Sexuality and Gender Issues.* Note how much of Professor Crenshaw's analysis (especially structural intersectionality) depends on the connections among people of color, poverty, and language. Feminist programs attacking rape, sexual harassment, and discrimination are not robust for the woman of color who is poor and does not speak English well. Query: Does the intersectionality thesis "work" for women of color who are well-educated, middle- or upperclass, and English-speaking? Consider Professor Hill as an example.

3. *Intersectionality and Sexual Orientation.* Like feminism, gaylaw has been predominantly white in its agenda and outlook. See Darren Lenard Hutchinson, " 'Gay Rights' for 'Gay Whites': Race, Sexual Identity, and Equal Protection Discourse," 85 *Cornell L. Rev.* 1358 (2000). Hutchinson broadens the concept of intersectionality into one that he calls *multidimensionality, i.e.,* the idea that a majority of people (the black male and the white woman, for example) share a mixture of privileging and disempowering traits, a phenomenon that ought to be figured into equal protection jurisprudence.

Whatever other dynamics apply, gay people of color have distinctive issues related to that identity. Tomás Almaguer develops the following contrast between Anglo and other ethnic Americans and Mexican Americans:

> Chicanos * * * have never occupied the social space where a gay or lesbian identity can readily become a primary basis of self-identity. This is due, in part, to their structural position at the subordinate ends of both the class and racial hierarchies, and in a context where ethnicity remains a primary basis of group identity and survival. Moreover, Chicano family life requires allegiance to patriarchal gender relations and to a system of sexual meanings that directly militate against the emergence of this alternative basis of self-identity. Furthermore, factors such as gender, geographical settlement, age, nativity, language usage and degree of cultural assimilation further prevent, or at least complicate, the acceptance of a gay or lesbian identity by Chicanos or Chicanas respectively. They are not as free as individuals situated elsewhere in the social structure to redefine their sexual identity in ways that contravene the imperatives of minority family life and its traditional gender expectations. * * *

Tomás Almaguer, "Chicano Men: A Cartography of Homosexual Identity and Behavior," in *The Lesbian and Gay Studies Reader* 255, 264 (Henry Abelove et al., eds., 1993).

Almaguer can be read to suggest that antigay discourse sediments differently in many minority communities than in mainstream ones. In many Hispanic communities in the United States, natural law tropes regarding women's roles and sodomy remain the dominant ways of thinking. So for a young Latina raised in a traditionalist community to identify as a "lesbian," she must work through the (religious) discourse she was raised with and then draw upon perhaps unfamiliar mainstream discourses. The danger of alienation from family and friends is different for her than for a young white woman in most U.S. cities or suburbs.

For a brilliant exploration of this theme, see Harlon Dalton, "AIDS in Blackface," 118 *Daedalus* 205 (1989). "[O]ne reason the black community has been slow in responding to AIDS is that many of us do not want to be associated with what is widely perceived as a gay disease." Because African Americans grew up in the shadow of a racist culture that viewed them as sexually degraded, there is a particular anxiety in black culture that its own sexual minorities be seized upon by whites to confirm their denigration of blacks generally. Moreover, Dalton suggests that "within the black community, internal homophobia has less to do with regulating sexual desire and affectional ties than with policing relations between the sexes. In this view, gay black men and lesbians are made to suffer because they are out of sync with a powerful cultural impulse to weaken black women and strengthen black men." He continues: "My suspicion is that openly gay men and lesbians evoke hostility in part because they have come to symbolize the strong female and the weak male that slavery and Jim Crow produced. * * * [L]esbians are seen as standing for the proposition that 'black men aren't worth shit.' More than even the 'no account' men who figure prominently in the repertoire of female blues singers, gay men symbolize the abandonment of black women. Thus, in the black community homosexuality carries more baggage than in the larger society."

POSTMODERN THEORY OF SEXUALITY, GENDER, AND THE LAW: SEXUALITY AND SEX AS SOCIAL CONSTRUCTS

This section presents a selection of theories that we have categorized for the sake of convenience as *postmodern*. The meaning of this widely-used term is contested, and it has become a term of derision, especially by people who do not know what it means. We confess that we are not entirely sure of a clear definition ourselves, but here we are deploying it to include a range of theories that understand "sexuality" and "gender" predominantly as productions of human discourse rather than as natural phenomena. Feminist theories such as those of Catherine MacKinnon and Gayle Rubin and critical race theories such as those of Kim Crenshaw might be characterized as postmodern, but we are reserving that label for theories that open up both terms more radically.

PART A. THE PHILOSOPHY OF MICHEL FOUCAULT

Mary McIntosh, "The Homosexual Role," 16 *Soc. Prob.* 182 (1968) asked, Why is it that "sexual orientation" is considered such an important object of study? She maintained that sexual orientation is a role created by society, and indeed created for socially regulatory purposes. McIntosh challenged the sexologists not as bad scientists (that was Kinsey's critique), but as bit players in a larger cultural drama of which they were but dimly aware.

McIntosh said that there is no transhistorical phenomenon that can be called "homosexuality." For most Americans, this is an astonishing statement. What about the Greeks? Weren't they "homosexuals"? McIntosh assures us that men and women of earlier times engaged in same-sex intimacy, sodomy, and the like. But the same physical acts have had radically different meanings at different points in time and in different cultures at the same time. A *sodomite* in the nineteenth century perceived himself much differently than the *pederast* of ancient Athens or the *homosexual* of today.

Much has been made in the last generation of McIntosh's thesis, most famously by the French philosopher Michel Foucault.[a] His three-volume *History of Sexuality* (published in English 1978, 1985, 1986) took and developed McIntosh's idea (without attribution) that "sexuality" per se was unknown in the ancient world and was the consequence of a confessional dialectic that has grown ever more intense in the modern world. Volume one of the *History* (the *Introduction*) treats the early modern and modern periods and maintains that sexuality itself is a consequence of an ongoing and increasingly focused attention to the body by priests, doctors, psychiatrists, and bureaucrats. Foucault explores the archaeology of sexuality (its genealogy as an idea) through several interrelated inquiries and critiques.

1. *Foucault's Critique of the Repressive Hypothesis*. One of Foucault's central insights was to challenge the conventional wisdom that the relationship between power and sex is one of repression. It is a staple of popular thinking that uptight or religious societies repressed sex, and that in the last several decades, sexual rebels have sought liberation from these edicts. Not so, said Foucault. He perceived a very different history.

Foucault started with the seventeenth-century Christian practice of the confessional. A traditional view might see the confessional only as a moment when the church exercises its power over the penitent, who is required to divulge any sins against ecclesiastical proscriptions. Foucault, however, describes the confessional as the practice that "prescribed as a fundamental duty the task of passing everything having to do with sex through the endless mill of speech." (*Introduction* 21.) This method of transforming sex into discourse became "a rule for everyone" and thus a prime example of what Foucault calls "an incitement" to talk about sex. "This is the essential thing: that Western man has been drawn for three centuries to the task of telling everything concerning his sex" (*id.* at 23). Thus, while laws and customs may have formally prohibited certain sexual behaviors and effectively limited sexual speech in many situations (between parent and child, for example), "at the level of discourses and their domains .. the opposite phenomenon occurred[:] ... a proliferation of discourses concerned with sex" (*id.* at 18).

The technique of generating "confessional" speech or sex-talk was later reinforced and expanded by mechanisms of power other than the church. Beginning in the eighteenth century, governments started to understand that they were dealing not just with subjects or citizens, but with a "population." At the heart of the issue of population was sex. Thus agencies of the state developed an interest in birth rates, age of marriage, illegitimacy and procreative practices. In short, sexual conduct began to be understood as having a direct relationship to the wealth and security of

---

a. The account of Foucault draws mainly from his *Introduction*, volume one of *History of Sexuality* (Robert Hurley trans. 1978), and from his essay "Afterword: The Subject and the Power," in *Beyond Structuralism and Hermeneutics* (Hubert L. Dreyfuss & Paul Rabinow eds., 1982). Particularly useful secondary sources are Vikki Bell, *Interrogating Incest: Feminism, Foucault and the Law* (1993); Celia Kitzinger, *The Social Construction of Lesbianism* (1987); David Macey, *The Lives of Michel Foucault* (1995).

nations. "It was essential that the state know what was happening with its citizens' sex, and the use they made of it, but also that each individual be capable of controlling the use he made of it. Between the state and the individual, sex became an issue, and a public issue no less; a whole web of discourses, special knowledges, analyses and injunctions settled upon it." (*Id.* at 26.)

Foucault cites the (French) school system of the 1700s as an example of an institutional system in which, on the surface, sex was eradicated but where, *sub rosa,* it was a driving force. "The space for classes, the shape of the tables, the planning of the recreation lessons, the distribution of the dormitories (with or without partitions, with or without curtains), the rules for monitoring bedtime and sleep periods—all this referred, in the most prolix manner, to the sexuality of children" (*Introduction* 28). It was deemed of paramount importance to monitor the children (boys) for any signs of sexuality, and to take all possible precautions to prevent masturbation. Because of the perceived dangers of masturbation (onanism), "devices of surveillance were installed; traps were laid for compelling admissions; inexhaustible and corrective discourses were imposed; parents and teachers were alerted, and left with the suspicion that all children were guilty, and with the fear of being themselves at fault if their suspicions were not sufficiently strong; they were kept in readiness in the face of this recurrent danger; their conduct was prescribed and their pedagogy recodified; an entire medico-sexual regime took hold of the family milieu" (*id.* at 42).

In the nineteenth century, medical discourse became the primary arena in which sexuality was penalized and stigmatized, yet also simultaneously incited, monitored, and commented upon. In a critical development, the mode of the confessional was medicalized, and in turn reconceptualized as therapeutic. Modern sexology acquired its professional status during the Victorian period. Officially, Victorians adhered to the "triple edict of taboo, nonexistence and silence" about sex. (*id.* at 3) But that era also witnessed an unprecedented explosion of detailed examination, analysis, and speculation about these supposedly taboo topics.

In sum, Foucault interpreted the history of sexuality not as a simple story of the repression of sex, but as a much more complicated process "that spreads [sex] over the surface of things and bodies, arouses it, draws it out and bids it speak, implants it in reality and enjoins it to tell the truth" (*id.* at 72).

2. *Systems of Power.* This is interesting, you may be thinking, but what about all those repressive laws? Foucault saw power systems as more complex than law, and rejected the underlying assumptions of a law centered view of the world. He critiqued the precepts of what he called "juridicodiscursive power" as naive. Power is not simply the state, he wrote, but resides in a multiplicity of interconnecting (and sometimes contradictory) systems. For example, he believed that the educational, religious, and medical systems exercised far greater power with respect to sexuality than did the law. Where others might see a social/sexual structure dichotomized as freedom and repression or the individual versus the state,

Foucault saw "a veritable 'technology' of sex" with multiple and conflicting players and effects. (*Introduction* 90.)

Foucault maintained that power comes from everywhere—from the bottom up and not just from the top down. He understood power as a complex web.

> It seems to me that power must be understood in the first instance as the multiplicity of force relations immanent in the sphere in which they operate and which constitute their own organization; as the process which, through ceaseless struggles and confrontations, transforms, strengthens, or reverses them; as the support which these force relations find in one another, thus forming a chain or a system, or on the contrary, the disjunctions and contradictions, which isolate them from one another; and lastly, as the strategies in which they take effect, whose general design or institutional crystallization is embodied in the state apparatus, in the formulation of the law, in the various social hegemonies. * * * [P]ower is not an institution, and not a structure; neither is it a certain strength we are endowed with; it is the name that one attributes to a complex strategical situation in a particular society. (*Id.* at 92–93.)

Systems of power relations ("force relations") enable and produce specific discourses, such as the discourses on sex. Discourses, or systems of understanding and practice, implement power relations, but also create points of resistance. "Discourse transmits and produces power; it reinforces it, but also undermines and exposes it, renders it fragile and makes it possible to thwart it." (*Id.* at 101.) A hegemonic (or dominant) discourse that presents homosexuality as an illness, for example, not only propagates that idea, but also can incite reaction, rebuttal, and rebellion.

Key to Foucault's theory is the belief that the operation of power is not simply prohibitory or negative. Power systems *produce* sexuality as well as prohibit it.

3.   Sexuality as a Discursive Production. As the "discursive explosion" regarding sex continued through the eighteenth and nineteenth centuries, its subjects (and objects) began to jell. Foucault perceived a gradual organization of power/knowledge around four subjects: the "hysterization" of women's bodies (in which women's bodies were analyzed "as being thoroughly saturated with sexuality"); a "pedagogization" of children's sex; "a socialization of procreative sex"; and "a psychiatrization of perverse pleasure." (*Introduction* at 104–105.) What occurred was nothing less than

> the very production of sexuality. Sexuality must not be thought of as a kind of natural given which power tries to hold in check, or as an obscure domain which knowledge tries gradually to uncover. It is the name that can be given to a historical construct: not a furtive reality that is difficult to grasp, but a great surface network in which the stimulation of bodies, the intensification of pleasures, the incitement to discourse, the formation of special knowledges, the strengthening of

controls and resistances, are linked to one another, in accordance with a few major strategies of knowledge and power. (*Id.* at 105–06.)

In other words, the very same regulatory discourse that is conventionally described as repressive actually *produced* what we understand as sexuality.

One specific example of this was the production of (the idea of) homosexuality. In analyzing the sexologists's study of "perverse pleasures" and what Foucault called "peripheral sexualities," he made his now famous observation dating the invention of homosexuality (as distinct from same-sex sexual practices) as a nineteenth century event:

> This new persecution of the peripheral sexualities entailed an *incorporation of perversions* and a new *specification of individuals.* As defined by the ancient civil or canonical codes, sodomy was a category of forbidden acts; their perpetrator was nothing more than the juridical subject of them. The nineteenth-century homosexual became a personage, a past, a case history, and a childhood. * * * Nothing that went into his total composition was unaffected by his sexuality. * * * The sodomite had been a temporary aberration; the homosexual was now a species. (*Id.* at 42–43, emphasis in the original.)

Consider also that some of the arguments advocating equality for gay people are framed in terms suggestive of a view of the homosexual as a distinct type of person. We tend to think of the *Hardwick* decision, for example, and a gay rights argument as extreme opposites. Foucault, himself a gay man, might critique both, however, as representing simply the flip sides of a coin, both equally trapped inside one discursive system.

We hope this discussion gives you some understanding of the complicated way in which sexual discourse operates, as well as the larger context in which Foucault comprehends this system. A further and important feature of that larger context is Foucault's tentative theory of sexuality as a dynamic system, and its implications for the future.

Before *sexuality* became an important system, *alliance* was the primary system for understanding and organizing households (in rural, nonwestern societies alliance is still typically the primary organizational system). In contrast to sexuality, a new and destabilizing system, alliance was a longstanding and homeostatic system: Its mechanism was to establish ties of blood and marriage, and its goal was to protect and reproduce the traditional patriarchal family (*Introduction* 105–06). The modern era may be characterized by the eclipse of the regime of alliance and its gradual supplantation by the regime of sexuality.

The family is the situs of this transition, and now its battleground. Premodern society viewed the family as the fundamental unit of society, and individuals were formed in the shadow of family ties. One's identity was framed in relation to one's parents, one's spouse, and kinship group. Where families had earlier left children to their own devices in exploring genitals and gender, bourgeois families of the early modern era became highly attentive to children's masturbation and so forth. The attention showered on this matter not only sexualized certain body parts, but also sexualized the family itself. Thus the family, the apex of alliance, became the birthplace of sexuality, which now often overshadows alliance as the basis of individual identity.

The discourse of sexuality has hardly abated in western culture, and Foucault saw its productiveness only multiplying in the future. Traditional ties of family and kinship will be evermore overtaken by ties of pleasure and corporality. Foucault believed that the future would dissolve many of the boundaries that we cleave to insistently now (such as the significance of sexual orientation) and would multiply the categories of pleasure. In his most visionary moment, he predicted "nothing less than a transgression of laws, a lifting of prohibitions, an irruption of speech, a reinstating of pleasure within reality, and a whole new economy in the mechanisms of power will be required." (*Introduction* 5.)

PROBLEM 5-2

STRATEGIES FOR CHALLENGING LAWS REGULATING SEXUALITY

Recall the issues we posed to a theoretically reconstituted Supreme Court in Problem 5-1: (a) criminalization of adultery and sex between adult first cousins; (b) sex-segregated education in a paramilitary college; and (c) same-sex marriage and polygamy. Aggregate the votes of our highly diverse Court—and then think about how Michel Foucault would critique the result and reasoning of the Court. We don't think it would be Foucauldian for us to ask for his "vote" in the cases. Instead, we are interested in how his vocabulary would understand the discourses involved in each case: What power dynamics does each law reflect? How does each law contribute to the construction of a particular understanding of sexuality or gender? How would the invalidation affect that discourse?

Let's assume that a divided Court would (a) strike down the adultery and first cousin statutes in an opinion by Richard Posner (dissent by John Finnis); (b) strike down the sex segregation and order VMI integrated in an opinion by Gayle Rubin (dissent as to invalidation by Finnis and as to remedy by Catharine MacKinnon); and (c) uphold the polygamy law while striking down the same-sex marriage bar in an opinion by Kimberlé Crenshaw (dissent as to same-sex marriage by Finnis). How would Foucault analyze each opinion?

PART B.   FEMINISM AND FOUCAULT[b]

Many American scholars have taken an interest in Foucault's work. The feminist treatment of Foucault has proven to be the most intellectually

b.   The works most helpful to us in this regard include Vikki Bell, *Interrogating Incest: Feminism, Foucault and the Law* (1993); Judith Butler, *Gender Trouble: Feminism and the Subversion of Identity* (1990); Susan Hekman, *Gender and Knowledge: Elements of a Postmodern Feminism* (1990); Carol Smart, *Feminism and the Power of Law* (1989); Ann Snitow et. al., *Powers of Desire: The Politics of Sexuality* (1984); Biddy Mar-

lively. Foucault's analysis of power relations simultaneously criticizes the feminist emancipation agenda, while providing fresh tools for the critical evaluation of patriarchy. The relationship between Foucault and feminism has not been one way. Feminists have presented some powerful challenges to Foucault's theory on sex, power, and truth, making it less contradictory for the effort. Consider the following lines of dialogue between feminists and Foucault.

To begin with, there is much that Foucault and leading feminist theories have in common, for both lines of thought are critical of the traditional wisdom about sex and sexuality. Foucault provides feminism another vocabulary for situating and problematizing the work of the early sexologists. Most of the early sexologists insisted that women's sexual pleasure is tied to the male penis. Both feminists and Foucault critique this claim as deriving from any "natural science" and insist that the thought must be linked with other power relations, such as the traditional subordination of women to men in western society. For Foucault as for most feminists, there is nothing unnatural about sex between two women, and the hysteria it creates in men is related to threats those men see to their power, specifically, their monopoly on female sexuality.

Foucault's thought is not very helpful, however, in ignoring the *gendering aspects of sexuality*. As Vikki Bell puts it,

> Foucault's central interest is with the production of the concept of sexuality and categories of sexuality ('homosexual', 'heterosexual', 'paedophiliac', etc.) through knowledge/power networks. By contrast, feminists are more interested in those knowledges which create a differential relationship between men and women, or that act against women as a group. Knowledges which suggest that women need men in order to experience sexual satisfaction, which situate lesbianism as a deviant sexual choice, which depict masculine sexuality as inherently predatory, have been considered by feminists not simply as powerful knowledges that constrain all individuals, but as powerful knowledges that differentially constrain women. Crucially, the central concern of feminism is the way in which these ways of understanding sexuality have operated to make women subordinate to men as individuals and as a group.

The major feminist criticism of Foucault's thesis on sexuality therefore is that he fails to consider what one might term the *gendering* aspects of sexuality. * * * What he fails to do is consider how the strategies of sexuality affect the relationship *between* men and women as gendered individuals. (Bell, *Interrogating Incest* 26–27.)

Foucault does not view the operation of power as so consistently oppressing one group as feminist theorists do. Recall Catharine Mac-

tin, "Feminism, Criticism and Foucault," and other essays in *Feminism and Foucault: Reflections on Resistance* (Irene Diamond & Lee Quinby eds. 1988); Nancy Hartsock, "Fou-   cault on Power: A Theory for Women?" in *Feminism/Postmodernism* (Linda J. Nickolson ed. 1990).

Kinnon's argument that the social construction of male and female sexuality is the key to gender oppression.

Foucault, in turn, poses a critique of early feminist theory, namely, its too simple understanding of power and its naive belief in truth. To the extent that some feminists believe that patriarchy unifies traditional power structures and that the feminist project is to overthrow patriarchy and thereby to liberate women's own true selves, Foucault would dissent. He argues that feminists have no better access to "truth" than the Victorians and that the feminist emancipatory project is merely the flip side of traditional views that sex is essential and univocal. In short, feminist resistance to the Victorians is trapped in basically the same vocabulary.

A different strain in early feminist thought, however, was grounded in radical challenges to the very sorts of fixed identity categories that Foucault found wanting. According to him,

> [T]he real strength of the women's liberation movements is not that of having laid claim to the specificity of their sexuality and the rights pertaining to it, but that they have actually departed from the discourse conducted within the apparatuses of sexuality. Ultimately, it is a veritable movement of de-sexualisation, a displacement effected in relation to the sexual centering of the problem, formulating the demand for forms of culture, discourse, language and so on, which are no longer part of that rigid assignation and pinning down to their sex which they had initially in some sense been politically obliged to accept in order to make themselves heard.

Michel Foucault, *Power/Knowledge: Selected Interviews and Other Writings* 219–20 (Colin Gordon ed. 1980). Note how Foucault's analysis mixes concepts of sex, sexuality, and, implicitly, gender.

Consider Judith Butler's elaboration. Sex for the Victorians was univocal insofar as there was a simple identity between a person and her sex— "one is one's sex" (Butler, *Gender Trouble* 94). The Victorians argued that sex was the "continuous cause and signification of bodily pleasures." Thus sex was biological and not social. This view produced a distorted understanding of sex, by essentializing it. For the social constructionist, sex is not a cause, but rather an effect of "an open and complex historical system of discourse and power." Sex is social, not biological; and feminism misses this by taking sex as the starting point of its analysis. By accepting sex as the root cause of female domination, some feminist theory fails to grasp that sex is merely an effect of female domination. Some feminists too quickly agree with the patriarch that sex is the reason men dominate women, for she or he should see that men dominate women through the creation of sex. By accepting this effect as a cause, feminism legitimates the regulatory strategy of patriarchy, and is thus self-defeating. (*Id.* at 94–95.)

A Foucauldian approach emphasizes a more complex understanding of power. Some feminist thought, especially in the early stages, seemed to operate under traditional views about power—what Foucault calls the *juridical* (or legal) model of power: power acts in negative (prohibitory) ways, repressing the illicit; power flows from a central hierarchical source; hence power can be overthrown by the powerless. If, as Foucault imagines, power is "omnipresent," productive rather than prohibitory, and normalizing rather than repressive, the feminist target (patriarchy) becomes more elusive and the role of the state (protect women against patriarchy) more ambiguous.

Butler's expansion of Foucault might be said to undermine the feminist agenda, basically by removing its subject. However theoretically attractive such a stance might be, its effect might be politically enervating. On the other hand, as Susan Hekman has argued, "the assumption that political action, to be valid, must be founded in absolute values is precisely the assumption that Foucault is challenging" (Hekman, *Gender and Knowledge* 180). The current situation of women is an "unstable truth" that can be the basis for political action and resistance, even if centuries from now our descendants might wonder why we became so anxious about gender as well as sexuality (recall the delphic conclusion of volume one of the *History of Sexuality*). Feminism might be viewed as a resistance discourse, which even if unstable is useful for an often silenced group to be heard (Bell 55–56). As Biddy Martin puts it,

> Our task is to deconstruct, to undo our own meanings and categories, the identities and the positions from which we intervene at any given point so as not to close the question of woman and discourse around new certainties and absolutes. We cannot afford to refuse to take a political stance 'which pins us to our sex' for the sake of abstract theoretical correctness, but we can refuse to be content with fixed identities or to universalize ourselves as revolutionary subjects. (Martin 16.)

PROBLEM 5–3

LAW, FOUCAULT, FEMINISM, RAPE, STATUTORY RAPE, AND INCEST

The criminal codes in virtually all the United States prohibit each of the following: rape (sexual assault), coercive sex against the will of one of the partners; statutory rape, where one of the partners is under the age of consent; and incest, where the partners are closely related. Consider the following case which involves all three of these issues, and consider further how this case illustrates the particular ways our culture has constructed sex and sexuality. Note that the defendant was charged with only one offense (incest), even though the facts also support a charge of rape.

State v. Marvin Kaiser
Washington Court of Appeals, 1983.
34 Wash.App. 559, 663 P.2d 839.

■ MUNSON, ACTING CHIEF JUDGE.

Marvin K. Kaiser appeals his incest conviction, RCW 9A.64.020. He contends the trial court erred in admitting his confession, the evidence was insufficient, improper evidence was admitted at trial, and the incest statute denied him equal protection. We affirm.

Mr. Kaiser was charged with having committed incest with his 16–year-old stepdaughter. On May 13 and 14, Mr. Kaiser met with a police detective to informally discuss the accusation. On May 15, 1981, Mr. Kaiser was advised of his rights as required by *Miranda v. Arizona*, 384 U.S. 436 (1966), and progeny. He indicated he wished to speak to an attorney. The questioning stopped; the detective made immediate arrangements for Mr. Kaiser to meet with a public defender who was present at the jail. Mr. Kaiser and the public defender discussed the charge for 20 to 25 minutes. Mr. Kaiser stated the public defender told him the crime was a felony and advised him not to make a statement.

Mr. Kaiser returned to the detective and decided to make a statement. The detective gave him the *Miranda* warnings from a printed form which Mr. Kaiser initialed and signed. The detective then taped an oral confession from Mr. Kaiser which also began with a waiver of all *Miranda* rights. Mr. Kaiser stated he entered the stepdaughter's bed against her will, disrobed her, engaged in full intercourse for a brief time, realized he had erred, and left. At the end of the statement, Mr. Kaiser signified the statement was true, he understood his *Miranda* rights and waived them, and no promises had been made. [The trial judge held that the confession was voluntary and therefore admissible against Kaiser, a finding the appeals court affirmed.] * * *

At the subsequent nonjury trial, the stepdaughter testified Mr. Kaiser had engaged in sexual intercourse against her wishes. She was asked whether her stepfather put his penis into her vagina. She replied that he had and that she knew this because of the pain. On cross examination, she was asked whether there was penetration. She replied, "I can't be sure."

Mr. Kaiser denied the event all together. He again explained the false statement was given to the detective to protect the family from publicity.

The stepdaughter's boyfriend testified she told him the following day that she had been raped by her stepfather. The boyfriend indicated she was distraught and cried for over an hour and a half before telling him; they later reported the incident to school officials.

The detective who received Mr. Kaiser's statement was asked by Mr. Kaiser's counsel whether he had recorded in any statement by the stepdaughter anything which showed penetration had occurred. From her statement, the detective testified she had told him Mr. Kaiser inserted his penis in her vagina. The detective testified he explained the terms to her prior to the statement and she stated she understood them.

The trial court found Mr. Kaiser guilty of incest, reasoning that where the stepdaughter's testimony was equivocal the confession was not. Because the trial court could not accept Mr. Kaiser's stated reasons for making a false statement, the court accepted the statement over the in-court testimony. The court found the stepdaughter's version to be more credible. * * *

Mr. Kaiser * * * contends the stepdaughter's answer on cross examination raised a reasonable doubt. Her testimony was not as equivocal as first appears. On direct, she gave no doubt penetration had occurred. She may not have known the meaning of the word "penetration" because there is a question of whether she knew the meaning of the word "erection". This confusion was not clarified.

Even if a doubt remained after her testimony, Mr. Kaiser's statement and the testimony of both the boyfriend and the detective bolstered her credibility. Although Mr. Kaiser's statement differed from the stepdaughter's testimony in the degree of violence, it essentially agreed on the specific act of intercourse. * * *

Mr. Kaiser finally contends the incest statute denies him equal protection of the law. His argument appears to be twofold: (1) because the "object of the statute was obviously to prevent a procreation of children which may be affected by the relationship of the parties who are closer than second cousins," the inclusion of stepchildren bears no rational relationship to a legitimate governmental objective; and (2) nonconsensual intercourse is punished until age 16 under the statutory rape statutes; equal protection is denied under the incest statute because even consensual intercourse is forbidden to age 18.

Historically, incest was prohibited by ecclesiastical canon; now, it is prohibited by statute. The statutory schemes differ; some states prevent illicit intercourse by consanguinity while others also include relation by affinity.

Prevention of mutated birth is only one reason for these statutes. The crime is also punished to promote and protect family harmony, to protect children from the abuse of parental authority, and because society cannot function in an orderly manner when age distinctions, generations, sentiments and roles in families are in conflict. Thus, the statute bears a rational relation to a legitimate governmental objective. The legislation bears a reasonable and substantial relationship to the health, safety, morals or welfare of the public. We hold the statute is therefore constitutional.

Mr. Kaiser notes consensual intercourse is not punishable after a female reaches age 16 except under the incest statute where even consensual intercourse is forbidden to age 18. He then asserts: "Had the defendant chosen merely to live with the mother of Connie, he would have incurred no penalties because of his act of intercourse with the child, . . ." Disregarding the fact that this intercourse was not consensual, and was therefore punishable as third degree rape, such a distinction would deny equal protection only if Mr. Kaiser could show the Legislature did not have a legitimate interest in discriminating between such individuals. As noted earlier, incest is a crime which affects the individuals, society, and, to a degree greater than other crimes, the family. The additional 2 years can be seen as an important protection for the family. The State has a legitimate interest in protecting children from parental abuse for an additional 2 years. Whether by consanguinity or affinity, parents have tremendous emotional and material leverage, even after a child reaches 16, which may not exist outside the home. The distinction is reasonable.

Mr. Kaiser's conviction is affirmed.

NOTES ON *KAISER*—FOUCAULT VERSUS FEMINISM

1. *The Incest Issue.* Incest is the tension point of Foucault's overlapping systems of individual identity: It is the key taboo in the system of kinship alliance, but the system of sexuality inspires and generates it as part of the family dynamics which literally inculcate sexuality. "[Incest] is manifested as a thing that is strictly forbidden in the family insofar as the latter functions as a deployment of alliance; but it is also a thing that is continually demanded in order for the family to be a hotbed of sexual incitement." (Foucault, *Introduction* 109.) Thus the incest taboo is not at all the oldfashioned idea moderns make it out to be—its intensity is owed to its central spot in both regimes, of sexuality and alliance. Note, for example, the centrality of the incest taboo for psychoanalysis; Freud is best known for his metaphorical statement of the relationship between family and sexuality—the Oedipus complex.

Consider the implications of Foucault's thought for *Kaiser* and for feminism. Foucault's theory of sexuality provides an interesting defense (only to incest, not to rape) and a fascinating problem with *Kaiser*. By making incest illegal, the state is announcing the convergence between the old regime of alliance and the new regime of sexuality: Both are threatened by incest, and their coinciding concerns give incest prohibitions their particular power. On the other hand, criminalizing incest, and making it the occasion for the drama of a court proceeding, ought to intensify the family as a situs for sexuality.

In *Kaiser*, the incest is between a father and a (step)daughter. This is the typical scenario, and its typicality has generated enormous feminist interest. Feminists have encouraged women and girls to tell their stories of family (father) abuse and have encouraged mothers and prosecutors to punish men (fathers) who have sex with daughters and stepdaughters. Foucault would question this strategy. Does it not yield the same sort of discourse that produces rather than suppresses sexuality? Is it possible that prohibitory laws make incest "sexy" for men like Marvin Kaiser? How would feminist theorists answer this charge? See Vikki Bell, *Interrogating Incest: Feminism, Foucault and the Law* ch. 4 (1993), for an excellent discussion.

It has been argued by feminist writers that the incest taboo is not quite the taboo that Foucault makes it out to be. Although the taboo seems to be a genuine deterrent to mother-son sex, fathers apparently have sex often with daughters and stepdaughters, albeit with great secrecy and often some degree of shame. See Judith Lewis Herman & Lisa Hirschman, *Father-Daughter Incest* (1981). Some feminist writers have conceptualized the asymmetrical incest taboo as reflecting the system by which men dominate women: The mother relinquishes her sexual feelings for the son, who enters into the father's world, while the father remains free to initiate the daughter into a sexualized world where men call the shots. See Elizabeth Ward, *Father-Daughter Rape* (1984). These feminists, therefore, understand incest differently from Foucault: Incest is important to the system of alliance, not just of family and kinship ties, but of a household which is dominated by men and whose denizens are sexually available to the paterfamilias.

Professor Bell believes that "the incest prohibition functions by making people consider the reaction their behaviour would receive. The imagined reaction may be somebody's reaction in particular, people's reaction in general, or the law's response. * * * On the other hand, MacKinnon's argument that the prohibition or illegality of acts can be 'part of their excitement potential' suggests that the 'prohibition of incest' as a discursive phenomenon may also be involved in the *commission* of incest." (Bell, *Interrogating Incest* 122.) Within this understanding, what role does *Kaiser*—the prosecution and a court decision affirming a conviction—play in the drama of the incest taboo?

2. *The Sex-with-Minors Issue.* In 1978, Foucault, Guy Hocquenghem, and Jean Danet proposed that consensual sex between adults and minors be legalized. See Foucault, *Politics, Philosophy, Culture: Interviews and Other Writings, 1977–1984* (Lawrence Kritzman ed. 1988). Their argument was that existing laws contributed to the child's fragile sexuality by setting it off limits, and deprives the child of the chance to explore her or his desires. Conversely, by creating and focusing on a special breed of criminal, the "child molester," the law is sexualizing a certain line and implicitly inviting people to cross over it—in derogation of the policy of protecting children. The three thinkers challenge the naturalness of the categories thus created ("vulnerable child," "child molester") and urge that the policy be abandoned.

Feminist theory has contributed importantly to the regulation of child abuse, and feminist discourse therefore is directly called into question by Foucault, Hocquenghem, and Danet. Feminist theory has tended to see all sex with children as akin to rape. "Adult-child sex is wrong because the fundamental conditions of consent cannot prevail in the relationship between an adult and a child." Emily Driver, "Introduction" to *Child Sexual Abuse: Feminist Perspectives* 5 (1989). If, as some feminists believe, there is a power disparity in all heterosexual relations, how much weight should be given to differences in age? Should relations between an adult woman and an underage male be treated the same or differently than relations between an adult man and an underage woman?

Bell believes that the Foucault critique is much more cogent than his prescription (Bell, *Interrogating Incest* 154–60). Once he descends into the realm of policy prescription, Foucault falls victim to all the questionable intellectual moves he criticized in *History of Sexuality*: giving too much credit to law as a directive force and ignoring the greater importance of other social forces, idealizing "freedom" as the absence of legal prohibition, and neglecting the impossible question of what "consent" even is. More important, Bell worries that the introduction of a consent defense into adult-child sex will create new and painful discursive possibilities. Testimony in ordinary abuse cases is traumatic enough for the child, and testimony by adult women (subject to vicious cross-examination to establish consent or acquiescence) is traumatic enough for women; consider the double trauma for a child pressed on issues of consent, invitation, and acquiescence. As Bell reminds the Foucauldians, sometimes lines cut off discourse.

3. *The Rape Issue.* Foucault was no defender of coerced sex, but he found perplexing the way in which rape laws privilege specific zones of the body. If Kaiser had struck his stepdaughter and knocked her teeth loose, he would be in much less legal trouble than if he had intercourse with her. One is assault, the other is sexual assault, which carries a much higher penalty and much greater social stigma. Foucault found such disparities ridiculous, for they gave too much significance to one orifice. See Foucault, *Politics, Philosophy, Culture* 201–02. Foucault resisted the way in which the deployment of sexuality—the way in which our sexuality is tied up with our identity—is so imperial in our laws as well as our lives.

Moreover, the higher penalty rests upon some fine distinctions. As *Kaiser* suggested, if there had been no "penetration" of the penis into the vagina, there would have been no rape (or statutory rape or incest). Apparently under Washington law, if Kaiser had forced his finger into his stepdaughter's vagina, he would not have been guilty of rape (other states do regulate this as sex, however). Foucault finds this just as ridiculous as before. "Sex" is not limited to penis-in-vagina, for it includes a panoply of pleasure-seeking touches. Foucault would both narrow sexuality's imperialism and expand what we mean by sexual pleasure.

Feminists tend to be more favorably impressed with this latter point than the former. See especially Monique Plaza, "Our Costs and Their Benefits," 4 *m/f* 31–32 (1980). While feminists do tend to see rape as violence and not just sex, they see it as an especially harmful kind of violence, contrary to Foucault. What he missed is the political dimension of rape's violence: Each rape is an assault against womanhood as well as woman, a marker for man's collective power to use and even erase woman. Like Bell, Plaza argues that Foucault neglects the insights of his own earlier work, namely, the social features of actions. A man punching another man is assault of a different nature than a man forcing his penis into a woman or even (Plaza agrees) punching a woman. The latter is more serious because of the other relations of power involved in man's hurting woman.

Judith Butler, Gender Trouble: Feminism and the Subversion of Identity

Pages 6–7, 22–23, 24–25 (1990).*

Although the unproblematic unity of "women" is often invoked to construct a solidarity of identity, a split is introduced in the feminist subject by the distinction between sex and gender. Originally intended to dispute the biology-is-destiny formulation, the distinction between sex and gender serves the argument that whatever biological intractability sex appears to have, gender is culturally constructed: hence, gender is neither the causal result of sex nor as seemingly fixed as sex. The unity of the subject is thus already potentially contested by the distinction that permits of gender as a multiple interpretation of sex.

If gender is the cultural meanings that the sexed body assumes, then a gender cannot be said to follow from a sex in any one way. Taken to its logical limit, the sex/gender distinction suggests a radical discontinuity between sexed bodies and culturally constructed genders. Assuming for the moment the stability of binary sex, it does not follow that the construction of "men" will accrue exclusively to the bodies of males or that "women" will interpret only female bodies. Further, even if the sexes appear to be unproblematically binary in their morphology and constitution (which will become a question), there is no reason to assume that genders ought to remain as two. * * * When the constructed status of gender is theorized as radically independent of sex, gender itself becomes a free-floating artifice, with the consequence that *man* and *masculine* might just as easily signify a female body as a male one, and *woman* and *feminine* a male body as easily as a female one.

* * * And what is "sex" anyway? Is it natural, anatomical, chromosomal, or hormonal, and how is a feminist critic to assess the scientific discourses which purport to establish such "facts" for us? * * * Is there a history of how the duality of sex was established, a genealogy that might expose the binary opinions as a variable construction? Are the ostensibly binary facts of sex discursively produced by various scientific discourses in the service of other political and social interests? If the immutable character of sex is contested, perhaps this construct called "sex" is as culturally constructed as gender; indeed, perhaps it was always already gender, with the consequence that the distinction between sex and gender turns out to be no distinction at all.

It would make no sense, then, to define gender as the cultural interpretation of sex, if sex itself is a gendered category. Gender ought not to be conceived merely as the cultural inscription of meaning on a pre-given sex (a juridical conception); gender must also designate the very apparatus of production whereby the sexes themselves are established. As a result, gender is not to culture as sex is to nature; gender is also the discursive/cultural means by which "sexed nature" or "a natural sex" is produced and established as "prediscursive," prior to culture, a politically neutral surface *on which* culture acts. * * *

Gender can denote a *unity* of experience, of sex, of gender, and desire, only when sex can be understood in some sense to necessitate gender—where gender is a psychic and/or cultural designation of the self—and desire—where desire is heterosexual and therefore differentiates itself through an oppositional relation to that other gender it desires. The internal coherence or unity of either gender, man or woman, thereby requires both a stable and oppositional heterosexuality. That institutional heterosexuality both requires and produces the univocity of each of the gendered terms that constitute the limit of gendered possibilities within an oppositional, binary gender system. This conception of gender presupposes not only a causal relation among sex, gender, and desire, but suggests as well that desire reflects or expresses gender and that gender reflects or expresses desire. The metaphysical unity of the three is assumed to be truly known and expressed in a differentiating desire for an oppositional gender—that is, in a form of oppositional heterosexuality. Whether as a naturalistic paradigm which establishes a causal continuity among sex, gender, and desire, or as an authentic-expressive paradigm in which some true self is said to be revealed simultaneously or successively in sex, gender, and desire, here "the old dream of symmetry," as [Luce] Irigaray has called it, is presupposed, reified, and rationalized.

This rough sketch of gender gives us a clue to understanding the political reasons for the substantializing view of gender. The institution of a compulsory and naturalized heterosexuality requires and regulates gender as a binary relation in which the masculine term is differentiated from the feminine term, and this differentiation is accomplished through the practices of heterosexual desire. The act of differentiating the two oppositional moments of the binary results in a consolidation of each term, the respective internal coherence of sex, gender, and desire. * * *

In this sense, *gender* is not a noun, but neither is it a set of free-floating attributes, for we have seen that the substantive effect of gender is performatively produced and compelled by the regulatory practices of gender coherence. Hence * * * gender proves to be performative—that is, constituting the identity it is purported to be. In this sense, gender is always a doing, though not a doing by a subject who might be said to preexist the deed. * * * There is no gender identity behind the expressions of gender; that identity is performatively constituted by the very "expressions" that are said to be its results.

Price Waterhouse v. Ann Hopkins

United States Supreme Court, 1989.
490 U.S. 228, 109 S.Ct. 1775, 104 L.Ed.2d 268.

■ BRENNAN, J., announced the judgment of the Court and delivered an opinion in which JUSTICE MARSHALL, JUSTICE BLACKMUN, and JUSTICE STEVENS join.

Ann Hopkins was a senior manager in an office of Price Waterhouse when she was proposed for partnership in 1982. She was neither offered nor denied admission to the partnership; instead, her candidacy was held for reconsideration the following year. When the partners in her office later refused to repropose her for partnership, she sued Price Waterhouse under Title VII, * * * charging that the firm had discriminated against her on the basis of sex in its decisions regarding partnership. Judge Gesell in the Federal District Court for the District of Columbia ruled in her favor on the question of liability, * * * and the Court of Appeals for the District of Columbia Circuit affirmed. * * * We granted certiorari to resolve a conflict among the Courts of Appeals concerning the respective burdens of proof of a defendant and plaintiff in a suit under Title VII when it has been shown that an employment decision resulted from a mixture of legitimate and illegitimate motives. * * *

Ann Hopkins had worked at Price Waterhouse's Office of Government Services in Washington, D.C., for five years when the partners in that office proposed her as a candidate for partnership. Of the 662 partners at the firm at that time, 7 were women. Of the 88 persons proposed for partnership that year, only 1—Hopkins—was a woman. Forty-seven of these candidates were admitted to the partnership, 21 were rejected, and 20—including Hopkins—were "held" for reconsideration the following year. Thirteen of the 32 partners who had submitted comments on Hopkins supported her bid for partnership. Three partners recommended that her candidacy be placed on hold, eight stated that they did not have an informed opinion about her, and eight recommended that she be denied partnership.

In a jointly prepared statement supporting her candidacy, the partners in Hopkins' office showcased her successful 2–year effort to secure a $25 million contract with the Department of State, labeling it "an outstanding performance" and one that Hopkins carried out "virtually at the partner level." Despite Price Waterhouse's attempt at trial to minimize her contribution to this project, Judge Gesell specifically found that Hopkins had "played a key role in Price Waterhouse's successful effort to win a multi-million dollar contract with the Department of State." Indeed, he went on, "[n]one of the other partnership candidates at Price Waterhouse that year had a comparable record in terms of successfully securing major contracts for the partnership."

The partners in Hopkins' office praised her character as well as her accomplishments, describing her in their joint statement as "an outstanding professional" who had a "deft touch," a "strong character, independence and integrity." Clients appear to have agreed with these assessments. At trial, one official from the State Department described her as "extremely competent, intelligent," "strong and forthright, very productive, energetic and creative." Another high-ranking official praised Hopkins' decisiveness, broad mindedness, and "intellectual clarity"; she was, in his words, "a stimulating conversationalist." Evaluations such as these led Judge Gesell to conclude that Hopkins "had no difficulty dealing with clients and her clients appear to have been very pleased with her work" and that she "was generally viewed as a highly competent project leader who worked long hours, pushed vigorously to meet deadlines and demanded much from the multidisciplinary staffs with which she worked."

On too many occasions, however, Hopkins' aggressiveness apparently spilled over into abrasiveness. Staff members seem to have borne the brunt of Hopkins' brusqueness. Long before her bid for partnership, partners evaluating her work had counseled her to improve her relations with staff members. Although later evaluations indicate an improvement, Hopkins' perceived shortcomings in this important area eventually doomed her bid for partnership. Virtually all of the partners' negative remarks about Hopkins—even those of partners supporting her—had to do with her "interpersonal skills." Both "[s]upporters and opponents of her candidacy," stressed Judge Gesell, "indicated that she was sometimes overly aggressive, unduly harsh, difficult to work with and impatient with staff."

There were clear signs, though, that some of the partners reacted negatively to Hopkins' personality because she was a woman. One partner described her as "macho"; another suggested that she "over-compensated for being a woman"; a third advised her to take "a course at charm school." Several partners criticized her use of profanity; in response, one partner suggested that those partners objected to her swearing only "because it's a lady using foul language." Another supporter explained that Hopkins "ha[d] matured from a tough-talking somewhat masculine hard-nosed mgr to an authoritative, formidable, but much more appealing lady ptr candidate." But it was the man who, as Judge Gesell found, bore responsibility for explaining to Hopkins the reasons for the Policy Board's decision to place her candidacy on hold who delivered the *coup de grace*: in order to improve her chances for partnership, Thomas Beyer advised, Hopkins should "walk more femininely, talk more femininely, dress more femininely, wear makeup, have her hair styled, and wear jewelry."

Dr. Susan Fiske, a social psychologist and Associate Professor of Psychology at Carnegie–Mellon University, testified at trial that the partnership selection process at Price Waterhouse was likely influenced by sex stereotyping. Her testimony focused not only on the overtly sex-based comments of partners but also on gender-neutral remarks, made by partners who knew Hopkins only slightly, that were intensely critical of her. One partner, for example, baldly stated that Hopkins was "universally disliked" by staff and another described her as "consistently annoying and irritating"; yet these were people who had had very little contact with Hopkins. According to Fiske, Hopkins' uniqueness (as the only woman in the pool of candidates) and the subjectivity of the evaluations made it likely that sharply critical remarks such as these were the product of sex stereotyping—although Fiske admitted that she could not say with certainty whether any particular comment was the result of stereotyping. Fiske based her opinion on a review of the submitted comments, explaining that it was commonly accepted practice for social psychologists to reach this kind of conclusion without having met any of the people involved in the decisionmaking process.

In previous years, other female candidates for partnership also had been evaluated in sex-based terms. As a general matter, Judge Gesell concluded, "[c]andidates were viewed favorably if partners believed they maintained their femin[in]ity while becoming effective professional managers"; in this environment, "[t]o be identified as a 'women's lib[b]er' was regarded as [a] negative comment." In fact, the judge found that in previous years "[o]ne partner repeatedly commented that he could not consider any woman seriously as a partnership candidate and believed that women were not even capable of functioning as senior managers—yet the firm took no action to discourage his comments and recorded his vote in the overall summary of the evaluations."

Judge Gesell found that Price Waterhouse legitimately emphasized interpersonal skills in its partnership decisions, and also found that the firm had not fabricated its complaints about Hopkins' interpersonal skills as a pretext for discrimination. Moreover, he concluded, the firm did not give decisive emphasis to such traits only because Hopkins was a woman; although there were male candidates who lacked these skills but who were admitted to partnership, the judge found that these candidates possessed other, positive traits that Hopkins lacked.

The judge went on to decide, however, that some of the partners' remarks about Hopkins stemmed from an impermissibly cabined view of the proper behavior of women, and that Price Waterhouse had done nothing to disavow reliance on such comments. He held that Price Waterhouse had unlawfully discriminated against Hopkins on the basis of sex by consciously giving credence and effect to partners' comments that resulted from sex stereotyping. Noting that Price Waterhouse could avoid equitable relief by proving by clear and convincing evidence that it would have placed Hopkins' candidacy on hold even absent this discrimination, the judge decided that the firm had not carried this heavy burden.

The Court of Appeals affirmed the District Court's ultimate conclusion, but departed from its analysis in one particular: it held that even if a plaintiff proves that discrimination played a role in an employment decision, the defendant will not be found liable if it proves, by clear and convincing evidence, that it would have made the same decision in the absence of discrimination. * * * Under this approach, an employer is not deemed to have violated Title VII if it proves that it would have made the same decision in the absence of an impermissible motive, whereas under the District Court's approach, the employer's proof in that respect only avoids equitable relief. We decide today that the Court of Appeals had the better approach, but that both courts erred in requiring the employer to make its proof by clear and convincing evidence.* * *

The District Court found that sex stereotyping "was permitted to play a part" in the evaluation of Hopkins as a candidate for partnership. Price Waterhouse disputes both that stereotyping occurred and that it played any part in the decision to place Hopkins' candidacy on hold. In the firm's view, in other words, the District Court's factual conclusions are clearly errone-ous. We do not agree. * * *

[Justice Brennan defended the trial court's reliance on Dr. Fiske's expert opinion about sex stereotyping.] Indeed, we are tempted to say that Dr. Fiske's expert testimony was merely icing on Hopkins' cake. It takes no special training to discern sex stereotyping in a description of an aggressive female employee as requiring "a course at charm school." Nor, turning to Thomas Beyer's memorable advice to Hopkins, does it require expertise in psychology to know that, if an employee's flawed "interpersonal skills" can be corrected by a soft-hued suit or a new shade of lipstick, perhaps it is the employee's sex and not her interpersonal skills that has drawn the criti-cism.

Price Waterhouse also charges that Hopkins produced no evidence that sex stereotyping played a role in the decision to place her candidacy on hold. As we have stressed, however, Hopkins showed that the partnership solicited evaluations from all of the firm's partners; that it generally relied very heavily on such evaluations in making its decision; that some of the partners' comments were the product of stereotyping; and that the firm in no way disclaimed reliance on those particular comments, either in Hop-kins' case or in the past. Certainly a plausible—and, one might say, inevitable—conclusion to draw from this set of circumstances is that the Policy Board in making its decision did in fact take into account all of the partners' comments, including the comments that were motivated by stereotypical notions about women's proper deportment.* * *

Nor is the finding that sex stereotyping played a part in the Policy Board's decision undermined by the fact that many of the suspect com-ments were made by supporters rather than detractors of Hopkins. A negative comment, even when made in the context of a generally favorable review, nevertheless may influence the decisionmaker to think less highly of the candidate; the Policy Board, in fact, did not simply tally the "yeses" and "noes" regarding a candidate, but carefully reviewed the content of the submitted comments. The additional suggestion that the comments were made by "persons outside the decisionmaking chain" * * *—and therefore could not have harmed Hopkins—simply ignores the critical role that partners' comments played in the Policy Board's partnership decisions.

Price Waterhouse appears to think that we cannot affirm the factual findings of the trial court without deciding that, instead of being overbear-ing and aggressive and curt, Hopkins is, in fact, kind and considerate and patient. If this is indeed its impression, petitioner misunderstands the theory on which Hopkins prevailed. The District Judge acknowledged that Hopkins' conduct justified complaints about her behavior as a senior manager. But he also concluded that the reactions of at least some of the partners were reactions to her as a *woman* manager. Where an evaluation is based on a subjective assessment of a person's strengths and weaknesses, it is simply not true that each evaluator will focus on, or even mention, the same weaknesses. Thus, even if we knew that Hopkins had "personality problems," this would not tell us that the partners who cast their evaluations of Hopkins in sex-based terms would have criticized her as sharply (or criticized her at all) if she had been a man. It is not our job to review the evidence and decide that the negative reactions to Hopkins were based on reality; our perception of Hopkins' character is irrelevant. We sit not to determine whether Ms. Hopkins is nice, but to decide whether the partners reacted negatively to her personality because she is a woman.

We hold that when a plaintiff in a Title VII case proves that her gender played a motivating part in an employment decision, the defendant may avoid a finding of liability only by proving by a preponderance of the evidence that it would have made the same decision even if it had not taken the plaintiff's gender into account. Because the courts below erred by deciding that the defendant must make this proof by clear and convincing evidence, we reverse the Court of Appeals' judgment against Price Waterhouse on liability and remand the case to that court for further proceedings.

■ [JUSTICE WHITE concurred only in the judgment. His analysis was relatively simple. *Mt. Healthy City School District Bd. of Educ. v. Doyle*, 429 U.S. 274 (1977), held that a public employee complaining of discharge in violation of his First Amendment rights had the burden of proving that constitutionally protected conduct was a "substantial factor" in the discharge decision. Justice White believed that the *Mt. Healthy* standard could be applied to Title VII cases without violence to the Court's precedents.]

■ [JUSTICE O'CONNOR also concurred only in the judgment. Like the plurality, she agreed to shift the burden of persuasion to employers once a Title VII plaintiff established that impermissible (sex) considerations were a "substantial factor" in an employment decision. Like the dissenters, she believed that this move was itself a "change in direction from some of our prior precedents" and sought to justify that change.]

■ JUSTICE KENNEDY, with whom THE CHIEF JUSTICE [REHNQUIST] and JUSTICE SCALIA join, dissenting.* * *

The ultimate question in every individual disparate-treatment case is whether discrimination caused the particular decision at issue. Some of the plurality's comments with respect to the District Court's findings in this case, however, are potentially misleading. As the plurality notes, the District Court based its liability determination on expert evidence that some evaluations of respondent Hopkins were based on unconscious sex stereotypes, and on the fact that Price Waterhouse failed to disclaim reliance on these comments when it conducted the partnership review. The District Court also based liability on Price Waterhouse's failure to "make partners sensitive to the dangers [of stereotyping], to discourage comments tainted by sexism, or to investigate comments to determine whether they were influenced by stereotypes." * * *

Although the District Court's version of Title VII liability is improper under any of today's opinions, I think it important to stress that Title VII creates no independent cause of action for sex stereotyping. Evidence of use by decisionmakers of sex stereotypes is, of course, quite relevant to the question of discriminatory intent. The ultimate question, however, is whether discrimination caused the plaintiff's harm. Our cases do not support the suggestion that failure to "disclaim reliance" on stereotypical comments itself violates Title VII. Neither do they support creation of a "duty to sensitize." As the dissenting judge in the Court of Appeals observed, acceptance of such theories would turn Title VII "from a prohibition of discriminatory conduct into an engine for rooting out sexist thoughts." * * *

The language of Title VII and our well-considered precedents require this plaintiff to establish that the decision to place her candidacy on hold was made "because of" sex. Here the District Court found that the "comments of the individual partners and the expert evidence of Dr. Fiske do not prove an intentional discriminatory motive or purpose," * * * and that "[b]ecause plaintiff has considerable problems dealing with staff and peers, the Court cannot say that she would have been elected to partnership if the Policy Board's decision had not been tainted by sexually based evaluations," * * * Hopkins thus failed to meet the requisite standard of proof after a full trial. I would remand the case for entry of judgment in favor of Price Waterhouse.

NOTE ON *HOPKINS* AND LAW'S INVOCATION OF GENDER

Hopkins might be criticized, as the dissent seems to do, for expanding a statutory ban on sex discrimination to include gender discrimination as well. (Title VII prohibits employment decisions "because of" the employee's "sex.") It appears that Ann Hopkins was discriminated against, not because women were considered unfit for the masculine world of accounting, but instead because she was perceived as too "mannish" a woman. Her story was not that her sex did not fit the job, but was more like her perceived gender did not fit her sex. See Ann Branigar Hopkins, *So Ordered: Making Partner the Hard Way* (1996) (Hopkins' own account of her treatment by Price Waterhouse, with ample references to trial and deposition testimony). Professor Butler's theory that sex and gender always work together provides some useful ways of thinking about this charge. The dissent insists on disaggregating gender from sex and only focusing on the latter; the plurality insists upon their interconnection. Butler maintains that sex cannot be coherently understood without gender, as well as vice versa.

After *Hopkins*, it appears that two slightly different kinds of discrimination might be remedied by Title VII: Price Waterhouse passed over Hopkins *either* because some partners didn't think women were capable of doing the job *or* because some partners were offended that this woman, however qualified, wasn't feminine enough for their tastes. In some ways, the second kind of discrimination (the kind Hopkins suffered) is more malignant, because it is so divorced from business necessity. Both kinds of discrimination are aimed at "gender stereotyping," either at the general level (women cannot do this job) or the specific (this woman can do the job, but she offends my sense of what a woman is). Can *Hopkins*, and Title VII, be read to create "an engine for rooting out sexist thoughts"? Should it? Does *Hopkins* solve what Katherine Franke (Chapter 3, Section 1) has called the "central mistake" of sex discrimination jurisprudence?

Does *Hopkins* create a claim for relief by "effeminate" men for job discrimination because they don't conform to gender stereotypes? See Mary Anne Case, "Disaggregating Gender from Sex and Sexual Orientation: The Effeminate Man in the Law and Feminist Jurisprudence," 105 *Yale L.J.* 1 (1995) (yes). If the mannish woman and the effeminate man can sue because the employer penalizes them for not conforming to gender stereotypes, can the lesbian or the gay man sue because she or he does not conform to the stereotypes that all women "need" men and that a man is not a "man" unless he has sex with women? Remember that this is an issue of statutory interpretation (Title VII of the Civil Rights Act of 1964), not constitutional law (the Equal Protection Clause). Does that make a difference? (See Chapter 8 for exploration of this and other Title VII issues.)

NOTES ON THE IMPLICATIONS OF BUTLER AND FOUCAULT FOR IDENTITY POLITICS AND EQUAL PROTECTION

1. *Goffman: The Management of "Spoiled Identities" and the Classical Model of Identity Politics.* Social scientists in the middle part of the twentieth century maintained that society and (in some instances) the state bear responsibility for individuals injured by the effect of *prejudice*, especially race-, religion-, and ethnicity-based prejudice. When society signals that certain traits are inferior or degraded, the individual internalizes that message and spends her entire lifetime struggling with that sense of inferiority. The social science appendix to the NAACP's brief in *Brown v. Board of Education* made this precise argument, and it was key to Chief Justice Warren's opinion for the Court. Feminist and gay rights litigators in cases like *Frontiero* (Chapter 3, Section 1) and *Watkins* (Chapter 3, Section 2B) made the same kinds of arguments: Cultural prejudices and stereotypes about women and gay people harmed individuals and were therefore deeply inconsistent with state obligations to afford "equal protection of the law."

Erving Goffman, *Stigma: Notes on the Management of Spoiled Identity* (1963) classically expressed this idea. "Stigmas" in our society include features such as homosexuality, minority religious views, mental and physical disabilities, etc. "In all of these various instances of stigma, * * * the same sociological features are found: an individual who might have been received easily in ordinary social intercourse possesses a trait that can obtrude itself upon attention and turn those of us whom he meets away from him, breaking the claim that his other attributes have on us." *Id.* at 6–7. Individuals thus stigmatized internalize society's views into their own identity understandings. "[A] discrepancy may exist between an individual's virtual and actual identity. This discrepancy, when known about or apparent, spoils his social identity; it has the effect of cutting him off from society and from himself so that he stands a discredited person facing an unaccepting world." *Id.* at 138. This is unfair to people who must manage "spoiled identities."

The classical model of identity politics—the civil rights movement and ensuing social movements for women, gay people, the disabled, and others—has maintained that certain variations (like race, skin color, now sex, and perhaps sexual orientation) from the norm are benign and ought not be the basis for social or legal stigma. As Goffman put it, identity politics rests upon the assumption that social mores or the law creates a rupture between the individual's virtual and actual identity; its claim is that many of these ruptures are illegitimate.

Pervasively driven by identity-based social movements, modern equal protection jurisprudence, starting no later than *Brown* and continuing with the sex discrimination cases and *Romer v. Evans*, suggests that the state cannot contribute to this degree of social stigma and that the state is empowered to regulate private acts of stigma-related discrimination. Reflecting the views of many social movement activists and of the judges filtering their arguments into constitutional doctrine, equal protection jurisprudence in the twentieth century was strongly *assimilationist*. Judges were inclined to eliminate legal discriminations based upon traits that were visible and immutable (race and sex), but not those based upon traits the Justices found invisible and possibly mutable (like sexual orientation). And when the state discriminated on the basis of act-based criteria or poverty, the Court was disinclined toward activism even when there was strong evidence of race- or sex-based effects. The message the Court was sending identity-based social groups was that they needed to work within the political process to achieve most of their goals.

2. *Foucault and Butler: Versions of the Social Constructionist Thesis as to Sex and Sexual Orientation—and Implications for the Classical Model of Identity Politics.* The classical model of identity politics and equal protection theory depends upon stable identity categories like people of color, women and men, and lesbians and gay men. Both Butler and Foucault ask us to reconsider the stability of sexuality and gender categories that social activists and judges alike take for granted. (Other theorists like Anthony Appiah and Ian Haney–López have called into question the stability of race-based categories.) How extensively they require that we reconsider categories is open to question. There are three readings that one might give to their claims (see Carole Vance, "Social Construction Theory: Problems in the History of Sexuality," in *Homosexuality, Which Homosexuality?* 13, 21 (Dennis Altman et al. eds. 1989)):

(a) The Weak Claim: Social Meaning Constructionism. The weakest reading of Butler and Foucault (and one that declines to go as far as either theorist) would accept *sex* and *sexual orientation* as stable biological categories and posit that the meaning of those categories and the normative

behavioral patterns associated with each vary across time and cultures. Throughout human history there are men and women, and men attracted to other men/women attracted to other women, but the social meaning and behavior appropriate for men and women have varied. The Athenians thought it obligatory for adult male citizens to marry women, but also appropriate for them to engage in anal sex with adolescent males (though only if the adult were the penetrator); it was highly appropriate for adult male Athenian citizens to be intimate friends, but generally inappropriate to engage in oral or anal sex with one another. In twentieth century American culture, men were expected to marry women, but it was considered highly inappropriate for them ever to engage in anal sex with other men. In contrast, American women had much more freedom than Athenian wives, including social freedom for unmarried women as the century wore on.

Consider the twentieth century category "cross-dressers" or "transvestites." *Cross-dressing* is a performative concept (Butler), a social construction (Foucault): it does not exist outside of the social meaning its activity creates. The category is a complete social construction, but one that builds on stable conceptions of man and woman: any man who dresses in the attire of a woman is a cross-dresser. The behavior and its normative acceptability changed drastically in twentieth century America. A woman in a tuxedo today is not a cross-dresser, but she would have been in 1920—not because she is no longer a woman, but because fashions and gender-normative dress codes have changed. Cross-dressing once was strongly associated with disapproved sexual "deviation," but so much less so today that openly straight people like Rudy Giuliani, Julie Andrews, and Dustin Hoffman have cross-dressed with success.

(b) The Strong Claim: Sexuality and Sex Are Socially Constructed. In *Gender Trouble* and *History of Sexuality*, respectively, the authors seem to take the position that both sex and sexuality are performative (Butler) and socially constructed (Foucault). Ontologically, there is no stable category of *man* or *woman*; society has created this binary, and it only has bite because people perform the categories so completely. Because man and woman are social categories, *homosexuality* and *heterosexuality* have no objective basis either. Indeed, according to Foucault, there is not an objective *sexuality* that people "have"; all that they "have" (at most) are urges and nervous systems that can be organized in a variety of ways by culture.

(c) The Moderate Claim: Sex and Sexual Orientation Are Socially Constructed in Part. A moderate claim "says that there may be a biological component to sex, but that we will never be sure what that biological component is, as we can only apprehend it through culture (that is, gender)." Kenji Yoshino, "Covering," 111 *Yale L.J.* 769, 868 (2002). Likewise, there may be a biological component to what we call homosexuality, but we will probably never be sure what that component is, as we can only apprehend it through culture (sex, gender, and sexuality). As even the weak

version of social constructionism maintains, the significance of one's biological sex or one's feelings for people of the same sex is completely cultural.

Under any of the three readings of Foucault and Butler, *identity* is socially constructed, imposed at least in part on individuals and not completely found within them. One's identity as a lesbian has a normative meaning and significance for which society is responsible (the weak version of their theory), and it may be that society is also responsible for the lesbian's understanding that she is "sexually attracted" to someone of the "same sex" rather than the "opposite sex" (the moderate or strong version). If the lesbian's identity is socially constructed, then culture bears much responsibility for that identity. Return to Goffman's idea that a spoiled identity creates a divide between one's actual and virtual identities. One punch line of social constructionist thought is that the actual and virtual identities may be indistinguishable. What implications does that harbor for equality theory? The next note considers one important implication.

3. *Yoshino: "Covering" as a Response to Spoiled Identities.* The state's response to traits considered socially malignant (homosexuality) or degraded (femininity, racial inferiority) has varied widely—ranging from campaigns of expulsion to incarceration to segregation to denigration. See Gordon Allport, *The Nature of Prejudice* (1954). Social psychologists like Allport and philosophers like Goffman worried that these campaigns harmed minorities by the wasteful responses they triggered in those whose identities were spoiled by social prejudice:

> The stigma and the effort to conceal it or remedy it become "fixed" as part of his personal identity. * * * [W]hen his differentness is not immediately apparent, and is not known beforehand (or at least not known by him to be known to the others) * * * [t]he issue is * * * of managing information about his failing. To display or not to display; to tell or not to tell; to let on or not to let on; to lie or not to lie; and in each case, to whom, how, when, and where. (Goffman, *Stigma* 138.)

Goffman is describing the phenomenon of *passing*. To avoid the disadvantages of stigma, women have passed as men, people of color have passed as white, Jews have passed as gentiles, Catholics have passed as Protestants, people with disease have passed as healthy, and gay people have passed as straight. Passing is often not wholly successful (the "deviant" is exposed), and even when it succeeds it exacts huge psychic costs for the individual. Social constructionist theory, however read, reinforces the traditional liberal view that society is responsible for those costs. So if a trait, like race or sex or sexual orientation, is not a legitimate basis for stigma, then it is impermissible for society to pressure individuals to hide their distinctiveness.

Social constructionist theory suggests a more radical approach, however. If classical identity politics and equal protection theory insist that minorities not have to pass as "normal" to receive the entitlements of the white heterosexual man, a performativist reading of stigma suggests that identity politics and equality theory should insist on more. To treat a person of color or woman or gay person differently from a straight white man is now an accepted violation of the equality norm; the minority or woman does not have to *pass* to receive the same treatment. But he or she does often have to *cover* to do so. The person of color who wears her hair in corn rows, the woman who does not wear dresses, and the gay man who does—all can be disciplined by society or even the law for not covering their difference and conforming to the norm accepted by traditional society. Yoshino, "Covering" draws from a moderate reading of Butler the idea that *woman* is a performative category whose socially constructed coherence rests just as much on dress, demeanor, and the like as on chromosomes and genitalia. Likewise, the *person of color* (or the black man, the Latina) is a performative category whose socially constructed coherence rests just as much on heritage, language, dress, and the like as on skin color. And the *lesbian, gay man, or bisexual* is performative in the same way.

The performative features of race, sex, and sexual orientation require equal protection law to consider the ways in which conformity as to behavior, attire, appearance, and language ought to be of concern. Mari Matsuda has pioneered the idea that language and appearance are just as important to antidiscrimination law as skin color and racial background. *E.g.,* Matsuda, "Accent Discrimination," 100 *Yale L.J.* 1329 (1991). By her account, the black woman who is pressured by her employer to cover her race by straightening her hair and changing her language is just as much deprived of her identity, and treated unequally, as the black woman pressured by her employer to pass as white. Yoshino extends this analysis to gay people as well. Judges may not agree with his conclusion, but they ought to consider how assimilative they want the Equal Protection Clause to be. "Civil rights practice, after all, is fundamentally about who has to change: The homosexual or the homophobe? The woman or the sexist? The racial minority or the racist?" Yoshino, "Covering," 938.

On the whole, Price Waterhouse was not asking Ann Hopkins to cover; it was asking her to *reverse cover*, to conform to conventional gender stereotypes. (The gay baseball superstar in Richard Greenberg's play *Take Me Out* receives some pressure to reverse cover; even his best friend on the team wonders why he's celibate and encourages him to have a boyfriend.) Yoshino argues that this should be a violation of Title VII, because the employer was asking Hopkins to hide her identity for reasons unrelated to her ability to do her job. What identity, exactly, was Hopkins being asked to cover? An identity as a tomboy (as she described herself)? If Hopkins's identity as a tomboy is protected by Title VII, can some of the fearful Price Waterhouse partners receive some Title VII consideration because they were, basically, sissies? Is there a slippery slope problem: Once identity is linked with conduct as well as traits, is there any natural stopping point for Title VII? Are there institutional reasons to let Congress revisit this slippery slope?

PART C. SOCIAL CONSTRUCTION, THE LAW, AND DISCOURSES OF DISEASE AND PRIVACY

Linda Singer, "Bodies—Pleasures—Powers"

differences: A Journal of Feminist Cultural Studies 45, 49–51, 53–54, 55–56 (1989).*

* * * The age of sexual epidemic demands a new sexual politics and, therefore, a rethinking of the relationship between bodies, pleasures, and powers beyond the call for liberation from repression. That is because, as Michel Foucault pointed out with a certain prescience, the power deployed in the construction and circulation of an epidemic, especially a sexual epidemic, functions primarily as a force of production and proliferation rather than as a movement of repression. The determination that a situation is epidemic is always, according to Foucault, a political determination (*The Birth of the Clinic 15*). Epidemics differ from diseases not in kind but in quantity. Hence the epidemic determination is in part a mathematical one, made by those with access to information and the authority to make and circulate such determinations. An epidemic emerges as a product of a socially authoritative discourse in light of which bodies will be mobilized, resources will be dispensed, and tactics of surveillance and regulation will appear to be justified. Foucault argues that a medicine of epidemic could only exist with supplementation by the police (*The Birth of the Clinic 15*). In this view, the construction of an epidemic situation has a strategic value in determining the configurations of what Foucault calls "bio-power," since the epidemic provides an occasion and a rationale for multiplying points of intervention into the lives of bodies and populations. For this reason, epidemics are always historically specific in a way that diseases are not, since the strategic imperatives motivating particular ways of coping with an epidemic always emerge as tactical responses to local utilities and circumstances. The construction of a sexual epidemic, as Foucault argues, provides an optimum site of intersection between individual bodies and populations. Hence sexual epidemic provides access to bodies and a series of codes for inscribing them, as well as providing a discourse of justification. When any phenomenon is represented as "epidemic," it has, by definition, reached a threshold that is quantitatively unacceptable. It is the capacity to make and circulate this determination, and to mobilize people in light of it, that constitutes the real political force of the discourse of sexual epidemic (Cindy Patton, *Sex and Germs: The Politics of AIDS* 51–66 [1985]). * * *

The history of the institutional responses to AIDS reveals how the politics of epidemics can work to solidify hegemonies. For years, gay activists and supporters lobbied for better funding for AIDS treatment and research, as the impact of the disease on their community increased. Such efforts went largely unrecognized and received little support from elected officials and health care professionals (Randy Shilts, *And the Band Played On* [1987]). It was not until the disease spread to other segments of the population and taxed health care resources that medical professionals began to speak of an epidemic. This indicates not only how power is operative in constructing epidemics but also how that construction can be used to organize attention, energy, and material support. * * *

The establishment of a connection between epidemic and transgression has allowed for the rapid transmission of the former to phenomena that are outside the sphere of disease. We are thus warned of the "epidemics" of teenage pregnancies, child molestation, abortion, pornography, and divorce. The use of this language marks all of these phenomena as targets for intervention because they have been designated as unacceptable, while at the same time reproducing the power that authorizes and justifies their deployment. According to this discourse, it is existing authority that is to be protected from the plague of transgressions. * * *

The limits of existing political discourse, as well as the urgency of the current situation, call for new forms of sexual political discourse, currency, and struggle. In this context, Foucault's work is especially helpful since his analysis of the proliferative operation of power supplements the limits of the repressive hypothesis, and offers the option of a strategic analysis which allows us to consider not only what is lost but also what is produced by the current organization of the sexual field which is itself a product of previous power deployments. This means that, counter to a logic which opposes erotic urgency and social utility or ghettoizes the sexual as some stable and invariable set of imperatives, Foucault's analysis demonstrates how the construction of each is dependent upon and made in light of the others, often, as in our age, with dire results which place our existence as a species in question. Part of the agenda for a sexual politics of epidemic will have to be a reconsideration of this "Faustian bargain," along with the generation of alternatives capable of mobilizing bodies sufficiently so as not to paralyze them in an economy of deprivation (Simon Watney, *Policing Desire* 123–35 [1987]). * * *

The underlying assumptions about the relationships among bodies, pleasures, and powers which make safe sex possible depend, at least indirectly, on Foucault's analysis and its destabilizing consequences. Safe sex presumes that pleasure and practice can be reorganized in response to overriding utilities and presumes, as well, the capacity of regimentary procedures to construct a body capable of taking pleasure in this new form of discipline. Unless bodies and pleasures are politically determined, they can not be redetermined, even in cases where that is what rational prudence would demand. The success of this strategy will thus depend not only on promulgating these techniques, but also on circulating a discourse that allows individuals to reconsider their bodies in a more liberatory and strategic way. What is new about the new sobriety is that its aesthetic of restraint is not represented in terms of a monastic economy of self-denial or obedience to some authoritative imperative, but is instead presented as a gesture of primary narcissism, a way of caring for and about oneself. Liberation, in this context, is relocated in an economy of intensification of control over one's body and one's position in sexual exchanges. * * *

Part of the change proffered by epidemic conditions is a shift in the relationship between knowledge and desire as they function in erotic situations. Specifically, knowledge of one's partner's physical condition and sexual history now becomes a prime object of concern. The erotic gaze is thus infected to some degree by the medical gaze which must learn to see sickness. The prudential aesthetic which characterizes the new sobriety creates specific forms of desire, like dating agencies, which promise matches with pre-screened AIDS-free partners.

Failing such elaborate screening procedures, and given the limits of their reliability, the ideology of safe sex encourages a reorganization of the body away from the erotic priorities with which it has already been inscribed. Specifically, safe sex advocates indulgence in numerous forms of non-genital contact and the re-engagement of parts of the body marginalized by an economy of genital primacy. It also entails a reconfiguration of bodies and their pleasures away from an ejaculatory teleology toward a more polymorphous decentered exchange, reviving and concretizing the critique of genital condensation begun over twenty years ago by sexual theorists like Marcuse and Firestone.

The new sobriety constructs a body well designed for the complexities of life in late capitalism, which requires a worker's body and a body of workers that are well-managed in the way a portfolio is well-managed, i.e., a body with flexible and diverse investments which maximize accumulated surplus as negotiable profits. The body constructed in the discourse of the new sobriety is inscribed with a discipline that is supposed to allow for more efficient functioning and control in both sex and work, in part, because this bodily regimen has been represented as an exercise in self-fulfillment and development which should be part of the well-managed enlightened life. * * *

NOTE ON AIDS AND NEW DISCOURSES OF THE BODY

As Singer's essay argues, law has become a focal point for AIDS discourse. Public health law has developed educational materials for doctors and the general population, as well as strategies for state intervention—including the closing of gay sex clubs in the 1980s. The National Institute of Health has invested in AIDS research, and periodic conferences of AIDS researchers generate headlines and new discussions of the disease. Public schools which were once ambivalent about whether they should teach children and adolescents sex education courses now believe that there must be some instruction but agonize over exactly what it should be. Discrimination against persons with AIDS (PWAs) is now legally regulated by the Americans with Disabilities Act and by state and local antidiscrimination laws.

In short, AIDS has created new categories of signification—categories which are restructuring the ways Americans understand their society and their own bodies. Singer maintains that AIDS is an occasion for redirecting the mechanisms by which the body is deployed for pleasure. By problematizing unprotected vaginal and anal sex, public health professionals and sex educators have, one might speculate, contributed to a latex sexuality, a focus on other body parts (nipples, necks, feet, etc.) as erogenous zones for more people, and so forth.

There is another discursive consequence, however. "[M]onogamy is coming back into its own, along with abstention, the safest sex of all. The virus in itself—by whatever name—has come to represent the moment of truth for the sexual revolution: as though God has once again sent his only beloved son to save us from our high-risk behavior. Who would have thought He would take the form of a virus: a viral Terminator ready to die for our sins." Paula Treichler, "AIDS, Homophobia and Biomedical Discourse: An Epidemic of Signification," 1 *Cultural Studies* 263 (1987). Traditionalists maintain that AIDS ought to be the occasion for a new discipline of the body that puts a lid back on sex outside of marriage. Even doctors might be contributing to a renewed discourse of sexual abstinence. Ralph Bolton, "AIDS and Promiscuity: Muddles in the Models of HIV Prevention," 14 *Medical Anthropology* 145 (1992), remarks on how obsessively the medical literature has associated HIV infection with number of sex partners, often explicitly using the term "promiscuity," even though the greater correlation is with unsafe sex practices and not number of partners.

Jed Rubenfeld, "The Right to Privacy"
102 *Harvard Law Review* 737, 783–84, 800 (1989).*

* * * The methodology heretofore universal in privacy analysis has begun with the question, "What is the state trying to forbid?" The proscribed conduct is then delineated and its significance tested through a preestablished conceptual apparatus: for its role in "the concept of ordered liberty," its status as a "fundamental" right, its importance to one's identity, or for any other criterion of fundamentality upon which a court can settle. Suppose instead we began by asking not what is being *prohibited*, but what is being *produced*. Suppose we looked not to the negative aspect of the law—the interdiction by which it formally expresses itself—but at its positive aspect: the real effects that conformity with the law produces at the level of everyday lives and social practices. * * *

* * * There *is* something fundamental at stake in the privacy decisions, but it is not the proscribed conduct, nor even the freedom of decision—it is not what is being taken away.

The distinctive and singular characteristic of the laws against which the right to privacy has been applied lies in their *productive* or *affirmative* consequences. There are perhaps no legal proscriptions with more profound, more extensive, or more persistent affirmative effects on individual lives than the laws struck down as violations of the right to privacy. Anti-abortion laws, anti-miscegenation laws, and compulsory education laws all involve the forcing of lives into well-defined and highly confined institutional layers. At the simplest, most quotidian level, such laws tend to *take over* the lives of the persons involved: They occupy and preoccupy. They affirmatively and very substantially shape a person's life; they direct a life's development along a particular avenue. These laws do not simply proscribe one act or remove one liberty; they inform the totality of a person's life.

The principle of the right to privacy is not the freedom to do certain, particular acts determined to be fundamental through some ever-progressing normative lens. It is the fundamental freedom not to have one's life too totally determined by a progressively more normalizing state. * * *

The danger, then, is a particular kind of creeping totalitarianism, an unarmed *occupation* of individuals' lives. That is the danger of which Foucault as well as the right to privacy is warning us: a society standardized and normalized, in which lives are too substantially or too rigidly directed. That is the threat posed by state power in our century. * * *

Most fundamentally, the prohibition against homosexual sex channels individuals' sexual desires into *reproductive* outlets. Although the prohibition does not, like the law against abortions, produce as an imminent consequence compulsory child-bearing, it nonetheless forcibly directs individuals into the pathways of reproductive sexuality, rather than the socially "unproductive" realm of homosexuality. These pathways are further guided, in our society, into particular institutional orbits, chief among which are the nuclear family and the constellation of practices surrounding a heterosexuality that is defined in conscious contradistinction to homosexuality. Indeed, it is difficult to separate our society's inculcation of a heterosexual identity from the simultaneous inculcation of a dichotomized complementarity of roles to be borne by men and women. Homosexual couples by necessity throw into question the allocation of specific functions—whether professional, personal, or emotional—between the sexes. It is this aspect of the ban on homosexuality—its central role in the maintenance of institutionalized sexual identities and normalized reproductive relations—that have made its *affirmative* or *formative* consequences, as well as the reaction against these consequences, so powerful a force in modern society. * * *

NOTE ON FOUCAULT, PRIVACY, AND RIGHTS DISCOURSE

A major point of agreement between feminism and Foucault is the recognition that sexuality functions as a power system ("the personal is political") and that it operates at multiple sites of power and resistance. Thus, for example, contested issues within a family, within a school or university, or within a profession are viewed as being just as much "politics" as an election or a policy protest. Does Rubenfeld's elaboration of a privacy doctrine undercut that proposition, by implicitly validating an anti-totalitarian defense only against the state?

Where does Foucauldian analysis leave the discourse of rights? Is the concept of an autonomous individual with a claim to a coherent, timeless body of rights obsolete and naive? If so, is paralysis the only outcome? For an analysis of the complexities of the dynamic between rights discourse and political organizing from a Marxist-feminist viewpoint, see Elizabeth Schneider, "The Dialectic of Rights and Politics: Perspectives from the Women's Movement," 61 *N.Y.U. L. Rev.* 589 (1986).

If Foucault and Rubenfeld are correct that law produces as well as restricts behaviors, should litigators use privacy doctrine in seeking intervention, and not just withdrawal, by the state? At least one scholar believes so:

> Rather than ask how individuals can be shielded from the exercise of state power, we should ask how state power might be invoked to restructure aspects of personal life in order to eliminate distorting factors in people's own interactions and personal decisionmaking.

Stephen Schnably, "Beyond *Griswold*: Foucauldian and Republican Approaches to Privacy," 23 *Conn. L. Rev.* 861, 870 (1991). The author goes on to conclude that the state should set the proper context for abortion counseling not merely by mandating that high quality, personalized counseling be made available, but also by providing funding for abortions and for day care, so that a woman's decision can be truly uncoerced. *Id.* at 940–41. How would a Foucauldian Constitution be structured?

CHAPTER 6

SEXUAL SPEECH

How we experience identity is a social as well as individual process. One develops as well as expresses one's identity through talking and associating with other people, creating texts, and forming groups and organizations. Indeed, the factors that are considered important enough to frame one's identity are socially constructed factors. Those of us who are left-handed do not consider that feature critical to our identities, in large part because society attaches no real significance to that characteristic. In our culture, being a man or a woman, an African American or an Asian American, or a Jew or an Italian are all identity characteristics in ways that left-handedness is not.

Sexual orientation is likewise a consequential factor because of the significance society attaches to it. It is sometimes visible, sometimes not. Because heterosexuality is considered the norm, its existence is assumed and often not noticed (at least officially) or remarked upon until one acts in some way to signal that it should not be assumed. Once that signal is communicated, however, sexual orientation can become highly visible, often dominating the perception of what is occurring. If we think of gender as biological sex, it is generally assumed to be a visible categorization. If we think of gender as performative of cultural roles, however, it too becomes sometimes visible, sometimes not, with its impact determined by whether a person's gender presentation correlates with our expectations for his or her biological sex. And it is gender performativity that, correctly or not, often signals sexual orientation. All in all, gender and sexuality seem to depend a great deal on expression.

Can majority groups invoke the power of the state to prevent unpopular identity groups from associating with one another, to penalize individuals who openly espouse an unpopular identity, or to condition state benefits on foregoing such speech? The First Amendment provides that "Congress shall make no law * * * abridging the freedom of speech, or of the press; or the right of the people peaceably to assemble, and to petition the Government for a redress of grievances." The Supreme Court has held that the Due Process Clause of the Fourteenth Amendment incorporates these protections against state as well as congressional laws. The First Amendment has been interpreted as a broad protection against state censorship and stands as a barrier to state intervention along these lines. How does the First Amendment regulate coming out or advocacy of the idea that homosexuality is normal or neutral? See Section 1. On what principles should the tension between protected coming out speech and the anti-gay views of equally protected associations, like the Boy Scouts, be resolved? See Section 2. Lastly, should sexualized expression, such as pornography or nude dancing, receive a lesser degree of constitutional protection than other expression? See Section 3. This chapter challenges you to devise a theory of the First Amendment and its appropriate role in mediating discourses of sexuality.

FROM OBSCENITY TO POLITICAL SPEECH

PART A. HISTORY

The strongest First Amendment protection is for "political" speech and publication. At the other end of the First Amendment spectrum is obscenity, which is categorically excluded from First Amendment protection. From the mid-nineteenth to the mid-twentieth century, positive speech about homosexuality and about sexuality outside of marriage was generally considered to be obscene. Obscenity laws were the primary mechanism used to suppress birth control materials (Chapter 2, Section 1). Some literary examples include:

- A New York court banned the classic lesbian novel *The Well of Loneliness* on the ground that "it seeks to justify the right of a pervert to prey upon normal members of a community and to uphold such relationship as noble and lofty. Although it pleads for tolerance, it does not argue for repression or moderation of insidious impulses." *People v. Friede*, 233 N.Y.S. 565, 567 (Mag. Ct. 1929) (ultimately overturned on appeal). The court quoted the main character as saying, " 'there's no shame in me.' "

- Other literary victims of the traditional obscenity test included *An American Tragedy, Lady Chatterly's Lover, God's Little Acre, Strange Fruit,* and *Memoirs of Hecate County.* An early watershed in the acceptance of explicit sexuality in serious literature came with Judge Augustus Hand's decision allowing the importation of James Joyce's *Ulysses. United States v. One Book Entitled "Ulysses,"* 72 F.2d 705 (2d Cir. 1934).

- Finally, in a case involving the film version of *Lady Chatterly's Lover*, the Supreme Court invalidated a New York statute that required the denial of a license to exhibit motion pictures "which are immoral in that they *portray* 'acts of sexual immorality as desirable, acceptable or proper patterns of behavior.' " *Kingsley International Pictures Corp. v. Regents of the University of the State of New York*, 360 U.S. 684, 687 (1959). The New York Court of Appeals had found that the film was not obscene, but that, taken as a whole, it "alluringly portrays adultery as proper behavior." The Supreme Court found that the propriety of adultery was an idea, the advocacy of which was protected.

As you read the cases that follow, consider what factors contributed to the process by which the lines blurred between political speech and sexual speech.

One, Inc. v. Otto Olesen

U.S. Court of Appeals for the Ninth Circuit, 1957.
241 F.2d 772, *reversed per curiam,* 355 U.S. 371 (1958).

■ ROSS, DISTRICT JUDGE.

[Responding to pressure from the Senate and the FBI, the U.S. Post Office confiscated copies of *One, Inc.*, the earliest continuously published homophile magazine in American history. The Post Office maintained that the magazine was nonmailable under 18 U.S.C. § 1461, which prohibits the Post Office from conveying or delivering "[e]very obscene, lewd, lascivious, or filthy book, pamphlet, picture, paper, letter, writing, print or other publication of an indecent character."]

* * * Our ultimate conclusion as to whether the magazine is mailable or not must be based upon the effect, or impact, that the wording of the various articles in the magazine have upon the reader. There is no precise pattern for reader reaction, so in determining whether the thought patterns created by the words employed in the magazine articles are obscene, lewd, lascivious, filthy or indecent, we must ascertain how other courts met the problem. * * *

* * * "The test of obscenity is whether the tendency of the matter is to deprave and corrupt the morals of those whose minds are open to such influence and into whose hands a publication of this sort may fall." "Would it * * * suggest or convey lewd thoughts and lascivious thoughts to the young and inexperienced?" * * *

Plaintiff, as publisher, states on the second page of the magazine that it is published for the purpose of dealing primarily with homosexuality from the scientific, historical and critical point of view-to sponsor educational programs, lectures and concerts for the aid and benefit of social variants and to promote among the general public an interest, knowledge and understanding of the problems of [sexual] variation. The story "Sappho Remembered," appearing on pages 12 to 15 of the magazine, the poem "Lord Samuel and Lord Montagu" on pages 18 and 19, and the information given on page 29 as to where to obtain "The Circle," a magazine "with beautiful photos," do not comport with the lofty ideals expressed on page 2 by the publishers.

The article "Sappho Remembered" is the story of a lesbian's influence on a young girl only twenty years of age but "actually nearer sixteen in many essential ways of maturity," in her struggle to choose between a life with the lesbian, or a normal married life with her childhood sweetheart. The lesbian's affair with her room-mate while in college, resulting in the lesbian's expulsion from college, is recounted to bring in the jealousy angle. The climax is reached when the young girl gives up her chance for a normal married life to live with the lesbian. This article is nothing more than cheap pornography calculated to promote lesbianism. It falls far short of dealing with homosexuality from the scientific, historical and critical point of view.

The poem "Lord Samuel and Lord Montagu" is about the alleged homosexual activities of Lord Montagu and other British Peers and contains a warning to all males to avoid the public toilets while Lord Samuel is "sniffing round the drains" of Piccadilly (London). The poem pertains to sexual matters of such a vulgar and indecent nature that it tends to arouse a feeling of disgust and revulsion. It is dirty, vulgar and offensive to the moral senses.

An article may be vulgar, offensive and indecent even though not regarded as such by a particular group of individuals constituting a small segment of the population because their own social or moral standards are far below those of the general community. Social standards are fixed by and for the great majority and not by or for a hardened or weakened minority.
* * *

It is difficult to determine if the article contained on page 29 under the caption "Foreign Books and Magazines That Will Interest You," is an advertisement for the magazine "The Circle" or is merely information given by the publisher of "One" to its readers as to where to obtain other books and magazines that may be of interest. Regardless, the situation is the same, if information is given as to where, or how, or from whom, or by what means, obscene or filthy material may be obtained. Although on its face the information in this article appears harmless, it cannot be said that the purpose is harmless. It is for the information of those who read the magazine and particularly the homosexuals. It conveys information to the homosexual or any other reader as to where to get more of the material contained in "One."

An examination of "The Circle" clearly reveals that it contains obscene and filthy matter which is offensive to the moral senses, morally depraving and debasing, and that it is designed for persons having lecherous and salacious proclivities.

[The court described stories in "The Circle" and found them similar to "Sappho Remembered," except that they related to the actions of "homosexuals" rather than "lesbians." The court held that "The Circle," like the other matter, was obscene, thereby rendering "One, Inc." nonmailable.]

NOTES ON THE CHANGE IN OBSCENITY LAW AND POSSIBLE GOALS OF THE FIRST AMENDMENT

1. *A New Test for Obscenity.* Ironically, at the very point the Ninth Circuit announced its decision, the Supreme Court was beginning to rethink the breadth of the obscenity exception to the First Amendment. The Supreme Court's per curiam decision in *One, Inc. v. Olesen*, 355 U.S. 371 (1958), reversed the decision that you just read. The Court's one-sentence opinion indicated that the lower court's decision was inconsistent with *Roth v. United States*, 354 U.S. 476 (1957), handed down six months earlier.

In *Roth*, the Court rejected the test of whether material tended to corrupt morals, which Americans had imported from Britain, where it was adopted in *Regina v. Hicklin*, L.R. 3 Q.B. 360 (1868). The *Roth* decision substituted two things for the *Hicklin* standard. First, the Court explicitly declared that obscenity as a category of expression lay outside the First Amendment:

> All ideas having even the slightest redeeming social importance—unorthodox ideas, controversial ideas, even ideas hateful to the prevailing climate of opinion—have the full protection of the guaranties, unless excludable because they encroach upon the limited area of more important interests. But implicit in the history of the First Amendment is the rejection of obscenity as utterly without redeeming social importance. * * * "*[S]uch utterances are no essential part of any exposition of ideas, and are of such slight social value as a step to truth that any benefit that may be derived from them is clearly outweighed by the social interest in order and morality * * *.*" (Emphasis added.) We hold that obscenity is not within the area of constitutionally protected speech or press.

354 U.S. at 489. Second, the Court adopted the forerunner of today's test for obscenity: "whether to the average person, applying contemporary community standards, the dominant theme of the material taken as a whole appeals to prurient interest." *Id.*

2. *Theories of the First Amendment.* Consider the constitutional policy basis, or bases, for the ultimate result in *One*. That is, what constitutional goals does the First Amendment potentially, or optimally, serve? Are those goals implicated in the Post Office's suppression of *One*? The following are some candidates nominated by various scholars and judges; consider these theories critically.

(a) *The Marketplace of Ideas.* According to John Stuart Mill, *On Liberty* (1857), truth or the best answer emerges from a competition in the marketplace of ideas. If some ideas are arbitrarily suppressed by the government, there will be a less robust public ventilation of ideas, and we shall be less likely to come to right answers and good policies. The Ninth Circuit's decision in *One* seems antithetical to a free marketplace of ideas, for Judge Ross is saying that there is *one* correct viewpoint about homosexuality (it is sick and abnormal), and any other viewpoint is simply wrong. Most educated people today would consider Judge Ross's position naive and ill-informed—and an example of where the First Amendment should have been invoked to head off premature closure in an important debate about the nature of homosexuality and same-sex intimacy. On the other hand, a marketplace of ideas metaphor may not always support a strong First Amendment. Consider our willingness in other settings to regulate dysfunctioning markets. The state can prohibit false commercial advertising, for example. Why can't the state prohibit "false advertising" about homosexuality?

(b) *Democracy Values.* Alexander Meiklejohn, *Free Speech and Its Relation to Self–Government* (1948), argues that channels of communication about political and social issues need to be kept open for democratic self-government to work well. He invokes the American tradition of the town meeting to valorize the First Amendment. While the Ninth Circuit's position in *One* might be criticized as cutting off the flow of relevant information to the body politic, it might be defended on the ground that it expunges information that most townspeople find disgusting (that being the point of obscenity regulations). Does "gross" speech contribute to democracy in action?

Lee Bollinger, *The Tolerant Society: Freedom of Speech and Extremist Speech in America* (1986), extends Meiklejohn's argument to maintain that the First Amendment is a check against people's tendency to be intolerant of those different from themselves or who espouse unfamiliar ideas. Insisting that the polity think twice before suppressing a community of different people, the First Amendment instantiates a norm of tolerance that contributes to a particularly robust and diverse polity. The Ninth Circuit's opinion is intolerant and therefore inconsistent with this vision, but is tolerance a value we want to press at any price? Should society "tolerate" a community of vandals on the grounds that they simply reflect another "perspective"? Would the tolerance idea require deregulation of prostitution?

(c) *Autonomy Values.* Speech and publication are primary methods by which people express, and oftentimes discover, their individuality and personhood. A libertarian would argue that the state must leave the individual alone when she is expressing or exploring personhood, unless there is evidence she is harming others. See Mill, *On Liberty* ch. 4. A communitarian could argue that the state should be encouraging individual flourishing. See Steven Shiffrin, *The First Amendment, Democracy, and Romance* (1990). The ethic of conformity reflected in the Ninth Circuit's opinion threatens to crush individual flourishing, yes?

Part B.   Coming Out Speech

Gay Students Organization of the University of New Hampshire v. Thomas Bonner

U.S. Court of Appeals for the First Circuit, 1974.
509 F.2d 652.

■ Coffin, Chief Judge.

The Gay Students Organization (GSO) was officially recognized as a student organization at the University of New Hampshire in May, 1973, and on November 9, 1973 the group sponsored a dance on campus. The dance itself was held without incident, but media coverage of the event and criticism by Governor Meldrim Thomson, Jr., led the University's Board of Trustees to reconsider its treatment of the organization. The next day,

November 10, 1973, the Board issued a "Position Statement" which indicated that the University would attempt to have determined the "legality and appropriateness of scheduling social functions by the Gay Students Organization" and which "directed that in the interim the University administration would schedule no further social functions by the Gay Students Organization until the matter is legally resolved." * * *

When the GSO requested permission to sponsor a play on December 7 and have a social function afterward, the University permitted the play but denied permission for the social function. The play was given as scheduled, and the GSO held a meeting following it. Sometime during the evening copies of two "extremist" homosexual publications were distributed by individuals over whom the GSO claims it had no control. Governor Thomson wrote an open letter to the trustees after the play, warning that if they did not "take firm, fair and positive action to rid your campuses of socially abhorrent activities" he would "stand solidly against the expenditure of one more cent of taxpayers' money for your institutions." Dr. Thomas N. Bonner, President of the University, then issued a public statement condemning the distribution of the homosexual literature and announcing that a repetition of the behavior would cause him to seek suspension of the GSO as a student organization. Bonner also revealed that he had "ordered that the current Trustee ban on GSO social functions be interpreted more strictly by administrative authorities than had been the case before December 7, 1973." * * *

* * * [W]e are conscious of the tension between deeply felt, conflicting values or moral judgments, and the traditional legal method of extracting and applying principles from decided cases. First, this case deals with a university attempting to regulate student activity—in the *in loco parentis* tradition which most judges, being over thirty, acknowledged without much question during their years of matriculation. Second, the campus group sought to be regulated stands for sexual values in direct conflict with the deeply imbued moral standards of much of the community whose taxes support the university.

The underlying question, usually not articulated, is whether, whatever may be Supreme Court precedent in the First Amendment area, group activity promoting values so far beyond the pale of the wider community's values is also beyond the boundaries of the First Amendment, at least to the extent that university facilities may not be used by the group to flaunt its credo. If visceral reactions suggest an affirmative answer, the next task for judges is to devise a standard which, while damping down the First Amendment on a university campus, is generally applicable and free from the dangers of arbitrariness. At this point troubles arise. How are the deeply felt values of the community to be identified? On an issue such as permissive abortion, the wider community may well be divided among those believing in "the right to life", those believing in "the right to control over one's body," and those who do not feel deeply either way. Assuming that "community-wide values" could be confidently identified, and that a university could limit the associational activity of groups challenging those values, such an approach would apply also to socialists, conscientious objectors, vivisectionists, those favoring more oil refineries. As to each group, there are sectors of the community to whom its values are anathema. Or, if values be limited to morals, the barrier would reach those attracted to pre-marital sex, atheism, the consumption of alcoholic beverages, esoteric heterosexual activity, violence on television, or dirty books. This is not to suggest that a university is powerless to proscribe either harmful activity or incitement of illegal activity, but it is to say that we are unable to devise a tolerable standard exempting this case at the threshold from general First Amendment precedents. * * *

Given this standard by which a university regulation should be judged, we now must ask whether, even though GSO was recognized as a campus organization, its members' right of association was abridged. * * * *Healy v. James,* [408 U.S. 169 (1972)] is controlling. It is true that there the university had refused to recognize the campus organization [Students for a Democratic Society (SDS)] altogether rather than denying it the use of campus facilities for certain activities. But the Court's analysis in *Healy* focused not on the technical point of recognition or nonrecognition, but on the practicalities of human interaction. While the Court concluded that the SDS members' right to further their personal beliefs had been impermissibly burdened by nonrecognition, this conclusion stemmed from a finding that the "primary impediment to free association flowing from nonrecognition is the denial of use of campus facilities for meetings and other appropriate purposes." The ultimate issue at which inquiry must be directed is the effect which a regulation has on organizational and associational activity, not the isolated and for the most part irrelevant issue of recognition *per se*.

Despite the language of *Healy* cited above, appellants argue that "social events" are not among the class of protected associational activities. One aspect of this argument is the suggestion that the ban on social events is permissible because other GSO activities such as discussions are allowed. A very similar contention was rejected in *Healy*. The university had pointed out that nonrecognition affected only on-campus activities, and that therefore the individuals wishing to form an SDS group could meet and distribute literature off campus, and even meet on campus if they did so informally. The Court was thus invited to find that the individuals were free to associate even though their on-campus activities were restricted. It held, however, that the other associational opportunities available to the individuals did not ameliorate significantly the disabilities imposed by the university. Once again, its standard was expressed in the clearest of terms—"[T]he Constitution's protection is not limited to direct interference with fundamental rights." Although the Supreme Court refused in *Healy* to characterize as insubstantial the impediments to association resulting from denial of access to campus bulletin boards and the school newspaper, that case could conceivably be read to shelter only those group efforts at self-promotion which utilize such conventional approaches.

There are, however, many other ways in which an organization might wish to go about attracting members and promoting its point of view. *Healy* has been interpreted to extend to the use of campus facilities for social events in the one case of which we are aware which has considered the issue. We are also led to this conclusion by the realization that efforts by a state to restrict groups other than the GSO to gatherings that were in no sense "social events" would be rejected out of hand. Even a lecture or discussion, which appear to be the only types of meetings which the appellants would allow the GSO to hold, becomes a social event if beer is served beforehand or coffee afterward. Teas, coffees and dinners form the backbone of many a political candidate's campaign, and yet these activities would seemingly be subject to prohibition. While a university may have some latitude in regulating organizations such as fraternities or sororities which can be purely social, its efforts to restrict the activities of a cause-oriented group like the GSO stand on a different footing. Considering the important role that social events can play in individuals' efforts to associate to further their common beliefs, the prohibition of all social events must be taken to be a substantial abridgment of associational rights, even if assumed to be an indirect one.

What we have been considering is appellants' contention that, so long as an association is allowed to meet, restrictions on some of its activities are permissible—i.e., that it is enough that the glass is half full. We now address appellants' contention that when we examine the other half of the glass, the activities barred by the campus regulation, we must conclude that the First Amendment offers no protection because the activities barred are not speech related. Putting aside for a moment the question of whether GSO social events constitute "speech" in their own right, we note the district court's conclusion, not disputed by appellants, that the GSO is a political action organization. The GSO's efforts to organize the homosexual minority, "educate" the public as to its plight, and obtain for it better treatment from individuals and from the government thus represent but another example of the associational activity unequivocally singled out for protection in the very "core" of association cases decided by the Supreme Court. Moreover, the activity engaged in by the GSO would be protected even if it were not so intimately bound up with the political process, for "it is immaterial whether the beliefs sought to be advanced by association pertain to political, economic, religious or cultural matters." *NAACP v. Alabama*, 357 U.S. at 460.

While we accept the district court's conclusion that the associational rights of GSO members have been impermissibly regulated, we cannot agree that their "more traditional First Amendment rights" have not been abridged as well. * * * Communicative conduct is subject to regulation as to "time, place and manner" in the furtherance of a substantial governmental interest, so long as the restrictions imposed are only so broad as required in order to further the interest and are unrelated to the content and subject matter of the message communicated. *Police Department v. Mosley*, 408 U.S. 92 (1972).

There can be no doubt that expression, assembly and petition constitute significant aspects of the GSO's conduct in holding social events. The GSO was created, as its Statement of Purpose attests, to promote the free exchange of ideas among homosexuals and between homosexuals and heterosexuals, and to educate the public about bisexuality and homosexuality. GSO claims that social events in which discussion and exchange of ideas can take place in an informal atmosphere can play an important part in this communication. It would seem that these communicative opportunities are even more important for it than political teas, coffees, and dinners are for political candidates and parties, who have much wider access to the media, being more highly organized and socially accepted. And beyond the specific communications at such events is the basic "message" GSO seeks to convey—that homosexuals exist, that they feel repressed by existing laws and attitudes, that they wish to emerge from their isolation, and that public understanding of their attitudes and problems is desirable for society.

Perhaps these claims, being self serving, fall short of establishing the speech-relatedness of GSO social events. But they receive the strongest corroboration from the interpretation placed on these events by the outside community, as related by appellants. Appellants have relied heavily on their obligation and right to prevent activities which the people of New Hampshire find shocking and offensive. In the brief for President Bonner and the University administrators we are told that the "activity of the GSO was variously labelled a spectacle, an abomination and similar terms of disapprobation" after the GSO dance on November 8, 1973; that the University has an obligation to prevent activity which affronts the citizens of the University and the town and which violates breach of the peace statutes; that the GSO dance constituted "grandstanding"; that recognition of the GSO inflamed a large segment of the people of the state; that the organization cannot be permitted to use its unpopularity without restriction to undermine the University within the state; and that "the ban on social functions reflects the distaste with which homosexual organizations are regarded in the State."

We do not see how these statements can be interpreted to avoid the conclusion that the regulation imposed was based in large measure, if not exclusively, on the content of the GSO's expression. It is well established that "above all else the First Amendment means that government has no power to restrict expression because of its message, its ideas, its subject matter, or its content." *Mosley*, 408 U.S. at 95. * * *

Another interest asserted by appellants is that in preventing illegal activity, which may include "deviate" sex acts, "lascivious carriage," and breach of the peace. But there has been no allegation that any such illegal acts took place at the GSO social events held on November 8 and December 7, 1973. Indeed, we emphasize the finding of the district court that "There were no official complaints about the dance, and no evidence was adduced to show that improper or illegal activities had taken place" at the dance. The only activity of even questionable legality discussed in the record involved the distribution of printed materials alleged to be obscene, and the district court found that no University of New Hampshire students were responsible for the distribution. Mere "undifferentiated fear or apprehension" of illegal conduct is not enough to overcome First Amendment rights, and speculation that individuals might at some time engage in illegal activity is insufficient to justify regulation by the state.

The University is by no means bereft of power to regulate conduct on campus. Not only may it act to prevent criminal conduct by policies focused on real and established dangers, but it can proscribe advocacy of illegal activities falling short of conduct, or conduct in itself noncriminal, if such advocacy or conduct is directed at producing or is likely to incite imminent lawless action. *Brandenburg v. Ohio*, 395 U.S. 444, 447 (1969).

Finally there is a residual power going beyond the prevention of criminal conduct and the kind of advocacy of such conduct we have described. In *Healy v. James*, the Supreme Court said that in a school environment, the power to prohibit lawless action is not limited to acts of a criminal nature: "Also prohibitable are actions which 'materially and substantially disrupt the work and the discipline of the school'." [*Healy*, 408 U.S. at 189, quoting *Tinker v. Des Moines Indep. Community Sch. Dist.*, 393 U.S. 503, 513 (1969).] We would assume that a university, so minded, would not be powerless to regulate public petting (heterosexual or otherwise), drinking in university buildings, or many other noncriminal activities which those responsible for running the institution rightly or wrongly think necessary "to assure that the traditional academic atmosphere is safeguarded." 408 U.S. at 194 n.24. Thus, if a university chose to do so, it might well be able to regulate overt sexual behavior, short of criminal activity, which may offend the community's sense of propriety, so long as it acts in a fair and equitable manner. The point in this case is that the district court has found no improper conduct, and it does not appear that the university ever concerned itself with defining or regulating such behavior. Defendants sought to cut back GSO's social activities simply because sponsored by that group. The ban was not justified by any evidence of misconduct attributable to GSO, and it was altogether too sweeping.
* * *

NOTES ON BONNER AND FIRST AMENDMENT DOCTRINE

1. *First Amendment Basics: If Protected Speech or Association, the State Cannot Engage in Content Discrimination.* Judge Coffin's decision in *Bonner* reflects standard First Amendment doctrine. The initial inquiry is whether the state is regulating protected expression, which includes association for expressive purposes. The next inquiry is what kind of regulation the state is engaged in. If the state regulation is just procedural (time, place, or manner), the state has substantial freedom, although it cannot impose unreasonable restrictions. If the state regulation is substantive (content-based), it can only do so if its regulation is narrowly tailored to meet a compelling state interest. This is an exceedingly hard test to pass.

2. *Student Organization Cases. Bonner* was an early example of the single most successful line of cases that gay rights advocates have brought: challenges to the denials of recognition of student organizations by universities. See *Gay and Lesbian Students Ass'n v. Gohn*, 850 F.2d 361 (8th Cir. 1988); *Gay Students Servs. v. Texas A & M Univ.*, 737 F.2d 1317 (5th Cir. 1984); *Gay Lib v. University of Mo.*, 558 F.2d 848 (8th Cir. 1977), cert. denied, 434 U.S. 1080 (1978); *Gay Alliance of Students v. Matthews*, 544 F.2d 162 (4th Cir. 1976); *Student Coalition for Gay Rights v. Austin Peay Univ.*, 477 F.Supp. 1267 (M.D.Tenn.1979); and *Wood v. Davison*, 351 F.Supp. 543 (N.D.Ga. 1972). What about the nature of the argument made in First Amendment cases might make courts hospitable to gay plaintiffs' claims, even in a time of widespread hostility to homosexuality?

Gay Law Students Association et al. v. Pacific Telephone and Telegraph Co.

California Supreme Court, 1979.
24 Cal.3d 458, 156 Cal.Rptr. 14, 595 P.2d 592.

■ TOBRINER, JUSTICE.

[Plaintiffs, four individuals and two associations organized to promote equal rights for homosexual persons, sued Pacific Telephone and Telegraph Company (PT & T), alleging that PT & T practiced discrimination against homosexuals in the hiring, firing and promotion of employees, and seeking both injunctive and monetary relief under the California Labor Code. The trial court sustained defendant's demurrer and held that California statutory law did not give plaintiffs a claim for relief. The California Supreme Court reversed.]

Over 60 years ago the California Legislature, recognizing that employers could misuse their economic power to interfere with the political activities of their employees, enacted Labor Code sections 1101 and 1102 to protect the employees' rights. Labor Code section 1101 provides that "No employer shall make, adopt, or enforce any rule, regulation, or policy: (a) Forbidding or preventing employees from engaging or participating in politics. . . . (b) Controlling or directing, or tending to control or direct the political activities of affiliations of employees." Similarly, section 1102 states that "No employer shall coerce or influence or attempt to coerce or influence his employees through or by means of threat of discharge or loss of employment to adopt or follow or refrain from adopting or following any particular course or line of political action or political activity." These sections serve to protect "the fundamental right of employees in general to engage in political activity without interference by employers."

These statutes cannot be narrowly confined to partisan activity. As explained in *Mallard v. Boring* (1960) 182 Cal.App.2d 390, 395: "The term 'political activity' connotes the espousal of a candidate *or a cause*, and some degree of action to promote the acceptance thereof by other persons." (Emphasis added.) The Supreme Court has recognized the political character of activities such as participation in litigation (*N.A.A.C.P. v. Button* (1963) 371 U.S. 415, 429), the wearing of symbolic armbands (*Tinker v. Des*

Moines School Dist. (1969) 393 U.S. 503), and the association with others for the advancement of beliefs and ideas (*N.A.A.C.P. v. Alabama* (1958) 357 U.S. 449).

Measured by these standards, the struggle of the homosexual community for equal rights, particularly in the field of employment, must be recognized as a political activity. Indeed the subject of the rights of homosexuals incites heated political debate today, and the "gay liberation movement" encourages its homosexual members to attempt to convince other members of society that homosexuals should be accorded the same fundamental rights as heterosexuals. The aims of the struggle for homosexual rights, and the tactics employed, bear a close analogy to the continuing struggle for civil rights waged by blacks, women, and other minorities.

A principal barrier to homosexual equality is the common feeling that homosexuality is an affliction which the homosexual worker must conceal from his employer and his fellow workers. Consequently one important aspect of the struggle for equal rights is to induce homosexual individuals to "come out of the closet," acknowledge their sexual preferences, and to associate with others in working for equal rights.

In light of this factor in the movement for homosexual rights, the allegations of plaintiffs' complaint assume a special significance. Plaintiffs allege that PT & T discriminates against "manifest" homosexuals and against persons who make "an issue of their homosexuality." The complaint asserts also that PT & T will not hire anyone referred to them by plaintiff Society for Individual Rights, an organization active in promoting the rights of homosexuals to equal employment opportunities. These allegations can reasonably be construed as charging that PT & T discriminates in particular against persons who identify themselves as homosexual, who defend homosexuality, or who are identified with activist homosexual organizations. So construed, the allegations charge that PT & T has adopted a "policy . . . tending to control or direct the political activities or affiliations of employees" in violation of section 1101, and has "attempt[ed] to coerce or influence . . . employees . . . to . . . refrain from adopting [a] particular course or line of political . . . activity" in violation of section 1102. * * *

■ RICHARDSON, JUSTICE, dissenting.

* * * [T]he complaint herein fails to allege *any* attempted control or coercion by PT & T of any employee or applicant with respect to any *"political"* activity whatever. Significantly, plaintiffs' appellate briefs do not even raise the point. They cite neither section 1101 nor 1102 in support of their complaint. The "political" argument has never been advanced nor apparently even thought of by either lawyers or litigants.

The gist of plaintiffs' allegations in the complaint herein is that plaintiffs have been damaged by reason of PT & T's alleged refusal to hire or promote "manifest homosexuals." As the "introduction" to the first amended complaint alleges, "PT & T has, since at least 1971, had an articulated policy of excluding homosexuals from employment opportunities with its organization." Again, in the "fact allegations" of the complaint, it is alleged that ". . . PT & T has maintained and enforced a policy of employment discrimination against homosexuals. . . . PT & T refuses to hire any 'manifest homosexual' which [*sic*] may apply to it for employment at any occupational level or category." Nowhere in the complaint, from beginning to end, do plaintiffs allege that PT & T's asserted policy of discrimination is directed toward any of plaintiffs' *political* activity or affiliations. Rather, plaintiffs contend, and the gravamen of their complaint is, that employment discrimination is based solely on the overt and manifest nature of their sexual orientation itself. * * *

NOTE ON *PT & T* AND "COMING OUT" AS POLITICAL ACTIVITY

1. *California Law.* Note the timing of the decision in *PT & T*, namely, the year after California voters rejected the Briggs Amendment, which would have banned advocates of gay rights from teaching in the public schools. The *Pacific Telephone* case was eventually settled with a $5 million payment to the plaintiff class and the adoption by defendant of an antidiscrimination policy. Arthur Leonard, *Sexuality and the Law* 417 (1992). In 1992, the legislature amended the Labor Code to add an explicit protection against discrimination based on sexual orientation. Cal. Lab. Code § 1102.1 (West 1993). Was the amendment necessary, in light of the *PT & T* precedent? Eventually, California added sexual orientation to the list of prohibited bases for discrimination in the state civil rights statute. Cal. Gov't Code §§ 12920, 12940 (West Supp. 2001). What might be some of the reasons why LGBT advocates continued to press for inclusion in the civil rights law, after they won inclusion in the Labor Code?

2. *The Personal As Political?* Under *PT & T*, would it be political speech to put a photograph of one's same-sex lover on one's desk at work? What about a photo of one's opposite-sex partner? How could the first act be political speech if the second is not also? Justice Tobriner's analysis links an individual's coming out to "the struggle of the homosexual community for equal rights." Can you frame an argument for transgender rights under the First Amendment?

3. *Don't Ask, Don't Tell.* Perhaps the harshest regime in U.S. law for penalizing coming out speech is the military's don't ask, don't tell policy. According to this policy, lesbians, gay men, and bisexuals might theoretically serve in the armed forces—but only if they do not self-identify as lesbian, gay, or bisexual and are not caught engaging in illegal sodomy. (See Chapter 7, Section 3, for an extended analysis.)

PART C.   "NO PROMO HOMO" RESTRICTIONS

National Gay Task Force v. Board of Education of the City of Oklahoma City

U.S. Court of Appeals for the Tenth Circuit, 1984.
729 F.2d 1270, affirmed by an equally divided Court, 470 U.S. 903 (1985).

■ LOGAN, CIRCUIT JUDGE.

The National Gay Task Force (NGTF), whose membership includes teachers in the Oklahoma public school system, filed this action in the district court challenging the facial constitutional validity of Okla. Stat. tit. 70, § 6–103.15. The district court held that the statute was constitutionally valid. On appeal NGTF contends that the statute violates plaintiff's members' rights to privacy and equal protection, that it is void for vagueness, that it violates the Establishment Clause, and, finally, that it is overbroad.

The challenged statute, Okla. Stat. tit. 70, § 6–103.15, provides:

"A. As used in this section:

1. 'Public homosexual activity' means the commission of an act defined in Section 886 of Title 21 of the Oklahoma Statutes [prohibiting sodomy], if such act is:

   a.   committed with a person of the same sex, and

   b.   indiscreet and not practiced in private;

2. 'Public homosexual conduct' means advocating, soliciting, imposing, encouraging or promoting public or private homosexual activity in a manner that creates a substantial risk that such conduct will come to the attention of school children or school employees; and

3. 'Teacher' means a person as defined in Section 1–116 of Title 70 of the Oklahoma Statutes.

B.   In addition to any ground set forth in Section 6–103 of Title 70 of the Oklahoma Statutes, a teacher, student teacher or a teachers' aide may be refused employment, or reemployment, dismissed, or suspended after a finding that the teacher or teachers' aide has:

1.   Engaged in public homosexual conduct or activity; and

2.   Has been rendered unfit, because of such conduct or activity, to hold a position as a teacher, student teacher or teachers' aide.

C.   The following factors shall be considered in making the determination whether the teacher, student teacher or teachers' aide has been rendered unfit for his position:

1.   The likelihood that the activity or conduct may adversely affect students or school employees;

2.   The proximity in time or place the activity or conduct to the teacher's, student teacher's or teachers' aide's official duties;

3.   Any extenuating or aggravating circumstances; and

4.   Whether the conduct or activity is of a repeated or continuing nature which tends to encourage or dispose school children toward similar conduct or activity."

The trial court held that the statute reaches protected speech but upheld the constitutionality of the statute by reading a "material and substantial disruption" test into it. We disagree. The statute proscribes protected speech and is thus facially overbroad, and we cannot read into the statute a "material and substantial disruption" test. Therefore, we reverse the judgment of the trial court.

We see no constitutional problem in the statute's permitting a teacher to be fired for engaging in "public homosexual activity." Section 6–103.15 defines "public homosexual activity" as the commission of an act defined in Okla. Stat. tit. 21, § 886, that is committed with a person of the same sex and is indiscreet and not practiced in private. * * *

The part of § 6–103.15 that allows punishment of teachers for "public homosexual conduct" does present constitutional problems. To be sure, this is a facial challenge, and facial challenges based on First Amendment overbreadth are "strong medicine" and should be used "sparingly and only as a last resort." *Broadrick v. Oklahoma*, 413 U.S. 601, 613 (1973). Nonetheless, invalidation is an appropriate remedy in the instant case because this portion of § 6–103.15 is overbroad, is "not readily subject to a narrowing construction by the state courts," and "its deterrent effect on legitimate expression is both real and substantial." *Erznoznik v. City of Jacksonville*, 422 U.S. 205, 216 (1975). Also, we must be especially willing to invalidate a statute for facial overbreadth when, as here, the statute regulates "pure speech."

Section 6–103.15 allows punishment of teachers for "public homosexual conduct," which is defined as "advocating, soliciting, imposing, encouraging or promoting public or private homosexual activity in a manner that creates a substantial risk that such conduct will come to the attention of school children or school employees." Okla. Stat. tit. 70, § 6–103.15(A)(2). The First Amendment protects "advocacy" even of illegal conduct except when "advocacy" is "directed to inciting or producing imminent lawless action and is likely to incite or produce such action." *Brandenburg v. Ohio*, 395 U.S. 444, 447 (1969). The First Amendment does not permit someone to be punished for advocating illegal conduct at some indefinite future time.

"Encouraging" and "promoting," like "advocating," do not necessarily imply incitement to imminent action. A teacher who went before the Oklahoma legislature or appeared on television to urge the repeal of the Oklahoma anti-sodomy statute would be "advocating," "promoting," and "encouraging" homosexual sodomy and creating a substantial risk that his or her speech would come to the attention of school children or school employees if he or she said, "I think it is psychologically damaging for people with homosexual desires to suppress those desires. They should act on those desires and should be legally free to do so." Such statements, which are aimed at legal and social change, are at the core of First Amendment protections. As in *Erznoznik*, the statute by its plain terms is not easily susceptible of a narrowing construction. The Oklahoma legislature chose the word "advocacy" despite the Supreme Court's interpretation of that word in *Brandenburg*. Finally, the deterrent effect of § 6–103.15 is both real and substantial. It applies to all teachers, substitute teachers, and teachers' aides in Oklahoma. To protect their jobs they must restrict their expression. Thus, the § 6–103.15 proscription of advocating, encouraging, or promoting homosexual activity is unconstitutionally overbroad. * * *

■ BARRETT, CIRCUIT JUDGE, dissenting. * * *

The majority, unlike the district court, holds that portion of the statute which allows "punishment" for teachers for advocating "public homosexual conduct" to be overbroad because it is "not readily subject to a narrowing construction by the state courts" and "its deterrent effect on legitimate expression is both real and substantial." I disagree. Sodomy is *malum in se*, i.e., immoral and corruptible in its nature without regard to the fact of its being noticed or punished by the law of the state. It is not *malum prohibitum*, i.e., wrong *only* because it is forbidden by law and not involving moral turpitude. It is on this principle that I must part with the majority's holding that the "public homosexual conduct" portion of the Oklahoma statute is overbroad.

Any teacher who advocates, solicits, encourages or promotes the practice of *sodomy* "in a manner that creates a substantial risk that such conduct will come to the attention of school children or school employees" is in fact and in truth *inciting* school children to participate in the abominable and detestable crime against nature. Such advocacy by school teachers, regardless of the situs where made, creates a substantial risk of being conveyed to school children. In my view, it does not merit any constitutional protection. There is no need to demonstrate that such conduct would bring about a material or substantial interference or disruption in the normal activities of the school. A teacher advocating the practice of sodomy to school children is without First Amendment protection. This statute furthers an important and substantial government interest, as determined by the Oklahoma legislature, unrelated to the suppression of free speech. The incidental restriction on alleged First Amendment freedom is no greater than is essential to the furtherance of that interest. * * *

The Oklahoma legislature has declared that the advocacy by teachers of homosexual acts to school children is a matter of statewide concern. The Oklahoma statute does not condemn or in any wise affect teachers, homosexual or otherwise, except to the extent of the non-advocacy restraint aimed at the protection of school children. It does not deny them any rights as human beings. To * * * require proof that advocacy of the act of sodomy will substantially interfere or disrupt normal school activities is a bow to permissiveness. To the same extent, the advocacy of violence, sabotage and terrorism as a means of effecting political reform held in *Brandenburg* to be protected speech unless demonstrated as directed to and likely to incite or produce such action *did not* involve advocacy of a crime *malum in se* to school children by a school teacher. * * *

NOTES ON *GAY TASK FORCE* AND THE FADING BOUNDARY BETWEEN SEXUAL SPEECH AND POLITICAL SPEECH

On review before the Supreme Court, the Justices split four to four; in that event, the court of appeals decision is affirmed. (Justice Powell took no part in the case because of illness. Leonard, *Sexuality and the Law* 616. The Tenth Circuit's decision remains the law of that circuit, but its affirmance by an equally divided Supreme Court means that it has no national precedential value.)

1. *The Briggs Initiative and Identity Speech.* The Oklahoma statute challenged in *NGTF* was identical in substance to a proposal popularly known as the Briggs Initiative for its sponsor, state Senator John Briggs, that was rejected by California voters. The campaign for and against the Briggs Initiative created the first large-scale consideration of a gay rights issue in electoral politics by focusing on what one of us has called "identity speech":

> [T]he Briggs Initiative was * * * framed in terms of banning a viewpoint, the "advocating" or "promoting" of homosexuality, rather than the exclusion of a group of persons. Lesbians and gay men easily fell within this proscription because to come out is to implicitly, or often explicitly, affirm the value of homosexuality. For that reason, a Briggs-style law could be used to target all lesbian and gay school employees who had expressed their sexual orientation, except in the most furtive contexts.

> The viewpoint target made the initiative more complicated, however. It threatened anyone, gay or straight, who voiced the forbidden ideas. Thus it simultaneously discriminated against gay people while extending its aim to everyone not gay who supported them.

> The proposed law did not merely include the two distinct elements of viewpoint bias and group classification. It merged them into one new concept. This merger—what I would describe as the formation of a legal construct of identity that incorporates both viewpoint and status—would come to dominate both the right-wing strategy against gay rights and the claims of the lesbian and gay community for equality.

> * * * The Briggs Initiative referendum campaign marked the moment when American politics began to treat homosexuality as something more than deviance, conduct, or lifestyle; it marked the emergence of homosexuality as an openly political claim * * *

Nan D. Hunter, "Identity, Speech and Equality," 79 *Va. L. Rev.* 1695, 1703–05 (1993).

2. *Category Contest.* Drafters of the Oklahoma statute at issue in *NGTF* labeled "encouraging," "promoting," and "advocating" of certain illegal conduct (sodomy) as "public homosexual conduct." What is the rhetorical strategy behind that phrase? Analyze its three components: What must be "public" for the behavior to be prohibited? Which Oklahoma statutes are and are not limited to "homosexual" activity? What is the "conduct" at issue?

By contrast, plaintiffs framed the statute as endangering pure political speech and relied on its potential scope extending to out-of-classroom speech. What if the statute had been limited to in-classroom speech or speech advocating illegal sexual acts?

3. *Off Duty Political Speech by Government Employees.* In *Pickering v. Board of Education*, 391 U.S. 563 (1968), the Supreme Court ruled that public employees can engage in speech critical of their employer's policies, so long as that speech does not diminish their efficiency on the job or disrupt the workplace. In general, that doctrine has protected gay employees. For example, in *Van Ooteghem v. Gray*, 654 F.2d 304 (5th Cir.1981), the court held that an assistant county treasurer could not be fired for addressing county commissioners as a citizen in favor of civil rights for lesbians and gay men. But courts have also drawn a line at more vivid forms of advocacy. See two cases, both in Chapter 8: *Singer v. U.S. Civil Service Commission* (gay man fired for "flaunting" his homosexuality by attempting to legalize gay marriage) and *Shahar v. Bowers* (lesbian denied job in state attorney general's office after participating in a wedding/commitment ceremony). Chapter 8 tackles the issue of the dynamic between speech and employment discrimination.

NOTE ON CONTENT—AND VIEWPOINT—BASED DISCRIMINATION

The *Bonner* and *NGTF* cases marked important turning points in courts applying the same First Amendment standard to advocacy of homosexuality as that applied to other forms of advocacy. Speech about homosexuality has emerged from its old categorization as obscenity (in *One, Inc.*, for example) and is now recognized as political speech. Using the principle of content or viewpoint neutrality in more recent cases, courts have struck down an Alabama law barring the use of public funds to support or recognize college LGBT student groups, *Gay Lesbian Bisexual Alliance v. Pryor*, 110 F.3d 1543 (11th Cir. 1997); and ruled that the Boston public transit authority could not refuse to display public service ads using sexually suggestive language to encourage safe sex, when it accepted equally risqué advertising for movies, *AIDS Action Committee of Massachusetts, Inc. v. Massachusetts Bay Transp. Authority*, 42 F.3d 1 (1st Cir. 1994).

IDENTITY AND VIEWPOINT

Identity can be constituted as much by what one is *not* as by what one *is*. The duality of identity formation often finds its way into the public arena, as when one group wants to self-identify in a context which threatens the self-identity of another group. When a group believes that exclusion of another group is central to its own coherency, norms of expression and anti-discrimination clash.

Gay Rights Coalition of Georgetown University Law Center et al. v. Georgetown University

District of Columbia Court of Appeals, en banc, 1987.
536 A.2d 1.

■ MACK, ASSOCIATE JUDGE.

In the District of Columbia, the Human Rights Act prohibits an educational institution from discriminating against any individual on the basis of his or her sexual orientation. Two student gay rights groups contend that Georgetown University violated this statutory command by refusing to grant them "University Recognition" together with equal access to the additional facilities and services that status entails. The University, relying on the trial court's factual finding that Georgetown's grant of "University Recognition" includes a religiously guided "endorsement" of the recipient student group, responds that the Free Exercise Clause of the First Amendment protects it from official compulsion to "endorse" an organization which challenges its religious tenets. Upholding the asserted constitutional defense, the trial court entered judgment in favor of Georgetown. The student groups appeal.

Our analysis of the issues differs from that of the trial court. At the outset, we sever the artificial connection between the "endorsement" and the tangible benefits contained in Georgetown's scheme of "University Recognition." With respect to the University's refusal to grant the status of "University Recognition," we do not reach Georgetown's constitutional defense. Contrary to the trial court's understanding, the Human Rights Act does not require one private actor to "endorse" another. Thus, Georgetown's denial of "University Recognition"—in this case a status carrying an intangible "endorsement"—does not violate the statute. Although affirming the trial court's entry of judgment for the University on that point, we do so on statutory rather than constitutional grounds.

We reach a contrary conclusion with respect to the tangible benefits that accompany "University Recognition." While the Human Rights Act does not seek to compel uniformity in philosophical *attitudes* by force of law, it does require equal *treatment*. Equality of treatment in educational institutions is concretely measured by nondiscriminatory provision of access to "facilities and services." D.C. Code § 1–2520 (1987). Unlike the "endorsement," the various additional tangible benefits that accompany a grant of "University Recognition" are "facilities and services." As such, they must be made equally available, without regard to sexual orientation or to any other characteristic unrelated to individual merit. Georgetown's refusal to provide tangible benefits without regard to sexual orientation violated the Human Rights Act. To that extent only, we consider the merits of Georgetown's free exercise defense. On that issue we hold that the District of Columbia's compelling interest in the eradication of sexual orientation discrimination outweighs any burden imposed upon Georgetown's exercise of religion by the forced equal provision of tangible benefits. * * *

There are two reasons why, as a matter of statutory construction, the Human Rights Act cannot be read to compel a regulated party to express religious approval or neutrality towards any group or individual. First, the statute prohibits only a discriminatory denial of access to "facilities and services" provided by an educational institution. D.C. Code § 1–2520 (1987). An "endorsement" is neither. The Human Rights Act provides legal mechanisms to ensure equality of *treatment*, not equality of *attitudes*. Although we fervently hope that nondiscriminatory attitudes result from equal access to "facilities and services," the Human Rights Act contains nothing to suggest that the legislature intended to make a discriminatory state of mind unlawful in itself. Still less does the statute reveal any desire to force a private actor to express an idea that is not truly held. The Human Rights Act demands action, not words. It was not intended to be an instrument of mind control. * * *

Second, as we have already pointed out, unless the language of the statute is plainly to the contrary, we must construe it so as to uphold its constitutionality. To read into the Human Rights Act a requirement that one private actor must "endorse" another would be to render the statute unconstitutional. The First Amendment protects both free speech and the free exercise of religion. Its essence is that government is without power to intrude into the domain of the intellect or the spirit and that only conduct may be regulated. Interpreting the Human Rights Act so as to require Georgetown to "endorse" the student groups would be to thrust the statute across the constitutional boundaries set by the Free Speech Clause and also, where sincere religious objections are raised, the Free Exercise Clause. Nothing in the statute suggests, let alone requires, such a result. * * *

Although the student groups were not entitled to summary judgment on the ground that Georgetown's denial of "University Recognition"—including an "endorsement"—violated the Human Rights Act, the statute does require Georgetown to equally distribute, without regard to sexual orientation, the tangible benefits contained in the same package. If discrimination appears from the record, this court may sustain the statutory ruling "on a ground different from that adopted by the trial court." Our review of the record reveals no genuine dispute that the tangible benefits were denied on the basis of sexual orientation. The Human Rights Act was violated to that extent.

The Human Rights Act cannot depend for its enforcement on a regulated actor's purely subjective, albeit sincere, evaluation of its own motivations. * * * It is particularly difficult to recognize one's own acts as discriminatory. Apart from organizations that failed to meet purely technical requirements such as a minimum membership, the record shows that Georgetown never denied "University Recognition" to a student group that was not mainly composed of persons with a homosexual orientation. Where, as here, those possessing characteristics identified by the legislature as irrelevant to individual merit are treated less favorably than others, the Human Rights Act imposes a burden upon the regulated actor to demonstrate that the irrelevant characteristic played no part in its decision. Georgetown failed to present facts that could show it was uninfluenced by sexual orientation in denying the tangible benefits. * * *

In denying GPGU's application for "University Recognition" Georgetown adverted to that group's expressed purpose (one of four) to "provide a forum for the development of responsible sexual ethics consonant with one's personal beliefs." That purpose is at odds with Roman Catholic teachings. But GRC's constitution contained no comparable statement; Georgetown's stated objection was to GRC's much broader intention to "[p]rovide lesbians and gay men entering the Law Center with information about Washington's gay community, including educational, cultural, religious, social and medical services." Because GRC's purposes include an asexual commitment to serving the broad range of needs experienced by homosexual students, but no statement as to the propriety of homosexual conduct, Georgetown's objection to that organization must to some extent have been prompted by the sexual orientation of its members.

That Georgetown's treatment of the gay student groups was not exclusively influenced by a specific objection to "purposes and activities" inconsistent with Roman Catholic dogma was further evidenced by Debbie Gottfried, the University's Director of Student Activities. In clarifying GPGU's status after it had obtained "Student Body Endorsement," but had failed to obtain "University Recognition," Gottfried wrote that the University would not change its position "on what it feels would be interpreted as endorsement and official support of *the full range of issues associated with this cause*." At no time has Georgetown defined what it meant by "the full range of issues" associated with the gay student groups, despite its insistence that Roman Catholic doctrine favors the provision of equal civil and political rights to homosexually oriented persons and that its religious objection was directed only to the promotion of homosexual conduct. Gottfried's statement was later repeated by Dean Schuerman, who wrote that the University would not lend its endorsement, support or approval to "the positions taken by the gay movement *on a full range of issues*" or "the major activities and issues which, *by definition*, are associated with a *gay organization*." Similarly, when Dean McCarthy turned down GRC's application at the Law Center, he wrote that the University would not lend its official subsidy and support to a gay law student organization because that "would be interpreted by many as endorsement of the positions taken by the gay movement on *a full range of issues*." Georgetown thus ascribed to the student groups not only "purposes and activities" which they may have had, but also a host of others automatically assumed to be a necessary attribute of their homosexual orientation. * * *

It is apparent from this correspondence, all of which was before Judge Braman when he granted summary judgment on the discrimination issue, that Georgetown's denial of tangible benefits was not closely tied to specific "purposes and activities" of the student groups promoting the homosexual conduct condemned by Roman Catholic doctrine. The conclusion is inescapable that the predominantly gay composition of the student groups played at least some role in their treatment by Georgetown. By objecting to the student groups' assumed connection, "by definition," to a "full range of issues" associated with the "gay movement," rather than to specific "purposes and activities" inconsistent with its Roman Catholic tradition, Georgetown engaged in the kind of stereotyping unrelated to individual merit that is forbidden by the Human Rights Act. In short, the record reveals no genuine doubt that Georgetown's asserted nondiscriminatory basis for its action was in fact tainted by preconceptions about gay persons. Georgetown did not apply "Recognition Criteria" on an equal basis to all groups without regard to the sexual orientation of their members. * * *

■ [CHIEF JUDGE PRYOR concurred in the result reached by Judge Mack. JUDGE NEWMAN wrote a concurring opinion, one section of which commanded a majority of the Court. He observed that the Human Rights Act protected against race, sex, and sexual orientation discrimination (etc.) with no differentiation as to the importance of eradicating each kind of discrimination. All three goals were of equal importance.]

■ BELSON, ASSOCIATE JUDGE, with whom NEBEKER, ASSOCIATE JUDGE, RETIRED, joins, concurring in part and dissenting in part. * * *

The Human Rights Act, by its plain language, does not prohibit discrimination against persons or groups based upon their advocacy. Rather, it prohibits discrimination against persons based upon their "sexual orientation" which, in the words of the statute, "means male or female homosexuality, heterosexuality and bisexuality, by preference or practice." D.C.Code § 1–2502(28) (1987). It follows that Judge Braman erred if he granted summary judgment against Georgetown on the theory that it violated the Act by denying recognition because of the groups' advocacy of homosexual life-styles.

* * * [A] construction of the Act that would prohibit a private actor from differentiating among persons based on their advocacy of ideas would not only be untrue to the Act, it would also abridge the first amendment's guarantees of free speech and, in this case, the free exercise of religion.

Judge Mack interprets the Act to prohibit the public and private educational institutions covered by it from engaging in certain types of conduct but, in an attempt to avoid conflict with the first amendment, she construes the Act not to reach the speech activities of a private institution. Judge Mack concludes that the Act therefore does not require one private actor to "endorse" another.

I would use a different analysis to determine whether Georgetown's denial of recognition to the student groups falls outside the scope of the Human Rights Act. I interpret the Act to prohibit adverse action taken against persons on the basis of their status as members of a protected class. The Act does not purport to prohibit actions taken against persons because of their promotion of ideas or activities (here, for example, promotion of ideas and conduct antithetical to Catholic teachings). Thus, in my view, if an entity covered by the Act fails to grant facilities and services to an individual because of his or her status as a member of a protected group, the Act is violated. In contrast, if an entity covered by the Act fails to provide facilities and services to an individual because of his or her promotion of ideas or activities, that conduct does not violate the Act. Furthermore, as developed below, a construction of the Act that would prevent a private actor from differentiating among others on the basis of the content of their speech would be unconstitutional, at least in the absence of a compelling state interest. Thus, a statutorily imposed requirement of neutrality toward the promotion of an idea, *viz.*, the morality of homosexual life-styles, would abridge first amendment rights. Similarly, an imposed duty either to endorse or to subsidize a position on that issue would also abridge those rights.

An analogy is illustrative. It could not seriously be suggested that the Human Rights Act could force a private, church-affiliated school to lend its endorsement or subsidy to a group that advocated or purposely facilitated fornication or adultery. Such a group, however, could argue that those activities reflect the group members' heterosexual orientation, an orientation that triggers the Act's protection to the same extent as does homosexual orientation. There can be no doubt that university authorities in such a case could recognize that the purposes and activities of an organization of this type would foster or promote acts that the Church deems immoral. While Catholic doctrine deems all homosexual acts immoral and only some heterosexual acts immoral, the principle is the same. Both this hypothetical group and the groups before us can properly be denied endorsement and subsidy by a religious institution because of their sponsorship and promotion of acts that the institution considers immoral, rather than on the basis of their members' status as homosexuals, heterosexuals, or bisexuals. See Tr. 541 (Georgetown would not subsidize activities of student "playboy" club); Tr. 628–30 (Georgetown would not support group that distributes information about abortion clinics to students). * * *

Even if there were a valid finding that Georgetown had violated the Human Rights Act, Georgetown should prevail in this litigation on the basis of its constitutional rights under the free speech and free exercise clauses of the first amendment. I discuss the constitutional issues here on the premise that Georgetown denied recognition to the student groups at least in large part because of the groups' sponsorship and promotion of ideas and activities. * * * Georgetown's concern over the groups' advocacy and speech activities permeated its consideration of the question of whether to grant them recognition. Therefore, Georgetown's right of free speech comes strongly into play. * * * Georgetown denied recognition "because recognition would be inconsistent with its duties as a Catholic institution." * * *

■ FERREN, ASSOCIATE JUDGE, with whom TERRY, ASSOCIATE JUDGE, joins, concurring in part and dissenting in part.

I continue to subscribe to the views expressed in the opinion of the division vacated by the en banc court, *Gay Rights Coalition of Georgetown University v. Georgetown University*, 496 A.2d 567, 587 (D.C.1985). Thus, I continue to believe that Georgetown University may not lawfully refuse to accord the plaintiff gay rights groups "University Recognition," which means (1) *status* equal to that of the other student groups formally recognized by the university, including permission to use the university name, and (2) the *tangible benefits* uniformly available to other recognized groups such as office space, supplies and equipment, a telephone, computer label and mailing services, student advertising privileges, financial counseling, and the opportunity to apply for lecture fund privileges and for other funding. I therefore concur, as far as it goes, in the result proposed by Judge Mack, joined by Chief Judge Pryor and Judge Newman, requiring the university to make the second category of (tangible) benefits available to the gay rights groups. But I respectfully dissent from the views of those three colleagues, as well as Judges Belson and Nebeker, who would deny the first category of (intangible) relief plaintiffs have requested. * * *

In contrast with Judge Mack, Judge Belson reads the Human Rights Act in a way that may not proscribe any of Georgetown's discriminatory conduct. He argues that the Act's reference to "sexual orientation" only forbids discrimination based on sexual "preference or practice," not discrimination based on "advocacy," meaning "promotion of ideas or activities." If Georgetown engaged only in the latter sort of discrimination, he says, it did not violate the Act. * * *

There is a * * * fundamental weakness of Judge Belson's analysis—of his unqualified proposition that the Act cannot be construed to forbid the suppression of "speech" or "advocacy." The distinction between discrimination based on advocacy and on status will not work. Part of who a person is, is what he or she says; to deny the right to speak is to deny an essential aspect of one's person. In this sense, therefore, an asserted right to discriminate against someone's advocacy of homosexuality is clearly a claimed right to discriminate against the person on the basis of one's sexual "preference" and thus "sexual orientation." D.C.Code §§ 1–2502(28),–2520(1) (1987). * * *

* * * I believe any effort to distinguish under the Act between legal discrimination against ideas and illegal discrimination against persons fails

to take into account that ideas—and advocacy—are an essential part of the person. But even if the distinction could be made, it is not easy to draw, in part because means capable of achieving the former may amount to the latter. I believe Judge Belson has overlooked, both in his analysis and in its application, the possibility that Georgetown's refusal to recognize the plaintiff groups, if only because of an aversion to their advocacy, is likely to be—indeed, inevitably is in the context of a university—an overly broad response that effectively discriminates against persons in violation of the Act. * * *

The fundamental [constitutional] question is: whether plaintiffs' request for "University Recognition"—meaning full citizenship as student groups at Georgetown University—may be denied, even though in violation of the Human Rights Act, because of Georgetown's first amendment rights. * * * I want to emphasize again that, on this record, "University recognition" or "endorsement" of the plaintiff student groups does not mean, explicitly or implicitly, a statement of approval—or even of neutrality-toward homosexuality, gay rights, or related matters. Because of the nature of the university, the Human Rights Act in no way compels Georgetown to take a position in violation of its right to free exercise of religious beliefs.

In context—and context is critically important—the Act only requires Georgetown not to discriminate against student groups that wish to express their own views in what I believe we may call, without fear of contradiction, a typical private university marketplace of ideas, which inherently stands for freedom of expression. * * * A legal requirement that Georgetown make its university-wide forum available on a nondiscriminatory basis to all student citizens of the university does not, in my view, imply in any way that the university corporation/administration itself can be reasonably identified with the views of any particular student organization or that the university, as such, has a position-pro, con, or neutral-on any particular message a student group happens to spread. The Human Rights Act, therefore, does not require Georgetown to espouse any view or to intimate even a neutral opinion. * * *

NOTES ON THE GEORGETOWN CASE

1. *Viewpoint as Constitutive of Identity.* "Notions of identity increasingly form the basis for gay and lesbian equality claims. Those claims merge not only status and conduct, but also viewpoint, into one whole. To be openly gay, when the closet is an option, is to function as an advocate as well as a symbol. The centrality of viewpoint to gay identity explains the logic behind what has become the primary strategy of anti-gay forces: the attempted penalization of those who 'profess' homosexuality, in a series of 'no promo homo' campaigns." Nan D. Hunter, "Identity, Speech and Equality," 79 *Va. L. Rev.* 1695, 1696 (1993). Imagine that a group of lesbian, gay and bisexual students had formed to seek and provide support for becoming heterosexual. Would Georgetown have been likely to charter the group? If so, wouldn't viewpoint (not identity) be the only explanation for its different treatment of the plaintiffs in this case? Conversely, imagine that heterosexual students seek to form a chapter of "Straight But Not Narrow." What result?

2. *Must One Choose Between Viewpoint and Identity?* Judge Ferren's opinion is a sophisticated attempt to tackle this dilemma. His central point is that "[e]ven if the Act were construed not to forbid discrimination against homosexual ideas, it unquestionably does forbid discrimination against homosexuals because of their ideas." Is that true? Is it illegal to discriminate against Latinos "because of their ideas"? Because of their ideas only about race or ethnicity? What *are* "homosexual ideas"?

Judge Mack's opinion also tackles the issue—and does so in a creative way. Responsive to the lesbian and gay plaintiffs' charge that they were being discriminated against because of their identity (and stereotypes based on that identity), she ruled that Georgetown had to give them equal access and services. Responsive to Georgetown's insistence that its identity as a Roman Catholic institution was tied up with its refusal to recognize an organization whose members opposed a fundamental moral teaching of that church, Judge Mack ruled that Georgetown did not have to recognize the student group. Is this an acceptable compromise? Are Judge Ferren's criticisms of the compromise cogent?

3. *The Subsequent History of the Georgetown Case.* Georgetown University withdrew its petition seeking Supreme Court review of the decision you read, and settled the lawsuit with the students. In 1989, Congress amended the Human Rights Act to exempt religious institutions from the prohibition against discrimination on the basis of sexual preference. Even after the amendment, however, the University adhered to its agreement with the students, and gay student groups have continued at both the main campus and at the Law Center.

NOTE ON THE RIGHT OF ASSOCIATION

Although the First Amendment does not explicitly protect rights of association, the Supreme Court held such rights protected by implication in *NAACP v. Alabama*, 357 U.S. 449 (1958). Justice Harlan's opinion reasoned that associational rights are prerequisites for rights to speak and publish that are explicitly protected. The Court disallowed a state's effort to obtain NAACP membership lists, because the disclosure of membership by an unpopular group would chill entry into the group. That sort of reasoning was just as applicable to homophile groups that had formed in the 1950s, particularly the Daughters of Bilitis and the Mattachine Society. Not only did the homophile groups promise to keep their membership hidden from the authorities, but many and perhaps most members of the group were disinclined to reveal their real names and identities to the group itself! Hence, even though *NAACP v. Alabama* did not involve lesbian and gay plaintiffs, its holding was critically important for homophile groups.

More recent cases have confirmed and broadened the associational feature of the First Amendment recognized in *NAACP*. "[T]he Court has recognized a right to associate for the purpose of engaging in those activities protected by the First Amendment—speech, assembly, petition for the redress of grievances, and the exercise of religion. The Constitution guarantees freedom of association of this kind as an indispensable means of preserving other individual liberties." *Roberts v. United States Jaycees*, 468 U.S. 609, 618 (1984). Under what circumstances, if any, can the state limit people's rights of association? Consider the following cases.

Kathryn Roberts v. United States Jaycees, 468 U.S. 609, 104 S.Ct. 3244, 82 L.Ed.2d 462 (1984). The Minnesota Human Rights Act, as amended in 1973, made it illegal for a "public accommodation" to "deny any person the full and equal enjoyment of the goods, services, facilities, privileges, advantages, and accommodations * * * because of race, color, creed, religion, disability, national origin or sex." The national Jaycees, a network of all-male civic clubs, disciplined its Minnesota chapters for admitting women pursuant to the state law, and the state courts held the national chapter in violation of the law. The Jaycees challenged the statute, as construed, on the ground that it violated the right of association in the First Amendment. The Supreme Court affirmed.

Justice Brennan's opinion for the Court recognized that "certain kinds of personal bonds have played a critical role in the culture and traditions of the Nation by cultivating and transmitting shared ideals and beliefs; they thereby foster diversity and act as critical buffers between the individual and the power of the State. * * * Protecting these relationships from unwarranted state interference therefore safeguards the ability independently to define one's identity that is critical to any concept of liberty." The core protection of this feature of the right of association is the family, "distinguished by such attributes as relative smallness, a high degree of selectivity in decisions to begin and maintain the affiliation, and seclusion from others in critical aspects of the relationship. * * * Conversely, an association lacking these qualities–such as a large business enterprise– seems remote from the concerns giving rise to the constitutional protection."

Under such a core-penumbra reasoning, the Jaycees were entitled to little special First Amendment protection, reasoned Justice Brennan. According to lower tribunals' findings of fact, the Jaycees were large and sprawling, relatively unselective in choosing members (essentially accepting everyone except women and a few other minorities), and unbonded in the interaction of members who remain strangers to one another. It was not clear that the Jaycees' interests triggered First Amendment protection.

In any event, infringements on even core associational rights can be justified by "regulations adopted to serve compelling state interests, unrelated to the suppression of ideas, that cannot be achieved through means significantly less restrictive of associational freedoms." Justice Brennan found the public accommodation law's "compelling interest in eradicating discrimination against its female citizens justifies the impact that application of the statute to the Jaycees may have on the male members' associational freedoms." He found it important that the statute did not discriminate "on the basis of viewpoint" and was not administered arbitrarily. Justice Brennan also emphasized the constitutional underpinnings of the state law.

There was no dissent, but **Justice O'Connor** concurred only in the Court's judgment. (**Justice Rehnquist** also concurred in the Court's judgment, but without stating his reasons.) She maintained that the majority's approach swept too broadly, threatening traditionalist associations for which some discrimination was important for the group's functioning—including the Girl Scouts. Nonetheless, she agreed with the Court that the anti-discrimination law could be constitutionally applied to the Jaycees—but because they were more like a public accommodation, indeed a commercial business, than a truly private organization. Her concurring opinion suggested that the more like a business the institution is, the less inclined courts should be to recognize First Amendment defenses against anti-discrimination laws.

The large majority of states and cities have statutes prohibiting discrimination by public accommodations (*e.g.*, hotels, restaurants) on the basis of race, ethnicity, religion, and sex or gender. Thirteen states plus the District of Columbia also prohibit discrimination by public accommodations on the basis of sexual orientation: California (initially as an interpretation of the Unruh Act, then by statute enacted in 2001); Connecticut (1991); the District of Columbia (regulation adopted 1973, statute 1977); Hawaii (limited scope, 1991); Maryland (2001); Massachusetts (enacted 1989, the statute at issue in *Hurley, infra*); Minnesota (1991); New Hampshire (1997); New Jersey (1991, the statute applied in *Dale, infra*); New Mexico (2003); New York (2003); Rhode Island (1995); Vermont (1991); and Wisconsin (1982). Dozens and probably hundreds of cities have similar prohibitions against public accommodation discrimination based on sexual orientation, including Baltimore (ordinance adopted 1988), Boston (1984), Chicago (1988), Cleveland (1984), Detroit (1979), Denver (1990), Los Angeles (1979), New Orleans (1991), New York City (1986), Philadelphia (1982), Portland (1991), St. Louis (1992), San Diego (1990), San Francisco (1978). Most of the statutes and ordinances define "public accommodation" broadly, and this breadth has generated not only questions of statutory interpretation, but also constitutional problems.

John Hurley v. Irish–American Gay, Lesbian and Bisexual Group of Boston

Supreme Court of the United States, 1995.
515 U.S. 557, 115 S.Ct. 2338, 132 L.Ed.2d 487.

■ JUSTICE SOUTER delivered the opinion of the Court.

[Since 1947, the South Boston Allied War Veterans Council, a private group, has been granted authority by the City of Boston to organize the annual St. Patrick's Day Parade, an event of special significance to people of Irish ancestry. Every year the Council has applied for and been granted a permit for the parade. In 1992, a court ordered the Council to include the

Irish–American Gay, Lesbian, and Bisexual Group of Boston (GLIB), the respondents. In 1993, GLIB sued the Council for violating the state law which prohibits discrimination on account of sexual orientation (*inter alia*) in the admission to a place of public accommodation. Relying on *Roberts*, the state courts interpreted the public accommodations law to require that GLIB be included and overruled the Council's claim that such an interpretation violated the First Amendment. The Supreme Court reversed.]

If there were no reason for a group of people to march from here to there except to reach a destination, they could make the trip without expressing any message beyond the fact of the march itself. Some people might call such a procession a parade, but it would not be much of one. Real "[p]arades are public dramas of social relations, and in them performers define who can be a social actor and what subjects and ideas are available for communication and consideration." S. Davis, *Parades and Power: Street Theatre in Nineteenth–Century Philadelphia* 6 (1986). Hence, we use the word "parade" to indicate marchers who are making some sort of collective point, not just to each other but to bystanders along the way. Indeed a parade's dependence on watchers is so extreme that nowadays, as with Bishop Berkeley's celebrated tree, "if a parade or demonstration receives no media coverage, it may as well not have happened." *Id.*, at 171. Parades are thus a form of expression, not just motion[.] * * *

The protected expression that inheres in a parade is not limited to its banners and songs, however, for the Constitution looks beyond written or spoken words as mediums of expression. Noting that "symbolism is a primitive but effective way of communicating ideas," *West Virginia Bd. of Ed. v. Barnette*, 319 U.S. 624, 632 (1943), our cases have recognized that the First Amendment shields such acts as saluting a flag (and refusing to do so), *id.*, at 632, 642, wearing an arm band to protest a war, *Tinker v. Des Moines Independent Community School Dist.*, 393 U.S. 503, 505–506 (1969), displaying a red flag, *Stromberg v. California*, 283 U.S. 359, 369 (1931), and even "[m]arching, walking or parading" in uniforms displaying the swastika, *National Socialist Party of America v. Skokie*, 432 U.S. 43 (1977). As some of these examples show, a narrow, succinctly articulable message is not a condition of constitutional protection, which if confined to expressions conveying a "particularized message," would never reach the unquestionably shielded painting of Jackson Pollock, music of Arnold Schönberg, or Jabberwocky verse of Lewis Carroll.

Not many marches, then, are beyond the realm of expressive parades, and the South Boston celebration is not one of them. Spectators line the streets; people march in costumes and uniforms, carrying flags and banners with all sorts of messages (e.g., "England get out of Ireland," "Say no to drugs"); marching bands and pipers play, floats are pulled along, and the whole show is broadcast over Boston television. To be sure, we agree with the state courts that in spite of excluding some applicants, the Council is rather lenient in admitting participants. But a private speaker does not forfeit constitutional protection simply by combining multifarious voices, or by failing to edit their themes to isolate an exact message as the exclusive subject matter of the speech. Nor, under our precedent, does First Amendment protection require a speaker to generate, as an original matter, each item featured in the communication. * * *

Respondents' participation as a unit in the parade was equally expressive. GLIB was formed for the very purpose of marching in it, as the trial court found, in order to celebrate its members' identity as openly gay, lesbian, and bisexual descendants of the Irish immigrants, to show that there are such individuals in the community, and to support the like men and women who sought to march in the New York parade. The organization distributed a fact sheet describing the members' intentions, and the record otherwise corroborates the expressive nature of GLIB's participation. In 1993, members of GLIB marched behind a shamrock-strewn banner with the simple inscription "Irish American Gay, Lesbian and Bisexual Group of Boston." GLIB understandably seeks to communicate its ideas as part of the existing parade, rather than staging one of its own. * * *

* * * The petitioners disclaim any intent to exclude homosexuals as such, and no individual member of GLIB claims to have been excluded from parading as a member of any group that the Council has approved to march. Instead, the disagreement goes to the admission of GLIB as its own parade unit carrying its own banner. Since every participating unit affects the message conveyed by the private organizers, the state courts' application of the statute produced an order essentially requiring petitioners to alter the expressive content of their parade. Although the state courts spoke of the parade as a place of public accommodation, once the expressive character of both the parade and the marching GLIB contingent is understood, it becomes apparent that the state courts' application of the statute had the effect of declaring the sponsors' speech itself to be the public accommodation. Under this approach any contingent of protected individuals with a message would have the right to participate in petitioners' speech, so that the communication produced by the private organizers would be shaped by all those protected by the law who wished to join in with some expressive demonstration of their own. But this use of the State's power violates the fundamental rule of protection under the First Amendment, that a speaker has the autonomy to choose the content of his own message. * * *

Petitioners' claim to the benefit of this principle of autonomy to control one's own speech is as sound as the South Boston parade is expressive. Rather like a composer, the Council selects the expressive units of the parade from potential participants, and though the score may not produce a particularized message, each contingent's expression in the Council's eyes comports with what merits celebration on that day. Even if this view gives the Council credit for a more considered judgment than it actively made, the Council clearly decided to exclude a message it did not like from the communication it chose to make, and that is enough to invoke its right as a private speaker to shape its expression by speaking on one subject while remaining silent on another. The message it disfavored is not difficult to identify. Although GLIB's point (like the Council's) is not wholly articulate, a contingent marching behind the organization's banner would at least bear witness to the fact that some Irish are gay, lesbian, or bisexual, and the presence of the organized marchers would suggest their view that people of their sexual orientations have as much claim to unqualified social acceptance as heterosexuals and indeed as members of parade units organized around other identifying characteristics. The parade's organizers may not believe these facts about Irish sexuality to be so, or they may object to unqualified social acceptance of gays and lesbians or have some other reason for wishing to keep GLIB's message out of the parade. But whatever the reason, it boils down to the choice of a speaker not to propound a particular point of view, and that choice is presumed to lie beyond the government's power to control. * * *

It might, of course, have been argued that a broader objective is apparent: that the ultimate point of forbidding acts of discrimination toward certain classes is to produce a society free of the corresponding biases. Requiring access to a speaker's message would thus be not an end in itself, but a means to produce speakers free of the biases, whose expressive conduct would be at least neutral toward the particular classes, obviating any future need for correction. But if this indeed is the point of applying the state law to expressive conduct, it is a decidedly fatal objective. Having availed itself of the public thoroughfares "for purposes of assembly [and] communicating thoughts between citizens," the Council is engaged in a use of the streets that has "from ancient times, been a part of the privileges, immunities, rights, and liberties of citizens." *Hague v. Committee for Industrial Organization*, 307 U.S. 496, 515 (1939) (opinion of Roberts, J.). Our tradition of free speech commands that a speaker who takes to the street corner to express his views in this way should be free from interference by the State based on the content of what he says. The very idea that a noncommercial speech restriction be used to produce thoughts and statements acceptable to some groups or, indeed, all people, grates on the First Amendment, for it amounts to nothing less than a proposal to limit speech in the service of orthodox expression. The Speech Clause has no more certain antithesis. While the law is free to promote all sorts of conduct in place of harmful behavior, it is not free to interfere with speech for no better reason than promoting an approved message or discouraging a disfavored one, however enlightened either purpose may strike the government. * * *

NOTE ON *HURLEY*, STATE ACTION, AND THE SPEECH–IDENTITY DIVIDE

1. *State Action.* GLIB had challenged the exclusions of gays on the basis of the First Amendment as well as the state public accommodations law. They lost their initial claim on the ground that the First Amendment (like the other individual rights protections of the Constitution) only applies to "state action" and there was no "state actor" in this case (the Veterans

Council being a private group). GLIB did not appeal this issue, and it was not before the Supreme Court.

Note how the dynamics of the litigation changes if GLIB is able to tag the Veterans Council as a state actor. The Council would then be in a dilemma: if it claims the parade is an expressive event it violates the First Amendment by excluding lesbian, gay, and bisexual speakers, but if it denies the expressiveness of a parade it has no defense to the public accommodations law.

2. *The Identity–Speech Dichotomy.* The Council contended that it excluded GLIB because of its expression. GLIB contended that it was excluded because of its members' sexual orientation. The state trial court found that GLIB was "excluded because of its values and its message, *i.e.*, its members' sexual orientation." It is not so easy to choose between these two, because for gay people the two are interconnected. Unlike race and sex, sexual orientation is ordinarily an invisible characteristic. If women march in this parade, they are conveying a message (women are Irish and proud of it!) by their very presence. Lesbians and gay men can only be known by more explicit signals. For them to participate in a parade in the same way that women participate, they need some device to uncloset themselves.

In the final question at oral argument, Justice Breyer asked the Council's attorney whether he thought GLIB's goal was identity or speech. Chester Darling, the attorney for the Council, exclaimed that it was "self-proclamation," expression, self-identity. Justice Breyer sighed wearily.

Boy Scouts of America, et al. v. James Dale

United States Supreme Court, 2000.
530 U.S. 640, 120 S.Ct. 2446, 147 L.Ed.2d 554.

■ CHIEF JUSTICE REHNQUIST delivered the opinion of the Court.

Petitioners are the Boy Scouts of America and the Monmouth Council, a division of the Boy Scouts of America (collectively, Boy Scouts). The Boy Scouts is a private, not for profit organization engaged in instilling its system of values in young people. The Boy Scouts asserts that homosexual conduct is inconsistent with the values it seeks to instill. Respondent is James Dale, a former Eagle Scout whose adult membership in the Boy Scouts was revoked when the Boy Scouts learned that he is an avowed homosexual and gay rights activist. The New Jersey Supreme Court held that New Jersey's public accommodations law requires that the Boy Scouts admit Dale. This case presents the question whether applying New Jersey's public accommodations law in this way violates the Boy Scouts' First Amendment right of expressive association. We hold that it does.

I.   James Dale entered scouting in 1978 at the age of eight by joining Monmouth Council's Cub Scout Pack 142. Dale became a Boy Scout in 1981 and remained a Scout until he turned 18. By all accounts, Dale was an exemplary Scout. In 1988, he achieved the rank of Eagle Scout, one of Scouting's highest honors.

Dale applied for adult membership in the Boy Scouts in 1989. The Boy Scouts approved his application for the position of assistant scoutmaster of Troop 73. Around the same time, Dale left home to attend Rutgers University. After arriving at Rutgers, Dale first acknowledged to himself and others that he is gay. He quickly became involved with, and eventually became the copresident of, the Rutgers University Lesbian/Gay Alliance. In 1990, Dale attended a seminar addressing the psychological and health needs of lesbian and gay teenagers. A newspaper covering the event interviewed Dale about his advocacy of homosexual teenagers' need for gay role models. In early July 1990, the newspaper published the interview and Dale's photograph over a caption identifying him as the copresident of the Lesbian/Gay Alliance.

Later that month, Dale received a letter from Monmouth Council Executive James Kay revoking his adult membership. Dale wrote to Kay requesting the reason for Monmouth Council's decision. Kay responded by letter that the Boy Scouts "specifically forbid membership to homosexuals." * * *

II. In *Roberts v. United States Jaycees*, 468 U.S. 609, 622 (1984), we observed that "implicit in the right to engage in activities protected by the First Amendment" is "a corresponding right to associate with others in pursuit of a wide variety of political, social, economic, educational, religious, and cultural ends." This right is crucial in preventing the majority from imposing its views on groups that would rather express other, perhaps unpopular, ideas. Government actions that may unconstitutionally burden this freedom may take many forms, one of which is "intrusion into the internal structure or affairs of an association" like a "regulation that forces the group to accept members it does not desire." *Id.*, at 623. Forcing a group to accept certain members may impair the ability of the group to express those views, and only those views, that it intends to express. Thus, "[f]reedom of association ... plainly presupposes a freedom not to associate." *Ibid.*

The forced inclusion of an unwanted person in a group infringes the group's freedom of expressive association if the presence of that person affects in a significant way the group's ability to advocate public or private viewpoints. *New York State Club Assn., Inc. v. City of New York*, 487 U.S. 1, 13 (1988). But the freedom of expressive association, like many freedoms, is not absolute. We have held that the freedom could be overridden "by regulations adopted to serve compelling state interests, unrelated to the suppression of ideas, that cannot be achieved through means significantly less restrictive of associational freedoms." *Roberts, supra*, at 623.

To determine whether a group is protected by the First Amendment's expressive associational right, we must determine whether the group engages in "expressive association." The First Amendment's protection of expressive association is not reserved for advocacy groups. But to come within its ambit, a group must engage in some form of expression, whether it be public or private.

Because this is a First Amendment case where the ultimate conclusions of law are virtually inseparable from findings of fact, we are obligated to independently review the factual record to ensure that the state court's judgment does not unlawfully intrude on free expression. The record reveals the following. The Boy Scouts is a private, nonprofit organization. According to its mission statement:

"It is the mission of the Boy Scouts of America to serve others by helping to instill values in young people and, in other ways, to prepare them to make ethical choices over their lifetime in achieving their full potential.

"The values we strive to instill are based on those found in the Scout Oath and Law:

"Scout Oath

"On my honor I will do my best

To do my duty to God and my country and to obey the Scout Law;

To help other people at all times;

To keep myself physically strong, mentally awake, and morally straight."

"Scout Law

"A Scout is:

Trustworthy Obedient

Loyal Cheerful

Helpful Thrifty

Friendly Brave

Courteous Clean

Kind Reverent."

Thus, the general mission of the Boy Scouts is clear: "[T]o instill values in young people." The Boy Scouts seeks to instill these values by having its adult leaders spend time with the youth members, instructing and engaging them in activities like camping, archery, and fishing. During the time spent with the youth members, the scoutmasters and assistant scoutmasters inculcate them with the Boy Scouts' values—both expressly and by example. It seems indisputable that an association that seeks to transmit such a system of values engages in expressive activity. See *Roberts, supra*, at 636 (O'Connor, J., concurring) ("Even the training of outdoor survival skills or participation in community service might become expressive when the activity is intended to develop good morals, reverence, patriotism, and a desire for self improvement.").

Given that the Boy Scouts engages in expressive activity, we must determine whether the forced inclusion of Dale as an assistant scoutmaster would significantly affect the Boy Scouts' ability to advocate public or private viewpoints. This inquiry necessarily requires us first to explore, to a limited extent, the nature of the Boy Scouts' view of homosexuality.

The values the Boy Scouts seeks to instill are "based on" those listed in the Scout Oath and Law. The Boy Scouts explains that the Scout Oath and Law provide "a positive moral code for living; they are a list of 'do's' rather than 'don'ts.'" The Boy Scouts asserts that "homosexual conduct is inconsistent with the values embodied in the Scout Oath and Law, particularly with the values represented by the terms 'morally straight' and 'clean.'"

Obviously, the Scout Oath and Law do not expressly mention sexuality or sexual orientation. And the terms "morally straight" and "clean" are by no means self defining. Different people would attribute to those terms very different meanings. For example, some people may believe that engaging in homosexual conduct is not at odds with being "morally straight" and "clean." And others may believe that engaging in homosexual conduct is contrary to being "morally straight" and "clean." The Boy Scouts says it falls within the latter category.

The New Jersey Supreme Court analyzed the Boy Scouts' beliefs and found that the "exclusion of members solely on the basis of their sexual orientation is inconsistent with Boy Scouts' commitment to a diverse and 'representative' membership ... [and] contradicts Boy Scouts' overarching objective to reach 'all eligible youth.'" 160 N.J., at 618, 734 A.2d, at 1226. The court concluded that the exclusion of members like Dale "appears antithetical to the organization's goals and philosophy." *Ibid.* But our cases reject this sort of inquiry; it is not the role of the courts to reject a group's expressed values because they disagree with those values or find them internally inconsistent.

The Boy Scouts asserts that it "teach[es] that homosexual conduct is not morally straight," and that it does "not want to promote homosexual conduct as a legitimate form of behavior." We accept the Boy Scouts' assertion. We need not inquire further to determine the nature of the Boy Scouts' expression with respect to homosexuality. But because the record before us contains written evidence of the Boy Scouts' viewpoint, we look to it as instructive, if only on the question of the sincerity of the professed beliefs. * * *

[The Court quotes BSA position statements on homosexuality.] This position statement was redrafted numerous times but its core message remained consistent. For example, a 1993 position statement, the most recent in the record, reads, in part:

> "The Boy Scouts of America has always reflected the expectations that Scouting families have had for the organization. We do not believe that homosexuals provide a role model consistent with these expectations. Accordingly, we do not allow for the registration of avowed homosexuals as members or as leaders of the BSA."

The Boy Scouts publicly expressed its views with respect to homosexual conduct by its assertions in prior litigation. For example, throughout a California case with similar facts filed in the early 1980's, the Boy Scouts consistently asserted the same position with respect to homosexuality that it asserts today. See *Curran v. Mount Diablo Council of Boy Scouts of America*, No. C 365529 (Cal. Super. Ct., July 25, 1991); 48 Cal. App. 4th 670, 29 Cal. Rptr. 2d 580 (1994); 17 Cal. 4th 670, 952 P. 2d 218 (1998). We cannot doubt that the Boy Scouts sincerely holds this view.

We must then determine whether Dale's presence as an assistant scoutmaster would significantly burden the Boy Scouts' desire to not "promote homosexual conduct as a legitimate form of behavior." Reply Brief for Petitioners 5. As we give deference to an association's assertions regarding the nature of its expression, we must also give deference to an association's view of what would impair its expression. That is not to say that an expressive association can erect a shield against antidiscrimination laws simply by asserting that mere acceptance of a member from a particular group would impair its message. But here Dale, by his own admission, is one of a group of gay Scouts who have "become leaders in their community and are open and honest about their sexual orientation." Dale was the copresident of a gay and lesbian organization at college and remains a gay rights activist. Dale's presence in the Boy Scouts would, at the very least, force the organization to send a message, both to the youth members and the world, that the Boy Scouts accepts homosexual conduct as a legitimate form of behavior.

Hurley is illustrative on this point. There we considered whether the application of Massachusetts' public accommodations law to require the organizers of a private St. Patrick's Day parade to include among the marchers an Irish–American gay, lesbian, and bisexual group, GLIB, violated the parade organizers' First Amendment rights. We noted that the parade organizers did not wish to exclude the GLIB members because of their sexual orientations, but because they wanted to march behind a GLIB banner. * * *

Here, we have found that the Boy Scouts believes that homosexual conduct is inconsistent with the values it seeks to instill in its youth members; it will not "promote homosexual conduct as a legitimate form of behavior." As the presence of GLIB in Boston's St. Patrick's Day parade would have interfered with the parade organizers' choice not to propound a particular point of view, the presence of Dale as an assistant scoutmaster would just as surely interfere with the Boy Scouts' choice not to propound a point of view contrary to its beliefs.

The New Jersey Supreme Court determined that the Boy Scouts' ability to disseminate its message was not significantly affected by the forced inclusion of Dale as an assistant scoutmaster because of the following findings:

> "Boy Scout members do not associate for the purpose of disseminating the belief that homosexuality is immoral; Boy Scouts discourages its leaders from disseminating any views on sexual issues; and Boy Scouts includes sponsors and members who subscribe to different views in respect of homosexuality." 160 N.J., at 612, 734 A.2d, at 1223.

We disagree with the New Jersey Supreme Court's conclusion drawn from these findings.

First, associations do not have to associate for the "purpose" of disseminating a certain message in order to be entitled to the protections of the First Amendment. An association must merely engage in expressive activity that could be impaired in order to be entitled to protection. For example, the purpose of the St. Patrick's Day parade in *Hurley* was not to espouse any views about sexual orientation, but we held that the parade organizers had a right to exclude certain participants nonetheless.

Second, even if the Boy Scouts discourages Scout leaders from disseminating views on sexual issues—a fact that the Boy Scouts disputes with contrary evidence—the First Amendment protects the Boy Scouts' method of expression. If the Boy Scouts wishes Scout leaders to avoid questions of sexuality and teach only by example, this fact does not negate the sincerity of its belief discussed above.

Third, the First Amendment simply does not require that every member of a group agree on every issue in order for the group's policy to be "expressive association." The Boy Scouts takes an official position with respect to homosexual conduct, and that is sufficient for First Amendment purposes. In this same vein, Dale makes much of the claim that the Boy Scouts does not revoke the membership of heterosexual Scout leaders that openly disagree with the Boy Scouts' policy on sexual orientation. But if this is true, it is irrelevant. The presence of an avowed homosexual and gay rights activist in an assistant scoutmaster's uniform sends a distinctly different message from the presence of a heterosexual assistant scoutmaster who is on record as disagreeing with Boy Scouts policy. The Boy Scouts has a First Amendment right to choose to send one message but not the other. The fact that the organization does not trumpet its views from the housetops, or that it tolerates dissent within its ranks, does not mean that its views receive no First Amendment protection.

Having determined that the Boy Scouts is an expressive association and that the forced inclusion of Dale would significantly affect its expression, we inquire whether the application of New Jersey's public accommodations law to require that the Boy Scouts accept Dale as an assistant scoutmaster runs afoul of the Scouts' freedom of expressive association. We conclude that it does. * * *

We recognized in cases such as *Roberts* and *Duarte* that States have a compelling interest in eliminating discrimination against women in public accommodations. But in each of these cases we went on to conclude that the enforcement of these statutes would not materially interfere with the ideas that the organization sought to express. * * *

In *Hurley*, we applied traditional First Amendment analysis to hold that the application of the Massachusetts public accommodations law to a parade violated the First Amendment rights of the parade organizers. Although we did not explicitly deem the parade in *Hurley* an expressive association, the analysis we applied there is similar to the analysis we apply here. We have already concluded that a state requirement that the Boy Scouts retain Dale as an assistant scoutmaster would significantly burden the organization's right to oppose or disfavor homosexual conduct. The state interests embodied in New Jersey's public accommodations law do not justify such a severe intrusion on the Boy Scouts' rights to freedom of expressive association. That being the case, we hold that the First Amendment prohibits the State from imposing such a requirement through the application of its public accommodations law.* * *

We are not, as we must not be, guided by our views of whether the Boy Scouts' teachings with respect to homosexual conduct are right or wrong; public or judicial disapproval of a tenet of an organization's expression does not justify the State's effort to compel the organization to accept members where such acceptance would derogate from the organization's expressive message. * * *

■ JUSTICE STEVENS, with whom JUSTICE SOUTER, JUSTICE GINSBURG, and JUSTICE BREYER join, dissenting. * * *

[I.] In this case, Boy Scouts of America contends that it teaches the young boys who are Scouts that homosexuality is immoral. Consequently, it argues, it would violate its right to associate to force it to admit homosexuals as members, as doing so would be at odds with its own shared goals and values. This contention, quite plainly, requires us to look at what, exactly, are the values that BSA actually teaches.* * *

To bolster its claim that its shared goals include teaching that homosexuality is wrong, BSA directs our attention to two terms appearing in the Scout Oath and Law. The first is the phrase "morally straight," which appears in the Oath ("On my honor I will do my best ... To keep myself ... morally straight"); the second term is the word "clean," which appears in a list of 12 characteristics together comprising the Scout Law. [The opinion quotes the Scout Handbook and the Scoutmaster Handbook on the meaning of those two phrases.]

It is plain as the light of day that neither one of these principles— "morally straight" and "clean"—says the slightest thing about homosexuality. Indeed, neither term in the Boy Scouts' Law and Oath expresses any position whatsoever on sexual matters. * * *

In light of BSA's self-proclaimed ecumenism, furthermore, it is even more difficult to discern any shared goals or common moral stance on homosexuality. Insofar as religious matters are concerned, BSA's bylaws state that it is "absolutely nonsectarian in its attitude toward ... religious training. The BSA does not define what constitutes duty to God or the practice of religion. This is the responsibility of parents and religious leaders." In fact, many diverse religious organizations sponsor local Boy Scout troops. Because a number of religious groups do not view homosexuality as immoral or wrong and reject discrimination against homosexuals, it is exceedingly difficult to believe that BSA nonetheless adopts a single particular religious or moral philosophy when it comes to sexual orientation. This is especially so in light of the fact that Scouts are advised to seek guidance on sexual matters from their religious leaders (and Scoutmasters are told to refer Scouts to them); BSA surely is aware that some religions do not teach that homosexuality is wrong.

II.   [The opinion criticizes the lack of clarity in portions of the 1978 position statement, including a reference to the Scouts' willingness to comply with anti-discrimination law.]

BSA's inability to make its position clear and its failure to connect its alleged policy to its expressive activities is highly significant. By the time Dale was expelled from the Boy Scouts in 1990, BSA had already been engaged in several suits under a variety of state antidiscrimination public accommodation laws challenging various aspects of its membership policy. Indeed, BSA had filed amicus briefs before this Court in two earlier right to associate cases (*Roberts* and *Duarte*) pointing to these very cases; it was clearly on notice by 1990 that it might well be subjected to state public accommodation antidiscrimination laws, and that a court might one day reject its claimed right to associate. Yet it took no steps prior to Dale's expulsion to clarify how its exclusivity was connected to its expression. It speaks volumes about the credibility of BSA's claim to a shared goal that homosexuality is incompatible with Scouting that since at least 1984 it had been aware of this issue indeed, concerned enough to twice file amicus briefs before this Court yet it did nothing in the intervening six years (or even in the years after Dale's expulsion) to explain clearly and openly why the presence of homosexuals would affect its expressive activities, or to make the view of "morally straight" and "clean" taken in its 1991 and 1992 policies a part of the values actually instilled in Scouts through the Handbook, lessons, or otherwise.

III.   BSA's claim finds no support in our cases. * * * [I]n *Jaycees*, we asked whether Minnesota's Human Rights Law requiring the admission of women "impose[d] any *serious burdens*" on the group's "collective effort on behalf of [its] *shared goals*." 468 U.S., at 622, 626–627 (*emphases added*). Notwithstanding the group's obvious publicly stated exclusionary policy, we did not view the inclusion of women as a "serious burden" on the Jaycees' ability to engage in the protected speech of its choice. Similarly, in *Rotary Club*, we asked whether California's law would "affect in any *significant* way the existing members' ability" to engage in their protected speech, or whether the law would require the clubs "to abandon their *basic goals*." 481 U.S., at 548 (*emphases added*). The relevant question is whether the mere inclusion of the person at issue would "impose any serious burden," "affect in any significant way," or be "a substantial restraint upon" the organization's "shared goals," "basic goals," or "collective effort to foster beliefs." Accordingly, it is necessary to examine what, exactly, are BSA's shared goals and the degree to which its expressive activities would be burdened, affected, or restrained by including homosexuals.

The evidence before this Court makes it exceptionally clear that BSA has, at most, simply adopted an exclusionary membership policy and has no shared goal of disapproving of homosexuality. BSA's mission statement and federal charter say nothing on the matter; its official membership policy is silent; its Scout Oath and Law–and accompanying definitions are devoid of any view on the topic; its guidance for Scouts and Scoutmasters on sexuality declare that such matters are "not construed to be Scouting's proper area," but are the province of a Scout's parents and pastor; and BSA's posture respecting religion tolerates a wide variety of views on the issue of homosexuality. Moreover, there is simply no evidence that BSA otherwise teaches anything in this area, or that it instructs Scouts on matters involving homosexuality in ways not conveyed in the Boy Scout or Scoutmaster Handbooks. In short, Boy Scouts of America is simply silent on homosexuality. There is no shared goal or collective effort to foster a belief about homosexuality at all–let alone one that is significantly burdened by admitting homosexuals.

As in *Jaycees*, there is "no basis in the record for concluding that admission of [homosexuals] will impede the [Boy Scouts'] ability to engage in [its] protected activities or to disseminate its preferred views" and New Jersey's law "requires no change in [BSA's] creed." And like *Rotary Club*, New Jersey's law "does not require [BSA] to abandon or alter any of" its activities. * * * [T]here is no evidence here that BSA's policy was necessary to—or even a part of—BSA's expressive activities or was ever taught to Scouts. * * * A State's antidiscrimination law does not impose a "serious burden" or a "substantial restraint" upon the group's "shared goals" if the group itself is unable to identify its own stance with any clarity.

IV. The majority pretermits this entire analysis. It finds that BSA in fact " 'teach[es] that homosexual conduct is not morally straight.' " This conclusion, remarkably, rests entirely on statements in BSA's briefs. Moreover, the majority insists that we must "give deference to an association's assertions regarding the nature of its expression" and "we must also give deference to an association's view of what would impair its expression." So long as the record "contains written evidence" to support a group's bare assertion, "[w]e need not inquire further." Once the organization "asserts" that it engages in particular expression, "[w]e cannot doubt" the truth of that assertion.

This is an astounding view of the law. I am unaware of any previous instance in which our analysis of the scope of a constitutional right was determined by looking at what a litigant asserts in his or her brief and inquiring no further. It is even more astonishing in the First Amendment area, because, as the majority itself acknowledges, "we are obligated to independently review the factual record." It is an odd form of independent review that consists of deferring entirely to whatever a litigant claims. But the majority insists that our inquiry must be "limited," because "it is not the role of the courts to reject a group's expressed values because they disagree with those values or find them internally inconsistent."

But nothing in our cases calls for this Court to do any such thing. An organization can adopt the message of its choice, and it is not this Court's place to disagree with it. But we must inquire whether the group is, in fact, expressing a message (whatever it may be) and whether that message (if one is expressed) is significantly affected by a State's antidiscrimination law. More critically, that inquiry requires our *independent* analysis, rather than deference to a group's litigating posture. Reflection on the subject dictates that such an inquiry is required.

Surely there are instances in which an organization that truly aims to foster a belief at odds with the purposes of a State's antidiscrimination laws will have a First Amendment right to association that precludes forced compliance with those laws. But that right is not a freedom to discriminate at will, nor is it a right to maintain an exclusionary membership policy simply out of fear of what the public reaction would be if the group's membership were opened up. It is an implicit right designed to protect the enumerated rights of the First Amendment, not a license to act on any discriminatory impulse. To prevail in asserting a right of expressive association as a defense to a charge of violating an antidiscrimination law, the organization must at least show it has adopted and advocated an unequivocal position inconsistent with a position advocated or epitomized by the person whom the organization seeks to exclude. If this Court were to defer to whatever position an organization is prepared to assert in its briefs, there would be no way to mark the proper boundary between genuine exercises of the right to associate, on the one hand, and sham claims that are simply attempts to insulate nonexpressive private discrimination, on the other hand. Shielding a litigant's claim from judicial scrutiny would, in turn, render civil rights legislation a nullity, and turn this important constitutional right into a farce. Accordingly, the Court's prescription of total deference will not do. * * *

V.   * * * BSA has not contended, nor does the record support, that Dale had ever advocated a view on homosexuality to his troop before his membership was revoked. Accordingly, BSA's revocation could only have been based on an assumption that he would do so in the future. But the only information BSA had at the time it revoked Dale's membership was a newspaper article describing a seminar at Rutgers University on the topic of homosexual teenagers that Dale attended.* * *

To be sure, the article did say that Dale was co-president of the Lesbian/Gay Alliance at Rutgers University, and that group presumably engages in advocacy regarding homosexual issues. But surely many members of BSA engage in expressive activities outside of their troop, and surely BSA does not want all of that expression to be carried on inside the troop. For example, a Scoutmaster may be a member of a religious group that encourages its followers to convert others to its faith. Or a Scoutmaster may belong to a political party that encourages its members to advance its views among family and friends. * * * From all accounts, then, BSA does not discourage or forbid outside expressive activity, but relies on compliance with its policies and trusts Scouts and Scoutmasters alike not to bring unwanted views into the organization. * * *

The majority, though, does not rest its conclusion on the claim that Dale will use his position as a bully pulpit. Rather, it contends that Dale's mere presence among the Boy Scouts will itself force the group to convey a

message about homosexuality–even if Dale has no intention of doing so.
* * *

Dale's inclusion in the Boy Scouts is nothing like the case in *Hurley*. His participation sends no cognizable message to the Scouts or to the world. Unlike GLIB, Dale did not carry a banner or a sign; he did not distribute any fact sheet; and he expressed no intent to send any message. If there is any kind of message being sent, then, it is by the mere act of joining the Boy Scouts. Such an act does not constitute an instance of symbolic speech under the First Amendment.

* * * Though participating in the Scouts could itself conceivably send a message on some level, it is not the kind of act that we have recognized as speech. Indeed, if merely joining a group did constitute symbolic speech; and such speech were attributable to the group being joined; and that group has the right to exclude that speech (and hence, the right to exclude that person from joining), then the right of free speech effectively becomes a limitless right to exclude for every organization, whether or not it engages in *any* expressive activities. That cannot be, and never has been, the law.

The only apparent explanation for the majority's holding, then, is that homosexuals are simply so different from the rest of society that their presence alone—unlike any other individual's—should be singled out for special First Amendment treatment. Under the majority's reasoning, an openly gay male is irreversibly affixed with the label "homosexual." That label, even though unseen, communicates a message that permits his exclusion wherever he goes. His openness is the sole and sufficient justification for his ostracism. Though unintended, reliance on such a justification is tantamount to a constitutionally prescribed symbol of inferiority. As counsel for the Boy Scouts remarked, Dale "put a banner around his neck when he ... got himself into the newspaper.... He created a reputation.... He can't take that banner off. He put it on himself and, indeed, he has continued to put it on himself." * * *

Furthermore, it is not likely that BSA would be understood to send any message, either to Scouts or to the world, simply by admitting someone as a member. Over the years, BSA has generously welcomed over 87 million young Americans into its ranks. In 1992 over one million adults were active BSA members. The notion that an organization of that size and enormous prestige implicitly endorses the views that each of those adults may express in a non-Scouting context is simply mind boggling. Indeed, in this case there is no evidence that the young Scouts in Dale's troop, or members of their families, were even aware of his sexual orientation, either before or after his public statements at Rutgers University. It is equally farfetched to assert that Dale's open declaration of his homosexuality, reported in a local newspaper, will effectively force BSA to send a message to anyone simply because it allows Dale to be an Assistant Scoutmaster. For an Olympic gold medal winner or a Wimbledon tennis champion, being "openly gay" per-haps communicates a message–for example, that openness about one's sexual orientation is more virtuous than concealment; that a homosexual person can be a capable and virtuous person who should be judged like anyone else; and that homosexuality is not immoral–but it certainly does not follow that they necessarily send a message on behalf of the organizations that sponsor the activities in which they excel. The fact that such persons participate in these organizations is not usually construed to convey a message on behalf of those organizations any more than does the inclusion of women, African–Americans, religious minorities, or any other discrete group. Surely the organizations are not forced by antidiscrimination laws to take any position on the legitimacy of any individual's private beliefs or private conduct. * * *

NOTES ON THE BOY SCOUTS CASE AND EXPRESSIVE IDENTITY LAW

1. *The Meaning of Outness.* The Court made two critical holdings as to the impact of the mere presence of an openly gay Scoutmaster. First, that "Dale's presence * * * would, at the very least, force the organization to send a message * * * that the Boy Scouts accepts homosexual conduct as a form of behavior." Second, that "the presence of an avowed homosexual and gay rights activist in an assistant scoutmaster's uniform sends a distinctly different message from the presence of a heterosexual assistant scoutmaster who is on record disagreeing with Boy Scouts policy." Do you agree? What are the ramifications of holding that compliance with an anti-discrimination law expresses a message? The dissent argues that mere presence "sends no cognizable message" and that the majority's ruling creates for an openly gay person a "label ... that permits his exclusion wherever he goes." For conflicting interpretations of the case, see Dale Carpenter, "Freedom of Expressive Association and Antidiscrimination Law After *Dale*: A Tripartite Approach," 85 *Minn. L. Rev.* 1515 (2001) (case was correctly decided; its central principle is important to lesbian and gay organizations); Richard Epstein, "The Constitutional Perils of Moderation: The Case of the Boy Scouts," 74 *S. Cal. L. Rev.* 119 (2000) (the Court ruled correctly but too narrowly; anti-discrimination laws should never apply to private associations that do not possess monopoly power); and Nan D. Hunter, "Accommodating the Public Sphere: Beyond the Market Model," 85 *Minn. L. Rev.* 1591 (2001) (the Court's unstated premises regarding sexuality and gender limited Dale's claim to full citizenship, which public accommodations laws have historically extended into the non-government realm). For an analysis of the conundrum that has arisen in the law because of its inability to harmonize equality claims with their intrinsic communicative elements, see Nan D. Hunter, "Expressive Identity: Recuperating Dissent for Equality," 35 *Harv. C.R-.C.L. L. Rev.* 1 (1999).

2. *The Meaning of* Hurley *After* Dale? Doctrinally, the decision turns on how the Court interprets *Hurley*. The majority relies primarily on *Hurley*'s exclusion of lesbian and gay marchers as support for the proposition that "forced inclusion" of an openly gay person would have the same impact as the inclusion sought by the lesbian, gay and bisexual Irish–American group in the St. Patrick's Day Parade. The dissent, including Justice Souter, who wrote the opinion in *Hurley*, argues that there is a "wide gulf" between *Dale* and *Hurley*. Do you think that the distinction is viable? How would you articulate a set of factors upon which courts could base rulings in future cases where openly lesbian, gay and bisexual persons seek to join organizations or participate in events?

3. *Gender as Subtext.* Although there is no sex discrimination argument as such used in *Dale*, gender is a subtextual issue in several respects. First, doctrinally, the parties argued over the applicability of cases like *Roberts*, in which women sought admission to previously male only clubs: Were the Scouts more like the Jaycees in *Roberts* or like the St. Patrick's Day Parade in *Hurley*? Does the presence of an openly gay person affect the BSA's expressive capacity more than the presence of women did for the Jaycees? Also, gender is a powerful cultural factor in the case. In their petition for certiorari, the Scouts argued that the presence of gay Scouts created a conflict with their message about "what it means to be a man." (If you're wondering why none of the Scouting cases involves the Girl Scouts, it is because they have never had an anti-lesbian policy.)

SEXUALLY EXPLICIT EXPRESSION

The endlessly recurring question in the law's treatment of sexually explicit speech has been whether sexual speech merits the protection accorded to nonsexual speech. Perhaps the starting point should be: Why not? That perspective, however, has never gained a majority within the Supreme Court. Start with first principles: Does protecting sexually explicit speech contribute to the goals of the First Amendment? (See Notes following *One, Inc., supra.*) Is eroticization a mode of advocacy?

NOTE ON OBSCENITY AND SEXUALLY EXPRESSIVE CONDUCT

Although the lines have blurred, as we saw in Section 1, the Supreme Court continues to assert a qualitative difference between sexual and political speech. In *Young v. American Mini Theatres, Inc.*, 427 U.S. 50, 70 (1976), for example, Justice Stevens' plurality opinion maintained that content-based regulation of sexual expression is permissible because "society's interest in protecting this type of expression is of a wholly different, and lesser, magnitude than the interest in untrammeled political debate." He continued:

> Whether political oratory or philosophical discussion moves us to applaud or to despise what is said, every schoolchild can understand why our duty to defend the right to speak remains the same. But few of us would march our sons and daughters off to war to preserve the citizens' right to see "Specified Sexual Activities" exhibited in the theaters of our choice.

Based on deeming it less valuable, courts have assigned sexual speech a lower rung on the hierarchy of First Amendment values. The only exception is Oregon, where the state supreme court ruled that obscenity was protected by the state constitution. *State v. Henry*, 732 P.2d 9 (Or. 1987).

Although a majority of the Supreme Court rejected Justice Stevens' view in *American Mini Theatres*, the Court's First Amendment doctrine nonetheless appears to depend upon the premise that sexual expression is less worthy than political expression. The Court allows government to regulate sexual expression in ways that it flatly forbids for political speech. Sexual expression can be zoned to remote parts of town, *City of Renton v. Playtime Theatres*, 475 U.S. 41 (1986), as well as *American Mini Theatres*; denied access to the airwaves until late at night, *FCC v. Pacifica Foundation*, 438 U.S. 726 (1978) (see Part C, *infra*), and even criminally suppressed if the community finds it simultaneously arousing, offensive, and valueless. By contrast, the state is generally barred from regulating political expression, even if a majority of the public finds it offensive, immoral, and without redeeming value. In *Cohen v. California*, 403 U.S. 15 (1971), for example, the Court protected a young man's expression of opposition to the Vietnam War through the phrase, "Fuck the Draft" on his jacket.

For 15 years after *Roth*, the Court's definition of obscenity evolved, but there was no majority on the Court in support of any single standard. In *Miller v. California*, 413 U.S. 15 (1973), Chief Justice Burger obtained a majority of five Justices for the following limits on state regulation:

> [W]e now confine the permissible scope of such regulation to works which depict or describe sexual conduct. That conduct must be specifically defined by the applicable state law, as written or authoritatively construed. A state offense must also be limited to works which, taken as a whole, appeal to the prurient interest in sex, which portray sexual conduct in a patently offensive way, and which, taken as a whole, do not have serious literary, artistic, political, or scientific value. *Id.* at 24.

The opinion gave as "plain examples of what a state statute could define for regulation * * * [p]atently offensive representations or descriptions of ultimate sexual acts, normal or perverted, actual or simulated" and "[p]atently offensive representations or descriptions of masturbation, excretory functions, and lewd exhibition of the genitals." Chief Justice Burger made clear that the state could only regulate representations of "patently offensive 'hard core' sexual conduct." What is hard core or patently offensive is to be ascertained by "applying contemporary community standards" of the state or area in which the representations are purveyed.

Note that under *Miller* the state can regulate depictions or representations of some sexual activity more rigorously than it can regulate the activity itself under the *Griswold–Loving–Lawrence* line of cases. This is an inversion of the First Amendment, which usually protects representation more than conduct.

How helpful is the *Miller* definition? Specifically, what exactly is "the prurient interest"? A Washington statute that defined prurient interest as "that which incites lasciviousness or lust" came before the Court in *Brockett v. Spokane Arcades, Inc.*, 472 U.S. 491 (1985). The appeals court had invalidated the statute on the ground that "it reached material that incited normal as well as unhealthy interest in sex." The Supreme Court reversed, ruling that any overbreadth was curable, in that the scope of the term "lust" could be construed to cover only "that which appeals to a shameful or morbid interest in sex." *Id.* at 504–05. Most remarkable is what is missing from the opinion—any attempt at defining "normal," "unhealthy," "shameful," or "morbid."

NOTE ON THE ELUSIVE PUBLIC–PRIVATE BOUNDARY

The Court held in *Stanley v. Georgia*, 394 U.S. 557 (1969), that the possession of obscene materials in one's home cannot be criminalized. The contrast between that holding and those discussed in this chapter starkly illustrates the fundamental role played by notions of a sharp break between public and private realms in the legal doctrine on sexual speech. A challenge to an Indiana law prohibiting public nudity triggered an attempt by the Court to map more precisely the bounds of those two realms and to justify the extremely anomalous result that, for obscene and other sexually explicit speech alone, expression that is private is entitled to greater protection than that which is public.

Barnes v. Glen Theatre, Inc., 501 U.S. 560, 111 S.Ct. 2456, 115 L.Ed.2d 504 (1991). Section 35–45–4–1 of the Indiana Code prohibited nudity in a public place and defined "nudity" to include wearing less than a G-string, not covering female breast nipples with "pasties," or showing male genitals "in a discernibly turgid state." This statute was the basis for prosecution of the Kitty Kat Lounge, where female go-go dancers took off all their clothes, and Glen Theatre, an adult bookstore offering booths where patrons could watch female strippers through glass windows. These defendants claimed that erotic dance, including nudity, involved "expressive conduct" protected by the First Amendment and therefore that the public nudity statute should not have been applied to their establishments.

Chief Justice Rehnquist's plurality opinion started with the premise that nude dancing can be "expressive conduct within the outer limits of the First Amendment, though we view it as only marginally so." He evaluated the public nudity regulation under the framework of *United States v. O'Brien*, 391 U.S. 367 (1968) (upholding rules against burning draft cards). The statute easily satisfied the *O'Brien* requirement that the law further a "substantial" governmental interest, namely, "protecting societal order and morality." The Chief Justice pointed to the laws of 47 states that regulated public indecency and, as authority, cited *Bowers v. Hardwick*. The Indiana law also met *O'Brien*'s requirement that the government interest be "unrelated to the suppression of free expression" because "[p]ublic nudity is the evil the State seeks to prevent, whether or not it is combined with expressive activity."

City of Erie, et al. v. Pap's A.M. tdba "Kandyland," 529 U.S. 277, 120 S.Ct. 1382, 146 L.Ed.2d 265 (2000). A Court majority agreed that governmental restrictions on public nudity should be evaluated by the *O'Brien* standard, with Justice Breyer joining the plurality Justices in *Barnes* to provide a fifth vote for that approach. Justices Scalia and Thomas concurred in the judgment, but argued that no First Amendment protection attached to nude dancing. Justice Souter continued to support the *O'Brien* standard, as he had in *Barnes*, but found that the government failed to adequately prove that harm actually results from nude dancing. Justices Stevens and Ginsburg dissented on the ground that enforcement of the law was directed only at certain forms of nude dancing, to the exclusion of "legitimate" theater.

David Cole, "Playing By Pornography's Rules: The Regulation of Sexual Expression"

143 *University of Pennsylvania Law Review* 111, 143–50, 176–77 (1994).*

* * * [In] *Barnes v. Glen Theatre, Inc.*, in which the Court upheld an Indiana "public nudity" statute that required nude dancers to wear pasties and a G-string. This case is about nothing but the public/private line; as Justice Scalia noted, "Indiana bans nudity in public places, but not within the privacy of the home." * * *

Rehnquist and Scalia reasoned that the state's interest in regulating public nudity was unrelated to expression because the state sought to protect "societal order and morality." Neither Justice explained, however, *how* public nudity harms public morality other than by virtue of what it expresses. Scalia insisted that the ban was unrelated to expression because it "generally" prohibited public nudity, irrespective of its message. But Scalia's use of "generally" is question-begging. The Indiana law does not "generally" prohibit all nudity, but singles out *public* nudity, that is, nudity communicated to others in public.

Ordinarily, where government selectively regulates public but not private conduct or expression, there is reason to suspect that the government is attempting to suppress the message communicated to the public, and strict scrutiny is triggered. In *Texas v. Johnson*, for example, the fact that the Texas statute prohibited only those flag burnings that would "seriously offend one or more persons likely to observe or discover" the conduct led the Court to conclude that the government's regulatory interest was related to the message that the conduct expressed, and therefore to apply stringent First Amendment scrutiny. By contrast, in *United States v. O'Brien*, the Court justified application of relaxed scrutiny to a statute prohibiting destruction of draft cards by noting that the law "does not distinguish between public and private destruction, and it does not punish only destruction engaged in for the purpose of expressing views." Like the flag burning statute in *Johnson* and unlike the draft card law in *O'Brien*, Indiana banned only *public* nudity, and did not attempt a *general* regulation of nudity.

Chief Justice Rehnquist justified his conclusion that the suppression of expression was not intended by claiming that "[p]ublic nudity is the evil the state seeks to prevent, whether or not it is combined with expressive activity." But public nudity has no effect on public morals except by virtue of what it expresses to those who see it: offensiveness, immodesty, sensuality, disrespect for social mores, etc. If public nudity expressed nothing, society would have no interest in suppressing it. It is only because public nudity is expressive that it is regulated. * * *

* * * [E]ach of the possibilities [for secondary harm] is inextricably tied to nude dancing's expressive character. If "the simple viewing of nude bodies" has any effect, it must be by virtue of what the nude bodies communicate visually. Similarly, if nude dancing attracts a crowd of predisposed men, it must be because they are drawn to what nude dancing communicates to them, unless one believes that nude dancers have some magnetic force of attraction irrespective of what they communicate. What is going on may not be "persuasive" in the strictly rational sense, but the First Amendment is not restricted to protecting rational persuasion.

Thus, all of the Justices in the *Barnes* majority strained mightily to reach the conclusion that the regulation at issue was unrelated to the suppression of expression. In an exchange with the *Barnes* dissenters, Justice Scalia provides a clue as to why the Justices were driven to such great lengths. The dissent had argued that the Indiana law was unconstitutional, at least as applied to nude barroom dancing, because such an application had nothing to do with avoiding offense to nonconsenting parties, and therefore "the only remaining purpose must relate to the communicative elements of the performance." Scalia responded:

> Perhaps the dissenters believe that "offense to others" *ought* to be the only reason for restricting nudity in public places generally, but there is no basis for thinking that our society has ever shared that Thoreauvian "you-may-do-what-you-like-so-long-as-it-does-not-injure-someone-else" beau ideal—much less for thinking that it was written into the Constitution.

Invoking the remarkable image of "60,000 fully consenting adults crowded into the Hoosier Dome to display their genitals to one another," Scalia maintained that such an event could be prohibited "even if there were not an offended innocent in the crowd." He argued that "[o]ur society prohibits, and all human societies have prohibited, certain activities not because they harm others but because they are considered, in the traditional phrase, '*contra bonos mores*,' *i.e.*, immoral," and one of those activities is public exposure of one's private parts.

Thus, Scalia not only accepts the public/private line, he makes it a moral imperative. But one might as easily say flag burning, criticizing one's elected leaders, and blasphemy are "immoral." The First Amendment usually demands more than a Latin phrase to justify the regulation of expression and specifically bars regulation based solely on a judgment that the expression is immoral. Thus, the majority was driven to find the Indiana statute "unrelated to expression" because it otherwise could not have upheld the law as a regulation of morals.

Left unstated is *how* requiring otherwise nude dancers to don pasties and G-strings will uphold the morals of the community. The moral difference between an entirely nude dancer and a dancer wearing pasties and a G-string is not immediately apparent. But the pasties and G-string do serve an important symbolic function: they insist that the law is present in this public space, very literally enforcing a line, albeit a very fine one. The thinness of the line is ultimately less important than the fact that the line exists. The statute regulates the public sphere precisely by demanding that dancers keep their "private parts" private, but only in the most minimal sense. Thus, the pasties and G-string are an apt metaphor for the regulation of sexual expression: they symbolically police the public sphere by barring certain "private" topics from surfacing, even as they permit (and possibly even increase the desirability of) *regulated* sexual expression in the public sphere. They reflect society's compromise on sexual expression: such expression may remain relatively free in the private sphere, but its public expression, although far from forbidden altogether, must be subject to legal regulation. The Court has in turn sanctioned that compromise, but in order to do so it has had to invert the First Amendment. * * *

[Cole then argues that what drives the society to regulate public expressions of sexuality is the need to impose limits on sexuality, "that which risks being beyond control * * * for the sake ultimately of the limit itself." Because pornography is dependent upon its taboo status for its appeal as well as its threat, this action by the state also helps to define what is sexy, with serious consequences for how all of us experience our sexuality. In developing this line of argument, Cole draws upon Michel Foucault's theory of sexuality as a discourse, and one that is the product of ostensibly repressive laws as well as normalizing social categories. See Chapter 5, Section 3.]

Although the public/private line is conventionally seen as essential to maintain the values of civilization, it plays an equally central role in the construction of sexuality. In large part, what makes sexual expression sexy in our culture is the potential for transgression, for abandonment of inhibitions, and for the play of fantasy. Social prohibitions ironically contribute to this conception of sexuality by constructing lines to transgress, inhibitions to abandon, and a "normal" reality against which fantasies may be played out. Pornographers play along with the lines society draws and even go further by drawing their own lines. Society regulates sexual expression because of its perceived dangers, yet without such regulation sexual expression might well lose some of its "dangerous" appeal.

Thus, while conventional accounts of sexual regulation portray the sex drive as an otherwise unrestrained libidinal instinct that must be contained, sublimated, and regulated to serve the interests of civilization, I have suggested that the sex drive is itself shaped by the regulatory lines we draw and precisely by the excitement that transgressing those taboos promises. The regulation of sexual expression reveals at bottom, not a struggle between social order and sexual anarchy, but a dynamic in which both law and sex are inextricably dependent on the drawing of lines. Paradoxically, then, sexual expression to some extent will always elude society's desperate attempts to regulate it, because sexual expression transforms whatever taboo is imposed into a fetish.

By our regulatory obsession we have constructed a very particular type of sexuality, one in which transgressing lines and violating taboos is central to sexual excitement. We should not (and most of us do not) assume that such a construction of sexuality is necessary or inevitable. But this construction of sexuality is so strongly determined in our culture—by the very regulations we impose—that it is difficult to conceive of sexuality in other than transgressive terms. This construction of sexuality limits the possibilities for alternative visions of sexuality, visions that are not delimited by the transgression of taboos. Both the traditional critics of pornography, who envision a sexuality characterized by love and devotion, and the feminist critics, who seek a sexuality predicated on equality between women and men, undermine their own causes by focusing on suppression as the means for achieving those ideals. They would do better *not* to seek to control sexual expression, but instead to participate in affirmative private and public exploration of alternative visions. In the end, not only the First Amendment, but sexuality itself, demand more speech, not less. More regulation and less speech will only ensure that we remain bound to a pornographic conception of sexuality.

PROBLEM 6–1

THE DWORKIN–MACKINNON PORNOGRAPHY ORDINANCES:
FEMINIST THEORIES FOR REGULATING SEXUAL SPEECH

In 1983, Andrea Dworkin and Catharine MacKinnon drafted, and the Minneapolis City Council passed, the first feminist anti-pornography ordinance, with the following stated purpose:

> The council finds that pornography is central in creating and maintaining the civil inequality of the sexes. Pornography is a systematic practice of exploitation and subordination based on sex which differentially harms women. * * *

Minneapolis Ordinance (Dec. 30, 1983; July 13, 1984), amending Minneapolis Code of Ordinances tit. 7, chs. 139 & 141.

The ordinance defined pornography as "the sexually explicit subordination of women, graphically depicted, whether in pictures or in words, that also includes one or more of the following:

(i) women are presented as dehumanized sexual objects, things, or commodities; or

(ii) women are presented as sexual objects who enjoy pain or humiliation; or

(iii) women are presented as sexual objects who experience sexual pleasure in being raped; or

(iv) women are presented as sexual objects tied up or cut up or mutilated or bruised or physically hurt; or

(v) women are presented in postures of sexual submission; or

(vi) women's body's parts—including but not limited to vaginas, breasts, and buttocks—are exhibited, such that women are reduced to those parts; or

(vii) women are presented as whores by nature; or

(viii) women are presented being penetrated by objects or animals; or

(ix) women are presented in scenarios of degradation, injury, abasement, torture, shown as filthy or inferior, bleeding, bruised, or hurt in a context that makes these conditions sexual.''

The mayor of Minneapolis twice vetoed the ordinance, but a similar one was later adopted by the city of Indianapolis. Both created civil law causes of action for monetary and injunctive relief against anyone who produced, sold, exhibited, or distributed ''pornography.''

Is this ordinance constitutional under *Miller*? Should there be a new exception to First Amendment protection for sexual speech? Consider the following materials.

Catharine MacKinnon, ''Pornography, Civil Rights, and Speech''

20 *Harvard Civil Rights–Civil Liberties Law Review* 1, 16–20, 22–24, 32–33, 26–27, 43–59 (1985).*

* * * In pornography, there it is, in one place, all of the abuses that women had to struggle so long even to begin to articulate, all the *unspeakable* abuse: the rape, the battery, the sexual harassment, the prostitution, and the sexual abuse of children. Only in the pornography it is called something else: sex, sex, sex, sex, and sex, respectively. Pornography sexualizes rape, battery, sexual harassment, prostitution, and child sexual abuse; it thereby celebrates, promotes, authorizes, and legitimizes them. More generally, it eroticizes the dominance and submission that is the dynamic common to them all. It makes hierarchy sexy and calls that ''the truth about sex'' or just a mirror of reality. Through this process, pornography constructs what a woman is as what men want from sex. This is what the pornography means. * * *

Pornography constructs what a woman is in terms of its view of what men want sexually, such that acts of rape, battery, sexual harassment, prostitution, and sexual abuse of children become acts of sexual equality. Pornography's world of equality is a harmonious and balanced place. Men and women are perfectly complementary and perfectly bipolar. Women's desire to be fucked by men is equal to men's desire to fuck women. All the ways men love to take and violate women, women love to be taken and violated. The women who most love this are most men's equals, the most liberated; the most participatory child is the most grown-up, the most equal to an adult. Their consent merely expresses or ratifies these preexisting facts.

The content of pornography is one thing. There, women substantively desire dispossession and cruelty. We desperately want to be bound, battered, tortured, humiliated, and killed. Or, to be fair to the soft core, merely taken and used. This is erotic to the male point of view. Subjection itself with self-determination ecstatically relinquished is the content of women's sexual desire and desirability. Women are there to be violated and possessed, men to violate and possess us either on screen or by camera or pen on behalf of the consumer. On a simple descriptive level, the inequality of hierarchy, of which gender is the primary one, seems necessary for the sexual arousal to work. Other added inequalities identify various pornographic genres or sub-themes, although they are always added through gender: age, disability, homosexuality, animals, objects, race (including anti-semitism), and so on. Gender is never irrelevant.

What pornography *does* goes beyond its content: It eroticizes hierarchy, it sexualizes inequality. It makes dominance and submission sex. Inequality is its central dynamic; the illusion of freedom coming together with the reality of force is central to its working. Perhaps because this is a bourgeois culture, the victim must look free, appear to be freely acting. Choice is how she got there. Willing is what she is when she is being equal. It seems equally important that then and there she actually be forced and that forcing be communicated on some level, even if only through still photos of her in postures of receptivity and access, available for penetration. Pornography in this view is a form of forced sex, a practice of sexual politics, an institution of gender inequality.

From this perspective, pornography is neither harmless fantasy nor a corrupt and confused misrepresentation of an otherwise natural and healthy sexual situation. It institutionalizes the sexuality of male supremacy, fusing the erotization of dominance and submission with the social construction of male and female. To the extent that gender is sexual, pornography is part of constituting the meaning of that sexuality. Men treat women as who they see women as being. Pornography constructs who that is. Men's power over women means that the way men see women defines who women can be. Pornography is that way. Pornography is not imagery in some relation to a reality elsewhere constructed. It is not a distortion, reflection, projection, expression, fantasy, representation, or symbol either. It is a sexual reality.

In Andrea Dworkin's definitive work on pornography, sexuality itself is a social construct gendered to the ground. Male dominance here is not an artificial overlay upon an underlying inalterable substratum of uncorrupted essential sexual being. Dworkin's *Pornography: Men Possessing Women* presents a sexual theory of gender inequality of which pornography is a constitutive practice. The way in which pornography produces its meaning constructs and defines men and women as such. Gender has no basis in anything other than the social reality its hegemony constructs. Gender is what gender means. The process that gives sexuality its male supremacist meaning is the same process through which gender inequality becomes socially real. * * *

There is a buried issue within sex discrimination law about what sex, meaning gender, is. If sex is a *difference*, social or biological, one looks to see if a challenged practice occurs along the same lines; if it does, or if it is done to both sexes, the practice is not discrimination, not inequality. If, by contrast, sex inequality is a matter of *dominance*, the issue is not the gender difference but the difference gender makes. In this more substantive, less abstract approach, the concern is whether a practice *subordinates* on the basis of sex. The first approach implies that marginal correction is needed; the second suggests social change. Equality to the first centers on abstract symmetry between equivalent categories; the asymmetry that occurs when categories are not equivalent is not inequality, it is treating unlikes differently. To the second approach, inequality centers on the substantive, cumulative disadvantagement of social hierarchy. Equality to the first is nondifferentiation; to the second, equality is nonsubordination. Although it is consonant with both approaches, our anti-pornography statute emerges largely from an analysis of the problem under the second approach.

To define pornography as a practice of sex discrimination combines a mode of portrayal that has a legal history—the sexually explicit—with an active term central to the inequality of the sexes—subordination. Among other things, subordination means to be placed in a position of inferiority or loss of power, or to be demeaned or denigrated. To be someone's subordinate is the opposite of being their equal. The definition does not include all sexually explicit depictions *of* the subordination of women. That is not what it says. It says, this which *does* that: the sexually explicit which subordinates women. To these active terms to capture what the pornography *does*, the definition adds a list of what it must also contain. This list, from our analysis, is an exhaustive description of what must be in the pornography for it to do what it does behaviorally. Each item in the definition is supported by experimental, testimonial, social, and clinical evidence. We made a legislative choice to be exhaustive and specific and concrete rather than conceptual and general, to minimize problems of chilling effect, making it hard to guess wrong, thus making self-censorship less likely, but encouraging (to use a phrase from discrimination law) voluntary compliance, knowing that if something turns up that is not on the list, the law will not be expansively interpreted. * * *

* * * It is [] vicious to suggest, as many have, that women like Linda Marchiano [the actress who portrayed "Linda Lovelace" in the movie, "Deep Throat"] should remedy their situations through the exercise of more speech. Pornography makes their speech impossible and where possible, worthless. Pornography makes women into objects. Objects do not speak. When they do, they are by then regarded as objects, not as humans, which is what it means to have no credibility. Besides, how Ms. Marchiano's speech is supposed to redress her injury, except by producing this legal remedy, is unclear since no amount of saying anything remedies what is being *done* to her in theatres and on home videos all over the world, where she is repeatedly raped for public entertainment and private profit. * * *

Received wisdom seems to be that because there is so little difference between convicted rapists and the rest of the male population in levels and patterns of exposure, response to, and consumption of pornography, pornography's role in rape is insignificant. A more parsimonious explanation of this data is that knowing exposure to, response to, or consumption of pornography will not tell you who will be reported, apprehended, and convicted for rape. But the commonalities such data reveal between convicted rapists and other men are certainly consistent with the fact that only a tiny fraction of rapes ever come to the attention of authorities. It does not make sense to assume that pornography has no role in rape simply because little about its use or effects distinguishes convicted rapists from other men, when we know that a lot of those other men *do* rape women; they just never get caught. In other words, the significance of pornography in acts of forced sex is one thing if sex offenders are considered deviants and another if they are considered relatively nonexceptional except for the fact of their apprehension and incarceration. * * *

To reach the magnitude of this problem on the scale it exists, our law makes trafficking in pornography—production, sale, exhibition, or distribution—actionable. Under the obscenity rubric, much legal and psychological scholarship has centered on a search for the elusive link between pornography defined as obscenity and harm. They have looked high and low—in the mind of the male consumer, in society or in its "moral fabric," in correlations between variations in levels of anti-social acts and liberalization of obscenity laws. The only harm they have found has been one they have attributed to "the social interest in order and morality." Until recently, no one looked very persistently for harm to women, particularly harm to women through men. The rather obvious fact that the sexes *relate* has been overlooked in the inquiry into the male consumer and his mind. The pornography doesn't just drop out of the sky, go into his head and stop there. Specifically, men rape, batter, prostitute, molest, and sexually harass women. Under conditions of inequality, they also hire, fire, promote, and grade women, decide how much or whether or not we are worth paying and for what, define and approve and disapprove of women in ways that count, that determine our lives.

If women are not just born to be sexually used, the fact that we are seen and treated as though that is what we are born for becomes something in need of explanation. If we see that men relate to women in a pattern of who they see women as being, and that forms a pattern of inequality, it becomes important to ask where that view came from or, minimally, how it is perpetuated or escalated. Asking this requires asking different questions about pornography than the ones obscenity law made salient. * * *

* * * Crucially, all pornography by our definition acts dynamically over time to diminish one's ability to distinguish sex from violence. The materials work behaviorally to diminish the capacity of both men and women to perceive that an account of a rape is an account of a rape. X-only materials, in which subjects perceive no force, also increase perceptions that a rape victim is worthless and decrease the perception she was

harmed. * * * Pornography can no longer be said to be just a mirror. It does not just reflect the world or some people's perceptions. It *moves* them. It increases attitudes that are lived out, circumscribing the status of half the population. * * *

Pornography stimulates and reinforces, it does not cathect or mirror, the connection between one-sided freely available sexual access to women and masculine sexual excitement and sexual satisfaction. The catharsis hypothesis is fantasy. The fantasy theory is fantasy. Reality is: Pornography conditions male orgasm to female subordination. It tells men what sex means, what a real woman is, and codes them together in a way that is behaviorally reinforcing. This is a real five-dollar sentence but I'm going to say it anyway: Pornography is a set of hermeneutical equivalences that work on the epistemological level. Substantively, pornography defines the meaning of what a woman is by connecting access to her sexuality with masculinity through orgasm. The behavior data show that what pornography means *is* what it does. * * *

Lisa Duggan, Nan D. Hunter, and Carole Vance, "False Promises: Feminist Anti–Pornography Legislation"

38 *New York Law School Law Review* 133 (1993) (Reprinted by permission from V. Burstyn, *Women Against Censorship* (1985)).

* * * Although proponents claim that the Minneapolis and Indianapolis ordinances represent a new way to regulate pornography, the strategy is still laden with our culture's old, repressive approach to sexuality. The implementation of such laws hinges on the definition of pornography as interpreted by the judiciary. The definition provided in the Minneapolis legislation is vague, leaving critical phrases such as "the sexually explicit subordination of women," "postures of sexual submission," and "whores by nature" to the interpretation of the citizen who files a complaint and to the judge who hears the case. The legislation does not prohibit just the images of rape and abusive sexual violence that most supporters claim to be its target, but instead drifts toward covering an increasingly wide range of sexually explicit material.

The most problematic feature of this approach is a conceptual flaw embedded in the law itself. Supporters of this type of legislation say that the target of their efforts is misogynous, sexually explicit, and violent representation, whether in pictures or words. Indeed, the feminist anti-pornography movement is fueled by women's anger at the most repugnant examples of pornography. But a close examination of the wording of the model legislative text, and examples of purportedly actionable material offered by proponents of the legislation in briefs defending the Indianapolis ordinance in a court challenge, suggests that the law is actually aimed at a range of material considerably broader than what the proponents claim is their target. The discrepancies between the law's explicit and implicit aims have been almost invisible to us because these distortions are very similar to distortions about sexuality in the culture as a whole. The legislation and supporting texts deserve close reading. Hidden beneath illogical transformations, non sequiturs, and highly permeable definitions are familiar sexual scripts drawn from mainstream, sexist culture that potentially could have very negative consequences for women.

[A] Venn diagram illustrates the three areas targeted by the law, and represents a scheme that classifies words or images that have any of three characteristics: violence, sexual explicitness, or sexism.

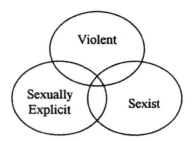

Clearly, a text or an image might have only one characteristic. Material can be violent but not sexually explicit or sexist: for example, a war movie in which both men and women suffer injury or death without regard to or because of their gender. Material can be sexist but not sexually explicit or violent. A vast number of materials from mainstream media—television, popular novels, magazines, newspapers—come to mind, depicting, for example, either distraught housewives or the "happy sexism" of the idealized family, with mom self-sacrificing, other-directed, and content. Finally, material can be sexually explicit but not violent or sexist: for example, the freely chosen sexual behavior depicted in sex education films or women's own explicit writing about sexuality.

As the diagram illustrates, areas can also intersect, reflecting a range of combinations of the three characteristics. Images can be violent and sexually explicit without being sexist—for example, a narrative about a rape in a men's prison, or a documentary about the effect of a rape on a woman. The latter example illustrates the importance of context in evaluating whether material that is sexually explicit and violent is also sexist. The intent of the maker, the context of the film, and the perception of the viewer together render a depiction of a rape sympathetic, harrowing, even educational, rather than sensational, victim-blaming, and laudatory.

Another possible overlap is between material that is violent and sexist but not sexually explicit. Films or books that describe violence directed against women by men in a way that clearly shows gender antagonism and inequality, and sometimes strong sexual tension, but no sexual explicitness, fall into this category—for example, the popular genre of slasher films in which women are stalked, terrified, and killed by men, or accounts of mass murder of women, fueled by male rage. Finally, a third point of overlap arises when material is sexually explicit and sexist without being violent— that is, when sex is consensual but still reflects themes of male superiority and female abjectness. Some sex education materials could be included in this category, as well as a great deal of regular pornography.

The remaining domain, the inner core, is one in which the material is simultaneously violent, sexually explicit, and sexist—for example, an image of naked woman being slashed by a knife-wielding rapist. The Minneapolis ordinance, however, does not by any means confine itself to this material.

To be actionable as pornography under the law, material must be judged by the courts to be "the sexually explicit subordination of women, graphically depicted whether in pictures or in words that also includes at least one or more" of nine criteria. Of these, only four involve the intersection of violence, sexual explicitness, and sexism, and then only arguably. Even in these cases, many questions remain about whether images with all three characteristics do in fact cause violence against women. And the task of evaluating material that is ostensibly the target of these criteria becomes complicated—indeed, hopeless—because most of the clauses that contain these criteria mix actions or qualities of violence with those that are not particularly associated with violence.

The section that comes closest to the stated purpose of the legislation is clause (iii): "women are presented as sexual objects who experience sexual pleasure in being raped." This clause is intended to cover depictions of rape that are sexually explicit and sexist; the act of rape itself signifies the violence. But other clauses are not so clear cut because the list of characteristics often mixes signs or by-products of violence with phenomena that are unrelated or irrelevant to judging violence.

Such a problem occurs with clause (iv): "women are presented as sexual objects tied up or cut up or mutilated or bruised or physically hurt." All these except the first, "tied up," generally occur as a result of violence. "Tied up," if part of consensual sex, is not violent and, for some practitioners, not particularly sexist. Women who are tied up may be participants in nonviolent sex play involving bondage, a theme in both heterosexual and lesbian pornography. Clause (ix) contains another mixed list, in which "injury," "torture," "bleeding," "bruised," and "hurt" are combined with phrases such as "degradation" and "shown as filthy or inferior," neither of which is violent. Depending on the presentation, "filthy" and "inferior" may constitute sexually explicit sexism, although not violence. "Degradation" is a sufficiently inclusive term to cover most acts of which a viewer disapproves.

Several other clauses have little to do with violence at all; they refer to material that is sexually explicit and sexist, thus falling outside the triad of characteristics at which the legislation is supposedly aimed. For example, movies in which "women are presented as dehumanized sexual objects, things, or commodities" may be infuriating and offensive to feminists, but they are not violent.

Finally, some clauses describe material that is neither violent nor necessarily sexist. Clause (v)—"women . . . in postures of sexual submission [or sexual servility, including by inviting penetration]"—and clause (viii)—"women ... being penetrated by objects or animals"—are sexually explicit, but not violent and not obviously sexist unless one believes that penetration—whether heterosexual, lesbian, or autoerotic—is indicative of gender inequality and female oppression. Similarly problematic are clauses that invoke representations of "women ... as whores by nature" and "women's body parts ... such that women are reduced to those parts." * * *

At its heart, this analysis implies that heterosexual sex itself is sexist, that women do not engage in it of their own volition, and that behavior pleasurable to men is intrinsically repugnant to women. In some contexts, for example, the representation of fellatio and multiple partners can be sexist, but are we willing to concede that they always are? If not, then what is proposed as actionable under the Indianapolis law includes merely sexually explicit representation (the traditional target of obscenity laws), which proponents of the legislation vociferously insist they are not interested in attacking. * * *

Certain troubling questions arise here, for if one claims, as some anti-pornography activists do, that there is a direct relationship between images and behavior, why should images of violence against women or scenarios of sexism in general not be similarly proscribed? Why is sexual explicitness singled out as the cause of women's oppression? For proponents to exempt violent and sexist images, or even sexist images, from regulation is inconsistent, especially since they are so pervasive. * * *

* * * [W]hat underlies this legislation, and the success of its analysis in blurring and exceeding boundaries, is an appeal to a very traditional view of sex: Sex is degrading to women. By this logic, any illustrations or descriptions of explicit sexual acts that involve women are in themselves affronts to women's dignity. In its brief, the City of Indianapolis was quite specific about this point: "The harms caused by pornography are by no means limited to acts of physical aggression. The mere existence of pornography in society degrades and demeans all women." Embedded in this view are several other familiar themes: that sex is degrading to women, but not to men; that men are raving beasts; that sex is dangerous for women; that sexuality is male, not female; that women are victims, not sexual actors; that men inflict "it" on women; that penetration is submission; that heterosexual sexuality, rather than the institution of heterosexuality, is sexist.

These assumptions, in part intended, in part unintended, lead us back to the traditional target of obscenity law: sexually explicit material. What initially appeared novel, then, is really the reappearance of a traditional theme. It is ironic that a feminist position on pornography incorporates most of the myths about sexuality that feminism has struggled to displace. * * *

Not only does pornography not cause the kind and degree of harm that can justify the restraint of speech, but its existence serves some social functions which benefit women. Pornographic speech has many, often anomalous, characteristics. Certainly one is that it magnifies the misogyny present in the culture and exaggerates the fantasy of male power. Another, however, is that the existence of pornography has served to flout conventional sexual mores, to ridicule sexual hypocrisy, and to underscore the importance of sexual needs. Pornography carries many messages other than woman-hating; it advocates sexual adventure, sex outside of marriage, sex for no reason other than pleasure, casual sex, anonymous sex, group sex, voyeuristic sex, illegal sex, public sex. Some of these ideas appeal to women reading or seeing pornography, who may interpret some images as legitimating their own sense of sexual urgency or desire to be sexually aggressive. Women's experience of pornography is not as universally victimizing as the ordinance would have it. * * *

Supporters of the anti-pornography ordinances both endorse the concept that pornographic speech contains no ideas or expressive interest, and at the same time attribute to pornography the capacity to trigger violent acts by the power of its misogyny. The City's brief in defense of the Indianapolis ordinance expanded this point by arguing that all sexually explicit speech is entitled to less constitutional protection than other speech. The anti-pornography groups have cleverly capitalized on this approach—a product of a totally nonfeminist legal system—to attempt, through the mechanism of the ordinances, to legitimate a new crusade for protectionism and sexual conservatism. * * *

NOTES ON THE FEMINIST DEBATE OVER REGULATING PORNOGRAPHY

1. *Unpacking the Arguments: Feminism and the Construction of Sexuality.* Both the "pro-censorship" and the "pro-sex" sides agree that sexuality is in fundamental ways socially constructed. Both agree that most commercial pornography at best ignores women's sexuality and at worst glorifies misogyny. Why such a bitter debate?

One historical analogy is the debate among women in the early twentieth century over whether to seek prohibition of alcohol. Although now often thought of as a silly, puritanical campaign to extinguish drinking, the temperance movement was led by committed feminists who documented the association of drunkenness with domestic violence. In both debates, women argued about what the real chain of causation was. (Does drinking/pornography lead to abuse? Would elimination of drinking/pornography substantially alleviate the problem?) More fundamentally, they also argued about using strategies designed to constrain male freedom versus strategies to expand the social space for women to act without conforming to traditional expectations.

Another way to analyze the pornography debate is to position the two feminist viewpoints in the context of existing legal doctrine on sexual speech. Both sides would de-privatize sexual speech. Rather than treating it as immoral under the obscenity approach, both see it as politically charged. The Dworkin–MacKinnon approach would continue to treat it as unique, however, albeit under a new rationale. The anti-censorship approach would abolish the separate, undervalued category of sexually explicit speech.

How do essentialist notions of male and female sexuality function in these arguments about pornography? Carlin Meyer argues in "Sex, Sin, and Women's Liberation: Against Porn–Suppression," 72 *Tex. L. Rev.* 1097, 1130–3, 1172–8 (1994), that the glorification of romantic love and its near saturation of popular culture have a more powerful and more insidious effect than does pornography on the construction of women's sexuality.

2. *Speech or Conduct? Public or Private?* Frederick Schauer, "Speech and 'Speech'—Obscenity and 'Obscenity': An Exercise in the Interpretation of Constitutional Language," 67 *Geo. L.J.* 899 (1979), argues that "the prototypical pornographic item on closer analysis shares more of the characteristics of sexual activity than of the communicative process. The pornographic item is in a real sense a sexual surrogate." Hence, he maintains that obscene representations are not "speech" at all, but rather "conduct" unprotected by the First Amendment. Schauer served on President Reagan's Pornography Commission, which issued a report reflecting these views. Consider how the feminist anti-pornography ordinance draws on that approach.

3. *What Are the Behavioral Effects of Viewing Pornography?* A key issue in the legal debate is whether exposure to certain materials induces criminal behavior. In a comprehensive review of the literature, three of the leading social scientists in the field concluded that "for the most part * * * sexually explicit images, per se, do not in the short run facilitate aggressive behavior against women, change attitudes about rape, or influence other forms of antiscoial behavior. Instead, the research indicates that it is the violent images fused with sexual images in some forms of pornography, or even the violent images alone, that account for many of the antisocial effects reported by social science researchers." Edward Donnerstein, Daniel Linz & Steven Penrod, *The Question of Pornography: Research Findings and Policy Implications* 2 (1987). What the researchers call violent or aggressive pornography has been shown to influence aggression toward women, at least in a laboratory situation, and to have negative effects on attitudes about women. *Id.* ch. 5. "It is important to note that materials that were merely sexual in nature had no effect on aggressive behavior." *Id.* at 98.

Is this the same material that the Indianapolis ordinance defined as pornography? Donnerstein, et al. define it as "depict[ions of] sexual coercion in a sexually explicit way," combined with a depiction of the female victim as initially resisting, then enjoying the rape. "[I]t is this unique feature of violent pornography—the presentation of the idea that women find sexual violence arousing—that plays an important role in producing violent pornography's harmful effects." *Id.* at 89.

Many of the materials that produce the most troubling effects are eroticized but not sexually explicit and thus would not fall within the ordinance's definition of pornography (nor within the category of obscenity). Research has found that exposure to "slasher films" (*e.g.*, *The Texas*

Chain Saw Massacre), in which graphic depictions of violence against women are mixed with erotic scenes, negatively affects men's responses to victims of sexual violence, at least in laboratory situations. *Id.* ch. 6.

Note the repeated emphasis in much of the advocates' discussion of pornography on images of bondage and sadomasochism (SM). Does SM imagery that depicts mutually desired bondage, for example, fall within the ordinance definition of pornography? Within the social scientists' definition of "violent" pornography?

American Booksellers Association, Inc. v. William Hudnut, III

U.S. Court of Appeals for the Seventh Circuit, 1985.
771 F.2d 323, *aff'd mem.*, 475 U.S. 1001 (1986).

■ EASTERBROOK, CIRCUIT JUDGE.

Indianapolis enacted an ordinance defining "pornography" as a practice that discriminates against women. "Pornography" is to be redressed through the administrative and judicial methods used for other discrimination. The City's definition of "pornography" is considerably different from "obscenity," which the Supreme Court has held is not protected by the First Amendment. * * *

"Pornography" under the ordinance is "the graphic sexually explicit subordination of women, whether in pictures or in words, that also includes one or more of the following:

(1) Women are presented as sexual objects who enjoy pain or humiliation; or

(2) Women are presented as sexual objects who experience sexual pleasure in being raped; or

(3) Women are presented as sexual objects tied up or cut up or mutilated or bruised or physically hurt, or as dismembered or truncated or fragmented or severed into body parts; or

(4) Women are presented as being penetrated by objects or animals; or

(5) Women are presented in scenarios of degradation, injury, abasement, torture, shown as filthy or inferior, bleeding, bruised, or hurt in a context that makes these conditions sexual; or

(6) Women are presented as sexual objects for domination, conquest, violation, exploitation, possession, or use, or through postures or positions of servility or submission or display."

Indianapolis Code § 16–3(q). The statute provides that the "use of men, children, or transsexuals in the place of women in paragraphs (1) through (6) above shall also constitute pornography under this section." The ordinance as passed in April 1984 defined "sexually explicit" to mean actual or simulated intercourse or the uncovered exhibition of the genitals, buttocks or anus. An amendment in June 1984 deleted this provision, leaving the term undefined.

The Indianapolis ordinance does not refer to the prurient interest, to offensiveness, or to the standards of the community. It demands attention to particular depictions, not to the work judged as a whole. It is irrelevant under the ordinance whether the work has literary, artistic, political, or scientific value. The City and many *amici* point to these omissions as virtues. They maintain that pornography influences attitudes, and the statute is a way to alter the socialization of men and women rather than to vindicate community standards of offensiveness. [Judge Easterbrook quoted from Catherine MacKinnon, "Pornography, Civil Rights and Speech," 20 *Harvard Civ.Rts.-Civ.L.Rev.* 1 (1985).]

Civil rights groups and feminists have entered this case as *amici* on both sides. Those supporting the ordinance say that it will play an important role in reducing the tendency of men to view women as sexual objects, a tendency that leads to both unacceptable attitudes and discrimination in the workplace and violence away from it. Those opposing the ordinance point out that much radical feminist literature is explicit and depicts women in ways forbidden by the ordinance and that the ordinance would reopen old battles. It is unclear how Indianapolis would treat works from James Joyce's *Ulysses* to Homer's *Iliad*; both depict women as submissive objects for conquest and domination.

We do not try to balance the arguments for and against an ordinance such as this. The ordinance discriminates on the ground of the content of the speech. Speech treating women in the approved way—in sexual encounters "premised on equality" (MacKinnon, *supra*, at 22)—is lawful no matter how sexually explicit. Speech treating women in the disapproved way—as submissive in matters sexual or as enjoying humiliation—is unlawful no matter how significant the literary, artistic, or political qualities of the work taken as a whole. The state may not ordain preferred viewpoints in this way. The Constitution forbids the state to declare one perspective right and silence opponents.

The ordinance contains four prohibitions. People may not "traffic" in pornography, "coerce" others into performing in pornographic works, or "force" pornography on anyone. Anyone injured by someone who has seen or read pornography has a right of action against the maker or seller.

Trafficking is defined in § 16–3(g)(4) as the "production, sale, exhibition, or distribution of pornography." The offense excludes exhibition in a public or educational library, but a "special display" in a library may be sex discrimination. Section 16–3(g)(4)(C) provides that the trafficking paragraph "shall not be construed to make isolated passages or isolated parts actionable."

"Coercion into pornographic performance" is defined in § 16–3(g)(5) as "[c]oercing, intimidating or fraudulently inducing any person . . . into performing for pornography. . . ." The ordinance specifies that proof of any of the following "shall not constitute a defense: I. That the person is a woman; ... VI. That the person has previously posed for sexually explicit pictures ... with anyone ...; ... VIII. That the person actually consented to a use of the performance that is changed into pornography; ... IX. That the person knew that the purpose of the acts or events in question was to make pornography; ... XI. That the person signed a contract, or made statements affirming a willingness to cooperate in the production of pornography; XII. That no physical force, threats, or weapons were used in the making of the pornography; or XIII. That the person was paid or otherwise compensated."

"Forcing pornography on a person," according to § 16–3(g)(5), is the "forcing of pornography on any woman, man, child, or transsexual in any place of employment, in education, in a home, or in any public place." The statute does not define forcing, but one of its authors states that the definition reaches pornography shown to medical students as part of their education or given to language students for translation. MacKinnon, *supra*, at 40–41.

Section 16–3(g)(7) defines as a prohibited practice the "assault, physical attack, or injury of any woman, man, child, or transsexual in a way that is directly caused by specific pornography."

For purposes of all four offenses, it is generally "not ... a defense that the respondent did not know or intend that the materials were pornography...." Section 16–3(g)(8). But the ordinance provides that damages are unavailable in trafficking cases unless the complainant proves "that the respondent knew or had reason to know that the materials were pornography." It is a complete defense to a trafficking case that all of the materials in question were pornography only by virtue of category (6) of the definition of pornography. In cases of assault caused by pornography, those who seek damages from "a seller, exhibitor or distributor" must show that the defendant knew or had reason to know of the material's status as pornography. By implication, those who seek damages from an author need not show this.

A woman aggrieved by trafficking in pornography may file a complaint "as a woman acting against the subordination of women" with the office of equal opportunity. A man, child, or transsexual also may protest trafficking "but must prove injury in the same way that a woman is injured...." Subsection (a) also provides, however, that "any person claiming to be aggrieved" by trafficking, coercion, forcing, or assault may complain against the "perpetrators." * * *

The office investigates and within 30 days makes a recommendation to a panel of the equal opportunity advisory board. The panel then decides whether there is reasonable cause to proceed and may refer the dispute to a conciliation conference or to a complaint adjudication committee for a hearing. The committee uses the same procedures ordinarily associated with civil rights litigation. It may make findings and enter orders, including both orders to cease and desist and orders "to take further affirmative action ... including but not limited to the power to restore complainant's losses. . . ." Either party may appeal the committee's decision to the board, which reviews the record before the committee and may modify its decision.

Under Indiana law an administrative decision takes effect when rendered, unless a court issues a stay. The board's decisions are subject to review in the ordinary course. Judicial review in pornography cases is to be de novo, which provides a second complete hearing. When the board finds that a person has engaged in trafficking or that a seller, exhibitor, or distributor is responsible for an assault, it must initiate judicial review of its own decision, and the statute prohibits injunctive relief in these cases in advance of the court's final decision. * * *

"If there is any fixed star in our constitutional constellation, it is that no official, high or petty, can prescribe what shall be orthodox in politics, nationalism, religion, or other matters of opinion or force citizens to confess by word or act their faith therein." *West Virginia State Board of Education v. Barnette*, 319 U.S. 624, 642 (1943). Under the First Amendment the government must leave to the people the evaluation of ideas. Bald or subtle, an idea is as powerful as the audience allows it to be. A belief may be pernicious—the beliefs of Nazis led to the death of millions, those of the Klan to the repression of millions. A pernicious belief may prevail. Totalitarian governments today rule much of the planet, practicing suppression of billions and spreading dogma that may enslave others. One of the things that separates our society from theirs is our absolute right to propagate opinions that the government finds wrong or even hateful. * * *

Under the ordinance graphic sexually explicit speech is "pornography" or not depending on the perspective the author adopts. Speech that "subordinates" women and also, for example, presents women as enjoying pain, humiliation, or rape, or even simply presents women in "positions of servility or submission or display" is forbidden, no matter how great the literary or political value of the work taken as a whole. Speech that portrays women in positions of equality is lawful, no matter how graphic the sexual content. This is thought control. It establishes an "approved" view of women, of how they may react to sexual encounters, of how the sexes may relate to each other. Those who espouse the approved view may use sexual images; those who do not, may not.

Indianapolis justifies the ordinance on the ground that pornography affects thoughts. Men who see women depicted as subordinate are more likely to treat them so. Pornography is an aspect of dominance. It does not persuade people so much as change them. It works by socializing, by establishing the expected and the permissible. In this view pornography is not an idea; pornography is the injury.

There is much to this perspective. Beliefs are also facts. People often act in accordance with the images and patterns they find around them. People raised in a religion tend to accept the tenets of that religion, often without independent examination. People taught from birth that black people are fit only for slavery rarely rebelled against that creed; beliefs coupled with the self-interest of the masters established a social structure that inflicted great harm while enduring for centuries. Words and images act at the level of the subconscious before they persuade at the level of the conscious. Even the truth has little chance unless a statement fits within the framework of beliefs that may never have been subjected to rational study.

Therefore we accept the premises of this legislation. Depictions of subordination tend to perpetuate subordination. The subordinate status of women in turn leads to affront and lower pay at work, insult and injury at home, battery and rape on the streets. In the language of the legislature, "[p]ornography is central in creating and maintaining sex as a basis of discrimination. Pornography is a systematic practice of exploitation and subordination based on sex which differentially harms women. The bigotry and contempt it produces, with the acts of aggression it fosters, harm women's opportunities for equality and rights [of all kinds]." Indianapolis Code § 16–1(a)(2).

Yet this simply demonstrates the power of pornography as speech. All of these unhappy effects depend on mental intermediation. Pornography affects how people see the world, their fellows, and social relations. If pornography is what pornography does, so is other speech. Hitler's orations affected how some Germans saw Jews. Communism is a world view, not simply a *Manifesto* by Marx and Engels or a set of speeches. Efforts to suppress communist speech in the United States were based on the belief that the public acceptability of such ideas would increase the likelihood of totalitarian government. Religions affect socialization in the most pervasive way. The opinion in *Wisconsin v. Yoder*, 406 U.S. 205 (1972), shows how a religion can dominate an entire approach to life, governing much more than the relation between the sexes. Many people believe that the existence of television, apart from the content of specific programs, leads to intellectual laziness, to a penchant for violence, to many other ills. The Alien and Sedition Acts passed during the administration of John Adams rested on a sincerely held belief that disrespect for the government leads to social collapse and revolution—a belief with support in the history of many nations. Most governments of the world act on this empirical regularity, suppressing critical speech. In the United States, however, the strength of the support for this belief is irrelevant. Seditious libel is protected speech unless the danger is not only grave but also imminent.

Racial bigotry, anti-semitism, violence on television, reporters' biases— these and many more influence the culture and shape our socialization. None is directly answerable by more speech, unless that speech too finds its place in the popular culture. Yet all is protected as speech, however insidious. Any other answer leaves the government in control of all of the institutions of culture, the great censor and director of which thoughts are good for us.

Sexual responses often are unthinking responses, and the association of sexual arousal with the subordination of women therefore may have a substantial effect. But almost all cultural stimuli provoke unconscious responses. Religious ceremonies condition their participants. Teachers convey messages by selecting what not to cover; the implicit message about what is off limits or unthinkable may be more powerful than the messages for which they present rational argument. Television scripts contain unarticulated assumptions. People may be conditioned in subtle ways. If the fact that speech plays a role in a process of conditioning were enough to permit governmental regulation, that would be the end of freedom of speech. * * *

Much of Indianapolis's argument rests on the belief that when speech is "unanswerable," and the metaphor that there is a "marketplace of ideas" does not apply, the First Amendment does not apply either. The metaphor is honored; Milton's *Aeropagitica* and John Stuart Mill's *On Liberty* defend freedom of speech on the ground that the truth will prevail, and many of the most important cases under the First Amendment recite this position. The Framers undoubtedly believed it. As a general matter it is true. But the Constitution does not make the dominance of truth a necessary condition of freedom of speech. To say that it does would be to confuse an outcome of free speech with a necessary condition for the application of the amendment.

A power to limit speech on the ground that truth has not yet prevailed and is not likely to prevail implies the power to declare truth. At some point the government must be able to say (as Indianapolis has said): "We know what the truth is, yet a free exchange of speech has not driven out falsity, so that we must now prohibit falsity." If the government may declare the truth, why wait for the failure of speech? Under the First Amendment, however, there is no such thing as a false idea, so the government may not restrict speech on the ground that in a free exchange truth is not yet dominant. * * *

We come, finally, to the argument that pornography is "low value" speech, that it is enough like obscenity that Indianapolis may prohibit it. Some cases hold that speech far removed from politics and other subjects at the core of the Framers' concerns may be subjected to special regulation. These cases do not sustain statutes that select among viewpoints, however. In *Pacifica* the FCC sought to keep vile language off the air during certain times. The Court held that it may; but the Court would not have sustained a regulation prohibiting scatological descriptions of Republicans but not scatological descriptions of Democrats, or any other form of selection among viewpoints.

At all events, "pornography" is not low value speech within the meaning of these cases. Indianapolis seeks to prohibit certain speech because it believes this speech influences social relations and politics on a grand scale, that it controls attitudes at home and in the legislature. This precludes a characterization of the speech as low value. True, pornography and obscenity have sex in common. But Indianapolis left out of its definition any reference to literary, artistic, political, or scientific value. The ordinance applies to graphic sexually explicit subordination in works great and small. The Court sometimes balances the value of speech against the costs of its restriction, but it does this by category of speech and not by the content of particular works. Indianapolis has created an approved point of view and so loses the support of these cases.

Any rationale we could imagine in support of this ordinance could not be limited to sex discrimination. Free speech has been on balance an ally of those seeking change. Governments that want stasis start by restricting speech. Culture is a powerful force of continuity; Indianapolis paints pornography as part of the culture of power. Change in any complex system ultimately depends on the ability of outsiders to challenge accepted views and the reigning institutions. Without a strong guarantee of freedom of speech, there is no effective right to challenge what is. * * *

Regina v. Donald Victor Butler, [1992] 1 S.C.R. 452, 89 D.L.R.4th 449 (Canada). Canada's obscenity law prohibits "any publication a dominant characteristic of which is the undue exploitation of sex, or of sex and any one or more of the following subjects, namely, crime, horror, cruelty and violence." The Canadian Supreme Court upheld the statute as not prohibiting the protection for free expression in the Canadian Charter by adopting a theory similar to that behind the Indianapolis ordinance. In Canada, unlike the U.S., hate speech is punishable by law, and the court analogized pornography to hate speech. The court ruled that Parliament could have had "a reasoned apprehension of harm" from materials that depicted "dehumanization in sexual relations."

A COMPARATIVE PERSPECTIVE: NOTES ON THE CANADIAN APPROACH TO SEXUAL SPEECH

1. *Similarities and Differences Between Canadian and American Free Expression Law.* Notwithstanding the distinct constitutional regimes, the same goals—free market of ideas, participation in the political process, personal autonomy—animate the judicial constructions in both countries. How would you analyze which legal regime is overall the better? Is it a risk of the Canadian regulation of hate speech and obscenity that constitutional protection will be too shallow when more oppressive censorship comes? Is a risk of the American approach that First Amendment absolutism will disable the government from needed regulations?

2. *Irony in the Canadian Approach: Feminist or Anti–Gay?* The first prosecution for obscenity initiated by Canadian police after the *Butler* ruling was against the owners of a gay bookstore for its sale of *Bad Attitude*, a lesbian sex magazine published in Boston. The store owners were found guilty, with the court ruling that the combination in one short story of "bondage in various forms, the pulling of hair, a hard slap and explicit sex" met the *Butler* test. *R. v. Scythes*, Ontario Court (Provincial Division) (Feb. 16, 1993) (unreported).

Lesbian and gay bookstores in Canada have been engaged in a long-running battle with Canadian Customs over the repeated confiscation of shipments of erotic or explicit books. The bookstores won a major victory in 2000 when the Canadian Supreme Court ruled that the customs agency had been systematically infringing their rights by targeting shipments to gay bookstores for sequestration. *Little Sisters Book and Art Emporium v. The*

Minister of Justice and Attorney General of Canada, 2000 SCC 69 (Can. Sup. Ct., 2000). However, the court refused to alter *Butler*'s definition of obscenity, despite the fact that Canadian Customs had relied on it to seize shipments of, *inter alia*, *Trash* by Dorothy Allison, *Querelle* by Jean Genet, *Macho Sluts* by Pat Califia and the cartoon book, *Hot Head Paisan*. For an in-depth description of the Canadian situation and a blow-by-blow account of the Little Sisters trial, see Janine Fuller & Stuart Blackley, *Restricted Entry: Censorship On Trial* (1995).

CHAPTER 7

U.S. MILITARY EXCLUSIONS AND THE CONSTRUCTION OF MANHOOD

No government institution has been more important in American history or more indicative of American attitudes about sexuality and gender than the U.S. armed forces. Yet despite the military's central role, service in the armed forces has been a selective obligation of citizenship: Only a minority of American citizens have ever been eligible for full military duty. The main exclusions have been ones that relate in some way or another to sexuality and gender: the exclusion and later segregation of people of color in the armed forces, a policy that ended in the 1950s (Section 1); the traditional exclusion of women from service and currently from combat positions, a policy under heavy fire for the last 20 years and perhaps on its way out (Section 2); and the current exclusion of lesbians, gay men, and bisexuals—still a robust policy as encoded in the famous "don't ask, don't tell" law (Section 3). Although each has had multiple meanings, one function they all share is policing the social understanding of "manhood."

A parallel project in this chapter will be to deepen the inquiry into equal protection law initiated in Chapter 3. The military's exclusions have focused on three classic discriminatory classifications: race, sex, and sexual orientation. Should the military, or any other branch of government, be able to classify and exclude along these lines without compelling justification? For most of our constitutional history, the answer has been "yes." Recently, race has become a suspect classification, and sex a quasi-suspect one if not a suspect one. As Chapter 3 indicated, sexual orientation is not a suspect classification requiring strict scrutiny under the U.S. Constitution. What should be its status? Do the reasons for scrutinizing race and sex classifications apply to sexual orientation? In addition, there are serious

First Amendment problems with the current military exclusion of open gays and lesbians.

Finally, this chapter will offer different angles on how manhood or masculinity is understood and valued in our society. The touchstone of sexuality and citizenship remains "the man." What does this mean? What is "manhood," and how does it relate to conceptions of citizenship?

RACIAL EXCLUSION AND SEGREGATION IN THE U.S. ARMED SERVICES

There is no more dramatic example of the link between citizenship and military service than the history of race in America. In *Dred Scott v. Sandford*, 60 U.S. 393 (1957), the primary evidence Chief Justice Roger Taney invoked to support the proposition that an African American could not be a "citizen" for federal diversity jurisdiction purposes was the fact that, since the 1790s, Congress had excluded men of African descent from the United States armed forces. *Id.* at 420. Section 1 of the Fourteenth Amendment overrode this part of the *Dred Scott* holding, but African Americans and other men of color continued to be excluded or segregated for several generations after Reconstruction. A central feature of the civil rights movement's politics of recognition for black Americans was an insistence that they serve in the military on the same terms and under the same conditions as white Americans. The story of this struggle has not been forgotten in the law, and it now follows. We start with Professor Karst's article, which not only presents a rich history of that struggle, but frames the entire chapter by demonstrating that the linkage between citizenship and military service also involves conceptions of what it has traditionally meant in the United States "to be a man."

Kenneth L. Karst, "The Pursuit of Manhood and the Desegregation of the Armed Forces"

38 *UCLA Law Review* 499–501, 502–08, 510–20 (1991).*

The statue of the Minuteman stands at the edge of the Lexington Battle Green as a reminder of the American tradition of the citizen soldier. From the Revolution onward, a great many Americans have believed that a citizen has the responsibility, in time of need, to serve in the armed forces. The same association of ideas also works in the other direction: when we amended the Constitution to lower the voting age to eighteen, one prominent slogan was, "If they're old enough to fight, they're old enough to vote." In the United States, as in Europe, citizenship and eligibility for military service have gone hand in hand. [Except that African Americans,

* Originally published in the *UCLA Law Review*. Copyright 1991, The Regents of the University of California. All Rights Reserved. Reprinted by permission.

women, and gays have been excluded or segregated for most of American history. Karst maintains that the three exclusions or segregations share a unifying theme.]

That unifying theme is the pursuit of manhood. Manhood, of course, has no existence except as it is expressed and perceived. The pursuit of manhood is an expressive undertaking, a series of dramatic performances. Masculinity is traditionally defined around the idea of power; the armed forces are the nation's preeminent symbol of power; and, not incidentally, "the Marines are looking for a few good men." The symbolism is not a side effect; it is the main point. From the colonial era to the middle of this century, our armed forces have alternately excluded and segregated blacks in the pursuit of manhood, and today's forms of exclusion and segregation are similarly grounded in the symbolism of masculine power. * * *

I.   The Problem of Manhood and the Ideology of Masculinity

The connections between military service and citizenship were well understood during the Civil War. Immediately after the first shots at Fort Sumter, black citizens began to volunteer for service in the Union Army and the militia. At first these efforts were rebuffed. By law Congress had limited membership in the militia to whites, and the Lincoln administration, still wooing the border states, feared that admitting blacks to the Army would send the signal that the Union's aim was not merely the preservation of the Union, but the abolition of slavery. Furthermore, some generals "feared that the presence of black soldiers in the army would create disharmony and drive away white volunteers." Working-class whites in Northern cities threatened violence to blacks who were proposing to organize military companies. To men at high and low levels in white society, black manhood suggested a new and disquieting form of rivalry, and so the Union cause had to be "a white man's war."

The issue of full citizenship for black people was never far below the surface of the question of black participation in the Army and the militia. Both slavery and lesser forms of racial discrimination were premised on an assumption, sometimes explicit and sometimes unspoken, that denied manhood—in the full sense of competence to be citizens—to black men. Then, as now, a citizen was a respected and responsible participant in society, and especially in society's decisions. "Manhood suffrage," a term commonly used in the era of Andrew Jackson, was not a slogan of universality; it excluded women and tribal Indians, and even in the North it typically excluded black men. Whites sometimes referred to black men as "degraded"; as George Fredrickson has remarked, the use of this term suggested "that there was some ideal of manhood from which the Negro had fallen or to which he might be raised."

In fact there was, and still is, an ideal of manhood. Historically the ideal, like the word itself, has embraced at least two meanings: masculinity and eligibility for equal citizenship. For most of our national history these meanings have been intertwined; a competence identified with masculinity has seemed a condition of full citizenship, and active participation in the community's public life has offered men reassurance of their masculinity. Because it is an abstract ideal, a construct of the mind, manhood in the sense of masculinity is in some measure unattainable; it can be pursued, but never wholly achieved. Yet, the achievement of manhood is seen by most men as essential to their identities. In combination, these elements are a recipe for anxiety. * * *

We are all consumers of images of manhood. According to these images a man is supposed to be: active; assertive; confident; decisive; ready to lead; strong; courageous; morally capable of violence; independent; competitive; practical; successful in achieving goals; emotionally detached; cool in the face of danger or crisis; blunt in expression; sexually aggressive and yet protective toward women. "Proving yourself" as a man can take many forms, but all of them are expressive, and all are variations on the theme of power. * * *

The heart of the ideology of masculinity is the belief that power rightfully belongs to the masculine—that is, to those who display the traits traditionally called masculine. This belief has two corollaries. The first is that the gender line must be clearly drawn, and the second is that power is rightfully distributed among the masculine in proportion to their masculinity, as determined not merely by their physical stature or aggressiveness, but more generally by their ability to dominate and to avoid being dominated. Both parts of the ideology contribute to the subordination of groups. This function is easy to see in efforts to express the gender line in sharp definition; the ideology of masculinity will be effective in assigning power only if those who are masculine are clearly identified. The second corollary of the ideology highlights the centrality of male rivalry. By making anxiety into an everyday fact of life, it leads nervous men to seek reassurances of their masculinity through group rituals that express domination over other groups. In combination these two beliefs purport to justify power by tautology, to ground the legitimacy of domination in domination itself.

In our country's history, the male-rivalry strand of the ideology of masculinity is repeatedly visible in the readiness of white men, and especially poor white men, to exclude black men from equal citizenship. During the Civil War the white men in the Northeast who were most visibly offended by the sight of blacks in uniform were recent immigrants from Ireland. Because they occupied the bottom of the employment ladder, they had little in the way of traditional masculine achievement to bolster their sense of self-worth. For the same reason they had much to fear from the competition of black laborers. Those fears modulated into opposition to the war when it became clear that the Union was fighting for emancipation, which would greatly increase their rivals' numbers. The Northern whites most bent on denying black men a traditional way of expressing manhood were those most in need of affirming their own. * * *

II.   Male Rivalry and the Double Battle of Black Soldiers

A.   *Race, Sex, and the Roots of White Male Anxiety*

In the eyes of Englishmen in the era of colonization, slavery implied something less than humanity, a status akin to that of a beast. This assumption was part of a logic that was circular; to complete the circle of justification, the defenders of black slavery argued that blacks were not fully human. Beneath the surface of these apologies lay both male rivalry and anxieties about self-definition. African men were thought by Europeans to be especially libidinous; it was easy for white men to project their own desires onto blacks, and to connect the need for control over blacks with the need to control themselves. This association was intensified in the American colonies as many white slaveholders came to exercise sexual privileges over female slaves; if white men's fears of slave revolts came to be associated with fears of black men's supposed sexual aggressiveness, no doubt one reason was the fear of retaliation. [Hence, the "militant South" was policed by all-white militias, where white men earned their chops by policing black men.]

Given this historical example, it was no wonder that the black men who volunteered to serve the Union in 1861 associated manhood and citizenship. Understandably, they believed that military service would allow them to be seen as men, as citizens. Once Northern blacks put on the uniform, they believed, it would be hard to deny them the vote. If Southern blacks were freed to serve as Union soldiers, the war would become a war to end slavery. Developments like these were just the recognitions of black manhood that many white men (especially working class whites) feared and that Frederick Douglass and other black leaders hoped for. As it happened, these recognitions came to pass—but only for a season. [By war's end, almost 200,000 black men had served as soldiers in the Union Army, including combat forces.]

* * * W. E. B. DuBois said it was the fact that the black man "rose and fought and killed" that enabled whites to proclaim him "a man and a brother.... Nothing else made Negro citizenship conceivable, but the record of the Negro soldier as a fighter." After the war three constitutional amendments and a package of Reconstruction civil rights acts not only abolished slavery, but promised black Americans equal citizenship, including the equal right to vote. Yet, formal citizenship was one thing, brotherhood quite another. * * * Black war veterans and black people generally learned that formal equality before the law could exist alongside the gravest sort of inequalities in fact. By the end of the century, racial discrimination remained a routine part of black people's experience in the North and West while the South had descended into the systematic racial subordination called Jim Crow.

A major motivating factor behind the Jim Crow segregation laws and the myriad social practices they reinforced was the pursuit of manhood among white men. As in the days of slavery, this pursuit translated into a need to deny, to repress, the manhood of black men. For "the militant South"—that is, for southern white men as a group—the humiliation of military defeat was compounded during twelve years of occupation by the Union army. By the late 1880s a sharp economic decline threatened the "family provider" function of large numbers of lower class white men, many of whom responded violently, removing black tenants from competition by driving them off desirable farm land. As economic recession deepened into depression, white violence against blacks intensified, taking new and more murderous forms. In the ensuing decades southern white lynch mobs and rioters would take thousands of black lives.

The problem of manhood was central in generating this violence. In the South, white men were supposed to be not only the providers for but the protectors of women. Then as now, the fears of losing, of not measuring up to the manly ideal, could turn men toward group action aimed at group domination. The rivalry of black men was seen in terms that were not just economic; it threatened a social status that had previously been awarded for whiteness alone. And if the day-to-day demonstrations of competence by liberated black men posed a problem for white male self-esteem, the abstraction of black manhood was frightening. This objectification originated in fear and grew on fear.

The political and social arrangements during the Reconstruction years and in the succeeding decade also threatened white Southern manhood by subjecting male-female relations to considerable strain. For the upper classes, the old chivalry was in tatters. But Southern white men of all stations in life shared a deeper anxiety about their ability to protect the women around them. At all levels of white society men had long exaggerated the sense that they were sexual aggressors. Not uncommonly they had been taught to believe that their sexuality was an animal urge that must be kept under strict control. Such a belief was heightened by the prevailing view of white women as symbols of purity who were anything but sexual beings. In this abstract, dehumanizing construction of womanhood, sex was at once a duty and a violation. For white men these beliefs were the seedbed for tension and guilt; they also translated readily into a nightmare of male rivalry.

When the anxiety about man-as-provider fused together with anxieties centered on sexuality, the combination was explosive. The abstract image of pure Southern womanhood became identified with a vision of white supremacy. The white woman, as the "perpetuator of [white] superiority's legitimate line," had to be kept remote from any sexual approach of the black man. The abstraction of black manhood was transformed into "the specific image of the black beast rapist." Anxious in the pursuit of manhood, a white man who joined a lynch mob could find three kinds of reassurance. He symbolically repressed the beast in himself; he found a sense of power in a ritual that expressed group domination; and he satisfied himself, in the safety of the crowd, that he was man enough to protect the women. Although only about one-third of all the lynchings of black men grew out of charges of rape, it was black-white rape that most whites specified as a justification of lynching in general. The explanation is plain: The image of black-white rape symbolized white men's self-doubt at the most primitive level.

B.   The Double Battle in the 20th Century

Even before World War I began, black leaders were calling for the Army to establish new black regiments and to train blacks to serve as officers. * * * The experience of black soldiers in Europe fell far short of these high hopes. All of them served in segregated units that quickly became a "dumping ground" for ineffective officers. Most black draftees were assigned to labor units. * * * When they returned home, black veterans encountered the same old racial discrimination in a new and virulent form. In the South, their very presence, as living symbols of black manhood, challenged the Jim Crow system at its psychic foundations. The result was a new wave of racial violence, including the lynching of black veterans in their Army uniforms.

After the war the Navy stopped enlisting blacks for general service, relegating black enlisted men to work as stewards. The Army explicitly reaffirmed its policy of racial segregation, and kept blacks ineligible for service as airplane pilots or radio signalmen. As another world war approached, black leaders had good reason for announcing that they would resist efforts to restrict black troops to labor units. * * *

More than 1,000,000 black men and about 4,000 black women served in the [armed] forces during [World War II]. Some 900,000 of the men served in the Army, about three-quarters of them in menial jobs such as "road building, stevedoring, laundry, and fumigating." Even the training of blacks for combat was exceptional; and in 1942, when someone suggested to General George Marshall, the Army Chief of Staff, that black troops be sent to fight in North Africa, he responded that the commanders there would object. As in the Civil War and World War I, blacks had to "fight for the right to fight." On this front, despite a steady drumbeat of criticism from black newspapers and black leaders, the services mostly resisted change.

Occasionally, however, those who were agitating for a racially inclusive military force could win a small victory. In 1942 the Navy announced that it would no longer limit black enlistees to messmen's duties, but would allow blacks to volunteer for general service—which, in this case, meant other support duties. By the end of the war, black enlistees constituted about four percent of the Navy and two and a half percent of the Marine Corps. Segregation remained the rule, however; given the problems of separation on shipboard, in 1944 the Navy established two ships with all-black crews. Soon thereafter a new Secretary of the Navy ordered integration of the crews on twenty-five auxiliary ships.

Around the same time the Army, which had not placed black combat troops in the line, was ordered to do so by a War Department that was reacting to political criticism. In Europe, when infantrymen became scarce, the Army inserted some black platoons into larger combat units. In the Army Air Force the black pilots of the segregated ninety-ninth Pursuit Squadron performed well. Even so, Army officials sought to minimize publicity about the achievements of black soldiers, to avoid blurring the Army's public image.

As the Navy's preposterous deployment of separate-but-equal vessels illustrated, the services' segregation policy was costly. New and separate units had to be organized and staffed, and separate training facilities had to be built; given the disparity in educational opportunities for blacks and whites before they entered the service, segregation prevented the most effective training and assignment of black soldiers and sailors. The main costs of segregation, however, lay in another dimension of human experience, one in which the problem of manhood was central. In 1941, before the attack on Pearl Harbor, William H. Hastie, an aide to Secretary of War Henry L. Stimson (and later the first black judge of the United States Court of Appeals), had written to his boss, criticizing the segregation of the Army in the strongest terms:

> [The segregationist] philosophy is not working.... In tactical units of the Army, the Negro is taught to be a fighting man[,] ... a soldier. It is impossible to create a dual personality which will be on the one hand a fighting man toward the foreign enemy, and on the other, a craven who will accept treatment as less than a man at home. One hears with increasing frequency from colored soldiers the sentiment that since they have been called to fight they might just as well do their fighting here and now.

General Marshall, asked to respond, had said that segregation was an established American custom, that "the level of intelligence and occupational skill of the Negro population is considerably below that of the white," and that "experiments within the Army in the solution of social problems are fraught with danger to efficiency, discipline, and morale."

The connection between this assessment and the historic anxieties of white men about the rivalry of black males is not hard to see. Marshall's unstated assumption was that white soldiers would lack confidence in blacks and be hostile to them, for they defined black men in general as incompetent and cowardly. Furthermore, integrating the Army would eventually result in placing black men in some positions of leadership; white soldiers would not accept this inversion of the historic racial definition of authority. Like all the Army's top leaders, Marshall had served in World War I and remembered the old accusations against black troops. But his assumption about the effect of integration on white attitudes proved mistaken. At the end of the war the Army took a survey of white soldiers who had served in combat alongside black platoons. At first, they said, they were resentful. But three-quarters of them said "their regard for the Negro had risen" as a result of the experience. By doing their jobs well, black soldiers expressed their competence and so, in this limited way, performed functions of education and persuasion. * * *

NOTES ON THE LEGALITY OF RACIAL SEGREGATION IN THE U.S. ARMED FORCES (1940s)[a]

Although there were limited experiments with desegregated units near the end of World War II, the armed forces remained officially segregated

---

a. The sources for this note are Richard Dalfiume, *Desegregation of the U.S. Armed Forces* (1969); Ulysees Lee, *The United States* *Army in World War II, Special Studies: The Employment of Negro Troops* (1966); Morris MacGregor, Jr., *Integration of the Armed*

through the end of the war. The Karst thesis suggests that desegregation would be very hard to accomplish in fact. Consider the following further context:

1. *The Uniform Resistance of the Top Brass to Desegregation.* Virtually all the nation's military leaders in the 1940s were opposed to racial integration. The military's top brass during World War II not only refused to integrate their armed forces, but were also reluctant to assign responsible duties to black units because of their "general consensus of opinion that colored units are inferior to the performance of white troops, except for service duties, * * * due to the inherent psychology of the colored race and their need for leadership" [Memo from General R.W. Crawford to General Eisenhower, Apr. 2, 1942, quoted in Dalfiume 60]. All the branches of the armed services in the 1940s concentrated African Americans in "service" branches because of the "general assumption within the armed forces that Negroes could perform only unskilled jobs and that they were particularly suited for labor units" [Dalfiume 61]. Recall General George Marshall's comment, quoted in the Karst article.

"The racist belief that the Negro was a natural coward was the real objection to integration by many in the Army" in 1949 [Dalfiume 188–89]. Lieutenant General Edward Almond wrote in 1941 that integration weakens the "efficiency" of the armed forces. "There is no question in my mind of the inherent difference in races. This is not racism—it is common sense and understanding. Those who ignore these differences merely interfere with the combat effectiveness of battle units." [Almond Letter, quoted in MacGregor 441.] The Army backed up such assertions by reference to polls taken in 1942 showing that more than 90% of the white soldiers supported segregated units, as did 30–40% of the black soldiers [MacGregor 40]. Similar evidence existed for the Navy. In 1940, Admiral W.R. Sexton wrote to the Secretary of the Navy that if "colored men" served in the Navy, "teamwork, harmony, and ship efficiency [would be] seriously handicapped" because of the attitudes of white sailors [*Blacks in the Military* 135].

2. *The Attitudes of Black and White Soldiers During World War II.* Why were attitudes so sour? Theoreticians such as Karst maintain that a large and maybe preponderant part of the tension between the races was sexual in nature. Quite by accident, we found internal military documents providing first-hand evidence regarding this thesis.[b] Even though U.S. forces in

Forces, 1940–1965 chs. 2–3 (1981); Bernard Nalty, *Strength for the Fight: A History of Black Americans in the Military* (1986); *Blacks in the Military: Essential Documents* (Bernard Nalty & Morris MacGregor, Jr. eds. 1981).

    The Army made this argument in 1949: "The soldier on the battlefield deserves to have, and must have, utmost confidence in his fellow soldiers. They must eat together, sleep together, and all too frequently die together. There can be no friction in their every-day living that might bring on failure in battle. A chain is as strong as its weakest link, and this is true of the Army unit on the battlefield." Quoted in Dalfiume 189 n.38.

    b. In gathering materials for another book project at the National Archives (Suitland, Maryland), we came across Army morale records that are based upon the Army's

Europe were racially segregated during World War II, strong racial tensions existed. In a 1942 survey, the Army found big problems at the two camps it surveyed which had significant percentages of African Americans. One-third of the soldiers in one of the camps emphasized "the Negro problem" in their morale surveys. The report reprinted the two most extreme statements:

> [One survey response:] Negro troops have the girls come down to camp and call for them. If anything will make a Southern's Blood run hot it is to see this happen. Things around this camp is getting pretty hot about these negro troops and white [English] girls. If it keeps on going as it is we will have a nice negro lynching down here and then things will be better.

> [A different response:] The Negro problem has been very poorly handled here. In my outfit it is now "the thing to hate" the negros. Every effort must be made to show the white soldiers that the negro soldiers are just members of our own army, fighting for the same "freedoms". Actually what is taking place in our army today is nothing more disgraceful than what Hitler is doing to minorities in Germany. I joined the American Army to fight against the persecution of minorities. I resent that our army actually practices the same type of persecution.

[G–1 Section, European Theatre of Operations, "Survey of Soldier Opinion, European Theatre of Operations, Sept. 14–26, 1942."]

Army censors read the mail of American soldiers stationed in Europe and reported on the racial concerns discussed in the letters home. African–American soldiers often reported loneliness in wholly white surroundings but sometimes also reported their surprise that the English were "swell" to them. The English women in particular were attracted to men of color. Some of the soldiers dated English women, and this raised the hackles of white soldiers to no end. Illustrative of the many letters are the following:

> [A black T/5 wrote:] Nowhere to go except to a show. I am not going to town at night. It is too dangerous. Our white soldiers make our life miserable and I do not want to come into a fight. In case that something should happen the colored fellow so and so would not get any justice.

> [A white private wrote:] I have seen nice looking white girls going with a coon. They think they are hot stuff. The girls here are so dumb it's pitiful. Wait till Georgia gets these *educated* negroes back there again.

> [A white corporal wrote:] Already we have found a little trouble here for ourselves. It seems that several outfits of colored troops preceded us over here and have succeeded pretty well in salting away the local

interviews with soldiers and, more interestingly, its reading the soldiers' mail to their lovers and families. The documents quoted in text can all be found in Record Group 338, Records of U.S. Army Commands, 1942 ff, European Theatre, Adjutant General's Section, Administrative Branch, Classified General Correspondence, 1942–44, 1945, Decimal File 250.1.

feminine pulchritude, what little there is of it. They have the natives convinced that they are "full blooded American Indians" and the girls really go for them in preference to the white boys, a fact that irks the boys no end, especially those of the outfit from the south. No doubt there will be some bloodshed in the near future.

[Base Postal Censor Morale Reports, September 1942, quoting from soldiers' mail.] These are only a few of the many comments picked up by military censors.

It was reported, also in 1942, that white officers in charge of a black unit stationed in Pennsylvania issued the following order: "any association between the colored soldiers and white women, whether voluntary or not, would be considered rape." The punishment for this offense was the death penalty. [Dalfiume 69.]

3.   *The Constitutional Status of Racial Segregation, 1940s.* When the Fourteenth Amendment to the Constitution was adopted in 1868, African Americans had served in the U.S. armed forces only in segregated units, and virtually all other institutions of public life also enforced some degree of segregation. When a challenge to Southern Jim Crow segregation reached the Supreme Court in 1896, the Court upheld the policy against equal protection challenge. The Court in *Plessy v. Ferguson*, 163 U.S. 537 (1896), justified the obvious racial classification on the ground that the law could not realistically "abolish distinctions based upon color, or to enforce social, as distinguished from political, equality, or a commingling of the two races upon terms unsatisfactory to either."

Starting in the 1910s, however, the Supreme Court was more receptive to challenges against racial discrimination. Upholding the conviction of a citizen for disobeying a curfew imposed only upon Japanese Americans, the Court in *Hirabayashi v. United States*, 320 U.S. 81, 100 (1943), stated: "Distinctions between citizens solely because of their ancestry are by their very nature odious to a free people whose institutions are founded upon the doctrine of equality. * * * [R]acial discriminations are in most circumstances irrelevant and therefore prohibited[.]" A bitterly divided Court in *Korematsu v. United States*, 323 U.S. 214 (1944), upheld the detention of Japanese Americans in prison camps. Still, the majority announced a key precept of equal protection law:

> [A]ll legal restrictions which curtail the civil rights of a single group are immediately suspect. That is not to say that all such restrictions are unconstitutional. It is to say that courts must subject them to the most rigid scrutiny. Pressing public necessity may sometimes justify the existence of such restrictions; racial antagonism never can. *Id.* at 216.

Korematsu is the first case to announce that racial classifications must be subjected to strict scrutiny: Courts will invalidate laws classifying on the basis of race unless the state shows it has a compelling goal and that the racial classification is necessary to achieve that goal (i.e., nonracial alternatives are not available). *Korematsu* also stands for the propositions that military necessity is the sort of state interest that can satisfy strict scrutiny and that the Court is typically deferential to the national government when it makes claims based upon national security, especially in wartime. Note, finally, that Japanese Americans, like African Americans, served in segregated military units during World War II. After World War II, the Court decided several very important race cases. Although the reasoning in each case was narrowly drawn, the pattern of decisions was friendly to claims against racial apartheid.

Under political pressure, President Harry Truman initiated a process for desegregating the armed forces in 1948. As he recalls it, see Merle Miller, *Plain Speaking: An Oral Biography of Harry S. Truman* 79 note (1974), every top military official he consulted was opposed to desegregation of the armed forces. On the other hand, the report of the President's Committee on Civil Rights had just condemned racial segregation in the military. The Committee found that "separate but equal" was a myth and condemned segregation generally. "Prejudice in any area is an ugly, undemocratic phenomenon," but "in the armed services where all men run the risk of death, it is particularly repugnant." President's Committee on Civil Rights, *To Secure These Rights* 41 (1947). The Committee rejected the view that the armed services could not be used for social experimentation, because it found that attitudes were inevitably formed or reformed in the caldron of battle, and that the military was the perfect place to "prove that the majority and minorities in our population can train and work and fight side by side in cooperation and harmony" [*id.* at 47].

NOTE ON THE TRUMAN ORDER AND THE PROCESS OF DESEGREGATING THE ARMED FORCES

In Executive Order 9981, issued on July 26, 1948, President Truman announced a policy of "equality of treatment and opportunity for all persons in the armed services without regard to race, color, religion or national origin. This policy shall be put into effect as rapidly as possible, having due regard to the time required to effectuate any necessary changes without impairing efficiency or morale." The order also created a Committee on Equality of Treatment and Opportunity in the Armed Services to work with each branch to implement the new norm. Charles Fahy was to be the Committee's chair.

The negotiations proceeded in different ways for different branches, given recent developments within each branch. The Air Force had developed its own plan for integration earlier in 1948, and that plan was immediately acceptable to the Fahy Committee; substantial integration was achieved in 1949. The Navy was at the same time committed to a policy of gradual integration, and the Fahy Committee was able to work out problems it had with the Navy's plans, yielding tangible policy commitments to integration in the Navy by mid–1949. The Army was committed to a separate but equal vision of equality. After years of negotiations, the Fahy Committee and the Army reached agreement on a new gradual integration policy on January 16, 1950. The Korean War speeded up the process of integration, and on October 30, 1954 the Secretary of Defense announced that the last racially segregated unit in the armed forces had been abolished.

Given officer opposition to integration as destructive of troop morale and unit cohesion, the Army conducted studies of the adjustment by troops to integration. The Army's G–1 study reported that integration of black soldiers into white combat units in Korea had been accomplished generally "without undue friction and with better utilization of manpower." Combat commanders "almost unanimously favor integration" [DA Personnel Research Team, "A Preliminary Report on Personnel Research Data" (July 28, 1951), quoted in MacGregor 441], a striking contrast to their pre-integration beliefs. Outside consultants also reviewed the situation, under the code name Project CLEAR. They reported that integration had not lowered white morale but greatly increased black morale; virtually all black soldiers supported integration, while white soldiers were not overtly hostile or were supportive; and in most instances white attitudes toward integration became more favorable with firsthand experience ["A Preliminary Report on the Utilization of Negro Manpower" (June 30, 1951), described in MacGregor 442].[c] These findings were pretty much the same as those of secret Army surveys conducted during World War II, when the Army had desegregated a few units, found few if any problems, and then suppressed the findings.

Reporter Lee Nichols interviewed members of all services in 1953. He found that blacks and whites were amazed at how smoothly integration actually proceeded once the armed services decided to do it, but that blacks and whites continued to have different attitudes about military policy and practice. Whites tended to expect blacks to "prove themselves" in their assignments, while blacks were often skeptical that equal opportunities were really available to them. Tensions between blacks and whites were later to be even more problematic during the Vietnam War, but on the whole observers of all stripes believe that racial integration of the armed forces has been relatively successful from the perspectives of whites, African Americans, and other people of color. Lee Nichols, *Breakthrough on the Color Front* (1954).

---

c. This was the preliminary report. A seven-volume final report was prepared in November 1951. It was later published under the title *Social Research and the Desegregation of the U.S. Army* (Leo Bogart ed. 1969).

THE EXCLUSION OF WOMEN FROM COMBAT

PART A.   A HISTORY OF WOMEN IN THE MILITARY, 1861–1971[a]

Officially, women, like African Americans, have been excluded from the armed services for most of our history and then have been segregated once the formal exclusion ended. (Unofficially, a surprising number of women-passing-as-men served in the American military, and in combat roles, during the nineteenth century. *E.g.*, Sarah Emma Edmonds Seelye, *Nurse and Spy* (1864).) Women were officially welcomed as nurses during the Civil War, an experience replicated in the Spanish–American War, but in both cases the women were viewed as civilian auxiliaries rather than as military personnel. World War I saw 34,000 women serve in the Nurse Corps of the various branches of service. The Navy started taking female yeomen in March 1917, but the Army refused to accept women. Congress in 1925 prohibited the Navy from enlisting women.

The issue of women in the armed services went no further until General George Marshall became Army Chief of Staff in 1939. Believing that the U.S. would be hard put to staff a war machine, Marshall insisted that women be considered for service. Pearl Harbor rendered Marshall's plan urgent. Congress created the Women's Army Auxiliary Corps (WAAC, later WAC when the Auxiliary dropped out) in May 1942, Public Law No. 77–554, and a similar bill for the Navy and Marines was enacted in July, Public Law No. 77–689 (creating the Navy Women's Reserve, later called WAVES, and the Marine Corps Women's Reserve). The Air Force also acquired a female auxiliary, called SPAR (for "Semper Paratus [sic]— Always Ready").

World War II created unprecedented personnel needs which transformed the women's auxiliaries. By 1944 women were performing a wide range of other military functions as well, including control tower operators, radio repair people and operators, air navigators, parachute riggers, gunner instructors, and engine mechanics. Most women, however, served in clerical jobs. General Eisenhower opposed women in the armed forces until he saw

a. For the account that follows, see Major General Jeanne Holm, USAF, *Women in the Military: An Unfinished Revolution* (1982); Judith Hicks Stiehm, *Arms and the Enlisted Woman* (1989); Linda Bird Francke, *Ground Zero: The Gender Wars in the Military* (1997); Lori Kornblum, "Women Warriors in a Men's World: The Combat Exclusion," 2 *L. & Inequality* 351 (1984).

how valuable they were in defending Britain, and after that he enthusiastically welcomed their support in the North African and then European Theatres. Previously skeptical male officers rated women successful soldiers. By the end of World War II, there were nearly 100,000 WACs, 86,000 WAVES, 18,000 Women Marines, and 11,000 SPARs, as well as over 18,000 nurses serving in the U.S. armed forces. Although most women as well as men were discharged after the war, General Eisenhower insisted that the WACs continue as a permanent part of the Army.

The post-war period was one of some consolidation and much retrenchment. Although the federal government established a permanent role for women when it enacted the Women's Armed Services Act of 1948, Public Law No. 80–625, this so-called "Integration Act" required segregation and marginalization of women in significant ways. The Act bestowed permanent military status on the women's corps and their members, but also imposed a 2% cap on the number of women who could serve in each branch, restricted the number of female officers and established a separate promotion list for women, set higher minimum ages for women wanting to enlist than were required for men, and allowed women to claim husbands or children as dependent only upon a showing of actual dependency (it was automatically assumed for the dependents of military men). Most important, the Act authorized the service Secretaries to assign women duties as they saw fit, provided that women could not be assigned flight or ship duties when the craft are "engaged in combat missions." This was a strange "integration," separate but deliberately unequal.

The situation evolved in more conservative directions after 1948, which turned out to be the high point for almost a generation. During the Korean War, women played less of a role than they did in World War II; they were no more than 1% of our troops in Korea. Relatedly, the training of military women grew increasingly obsessed with maintaining their ladylike image. "Hair styles had to be fashionable but 'conservative' and 'appropriate' to the uniform. Elaborate beehives and large boufants were frowned upon but were preferable to very short 'mannish' styles (there must be no appearance of lesbianism). According to Navy regulation, 'Hair shall be arranged and shaped to present a conservative, feminine appearance.' " (Holm 181–82.) The military's fetishism about appearance led to elaborate debates and regulations about skirt length (below the knee), pumps (in) versus boots (out), and hats and gloves (mandatory for most occasions).

The war in Vietnam created a substantial demand for women in a full range of military jobs. At the same time, the women's liberation movement questioned women's severely unequal treatment. In Public Law No. 90–130, Congress removed the formal restrictions on promotion of women. The Tet offensive in 1968 saw women perform valorously and valuably; opposition to women's service among male officers and soldiers eroded. "[The] belief that the frail (or fair) sex will tremble at the first sign of trouble is not true. * * * I observed the female military members performing their duties no different than anyone else." [Quoted in Holm 237.]

The military's policy of separate but unequal imploded after 1972, and a series of interconnected policies were terminated: segregation in procurement and training, gender quotas for promotions (stealthily continued after 1967), unequal family policies, and some of the paternalism. Some of these changes were made in anticipation of adoption of the ERA, which supporters and opponents agreed would require the armed services to end their formal discrimination against women in the draft and even in combat duty. Other changes were in response to aggressive congressional pressure. Yet other changes were made, apparently, in response to lawsuits and Supreme Court doctrine, which in the early 1970s was evolving rather rapidly.

PART B.   PARTIAL INTEGRATION OF WOMEN IN THE ARMED FORCES, 1971–81

Before 1971, the U.S. Supreme Court had never invalidated a statute because it discriminated against women or relied on a sex-based classification. The first decision to do so, *Reed v. Reed*, 404 U.S. 71 (1971), invalidated an Idaho statute preferring men over women as executors of estates. The next major case involved one of the policies established in the Integration Act of 1948. (See Chapter 3, Section 1 for an introduction to the Supreme Court's evolving scrutiny of sex-based classifications and the arguments for and against the heightened scrutiny given such classifications since the mid–1970s.)

Sharon Frontiero and Joseph Frontiero v. Elliott Richardson

United States Supreme Court, 1973.
411 U.S. 677, 93 S.Ct. 1764, 36 L.Ed.2d 583.

[Excerpted in Chapter 3, Section 1]

PROBLEM 7–1

CONSTITUTIONAL ISSUES FOR WOMEN IN THE MILITARY, AFTER FRONTIERO

(A) All–Male Service Academies. West Point, the Naval Academy, and the Air Force Academy had always been exclusively male. In 1972, Senator Jacob Javits nominated a woman for the Naval Academy, which refused to consider her. Deputy Secretary of Defense William Clements, Jr. categorically rejected the Javits proposition: "Training cadets at the Academies is expensive, and it is imperative that these opportunities be reserved for those with potential for combat roles." Javits' nominee sues the Naval Academy after *Frontiero*. What arguments should the plaintiff make? How would a court rule? See *Waldie v. Schlesinger*, 509 F.2d 508 (D.C.Cir. 1974).[b]

(B) The Combat Exclusions. In 1977, 10 U.S.C. § 6015 (subsequently amended), provided that "women may not be assigned to duty in aircraft that are engaged in combat missions nor may they be assigned to vessels of the Navy other than hospital ships and transports." This was a statutory exclusion applicable to the Navy and Air Force; the Army by its own regulations excluded women from combat in 1972. In 1976, a Supreme Court majority held that sex-based classifications are subjected to an intermediate version of heightened scrutiny. See *Craig v. Boren*, 429 U.S. 190 (1976) (Chapter 3, Section 1). What arguments can be made against the combat exclusion after *Craig*? See *Owens v. Brown*, 455 F.Supp. 291 (D.D.C.1978) (a successful lawsuit).

(C) Registration for the Draft. Responding to Soviet aggression in Afghanistan, President Carter in February 1980 requested congressional authority to register women as well as men for the draft. Many legislators opposed this request, on grounds of (1) the limited number of noncombat jobs available to women, (2) the strain on training resources if equal numbers of women were introduced, and (3) the many ancillary issues that needed to be addressed (*e.g.*, the draft status of mothers). After extensive hearings, both House and Senate rejected the President's proposal by large margins. The District Court for the Eastern District of Pennsylvania rules that the new policy is unconstitutional. The Supreme Court stays the lower court injunction and accepts the case for immediate appeal. How will it rule? How should it rule? Read the next case.

Bernard Rostker v. Robert Goldberg et al.

United States Supreme Court, 1981.
453 U.S. 57, 101 S.Ct. 2646, 69 L.Ed.2d 478.

■ Justice Rehnquist delivered the opinion of the Court.

The question presented is whether the Military Selective Service Act, 50 U.S.C. App. § 451 *et seq.* (1976 ed. and Supp. III), violates the Fifth Amendment to the United States Constitution in authorizing the President to require the registration of males and not females.

Congress is given the power under the Constitution "To raise and support Armies," "To provide and maintain a Navy," and "To make Rules for the Government and Regulation of the land and naval Forces." Art. I, § 8, cls. 12–14. Pursuant to this grant of authority Congress has enacted the Military Selective Service Act, 50 U.S.C. App. § 451 *et seq.* (1976 ed. and Supp. III) (the MSSA or the Act). Section 3 of the Act, 62 Stat. 605, as

b. Public Law No. 94–106 (Oct. 1975), statutorily integrated the academies, with the first women admitted for the 1976–77 school year. For two divergent factual as well as normative accounts of gender integration at the Air Force Academy, compare Judith Hicks Stiehm, *Bring Me Men and Women: Mandated Change at the United States Air Force Academy* (1981), with Brian Mitchell, *Weak Link: The Feminization of the American Military* (1989).

amended, 50 U.S.C. App. § 453, empowers the President, by proclamation, to require the registration of "every male citizen" and male resident aliens between the ages of 18 and 26. The purpose of this registration is to facilitate any eventual conscription: pursuant to § 4(a) of the Act, 62 Stat. 605, as amended, 50 U.S.C. App. § 454 (a), those persons required to register under § 3 are liable for training and service in the Armed Forces. The MSSA registration provision serves no other purpose beyond providing a pool for subsequent induction. * * *

This is not * * * merely a case involving the customary deference accorded congressional decisions. The case arises in the context of Congress' authority over national defense and military affairs, and perhaps in no other area has the Court accorded Congress greater deference. * * *

The Solicitor General argues, largely on the basis of the foregoing cases emphasizing the deference due Congress in the area of military affairs and national security, that this Court should scrutinize the MSSA only to determine if the distinction drawn between men and women bears a rational relation to some legitimate government purpose, and should not examine the Act under the heightened scrutiny with which we have approached gender-based discrimination [*Craig*]. We do not think that the substantive guarantee of due process or certainty in the law will be advanced by any further "refinement" in the applicable tests as suggested by the Government. Announced degrees of "deference" to legislative judgments, just as levels of "scrutiny" which this Court announces that it applies to particular classifications made by a legislative body, may all too readily become facile abstractions used to justify a result. In this case the courts are called upon to decide whether Congress, acting under an explicit constitutional grant of authority, has by that action transgressed an explicit guarantee of individual rights which limits the authority so conferred. Simply labeling the legislative decision "military" on the one hand or "gender-based" on the other does not automatically guide a court to the correct constitutional result.

No one could deny that under the test of *Craig* v. *Boren*, the Government's interest in raising and supporting armies is an "important governmental interest." Congress and its Committees carefully considered and debated two alternative means of furthering that interest: The first was to register only males for potential conscription, and the other was to register both sexes. Congress chose the former alternative. When that decision is challenged on equal protection grounds, the question a court must decide is not which alternative it would have chosen, had it been the primary decision-maker, but whether that chosen by Congress denies equal protection of the laws.

Nor can it be denied * * * that judicial deference to such congressional exercise of authority is at its apogee when legislative action under the congressional authority to raise and support armies and make rules and regulations for their governance is challenged. As previously noted, deference does not mean abdication. The reconciliation between the deference due Congress and our own constitutional responsibility is perhaps best instanced in *Schlesinger* v. *Ballard*, 419 U.S., at 510, where we stated:

> "This Court has recognized that 'it is the primary business of armies and navies to fight or be ready to fight wars should the occasion arise.' [*U.S. ex rel.*] *Toth* v. *Quarles*, 350 U.S. 11, 17. The responsibility for determining how best our Armed Forces shall attend to that business rests with Congress, see U.S. Const., Art. I, § 8, cls. 12–14, and with the President. See U.S. Const., Art. II, § 2, cl. 1. We cannot say that, in exercising its broad constitutional power here, Congress has violated the Due Process Clause of the Fifth Amendment." * * *

The MSSA established a plan for maintaining "adequate armed strength . . . to insure the security of [the] Nation." 50 U.S.C. App. § 451(b). Registration is the first step "in a united and continuous process designed to raise an army speedily and efficiently," *Falbo* v. *United States*, 320 U.S. 549, 553 (1944), and Congress provided for the reactivation of registration in order to "provid[e] the means for the early delivery of inductees in an emergency." S. Rep. No. 96–826, at 156. * * * Congress rather clearly linked the need for renewed registration with its views on the character of a subsequent draft. * * * As Senator Warner put it, "I equate registration with the draft." *Hearings on S. 2294*, at 1197. * * *

Congress determined that any future draft, which would be facilitated by the registration scheme, would be characterized by a need for combat troops. The Senate Report explained, in a specific finding later adopted by both Houses, that "[i]f mobilization were to be ordered in a wartime scenario the primary manpower need would be for combat replacements." S. Rep. No. 96–826, p. 160 (1980); see *id.*, at 158. * * *

Women as a group, however, unlike men as a group, are not eligible for combat. * * * In the words of the Senate Report:

> "The principle that women should not intentionally and routinely engage in combat is fundamental, and enjoys wide support among our people. It is universally supported by military leaders who have testified before the Committee. . . . Current law and policy exclude women from being assigned to combat in our military forces, and the Committee reaffirms this policy." S. Rep. No. 96–826, *supra*, at 157.

The Senate Report specifically found that "[w]omen should not be intentionally or routinely placed in combat positions in our military services." *Id.*, at 160. See S. Rep. No. 96–226, *supra*, at 9. The President expressed his intent to continue the current military policy precluding women from combat, and appellees present their argument concerning registration against the background of such restrictions on the use of women in combat. * * *

The existence of the combat restrictions clearly indicates the basis for Congress' decision to exempt women from registration. The purpose of registration was to prepare for a draft of combat troops. Since women are excluded from combat, Congress concluded that they would not be needed in the event of a draft, and therefore decided not to register them. * * *

The District Court stressed that the military need for women was irrelevant to the issue of their registration. As that court put it: "Congress could not constitutionally require registration under the MSSA of only black citizens or only white citizens, or single out any political or religious group simply because those groups contain sufficient persons to fill the needs of the Selective Service System." This reasoning is beside the point. The reason women are exempt from registration is not because military needs can be met by drafting men. This is not a case of Congress arbitrarily choosing to burden one of two similarly situated groups, such as would be the case with an all-black or all-white, or an all-Catholic or all-Lutheran, or an all-Republican or all-Democratic registration. Men and women, because of the combat restrictions on women, are simply not similarly situated for purposes of a draft or registration for a draft.

Congress' decision to authorize the registration of only men, therefore, does not violate the [Equal Protection component of the Fifth Amendment's] Due Process Clause. The exemption of women from registration is not only sufficiently but also closely related to Congress' purpose in authorizing registration. The fact that Congress and the Executive have decided that women should not serve in combat fully justifies Congress in not authorizing their registration, since the purpose of registration is to develop a pool of potential combat troops. * * *

■ [The dissenting opinion of JUSTICE WHITE (joined by JUSTICE BRENNAN) is omitted.]

■ JUSTICE MARSHALL, with whom JUSTICE BRENNAN joins, dissenting. * * *

The Government does not defend the exclusion of women from registration on the ground that preventing women from serving in the military is substantially related to the effectiveness of the Armed Forces. Indeed, the successful experience of women serving in all branches of the Armed Services would belie any such claim. Some 150,000 women volunteers are presently on active service in the military, and their number is expected to increase to over 250,000 by 1985. At the congressional hearings, representatives of both the Department of Defense and the Armed Services testified that the participation of women in the All–Volunteer Armed Forces has contributed substantially to military effectiveness. * * *

* * * [The majority] states that "Congress determined that any future draft, which would be facilitated by the registration scheme, would be characterized by a need for combat troops." The Court then reasons that since women are not eligible for assignment to combat, Congress' decision to exclude them from registration is not unconstitutional discrimination inasmuch as "[m]en and women, because of the combat restrictions on women, are simply not similarly situated for purposes of a draft or registration for a draft." There a certain logic to this reasoning, but the Court's approach is fundamentally flawed.

* * * The relevant inquiry under the *Craig v. Boren* test is not whether a *gender-neutral* classification would substantially advance important governmental interests. Rather, the question is whether the gender-

based classification is itself substantially related to the achievement of the asserted governmental interest. Thus, the Government's task in this case is to demonstrate that excluding women from registration substantially furthers the goal of preparing for a draft of combat troops. Or to put it another way, the Government must show that registering women would substantially impede its efforts to prepare for such a draft. Under our precedents, the Government cannot meet this burden without showing that a gender-neutral statute would be a less effective means of attaining this end. As the court explained in *Orr v. Orr*, 440 U.S. [268, 283 (1979)] (emphasis added):

> "Legislative classifications which distribute benefits and burdens on the basis of gender *carry the inherent risk of reinforcing sexual stereotypes about the 'proper place' of women and their need for special protection. . . .* Where, as here, the [Government's] . . . purposes are as well served by a gender-neutral classification as one that gender classifies and therefore carries with it the baggage of sexual stereotypes, the [Government] cannot be permitted to classify on the basis of sex."

In this case, the Government makes no claim that preparing for a draft of combat troops cannot be accomplished just as effectively by *registering* both men and women but *drafting* only men if only men turn out to be needed. Nor can the Government argue that this alternative entails the additional cost and administrative inconvenience of registering women. This Court has repeatedly stated that the administrative convenience of employing a gender classification is not an adequate constitutional justification under the *Craig v. Boren* test.

The fact that registering women in no way obstructs the governmental interest in preparing for a draft of combat troops points up a second flaw in the Court's analysis. The Court essentially reduces the question of the constitutionality of male-only *registration* to the validity of a hypothetical program for *conscripting* only men. The Court posits a draft in which *all* conscripts are either assigned to those specific combat posts presently closed to women or must be available for rotation into such positions. By so doing, the Court is able to conclude that registering women would be no more than a "gestur[e] of superficial equality," since women are necessarily ineligible for every position to be filled in its hypothetical draft. If it could indeed be guaranteed in advance that conscription would be reimposed by Congress only in circumstances where, and in a form under which, all conscripts would have to be trained for and assigned to combat or combat rotation positions from which women are categorically excluded, then it could be argued that registration of women would be pointless.

* * * [Such an] argument rests on a premise that is demonstrably false. As noted, the majority simply assumes that registration prepares for a draft in which *every* draftee must be available for assignment to combat. But the majority's draft scenario finds no support in either the testimony before Congress, or more importantly, in the findings of the Senate Report. Indeed, the scenario appears to exist only in the Court's imagination, for

even the Government represents only that "in the event of mobilization, *approximately two-thirds* of the demand on the induction system would be for *combat skills.*" Brief for Appellant 29 (emphasis added). [Justice Marshall then demonstrated, from the Senate Report, that Congress itself assumed that only most, and not all, of those registered would ever be drafted, and that most, but not all, of the draftees would serve in combat roles.]

* * * All four Service chiefs agreed that there are no military reasons for refusing to register women, and uniformly advocated requiring registration of women. The military's position on the issue was summarized by then Army Chief of Staff General Rogers: "[W]omen should be required to register for the reason that [Marine Corps Commandant] General Wilson mentioned, which is in order for us to have an inventory of what the available strength is within the military qualified pool in this country."
* * *

NOTE ON *ROSTKER* AND JUDICIAL DEFERENCE TO EXECUTIVE AND CONGRESSIONAL MILITARY POLICIES

The Court's decision in *Rostker* is hard to square with the *Craig* test, especially as applied in the VMI and other cases (Chapter 3, Section 1). Although the Court invoked important state goals, the connection between those goals and the sex-based classification was questionable; the goals could easily have been achieved with a registration system including women. Moreover, the sex-based scheme also tracked traditional stereotypes (male warriors protecting women-folk; nurturing mother, wandering father). Finally, the most plausible current justification for the exclusion of women was that a simple sex-based scheme was easier or cheaper to administer—but *Craig* and other precedents had specifically rejected ease-of-administration as a justification for sex-based classifications.

One might say that *Rostker* was just a mistake, superseded by the Court's tougher post–1981 sex discrimination jurisprudence, but there is no evidence a majority of the Supreme Court views *Rostker* with any such skepticism. And, from an institutionalist perspective, the decision can be defended. The federal judiciary defers to Congress and the President with regard to matters of military and immigration policies. *Deference* to another institution's line-drawing means that the Court will give the institution some latitude to make decisions the Court would not have made—or would not allow other institutions to make.[c] (The Court does not *defer* to another institution's policy if the Justices *agree* with the policy or its constitutionality.) The Court might defer to the other institution in three different ways:

c. The classic example of deference to military policies is *Goldman v. Weinberger*, 475 U.S. 503 (1986), which upheld the Army's dress code (barring unauthorized head gear) as applied to bar a Jewish officer from wearing a yarmulke while in uniform. Such a rule would surely have been invalidated if enforced by the state as an employer outside of the military context, but a divided Court upheld the application against First Amendment attack.

(1) by accepting its normative understanding of its proper or acceptable *ends*, (2) by giving it leeway in the choice of *means* through which it pursues its ends, or (3) by giving it the benefit of the doubt as to factual assertions needed to connect proper ends with sex-based means. Recall *Korematsu* and *Hirabayashi*, where the Court gave Congress and the President leeway to adopt race-based national security policies and credited questionable military assertions about the presumptive disloyalty of Japanese Americans.

Deference can be justified on grounds of the other institution's (1) greater democratic legitimacy as a forum for making important value choices, (2) greater competence in drawing lines in a particular policy arena, or (3) implicit or explicit constitutional authorization to have primacy in making such decisions. All three justifications might apply to a President-Congress military policy, to wit: (1) The President and Congress are elected by and accountable to the people; their decisions in dealing with military and foreign affairs are intensely scrutinized by the media and within the political process, and the effects of their decisions are often easy to trace back to the decisionmakers. (2) Federal judges concede that they have little competence in military policy, which often rests upon secret and fast-changing intelligence as well as important judgments about how to manage the armed forces most effectively. That the armed forces are a *specialized total community* makes judicial interference even more risky. (3) The Constitution vests those institutions with unique authority to create and command the armed forces, with little or no textual role for the Court. (Consider problems with each of these arguments for deference in *Rostker* itself.)

The degree of deference accorded Congress in *Rostker* could well have saved the federal armed forces statute struck down in *Frontiero*, a leading sex discrimination precedent. How can the two decisions be reconciled? *Query* also: Before 1948, the Defense Department followed a policy of race-based segregation in our armed forces; the main justification was that integration would undermine unit cohesion and morale, because white soldiers were uncomfortable with, and often hostile to, black soldiers. Had President Truman not ended the policy in 1948, would the Supreme Court have invalidated the de jure segregation in the armed forces after *Brown* and *Bolling*? Or would the Court have deferred?

An issue the Court did not resolve (because plaintiffs did not raise or contest it) in *Rostker* was whether the exclusion of women from combat positions in the armed services was valid or whether such exclusion violated notions of equal protection. Judge John Sirica had struck down 10 U.S.C. 6015, as applied to prevent Navy women from serving at sea. *Owens v. Brown*, 455 F.Supp. 291 (D.D.C.1978) (see Problem 7–1B). Should groups critical of the military's policies have first attacked the exclusion from combat, and then the registration requirements? Does *Rostker* abrogate *Owens*?

PART C.   WOMEN'S COMBAT EXCLUSION AND SEXUAL HARASSMENT AFTER 1981

Although submerged in *Rostker*, the exclusion of women from combat-related positions in the military was already on the national agenda when the Court delivered its much-criticized opinion. While a recurring theme of the history of women in uniform has been the belief that women should not serve in combat positions, military spokesmen were not called upon to defend the exclusion until the 1970s. To this day, they are still struggling to justify it.

Early defenders of the exclusion emphasized "real differences" between women and men in terms of strength (especially lifting and throwing ability) and speed. In hand-to-hand combat, units having women would be at a disadvantage. These arguments seem like pink herrings. If strength is the key factor, then make combat roles turn on strength tests that women as well as men can take to qualify for combat duties. No one disputes that many women are stronger than many men. Moreover, in the technologically sophisticated armed services, hand-to-hand combat is no longer the norm. Many women possess the physical skills for flying airplanes and deploying equipment that men do, and women may have a comparative advantage in some physical skills (possibly stamina) that are more relevant than the ability to bench press 300 pounds.

Relatedly, early defenders of the exclusion maintained that women are not as "aggressive" as men and could not take the stress of combat. They produced no data to support any such claim, however. In fact, the experience of World War II, Korea, and Vietnam suggested that women can handle stress as well or better than men. Critics of the foregoing arguments also reminded the military officials that eerily similar arguments have been advanced against opening any profession to women, from law to the presidency: women are "naturally" less aggressive or able to handle stress and the real world than men. So, too, eerily similar arguments had been advanced against racial integration in the 1940s: African Americans were "naturally" less aggressive or intelligent (or both) than white soldiers. All of these earlier arguments have been discredited by historical experience, and their repeated invocation ought to have diminished credibility.

These arguments were surrogates for deeper concerns. The Superintendent of the Air Force Academy explained that opening combat or even leadership roles to women "offends the dignity of womanhood and ignores the harsh realities of war. * * * Fighting is a man's job and should remain so." General Robert H. Barrow, former Commandant of the Marine Corps, had this to say:

> War is man's work. Biological convergence on the battlefield would not only be dissatisfying in terms of what women could do, but it would be an enormous psychological distraction for the male who wants to think that he's fighting for that woman somewhere behind, not up there in

the same foxhole with him. It tramples the male ego. When you get right down to it, you have to protect the manliness of war.

We got this quote from the Karst article that opened this chapter (38 *UCLA L. Rev.* at 534). Consistent with his overall thesis, Karst argues that the exclusion of women from combat serves the symbolism of Victorian masculinity: men protect women and the family from the outside enemy, a trope that would be disrupted by women fighting for their own protection; war is the greatest test as well as crucible of manhood, a bit of male bonding that would be undermined by women in the foxhole; men are by nature aggressive fighters, in contrast to nurturing passive women. These images are increasingly recognized as stereotypes, and after *Frontiero* it is perilous to ground military policy on such obvious stereotypes. The manliness-of-war argument is losing its appeal and is legally dangerous besides. Is there any refuge for the military's reluctance to allow women to serve in combat roles? Although the author opposes the combat exclusion, the following excerpt is a particularly useful statement of the male-bonding/unit cohesion objection.

Mady Wechsler Segal, "The Argument for Female Combatants"

In *Female Soldiers: Combatants or Noncombatants?* 267, 278–81.
Nancy Loring Goldman, Editor, 1982.*

The willingness to engage in actual combat, to kill and to risk being killed, depends upon a very strong devotion to the group. This commitment to the group is seen as depending, among other motivations, on male bonding. The presence of women would interfere with the process of devotion of men to each other, as women are outsiders who are not privy to the male subculture. There may also be competition among the men for the sexual favors of the women. No real evidence exists to support or refute these arguments. One point is clear: if men believe that women are not part of their group and that they cannot function with women around, this belief will disrupt such functioning and may hinder actual ability to cope with the stress of combat, thereby serving as a self-fulfilling prophecy.

Let me offer an additional explanation for men's resistance to allowing women in combat units. I conjecture that there is a psychological differentiation between the "real world" and combat that enables some men to survive the enormous psychological stress of combat. One survives by preserving a mental picture of the normal world back home to which one will return from the horror world of combat. One is engaged in an elaborate game * * * and when the game is over, one can go home to an intact world. One of the major components of the world back home is women, "our women," who are warm, nurturant, ultra-feminine, and objects of sexual fantasy. Women (at least "our women") are not a part of war. Indeed, one of the reasons for fighting is to protect our women and the rest of what is in that image of the world back home. If we allow these women into combat with us, then this psychological differentiation cannot be maintained, and we lose this psychological defense. * * *

If these speculations are accurate, I do not know precisely what effect women in combat would have on combat unit cohesion. I suspect that the effects have already been felt in military units that used to be all male but now have women, including the academies. Various processes of social change resulting from gender integration have probably already begun and will continue to proceed in creating new styles of interaction in face-to-face working units. It is certainly hoped that women's presence in groups will not automatically result in low cohesion. New images of the "real world back home" may supplant the old ones. The new images may then serve the same psychological functions.

The concern that women in combat units will reduce unit cohesion is reminiscent of arguments that have been used in the past to justify excluding women from other occupations. It was not so long ago that women were excluded from law, medicine, police work, and fire fighting (to name a few). This exclusion was based partly on women's supposed inability as individuals to perform the jobs adequately and partly on the potential disruption of men's interpersonal relations if women were included. While such arguments were accepted in the past, they have now been shown to be fallacious. * * *

Even outside of combat situations, there are certain interpersonal problems already existing in the military that deserve attention. The lack of acceptance of women by many military men creates problems for the women. As in other predominantly male settings, military women often face prejudice from male superiors, peers, and subordinates and face certain male behavior that creates stress for the women. Such behavior includes differential treatment of women that interferes with their job performance and sexual harassment of varying degrees.[d] These problems also exist in institutional settings other than the military, but they must be addressed in the military before women can function most effectively.

The interpersonal problems associated with gender integration of previously all-male settings * * * are similar to problems that were experienced in the process of racial integration of the U.S. armed forces. * * * In the first half of this century, black men were underrepresented in the military and were largely excluded from combat jobs. * * *

* * * Many of the arguments being advanced to justify exclusion of women from combat are reminiscent of those used in the past to bar black men from combat. * * *

---

d. [Eds.] This is an understatement, as subsequent events and studies have revealed, most notably the Tailhook scandal. See Military Personnel and Compensation Subcomm. and Defense Policy Panel of the House Comm. on Armed Services, 102d Congress, 2d Session, Report, *Women in the Military: The Tailhook Affair and the Problem of Sexual Harassment* (Sept. 14, 1992).

The cohesion of military units in general and combat units in particular, need not be based on the exclusion of women. The bonds that tie soldiers to their groups often derive from respect for their fellow group members, based on performance that contributes to the goals of the group (including survival). Such mutual interdependence and affective regard can develop in mixed gender groups. DeFleur's study of the Air Force Academy shows that over the course of the first four years of gender integration, there has been some increase in male acceptance of and interaction with the women. Women are far from being fully accepted and integrated [as of 1982], however, a situation at least partially attributable to the lack of interdependence among cadets.

Intragroup cohesion also depends on having a definition of those who are considered outsiders by the group. Such exclusions need not include all women, just as they need not include all members of other categories, for example, college men or blacks. Rather, women who are seen as poor soldiers (or as not being soldiers) are excluded, while women who are seen as good combat soldiers can be fully integrated into the group. * * *

NOTE ON CONGRESSIONAL RESPONSE TO THE DEMAND FOR A COMBAT ROLE FOR WOMEN

In 1991, Congress repealed the statutory limitation on assignment of women to combat aircraft (part of § 6015). Public Law No. 102–190, § 531, 105 Stat. 1365. Congress also established a commission to assess the laws and policies restricting women from combat in general. *Id.* § 541. The commission recommended against participation of women in ground combat, but favored a more flexible policy in other contexts. Following this latter idea, Secretary of Defense Les Aspin opened combat aircraft assignments to women. In 1995, Congress repealed § 6015, the statutory restriction on the assignment of women in the Navy and Marine Corps. Public Law No. 103–160, § 541, 107 Stat. 1659. The statute also authorized the Secretary of Defense to change military personnel policies in order to make available to female members of the armed forces assignment to any type of combat unit, class of combat vessel, or type of combat platform that is not open to such assignments, but the Secretary must, not less than 30 days before such change is implemented, transmit to the Committees on Armed Services of the Senate and House of Representatives notice of the proposed change in personnel policy. (*Id.* § 542, 107 Stat. 1659–60.) In addition, § 543(a) of the statute requires gender-neutral occupational standards:

GENDER NEUTRALITY REQUIREMENT. In the case of any military occupational career field that is open to both male and female members of the Armed Forces, the Secretary of Defense-

(1) shall ensure that qualification of members of the Armed Forces for, and continuance of members of the Armed Forces in, that occupational career field is evaluated on the basis of common, relevant performance standards, without differential standards or evaluation on the basis of gender;

(2) may not use any gender quota, goal, or ceiling except as specifically authorized by law; and

(3) may not change an occupational performance standard for the purpose of increasing or decreasing the number of women in that occupational career field. (107 Stat. 1661.)

In 1994 a subcommittee of the House Armed Services Committee held hearings which explored people's attitudes about women in combat.[e] A Youth Tracking Study on opinions of women in combat had some interesting findings. Respondents aged 16 to 21 were asked whether policy should be changed to allow women to volunteer for combat assignments. In 1988, 47% of the male and 42% of the female respondents favored the change, with only 27% and 26%, respectively, opposed. (The rest were neutral.) By 1993, support had risen to 60% among males and 69% among females, with 18% and 11% opposed. See *April 1994 Hearings* 82. In 1992, another interesting question was added: "If you knew women in the military would serve under the same conditions as men, how would this effect your attitude toward enlistment?" Almost three-quarters of the male respondents and almost two-thirds of the female respondents said it would have no effect; just under 18% of the men and under 30% of the women said it would make them less likely to join (*id.* at 81).

In accordance with popular opinion and new congressional dictates, Secretary of Defense Les Aspin in January 1994 lifted the "risk rule" that had blocked women from serving in units which had a high probability of engaging in combat. This change opened more than 250,000 positions to women; now over 80% of the total jobs in the armed services are open to women, including 99% of Air Force and 94% of all Navy positions. See Madeline Morris, "By Force of Arms: Rape, War, and Military Culture," 45 *Duke L.J.* 651, 736–37 (1996). Many restrictions remain in place: women are not allowed to serve in units that engage in direct ground combat, including infantry, field artillery, and armor, and they are also excluded from special operations units such as the Green Berets, the Delta Force, and the Rangers. And even though women have become *eligible* for new posts, they have only just begun to actually serve in them. For example, by the end of 2001, only 16 of the Air Force's 759 bomber pilots, and only 43 of the Air Force's 3,500 fighter pilots were women.

Nonetheless, women are serving in new roles, and they are serving with distinction. In the 2002 war in Afghanistan, women participated in numerous bombing campaigns and were even put in command of two ships that the Navy sent to the region. In the 2003 war in Iraq, women participated in the ground war and suffered both casualties and fatalities; in addition, women were captured by the Iraqi forces and held until the war ended.

e. *Recruiting and Expanded Role for Women in the Military: Hearings Before the Subcomm. on Military Forces and Personnel* of the House Comm. on Armed Services, 103d Congress, 2d Session (Apr., July, 1994) [referred to in text as "*April 1994 Hearings*"].

PROBLEM 7–2

THE LEGALITY OF CURRENT POLICY EXCLUDING WOMEN FROM COMBAT

You are an attorney representing Private Jane Able, a soldier in the Army; under current Army rules, she cannot serve in front-line combat units, what the Defense Department calls "direct ground combat." About a third of the positions in the Army fall within this category, and Able's prospects of promotion are significantly diminished by the bar. She wants to sue the Secretary of the Army to require him to allow qualified women to serve in front-line combat units. You have uncovered the foregoing congressional materials, as well as the following government reports evaluating women's performance during the Persian Gulf War of 1991.

The General Accounting Office (GAO) in 1993 issued a report on women's combat or near-combat roles during the 1991 war. GAO, *Women in the Military: Deployment in the Persian Gulf War* (July 1993). Based upon its on-site interviews and observations, the team of GAO experts made the following findings: (1) Women were an integral part of military service operations, including combat operations, during that war. "Perceptions of favoritism, the tendency of men to want to protect women, and comparable award recognition generally were not considered impediments to the effective operation of mixed-gender units." *GAO Report* 15. (2) Women and men operated effectively under the same deployment conditions, including conditions of stress and little privacy. Neither men nor women appreciated the lack of privacy, but both groups handled the inconveniences well. Also, "women's health and hygiene issues were inconsequential." *Id.* at 29. (3) Gender homogeneity was not a prerequisite to unit cohesion. "Discipline problems during the deployment were considered to be infrequent, and women were more likely to be seen as having a positive or neutral effect on interpersonal friction than a negative one." *Id.* at 38. "The theory that only men can bond is misleading. Individuals who experience a crisis bond because of the crisis—not because they are women or men." *Id.* at 40.

These conclusions were substantially replicated in Margaret Harrell & Laura Miller, *New Opportunities for Military Women: Effects Upon Readiness, Cohesion, and Morale* (RAND 1997). The RAND study also reported several concerns. First, men seemed to resent what they perceived as double standards in service, such as different physical standards for women or an inclination on the part of leaders not to demand as much of women. Second, morale problems sometimes were created by dating and sexual relationships among soldiers, even those not forbidden by regulations. Third and most seriously, sexual harassment continued to be cited as a morale problem (see research below).

How should you craft your arguments on behalf of Able? What legal authorities should you deploy, and how should you use them? How do you answer the deference-to-the-military argument and distinguish *Rostker*? Does your case have any significant chance of success? What strategies would enhance your odds of prevailing? What tack do you think the Defense Department lawyers will take?

Department of Defense, Directive 1350.2, "The Defense Military Equal Opportunity Program," Available At http://web7.whs.osd.mil/Pdf/d13502p.pdf (As Modified May 7, 1997).

This Directive creates a "Department of Defense Military Equal Opportunity (MEO) Program," which carries out a policy against discrimination based on "race, color, religion, sex or national origin." The anti-discrimination policy includes a rule against sexual harassment. Paragraph E2.1.15 defines "sexual harassment" as "[a] form of sex discrimination that involves unwelcome sexual advances, requests for sexual favors, and other verbal or physical conduct of a sexual nature when:

    a.   Submission to such conduct is made explicitly or implicitly a term or condition of a person's job, pay, or career, or

    b.   Submission to or rejection of such conduct by a person is used as a basis for career or employment decisions affecting that person, or

    c.   Such conduct has the purpose or effect of unreasonably interfering with an individual's work performance or creates an intimidating, hostile, or offensive working environment."

This definition of sexual harassment is taken from the EEOC's 1980 Guidelines regulating sexual harassment in the civilian workplace, pursuant to Title VII of the Civil Rights Act of 1964 (Chapter 8, Section 1 of this Casebook). See Michael Noone, "Chimera or Jackalope? Department of Defense Efforts to Apply Civilian Sexual Harassment Criteria to the Military," 6 *Duke J. Gender L. & Pol'y* 151 (1999) (critical of this borrowing). Each of the branches of the armed forces has implemented this Directive through its own regulations.

The evidence is plentiful that this Directive is often violated. Both the GAO and RAND reports regarding the role of women in the 1991 Gulf War found that sexual harassment of female by male soldiers was a significant problem. Since those reports, there have been publicized incidents that have dramatized the problem and pressed the Defense Department to address it more systematically (and with formal legal rules and regulations). The following Notes systematically explore the documented problem and the proposed policy responses.

NOTES ON SEXUAL HARASSMENT IN THE U.S. ARMED FORCES: SHOULD SEX–INTEGRATED TRAINING BE RECONSIDERED?

On November 7, 1996, the U.S. Army announced that three soldiers at the Aberdeen Proving Ground in Maryland faced court-martial charges stemming from alleged sexual misconduct with female recruits. Among those accused of harassing conduct was Staff Sergeant Delmar Simpson. He was charged with nine counts of rape, three counts of forcible sodomy, and other serious offenses. The rape charges were based on accusations that

Simpson abused his authority to require sex from female soldiers under his charge. Found guilty by a military jury, he was sentenced to 25 years in prison—a penalty some observers criticized as too harsh and others faulted as too lenient. This case triggered a series of media reports and an investigation by the Army, which proposed reforms the next year.

The Army's heightened sensitivity to sexual discrimination and harassment has provoked various concerns and even backlashes. At Aberdeen itself, some male soldiers reacted to the scandal by adopting informal rules against any unmonitored interaction with female soldiers, thereby marginalizing women even more than before. See Diane Mazur, "The Beginning of the End for Women in the Military," 48 *Fla. L. Rev.* 461 (1996). That all of the Aberdeen defendants ultimately accused were black men and most of the accusers were white women provoked concern from civil rights groups that the prosecutions were racially selective. *E.g.*, Patti Giuffre & Christine Williams, "Boundary Lines: Labeling Sexual Harassment in Restaurants," 8 *Gender & Soc'y* 378, 387–97 (1994).

Feminists worried that the publicity surrounding the mushrooming Aberdeen scandal created a "gender panic." See generally Martha Chamallas, "The New Gender Panic: Reflections on Sex Scandals and the Military," 83 *Minn. L. Rev.* 305 (1998), cites the prosecution of Lieutenant Kelly Flinn for adultery. Flinn's memoir concluded: "[M]aybe * * * this was a way of saying, without having to say it, that women have no place in the military: let them in and all hell breaks loose." Kelly Flinn, *Proud to Be* 206 (1997). That may be an overstatement, but there is some evidence that the scandal made many male soldiers restive. According to 1999 survey data, nearly half of enlisted personnel believed that regulations governing fraternization and sexual harassment were applied unevenly (with overwhelming majorities suggesting that women are favored), while more than a third of respondents suggested that regulations covering adultery were applied unevenly and to the benefit of female soldiers.

In the wake of the Aberdeen scandal, Senator Rick Santorum and others concluded that the armed forces' "experiment" with integrated training of women and men had failed. Defense Secretary William Cohen appointed a special panel charged with reviewing sex-integrated training. On December 16, 1997, after visiting 17 military installations and interviewing more than 2000 military personnel, the Federal Advisory Committee on Gender–Integrated Training and Related Issues issued its report to Secretary Cohen. Despite concluding that "gender-integrated training must continue to be an important element of the training program," the Committee proposed a number of changes designed to limit the extent of such training, including the establishment of separate barracks for male and female recruits and the organization of same-sex platoons, divisions, and flights—the core "operational training units" relied upon in basic training to teach recruits team-building, unit cohesion, and discipline.

Critics like Professor Chamallas charged that, if adopted, the Committee's proposal would represent a significant regression in military policy. Chamallas maintains that proposals for sex resegregation would not only set back women's integration into the armed forces and its power structure, but would also fuel the fires of sexual harassment. In civilian contexts, Professor Vicki Schultz, "Telling Stories About Women and Work: Judicial Interpretations of Sex Segregation in the Workplace in Title VII Cases Raising the Lack of Interest Argument," 103 *Harv. L. Rev.* 1749 (1990), and "Reconceptualizing Sexual Harassment," 107 *Yale L.J.* 1683 (1998), argues that the structure and ideology of the workplace drive sexual harassment. In particular, a workplace with a few token women working in marginalized (and sex-stereotyped) positions is a workplace that is *most* likely to have sexual harassment. In contrast, a workplace with a fair number of women, working in a variety of positions (including positions of power and others not traditionally occupied by women), is one that for structural reasons is not going to have as much sexual harassment. See also Kathryn Abrams, "The New Jurisprudence of Sexual Harassment," 83 *Cornell L. Rev.* 1169 (1998); Anita Bernstein, "Treating Sexual Harassment with Respect," 111 *Harv. L. Rev.* 445 (1997); Martha Chamallas, "Structuralist and Cultural Domination Theories Meet Title VII: Some Contemporary Influences," 92 *Mich. L. Rev.* 2370 (1994).

Chamallas, "New Gender Panic," 324–32, draws from this literature the conclusion that women will inevitably be harassed and denigrated within the armed forces unless structural changes are made—especially increasing the numbers of women beyond token amounts and increasing women's access to power positions. Indeed, the Defense Department's own data supported that proposition. The Marine Corps had the lowest percentage of women and was in the 1990s the only branch to have sex-segregated basic training—yet it had the highest level of reported sexual harassment. The Navy had the most sex-integrated basic training—yet was most successful in reducing the reported levels of harassment.[f]

Resegregation would not only fail to address these structural concerns but would, Chamallas worries, represent a symbolic and probably practical backwards step. It would be a signal to the armed forces to de-emphasize the recruitment of women (the Army and Navy in 1994 aimed at achieving a female enlistment rate of 18%). More deeply, sex-segregated training would further undermine women's abilities to achieve leadership positions within the armed services. It is hard to doubt the feminist wisdom that fair and equal treatment of women in the workforce—including military ones— is harder if not impossible if women are not in supervisory and leadership positions, including positions where they exercise leadership over men. Chamallas, "New Gender Panic," 328–30 (citing the empirical literature). The feminist bottom line: Under tokenism theory, "more thorough integration of women into all aspects of military life, including positions

f. These startling facts are discussed in the statement of Nancy Duff Campbell, Co-President of the National Women's Law Center on Gender–Integrated Training, which was presented to the Senate subcommittee. See *Gender-Integrated Training and Related Matters: Hearing Before the Subcomm. on Personnel of the Senate Comm. on Armed Servs.*, 105th Cong., 1st Sess. 40 ff. (1997).

designated as combat positions, would appear to be the best response to Aberdeen.'' *Id.* at 332.

As you can see, the problem of sexual harassment in the armed forces must be considered among the most serious problems that institution faces. And experts are divided as to exactly what should be done to handle the problem of sexual harassment in the armed forces. Those of us who have never served in the armed forces are at a particular disadvantage in opining as to solutions, but give it a try: If you could tell the armed forces to make one big change in response to the sexual harassment problem, what would your recommendation be?

THE MILITARY'S EXCLUSION OF LESBIANS, GAY MEN, AND BISEXUALS

PART A. ORIGINS OF THE ARMED FORCES' EXCLUSION OF GAY PEOPLE[a]

In 1778, the Continental Army was fortunate to receive Baron Frederich Wilhelm Ludolf Gerhard Augustin von Steuben of Prussia, the drillmaster who retrained General Washington's Army at Valley Forge and literally rewrote the Americans' manual on discipline and order. Ironically, von Steuben was available for American service because he had in late 1777 been accused of "having taken familiarities with young boys which the law forbids and punishes severely" in Prussia, and was in danger of being prosecuted (Shilts, *Conduct Unbecoming* 8–9). The further irony is that at the very moment von Steuben rescued the struggling American cause, the Continental Army court-martialed and executed Lieutenant General Gotthold Frederick Enslin for engaging in the "abominable crime against nature" with Private John Monhart.

Article 93 of the Articles of War of 1916 prohibited assault to commit a felony, apparently including assault to commit sodomy. The Articles of War adopted by Congress in 1920 enumerated sodomy as a separate offense under Article 93. Act of June 4, 1920, 41 Stat. 787. Various other wartime statutes prohibited lewd practices in or near U.S. military bases. Note that these newly specified regulations coincided with popular and medical perceptions that a new species of human—"sex perverts" or "degenerates"—could be defined by their desire to engage in sodomy with people of their own sex (usually men).

The first celebrated event in this new era of military regulation was the Newport Naval Training Station scandals of 1919–20 (Murphy, *Perverts*

a. Our discussion draws from Allan Bérubé, *Coming Out Under Fire: The History of Gay Men and Women in World War Two* (1992); William Eskridge, Jr., *Gaylaw: Challenging the Apartheid of the Closet* chs. 1–2 (1999); Leisa Meyer, *Creating G.I. Jane: Sexuality and Power in the Women's Army Corps During World War II* (1996); Lawrence Murphy, *Perverts by Official Order: The Campaign Against Homosexuality by the United States Navy* (1988); Randy Shilts, *Conduct Unbecoming: Lesbians and Gays in the U.S. Military—Vietnam to the Persian Gulf* (1993); Major Jeffrey Davis, "Military Policy Toward Homosexuals: Scientific, Historical, and Legal Perspectives," 131 *Military L. Rev.* 55 (1991).

by Official Order). In 1919, Lieutenant Erastus Hudson authorized a sting operation whereby undercover operatives ferreted out "sex perverts" among the hospital and other military personnel at Newport, as well as among the townsfolk. A board of inquiry in March 1919 assembled the evidence against a couple of dozen defendants, most of whom were arrested and court-martialed on charges of conduct unbecoming a soldier (before the 1920 Articles made sodomy an offense). This was the first military investigation to integrate military vice with the surrounding community, to focus on gangs of "perverts" and assemble evidence by infiltrating the gangs with undercover operatives, and to use the testimony of each accused person to implicate other "perverts" if possible. Newport was the first homosexual witch-hunt in the U.S. armed forces.

Congress expressed outrage that military personnel were committing unnatural acts in order to procure evidence of sodomy. There were few courts-martial for sodomy after that. Section VIII of the separation regulations ("inaptness or undesirable habits or traits of character") became the mechanism by which homosexuals were quietly drummed out of the service, albeit in very small numbers. The difficulty of expulsion also suggested the importance of pre-induction screening. In 1921, Army Regulation 40–105 announced that recruits could be rejected for evidence of medical defects or diseases, including physical or moral "degeneration." The "degenerate" individual could be identified by stigmata such as "indecency" and "sexual perversion." The regulation also excluded recruits who showed signs of "constitutional psychopathic state," including "sexual psychopathy," which made them "incapable of attaining a satisfactory adjustment to the average environment of civilized society." (Eskridge, *Gaylaw*.)

The creation of homosexuality as a legal and medical rather than just a moral phenomenon came to have great significance during World War II. With the war came the draft, the need to enlist large numbers of men, and arguments from the psychiatric community that homosexuality should be treated as an illness rather than as a crime (Bérubé, *Coming Out Under Fire* ch. 1). Medical Circular No. 1 was issued by the Selective Service on November 7, 1940, explaining psychiatry to the 30,000 volunteer physicians at local draft boards; homosexuality was not mentioned. The Service revised the Circular in 1941 and included "homosexual proclivities" in the list of disqualifying "deviations." The Army listed "homosexual persons" among those to be rejected because of "psychopathic personality disorders." The Navy sought to screen out people "whose sexual behavior is such that it would endanger or disturb the morale of the military unit."

The Army's 1942 mobilization regulations contained instructions on "Sexual Perversions" (Bérubé 19). These regulations, published in final form in 1943, were in place for the remainder of the war. "Persons habitually or occasionally engaged in homosexual or other perverse sexual practices" were "unsuitable for military service" as was anyone having "a record as a pervert." "Homosexuals" could be recognized by "feminine body characteristics" or "effeminacy in dress and manner" or "patulous [expanded] rectum." The regulations rejected physically normal but personally "effeminate" men because they "would become subject to ridicule and 'joshing' which will harm the general morale and will incapacitate the individuals." During the course of the war, 18,000,000 Americans were inducted; fewer than 5,000 were rejected for homosexuality. Clearly, little effort was made to open every closet door.

The detection of lesbians was even more lax. Because women did not serve in the military in large numbers before World War II, there were not in place preexisting alarms about sexual deviation. Hence, lesbians were almost always able to enter the armed forces undetected. A good many women joined up *because* they "wanted to be with all those women," as Phillis Abry recalls (Bérubé 28). Although WAC and WAVE top brass pressed for better screening to keep their forces from becoming dominated by lesbians, the need for personnel and the lack of direction rendered the screening a porous sieve indeed. Only in 1944, near the end of the war, were regulations issued to detect lesbians.

Although thousands of military personnel engaged in homosexual activities during the war, there was little enforcement of the homosexual exclusion. The only big scandal was the investigation of lesbian activity at the WAC training center at Fort Oglethorpe, Georgia (Meyer, *G.I. Jane*). Upon complaint of a concerned mother, Lieutenant Colonel Birge Holt and Captain Ruby Herman conducted an investigation and uncovered mountains of letters and testimony involving explicit same-sex intimacy at Fort Oglethorpe. But only a couple of women were discharged, and the investigators invoked a series of War Department medical circulars to justify retention of most involved. The investigators targeted women who not only engaged in sexual relations with other women, but who also transgressed gender roles through cross-dressing and the like.

The leniency shown by the military during World War II ended soon after the war did. The period 1947–53 saw an aggressive enforcement of the homosexuality exclusion. The Army's post-war policy had some flexibility to retain people with "homosexual tendencies," but generally operated under a simple principle: "True, confirmed, or habitual homosexual personnel, irrespective of sex, will not be permitted to serve in the Army in any capacity and prompt separation of known homosexuals from the Army is mandatory." AR 600–443, § I, & 2 (April 10, 1953). From 1953 into the 1970s more than a thousand people were discharged from the armed forces each year on grounds of homosexuality. Many more were negotiated out quietly and do not appear on the record books.

The main concern voiced about homosexuals by the military in the 1950s was their presumed disloyalty, although the discourse of sick or predatory homosexuals remained robust. A standard script was that homosexuals would be particularly susceptible to blackmail: Their status was so repugnant that Communists would be able to extract secret information out of them by threat of exposure. A 600–page internal Navy report compiled by Admiral Crittenden debunked the security and blackmail argument in 1957, but the Navy only suppressed the Crittenden Report and maintained its public stance. Periodically, there would be witch-hunts to find and expel lesbians and gay men; in the 1960s, these "suspected homosexuals" either left quietly or denied the charges, increasingly reliant on the advice of attorneys or paralegals who knew and could exploit the military's rules and procedures.

PART B.   THE GAY EXCLUSION UNDER LEGAL FIRE, 1976–93

Before the Stonewall riots (1969), expulsions of homosexuals from the armed forces were the result of military investigations. The witch hunts continued after 1969, but a new breed of soldier came to the fore—the person who openly conceded her or his homosexuality and sued the armed forces to stay in. In *Matlovich v. Secretary of the Air Force*, 591 F.2d 852 (D.C.Cir.1978); *Berg v. Claytor*, 591 F.2d 849 (D.C.Cir.1978), the D.C. Circuit declined to hold the military's gay exclusions unconstitutional but held instead that the military vested illegal discretion with officials enforcing the exclusionary policy. Specifically, the services allowed for retention of homosexuals where appropriate but did not define when retention would be appropriate. Because Leonard Matlovich and Copy Berg had exemplary service records and no evidence of misconduct, it was not clear why they should not have fallen under the exception.

Ironically, these successful lawsuits led to a hardening of the military's policy. The Department of Defense in the waning days of the Carter Administration decided not to compromise the homosexuality exclusion and instead issued a new series of directives that were carried over by the new Reagan Administration. Directive 1332.14.1.H provided that enlisted personnel who were admitted homosexuals or engaged in homosexual activities or joined in a same-sex marriage would be separated from the service, unless they could show that they were really heterosexuals who had slipped up. Directive 1332.30.1.H applied the same precept to officers. The new directives stimulated a new series of lawsuits and court decisions, most of which upheld the directives.

Perry J. Watkins v. United States Army

United States Court of Appeals for the Ninth Circuit, 1988.
847 F.2d 1329, *vacated*, 875 F.2d 699 (1989).

[Excerpted in Chapter 3, Section 2B]

Joseph Steffan v. William J. Perry

United States Court of Appeals for the District of Columbia Circuit, *en banc*, 1994.
41 F.3d 677.

■ SILBERMAN, J., [delivered the opinion for the en banc Court.] * * *

[Joseph Steffan] enrolled in the Naval Academy in 1983. He successfully completed three of his four years of training, and consistently ranked near the top of his class. During his senior year, Steffan admitted privately that he was gay. At a performance board, Steffan was asked, "I'd like your word, are you a homosexual?" He replied, "Yes, sir." Based on this hearing the Performance Board recommended to the Commandant of the Academy that "Steffan be separated from the Naval Academy due to insufficient aptitude for commissioned service." Steffan was separated and subsequently sued for reinstatement. He maintained that the Naval Academy regulations requiring separation for simply being "homosexual" were unconstitutional, as were the underlying Department of Defense regulations. DOD Directive 1332.14.H.1.a, 32 C.F.R. Pt. 41, App. A (1991) (superseded).[b]

[A panel of the D.C. Circuit found the separation and the DOD Directive unconstitutional, *Steffan v. Aspin*, 8 F.3d 57 (1993), but the en banc court upheld the separation. Judge Silberman's opinion commanded an en banc majority for the following discussion of the constitutionality of the Naval Academy regulations, which were very similar to the DOD Directive. We have omitted his discussion of Steffan's procedural obstacles in challenging the Department of Defense Directive.]

* * * [W]e are required to ask two questions of the [Naval Academy] regulations. First, are they directed at the achievement of a legitimate governmental purpose? Second, do they rationally further that purpose? The first of these questions is not even in dispute in this case. * * * Steffan concedes that the military may constitutionally terminate service of all those who engage in homosexual conduct—wherever it occurs and at whatever time the conduct takes place. Counsel at oral argument further admitted, in connection with a discussion focused on the DOD Directives, that the military could ban even those who reveal an "intention" to engage in such conduct. It is common ground, then, that the regulations would be serving a legitimate purpose by excluding those who engage in homosexual conduct or who intend to do so.

The dispute between the parties is thus limited to the question whether the regulations (focusing now on the Academy regulations), by requiring the discharge of those midshipmen who describe themselves as homosexual—whether or not the Academy has information establishing that an individual has engaged in homosexual conduct or intends to do so— are rational. Steffan first argues that there is no necessary factual connection between such self-description and such conduct. But Steffan relies primarily on a more subtle and novel argument. Even if the government could rationally, as a factual matter, draw a connection between the statement and the conduct, other legal considerations prevent the government from so doing. The military may not, according to Steffan, "punish" homosexuals solely on the basis of their "status." Nor may the military presume that self-declared homosexuals will actually engage in homosexual

---

b. [Eds.] The Directives mandated that a "member shall be separated ... if one or more of the following approved findings is made." 1332.14.H.1.c. One such finding was that "[t]he member has stated that he or she is a homosexual ... unless there is a further finding that the member is not a homosexual." 1332.14.H.1.c.(2). And the term "homosexual" is defined as "a person, regardless of sex, who engages in, desires to engage in, or intends to engage in homosexual acts." 1332.14.H.1.b.(1).

conduct, for such conduct is illegal under the Code of Military Justice. (Sodomy is prohibited under 10 U.S.C. § 925 (1988).) Such a presumption—that someone will actually break the law—is inconsistent, he argues, with our legal traditions.

We consider first whether the Academy regulation has a rational factual basis. The appropriate question, it seems to us, is whether banning those who admit to being homosexual rationally furthers the end of banning those who are engaging in homosexual conduct or are likely to do so. The Academy can treat someone who intends to pursue homosexual conduct in the same manner as someone who engages in that conduct, because such an intent is a precursor to the proscribed conduct and makes subsequent homosexual conduct more likely than not. And the military may reasonably assume that when a member states that he is a homosexual, that member means that he either engages or is likely to engage in homosexual conduct. The inference seems particularly valid in this case because Steffan made no attempt to clarify what he meant by the term. He did not specify (nor was he asked by the Board) whether he had engaged in homosexual conduct in the past, whether he was presently engaged in homosexual conduct, whether he intended to engage in homosexual conduct in the future, or whether all three were true. * * *

Admittedly, it is conceivable that someone would describe himself as a homosexual based on his orientation or tendencies (and, perhaps, past conduct), notwithstanding the absence of any ongoing conduct or the probability of engaging in such conduct. That there may be exceptions to the assumption on which the regulation is premised is irrelevant, however, so long as the classification (the regulation) in the run of cases furthers its purpose, and we readily conclude that it does. * * * The rule of law presupposes the creation of categories.

The military thus may rely on presumptions that avoid the administratively costly need to adduce proof of conduct or intent, so long as there is a rational basis for believing that the presumption furthers that end. And the military certainly furthers its policy of discharging those members who either engage in, or are likely to engage in, homosexual conduct when it discharges those who state that they are homosexual. The special deference we owe the military's judgment necessarily affects the scope of the court's inquiry into the rationality of the military's policy. Whether a certain course of conduct is rational does not depend solely upon the degree of correlation that exists between a surface characteristic and a corresponding hidden trait. For the question whether the degree of correlation justifies the action taken—i.e., whether it is rational—necessarily depends on one's assessment of the magnitude of the problem the action seeks to avoid. The military is entitled to deference with respect to its estimation of the effect of homosexual conduct on military discipline and therefore to the degree of correlation that is tolerable. Particularly in light of this deference, we think the class of self-described homosexuals is sufficiently close to the class of those who engage or intend to engage in homosexual conduct for the military's policy to survive rational basis review.

Because removing from the military all those who admit to being homosexual furthers the military's concededly legitimate purpose of excluding from service those who engage in homosexual conduct, Steffan's argument at bottom must be based on the notion that the classification drawn by the military is impermissibly over-inclusive—that the military may not presume that all admitted homosexuals will engage in homosexual conduct because some homosexuals would not. However, courts are compelled under rational-basis review to accept a legislature's generalizations even when there is an imperfect fit between means and ends. A classification does not fail rational-basis review because it " 'is not made with mathematical nicety or because in practice it results in some inequality.' The problems of government are practical ones and may justify, if they do not require, rough accommodations—illogical, it may be, and unscientific." [*Heller v. Doe*, 113 S.Ct. 2637, 2643 (1993).]

Steffan seeks to end-run this analysis by arguing that a prohibition triggered simply by an admission of homosexuality is one based on "status" rather than conduct, and therefore is legally impermissible regardless of its rational relationship, as a factual matter, to the military's objective. * * *

It is true that the Constitution forbids criminal punishments based on a person's qualities—we assume that this is what is meant by "status"—rather than on his or her conduct. See *Robinson v. California*, 370 U.S. 660 (1962). Yet, this proposition has never meant that employment decisions—which is what this case is about—cannot be made on such a basis. One cannot be put in jail for having been born blind (although a blind person who drives a truck and kills someone could be jailed for his act). But it obviously would be constitutional for the military to prohibit blind people from serving in the armed forces, even though congenital blindness is certainly a sort of "status." The logic of Steffan's argument and of the original panel's decision—that "America's hallmark" prohibits "punishment" (which term is meant to encompass discharge decisions) based on a person's "status"—would mean that the military acts unconstitutionally if it refuses to enlist blind individuals.

It is asserted that one does not choose to be homosexual and that therefore it is unfair for the military to make distinctions on that basis. But whether or not one's homosexuality is genetically predetermined, one's height certainly is. Steffan conceded at oral argument that the Navy's maximum height restrictions are constitutional because they rationally further a legitimate naval purpose. That concession amounts to an admission that employment decisions based on a person's characteristics are subject to the same analysis as decisions based on a person's conduct. Both are tested to see whether they rationally further a legitimate purpose.

The controversy before us is quite analogous to *Massachusetts Bd. of Retirement v. Murgia*, 427 U.S. 307 (1976) (per curiam), in which the Supreme Court upheld a mandatory retirement age of 50 for police officers on the grounds that the classification rationally furthered the government's purpose of excluding those who lacked the physical conditioning to be officers. In other words, the Court upheld a classification based on "status"—after all, a classification based on age turns on how old someone is, not on what he can do—that was aimed prophylactically at preventing the risk of unsatisfactory conduct. The connection between homosexuality and homosexual conduct is at least as strong (indeed, it seems much stronger) as the relationship upheld in *Murgia* between age—a paradigmatic "status"—and unsatisfactory job performance. * * *

The separate opinions of JUDGE BUCKLEY, JUDGE RANDOLPH, and JUDGE GINSBURG are omitted.

■ CIRCUIT JUDGE WALD [joined by CHIEF JUDGE EDWARDS and JUDGE ROGERS], dissenting.

[Judge Wald objected to the majority's transformation of Steffan's case into one involving homosexual conduct.] The linchpin of the court's transformation strategy is its assertion that "a statement that one is a homosexual" may be "used by the Navy as a proxy for homosexual conduct—past, present, or future." We disagree in the most fundamental way with that claim, and believe that in the military context, where homosexual conduct results in automatic discharge or imposition of criminal sanctions, it is inherently unreasonable to equate an admission of homosexual identity with commission of or intent to engage in homosexual conduct. * * *

* * * Inferring future homosexual conduct from an admission of homosexuality presents the now-familiar "propensity" issue—whether the admission itself indicates that an individual will "one day" actually engage in proscribed homosexual conduct. [Judge Wald argues from the DOD Directive and the Department's interpretation of the Directive that the government as well as Steffan recognize the difference between homosexual "orientation" and homosexual "conduct." See also the Problem following this case, which describes the new "don't ask, don't tell" law.]

Given, then, that homosexual orientation and conduct are analytically distinct concepts, the "propensity" question reduces to whether an admission of homosexuality alone, without elaboration of any kind, may rationally give rise to an inference that a particular individual will "one day" engage in homosexual conduct, regardless of the inhibitions of his or her environment. Neither the majority nor the government offers any indication that such a presumption is rooted in reality. The government's brief baldly claims that there is a "sound factual connection between the proved and inferred facts," but offers no further support for this proposition. At oral argument, the government repeatedly relied on the incantation that the "nature of human sexuality" supported the inference. * * *

* * * The government's contention in this case smacks of precisely the sort of stereotypical assessment forbidden by *Stanton* and *Reed*; at bottom, the government and the majority seem to be saying that gay servicemembers—unlike heterosexuals—must be presumed incapable of controlling their sexual "desires" in conformity with the law. While the government is not obliged to offer evidence to support the rationality of an inference, neither are courts obliged to accept the naked assertion of an untenable position.

The irrationality of the government's inference is particularly patent in the military, where homosexual conduct is grounds for automatic discharge and, in the case of homosexual sodomy, punishable by incarceration. Indeed, it is much more reasonable to infer that a servicemember who admits to "homosexuality" will thereafter assiduously forego homosexual conduct. After all, servicemembers are surely aware that statements of homosexual orientation or desire will trigger close scrutiny of their subsequent behavior for evidence of homosexual "conduct" or "intent," as indeed occurred in Steffan's case. It would be foolhardy for servicemembers to freely admit "homosexuality," unless they were quite confident that no additional evidence of conduct or intent existed. * * *

The Supreme Court has repeatedly emphasized that even prior conduct does not demonstrate a "propensity" to engage in the same actions after they later become illegal. See, e.g., *Jacobson v. United States*, 503 U.S. 540 (1992) ("Evidence of predisposition to do what once was lawful is not, by itself, sufficient to show predisposition to do what is now illegal, for there is a common understanding that most people obey the law even when they disapprove of it."). And if prior conduct does not permit an inference regarding future conduct, such a conclusion is still less justifiable when based on mere orientation or "desire." "[A] person's inclinations and 'fantasies . . . are his own and beyond the reach of government'. . . . " *Id.* (quoting *Paris Adult Theatre I v. Slaton*, 413 U.S. 49, 67 (1973)). Indeed, as Justice Marshall wrote in *Stanley v. Georgia*, 394 U.S. 557, 565 (1969) [excerpted in Chapter 2, Section 1B], "Our whole constitutional heritage rebels at the thought of giving government the power to control men's minds." Clearly the Navy may not exercise this power over the minds of servicemembers by discharging them on the basis of inquiries about "homosexuality." * * *

The majority's attempt to analogize this case to *Massachusetts Bd. of Retirement v. Murgia*, 427 U.S. 307 (1976), upholding a mandatory retirement age of 50 for police officers on the ground that it rationally furthered a legitimate purpose of excluding officers lacking necessary physical fitness, misses the mark, as do its other examples of height and blindness disqualifications from government service. Of course the Navy can exclude individuals based on disqualifying physical or mental characteristics beyond their control. It is, however, an altogether different proposition to predicate exclusion on the assumption that certain individuals will not exert their will to prevent mere "desires" from translating into illegal actions.

To put the argument plainly, there is nothing a blind or tall person can do to negate those characteristics that disqualify him from military service. There is no will power that will spare an aging person the eventual loss of physical ability. And certainly there is no way that these people merely by conforming to the law can qualify for military service. But a servicemember who has homosexual desires can; he need only refrain from engaging in prohibited homosexual conduct, and by the Navy's own admission he will be as "fit" as the next person. Since a decision not to act is within the control of the individual servicemember—unlike the "decision" whether to age or be blind—it is not rational to assume that he will choose to engage in conduct that would subject him to discharge or even incarceration. * * *

NOTES ON *WATKINS* AND *STEFFAN* AND THE "OLD" EXCLUSION OF GAYS FROM THE MILITARY

Note how Judge Norris (*Watkins*) and Judge Wald (dissenting in *Steffan*) view the constitutional issue through the prism of identity—while Judge Reinhardt (dissenting in *Watkins*) and Judge Silberman (*Steffan*) view the constitutional issue through the prism of (illegal) conduct. Is there any neutral way to arbitrate their difference in perspective?

Deference might be one means of arbitration: Because the military views the gay exclusion through the lens of conduct, a reviewing court required to show deference must at least consider that perspective and ought presumptively to adhere to it. History might be another means of arbitration: Gay people seeking to serve openly in the military are engaged in the same kind of politics of recognition and civic engagement that people of color and women engaged in earlier in the century; unless there is any basis for distinguishing among the three groups, the claims of gay people ought to be accommodated. But this lesson of history might be trumped by the further lesson that it was the political branches and not the judicial branch that accomplished the integration.

Does the Supreme Court's opinion in *Lawrence* (Chapter 4), which overruled *Hardwick*, create problems for Judge Silberman's deployment of illegal conduct as a justification for a status-based discrimination. Does the UCMJ's criminalization of consensual sodomy survive *Lawrence*? (You might want to differentiate between sodomy on government property, such as the barracks, and that on private property in thinking about this issue.) This issue is now being litigated, with military appeals judges skeptical that all consensual sodomy can still be regulated, even under military law. If it does not, does Judge Silberman's syllogism collapse? Is there any other justification for the ban if the government cannot use it as a basis for purging the armed forces of illegal sodomites?

Even under Judge Silberman's assumptions, there is an important conundrum: a statement that "I am a heterosexual" is almost as probative evidence that one has and will commit illegal sodomy, as the statement "I am a homosexual." Studies have found that three-quarters of the American heterosexual population have engaged in active oral sex, three quarters receptive oral sex, and more than a fifth anal sex. *E.g.*, Edward Laumann et al., *The Social Organization of Sexuality: Sexual Practices in the United States* 98–99 (1994). Does this mean that open heterosexuals—the large majority of them sodomites by the government's inference—should be kicked out? (Hint: Of course not!) If not, are equal protection concerns heightened? Consider Justice O'Connor's concurring opinion in *Lawrence* (Chapter 4).

PART C.   DON'T ASK, DON'T TELL, 1993–

President Clinton in January 1993 announced his intention to end the exclusion of bisexuals, lesbians, and gay men by executive order. Facing a firestorm of protest from various quarters and blindsided by his own Joint Chiefs of Staff, the President immediately agreed with Senator Sam Nunn, the Chair of the Senate Armed Services Committee, and General Colin Powell, the Chair of the Joint Chiefs of Staff, to postpone any executive order until after Congress had studied the matter in a series of House and Senate hearings.

Policy Concerning Homosexuality in the Armed Forces: Hearings Before the Senate Committee on Armed Services

103d Congress, 2d Session. 595–97, 599–602, 606–09, 618–19 (May 11, 1993).

[Retired General H. Norman] SCHWARZKOPF: * * * Let me first state that my position on this matter is not based on any kind of moral outrage over what many consider immoral conduct. Also, I would like to state I am a very strong advocate of our Constitution's provisions for individual rights, and therefore my position is not a condemnation of anyone's right to choose their sexual orientation.

That said, I must say that I am opposed to an executive order lifting the ban on homosexuals in the military service, and my opposition grows out of honest concern for the impact that such a measure would have on the men and women of our Armed Forces and the resultant reduction in our Nation's ability to protect our vital interest.

The Armed Forces' principal mission is not to be instruments of social experimentation. The first, foremost, and all eclipsing mission of our military is to be ready to fight our Nation's wars and when called upon to do so to win those wars.

We send our troops into battle for God, country, and mom's homemade apple pie, but study after study of many different wars on many different battlefields time and time again come to the same conclusion.

What keeps soldiers in their foxholes rather than running away in the face of mass waves of attacking enemy, what keeps the marines attacking up the hills under withering machine gun fire, what keeps the pilots flying through heavy surface-to-air missile fire to deliver the bombs on targets, is the simple fact that they do not want to let down their buddies on the left or the right.

They do not want to betray their unit and their comrades with whom they have established a special bond through shared hardship and sacrifice not only in the war but also in the training and the preparation for the war.

It is called unit cohesion, and in my 40 years of army service in three different wars I have become convinced that it is the single most important factor in a unit's ability to succeed on the battlefield. Anyone who disputes this fact may have been to war, but certainly never led troops into battle.

Whether we like it or not, in my years of military service I have experienced the fact that the introduction of an open homosexual into a small unit immediately polarizes that unit and destroys the very bonding that is so important for the unit's survival in time of war.

For whatever reason, the organization is divided into a majority who oppose, a small minority who approve, and other groups who either do not care or just wish the problem would go away, and I do not find this surprising, given the divisiveness that I have encountered in our Nation in the past year. The attitudes of our servicemen and women simply reflect, in my opinion, the attitudes that I have encountered in the American people.

Do not get me wrong, please. I am not saying that homosexuals have not served honorably in our Armed Forces in the past. Of course they have, and I am quite sure that they will in the future, although I candidly must say that I completely reject the grossly overinflated numbers quoted by some organizations.

However, in every case that I am familiar with, and there are many, whenever it became known in a unit that someone was openly homosexual, polarization occurred, violence sometimes followed, morale broke down and unit effectiveness suffered. Plain and simply, that has been my experience.

[The General also said that the volunteer army is possible only because the military has, thus far, enjoyed a highly qualified poor of volunteers.] Will this same pool of high quality young men and women be available to us if the ban on homosexuals in the military is lifted? If what I am told by young men and women who talked to me is indicative, the answer is no. If what I am told by countless parents is indicative, the answer is clearly no.

What about those men and women already serving? Are they going to stick with us like they have in the past? There is little doubt that we will lose quite a few of them. The result of this decrease in quality of enlistees and reenlistees can only result in a decrease in the quality of our armed forces.

Often, various precepts of our Constitution clash. This has clearly been the case in the military. We have excluded people from serving due to height, weight, sex, mental capacity, and physical disability. We even retire brilliant, handsome, erudite general officers after 35 years of service. [Laughter.]

I mean, this is clearly a case of age discrimination. [Laughter.]

These exclusions have been contested over and over in the courts, and the decisions have been universally the same. The interest of the defense of our Nation has prevailed.

One last point. Our Armed Forces are already under severe pressure from ongoing deep budget cuts, resultant force drawdowns, inactivations and base closures, and what some call draconian personnel reductions in force, viewed by many as a breach of an implicit social contract.

Yet many who advocate lifting the ban on homosexuals in the military blithely say we can overcome all of the problems I have raised by ordering already overburdened military leaders at all levels to "institute training for all personnel on the acceptance of homosexual or bisexual orientation or conduct," even when a large majority of the leaders and the troops have clearly stated, "they oppose allowing homosexuals in the military" and "believe gays serving openly in the military would be very disruptive to discipline."

The military establishment is not fragile, but in my mind such actions would be seriously overloading their plate. They will faithfully try and execute the orders of their civilian leaders, but their hearts simply will not be in it. To me, they will be just like many of the Iraqi troops who sat in the deserts of Kuwait forced to execute orders they did not believe in.

And what about our troops' rights? Are we really ready to do this to the men and women of our Armed Forces and to risk a possible decrease in our Nation's ability to defend itself simply to force our servicemen and women to accept a lifestyle of a very well-organized, well-financed, and very vocal, but what turns out to be a very small minority of our society? I personally sincerely hope not. * * *

[Marine Colonel Frederick C.] PECK: * * * I have returned last Wednesday from Somalia. I spent 5 months in Somalia, and then a month before that in Kenya, working on the airlift in Operation Provide Relief, and then Restore Hope. * * *

[There,] the grunts lived like grunts always do. We found wherever we could to throw down a bedroll, in abandoned buildings, or in worst cases, out in places like Badar and Baidoa, just digging a hole in the ground and putting a poncho over it. And when it rained out there, it got pretty miserable. Not to bore you with details, but the facilities were primitive; I am talking about toilet facilities. At first they were holes in the ground, and then they were improved to plywood 2–holers. You know, real fancy accommodations. And they never got much better than that. * * *

I have to tell you that among the troops out there, Topic A was this topic that we are discussing right here. And I also have to say that I served alongside, directly alongside, the Canadians and the Australians, who have had recent experience of their Legislatures dropping the ban. * * * [L]et me tell you that, amongst the Australians and the Canadians, how they handled it, how the troops handled it: And that is by intimidation.

They said no gays would dare assert themselves, where they were; and it would be barracks justice, and a very inhospitable environment for anyone who stepped forward. So they did not have a problem, because no one came out of the closet; no one was stepping forward, and it was very easy for them to deal with. I do not advocate that as necessarily the right way to deal with things, I just want to tell you how it is, and how I saw it. * * *

[The witness describes his tour of duty with the Marines' "Hollywood Liaison Office."] I worked with a lot of people in Hollywood whose sexual orientations and a lot of other things about their personal lifestyles were much, much different than my own. I think I was successful there. * * * And I am saying this to tell you that I am not a homophobe, I am not the kind of person who has led some cloistered, sheltered military life, who has never had to deal with the homosexuals before. I have worked with them all the time. I can work with homosexuals, shoulder to shoulder.

But I do not think I can live with them and coexist with them in a military environment. It is one thing to share an office with someone, it is quite another thing to share a lifestyle; and that is what the military is: It is a way of life.

When you go to someplace like Somalia, there is not any off-duty time. It is not like working inside the beltway at the Pentagon where at the end of the day you go home. Your workplace is your living space, it is your home. And when you want to take someone of a different sexual orientation into that, let me tell you, think about what it would be in your personal, in your personal life. If you took someone of a different sexual orientation in, to live in your home, and how it would effect the way you carried out your daily life. * * *

I have three sons, I wrote to Senator Nunn and in my letter, and if the ban on gays and lesbians serving in the military were to be dropped, I would counsel all three of my sons to stay out of the military. Absolutely.

My oldest son, Scott, is a student at the University of Maryland, he is just about to graduate. If he were to walk into a recruiter's office, it would be the recruiter's dream come true[!] He is 6 foot 1, blue-eyed, blonde hair, great student.

I have not been the greatest father to him, I will confess that. His mother and I divorced when he was 6 years old. She later died of cancer, lymphoma, when he was 16. He has had a rough life, but he has come through it. And he has persevered, he switched colleges, switched majors, had the problems that most teenagers have growing up. But if he were to go and seriously consider joining the military, I would have to, number 1, personally counsel against it, and number 2, actively fight it.

Because my son, Scott, is a homosexual; and I do not think there is any place for him in the military. I love him; I love him as much as I do any of my sons. I respect him, I think he is a fine person; but he should not serve in the military. And that is the strongest testimonial I think I can give. I am the father of a homosexual boy, a young man, and I do not think he should serve in the military.

I spent 27 years of my life in the military, and I know what it would be like for him if he went in. And it would be hell. And if we went into combat, which as the General said is the whole purpose for us being here, he would be at grave risk if he were to follow in my footsteps as a infantry platoon leader or a company commander. I would be very fearful that his life would be in jeopardy from his own troops.

* * * [T]here are people who would put my son's life at risk in our own Armed Forces. * * *

Chairman [Samuel] NUNN: * * * [L]et me ask each of you this question. There are some who see this as a civil rights issue, or as an issue that is comparable to the debate about women and their role in the military, and certainly we hear over and over again that the same arguments are used against admitting openly gays and lesbians in the military as were used back in the 1940s and 1950s about the admission of blacks into integrated units in the military.

How would each of you respond to the general question as to whether you see an analogy between this debate and the debate that occurred in the civil rights era back in the forties and fifties, and also the question of women? * * *

Colonel PECK. * * * I think if someone declares their homosexuality that that is a statement that defines a behavior. It certainly connotes a behavior. If I say I am black or I am white or Jewish or Protestant or Catholic, it does not necessarily indicate how I am going to behave. But it does indicate a behavior if I say I am homosexual.

When I think of the analogy of race, I find that somewhat offensive. If I could use another analogy, it would be much akin to someone in the military saying I am a racist. Making that statement and then following up with, but I will not let my racial attitudes interfere with my behavior. You certainly would not expect the troops that had to follow that person to respect them or trust them. If the person says they are a racist, anyone of color or of the wrong ethnicity or religion working for him or her would be immediately suspect.

And it is the same analogy that I would have about someone who comes out and declares openly that they are gay or lesbian in the military. Once they do that, I think they compromise their position and it certainly has limited their effectiveness. * * *

General SCHWARZKOPF: There is certainly an analogy, but I do not agree that it is applicable here.

First of all, I do not think it is any secret that Colin Powell and my deputy, Cal Waller, have both said that there is no analogy, and they are certainly capable of speaking, since they entered the Armed Forces during that time and lived through a great deal of it. And I value their judgment greatly in this matter.

Second, we have a distinction between something that a person is born with and a chosen conduct. I know of no medical study anywhere that has validly proved that people are born homosexual. It is a question of choice of conduct in their case. An African American is born black and they are black, and they are going to continue to be black. And they are going to continue to be African Americans, and they have no choice in the matter whatsoever.

I think there is a very important point that we ought to remember, though. In 1953, I believe the statistic was that at the time the orders were issued to integrate our armed services, 30 percent of the people within the military were against the integration. Today, we have 78 or 80 percent of the people in the military against bringing homosexuals in. There is a rather considerable difference in the opinions of the people within our Armed Forces with regard to that issue.

I would also say that at that time I think there was a majority of the American people that were very much in favor of integration of African Americans into our Armed Forces and, indeed, into our society. And my experience has been that it is just the opposite today. The majority of the American people are not in favor of the integration of homosexuals—a lifting of the ban on open homosexuality. * * *

Major [Kathleen] BERGERON: * * * I do not see an analogy to either the race issue or the women's issue. I think color and gender are benign physical characteristics, as the General [Colin Powell] has said, that someone is born with. They do not have a behavior that has the potential to affect other people and the people around them. And I personally resent the analogy to the females or to gender because the issue, and the issue that we are currently still struggling with in the military, I think, is a question of capabilities, and where women are going to be deployed * * *.

So, I do not see analogy with either one. * * *

General SCHWARZKOPF: Mr. Chairman, may I comment on the female issue also? * * *

We discriminate against women in the Armed Forces today, period. It is simply because we have come to a judgment that there are certain organizations where the defense of the nation will suffer if you made it 50/50. And because of that we have adopted combat exclusion rules.

Now, some of them have been lifted, but a lot of them continue to be in effect for the very reason that we are interested in the defense of our Nation. So, yes, we have brought women in, and they do an outstanding job serving in our Armed Forces. But they are discriminated against. They are allowed to only serve in certain positions under certain circumstances, because we worry about the defense of our Nation, which is the foremost precept.

That just happens to be a matter of fact. And so, to say that this is an analogous issue to black Americans or to females, I think it completely misses the point that always, in every case, we have been looking at what's best for the defense of the Nation. * * *

Senator LEVIN: * * * Now let me get to the question that is the heart of the matter. Whether or not if someone is in the military, * * * and they say I am a homosexual, that that person should be removed. They do not say that they have engaged in homosexual activity. They simply say I am a homosexual. That would be enough, for you, to remove that person from the military.

General SCHWARZKOPF: Right, because that would polarize the organization. * * *

Senator LEVIN: * * * You said that the statement I am a homosexual, that is conduct in your book.

General SCHWARZKOPF: Of course. It also happens to be the DOD test today.

NOTE ON THE AFTERMATH OF THE GAYS IN THE MILITARY HEARINGS: DON'T ASK, DON'T TELL

General Schwarzkopf and Colonel Peck were effective witnesses, and Peck's was the most dramatic testimony of the hearings. Is there any cogent response to the heartfelt confession of a father who felt so strongly about the issue that he would not only steer his son away from a career he loved, but was willing to "out" that son on national television? What are the implications of his uncontradicted assertion that straight soldiers might kill an openly gay soldier? (When supporters of the ban made the same point in House committee hearings, Committee Chair Ron Dellums expressed outrage that this would be tolerated in an organization that prides itself on discipline.)

On July 17, President Clinton endorsed Senator Nunn's "don't ask, don't tell" approach, and in the next week both House and Senate held hearings on the new policy. Senator Nunn's Armed Services Committee assembled Secretary of Defense Leslie Aspin and the entire Joint Chiefs of Staff for a hearing on the new policy. The most dramatic point was when Senator Dan Coats (R–Ind.) polled the Joint Chiefs with the inquiry, "Is homosexuality incompatible with military service?" The response of the Joint Chiefs was split: General Colin Powell (the Chair of the Joint Chiefs), Admiral David Jeremiah (Navy), and General Merrill McPeak (Air Force) responded, *Open homosexuality* in a unit setting is incompatible with military service. Three other Joint Chiefs—General Carl Mundy (Marines), General Gordon Sullivan (Army), and Admiral Frank Kelso II (Naval Operations)—responded, *Homosexuality* is incompatible.

With the support of the President, Congress in Public Law No. 103–160, § 571(a)(1), 107 Stat. 1670, added the following new provision, codified at 10 U.S.C. § 654:

(a) Findings. Congress makes the following findings: * * *

(4) The primary purpose of the armed forces is to prepare for and to prevail in combat should the need arise.

(5) The conduct of military operations requires members of the armed forces to make extraordinary sacrifices, including the ultimate sacrifice, in order to provide for the common defense.

(6) Success in combat requires military units that are characterized by high morale, good order and discipline, and unit cohesion.

(7) One of the most critical elements in combat capability is unit cohesion, that is, the bonds of trust among individual service members that make the combat effectiveness of a military unit greater than the sum of the combat effectiveness of the individual unit members.

(8) Military life is fundamentally different from civilian life in that-

    (A) the extraordinary responsibilities of the armed forces, the unique conditions of military service, and the critical role of unit cohesion, require that the military community, while subject to civilian control, exist as a specialized society; and

    (B) the military society is characterized by its own laws, rules, customs, and traditions, including numerous restrictions on personal behavior, that would not be acceptable in civilian society.

(9) The standards of conduct for members of the armed forces regulate a member's life for 24 hours each day beginning at the moment the member enters military status and not ending until that person is discharged or otherwise separated from the armed forces.

(10) Those standards of conduct, including the Uniform Code of Military Justice, apply to a member of the armed forces at all times that the member has a military status, whether the member is on base or off base, and whether the member is on duty or off duty.

(11) The pervasive application of the standards of conduct is necessary because members of the armed forces must be ready at all times for worldwide deployment to a combat environment.

(12) The worldwide deployment of United States military forces, the international responsibilities of the United States, and the potential for involvement of the armed forces in actual combat routinely make it necessary for members of the armed forces involuntarily to accept living conditions and working conditions that are often spartan, primitive, and characterized by forced intimacy with little or no privacy.

(13) The prohibition against homosexual conduct is a long-standing element of military law that continues to be necessary in the unique circumstances of military service.

(14) The armed forces must maintain personnel policies that exclude persons whose presence in the armed forces would create an unacceptable risk to the armed forces' high standards of morale, good order and discipline, and unit cohesion that are the essence of military capability.

(15) The presence in the armed forces of persons who demonstrate a propensity or intent to engage in homosexual acts would create an unacceptable risk to the high standards of morale, good order and discipline, and unit cohesion that are the essence of military capability.

(b) Policy. A member of the armed forces shall be separated from the armed forces under regulations prescribed by the Secretary of Defense if one or more of the following findings is made and approved in accordance with procedures set forth in such regulations:

(1) That the member has engaged in, attempted to engage in, or solicited another to engage in a homosexual act or acts unless there are further findings, made and approved in accordance with procedures set forth in such regulations, that the member has demonstrated that-

(A) such conduct is a departure from the member's usual and customary behavior;

(B) such conduct, under all the circumstances, is unlikely to recur;

(C) such conduct was not accomplished by use of force, coercion, or intimidation;

(D) under the particular circumstances of the case, the member's continued presence in the armed forces is consistent with the interests of the armed forces in proper discipline, good order, and morale; and

(E) the member does not have a propensity or intent to engage in homosexual acts.

(2) That the member has stated that he or she is a homosexual or bisexual, or words to that effect, unless there is a further finding, made and approved in accordance with procedures set forth in the regulations, that the member has demonstrated that he or she is not a person who engages in, attempts to engage in, has a propensity to engage in, or intends to engage in homosexual acts.

(3) That the member has married or attempted to marry a person known to be of the same biological sex. * * *

(e) Rule of Construction. Nothing in subsection (b) shall be construed to require that a member of the armed forces be processed for separation from the armed forces when a determination is made in accordance with regulations prescribed by the Secretary of Defense that-

(1) the member engaged in conduct or made statements for the purpose of avoiding or terminating military service; and

(2) separation of the member would not be in the best interest of the armed forces.

(f) Definitions. In this section:

(1) The term "homosexual" means a person, regardless of sex, who engages in, attempts to engage in, has a propensity to engage in, or intends to engage in homosexual acts, and includes the terms "gay" and "lesbian."

(2) The term "bisexual" means a person who engages in, attempts to engage in, has a propensity to engage in, or intends to engage in homosexual and heterosexual acts.

(3) The term "homosexual act" means-

(A) any bodily contact, actively undertaken or passively permitted, between members of the same sex for the purpose of satisfying sexual desires; and

(B) any bodily contact which a reasonable person would understand to demonstrate a propensity or intent to engage in an act described in subparagraph (A).

On December 21, 1993, Secretary Aspin issued a memorandum and Directives concerning the implementation of the new policy. Memorandum from Secretary Aspin to the Secretaries of the Military Departments et al. (Dec. 21, 1993). They provided that an applicant to become a member will not be asked about his or her sexual orientation, that "homosexual orientation is not a bar" to "service entry or continued service," but that "homosexual conduct" is. Such "conduct" includes not only homosexual "acts" but also a statement by a member or applicant that "demonstrates a propensity or intent to engage" in such acts. A statement that demonstrates the "propensity" will thus require separation unless the member rebuts a presumption that he or she engages or intends to engage in "homosexual acts" or has a "propensity" to do so. Directives 1332.14 (separations [*i.e.*, discharge] of enlisted personnel), 1332.30 (separations of officers), and 1304.26 (enlistment).

Department of Defense Directive Number 1332.14. Enlisted Administrative Separations.

December 1993.

H.   *Homosexual Conduct.*

1.   Basis.

a.   Homosexual conduct is grounds for separation from the Military Services. Homosexual conduct includes homosexual acts, a statement by a member that demonstrates a propensity or intent to engage in homosexual acts, or a homosexual marriage or attempted marriage. A statement by a member that demonstrates a propensity or intent to engage in homosexual acts is grounds for separation not because it reflects the member's sexual orientation, but because the statement indicates a likelihood that the member engages in or will engage in homosexual acts. Sexual orientation is considered a personal and private matter, and homosexual orientation is not a bar to continued service unless manifested by homosexual conduct.

b.   A member shall be separated under this section if one or more of the following approved findings is made:

(1) The member has engaged in, attempted to engage in, or solicited another to engage in a homosexual act or acts, unless there are approved further findings that:

(a) Such acts are a departure from the member's usual and customary behavior;

(b) Such acts under all circumstances are unlikely to recur;

(c) Such acts were not accomplished by use of force, coercion, or intimidation;

(d) Under the particular circumstances of the case, the member's continued presence in the Armed Forces is consistent with the interest of the Armed Forces in proper discipline, good order, and morale; and

(e) The member does not have a propensity or intent to engage in homosexual acts.

(2) The member has made a statement that he or she is a homosexual or bisexual, or words to that effect, unless there is a further approved finding that the member has demonstrated that he or she is not a person who engages in, attempts to engage in, has a propensity to engage in, or intends to engage in homosexual acts. A statement by a Service member that he or she is a homosexual or bisexual, or words to that effect, creates a rebuttable presumption that the Service member engages in homosexual acts or has a propensity or intent to do so. The Service member shall be advised of this presumption and given the opportunity to rebut the presumption by presenting evidence that he or she does not engage in homosexual acts and does not have a propensity or intent to do so. Propensity to engage in homosexual acts means more than an abstract preference or desire to engage in homosexual acts; it indicates a likelihood that a person engages in or will engage in homosexual acts. In determining whether a member has successfully rebutted the presumption that he or she engages in or has a propensity or intent to engage in homosexual acts, some or all of the following may be considered:

(a) whether the member has engaged in homosexual acts;

(b) the member's credibility;

(c) testimony from others about the member's past conduct, character, and credibility;

(d) the Nature and circumstances of the member's statement;

(e) any other evidence relevant to whether the member is likely to engage in homosexual acts.

This list is not exhaustive; any other relevant evidence may also be considered.

(3) The member has married or attempted to marry a person known to be of the same biological sex (as evidence by the external anatomy of the persons involved).

2. *Burden of Proof.* * * * [Refers to H.4.e. and f., which provide as follows:

e. The member shall bear the burden of proving, by a preponderance of the evidence, that retention is warranted under the limited circumstances described in paragraph H.1.b. except in cases where the member's conduct was solely the result of a desire to avoid or terminate military service.

f. Findings regarding whether or not retention is warranted under the limited circumstances of paragraph H.1.b. are required if the member clearly and specifically raises such limited circumstances.] * * *

HYPOTHETICAL TEACHING SCENARIOS * * *

The following hypothetical scenarios are for training purposes only. They are not meant to prescribe "correct" outcomes, but to illustrate how relevant personnel should approach issues that may arise under the DoD policy on homosexual conduct in the Armed Forces. * * *

2. *Situation*: An officer observes two male junior enlisted Service members walking and holding hands while off-duty and on liberty. The Service members are wearing civilian clothes and are in an isolated wooded park and, except for the officer, they are alone. He reports the incident to the commanding officer (CO) and adds that he is surprised to find out they appear to be homosexuals. He asks the CO what he proposes to do about the incident. The CO decides he will call the two Service members into his office, separately, and ask them about the officer's observations.

Issue: Was the CO's action appropriate? If not, what action should he have taken?

Discussion: The officer's observation of the two enlisted Service members walking and holding hands in the park constitutes credible information of homosexual conduct if the officer is someone the CO otherwise trusts and believes. The two Service members' hand-holding in these circumstances indicates a homosexual act and therefore the commanding officer may follow-up and inquire further. Probably, the extent of the inquiry will be two confidential one-on-one conferences between the CO and the two Service members to inquire into the incident.

Before the Service members are asked to discuss or explain the incident, the CO should advise them of the military's policy on homosexual conduct. Should they decline to discuss the matter, the questioning should stop. At that point, the CO may consider other relevant information and decide whether to initiate administrative separation actions based on the information he possesses. * * *

12. *Situation*: An enlisted Service member states to his commanding officer that he is a homosexual. He also tells this to several other enlisted members. An Administrative Discharge Board is convened. At the Board hearing, the member does not dispute that he stated on several occasions that he is a homosexual. He promises, however, that he will not engage in any homosexual acts during the remainder of his term of enlistment. The member presents no other evidence.

Issue: How should the Board consider whether the Service member has successfully rebutted the presumption?

Discussion: A statement by a Service member that he or she is a homosexual creates a rebuttable presumption that the member engages in or has a propensity or intent to engage in homosexual acts. This means that the statement itself is evidence that the member engages in or is likely to engage in homosexual acts. If the member fails to demonstrate that he or she in fact does not engage in homosexual acts and is not likely to do so, he or she may be discharged. * * *

If the only evidence that the member presented was his promise that he would not engage in any homosexual acts during the remainder of his term of enlistment, the Board would determine whether that promise, in light of the Board's assessment of the member's credibility and the nature and circumstances of his statements that he was a homosexual, was sufficient to demonstrate that he does not engage in homosexual acts and is not likely to do so. * * *

PROBLEM 7–3

APPLICATIONS OF DON'T ASK, DON'T TELL

(A) Hand–Holding. Assume that the Board in Hypothetical Situation No. 2 separates the two men based on the evidence of hand-holding. Both men deny they are homosexuals, and there is no evidence of other conduct. The men sue to remain in the Army. You are a federal district judge. How do you rule, and why?

(B) Hanging Out at a Lesbian Bar. A servicewoman has been observed on three occasions leaving a bar known to cater to a lesbian clientele. On one occasion she left with another woman, but there was no evidence of intimacy between the two. Are these sightings the basis for separation? Should the commanding officer commence an investigation? This problem is adapted from Hypothetical Situation No. 3 (omitted in our excerpt).

(C) Confessions of Status. Assume that the Board in Hypothetical No. 12 separates the man based only upon his verbal statement and without any evidence of homosexual activities. Would a judge sustain this action? Read the next cases.

NOTE ON DISCHARGES UNDER THE DON'T ASK, DON'T TELL REGIME

As you can see from the foregoing account, the new policy is riddled with compromises and uncertainties for service personnel. An excellent collection of essays on the new policy in operation is *Don't Ask, Don't Tell: Debating the Gay Ban in the Military* (Aaron Belkin & Geoffrey Bateman eds. 2003). Moreover, the Servicemembers Legal Defense Network (SLDN), founded by Dixon Osburn and Michelle Benecke in the wake of the 1993 statute, has monitored the don't ask, don't tell policy since its inception and has produced a series of useful and fact-filled reports on the implementation of the policy. The SLDN report for 2003 contains the following data on discharges of lesbian, gay, and bisexual personnel from the armed forces in the last 23 years. From 1980 to 1982, the number of discharges steadily increased, from 1854 to 1998, and then declined almost every year after that, to 1660 in 1985, then down to 941 in 1990. The discharges reached rock bottom at 617 in 1994—and then started climbing again, to 772 (1995), 870 (1996), 1007 (1997), 1163 (1998), 1046 (1999), 1212 (2000), and 1273 (2001). Since 2001, the numbers have been falling again, to 906 (2002) and lower during the Iraq War (2003–??).

Several points are suggested by this and other data. The first is that, overall, the number of gay-related discharges has gone down over the last twenty years; the decline is less remarkable in light of the fact that the size of the U.S. armed forces has declined from just over two million soldiers in 1980 to 1.4 million in 2002. Still, the rate of discharge has declined from about 9 people dismissed for every 10,000 soldiers in 1980 to about 6 people dismissed per 10,000 soldiers in 2002. Periods of war (1990–91 and 2002) have been associated with dips in the discharge rates.

Second, the rate of discharge has been much higher for women and racial minorities than for white male personnel. Although women have constituted between 10% and 15% of military personnel for this period, they have constituted between 20% and 31% of the gay-related discharges. African–American women have been discharged at a rate almost three times their percentage of the military, and Latinas have also been discharged in numbers disproportionate to their overall force. See Sevicemembers Legal Defense Network, *Conduct Unbecoming: The Ninth Annual Report on "Don't Ask, Don't Tell, Don't Pursue, Don't Harass"* 43–44 (2003).

Third, the rate of discharge spiked up after the implementation of the "don't ask, don't tell" policy. Ironically, a policy that was billed as a liberalization saw a doubling of the number of discharges between 1994 and 2001, a trend that is more remarkable in light of the fact that the total number of women and men in the armed forces declined sharply in that period. Consider the ways that theories of sexuality, gender, and the law help us understand the odd history of gay-related discharge numbers. (The Defense Department claims that the decline owes much to personnel who are "outing" themselves in order to exit the armed forces.)

1. *Feminist Theories.* Feminist theory would understand the discharge numbers in light of women's changing role in the armed forces; some feminists would consider this to the primary reason for continued gay-bashing discharges. During a period in which women are becoming more prominent in the armed forces, but are still not present in more than token numbers in command positions, men will be particularly resentful. The time-tested means for men to resist women's entry into traditional male domains are sexual harassment (Chamallas, "The New Gender Panic") and lesbian-baiting (Michelle Beinecke & Kristin Dodge, "Military Women in Nontraditional Fields: Casualties of the Armed Forces' war on Homosexuals," 13 *Harv. Women's L.J.* 215 [1990]). This kind of boys culture hazing was hard to control in the 1990s, in part because many commanders did not agree with what they perceived as the pro-gay "don't ask, don't tell" policy, as well as what they perceived as the effeminization of the armed forces. How would Catharine MacKinnon and Gayle Rubin (feminist theorists presented in Chapter 5, Section 2A) approach this problem?

2. *Prejudice Theory.* Elisabeth Young–Bruehl, *Anatomy of Prejudices* (1996) suggests that official policy is not going to change people's prejudices if they serve important emotional functions, as homophobia does. She makes the fascinating observation that the 1993 don't ask, don't tell compromise served the interests of *hysterical homophobes* (people who project onto homosexuals their own unacceptable sexual feelings) but not other kinds: "Homosexuals may remain in the military, available for actual or fantasy sexual service, but must be secret, closeted. For *obsessionals*," people who believe that homosexuals secretly conspire to undermine institutions and mores dear to them, "this compromise is a horrible opening of the door to infiltration, an invitation to rapists, and for *narcissists* it is a dreadful blurring of boundaries, a defeat for the project of establishing self-definitional spheres." (*Id.* at 158–59.) If she is right, then obsessional and narcissistic homophobes might be expected to undermine don't ask, don't tell by continuing to ask, and perhaps by asking with even greater intensity. This might help explain the continuing witch-hunts during the Clinton Administration.

3. *Social Constructionist Theory.* Michel Foucault and Judith Butler suggest another kind of explanation for the high discharge rates of the 1990s: the highly visible debate about gays in the military itself creates a discourse of silent-but-intense super-scrutiny that is more harmful for closeted lesbian and gay personnel than the old policy was. Gay rights advocates themselves have *sexualized* the armed forces in ways that put the unmarried, the slightly unconventional, the loner on the spot in ways that they were not before the public debate. Some military gays believe that the Perry Watkins case and the 1993 debate among the White House, Congress, and the Defense Department created a false picture of the armed forces as pervasively sexualized. *E.g.*, Jennifer Egan, "Uniforms in the Closet," *N.Y. Times Mag.*, June 28, 1998, at 26–31, 40, 48, 56; Diane Mazur, "The Unknown Soldier: A Critique of 'Gays in the Military' Scholarship and Litigation," 29 *U. Calif. Davis L. Rev.* 223 (1996). If that is so, it empowers military homophobes in ways the pre–1993 policy did not, for the homosocial armed forces has a strong incentive in a sex-ambivalent and gay-negative society to purge itself of suspicions of sexual randiness and homosexuality.

Lt. Paul Thomasson, USN v. William J. Perry, 80 F.3d 915 (4th Cir. 1996) (en banc). A fractured Fourth Circuit held that § 654(b) was constitutionally applied to expel Lt. Paul Thomasson after he declared his homosexuality and then refused to offer evidence to rebut the presumption he had engaged in homosexual acts. Nine judges joined the majority opinion of Chief Judge J. Harvie **Wilkinson**, which followed *Steffan*: Courts should defer to the political branches on military issues, and such deference includes the armed forces' judgment that statements of homosexuality are plausible evidence of illegal sodomy, and that open homosexuality within the military context undermines morale and unit cohesion. Four judges joined Judge K.K. **Hall**'s opinion dissenting from this holding, for reasons similar to Judge Wald's dissent in *Steffan*.

Six judges joined a concurring opinion by Judge Michael **Luttig**, who adopted an argument advanced by the Family Research Council, that the Department of Defense regulations are invalid. "The requirement that, in order to be discharged, one must at least demonstrate a likelihood to engage in homosexual acts exists only in a regulation promulgated by the Administration, ostensibly in implementation of the statute. That regulation redefines the statutory term 'propensity' so that only those homosexual service members who are *likely* to engage in homosexual acts will be discharged. Through this regulation the Administration has effectively secured the very policy regarding military service by homosexuals that it was denied by the Congress." In short, the gays in the military flap of 1993 ended up recodifying the prior policy, and the Clinton Administration's spin is contrary to the statute.

As evidence for this position, Judge Luttig relied on the structure of § 654(b)(2), which says personnel shall be separated if they state they are homosexual; the proviso ("unless") only allows personnel to stay in if they can persuade the armed forces that they are really *not* homosexual. Hence, Judge Luttig interpreted § 654(b)(2)'s exception for a soldier who can show that he or she is *not* a person with "propensity to engage in, or intends to engage in homosexual acts," to apply only to the *heterosexual who misspoke*, and not to the *celibate homosexual*. Judge Luttig argued that this reading is reinforced by § 654(b)(1), which allows a *heterosexual who slipped* and engaged in one homosexual act ("I was drunk and didn't know what I was doing and will never do it again") to stay in the armed forces, so long as he or she can persuade the military that he or she really is a heterosexual. Hence, Judge Luttig would have invalidated the regulation, in part, but would still have expelled Thomasson based upon the statute itself.

Although only six of the twelve participating judges joined Judge Luttig, none of the Fourth Circuit judges responded to his arguments. Is there a response? Assume the regulation is invalid, and that "homosexuals" are excluded from service merely because of their status. Is Judge Luttig right that this is a constitutional policy? In light of *Romer v. Evans*?

NOTE ON DON'T ASK, DON'T TELL CONSTITUTIONAL CHALLENGES AND THE DEFERENCE ISSUE

Thomasson has emerged as the leading case evaluating the don't ask, don't tell policy, but *Thomasson* and its progeny have added little to the analytical debate between the majority and dissent in *Steffan, supra*. Every federal court of appeals has thus far upheld the policy, albeit usually in the face of forceful dissenting opinions. See *Able v. United States*, 88 F.3d 1280 (2d Cir. 1996), *on remand*, 968 F.Supp. 850 (E.D.N.Y. 1997), *rev'd*, 155 F.3d 628 (2d Cir. 1998); *Richenberg v. Perry*, 97 F.3d 256 (8th Cir. 1996); *Holmes v. California Army Nat'l Guard*, 124 F.3d 1126 (9th Cir.1997). The Second, Fourth, Eighth, and Ninth Circuits have basically agreed with *Steffan*'s analytical structure for disposing of the First Amendment and Equal Protection Clause problems with penalizing a soldier because she says she is gay: The statement "I am gay/lesbian" is not being punished *per se*, but is only being used as evidence that the declarant presumptively commits "homosexual acts" (sodomy) criminal under the Uniform Code of Military Justice.

Dissenting opinions by Judges K.K. Hall (*Thomasson*), Richard Arnold (*Richenberg*), and Stephen Reinhardt (*Holmes*; compare his dissent in *Watkins*) followed Judge Patricia Wald's *Steffan* dissent in arguing that there is no rational basis for believing that the openly lesbian soldier is *more likely* to engage in illegal behavior than her openly straight male colleague, who is more likely to have engaged in illegal sexual harassment, illegal rape, illegal anal sex and is almost as likely to have engaged in illegal oral sex as well. The dissenters' arguments have certainly received a constitutional boost from the Supreme Court's decisions in *Romer* and *Lawrence*.

The circuit court majorities have responded with the deference argument: The armed forces have to make broad categorical judgments, excluding sight-impaired people as well as gays for example, and courts should not interfere with those judgments, especially those that go to the unit cohesion and morale features central to the military mission. Recall that the Supreme Court bent over backwards to defer to political and military judgments on an issue of blatant sex discrimination in *Rostker*. Does the deference argument survive *Lawrence*? In dissent, Justice Scalia opined that it did not. Is he right? Explore the deference issue in greater detail.

1. *Issues of Fact versus Issues of Law.* Perhaps deference is most appropriate as to issues of fact, such as the Administration's idea that statements of homosexuality are evidence of sodomy, which is illegal under the Uniform Code of Military Justice. This is actually quite true, but recall that the statement "I am a heterosexual" is just as probative evidence that one has and will commit sodomy in violation of the Code. Laumann et al., *Sexual Practices in the United States* 98–99. The issue of deference, therefore, does not relate to a matter of fact (homosexuals are prone to commit illegal sodomy), but relates to a matter of discrimination law (why does the military treat presumptive heterosexual sodomites differently?).

2. *Does a Historical Pattern of "Crying Wolf" Matter? What About Evidence from Experts within the Military?* As to military judgments that gay people would disrupt unit cohesion, the military used that to justify racial segregation and exclusion of women from a broad range of military positions. The available evidence, recounted in this chapter, suggests that the military was crying "wolf" both times. Is the gay/lesbian exclusion the third "wolf"? Return to Ken Karst's article on military service and the construction of manhood. His overall argument seems to be that the race, sex, and sexual orientation exclusions have been inspired by similar prejudices and were long justified by the same kinds of inaccurate stereotypes and institutionalist logic. The logic of his article is that the gay exclusion should follow the path of the race and sex ones—revocation.

A number of expert studies by executive branch consultants lend support to Karst's argument. The most detailed study was that of the RAND Institute for the Department of Defense in 1993. Consistent with prior findings by the Government Accounting Office and the Defense Personnel Security Research and Education Center, RAND concluded: "concerns about the potential effect of permitting [open] homosexuals to serve in the military are not groundless, but the problems do not appear insurmountable, and there is ample reason to believe that heterosexual and homosexual personnel can work together effectively."[c] Do the views of people like retired General Schwarzkopf suffice to justify the policy in light of this evidence to the contrary?

3. *Experience in Other Countries.* Almost all of our NATO and North American allies have revoked their exclusions of gay people from their armed forces. The Center for the Study of Sexual Minorities in the Military at the University of California, Santa Barbara has studied the transitions from gay-exclusionary to gay-inclusionary armed forces in a wide range of countries. The Center's studies have concluded that the transitions went much more frictionlessly than anticipated. Generally, some but not many soldiers "came out" as lesbian or gay, but predicted problems with morale and unit cohesion did not materialize. *E.g.*, Aaron Belkin & Jason McNichol, *The Effects of the 1992 Lifting of Restrictions on Gay and Lesbian Service in the Canadian Forces: Appraising the Evidence* (April 2000); Aaron Belkin & Melissa Levitt, *The Effects of Lifting of Restrictions on Gay and Lesbian Service in the Israeli Forces: Appraising the Evidence* (June 2000).

Consider the relevance of the experience of other countries. One might question their relevance, as General Schwartzkopf did in the 1993 Senate hearings, on grounds that the armed forces of other countries are not comparable to ours or that it is too early to tell what effects the policy changes have had. Most of the other countries are not nearly so socially homophobic as the United States is; what might fly in gay-friendly Canada and The Netherlands might not in the United States. Finally, inclusion of gays in the military has generally been accomplished by the political branches, and not the courts, in other countries. On the other hand, the pervasiveness of the unit cohesion argument against gays in the military and its uniform failure to predict post-integration events might count for something.

Responding to a decision declaring its exclusion violative of the European Convention on Human Rights, see *Lustig-Prean v. United Kingdom*, 29 EHRR 548 (Eur. Ct. Human Rights, 1999), the United Kingdom, a

---

c. RAND, National Defense Research Institute, Report to the Office of the Secretary of Defense, *Sexual Orientation and U.S. Military Personnel Policy: Options and Assessment* 329–30 (1993). See also U.S. General Accounting Office, Report to Congressional Requestors, *Defense Force Management:* *DOD's Policy on Homosexuality* (June 1992); Theodore Sarbin & Kenneth Karois, Defense Personnel Security Research and Education Center, *Nonconforming Sexual Orientations and Military Suitability* (Dec. 1988), reprinted in *Gays in Uniform: The Pentagon's Secret Reports* (Kate Dyer ed. 1990).

country not known as gay-friendly, opened military service to openly lesbian, gay, and bisexual persons. Reportedly, the new policy has been implemented without any troubles. See Aaron Belkin & R.L. Evans, *The Effects of Including Gay and Lesbian Soldiers in the British Armed Forces: Appraising the Evidence* (Center for the Study of Sexual Minorities in the Military Nov. 2000). There is no evidence that the service of openly lesbian or gay soldiers interfered in any way with British troops' morale in the Iraq War.

NOTE ON HARASSMENT OF GENDER AND SEXUAL MINORITIES IN THE ARMED FORCES

The Servicemembers Legal Defense Network (SLDN) has documented anti-gay harassment and other forms of violence, including murders of suspected gay personnel, within the armed forces. On July 5, 1999, Private Barry Winchell was murdered in his sleep by two soldiers who had been among those who regularly harassed him as a suspected "fag." (Only one of the two soldiers was convicted of the murder; the second soldier received a lenient plea bargain.) Investigations in the wake of his murder found that anti-gay "banter" was routine in Fort Campbell, where Winchell was posted, and that repeated harassment of the private went unpunished by superior officers who were aware of it. Winchell's parents have filed wrongful death claims against the Army under the Military Claims Act.

In the wake of unfavorable publicity surrounding the Winchell murder, the Defense Department's Inspector General conducted a survey of 75,000 service personnel; its report, issued in March 2000, revealed that 80% had heard anti-gay remarks within the last year, 37% had witnessed or experienced anti-gay harassment, and 5% had witnessed or experienced anti-gay assaults. 85% of the respondents reported that the officers in charge took no action to stop the harassment. In July 2000, a DOD working group published an *Anti-Harassment Action Plan*, with thirteen recommendations. The Department approved the findings and drafted a Directive on the matter of harassment. Each of the service branches (Army, Navy, Air Force, Marine Corps) has developed and implemented its own regulations and directives. Probably in response to better training and less tolerance of harassment, reported incidents have steadily declined from 1998 to 1999 to 2000 to 2001.

The Army, the branch with which Private Winchell was associated, took the lead in developing rules against harassment. In a Directive entitled "Dignity and Respect for All," ALARACT008/00 (Jan. 2000), the Army took the position that, "Harassment of soldiers for any reason, to include perceived sexual orientation, will not be tolerated." According to SLDN, the decline in antigay harassment in 2000 was most pronounced in the Army and was due in part to the new intolerant policy toward antigay harassment. Nonetheless, there were still plenty of episodes.

*

CHAPTER 8

SEXUALITY, GENDER, AND THE LAW IN THE WORKPLACE

What does it mean to talk about "sexuality in the workplace"? Or "gender in the workplace"? Some possibilities include:

- the visible manifestation of sexuality, the traditional example being pregnancy and a more recent example being AIDS;

- persons whose status is sexualized by society, even without visible manifestations (gay men, lesbians);

- the choreographed display of gendered ideals, such as a waitress' wearing tight, body-revealing clothing, or their confusion, such as a man's wearing such clothing;

- eroticized behavior, exhibiting one's sexuality in the workplace;

- the use of sexuality to gain advantages in the workplace (*e.g.*, sleeping your way to the top);

- the use of sexuality as a mechanism of harassment, usually to dominate the space and dynamics of the workplace by those traditionally empowered.

All of these meanings emerge in the cases and other materials that you will read in this Chapter. Much of the law in this field implicitly seeks the purging of sexuality from the workplace. Is this merely an appropriate, rational suppression of eroticization from an arena in which it does not belong? Consider the following perspectives.

Rosemary Pringle, Sexuality at Work

From *Secretaries Talk* (1988).*

If the boss-secretary relation is organised around sexuality and family imagery this seems to place it outside the modern bureaucratic structures that are a feature of all large organisations. The relationship is often conceptualised either as archaic or as marginal to the workings of bureaucracy "proper". It is argued here that, on the contrary, the boss-secretary relationship is the most visible aspect of a pattern of domination based on desire and sexuality. Far from being an exception, it vividly illustrates the workings of modern bureaucracies. Gender and sexuality are central not only in the boss-secretary relation but in all workplace power relations.

Two bodies of theory are important to the development of this argument. A variety of feminist analyses, particularly of sexual harassment, indicate the ubiquity of coercive sexual encounters in the workplace; and theorists such as Marcuse and Foucault have indicated, in their different ways, the connections between sexual *pleasure* and the operations of *power*. By contrast, most organisation theory continues to treat sexuality and gender as marginal or incidental to the workplace. In doing so, however, it expresses a widely held view that while gender was central to "traditional" social relations it has become outmoded in "modern" society which is more concerned with "personhood". Since degendering is implicit in the modernist emphasis on rationality and in the development of liberal democratic institutions, it is important to start by considering the ways in which gender is suppressed in the main texts.

For Weber, bureaucracy is progressive in that it breaks down the old patriarchal structures and removes the arbitrary power held by fathers and masters in traditional society. He distinguishes between traditionalism, which is patriarchal, and the rational-legal order of the modern world which promises the end of tyranny and despotism and the development of liberal democracy. All attempts to theorise bureaucracy have been carried out in the shadow of Weber's classical account. He still sets the terms of the dominant frameworks for studies of power and organisations. Although the limits of his theory have been clearly shown in more than half a century of organisation studies, Weber's version retains a powerful ideological hold. People's views of how organisations actually do work and how they "ought" to work are still filtered through Weber and the theory becomes, in some sense, a self-fulfilling prophecy.

Weber has been given a favourable reading by liberal feminists because he does appear to provide a basis for understanding breakdown of patriarchal relations. Equal Employment Opportunity and Affirmative Action plans, for example, emphasize the importance of excluding "private" considerations and insist on the impersonal application of rules. Secretaries, it is thought, should ignore or reject the sexual and familial images and focus on skills and career ladders. The implication here is that secretarial work should be "rationalized", made to fit the bureaucratic pattern. In her broadly liberal feminist analysis, *Men and Women of the Corporation* [1977], Rosabeth Moss Kanter denies that gender or sexuality have much explanatory potential. She observes that "what look like sex differences may really be power differences" and that "power wipes out sex" [pp. 201–12]. In this framework the problem for secretaries is that they lack power; they are caught up in an old-fashioned patriarchal relationship that is out of kilter with "modern" business practices. The question then becomes how can individual secretaries remove themselves from these backwaters and place themselves on the management ladder? Kanter's very lucid analysis of the power structure is designed to help individuals articulate their positions and thereby improve their own manoeuvering for power.

According to Weber, the overriding concerns of bureaucratic organisations are efficiency and consistency in the application of rules. Authority established by rules stands in contrast to the "regulation of relationships through individual privilege and bestowals of favour" which characterizes patrimonialism. Traditional forms of domination are based on the household unit and are patriarchal in the direct sense that the father, as head of the family, possesses authority. In larger forms of traditional organisation authority is patrimonial, that is, it takes the form of personal allegiance to the master. In bureaucracy, by contrast, loyalty is to an office not to a particular person. Impersonality and the separation of the public and private spheres distinguish bureaucracy from traditionalism. As theorised by Weber, bureaucracy "has a 'rational' character: rules, means, ends, and matter-of-factness dominate its bearing. . . . The march of bureaucracy has destroyed structures of domination which had no rational character, in the special sense of the term."

According to Weber's "ideal type", bureaucracies are based on impersonality, functional specialisation, a hierarchy of authority and the impartial application of rules. There are well-defined duties for each specialised position and recruitment takes place on criteria of demonstrated knowledge and competence. Authority is held in the context of strict rules and regulations and graded hierarchically with the supervision of lower offices by higher ones. Authority established by rules stands in contrast to the "regulation of relationships through individual privileges and bestowals of favor" which characterised traditional structures. Above all there is a separation of the public world of rationality and efficiency from the private sphere of emotional and personal life.

The boss-secretary relationship runs against every one of these criteria. By having direct access to the powerful, secretaries are outside the hierarchy of authority. Far from being specialised, they can be called upon to do just about anything, and their work may overlap with that of their bosses. The relationship is based on personal rapport, involves a degree of intimacy, day-to-day familiarity and shared secrets unusual for any but lovers or close friends, and is capable of generating intense feelings of loyalty, dependency and personal commitment. How are we to explain this least "bureaucratic" of relationships? Is it merely an exception or does its existence suggest problems with the way bureaucracy itself has been theorised? * * *

It remains important to analyse the discourse of "bureaucratic rationality" as it affects men and women. This involves not so much a rejection of Weber as a rereading designed to bring out the underlying assumptions. It can be argued that while the rational-legal or bureaucratic form presents itself as gender-neutral, it actually constitutes a new kind of patriarchal structure. The apparent neutrality of rules and goals disguises the class and gender interests served by them. Weber's account of "rationality" can be interpreted as a commentary on the construction of a particular kind of masculinity based on the exclusion of the personal, the sexual and the feminine from any definition of "rationality". The values of instrumental rationality are strongly associated with the masculine individual, while the feminine is associated with that "other" world of chaos and disorder. This does not mean that men are in fact "rational" or that women are "emotional" but rather that they learn to recognise themselves in these conceptions.

It may be argued that "rationality" requires as a condition of its existence the simultaneous creation of a realm of the Other, be it personal, emotional, sexual or "irrational". Masculine rationality attempts to drive out the feminine but does not exist without it. "Work" and "sex" are implicitly treated as the domains of the "conscious" and the "unconscious". But far from being separate spheres the two are thoroughly intertwined. Despite the illusion of ordered rationality, workplaces do not actually manage to exclude the personal or sexual. Rather than seeing the presence of sexuality and familial relations in the workplace as an aspect of traditional, patriarchal authority, it makes more sense to treat them as part of modern organisational forms. I am concerned here not with "actual" families but with the family symbolism that structures work as well as personal relationships. The media, advertising and popular culture are saturated in such imagery, which provides a dominant set of social meanings in contemporary capitalist society. * * *

If we accept that a series of discourses on sexuality underpin bureaucratic control, it is possible to see secretaries not as marginal but as paradigmatic of how that power operates. Thus the boss-secretary relation need not be seen as an anomalous piece of traditionalism or of an incursion of the private sphere, but rather as a site of strategies of power in which sexuality is an important though by no means the only dimension. Far from being marginal to the workplace, sexuality is everywhere. It is alluded to in dress and self-presentation, in jokes and gossip, looks and flirtations, secret affairs and dalliances, in fantasy, and in the range of coercive behaviours that we now call sexual harassment. Rather than being exceptional in its sexualisation, the boss-secretary relation is an important nodal point for the organisation of sexuality and pleasure. This is no less true when the boss happens to be a woman.

Sex at work is very much on display. It is undoubtedly true that for both men and women sexual fantasies and interactions are a way of killing time, of giving a sense of adventure, of livening up an otherwise boring day. As Michael Korda put it, "the amount of sexual energy circulating in any office is awe-inspiring, and given the slightest sanction and opportunity it bursts out". Marcuse was one of the first to recognise the pervasiveness of sexuality in the workplace and to try to theorise it. He recognised that it was not just an instance of incomplete repression but was encouraged as a means of gratification in otherwise boring jobs. If open-plan offices are about surveillance they are also, he suggests, about controlled sex.

Marcuse introduced the concept of "repressive desublimation" to explain how people were being integrated into a system which in its sweeping rationality, which propels efficiency and growth, is itself irrational. He pointed to the ways in which, without ceasing to be an instrument of labour, the body is allowed to exhibit its sexual features in the everyday work world and in work relations. . . . The sexy office and sales girls, the handsome, virile junior executive and floor worker are highly marketable commodities, and the possession of suitable mistresses . . . facilitates the career of even the less exalted ranks in the business community. . . . Sex is integrated into work and public relations and is thus made susceptible to (controlled) satisfaction. . . . But no matter how controlled . . . it is also gratifying to the managed individuals. . . . Pleasure, thus adjusted, generates submission.

In Foucault's account, sexuality in the workplace is not simply repressed or sublimated or subjected to controlled expression. It is actively produced in a multiplicity of discourses and interactions. Modern Western societies have accumulated a vast network of discourses on sex and pleasure. We expect to find pleasure in self-improvement in both our work and non-work activities. Purposive activity operates not through the denial of pleasure but its promise: we will become desirable. * * *

The difficulty with both Marcuse and Foucault is that they are gender-blind. While they establish the centrality of sexuality in the workplace, they pay very little attention to gender. Marcuse presumes that men and women are equally and similarly oppressed, ignoring the ways that women are required to market sexual attractiveness to men. Foucault acknowledges gender struggles but does not afford them any priority or permanence. Central to his work is the idea that there is no constant human subject or any rational course to history. If there is no human subject, then for Foucault there is no gendered subject. Feminist struggles are, like any others, merely immediate responses to local and specific situations. Foucault's account of power is counterposed to any binary opposition between rulers and ruled. Though he underplays the significance of gender, he does provide the basis for developing a more dynamic and fluid conception of power relations between men and women. "Male power" is not simply and unilaterally imposed on women—gender relations are a process involving strategies and counter-strategies of power.

Where organisation theorists have maintained a division between sex and work, women are left in little doubt that the two go together. Women are constantly aware of sexual power structures and the need to put up barriers against men. Though they might enjoy male company and male jokes they are careful to limit their participation and to make it clear to men "how far they can go". Many secretaries have chosen their current jobs on the basis of minimising any further experiences of sexual harassment. One head office, nicknamed the "twenty five year club" because of the length of time most of the managers had been there, was regarded as something of a refuge. If there was no sexual excitement on the sixteenth floor, at least there was no danger.

Vicki Schultz, "The Sanitized Workplace"

112 Yale Law Journal 2061, 2158–60, 2191 (2003)*

* * * [F]or many employees, the determination of whether certain sexual behaviors are offensive (or perhaps even "sexual") turns on who is engaging in it. Such findings are not surprising, for they confirm the general insight that workplace sexuality is given meaning within organizational context. As a result, the same sexual conduct that would be tolerated—or even welcomed—from coworkers of a similar status may well be labeled sexual harassment if it is engaged in by coworkers of a different status, particularly if they are perceived as part of a social group culturally marked as "sexual."

In a recent study of waiters in restaurants that employ equal numbers of men and women, for example, the researchers found that, as in many restaurants, their subjects worked in cultures that were highly sexualized. In the restaurants where they worked:

> [S]exual joking, touching, and fondling were common, everyday occurrences. . . . For example, when asked if he and other waitpeople ever joke about sex, one waiter replied, "about 90% percent of [the jokes] are about sex." According to a waitress, "at work . . . [we're] used to patting and touching and hugging." Another waiter said, "I do not go through a shift without someone . . . pinching my nipples or poking me in the butt or grabbing my crotch. . . . It's just what we do at work."

True to our earlier observations, in these gender-integrated workplaces, the women as well as the men said they enjoyed the sexualized interactions; they actively participated in the ritualized displays of heterosexuality with their male coworkers, and did not consider their sexual advances improper. Yet, when some of the Mexican men, who were concentrated in positions as kitchen cooks and busing staff, made identical sexual overtures, the white waitresses were quick to take offense and to label the conduct sexual harassment. * * *

Several of the white waitresses admitted that they felt comfortable engaging in sexual banter and touching with the other waitpeople (who were predominantly white), but not with the Mexican workers. In the racial and occupational hierarchy of the restaurant culture, the white women

* Reprinted by permission of the Yale Law Journal.

closed ranks against the Mexican men as sexual harassers, whom they perceived as too beneath them to be assuming sexual familiarities.

In addition to these racial/status differences, the researchers found that sexual orientation mattered to how sexual conduct was perceived. Male waiters who saw themselves as heterosexual characterized sexual horseplay and conversation as "sexual harassment" when it came from openly gay men, even though the waiters welcomed similar interactions with other straight men. One of the straight men objected to a gay coworker touching him on the rear end, for example, and another expressed discomfort about a gay baker talking about his sexual experiences and desires. Yet, these same men conceded that similar sexual conversation and horseplay from straight men didn't bother them, and bragged that they themselves initiated such interactions. In the eyes of many of the straight men, the gay men were marked as potential sexual harassers from the beginning. Thus, any expression of sexuality by gay men became a self-fulfilling prophecy—a confirmation of the misplaced sexual desire they were expected to embody and enact. * * *

These results are disheartening, but they are not surprising. * * * Within many sectors of American society, members of stigmatized minority groups are stereotyped as overly—even pathologically—"sexual." African-American men have learned not to participate in the sexual banter and horseplay of predominantly white organizations, or else risk threatening organizational power relations. Black women, too, must downplay their sexuality—and even their sexual attractiveness—or else risk bringing unwanted attention to themselves. Gay men and lesbians often feel pressure to suppress information about their personal lives in the workplace to protect themselves from stigma, and other sexual minorities occupy an even lower place on the hierarchy of sexual propriety. Working-class men of all races are seen as crude and vulgar, especially when they engage in sexual displays toward their female "betters." Even white working-class women are often considered bad girls whose bawdy sexuality places them outside the bounds of respectability and protection. * * *

Debate on the Employment Non–Discrimination Act [ENDA]

United States Senate, September 10, 1996.
142 *Cong. Rec.* S10137.

MR. NICKLES:

[The proposed legislation would bar sexual orientation discrimination.] ENDA threatens to make sexuality an issue where it has never been an issue before. Currently, most employers don't know about their employees' sexual orientation and don't care. ENDA will help put an end to that. Some employers do care, and ENDA will put an end to that, too. ENDA is about sexuality, but it is not about privacy. ENDA is about going public.

SECTION 1

SEX DISCRIMINATION

PART A. DISCRIMINATION BY THE GOVERNMENT

A dominant historical theme of Anglo–American law has been the state's willingness to exclude sexualized minorities from the workplace. The first, and longest lived, exclusion was of women. Women's exclusion from jobs and from the professions was invisible for most of American history, so "natural" did it seem that women's "place" was in the home. It was not until the mid-nineteenth century that women became a sufficiently serious employment threat that unstated, implicit exclusions of women from jobs came to be stated and explicit. At the same time, the New Women started pressing their claims in court. After the adoption of the Fourteenth Amendment in 1868, women had colorable claims that their exclusions by the state were unconstitutional.

Myra Bradwell's application for a license to practice law was denied by the Illinois Supreme Court solely because she was a (married) woman. The U.S. Supreme Court affirmed this judgment against attack in *Bradwell v. Illinois*, 83 U.S. (16 Wall.) 130 (1873). The Court held that Bradwell's exclusion did not violate the Privileges or Immunities Clause. Justice Bradley, speaking for himself and Justices Swayne and Field, concurred in the judgment on broad grounds, reflecting a widely held theory of sex and gender:

> [T]he civil law, as well as nature herself, has always recognized a wide difference in the respective spheres and destinies of man and woman. Man is, or should be, woman's protector and defender. The natural and proper timidity and delicacy which belongs to the female sex evidently unfits it for many of the occupations of civil life. The constitution of the family organization, which is founded in the divine ordinance, as well as in the nature of things, indicates the domestic sphere as that which properly belongs to the domain and functions of womanhood. The harmony, not to say identity, of interests and views which belong, or should belong, to the family institution is repugnant to the idea of a woman adopting a distinct and independent career from that of her husband. So firmly fixed was this sentiment in the founders of the common law that it became a maxim of that system of jurisprudence that a woman had no legal existence separate from her husband. * * *

> It is true that many women are unmarried and not affected by any of the duties, complications, and incapacities arising out of the married state, but these are exceptions to the general rule. The paramount destiny and mission of woman are to fulfil the noble and benign offices

434

of wife and mother. This is the law of the Creator. And the rules of civil society must be adapted to the general constitution of things, and cannot be based upon exceptional cases.

The humane movements of modern society, which have for their object the multiplication of avenues for woman's advancement, and of occupations adapted to her condition and sex, have my heartiest concurrence. But I am not prepared to say that it is one of her fundamental rights and privileges to be admitted into every office and position, including those which require highly special qualifications and demanding special responsibilities. * * *

After *Bradwell*, constitutional litigation over sex discrimination issues continued under the Due Process Clause of the Fourteenth Amendment. The due process cases involved industry attacks on legislation providing workplace protections for women. Early in the women's rights movement, Elizabeth Cady Stanton and Susan B. Anthony had advocated equal pay for equal work, eight hour days, and better workplace conditions for women. The mainstream unions after the turn of the century tended to fight for maximum hour laws mainly for women and children, arguably as a way to prevent women from competing on equal terms with men in the workplace. As a result of this and many other factors, women—who constituted about one-fifth of the workforce at the turn of the century—tended to be segregated into "women's work," jobs reflecting home-based values (teaching, helping, nurturing).

Hence, "protective" legislation was often favored by male workers as a way to channel women into "women's work" and away from competition with men. Thus, when Oregon's law setting maximum hours for women was challenged, the main supporters of the law were the state, the National Consumers' League, and its chief theoretician and advocate, Louis Brandeis. Notwithstanding its precedents protecting employer-employee "liberty of contract," the Supreme Court unanimously upheld the law, based upon the state's compelling interest in protecting women:

> That woman's physical structure and the performance of maternal functions place her at a disadvantage in the struggle for subsistence is obvious. * * * [B]y abundant testimony of the medical fraternity continuance for a long time on her feet at work, repeating this from day to day, tends to injurious effects upon the body, and as healthy mothers are essential to vigorous offspring, the physical wellbeing of woman becomes an object of public interest and care in order to preserve the strength and vigor of the race.

> Still again, history discloses the fact that woman has always been dependent upon man. * * * As minors * * * she has been looked upon in the courts as needing especial care that her rights may be preserved. * * * Differentiated by these matters from the other sex, she is properly placed in a class by herself, and legislation designed for her protection may be sustained even when like legislation is not necessary for men and could not be sustained. It is impossible to close one's eyes

to the fact that she still looks to her brother and depends upon him. * * *

Muller v. Oregon, 208 U.S. 412, 421 (1908). Most middle-class progressive groups applauded these decisions, and the NCL's "Brandeis brief" and its detailed empirical policy arguments became a new standard for influencing the Court.

Yet in the wake of *Muller*, many women came to oppose protective legislation, arguing that "unequal wages and bad factory conditions, and not special laws for adult women workers, are the things in which we should all interest ourselves. * * * When we limit women's opportunities to work, we simply create more poverty, and we postpone the day when equal pay for equal work will be universal." Views of Rheta Childe Dorr, *Good Housekeeping*, Sept. 1925, at 156 ff.

Like the due process cases, the equal protection cases involved statutes that "protected" women in traditional "women's" occupations, while excluding or restricting them from traditional "men's" occupations. In *Goesaert v. Cleary*, 335 U.S. 464 (1948), for example, the Court upheld a statute allowing a woman to work as a bartender only if she were the wife or daughter of the bar owner. *Goesaert* approached the problem as simply a matter of rationality review: "The Constitution does not require legislatures to reflect sociological insight, or shifting social standards, any more than it requires them to keep abreast of the latest scientific standards." Before 1974, no Supreme Court case invalidated a government employment policy that discriminated based on sex.

Of course, that first case, *Frontiero* (Chapter 3), was the Court's introduction to claims for "heightened" scrutiny for an employment statute discriminating on the basis of sex. Responding to the women's rights movement, the Court later struck down many sexbased employment discriminations. But the Court also adopted a rule for all Equal Protection Clause cases that plaintiffs had to demonstrate an intent to discriminate, in *Personnel Administrator of Massachusetts v. Feeney*, 442 U.S. 256 (1979) (Chapter 3).

After the enactment of Title VII in 1964, most challenges to discriminatory employment policies alleged violations of that statute, rather than of the Constitution. (Feeney brought only a constitutional challenge because Title VII contains an exemption for veterans preference systems.) One major advantage of the statutory claim for plaintiffs alleging discrimination is that its scope includes discriminatory effects, regardless of intent.

PART B. DISCRIMINATION ON THE BASIS OF PREGNANCY

1. *CONSTITUTIONAL CLAIMS*

One of the persistent problems in equal protection jurisprudence has been how to analyze pregnancy—as inextricably intertwined with gender or as coincidental medical condition. The issue arose in a series of cases litigated in the late 1960s and early 1970s against school boards, which were not then covered by Title VII. School districts at that time commonly had mandatory leave policies, forcing pregnant teachers to resign their position at least four to five months before the expected birth. As was noted in the case which reached the Supreme Court, *Cleveland Board of Education v. LaFleur*, 414 U.S. 632, 653 (1974) (Powell, J., concurring), "The records before us abound with proof that a principal purpose behind the adoption of the regulations was to keep visibly pregnant teachers out of the sight of schoolchildren." Insurance coverage, however, proved to be a more difficult issue than firing.

Dwight Geduldig v. Carolyn Aiello, 417 U.S. 484, 94 S.Ct. 2485, 41 L.Ed.2d 256 (1974). California's disability insurance program paid benefits to persons in private employment temporarily unable to work because of a physical disability not covered by worker's compensation. The program excluded disabilities associated with pregnancy from coverage (but covered some less costly conditions that occur only in men). The Court held that the exclusion was constitutional. The case elicited two diametrically opposed views of how the law should define equality when addressing differences that are both related to biology and produced by the processes of social construction, the recurring conundrum of sex discrimination law.

Justice Stewart's opinion for the Court found that the program did not discriminate based on sex:

California does not discriminate with respect to the persons or groups which are eligible for disability insurance protection under the program. The classification challenged in this case relates to the asserted under-inclusiveness of the set of risks that the State has selected insure. Although California has created a program to insure most risks of employment disability, it has not chosen to insure all such risks, and this decision is reflected in the level of annual contributions exacted from participating employees. * * *

These policies provide an objective and wholly noninvidious basis for the State's decision not to create a more comprehensive insurance program than it has. There is no evidence in the record that the selection of the risks insured by the program worked to discriminate against any definable group or class in terms of the aggregate risk protection derived by that group or class from the program. There is no risk from which men are protected and women are not. Likewise, there is no risk from which women are protected and men are not.

In a footnote, the Court added: "The program divides potential recipients into two groups—pregnant women and nonpregnant persons. While the first group is exclusively female, the second includes members of both sexes. The fiscal and actuarial benefits of the program thus accrue to members of both sexes." Indeed, noted Justice Stewart, the overall annual claim rate and claim cost were greater for women than for men.

In the absence of a classification that discriminated based on sex, the Court found that the exclusion was rationally related to the program's financial structure and cost containment goals, particularly to whether it would remain self-supporting without needing to increase the cost of premiums or rely on revenue raised by taxes.

Three dissenting Justices (Brennan, Douglas, Marshall) argued that the program did discriminate "by singling out for less favorable treatment a gender-linked disability peculiar to women," and that a more exacting scrutiny was required to justify any such discrimination, under *Reed* and *Frontiero* (the latter just decided). They would have required the benefits system to treat pregnancy the same as any other temporarily disabling condition.

The Court's decision in *Geduldig* remains good law as an analysis of equal protection doctrine applicable to discrimination based on pregnancy. As a practical matter, adoption of the Pregnancy Discrimination Act, *infra*, sapped *Geduldig* of much its effect in the workplace. Because of the existence of that statutory protection, subsequent litigation has largely ignored the constitutional dimensions of pregnancy-based policies. However, the debate continued over whether coverage of pregnancy-related conditions should be treated as an essential part of the norm for health insurance policies or as an add-on.

2. STATUTORY CLAIMS

Following the reasoning of *Geduldig* on its constitutional claim, the Supreme Court held in *General Electric v. Gilbert*, 429 U.S. 125 (1976), that pregnancy-based discrimination also does not constitute sex-based discrimination under Title VII, because although only women can become pregnant, the class of "nonpregnant persons" includes both women and men. In 1978, Congress responded to the Court's decision by amending Title VII to "prohibit sex discrimination on the basis of pregnancy." The amendment, entitled the Pregnancy Discrimination Act ("PDA"), added this language:

> The terms "because of sex" or "on the basis of sex" include, but are not limited to, because of or on the basis of pregnancy, childbirth, or related medical conditions; and women affected by pregnancy, childbirth, or related medical conditions shall be treated the same for all employment-related purposes, including receipt of benefits under fringe benefit programs, as other persons not so affected but similar in their ability or inability to work * * *.

42 U.S.C.A. § 2000e(k). This provision "made clear that, for all Title VII purposes, discrimination based on a woman's pregnancy is, on its face, discrimination because of her sex." The Supreme Court in *Newport News Shipbuilding and Dry Dock Co. v. EEOC*, 462 U.S. 669 (1983), held that the 1978 amendment not only overrode the *Gilbert* result, but overruled *Gilbert*'s approach to sex discrimination in the context of pregnancy.

NOTE ON THE EQUAL TREATMENT/SPECIAL TREATMENT DEBATE AND THE PDA'S APPLICATION TO PREGNANCY–BASED PROTECTIONS

Although the PDA fixed the problem created by the *GeduldigGilbert* line of cases, it also set the stage for one of the most contentious feminist debates of the 1980s. The intent behind the enactment of the PDA was to equalize "up," by forcing employers to include pregnancy in their comprehensive health insurance coverage and medical leave policies. At least theoretically, it is always possible to also equalize "down," which in this instance would have meant denying such coverage to everyone, for all conditions. As a practical matter, workers who already had health insurance and sick leave could be counted on to oppose such a proposal by employers; and, in a reasonably competitive market for labor, most companies would not want to be seen as such an unattractive employer. For small businesses, however, these assumptions did not necessarily hold true, especially for the issue of sick leave. Responding to business concerns opposing a mandate requiring medical leave for all workers but persuaded by women's rights advocates that California should amend its state law to counter the effect of *Gilbert*, the California legislature enacted the following statute while the PDA was still pending in Congress:

> It shall be an unlawful employment practice unless based upon a bona fide occupational qualification: * * * (b) For any employer to refuse to allow a female employee affected by pregnancy, childbirth, or related medical conditions * * * (2) To take a leave on account of pregnancy for a reasonable period of time; provided, such period shall not exceed four months * * *. Reasonable period of time means that period during which the female employee is disabled on account of pregnancy, childbirth, or related medical conditions. * * *

Cal. Gov't Code Ann. § 12945(b)(2) (West 1980).

When Lillian Garland sought to return from her pregnancy leave in 1982, her employer, California Federal Savings & Loan Association, informed her that it had not saved her position. She charged the bank with violating the California statute, and it sought a declaration that the California statute was invalid as inconsistent with and preempted by the PDA. The bank argued that it treated male and female workers identically and thus was in compliance with the PDA and that the pregnancy leave mandated by the state statute would force it to treat pregnant workers differently, which the PDA prohibited.

Feminists filed briefs on all sides of the case, and scholars engaged in lengthy debates in the pages of law reviews. The group that became known as the "special treatment" advocates argued in support of the California statute, reasoning that its effect was to produce an outcome that put women on equal footing with men, even if it violated formal strictures of equality in doing so. Pregnancy had been excluded from coverage and leave policies because the underlying norm was the male worker, they reasoned. The California approach guaranteed that women's life experiences, including pregnancy, had to be treated also as the norm. Without the promise that they could return to their jobs after childbirth, women could never achieve equality in the workforce. Professor Christine Littleton and others authored a brief for the Coalition for Reproductive Equality in the Workplace which supported the California law.

The "equal treatment" feminists saw that approach as a trap. For decades, protectionist labor laws had been enacted with the purported goal of helping women, but had functioned only to help keep them in their place. A California-style system would reinforce the old notion that women were more expensive as workers and generated bothersome special rules, ultimately hurting women. Such laws would also reinforce and perpetuate the assumption that children were women's concern and responsibility; a father who sought to spend even one day caring for an infant could be fired for doing so. Joan Bertin and others authored a brief for the American Civil Liberties Union opposing the California law and arguing that it was preempted. Professors Wendy Webster Williams and Susan Deller Ross, authors of the PDA, wrote a brief for the National Organization for Women and the Women's Legal Defense Fund, arguing that the benefits of the California law should be extended to men in order to meet the requirements of the PDA.

At a more theoretical level, feminists disagreed over *how* special pregnancy and childbirth are; do they amount to a "real" difference? The text of the PDA reflects the position that the experience of giving birth is analogous to any number of other temporarily disabling conditions. Some special treatment feminists characterized insistence on that analogy as assimilationism. At bottom, this was a debate about the extent to which the meaning of pregnancy was a social construct, and an intense battle over what was the best strategy to advance the interests of most women, in both the long term and the short term.

California Federal Savings and Loan Assoc. v. Mark Guerra

Supreme Court of the United States, 1987.
479 U.S. 272, 107 S.Ct. 683, 93 L.Ed.2d 613.

■ JUSTICE MARSHALL delivered the opinion of the Court. * * *

In order to decide whether the California statute requires or permits employers to violate Title VII, as amended by the PDA, or is inconsistent with the purposes of the statute, we must determine whether the PDA prohibits the States from requiring employers to provide reinstatement to pregnant workers, regardless of their policy for disabled workers generally.

Petitioners argue that the language of the federal statute itself unambiguously rejects California's "special treatment" approach to pregnancy discrimination, thus rendering any resort to the legislative history unnecessary. They contend that the second clause of the PDA forbids an employer to treat pregnant employees any differently than other disabled employees. Because " '[t]he purpose of Congress is the ultimate touchstone' " of the preemption inquiry, however, we must examine the PDA's language against the background of its legislative history and historical context. * * *

* * * By adding pregnancy to the definition of sex discrimination prohibited by Title VII, the first clause of the PDA reflects Congress' disapproval of the reasoning in *Gilbert*. Rather than imposing a limitation on the remedial purpose of the PDA, we believe that the second clause was intended to overrule the holding in *Gilbert* and to illustrate how discrimination against pregnancy is to be remedied. * * * [W]e agree with the Court of Appeals' conclusion that Congress intended the PDA to be "a floor beneath which pregnancy disability benefits may not drop—not a ceiling above which they may not rise."

The context in which Congress considered the issue of pregnancy discrimination supports this view of the PDA. Congress had before it extensive evidence of discrimination *against* pregnancy, particularly in disability and health insurance programs like those challenged in *Gilbert* * * *. The Reports, debates, and hearings make abundantly clear that Congress intended the PDA to provide relief for working women and to end discrimination against pregnant workers. In contrast to the thorough account of discrimination against pregnant workers, the legislative history is devoid of any discussion of preferential treatment of pregnancy, beyond acknowledgments of the existence of state statutes providing for such preferential treatment. Opposition to the PDA came from those concerned with the cost of including pregnancy in health and disability-benefit plans and the application of the bill to abortion, not from those who favored special accommodation of pregnancy. * * *

Title VII, as amended by the PDA, and California's pregnancy disability leave statute share a common goal. The purpose of Title VII is "to achieve equality of employment opportunities and remove barriers that have operated in the past to favor an identifiable group of . . . employees over other employees." *Griggs v. Duke Power Co.*, 401 U.S. 424, 429–430 (1971). Rather than limiting existing Title VII principles and objectives, the PDA extends them to cover pregnancy. As Senator Williams, a sponsor of the Act, stated: "The entire thrust . . . behind this legislation is to guarantee women the basic right to participate fully and equally in the workforce, without denying them the fundamental right to full participation in family life." 123 Cong. Rec. 29658 (1977).

Section 12945(b)(2) also promotes equal employment opportunity. By requiring employers to reinstate women after a reasonable pregnancy disability leave, § 12945(b)(2) ensures that they will not lose their jobs on account of pregnancy disability. * * * By "taking pregnancy into account," California's pregnancy disability-leave statute allows women, as well as men, to have families without losing their jobs.

We emphasize the limited nature of the benefits § 12945(b)(2) provides. The statute is narrowly drawn to cover only the period of *actual physical disability* on account of pregnancy, childbirth, or related medical conditions. Accordingly, unlike the protective labor legislation prevalent earlier in this century, § 12945(b)(2) does not reflect archaic or stereotypical notions about pregnancy and the abilities of pregnant workers. A statute based on such stereotypical assumptions would, of course, be inconsistent with Title VII's goal of equal employment opportunity. * * *

■ [The concurring opinions of JUSTICES STEVENS and SCALIA are omitted.]

■ JUSTICE WHITE, with whom THE CHIEF JUSTICE [REHNQUIST] and JUSTICE POWELL join, dissenting. * * *

The second clause [of the PDA] could not be clearer: it mandates that pregnant employees "shall be treated the same for all employment-related purposes" as nonpregnant employees similarly situated with respect to their ability or inability to work. This language leaves no room for preferential treatment of pregnant workers. * * *

Contrary to the mandate of the PDA, California law requires every employer to have a disability leave policy for pregnancy even if it has none for any other disability. An employer complies with California law if it has a leave policy for pregnancy but denies it for every other disability. On its face, § 12945(b)(2) is in square conflict with the PDA and is therefore preempted. Because the California law permits employers to single out pregnancy for preferential treatment and therefore to violate Title VII, it is not saved by § 708 which limits preemption of state laws to those that require or permit an employer to commit an unfair employment practice.

The majority nevertheless would save the California law on two grounds. First, it holds that the PDA does not require disability from pregnancy to be treated the same as other disabilities; instead, it forbids less favorable, but permits more favorable, benefits for pregnancy disability. The express command of the PDA is unambiguously to the contrary, and the legislative history casts no doubt on that mandate.

The legislative materials reveal Congress' plain intent not to put pregnancy in a class by itself within Title VII, as the majority does with its "floor ... not a ceiling" approach. The Senate Report clearly stated:

> "By defining sex discrimination to include discrimination against pregnant women, the bill rejects the view that employers may treat pregnancy and its incidents as *sui generis*, without regard to its functional comparability to other conditions. Under this bill, the treatment of pregnant women in covered employment must focus not on their condition alone but on the actual effects of that condition on their ability to work. Pregnant women who are able to work must be permitted to work on the same conditions as other employees; and when they are not able to work for medical reasons, they must be accorded the same rights, leave privileges and other benefits, as other workers who are disabled from working."

[S.Rep. No. 95–331, p. 4 (1977).] * * *

The majority correctly reports that Congress focused on discrimination against, rather than preferential treatment of, pregnant workers. There is only one direct reference in the legislative history to preferential treatment. Senator Brooke stated during the Senate debate: "I would emphasize most strongly that S. 995 in no way provides special disability benefits for working women. They have not demanded, nor asked, for such benefits. They have asked only to be treated with fairness, to be accorded the same employment rights as men." [123 Cong.Rec. 29664 (1977).] Given the evidence before Congress of the widespread discrimination against pregnant workers, it is probable that most Members of Congress did not seriously consider the possibility that someone would want to afford preferential treatment to pregnant workers. The parties and their *amici* argued vigorously to this Court the policy implications of preferential treatment of pregnant workers. In favor of preferential treatment it was urged with conviction that preferential treatment merely enables women, like men, to have children without losing their jobs. In opposition to preferential treatment it was urged with equal conviction that preferential treatment represents a resurgence of the 19th-century protective legislation which perpetuated sex-role stereotypes and which impeded women in their efforts to take their rightful place in the workplace. See, *e.g.*, *Muller*; *Bradwell* (Bradley, J., concurring). It is not the place of this Court, however, to resolve this policy dispute. Our task is to interpret Congress' intent in enacting the PDA. Congress' silence in its consideration of the PDA with respect to preferential treatment of pregnant workers cannot fairly be interpreted to abrogate the plain statements in the legislative history, not to mention the language of the statute, that equality of treatment was to be the guiding principle of the PDA. * * *

NOTE ON SUBSEQUENT PARENTAL LEAVE LEGISLATION

Throughout the 1980s and early 1990s, women's rights advocates sought a law guaranteeing leave for both parents. Several such bills passed Congress, but were killed by presidential veto. In 1993, the Family and Medical Leave Act (FMLA) became law. Under it, all employers of 50 or more workers have to offer employees up to 12 weeks of unpaid leave, with continuation of health benefits and a right to return to the same or similar job, in order for the worker to care for a newly-born or newly-adopted child, to deal with a serious health problem of his own, or to care for a spouse, child, or parent of the employee who has a serious health problem.

In **Nevada Department of Human Resources v. William Hibbs, 538 U.S. 721, 123 S.Ct. 1972, 155 L.Ed.2d 953 (2003)**, the Supreme Court upheld the FMLA against a challenge which would have barred suits against state governments as employers, on the ground that the FMLA's scope exceeded Congress's authority to abrogate the sovereign immunity of the states. The Court found that Congress properly exercised its power under Section 5 of the Fourteenth Amendment to redress violations of the Equal Protection Clause. In so doing, **Chief Justice Rehnquist**'s opinion for the Court adopted this analysis:

"Stereotypes about women's domestic roles are reinforced by parallel stereotypes presuming a lack of domestic responsibilities for men. Because employers continued to regard the family as the woman's domain, they often denied men similar accommodations or discouraged them from taking leave. These mutually reinforcing stereotypes creat-ed a self-fulfilling cycle of discrimination that forced women to contin-ue to assume the role of primary family caregiver, and fostered employers' stereotypical views about women's commitment to work and their value as employees. Those perceptions, in turn, Congress reasoned, lead to subtle discrimination that may be difficult to detect on a case-by-case basis. * * *

"By creating an across-the-board, routine employment benefit for all eligible employees, Congress sought to ensure that family-care leave would no longer be stigmatized as an inordinate drain on the work-place caused by female employees, and that employers could not evade leave obligations simply by hiring men. By setting a minimum stan-dard of family leave for *all* eligible employees, irrespective of gender, the FMLA attacks the formerly state-sanctioned stereotype that only women are responsible for family caregiving, thereby reducing employ-ers' incentives to engage in discrimination by basing hiring and pro-motion decisions on stereotypes. * * * [T]he FMLA is narrowly target-ed at the fault line between work and family—precisely where sex-based overgeneralization has been and remains strongest * * *."

The Court cited data stating that the overwhelming majority of workers who take leave upon the arrival of a child are women, even though men are equally entitled to do so. In law firms, for example, although many now have a "mommy track," there is in practice no "daddy track." Where does this leave the special treatment/equal treatment debate?

Other aspects of differential treatment based on pregnancy also contin-ue to arise in the law. One with particular relevance to our concerns is how an unmarried woman's decision to have a child affects her in the work-place. A number of courts have affirmed that a woman's claim of pregnan-cy-based discrimination by a business employer is no less valid because she is unmarried. *Nelson v. Wittern Group*, 140 F.Supp.2d 1001 (S.D.Iowa 2001); *Strickland v. Prime Care of Dothan*, 108 F.Supp.2d 1329 (M.D.Ala. 2000); *Hargett v. Delta Automotive*, 765 F.Supp. 1487 (N.D.Ala. 1991). Other kinds of defendants, however, have asserted a countervailing right to exclude unmarried pregnant women from the workplace.

Crystal Chambers v. Omaha Girls Club, Inc.

U.S. Court of Appeals for the Eighth Circuit, 1987.
834 F.2d 697, *rehearing en banc denied*, 840 F.2d 583 (1988).

■ WOLLMAN, CIRCUIT JUDGE:

[The Omaha Girls Club is a private, non-profit corporation that offers programs designed to assist young girls between the ages of eight and eighteen to maximize their life opportunities through creating trusting relationships among girls and with adult mentors. Among the Club's many activities are programs directed at pregnancy prevention. Most of the girls and staff members who participate in this and other programs in two

Omaha locations are African American. One of the Club's "role model rules" is a ban of single-parent pregnancies among its staff members. Crystal Chambers, a black single woman, was employed by the Club as an arts and crafts instructor at the Club's North Omaha facility. The Club terminated her when she became pregnant, a violation of the role model rule. Chambers challenged the rule against single-mother pregnancies as a "disparate treatment" in violation of Title VII, as amended by the PDA, and as having a "disparate impact" on African American women, in violation of Title VII's ban on race discrimination. Her claims were dismissed by the trial court.]

* * * [As to the race discrimination claim:] The district court found that the role model rule is justified by business necessity because there is a manifest relationship between the Club's fundamental purpose and the rule. Specifically, the court found:

> The Girls Club has established by the evidence that its only purpose is to serve young girls between the ages of eight and eighteen and to provide these women with exposure to the greatest number of available positive options in life. The Girls Club has established that teenage pregnancy is contrary to this purpose and philosophy. The Girls Club established that it honestly believed that to permit single pregnant staff members to work with the girls would convey the impression that the Girls Club condoned pregnancy for the girls in the age group it serves. The testimony of board members * * * made clear that the policy was not based upon a morality standard, but rather, on a belief that teenage pregnancies severely limit the available opportunities for teenage girls. The Girls Club also established that the policy was just one prong of a comprehensive attack on the problem of teenage pregnancy. The Court is satisfied that a manifest relationship exists between the Girls Club's fundamental purpose and its single pregnancy policy.

The court also relied in part on expert testimony to the effect that the role model rule could be helpful in preventing teenage pregnancy. Chambers argues, however, that the district court erred in finding business necessity because the role model rule is based only on speculation by the Club and has not been validated by any studies showing that it prevents pregnancy among the Club's members. * * *

We believe that "the district court's account of the evidence is plausible in light of the record viewed in its entirety." Therefore, we cannot say that the district court's finding of business necessity is clearly erroneous. The district court's conclusion on the evidence is not an impermissible one. Although validation studies can be helpful in evaluating such questions, they are not required to maintain a successful business necessity defense. Indeed, we are uncertain whether the role model rule by its nature is suited to validation by an empirical study. * * *

[As to the pregnancy discrimination claim:] No violation of Title VII exists, however, if the employer can show that the challenged employment practice is a bona fide occupational qualification (BFOQ). * * *

The BFOQ exception is " 'an extremely narrow exception to the general prohibition of discrimination on the basis of sex.' " * * * [Courts] have noted the existence of several formulations for evaluating whether an employment practice is a BFOQ. The formulations include: whether " 'the essence of the business operation would be undermined' " without the challenged employment practice; whether safe and efficient performance of the job would be possible without the challenged employment practice; and whether the challenged employment practice has " 'a manifest relationship to the employment in question.' "

Although the district court did not clearly conclude that the role model rule qualified as a BFOQ, several of the court's other findings are persuasive on this issue. The court's findings of fact, many of which are relevant to the analysis of a potential BFOQ exception, are binding on this court unless clearly erroneous. The facts relevant to establishing a BFOQ are the same as those found by the district court in the course of its business necessity analysis. As already noted, the district court found that the role model rule has a manifest relationship to the Club's fundamental purpose and that there were no workable alternatives to the rule. Moreover, the district court's finding of business necessity itself is persuasive as to the existence of a BFOQ. This court has noted that the analysis of a BFOQ "is similar to and overlaps with the judicially created 'business necessity' test." The various standards for establishing business necessity are quite similar to those for determining a BFOQ. Indeed, this court has on different occasions applied the same standard—"manifest relationship"—to both business necessity and BFOQ. Inasmuch as we already have affirmed the district court's finding of business necessity as not clearly erroneous, we feel compelled to conclude that "[i]n the particular factual circumstances of this case," the role model rule is reasonably necessary to the Club's operations. Thus, we hold that the role model rule qualifies as a bona fide occupational qualification. * * *

■ McMILLAN, CIRCUIT JUDGE, dissenting. * * *

* * * I would reject the BFOQ or business necessity exceptions offered by OGC because there is no evidence to support a relationship between teenage pregnancies and the employment of an unwed pregnant instructor, and therefore I am left with the definite and firm conclusion that the district court made a mistake.

The district court, and now this court, accepts without any proof OGC's assumption that the presence of an unwed pregnant instructor is related to teenage pregnancies. OGC failed to present surveys, school statistics or any other empirical data connecting the incidence of teenage pregnancy with the pregnancy of an adult instructor. OGC also failed to present evidence that other girls clubs or similar types of organizations employed such a rule. OGC instead relied on two or three highly questionable anecdotal incidents to support the rule. * * * Instead of requiring OGC to demonstrate a reasonable relationship between teenage pregnancy and the employment of single pregnant women, the district court accepted the beliefs and assumptions of OGC board members. * * *

Neither an employer's sincere belief, without more, (nor a district court's belief), that a discriminatory employment practice is related and necessary to the accomplishments of the employer's goals is sufficient to establish a BFOQ or business necessity defense. The fact that the goals are laudable and the beliefs sincerely held does not substitute for data which demonstrate a relationship between the discriminatory practice and the goals. The district court, recognizing that there was no data to support such a relationship, should have held that OGC failed to carry its burden of showing a BFOQ or business necessity. * * *

NOTE ON *CHAMBERS* AND CRITICAL RACE THEORY

Chambers is an excellent example of a case in which issues pertaining to gender and sexuality are "raced." The plaintiff uses race as part of her claim, asserting successfully that the role model policy has a disparate impact on African-American women. But the fact that both she and her charges are African American seems to strengthen the defendant's argument about the extent to which the role model effect actually operates. Would such an effect be accepted if the adult and the teenagers were all white? If the adult were African American, but the girls were white?

Professor Regina Austin sees *Chambers* as a battle over racialized meanings of sexuality. Noting that most of the teenagers' own mothers were not married, Austin reads a deeper meaning into the case:

> Although Crystal Chambers' firing was publicly justified on the ground that she would have an adverse impact on the young Club members, it is likely that the Club in part sacked her because she resisted its effort to model her in conformity with white and middle-class morality. In its struggles against the culture of the girls' mothers, Crystal Chambers, employee and arts and crafts instructor, was supposed to be on the Club's side. But like a treasonous recruit, Crystal turned up unmarried and pregnant. As such, she embodied the enemy. If the Club could not succeed in shaping and restraining the workers whose economic welfare it controlled, how could it expect to win over the young members and supplant their mothers' cultural legacy? * * *
>
> The critique of the images of black women whites have historically promoted is relevant to the assessment of the treatment accorded contemporary role models. Role models are supposed to forgo the vices of Jezebel and exhibit the many virtues of Mammy. The case of Crystal Chambers illustrates this quite well. When Crystal Chambers refused to subordinate her interest in motherhood to the supposed welfare of the Club girls, she essentially rejected the Club's attempt to impose upon her the "positive" stereotype of the black female as a repressed, self-sacrificing, nurturing woman whose heart extends to other people's children because she cannot (or should not) have kids of her own. Instead, like a Jezebel, Crystal Chambers "flaunted" her sexuality and reproductive capacity, but, unlike her counterpart in slavery, she did so in furtherance of her own ends, in defiance of her white employers, and

in disregard of a rule that forbade her from connecting with a man outside of the marriage relationship.

Regina Austin, "Sapphire Bound!" 1989 *Wis.L.Rev.* 539, 557, 571.

PART C.   DISCRIMINATION ON THE BASIS OF GENDER STEREOTYPES

In Chapter 3, Section 3, you explored the interconnections between gender and sexuality mostly in constitutional cases, but as the text points out, the bulk of the judicial analysis which is emerging on this point has come out of statutory, primarily Title VII, case law, simply because there are so many more cases litigated on statutory, rather than constitutional, grounds. We now return to the fascinating project of sorting out the sexuality-gender dynamic, specifically in Title VII law.

How should a statute that prohibits discrimination "because of . . . sex" should be interpreted when sexual speech or behavior manifests itself in the workplace; or, when plaintiffs, women or men, are treated adversely because of how they conform, or not, to cultural norms and expectations associated with femaleness or maleness? Sometimes, but not always, the cases involve persons who are, or are perceived to be, gay. Does that mean that what this subcategory of cases "really" involve is sexual orientation, not sex? Can such cases ever *not* involve sex discrimination? Could such an interpretation be squared with the Congressional intent behind Title VII? Are the answers to these questions different when the plaintiff is transgender? Analyze the following problem which we have adapted from I. Bennett Capers, Note, "Sex(ual) Orientation and Title VII," 91 *Colum. L. Rev.* 1158 (1991).

PROBLEM 8–1

ALICE, BOB, AND CALVIN

Given the language, history, and purposes of Title VII's prohibition of job discrimination on the basis of "sex," which if any of the following hypothetical associates has a claim for relief under Title VII?

Alice, Bob, and Calvin are sixth-year associates at a law firm. All three are up for partnership. A, B, and C are the top three associates in terms of billable hours and generation of business, and their work evaluations are also the tops. Yet the partnership decides to deny them promotion.

A, B, and C all file Title VII complaints, making the following allegations: Alice claims that she was rejected because her "tough macho behavior" and "unladylike language" ruffled the all-male partnership. Bob was told that the partners consider him "too soft" and joked that he "has lace in his jockey shorts." Calvin, star of the firm's basketball team, claims that he was rejected because he is openly gay.

Your starting point should be to reread a case in Chapter 5; then consider one of the most recent Court of Appeals rulings on this question.

Price Waterhouse v. Ann B. Hopkins

United States Supreme Court, 1989.
490 U.S. 228, 109 S.Ct. 1775, 104 L.Ed.2d 268.

[Excerpted in Chapter 5, Section 3]

Jimmie L. Smith v. City of Salem, Ohio

United States Court of Appeals for the Sixth Circuit, 2004.
378 F.3d 566.

■ Circuit Judge Cole

* * * In his complaint, Smith asserts Title VII claims of retaliation and employment discrimination "because of . . . sex." The district court dismissed Smith's Title VII claims on the ground that he failed to state a claim for sex stereotyping pursuant to *Price Waterhouse v. Hopkins.* The district court implied that Smith's claim was disingenuous, stating that he merely "invokes the term-of-art created by *Price Waterhouse,* that is, 'sex-stereotyping,' " as an end run around his "real" claim, which, the district court stated, was "based upon his transsexuality." The district court then held that "Title VII does not prohibit discrimination based on an individual's transsexualism." * * *

* * * As Judge Posner has pointed out, the term "gender" is one "borrowed from grammar to designate the sexes as viewed as social rather than biological classes." Richard A. Posner, Sex and Reason, 24–25 (1992). The Supreme Court made clear that in the context of Title VII, discrimination because of "sex" includes gender discrimination: "In the context of sex stereotyping, an employer who acts on the basis of a belief that a woman cannot be aggressive, or that she must not be, has acted on the basis of gender." *Price Waterhouse* at 250. The Court emphasized that "we are beyond the day when an employer could evaluate employees by assuming or insisting that they matched the stereotype associated with their group." *Id.* at 251.

Smith contends that the same theory of sex stereotyping applies here. His complaint sets forth the conduct and mannerisms which, he alleges, did not conform with his employers' and co-workers' sex stereotypes of how a man should look and behave. Smith's complaint states that, after being diagnosed with GID [gender identity disorder], he began to express a more feminine appearance and manner on a regular basis, including at work. The complaint states that his co-workers began commenting on his appearance and mannerisms as not being masculine enough; and that his supervisors at the Fire Department and other municipal agents knew about this allegedly unmasculine conduct and appearance. The complaint then describes a high-level meeting among Smith's supervisors and other municipal officials regarding his employment. Defendants allegedly schemed to compel Smith's resignation by forcing him to undergo multiple psychological evaluations of his gender non-conforming behavior. The complaint makes clear that these meetings took place soon after Smith assumed a more feminine appearance and manner and after his conversation about this with Eastek. * * * In short, Smith claims that the discrimination he experienced was based on his failure to conform to sex stereotypes by expressing less masculine, and more feminine mannerisms and appearance. * * *

After *Price Waterhouse,* an employer who discriminates against women because, for instance, they do not wear dresses or makeup, is engaging in sex discrimination because the discrimination would not occur but for the victim's sex. It follows that employers who discriminate against men because they *do* wear dresses and makeup, or otherwise act femininely, are also engaging in sex discrimination, because the discrimination would not occur but for the victim's sex.

Yet some courts have held that this latter form of discrimination is of a different and somehow more permissible kind. For instance, the man who acts in ways typically associated with women is not described as engaging in the same activity as a woman who acts in ways typically associated with women, but is instead described as engaging in the different activity of being a transsexual (or in some instances, a homosexual or transvestite). * * *

Such analyses cannot be reconciled with *Price Waterhouse,* which does not make Title VII protection against sex stereotyping conditional or provide any reason to exclude Title VII coverage for non sex-stereotypical behavior simply because the person is a transsexual. As such, discrimination against a plaintiff who is a transsexual-and therefore fails to act and/or identify with his or her gender-is no different from the discrimination directed against Ann Hopkins in *Price Waterhouse,* who, in sex-stereotypical terms, did not act like a woman. Sex stereotyping based on a person's gender non-conforming behavior is impermissible discrimination, irrespective of the cause of that behavior; a label, such as "transsexual," is not fatal to a sex discrimination claim where the victim has suffered discrimination because of his or her gender non-conformity. Accordingly, we hold that Smith has stated a claim for relief pursuant to Title VII's prohibition of sex discrimination. * * *

NOTE ON *HOPKINS* AND TITLE VII'S APPLICATION TO GENDER STEREOTYPE DISCRIMINATION

Professor Mary Anne Case summarizes the state of the law on gender discrimination in the following chart:

TABLE 1. ANALYSIS OF GENDER DISCRIMINATION CLAIMS UNDER TITLE VII

	SEX OF EMPLOYEE	GENDER OF EMPLOYEE	GENDER OF JOB	EMPLOYER DEMAND	ANALYSIS & RESULT UNDER TITLE VII
1	Female	Masculine	Masculine (e.g., accountant) or none	Act more femininely[1]	Disparate treatment: *Price Waterhouse v. Hopkins*
2	Male	Feminine	Feminine (e.g., nursery school teacher) or none	Act more masculinely[2]	Disparate treatment: result governed by *Hopkins*: impermissible sex stereotyping
3	Female	Feminine	Masculine (e.g., commission salesperson) or none	Act more masculinely[2]	Disparate impact: once employee shows that requiring masculine or disfavoring feminine qualities has disparate impact on females, who are disproportionately feminine and not masculine, employer must then show that requiring masculine or disfavoring feminine characteristics is job-related and consistent with business necessity
4	Male	Feminine	Masculine	Act more masculinely[2]	*Ius tertii* claim, raising argument made by feminine woman in row 3 above
5	Male	Masculine	Feminine (e.g., Jenny Craig counselor)	Act more femininely[1]	Disparate impact: analysis is mirror image of row 3 above
6	Female	Masculine	Feminine	Act more femininely[1]	Analysis is mirror image of row 4 above

Notes:

[1]"Act more femininely" is here a shorthand for, e.g., the advice given Ann Hopkins to "walk more femininely, talk more femininely, dress more femininely, wear make-up, have [your] hair styled, . . . wear jewelry" and go to "charm school." 490 U.S. at 235 (1989).

[2]Or act less femininely. Both phrases are shorthand for the reverse of the advice given Hopkins, e.g., take off your makeup and jewelry, cut your hair short and go to assertiveness training class.

Mary Anne C. Case, "Disaggregating Gender from Sex and Sexual Orientation: The Effeminate Man in the Law and Feminist Jurisprudence," 105 *Yale L.J.* 1, 5 (1995). Where would *Smith* fit? As this book goes to press in 2005, *Smith* remains a minority opinion in the federal courts, and the Supreme Court has not addressed the question of whether non-masculine men are covered by Title VII. Is it a better strategy for advocates for equal job rights for transgender people to argue that they are already protected by laws prohibiting sex discrimination, or to argue that new laws specific to transgender discrimination are necessary?

Multiple aspects of gender arise in employment discrimination litigation. Women face job barriers that are about sex, but not only about sex. In one of the earliest cases brought under Title VII, the Supreme Court rejected the employer's attempt to justify a policy of not hiring women with small children by arguing that it was not sex discrimination, but "sex plus." *Phillips v. Martin Marietta*, 400 U.S. 542 (1971). One can conceptualize many of the cases raising claims related to gender as "sex plus" cases: they involve issues related to anatomic sex plus gender stereotypes.

Another level of complexity results when a plaintiff faces assumptions about what behavior is to be expected from women of certain racial or ethnic groups. Courts have a mixed record—sometimes recognizing the compounding effects of such stereotypes, sometimes dismissing cases because plaintiffs fail to establish that the employer discriminated against either women as a group (because other women were employed) or that racial or ethnic group as a group (because males in the group were employed). See Kathryn Abrams, "Title VII and the Complex Female Subject," 92 *Mich. L. Rev.* 2479 (1994); Devon Carbado & Mitu Gulati, "Working Identity," 85 *Cornell L. Rev.* 1259 (2000) and "The Fifth Black Woman," 11 *J. of Contemp. Legal Issues* 701 (2001); Kimberlé Crenshaw, "Demarginalizing the Intersection of Race and Sex," 1989 *U. Chi. Legal F.* 139.

SEXUAL ORIENTATION DISCRIMINATION

PART A. DISCRIMINATION BY THE GOVERNMENT

The primary, current as well as historical, example of job discrimination on the basis of sexual orientation by a governmental entity is the U.S. armed forces, a story told and examined in Chapter 7. Consider the parallel history of U.S. Civil Service and state civil service policies.

1. THE BIRTH OF A CIVIL RIGHTS MOVEMENT

David Johnson, "Homosexual Citizens: Washington's Gay Community Confronts the Civil Service"

Washington History, Fall/Winter 1994–95, at 45–51, 53, 55–57, 59–61.*

It was 2:00 a.m. on a Tuesday night in the fall of 1963, and Washington's principal downtown gay bars, the Chicken Hut and the Derby Room, had just closed. On his way home, Clifford Norton, a budget analyst with the National Aeronautics and Space Administration, decided to drive by nearby Lafayette Park, a popular meeting and trysting site for gay men since the early part of the century. Seeing Madison Proctor standing on the corner, Norton stopped his car, rolled down the window and struck up a conversation. After inviting Proctor home for a drink, he drove him to his nearby parked car. Norton then drove home to his Southwest Washington apartment, and Proctor followed. When they arrived, however, they discovered they had been followed by two District of Columbia police officers assigned to the Morals Division. Outside the parking lot, the officers questioned Norton and Proctor about their interaction at the park and, because they had trailed them at speeds exceeding 45 miles per hour, brought the two in to police headquarters on a "traffic violation."

At headquarters, Roy Blick, chief of the Morals Division, interrogated Norton and Proctor for two hours concerning their activities that night and their sexual histories in general. "How long have you been a homosexual?" Blick repeatedly asked the NASA employee. Norton refused to answer. Blick eventually relented and issued Norton only a traffic summons. But

---

* Reprinted with permission of *Washington History.* For a more detailed examination of this history, see David K. Johnson, *The Lavender Scare: The Cold War Persecution of Gays and Lesbians in the Federal Government* (2004).

453

since Norton had revealed his place of employment, Blick telephoned NASA's security director, who came to police headquarters and continued to interrogate Norton about his sexual history until 6:30 a.m. Several days later, despite a 15–year record of exemplary government service, NASA discharged Norton for "immoral, indecent and disgraceful conduct." Although they acknowledged that issues of national security were not involved, NASA officials claimed that a recurrence of this type of activity might "embarrass" the agency. The Civil Service Commission concurred and determined that Norton's dismissal would promote "the efficiency of the service."

The attempt to ferret gay men and lesbians from the federal civil service is commonly associated with the anti-Communist witch hunts of the McCarthy era. But the "purge of the perverts" actually began before McCarthy made headlines with his attacks on the State Department and continued long after his death in 1957. Norton's detention and subsequent dismissal was only one of thousands of similar incidents that occurred in Washington from the late 1940s through the late 1960s. Washington's gay community reluctantly found itself on the front lines as the government attempted to eliminate sexual deviants from the ranks of the Civil Service reputedly to protect "national security."

Despite the heated rhetoric of the McCarthy era, the purge had little to do with national security. Instead, it reflected an underlying anxiety over the bureaucratization and urbanization of Washington, changes largely precipitated by the New Deal and World War II.

Norton's otherwise routine 1963 arrest marked a turning point in the hostile relationship between the city's gay community and the federal government. A closeted middle-aged gay man, Norton was no activist, but he had heard about a new organization of gays and lesbians called the Mattachine Society of Washington. Founded in 1961 by a handful of gay men, some of whom had been fired similarly from the federal government, Mattachine of Washington had received considerable publicity in the local press. The group helped Norton contest his dismissal * * *. Norton's case demonstrates how, by the early 1960s, Washington's gay community was beginning to fight back.

The issue of gays in government first came to public attention in 1950. In February, just days after Senator McCarthy made national headlines with his claim that 205 Communists (later reduced to 57) were working for the State Department, the under secretary of state for security revealed that 91 homosexuals had been fired. By that summer Washington had "gone crazy," according to Saturday Evening Post reporters Joseph and Stewart Alsop, with congressional leaders railing about Communists and sexual deviants infiltrating the government. Fear and suspicion gripped the city, as numerous "good men" quit the government, and many who stayed, even powerful U.S. senators, presumed that their telephone lines were tapped. * * *

* * * Under congressional pressure, the dismissals spread beyond the State Department. Throughout the executive branch, hundreds of civil

servants were called in by their agency's personnel officer. Thousands lived in dread that they too would be summoned. The routine was always the same. Employees knew that it had nothing to do with loyalty or subversion; nonetheless they could expect to lose their jobs. "Information has come to our attention indicating that you are a homosexual," the interrogator would begin. "What comment do you care to make?" Regardless of the response, the civil servant was usually granted "the opportunity" to resign quietly.

By November 1950, an additional 400 federal civil servants across the country had resigned or were fired following such interviews. By the end of the decade the number was in the thousands. Suspicion shrouded anyone who left the government. A *New Yorker* cartoon depicted a man explaining to a potential employer, "It's true, sir, that the State Department let me go, but that was solely because of incompetence." * * *

The question senators wanted answered that summer was, "Who put the 91 homosexuals in our State Department?" The question implied that "an unseen master hand" had placed them there in order to weaken America's foreign policy apparatus. Homosexuals were not assumed to be Communists—although some observers would come to equate the two—but they were thought to be vulnerable to blackmail and therefore to pose a "security risk." Homosexuals might not be intrinsically disloyal, but they could be used by those who were, so the thinking went. * * *

Although the rhetoric fueling much of the hysteria over gays in the government in the 1950s centered on the alleged threat to national security, this was never an issue in any actual dismissals. A combination of congressional actions and executive orders did increase the power of the Civil Service Commission and of the various agencies themselves to dismiss federal employees determined to be "security risks." The Eisenhower administration even issued an executive order banning the government from employing anyone guilty of "sexual perversion." Still, none of these measures were used against suspected homosexuals. If the alleged gay man or lesbian did not simply resign, he or she was generally dismissed for "immoral conduct," a disqualification that had been included in civil service regulations since the administration of Theodore Roosevelt. An even earlier Department of the Interior prohibition on immorality led to the termination of gay poet Walt Whitman's employment in 1865. The purges of the 1950s represented more a change in rhetoric and enforcement than in government policy. * * *

The 1940 revelation that Roosevelt was harboring at least one homosexual in a key administration position gave critics another angle of attack. Under–Secretary of State Sumner Welles was a friend of Roosevelt's and, like the president, came from a wealthy eastern family. Because of this close connection, Welles served as the de facto head of the department, with more influence over foreign policy than Secretary of State Cordell Hull. But then, in 1940, complaints that Welles had made "lewd homosexual advances" to several African–American railroad porters fell into the hands of his enemy, U.S. Ambassador to France William Bullitt. For two years,

Roosevelt resisted firing Welles, but when Bullitt leaked the information to Republican Senator Ralph O. Brewster of Maine, who threatened to launch a Senate probe, the president was forced to seek his resignation. The press reported the resignation as the result of a power struggle with Secretary Hull, but Washington insiders knew that was only half the story.

Although foreign service officers had long been denounced as "cookie pushers in striped pants," no one did more to link the New Deal and the State Department with homosexuality than Welles. In 1950, when the issue of gays in the State Department came out in the press, several journalists pointed somewhat obliquely to Welles as the origin of the problem. * * * Many saw Sumner Welles, abetted by his friend President Roosevelt, as the center of a gay fifth column threatening the integrity of the government. * * *

* * * Critics of the New Deal believed that the large increase in the federal bureaucracy under the Roosevelt administration offered a haven for deviants. "The exceptional ones" may go to New York and Hollywood, [journalists] argued, but the more mediocre queers were attracted by the security of the Civil Service. "If you're wondering where your wandering semiboy is tonight, he's probably in Washington," they warned the nation.

In the "mediocrity and virtual anonymity of commonplace tasks" within the federal bureaucracy, they theorized, "the sexes—all four of them—are equal in the robot requirements and qualifications." Not only had the Civil Service erased gender distinctions, but "there is no color line, no social selectivity; not even citizenship is always a prerequisite." The rising scope and power of government bureaucracy was seen as somehow emasculating society, creating a world of gender-neutral bureaucrats. Like Communism itself, bureaucracy raised the specter of a face-less, gender-less, family-less welfare state. Homosexual civil servants were seen as the natural conclusion of this frightening trend. * * *

The total number of gays and lesbians affected by the purge cannot be calculated. However, some published figures give a sense of its impact. In the two years between May 1953 and June 1955, more than 800 federal employees nationwide either resigned or were terminated with "files contain[ing] information indicating sex perversion," according to documents submitted to Senate investigators. Many more dismissals occurred on an informal undocumented basis, ostensibly to protect the reputation of the employee. Other gay and lesbian civil servants resigned before their sexual orientation was discovered. Ray Mann, for example, decided to leave the State Department in the summer of 1954 because "being unmarried, I just didn't think my future lay in working for the U.S. government in the McCarthy era." Large numbers of applicants were also rejected because of their sexual orientation, and thousands of men and women were discharged from the military, where the sexual witch hunt was even more severe.

The impact was not limited to federal employees. Millions of private-sector employees worked for government contractors who required security clearances. Other private industries adopted the policies of the federal government—the nation's largest single employer—even though they had no direct federal contracts. * * *

Only slowly did any effort at collective political resistance emerge. Even Frank Kameny, who in 1957 became one of the first to fight his dismissal from the Civil Service, initially distanced himself from the charge of homosexuality, asking that he be examined as an individual and not be judged like other homosexuals. But by 1960, when his case reached the U.S. Supreme Court, Kameny realized that it was not about him as an individual at all. In petitioning the court for a writ of certiorari—his attorney having abandoned the case—Kameny charged that he, along with 15 million other Americans, was being treated as a second-class citizen. He was not being persecuted for illegal conduct but for his sexual identity. This was "no less illegal," he argued, "than discrimination based on religious or racial grounds." * * *

When the Supreme Court declined to hear his case in 1961, Kameny began casting about for others who might join his cause. Social contacts at gay bars and parties helped, but a mailing list of the Mattachine Society of New York provided the largest group of supporters. In August 1961, New York Mattachine set up an organizational meeting at the Hay–Adams Hotel for those interested in forming a group in Washington. Among the approximately 16 men in the room that night was Lieutenant Louis Fochet of the Metropolitan Police Department's Morals Division. Ron Balin, who recognized Fochet, alerted Kameny. During the discussion period after a formal presentation by Mattachine of New York, Kameny rose and said, "I understand that there is a member of the Metropolitan Police Department here. Could he please identify himself and tell us why he's here?" Fochet, visibly flustered, explained that he had been invited and quickly left. Kameny's conduct at this initial organizational meeting set the tone for the future activities of what became the Mattachine Society of Washington (MSW). * * *

In contrast to the secretive genesis of almost all previous gay organizations, MSW distributed press releases announcing its formation to every member of Congress, President Kennedy, and the Cabinet. But while coming out publicly, MSW simultaneously wrapped itself metaphorically in the American flag. In the organization's constitution, hammered out in the fall of 1961, the group based its objectives on the two founding documents of American democracy, dedicating itself to "act by any lawful means . . . to secure for homosexuals the right to life, liberty, and the pursuit of happiness, as proclaimed for all men by the Declaration of Independence and . . . the basic rights and liberties established by the word and spirit of the Constitution of the United States." They were coming out not just as homosexuals but as "homosexual citizens."

Because they were fighting for their rights as American citizens, MSW members adopted the methods of traditional reform groups, particularly those of the civil rights movement. As an advocacy group, MSW modeled itself after the National Association for the Advancement of Colored People (NAACP) and the American Civil Liberties Union (ACLU). It sought meetings with government officials, shepherded test discrimination cases through the courts, leafleted government buildings with pamphlets on how to handle an arrest or federal interrogation, and publicized its cause wherever possible. [Conservatively dressed MSW members picketed the headquarters of the Commission on June 26, 1965, the first such protest by a homophile organization.]

Perhaps even more intimidating to the Civil Service Commission than gay and lesbian protesters was a June 1965 court victory for Bruce Scott, MSW's secretary. Based on a 1947 arrest for loitering in Lafayette Park, Scott had been fired from the Department of Labor in 1956 after 17 years of service. When he reapplied to the department in 1962, he was again judged unsuitable, but with the help of MSW and the ACLU he filed suit. As the *Washington Post* pointed out in an editorial supporting Scott's lawsuit, "no specific act of immoral conduct was charged against him." The U.S. Court of Appeals [for the District of Columbia Circuit] overturned his disqualification, charging that the commission "may not rely on a determination of 'immoral conduct' based only on such vague labels as 'homosexual' or 'homosexual conduct' as a ground for disqualifying [Scott]." The court demanded for the first time that the commission define its terms and explain the rationale behind its policy.

After publicity over the pickets and its defeat in the Scott case, the commission finally agreed to meet with Mattachine representatives in the fall of 1965. In September Lawrence Meloy, Civil Service Commission general counsel, and Kimbell Johnson, director, Bureau of Personnel Investigations, met with five MSW members at the commission's headquarters. At the conclusion of the hour-and-a-half long meeting, the commission representatives requested that MSW submit a formal statement of its position and promised a response.

As a result of this exchange, the commission made the first attempt to explain its position on homosexuality * * *. In his letter to MSW, Chairman Macy claimed that the commission did not discriminate against a class of people but simply excluded individuals based on illegal or immoral conduct when it became public, such as through an arrest record or general "notoriety." As long as one did not "publicly proclaim that he engages in homosexual conduct" or "that he prefers such relationships," Macy asserted that the commission would not pry into an individual's private life. However, the commission did have to consider how the public would react to transacting government business with "a known or admitted sexual deviate."

By requiring federal employees to keep their homosexual behavior hidden, the commission's letter was an admonition to gay and lesbian employees: stay in the closet. In a 1969 interview Kimbell Johnson stated that many people continued to view the presence of known homosexuals in government service as "repugnant" and that the commission therefore disqualified them "in order to retain public confidence." Lesbians were less likely to be investigated because the public finds them "less repugnant." The issue of vulnerability to blackmail was never mentioned. The commission was not concerned with security but with its own image. The Civil Service did not want to be seen as a haven for deviants as it had been portrayed in the 1950s by critics of the New Deal. * * *

2. *The Saga of the Civil Service*

Norton contested his discharge from NASA, but a Civil Service Appeals Examiner and the Board of Appeals and Review agreed with NASA's conclusions that Norton engaged in "immoral, indecent, and disgraceful conduct." Norton subsequently filed an action for reinstatement in District Court. The Court granted defendant's motion for summary judgment, and Norton appealed.

Clifford Norton v. John Macy et al.

U.S. Court of Appeals for the District of Columbia Circuit, 1969.
417 F.2d 1161.

■ Bazelon, Chief Judge.

Appellant, a former GS–14 budget analyst in the National Aeronautics and Space Administration (NASA), seeks review of his discharge for "immoral conduct" and for possessing personality traits which render him "unsuitable for further Government employment." As a veterans preference eligible, he could be dismissed only for "such cause as will promote the efficiency of the service." Since the record before us does not suggest any reasonable connection between the evidence against him and the efficiency of the service, we conclude that he was unlawfully discharged. [Judge Bazelon recounted the facts of Norton's nocturnal escapade, his interrogation and arrest, and discharge from government service.]

Congress has provided that protected civil servants shall not be dismissed except "for such cause as will promote the efficiency of the service." The Civil Service Commission's regulations provide that an appointee may be removed, *inter alia,* for "infamous * * *, immoral, or notoriously disgraceful conduct" and for "any * * * other disqualification which makes the individual unfit for the service." We think—and appellant does not strenuously deny—that the evidence was sufficient to sustain the charge that, consciously or not, he made a homosexual advance to Procter. Accordingly, the question presented is whether such an advance, or appellant's personality traits as disclosed by the record, are "such cause" for removal as the statute requires.

* * * The Government's obligation to accord due process sets at least minimal substantive limits on its prerogative to dismiss its employees: it forbids all dismissals which are arbitrary and capricious. These constitutional limits may be greater where, as here, the dismissal imposes a "badge of infamy," disqualifying the victim from any further Federal employment, damaging his prospects for private employ, and fixing upon him the stigma of an official defamation of character. The Due Process Clause may also cut deeper into the Government's discretion where a dismissal involves an

intrusion upon that ill-defined area of privacy which is increasingly if indistinctly recognized as a foundation of several specific constitutional protections. Whatever their precise scope, these due process limitations apply even to those whose employment status is unprotected by statute. * * *

Preliminarily, we must reject appellee's contention that once the label "immoral" is plausibly attached to an employee's off-duty conduct, our inquiry into the presence of adequate rational cause for removal is at an end. A pronouncement of "immorality" tends to discourage careful analysis because it unavoidably connotes a violation of divine, Olympian, or otherwise universal standards of rectitude. * * *

We are not prepared to say that the Commission could not reasonably find appellant's homosexual advance to be "immoral," "indecent," or "notoriously disgraceful" under dominant conventional norms. But the notion that it could be an appropriate function of the federal bureaucracy to enforce the majority's conventional codes of conduct in the private lives of its employees is at war with elementary concepts of liberty, privacy, and diversity. And whatever we may think of the Government's qualifications to act *in loco parentis* in this way, the statute precludes it from discharging protected employees except for a reason related to the efficiency of the service. Accordingly, a finding that an employee has done something immoral or indecent could support a dismissal without further inquiry only if all immoral or indecent acts of an employee have some ascertainable deleterious effect on the efficiency of the service. The range of conduct which might be said to affront prevailing mores is so broad and varied that we can hardly arrive at any such conclusion without reference to specific conduct. Thus, we think the sufficiency of the charges against appellant must be evaluated in terms of the effects on the service of what in particular he has done or has been shown to be likely to do. * * *

* * * The NASA official who fired him, Mr. Garbarini, testified that * * * [his] advisers told him that dismissal for any homosexual conduct was a "*custom* within the agency," and he decided to follow the custom because continued employment of appellant might "turn out to be embarrassing to the agency" in that "if an incident like this occurred again, it could become a public scandal on the agency."

Thus, appellee is now obliged to rely solely on this possibility of embarrassment to the agency to justify appellant's dismissal. The assertion of such a nebulous "cause" poses perplexing problems for a review proceeding which must accord broad discretion to the Commission. We do not doubt that NASA blushes whenever one of its own is caught *in flagrante delictu*; but if the possibility of such transitory institutional discomfiture must be uncritically accepted as a cause for discharge which will "promote the efficiency of the service," we might as well abandon all pretense that the statute provides any substantive security for its supposed beneficiaries. A claim of possible embarrassment might, of course, be a vague way of referring to some specific potential interference with an agency's performance; but it might also be a smokescreen hiding personal antipathies or moral judgments which are excluded by statute as grounds for dismissal. A reviewing court must at least be able to discern some reasonably foreseeable, specific connection between an employee's potentially embarrassing conduct and the efficiency of the service. Once the connection is established, then it is for the agency and the Commission to decide whether it outweighs the loss to the service of a particular competent employee.

In the instant case appellee has shown us no such specific connection. Indeed, on the record appellant is at most an extremely infrequent offender, who neither openly flaunts nor carelessly displays his unorthodox sexual conduct in public. Thus, even the potential for the embarrassment the agency fears is minimal. We think the unparticularized and unsubstantiated conclusion that such possible embarrassment threatens the quality of the agency's performance is an arbitrary ground for dismissal.

Lest there be any doubt, we emphasize that we do not hold that homosexual conduct may never be cause for dismissal of a protected federal employee. Nor do we even conclude that potential embarrassment from an employee's private conduct may in no circumstances affect the efficiency of the service. What we do say is that, if the statute is to have any force, an agency cannot support a dismissal as promoting the efficiency of the service merely by turning its head and crying "shame."

■ TAMM, CIRCUIT JUDGE dissenting:

* * * I would affirm. To do otherwise would implicate me in the setting of precedent for the proposition that off-duty homosexual conduct, coupled with a capacity for "blacking out" while intoxicated, bears no real relationship to the functioning of an efficient service within a government agency. Homosexuals, sadly enough, do not leave their emotions at Lafayette Square and regardless of their spiritual destinies they still present targets for public reproach and private extortion. I believe this record supports the finding that this individual presents more than a potential risk in this regard and that his termination will serve the efficiency of the service. Despite the billows of puffery that continue to float out of recent opinions on this subject, I believe that the theory that homosexual conduct is not in any way related to the efficiency and effectiveness of governmental business is not an evil theory—just a very unrealistic one.

NOTES ON *NORTON* AND GOVERNMENT EMPLOYMENT

1. *Subsequent Civil Service Developments.* The principle in *Norton* (that a gay or lesbian person cannot be fired without a showing that there is a "nexus" between sexual orientation and job fitness) has been codified, first by administrative policy guidance and then by statute. A Civil Service Bulletin dated December 21, 1973, instructed supervisors:

> You may not find a person unsuitable for Federal employment merely because that person is a homosexual or has engaged in homosexual acts, nor may such exclusion be based on a conclusion that a homosexual person might bring the public service into contempt. You are,

however, permitted to dismiss a person or find him or her unsuitable for Federal employment where the evidence establishes that such person's homosexual conduct affects job fitness—excluding from such consideration, however, unsubstantiated conclusions concerning possible embarrassment to the Federal service.

In 1975, the Commission promulgated formal regulations to the same effect, 5 C.F.R. § 731.202(b). In 1978, the statute governing the Civil Service was amended to add the following:

Any employee who has authority to take, direct others to take, recommend or approve any personnel action, shall not, with respect to such authority—* * * (10) discriminate for or against any employee or applicant for employment on the basis of conduct which does not adversely affect the performance of the employee or applicant or the performance of others * * *

5 U.S.C.A. § 2302(b)(10). This language has been officially interpreted to preclude civil service discrimination on the basis of sexual orientation. In 1998, President Clinton amended Executive Order No. 11,478, which mandates antidiscrimination protections for federal government employees, by adding sexual orientation to the list of prohibited bases for discrimination. Executive Order No. 13,087 (May 29, 1998).

2. *Security Clearances.* The "security risk" rationale continued for two decades to be cited as the primary rationale for excluding lesbian, gay, and bisexual employees by some federal agencies exempted from the normal civil service rules, most prominently the Federal Bureau of Investigation and the Central Intelligence Agency. The FBI's exclusionary policy was upheld in *Padula v. Webster*, 822 F.2d 97 (D.C.Cir.1987). In addition, it was used to justify separate and more stringent investigations of hundreds of thousands of federal and private sector workers who have needed security clearances in order to obtain jobs or promotions. See *High Tech Gays v. Defense Industrial Security Clearance Office*, 895 F.2d 563 (9th Cir.1990).

In 1995, President Clinton signed an Executive Order prohibiting discrimination based on sexual orientation in the granting of security clearances. Executive Order No. 12968, 60 Fed.Reg. 40245 (Aug. 7, 1995). The Order ended the practice by federal agencies of automatically subjecting lesbian and gay applicants for clearances to an extensive background investigation on that basis alone.

3. *State Law.* Most state government workers are protected against sexual orientation discrimination: 25 states plus the District of Columbia prohibit such discrimination, either by statute or Executive Order.

John Singer v. U.S. Civil Service Commission

U.S. Court of Appeals for the Ninth Circuit, 1976.
530 F.2d 247, *vacated,* 429 U.S. 1034, 97 S.Ct. 725, 50 L.Ed.2d 744 (1977).

■ Jameson, District Judge. * * *

On August 2, 1971, Singer was hired by the Seattle Office of the Equal Employment Opportunity Commission (EEOC) as a clerk typist. Pursuant to 5 C.F.R. § 315.801 *et seq.,* he was employed for one year on probationary status, subject to termination if "his work performance or conduct during this period (failed) to demonstrate his fitness or his qualifications for continued employment" (§ 315.804). At the time he was hired Singer informed the Director of EEOC that he was a homosexual.

On May 12, 1972, an investigator for the Civil Service Commission sent a letter to Singer inviting him "to appear voluntarily for an interview to comment upon, explain or rebut adverse information which has come to the attention of the Commission" as a result of its investigation to determine Singer's "suitability for employment in the competitive Federal service." The interview was set for May 19. Singer appeared at the appointed time with his counsel. Singer was advised that the investigation by the Commission disclosed that "you are homosexual. You openly profess that you are homosexual and you have received widespread publicity in this respect in at least two states." Specific acts were noted, which may be summarized as follows:

(1) During Singer's previous employment with a San Francisco mortgage firm Singer had "flaunted" his homosexuality by kissing and embracing a male in front of the elevator in the building where he was employed and kissing a male in the company cafeteria;

(2) The *San Francisco Chronicle* wrote an article on Singer in November of 1970 in which he stated his name and occupation and views on "closet queens";

(3) At the Seattle EEOC office Singer openly admitted being "gay" and indicated by his dress and demeanor that he intended to continue homosexual activity as a "way of life";

(4) On September 20, 1971, Singer and another man applied to the King County Auditor for a marriage license, which was eventually refused by the King County Superior Court;

(5) As a result of the attempt to obtain the marriage license Singer was the subject of extensive television, newspaper and magazine publicity;

(6) Articles published in the Seattle papers of September 21, 1971 included Singer's identification as a typist employed by EEOC and quoted Singer as saying, in part, that he and the man he sought to marry were "two human beings who happen to be in love and want to get married for various reasons"; * * *

[By a letter dated June 26, 1972 the Chief of the Investigations Division of the Seattle office of the Civil Service Commission notified Singer that by reason of his "immoral and notoriously disgraceful conduct" he was disqualified under the Civil Service Regulations, 5 C.F.R. § 731.201(b). The letter stated: "The information developed by the investigation, taken with your reply, indicate that you have flaunted and broadcast your homosexual activities and have sought and obtained publicity in various media in pursuit of this goal. * * * Your activities in these matters are those of an advocate for a socially repugnant concept. * * * In determining that your employment will not promote the efficiency of the service, the Commission has considered such pertinent factors as the potential disruption of service efficiency because of the possible revulsion of other employees to homosexual conduct and/or their apprehension of homosexual advances and solicitations; the hazard that the prestige and authority of a Government position will be used to foster homosexual activity, particularly among youth; the possible use of Government funds and authority in furtherance of conduct offensive to the mores and law of our society; and the pos]sible embarrassment to, and loss of public confidence in, your agency and the Federal civil service."

* * * The leading case is *Norton v. Macy* * * *. The court noted, however, that homosexual conduct cannot be ignored as a factor in determining fitness for federal employment since it might "bear on the efficiency of the service in a number of ways." More specifically the court said: "If an employee makes offensive overtures while on the job, or if his conduct is notorious, the reactions of other employees and of the public with whom he comes in contact in the performance of his official functions may be taken into account. Whether or not such potential consequences would justify removal, they are at least broadly relevant to 'the efficiency of the service.' " * * *

We conclude from a review of the record in its entirety that appellant's employment was not terminated because of his status as a homosexual or because of any private acts of sexual preference. The statements of the Commission's investigation division, hearing examiner, and Board of Appeals make it clear that the discharge was the result of appellant's "openly and publicly flaunting his homosexual way of life and indicating further continuance of such activities," while identifying himself as a member of a federal agency. The Commission found that these activities were such that "general public knowledge thereof reflects discredit upon the Federal Government as his employer, impeding the efficiency of the service by lessening public confidence in the fitness of the Government to conduct the public business with which it was entrusted."

The Subsequent History of Singer's Case. The Ninth Circuit opinion was vacated by the Supreme Court, which remanded the case to the Civil Service Commission for reconsideration in light of new Civil Service regulations adopted during the pendency of the case. In 1978, the Federal Employee Appeals Authority (FEAA) canceled the personnel action that caused Singer's dismissal. The FEAA found a "complete absence of any evidence which indicates that appellant's presence on the rolls of the agency impeded the agency's ability to carry out its missions" and concluded that the dismissal had been based on "unsubstantiated conclusions." Rhonda Rivera, "Sexual Preference Law," 30 *Drake L. Rev.* 317–18 (1980–81).

Robin Joy Shahar v. Michael Bowers

U.S. Court of Appeals, Eleventh Circuit, 1997 (en banc).
114 F.3d 1097, *cert. denied*, 522 U.S. 1049, 118 S.Ct. 693, 139 L.Ed.2d 638 (1998).

■ CIRCUIT JUDGE EDMONDSON:

In this government employment case, Plaintiff–Appellant contends that the Attorney General of the State of Georgia violated her federal constitutional rights by revoking an employment offer because of her purported "marriage" to another woman. The district court concluded that Plaintiff's rights had not been violated. We affirm. * * *

[II.] Even when we assume, for argument's sake, that either the right to intimate association or the right to expressive association or both are present, we know they are not absolute. * * * Georgia and its elected Attorney General also have rights and duties which must be taken into account, especially where (as here) the State is acting as employer. * * * We also know that because the government's role as employer is different from its role as sovereign, we review its acts differently in the different contexts. In reviewing Shahar's claim, we stress that this case is about the government acting as employer.

* * * We conclude that the appropriate test for evaluating the constitutional implications of the State of Georgia's decision—as an employer—to withdraw Shahar's job offer based on her "marriage" is the same test as the test for evaluating the constitutional implications of a government employer's decision based on an employee's exercise of her right to free speech, that is, the *Pickering* balancing test. [In *Pickering v. Board of Education*, the Supreme Court ruled that a public employee has a First Amendment right to speak out on matters of public concern, unless her employer can demonstrate a stronger, countervailing interest in promoting the effective functioning of the workplace by limiting the employee's speech.]

* * * [G]overnment employees who have access to their employer's confidences or who act as spokespersons for their employers, as well as those employees with some policy making role, are in a special class of employees and seldom prevail under the First Amendment in keeping their jobs when they conflict with their employers. * * *

Put differently, the government employer's interest in staffing its offices with persons the employer fully trusts is given great weight when the pertinent employee helps make policy, handles confidential information or must speak or act—for others to see—on the employer's behalf. Staff Attorneys inherently do (or must be ready to do) important things, which require the capacity to exercise good sense and discretion (as the Attorney General, using his considered judgment, defines those qualities): advise about policy; have access to confidential information (for example, litigation strategies); speak, write and act on behalf of the Attorney General and for the State. * * *

As both parties acknowledge, this case arises against the backdrop of an ongoing controversy in Georgia about homosexual sodomy, homosexual marriages, and other related issues, including a sodomy prosecution—in which the Attorney General's staff was engaged—resulting in the well known Supreme Court decision in *Bowers v. Hardwick*. When the Attorney General viewed Shahar's decision to "wed" openly—complete with changing her name—another woman (in a large "wedding") against this background of ongoing controversy, he saw her acts as having a realistic likelihood to affect her (and, therefore, the Department's) credibility, to interfere with the Department's ability to handle certain kinds of controversial matters (such as claims to same sex marriage licenses, homosexual parental rights, employee benefits, insurance coverage of "domestic partners"), to interfere with the Department's efforts to enforce Georgia's laws against homosexual sodomy, and to create other difficulties within the Department which would be likely to harm the public perception of the Department. [Eds.: The Georgia Supreme Court ruled that the state's sodomy law was unconstitutional in the year following this decision. *Powell v. State* (Chapter 2).]

In addition, because of Shahar's decision to participate in such a controversial same sex "wedding" and "marriage" and the fact that she seemingly did not appreciate the importance of appearances and the need to avoid bringing "controversy" to the Department, the Attorney General lost confidence in her ability to make good judgments for the Department.

Whatever our individual, personal estimates might be, we—as we observe throughout this opinion—cannot say that the Attorney General's worries and view of the circumstances that led him to take the adverse personnel action against Shahar are beyond the broad range of reasonable assessments of the facts.

* * * To decide this case, we are willing to accord Shahar's claimed associational rights (which we have assumed to exist) substantial weight. But, we know that the weight due intimate associational rights, such as, those involved in even a state authorized marriage, can be overcome by a government employer's interest in maintaining the effective functioning of his office.

In weighing her interest in her associational rights, Shahar asks us also to consider the "non employment related context" of her "wedding" and "marriage" and that "[s]he took no action to transform her intimate association into a public or political statement." * * *

If Shahar is arguing that she does not hold herself out as "married," the undisputed facts are to the contrary. Department employees, among many others, were invited to a "Jewish, lesbian feminist, out door wedding" which included exchanging wedding rings: the wearing of a wedding ring is an outward sign of having entered into marriage. Shahar listed her "marital status" on her employment application as "engaged" and indicated that her future spouse was a woman. She and her partner have both legally changed their family name to Shahar by filing a name change petition with the Fulton County Superior Court. They sought and received the married rate on their insurance. And, they, together, own the house in which they cohabit. These things were not done secretly, but openly.

Even if Shahar is not married to another woman, she, for appearance purposes, might as well be. We suppose that Shahar could have done more to "transform" her intimate relationship into a public statement. But after (as she says) "sanctifying" the relationship with a large "wedding" ceremony by which she became—and remains for all to see—"married," she has done enough to warrant the Attorney General's concern. He could conclude that her acts would give rise to a likelihood of confusion in the minds of members of the public: confusion about her marital status and about his attitude on same sex marriage and related issues. * * *

* * * Shahar says that by taking into account these concerns about public reaction, the Attorney General impermissibly discriminated against homosexuals; and she refers us to the Supreme Court's recent decision in *Romer v. Evans.* (Chapter 3)

* * * *Romer* is about people's condition; this case is about a person's conduct. And, *Romer* is no employment case. Considering (in deciding to revoke a job offer) public reaction to a future Staff Attorney's conduct in taking part in a same sex "wedding" and subsequent "marriage" is not the same kind of decision as an across the board denial of legal protection to a group because of their condition, that is, sexual orientation or preference. * * *

NOTES ON *SHAHAR*

1. *The Meanings of Marriage.* One of the undertones of the majority decision is the implication not only that Shahar's relationship is something less than a real marriage (hence the quotation marks), but also that her actions in having such a ceremony provide evidence of the likelihood of loss of public confidence in the office of the Attorney General. Compare this case to *Singer*. Is *Shahar* another example of penalizing the "flaunting" of one's sexuality? Again, consider possible limits to the impact of *Lawrence*: could Bowers have taken the same action after *Lawrence*, arguing that Shahar could not be trusted to enforce and apply marriage-related law, regardless of the state of sodomy law?

2. *Postscript*: In the week after the *en banc* decision was handed down, Michael Bowers announced that he had carried on an adulterous affair for more than a decade with a woman who previously had worked in his office. Bowers had recently resigned as Attorney General and announced his candidacy for the Republican nomination for Governor of Georgia. Adultery is a crime in Georgia. News reports quoted Bowers as saying that "living in a situation of immorality while enforcing the law against somebody * * * [is] hypocritical morally," but also that he had no second thoughts about his decisions to defend the state's sodomy law and to fire Shahar. Kevin Sack, "Georgia Candidate for Governor Admits Adultery and Resigns Commission in Guard," N. Y. Times, June 6, 1997, p. A29. Meanwhile, Robin Shahar became an assistant city attorney for the City of Atlanta.

Wendy Weaver v. Nebo School District, et al.

U.S. District Court for the District of Utah, 1998.
29 F.Supp.2d 1279.

■ SENIOR DISTRICT JUDGE JENKINS.

* * * For the past nineteen years, plaintiff Wendy Weaver has been a teacher at Spanish Fork High School in the Nebo School District. Ms.

Weaver, a tenured faculty member since 1982, teaches psychology and physical education. Her reputation as an educator at Spanish Fork is unblemished: she has always been considered an effective and capable teacher, her evaluations range from good to excellent, and she has never been the subject of any disciplinary action.

In addition to her teaching responsibilities, Ms. Weaver has served as the girl's volleyball coach since 1979. She has been effective in this endeavor, leading the team to four state championships. * * *

In the late spring and early summer of 1997, Ms. Weaver began preparing for the upcoming school volleyball season—as she did in the past—by organizing two summer volleyball camps for prospective team players. As usual, these camps were to be held at Spanish Fork High School in June and July of 1997. Ms. Weaver telephoned prospective volleyball team members to inform them of the camp schedules. One of the calls [made in June] went to a senior team member. During the conversation, the team member asked Ms. Weaver. "Are you gay"? Ms. Weaver truthfully responded, "Yes." The team member then told Ms. Weaver that she would not play on the volleyball team in the fall. On July 14, 1997, the team member and her parents met with defendants Almon Mosher, Director of Human Resources for the Nebo School District, and Larry Kimball, Director of Secondary Education for the Nebo School District, and told them that Ms. Weaver told them that she is gay and that the team member decided she would not play volleyball. * * *

[The court then summarizes series of calls to the principal and district officials, beginning before the July 14 conversation, in which questions were raised about Weaver's sexual orientation. The consultations which followed culminated in letters to Weaver directing her not to discuss her sexual orientation with students in any setting "because you are always perceived by the student as a teacher, authority figure and role model." Weaver challenged the decision not to renew her contract as volleyball coach on both First Amendment and Equal Protection grounds. The court addressed the First Amendment issue, using the *Pickering* test also used by the Eleventh Circuit in *Shahar*, *supra*. The court found that the speech concerned a topic of public concern.]

Turning to the second step [in the *Pickering* test], the court must next determine whether the School District's "interests" outweigh Ms. Weaver's "interests" in acknowledging her sexual orientation and living her life openly as a lesbian. The School District must demonstrate that allowing Ms. Weaver to speak about her sexual orientation would result in a "material and substantial interference or disruption" in the normal activities of the school.

It is clear to this court that on this record no such showing has been made nor can be made.

The defendants point to the several inquiries and complaints they received from some members of the community regarding Ms. Weaver's sexual orientation as evidence of a sufficient "disruption" to justify its efforts to restrict Ms. Weaver's speech. As the record now stands, however, it cannot be said that "her speech" caused a material or substantial disruption. As counsel for Ms. Weaver aptly noted, one of the duties a school administrator undertakes is the handling of student, faculty, parent, and community complaints. Ms. Weaver continued to teach her classes without any problems. Indeed, the defendants have been unable to point to any actual disruptive events since Ms. Weaver's sexual orientation became public knowledge.

The statement from a student and volleyball team member that she felt uncomfortable about playing for Ms. Weaver, and that she would not play volleyball in her senior year, is just that. While this student's actions may have interrupted her own activities, there is no evidence that the activities of the school were in any way disrupted. It cannot be said that a single student's decision not to take part in a wholly voluntary extracurricular activity can support a showing of a "material and substantial" disruption in the school's activities. * * *

The July 22 letter does not limit [its] restrictions to speech made in the classroom or during any school-sponsored functions a limitation that all parties now seem to agree would be reasonable. Instead, these restrictions limit Ms. Weaver's ability to speak on her sexuality outside of the school, as, for example, when meeting a parent of a student in the supermarket, or when speaking at dinner with a friend who may be a staff member at the school, or even when speaking with her own children, who are students in the School District. Moreover, under the broad restrictions contained in the July 22 letter, Ms. Weaver could violate its terms if she is spotted by some student, parent, or staff member while walking hand-in-hand with another in the seclusion of her own yard. By restricting Ms. Weaver's speech outside the classroom, these restrictions are unconstitutionally overbroad. * * *

Notably, it was only Ms. Weaver who received a letter restricting her speech. The School District concedes that no other teachers have received such a letter limiting their speech on matters of sexual orientation. * * * Because the restrictions imposed on Ms. Weaver * * * only targeted speech concerning homosexual orientation and not heterosexual orientation, the restrictions are properly considered viewpoint restrictions. * * *

[The court next addressed the Equal Protection issue.] * * * In *Romer* [*v. Evans*], the [Supreme] Court noted that under the ordinary deferential equal protection standard—that is, rational basis—the Court would "insist on knowing the relation between the classification adopted and the object to be obtained." * * * Noting that the "inevitable inference" that arises from a law of this sort is that it is "born of animosity toward the class of persons affected," the Court described the amendment as "a status-based enactment divorced from any factual context from which we could discern a relationship to legitimate state interests." * * *

The question then is whether bias concerning Ms. Weaver's sexual orientation furnishes a rational basis for the defendants' decision not to assign her as volleyball coach. The "negative reaction" some members of the community may have to homosexuals is not a proper basis for discriminating against them. So reasoned the Supreme Court in the context of race. *See, e.g., Brown v. Board of Educ.*, 347 U.S. 483, 495 (1954). If the community's perception is based on nothing more than unsupported assumptions, outdated stereotypes, and animosity, it is necessarily irrational and under *Romer* and other Supreme Court precedent, it provides no legitimate support for the School District's decisions.

The record now before the court contains no job-related justification for not assigning Ms. Weaver as volleyball coach. Nor have the defendants demonstrated how Ms. Weaver's sexual orientation bears any rational relationship to her competency as teacher or coach, or her job performance as coach—a position she has held for many years with distinction. As mentioned earlier, it is undisputed that she was an excellent coach and apparently, up until the time her sexual orientation was revealed, the likely candidate for the position. Principal Wadley's decision not to assign Ms. Weaver (a decision reached after consulting with the other defendants) was based solely on her sexual orientation. Absent some rational relationship to job performance, a decision not to assign Ms. Weaver as coach because of her sexual orientation runs afoul of the Fourteenth Amendment's equal protection guarantee.

Although the Constitution cannot control prejudices, neither this court nor any other court should, directly or indirectly, legitimize them. Indeed, as the Supreme Court has recently admonished, " '[i]f the constitutional conception of "equal protection of the laws" means anything, it must at the very least mean that a bare ... desire to harm a politically unpopular group cannot constitute a legitimate governmental interest.' " *Romer*, 517 U.S. at 634 [quotation omitted]. Nor can public officials avoid their constitutional duty by "bowing to the hypothetical effects of private ... prejudice that they assume to be both widely and deeply held." *Palmore [v. Sidotti]*, 466 U.S. 429, 433 (1984) (quotation omitted). Simply put, the private antipathy of some members of a community cannot validate state discrimination. Because a community's animus towards homosexuals can never serve as a legitimate basis for state action, the defendants' actions based on that animus violate the Equal Protection Clause. * * *

[As relief, the court ordered payment of $1,500 in money damages, the removal of both letters from her file, and directed the School District to offer the plaintiff the girl's volleyball coaching position.]

Postscript. The school district in *Weaver* elected not to appeal. Angry parents sued the state education department and Weaver. They asserted that the department was acting illegally by failing to suspend her certification and sought to require the local district to fire her. They alleged a number of infractions by Weaver, including violation of the state's sodomy law. The Utah Supreme Court dismissed the complaint on the grounds that the parent plaintiffs had not raised a justiciable controversy, but were seeking merely an advisory opinion in the form of a declaratory judgment. *Miller v. Weaver*, 66 P.3d 592 (Utah 2003).

NOTES ON CONSTITUTIONAL CLAIMS FOR EQUALITY

1. *Easing the Double Bind? Shahar* and *Weaver* address many of the issues that arise when coming out speech occurs in the workplace. They illustrate the extent to which equality and expression concepts are interwoven in sexual orientation case law. Both date from the same post-*Romer v. Evans*, but pre-*Lawrence v. Texas* era, yet they come to sharply different results. Are they distinguishable, or simply contradictory?

2. *The Necessary Reliance on Constitutional Claims.* Unlike sex discrimination, sexual orientation discrimination in the workplace is not prohibited by a federal civil rights law. In Section 3, *infra*, we will consider the emerging law of the various states and municipalities that have antidiscrimination statutes. But outside those states or cities, federal and state *constitutional* law is usually the only basis for a claim of employment discrimination. One result is that the body of Equal Protection law that you studied in Chapter 3, Sections 2 and 3, is likely to govern a large number of workplace-related lawsuits.

3. *State Constitutional Law.* Similarly, in states without antidiscrimination laws that cover sexual orientation, litigants may assert claims based on the meaning of equal protection under their *state* constitutions as well as under the federal constitution. See *Tanner v. Or. Health Sci. Univ.*, Section 3 *infra*. Does this bring to mind some of the litigation strategies used by gay rights advocates seeking privacy rights after *Hardwick* and before *Lawrence*?

PART B.   DISCRIMINATION BY PRIVATE ENTITIES

The city of East Lansing, Michigan, enacted the first civil rights law covering sexual orientation discrimination in 1972. In 1974, Representative Bella Abzug introduced the first bill in Congress to prohibit such discrimination as a matter of federal law, which would have added sexual orientation to the 1964 Civil Rights Act. As of 2005, 15 states plus the District of Columbia have statutes prohibiting discrimination based on sexual orientation in both private and public sector workplaces. An interesting perspective on the state of state law is that, at the time the Supreme Court decided *Lawrence v. Texas*, the same number of states had civil rights statutes as had sodomy laws. In addition, there are statutes or executive orders in 10 other states that bar such discrimination solely against public sector employees. These provisions may be enforceable only administratively, and provide neither legal or equitable rights enforceable in court. At the local level, more than 150 cities and counties have ordinances prohibiting job discrimination because of sexual orientation, either generally or just for municipal employment. There is still no federal statute.

In the final part of this section, we turn to what has generated almost as many statutes as the basic antidiscrimination guarantee: the issue of allowing benefits for partners of unmarried (sometimes gay only) employees. In 1980, not a single employer in the U.S. offered benefits to domestic partners of employees. Now, thousands do. The dramatic difference is a result of a combination of litigation, legislation, and voluntary adoption of benefits policies by corporate America, especially in certain industries. Eleven states plus the District of Columbia offer domestic partner coverage to their own employees.

1. THE CASE FOR SEXUAL ORIENTATION ANTI-DISCRIMINATION LAWS

In the legislative debates about whether civil rights laws should include sexual orientation, a series of issues recur, including whether lesbians and gay men need protection against workplace discrimination; and whether such laws are either used enough to make a difference, or, alternatively, would be used so often that employers' cost of doing business would increase.

In Congress, a principal objection to ENDA has been that lesbians, gay men, and bisexuals are more affluent than other groups covered by antidiscrimination laws, and therefore in no need of civil rights protections. The image of gay people as more affluent than others is fairly widespread. It was a minor theme of Justice Scalia's dissent in *Romer v. Evans* [Chapter 3, Section 2] and hinted at by his references to "elites" in his dissent in *Lawrence v. Texas* [Chapter 4, Section 1]. Is it true? The issue is laced with many variables. As a threshold question, there is the difference between incomes and patterns of expenses. Lesbian or gay couples are less likely to have children than heterosexual couples, and there could easily be different spending patterns in households with children than in households without children. The discrimination issue, however, would need to be answered by examining whether the incomes are different.

Economist Lee Badgett of the University of Massachusetts has done the most extensive research on and analysis of economic discrimination questions. Using random sample data pooled from surveys conducted by the University of Chicago, Professor Badgett created a master data set, which showed the annual average earnings of employees by sex and sexual orientation as follows (in 1991 dollars):

> Heterosexual Men $28,680
>
> Homosexual/Bisexual Men $21,258
>
> Heterosexual Women $19,738
>
> Homosexual/Bisexual Women $21,331

These were the averages computed after a multiple regression analysis controlled for differences in education, race, urban residence, age, geographic region, marital status, and occupational category. Only fulltime workers were compared.

The data reveal two different patterns. Gay and bisexual men earn on the average 35 per cent less than heterosexual men, a gap that is statistically significant. Professor Badgett could find no factor other than discrimination which appeared to account for this differential, since on background factors like father's educational level and quality of schooling, there was no difference between the groups of men. For women, the gap was much less (not statistically significant), and took the other direction: lesbians and bisexual women earned on the average 11 per cent more than heterosexual women. Additional wage regression studies based on other data sets have all reached the same core conclusion: significant income disadvantage for gay and bisexual men; no disadvantage, and possibly a small advantage, for lesbian and bisexual women. Of course, economic data cannot explain why sexual orientation correlates so strongly with income gaps among male workers as a group, and not with income differentials among female workers. It appears, however, that if one measures discrimination by differentials in wages, gay and bisexual men suffer a sharp penalty for their sexual orientation, while all groups of women earn incomes that are significantly lower than those of heterosexual men. A similar dynamic operates as to race: white women earn more, but only slightly more, than African–American women; but African–American men earn significantly less than white men.

Another concern, raised by employers, is that ENDA would flood the courts with complaints by lesbian and gay employees. The most comprehensive data as to the number of complaints filed under existing laws prohibiting job discrimination based on sexual orientation were collected by the General Accounting Office in response to requests from Senator James Jeffords, a cosponsor of ENDA and chair of the Senate Committee on Labor and Human Resources, to which ENDA had been referred. The first GAO Report covered data from 1992 to 1997 in 11 states and the District of Columbia. The second updated the first, adding data from between 1997 and 2000. Both reports found that the absolute number of complaints of sexual orientation filed in each state was small, ranging from a low of two per year in smaller states to a high of 173 during one year in California. Both reports also found that the percentage of all discrimination complaints which alleged sexual orientation discrimination was low, ranging from one percent to three per cent.

The proponents of ENDA hailed the results, arguing that the GAO studies proved that the number of complaints filed under a federal statute also likely would be small, thus unlikely to significantly increase either annual costs for employers or the caseload in the courts. Opponents questioned whether, if the number of cases would be so small, there was really a need for a federal statute.

William Rubenstein points out that neither the absolute numbers nor the percentage of total complaints is meaningful without knowing the number of lesbian and gay male workers relative to the total workforce.[a] In

---

a. William B. Rubenstein, "Do Gay Rights Laws Matter?: An Empirical Assessment," 75 *S. Calif. L. Rev.* 65 (2001).

order to answer that question, Rubenstein computed population-adjusted complaint rates for each of the states studied by the GAO, for sexual orientation, race, and sex discrimination complaints. Using an estimate that lesbians and gay men comprise five percent of the workforce, he found that the rate of sexual orientation complaints in most states roughly paralleled the rate of sex discrimination complaints, after adjusting for the number of women in the workforce.

Even on their face, the GAO data raise as many questions than they answer. It is striking that states with wide variances in total populations report similar numbers of discrimination complaints. For example, the two states in the GAO Reports with the closest number of sexual orientation complaints were California, which reported 151, 127 and 154 such complaints in the last three years studied, and Massachusetts, which reported 148, 169 and 113 complaints in those years. Yet the 1990 population of California was approximately five times that of Massachusetts.

In addition to possible demographic factors, major differences in enforcement regimes may help explain these variations. Federal and state (or local) laws differ significantly in remedies, procedures and public awareness of the laws. For example, the GAO reported that three of the state laws studied did not provide for a private right of action. Persons with complaints of sexual orientation discrimination might conclude that pursuing only an administrative agency complaint would not be worth the effort or expense. (Municipal antidiscrimination laws also often do not include a private right of action, and generally provide fewer remedies.)

2.   SEXUAL ORIENTATION ANTI-DISCRIMINATION LAWS, AS APPLIED

Lawrence Lane v. Collins & Aikman Floorcoverings, Inc., Jeff Raabe, John Shearer

U.S. District Court for the Southern District of New York, 2001.
2001 WL 1338918, 87 Fair Empl.Prac.Cas. (BNA) 449.

■ BERMAN, J.

Plaintiff Lawrence B. Lane ("Plaintiff" or "Lane") has brought an action against his former employer, Collins & Aikman Floorcoverings, Inc. ("Collins & Aikman" or "C & A"), and Collins & Aikman supervisors Jeff Raabe ("Raabe") and John Shearer ("Shearer") (collectively, "Defendants"), alleging that Defendants discharged Lane from employment and subjected him to a hostile work environment in violation of the New York City Administrative Code § 8–101 et seq. on the basis of Lane's sexual orientation. * * *

Collins & Aikman, headquartered in Dalton, Georgia, manufactures, markets and sells commercial flooring systems. Collins & Aikman's product is marketed and sold through ten (10) regions; each region is managed by a Regional Manager; and each region is divided into territories assigned to a territorial Account Manager.

On June 23, 1997, Lane was hired by Collins & Aikman as the New York Regional Manager. Lane reported to Shearer (Eastern Area Vice President) who, in turn, reported to Raabe (Vice President Sales). Lane's responsibilities included "overseeing the sales of the New York Region, improving those sales, and recruiting, hiring, and supervising the Account Managers in the New York Region." At the time Lane was hired, the New York Region was viewed by management as "dysfunctional." Shearer evaluated Lane's performance in or about October 1997, noting that "Lane was 'doing an outstanding job based on his short tenure,' but that several areas needed improvement. . . ."

Plaintiff alleges that for the first 21 months after he began to work at Collins & Aikman he often received praiseworthy comments for his performance, *e.g.* "doing a terrific job" . . . "assembled a great team" . . . "people like you who are committed to excellence." He further asserts that, at the time he received this positive feedback, "the persons providing the feedback were not aware of plaintiff's sexual orientation." Plaintiff also alleges that at C & A meetings, among other times, "homophobic jokes and banter . . . made about the sexual proclivities of gay men and the supposed risk to heterosexual men of having gays around . . . were commonplace" and that "various managers affected limp wrists and lisps as a way of making fun of gays." * * *

On June 24, 1999, Raabe and Shearer met with Lane to discuss Lane's job performance. They informed Lane that he was not accomplishing a critical phase of his job, *i.e.*, building a team in the New York region and, as a result, his "job was in jeopardy." The parties dispute whether either Raabe or Shearer was aware of Lane's sexual orientation at the time of this meeting. Lane contends that Shearer knew no later than July 13, 1999 that Lane was gay, after Picaroni [an account manager] told Shearer that Lane had made a "confession" during a dinner meeting between Picaroni and Lane the previous night.

* * * In August 1999, the decision was made at Collins & Aikman headquarters to terminate Plaintiff. On September 1, 1999 Shearer and Raabe fired Lane "because of the sales numbers in the New York Region, because of [Shearer's] concern that [Shearer] was not receiving proper information from Lane, and because Lane could not build or keep a team together." * * *

Defendants contend that "it is undisputed that when Raabe and Shearer met with Lane on June 24, 1999 . . . and warned Lane that his job was in jeopardy . . . neither Shearer nor Raabe was aware of Lane's sexual orientation" to suggest Lane's termination could not have involved discrimination. "Shearer became aware of the *possibility* that Lane might be gay on July 13, 1999" as a result of a conversation between Shearer and Picaroni. (emphasis in [Defendants' brief]). As noted, Plaintiff disputes this contention, stating that Shearer or Raabe may earlier have been aware that he was gay because, among other things, of his conduct and dress. [Plaintiff referenced his trips to Fire Island, his wearing of a "pinky" ring, and his refusal to partake in "antigay banter;" he also alleged that he was told, "you know that the whole region knows that you're gay...."] * * * Plaintiff argues that Shearer's own conduct in the workplace [e.g., making antigay comments] is prima facie evidence of Shearer's own homosexual bias. * * *

Plaintiff [also] alleges that Defendants subjected him "to a hostile work environment permeated with harassment based on sexual orientation" in violation of the New York City Administrative Code. * * *

Lane was employed with Collins & Aikman for approximately two years. During that time, he identified "at least six incidents where homophobic statements, gestures or both were made in his presence." The incidents included: (i) "wrist dropping, lisping [and] role playing gay kind of thing" during "down time" at a company meeting, and (ii) a co-employee's comment about a Regional Manager's butt followed by a "role-playing, fag kind of thing" at an informal company dinner in Chattanooga. Comments were allegedly made by several employees at C & A company meetings. Lane did not report any of these incidents to senior management.

* * * Plaintiff's hostile work environment claim cannot withstand Defendant's summary judgment motion. * * * First, the conduct complained of consisted of infrequent, isolated comments and gestures. Second, the alleged conduct—while certainly inappropriate—was neither (legally) "severe," nor strongly condemnatory. Third, the conduct complained of was not physically threatening. Fourth, Plaintiff presents no (compelling) evidence that the conduct reasonably interfered with his work. * * * Fifth, Plaintiff has offered only limited testimony about any psychologically harmful effects he experienced. Considering the "totality of the circumstances," the workplace Plaintiff describes cannot, as a matter of law, be said to be "permeated with discriminatory intimidation, ridicule, and insult that is sufficiently pervasive to alter the conditions of [Plaintiff's] employment and create an abusive working environment."

[The court ruled that Plaintiff had produced sufficient evidence to go to trial on his claim of employment discrimination, but granted judgment to Defendant on the claim of hostile work environment.]

3.   COVERAGE OF BENEFITS FOR DOMESTIC PARTNERS

There has been an explosion in the number of workplaces that offer partner benefits to their employees. According to *The State of the Workplace* (published by HRC) there were 7,149 employers in all sectors of the economy that offered partner as well as spousal benefits as of the end of 2003. Of those, roughly two-thirds made the benefits available to both opposite- and same-sex couples; the other one-third limited the benefits to same-sex couples. The materials in this Part trace the legal issues first through litigation, then legislation. As you compare *Ross* and *Tanner*, notice how important the standard of review is, especially as to whether plaintiffs must demonstrate that defendants *intended* to discriminate based on sexual orientation.

Mary Ross v. Denver Department of Health and Hospitals

Colorado Court of Appeals, 1994.
883 P.2d 516.

■ JUDGE KAPELKE.

This is an appeal from a judgment of the district court reversing the determination of the Denver Career Service Board (Board) that plaintiff, Mary K. Ross, was not entitled to receive family sick leave benefits to care for her same-sex domestic partner. We reverse and remand with directions.
* * *

The eligibility for sick leave benefits to take care of other persons is prescribed in C.S.A. Rule 11–32, which provides, in pertinent part, that "sick leave may be used ... for necessary care and attendance during sickness ... of a member of the employee's immediate family." * * *

As Ross acknowledges, a same-sex partner does not fall within the agency's definition of "immediate family." Nevertheless, before both the hearings officer and the district court, Ross successfully argued that the family definition in C.S.A. Rule 1 has been superseded and, in effect, invalidated by the agency's promulgation of C.S.A. Rule 19–10(c), which [prohibits discrimination based on sexual orientation.]

Thus, the dispositive [issue is] * * * whether the denial of sick leave benefits to Ross was an action resulting in discrimination because of her sexual orientation. * * *

There is no evidence that Ross' employer singled her out and treated her differently than it would have treated a similarly situated heterosexual employee. Nor is there any evidence that the Department's decision to deny Ross' request for sick leave was motivated by discriminatory animus. * * *

We conclude that the Board's interpretation of its rules was reasonable and that the regulatory definition of "immediate family" does not impermissibly discriminate against Ross by reason of her sexual orientation. The definition in the rule applies equally to heterosexual and homosexual employees and thus does not discriminate on the basis of sexual orientation. * * *

Ross was not denied family sick leave benefits to care for her same-sex partner because she is homosexual. An unmarried heterosexual employee also would not be permitted to take family sick leave benefits to care for his or her unmarried opposite-sex partner. Thus, the rule does not treat homosexual employees and similarly situated heterosexual employees differently. *See Hinman v. Department of Personnel Administration*, 213 Cal. Rptr. 410 (Cal.Ct.App.1985); *Phillips v. Wisconsin Personnel Commission*,

482 N.W.2d 121 (Wis.App.1992). [Both cases held that similar rules differentiate based on marital status, not sexual orientation.] * * *

We recognize that under current Colorado law, a homosexual's same-sex partner cannot be a "spouse" and therefore cannot be considered part of the partner's "immediate family" under the present definition in C.S.A. Rule 1. Ross urges that her inability to marry her same-sex partner thus distinguishes her situation from that of an unmarried heterosexual employee. That distinction, however, does not alter our conclusion that the Career Service Rules do not discriminate on the basis of sexual orientation. In this regard, Ross' concern is with a perceived unfairness of the state's marital laws. The decision to change the marriage laws to permit same-sex marriages, however, is a matter for the legislature, not the courts. * * *

Postscript. Two years after this decision, Denver adopted an ordinance that extended health insurance benefits to the partners of lesbian and gay city employees. James Brooke, "Denver Extends Health Coverage to Partners of Gay Employees," *New York Times*, Sept. 18, 1996, at A17.

Christine Tanner v. Oregon Health Sciences University

Oregon Court of Appeals, 1998.
157 Or.App. 502, 971 P.2d 435.

■ PRESIDING JUDGE LANDAU.

Plaintiffs are three lesbian nursing professionals employed by Oregon Health Science University's (OHSU) and their unmarried domestic partners. Each of the couples has enjoyed a long-term and committed relationship, which each wishes to continue for life. Each of the couples would be married if Oregon law permitted homosexual couples to marry.

All three OHSU employees applied for medical and dental insurance benefits for their domestic partners. The OHSU benefits manager refused to process the applications on the ground that the domestic partners of the employees did not meet the State Employees' Benefits Board (SEBB) eligibility criteria. [SEBB rules permitted employees to purchase insurance coverage for "family members;" unmarried domestic partners of employees did not qualify as "family members."] * * *

* * * [W]e must determine whether the fact that the privileges and immunities are not available to that class [of gay people] may be justified by genuine differences between the class and those to whom the privileges and immunities are made available. Stated perhaps more plainly, we must determine whether the fact that the domestic partners of homosexual OHSU employees cannot obtain insurance benefits can be justified by their homosexuality. The parties have suggested no such justification, and we can envision none.

OHSU's defense is that it determined eligibility for insurance benefits on the basis of marital status, not sexual orientation. According to OHSU, the fact that such a facially neutral classification has the unintended side effect of discriminating against homosexual couples who cannot marry is not actionable under Article I, section 20. [However,] Article I, section 20, does not prohibit only intentional discrimination. [By comparison, under the federal Constitution, an equal protection violation will be found only upon proof of intentional discrimination. *Washington v. Davis*, 426 U.S. 229 (1976).]

* * * OHSU has taken action with no apparent intention to treat disparately members of any * * * class of citizens. Nevertheless, its actions have the undeniable effect of doing just that. * * * OHSU's intentions in this case are not relevant. What is relevant is the extent to which privileges or immunities are not made available to all citizens on equal terms.

OHSU insists that in this case privileges and immunities are available to all on equal terms: All *married* employees—heterosexual and homosexual alike—are permitted to acquire insurance benefits for their spouses. That reasoning misses the point, however. Homosexual couples may not marry. Accordingly, the benefits are not made available on equal terms. They are made available on terms that, for gay and lesbian couples, are a legal impossibility.

We conclude that OHSU's denial of insurance benefits to the unmarried domestic partners of its homosexual employees violated Article I, section 20, of the Oregon Constitution * * *

NOTE ON EQUAL BENEFITS LEGISLATION

In general, the legislation requiring partner benefits was first enacted at the municipal level, followed by state laws. At the end of 2002, there were approximately 140 governmental entities in addition to the nine states which offered such benefits to their employees. None of the laws covered private sector workplaces, however, because a federal law governs virtually all private employer benefit plans, and preempts contrary state or local laws.

Several cities—including San Francisco, Los Angeles, Minneapolis, Seattle and Oakland—have taken the campaign to require partner benefits a step further by enacting Equal Benefits Ordinances. EBOs require all entities, including private sector businesses, that contract with the particular city to grant the same benefits to their employees' domestic partners as to employees' spouses. It is EBOs that have led to the sharp increase in the number of workplaces that offer partner benefits. California enacted a statewide EBO that will take effect in 2007.

SECTION 3

SEXUAL HARASSMENT DISCRIMINATION UNDER TITLE VII

The language of Title VII broadly prohibits employment discrimination "because of * * * sex." Under this broad umbrella, two kinds of sexual harassment claims have developed. In the earliest cases, plaintiffs alleged that as a condition of employment, they were subjected to quid pro quo sexual harassment because of their sex. In a typical *quid pro quo* case, a plaintiff alleges that her boss or supervisor required her to have sex with him (or continue a previous consensual relationship) as a condition for not being fired, receiving satisfactory job performance evaluations, gaining choice job assignments, or earning promotions.

As the agency responsible for enforcement of Title VII, the Equal Employment Opportunity Commission issued "Guidelines On Discrimination Because Of Sex," codified at 29 C.F.R. ch. XIV § 1604.45 Fed. Reg. 25,024 (Apr. 11, 1980). Section 1604.11(a)(1) and (2) defined *quid pro quo* sexual harassment as prohibited conduct. EEOC added as subsection (3) a provision that sexual harassment conduct which creates an "intimidating, hostile, or offensive working environment" because of an employee's sex is also a form of prohibited sex discrimination. In *Meritor Sav. Bank, FSB v. Vinson*, 477 U.S. 57 (1986), the Supreme Court unanimously adopted the EEOC position that sexual discrimination which creates a hostile or abusive work environment is a violation of Title VII. The Court then laid out the framework necessary to prove this type of sexual harassment claim:

> To prevail on a hostile environment claim, plaintiff must establish: (1) she belongs to a protected group, (2) she was subject to unwelcome sexual harassment, (3) the harassment was based on sex, (4) the harassment affected a "term, condition, or privilege" of employment, and (5) the employer knew or should have known of the harassment in question and failed to take proper remedial action.

As you will see in *Burns, infra*, some cases continue to center on the key element of (2), "unwelcomeness."

Today, two new forms of sexual harassment claims have emerged: those in which both the harasser and harassee are of the same sex, and those in which an employee is harassed because she or he violates gender or sexuality norms. How should such cases be analyzed under the EEOC's guidelines? Under *Hopkins*?

480

Lisa Ann Burns v. McGregor Electronic Industries, Inc.

U.S. Court of Appeals for the Eighth Circuit, 1992.
955 F.2d 559.

■ WOLLMAN, CIRCUIT JUDGE. * * *

On August 30, 1985, Burns filed a complaint alleging constructive discharge from her employment with McGregor, a stereo speaker manufacturer employing fifty to seventy-five workers. She sought back pay, reinstatement, and all other related relief. Burns had worked at McGregor during three separate periods: October 14, 1980 through August 10, 1981; September 15, 1981 through June 20, 1983; and September 26, 1983 through July 19, 1984.

McGregor, which is located in McGregor, Iowa, is owned by Paul Oslac, a resident of Chicago, Illinois. Burns testified that during her first period of employment with McGregor, manager-trainee Marla Ludvik often made sexual comments as Burns left the restroom, such as "have you been playing with yourself in there?" Ludvik also made almost daily comments to other workers that she did not think Burns took douches, that she saw Burns riding in Oslac's car, and that Burns was going out with Oslac. Ludvik tried to convince Burns to date male employees. Supervisors Cleo Martin and Eldon Rytilahti heard Ludvik's remarks. Burns complained to Martin and to Mary Jean Standford, then the plant manager, but nothing changed.

The plant consisted of assembly lines in the basement and on the main floor, an office, a laboratory, and a third floor apartment used by Oslac when he visited the plant. Burns testified that Oslac showed her advertisements for pornographic films in *Penthouse* magazine, talked about sex, asked her to watch pornographic movies with him, and made lewd gestures, such as ones imitating masturbation. A former worker, Kim Heisz, saw one of Oslac's gestures. Oslac asked Burns for dates at least once a week. She gave him excuses rather than direct refusals because, she testified, she feared the loss of her job. She stated that his behavior made her angry, upset, and "real nervous," and that sometimes she would cry at work or at home. Burns also testified that there was no one above Oslac to whom she could complain; and that although she received no complaints, her work slowed down and she started dropping assembly parts. She voluntarily left McGregor on August 10, 1981.

Burns returned on September 15, 1981, because, she maintained, she needed the work. The newly-hired plant manager, Virginia Kelley, placed her in a higher-paying quality control job. Burns testified that during this period Oslac visited the plant from 11:00 a.m. Monday until 9:00 a.m. Tuesday of each week and that he spent most of this time with her. He continued to ask for dates and wanted to engage in oral sex so she would "be able to perform [her] work better." When Burns refused a date, Oslac told her, "I'm tired of your fooling around and always turning me down. You must not need your job very bad." Believing that Oslac intended to fire her, she accepted an invitation to dinner at his apartment on the condition that her mother would join them. Burns testified that her mother refused to go, so her father, Daniel Burns, went with her. As the district court found, Oslac appeared shocked when Burns' father appeared at the dinner with Burns. After the meal, Daniel Burns told Oslac he knew what was going on and for Oslac "to leave the girls alone at work."

Burns further testified that during her second period of employment Ludvik, who was then a supervisor, circulated a petition to have Burns fired because nude photographs of her, taken by her father, appeared in two motorcycle magazines—*Easyrider* and *In the Wind*. One full frontal view of Burns revealed a pelvic tatoo; two photographs highlighted jewelry attached to her pierced nipples. Burns testified that she had willingly allowed her father to do the piercing and photography. She did not take copies of the magazines into the plant. Former employee Deborah Johnson testified that she saw Ludvik showing employees the magazine and the petition. Burns testified that after Oslac learned about the nude photos from Ludvik, he told her, "They're ganging up on you and trying to get rid of you. If you don't go out with me, I might just let them do it." Oslac then asked Burns to pose nude for him in the plant in return for overtime pay.

Burns further testified that she was humiliated by plant gossip that she was Oslac's girlfriend; that supervisor June Volske tried to get her to sit on Oslac's lap, to go out with him, or to go up to his apartment; and that coworker Eugene Ottaway called her vulgar names. She complained to Kelley, who appeared to try to "do something" for a period of time, and to Kelley's successor. Burns testified that her second period of employment was "hostile" and "extremely worse" than the first. She quit again on June 20, 1983.

Burns returned to McGregor for the third time on September 26, 1983, because, she said, Kelley had returned to the plant and because she needed work to support herself, her father, and her brother. When Burns expressed concerns about Oslac's behavior, Kelley assured her that Oslac would no longer enter the plant. Oslac continued to visit Burns, although he did not spend as much time with her as he had previously. According to Burns, he repeatedly asked her to go out, pose nude, and watch pornographic movies. On one occasion when other employees were present, Oslac threw his arm around her, cupped his hand as if to grab her breast, and said, "Well, I see I got you back, lover." He also gave her an *Easyrider* calendar.

Oslac had not visited the plant within the four to six weeks preceding Burns' last day, July 19, 1984. On that day, Burns asked Ottaway to move stacks of speakers, and he refused. Burns reported this to a supervisor, who instructed Ottaway to move the speakers. Ottaway then pushed and shoved the stacks, all the while calling Burns a series of vulgar names similar to those he admitted to having called her on other occasions, and placed the speakers so high she could not reach them. When Burns asked him to make the stacks lower, Ottaway threw the speakers across the room. Burns began crying and tried to get a supervisor to stop Ottaway, but the supervisor did nothing. Burns left work and did not return.

Burns testified that the overall work environment was "hostile and offensive." She testified that during the last six weeks of her third period of employment at McGregor she overheard Ottaway tell a fellow worker that "he should throw [Burns] over the [conveyor] belts" and commit an act of sodomitic intercourse upon her. Called as a witness for McGregor, Ottaway denied making the statement attributed to him by Burns about "throwing her over the belts." He admitted on direct examination, however, that he had called Burns names—"anything nasty." He testified that Burns had responded by calling him similar names. He further testified that during the speaker-throwing incident on July 19, 1984, he was angry at Burns and had "called her every name in the book." [Other witnesses confirmed that Ottaway called Burns abusive names and that Oslac routinely touched women in improper ways and make lewd gestures while in the plant.]

Testifying by way of deposition, Oslac denied Burns' allegations. He testified that he had invited Burns and her father to dinner at his apartment because Burns was planning to quit and that he convinced her father to talk her into staying. He claimed that he never talked to Burns at all during her last period of employment. He admitted spending quite a bit of time in her testing booth during her second period of employment, but said that Burns needed a lot of encouragement. He admitted showing several workers a bruise, but said that he pulled his pant leg up to do so and did not drop his pants to his knees. He claimed that the *Easyrider* calendar was given to him by Burns, not the other way around.

On the basis of this and other testimony, the district court indicated that it had some difficulty in determining what actually went on at McGregor because "rumor and gossip ran rampant." The court found that several forces contributed to Burns' decision to quit her job: the general working conditions; gossip about the nude photos (and the resulting treatment by coemployees); unwanted sexual advances by Oslac; and the sexually-charged name-calling during the running dispute with other employees about moving and stacking speakers. The district court found "the primary reason [Burns quit] was the incident on the last day during which she and Eugene Ottaway got into a violent name-calling argument and speakers were knocked about."

The district court found that the sexual harassment that Burns received from her coworkers peaked during the second period of employment and resulted from the publication of the nude photos. The court found that there was little or no sexual harassment directed toward Burns by her coworkers during her third period of employment at McGregor. The court found that "[i]n view of [Burns'] willingness to display her nude body to the public in Easy Riders publications, crude magazines at best, her testimony that she was offended by sexually directed comments and Penthouse or Playboy pictures is not credible." The court stated that it had no doubt that Oslac had made unwelcome sexual advances to Burns during her first two employment periods, but that Burns had exaggerated the severity and pervasiveness of the harassment and its effect upon her. The district court concluded that, in light of the whole record and the totality of the circumstances, Burns had failed to prove "by a preponderance of credible evidence" that the sexual harassment was sufficiently severe or pervasive to alter the conditions of her employment and create an abusive work environment, citing *Meritor Savings Bank v. Vinson*, 477 U.S. 57, 66 (1986). * * *

* * * The district court had "no doubt" that Oslac made unwelcome sexual advances toward Burns during the first two periods she was employed, but found that there were few opportunities for Oslac to see her during the third period. The court also found that Burns lacked credibility when she testified that she was offended by the pornographic pictures and by the sexual comments.

The threshold for determining that conduct is unwelcome is "that the employee did not solicit or incite it, and the employee regarded the conduct as undesirable or offensive." The district court's finding that Oslac's advances were unwelcome necessarily required the district court to believe Burns' testimony that Oslac's behavior was offensive to her. Thus, the district court's finding that Oslac made unwelcome advances toward Burns and its finding that Burns was not credible when she stated that Oslac's behavior was offensive appear on their face to be internally inconsistent.

There is no evidence in the record that Burns solicited any of the conduct that occurred. However, the gossip, lewd talk, and the petition all occurred after the nude photographs of Burns appeared. These incidents were incited by the nude photographs and must be considered separately from Oslac's conduct. His conduct occurred both before and after Burns appeared in the magazines and did not change in kind or intensity after the appearance of the photos, though his advances tapered off during Burns' third period of employment. Eugene Ottaway's conduct and that of Burns' supervisors must also be analyzed separately from the conduct that occurred after Burns appeared nude. Ludvik, a plant supervisor, made inappropriate sexual and personal remarks and encouraged Burns to go out with Oslac, both before and after the nude pictures appeared. When Burns complained to supervisors about Oslac's behavior, she received either no response or promises that were not kept. Ottaway, according to the record, knew of the nude pictures and harassed Burns about them, but he also called Burns and other employees names of a sexual nature. Burns' complaints to her supervisor about Ottaway's conduct bore no results. The district court should, on remand, take all of this conduct into account as part of the "totality of the circumstances" in determining whether Burns found the conduct unwelcome. "The correct inquiry is whether [the plaintiff] by her conduct indicated that the alleged sexual advances were unwelcome[.]" *Meritor*, 477 U.S. at 68.

Evidence regarding a plaintiff's sexually provocative speech or dress is relevant "in determining whether he or she found particular sexual advances unwelcome." *Id.* at 69. Thus, in making the determination as to whether the conduct directed at Burns was unwelcome, the nude photo evidence, though relating to an activity engaged in by Burns outside of the work place, may be relevant to explain the context of some of the comments and actions directed by Oslac and coworkers to Burns.

Last, the district court found that the harassment Burns underwent was not so severe or pervasive that it affected a term, condition or privilege of employment. To affect a "term, condition, or privilege" of employment within the meaning of Title VII, the harassment "must be sufficiently severe or pervasive 'to alter the conditions of [the victim's] employment and create an abusive working environment.'" *Id.* at 67. The E.E.O.C. guidelines state that conduct is prohibited by Title VII where it "has the purpose or effect of unreasonably interfering with an individual's work performance *or* creating an intimidating, hostile, or offensive working environment." 29 C.F.R. § 1604.11(a)(3) (emphasis added). In approving this language, the Supreme Court cited cases involving racial discrimination and stated that "[o]ne can readily envision working environments so heavily polluted with discrimination as to destroy completely the emotional and psychological stability of [the] workers." *Meritor*, 477 U.S at 66. The court went on to state that "[n]othing in Title VII suggests that a hostile environment based on discriminatory *sexual* harassment should not be likewise prohibited." *Id.* (emphasis in original).

The district court reasoned that a person who would appear nude in a national magazine could not be offended by the behavior which took place at the McGregor plant. It also believed that Burns had exaggerated the severity and pervasiveness of the harassment and its effect on her. Again, these findings are at odds with the district court's finding that Oslac's advances were unwelcome.

We believe that a reasonable person would consider the conduct of Oslac and Burns' supervisors to be sufficiently severe or pervasive to alter the conditions of employment and create an abusive work environment. Burns testified that she was offended by the pictures in the pornographic magazines because they depicted couples engaged in various acts of sexual intercourse. She testified that she found Oslac's sexual advances and Ludvik's and Ottaway's comments humiliating and degrading. Burns continually complained to different supervisors, and she quit three separate times when she could no longer tolerate the conduct. The question is whether Burns has shown she is an "affected individual," that is, whether she was at least as affected as the reasonable person under like circumstances. On remand, the district court must determine whether Burns was as affected as that hypothetical "reasonable person." * * *

NOTES ON "TRADITIONAL" SEXUAL HARASSMENT

1. *Who's the Norm?* In *Burns*, the appeals court finds that a reasonable person would have found the alleged conduct to have been sufficiently severe to contaminate the workplace, but remands for the district court to determine whether Burns was herself a reasonable person for purposes of that inquiry. Should such an assessment be subjective or objective? What if the evidence proved that she had been raised in a very sheltered environment and thus became extremely upset even by non-severe actions?

2. *Meanings of "Sex."* The district court in *Burns* found that "the harassment, because it was sexual, was based on [plaintiff's] sex." Does the word "sex" in that sentence mean sexual conduct, sexual desire or sexual category? In general, in heterosexual cases, courts have reasoned that because the defendant wanted to have sex (conduct), and is implicitly presumed to be heterosexual (desire), he (in the typical case) targets the victim based on her (anatomic) sex (category). Generally, the same analysis works when the hostile conduct or speech is sexualized but not expressive of desire to have sex. For example, calling someone a sexual epithet would usually be related to his or her anatomic sex because most such epithets apply only to women or only to men. What if the conduct was sexualized but not necessarily linked to gender? Consider Marla Ludvik's conduct in showing others the photographs of Burns: would Burns have to prove that Ludvik would not have displayed nude photographs of a male worker whom she disliked? Or was it the sexualized nature of the insult that made that an act of sex discrimination? Should that count as sex discrimination?

3. *Feminist Critiques of Sexual Harassment Law.* Professor Vicki Schultz criticizes sexual harassment case law for both under- and over-inclusiveness. Vicki Schultz, "Reconceptualizing Sexual Harassment," 107 *Yale L.J.* 1683 (1998). As to the former, she argues that courts have conflated gender harassment and sexual abuse. As a result, the law misses much of the worst harassment of women because it isn't sexual. Gender-based, non-sexual insults ("you don't look like a mechanic") undermine women's competence and authority. What they have in common with sexualized harassment such as that in *Burns,* Schultz argues, is that the victim's very womanness is used as evidence of her inadequacy.

Sexual harassment law is also overinclusive, Schultz says, because judges often tend to assume that all sexualized conduct or speech is discriminatory. She elaborates on this point in "The Sanitized Workplace," excerpted in the Introduction to this Chapter. She proposes that feminist lawyers concentrate on ending gender-segregated or gender-imbalanced workplaces. When women workers have achieved critical mass in a particular workplace, research shows that they exercise sufficient power to informally establish the norms for sexualized interaction.

Medina Rene v. MGM Grand Hotel, Inc.

U.S. Court of Appeals for the Ninth Circuit, *en banc,* 2002.
305 F.3d 1061, *cert. denied,* 538 U.S. 922 (2003).

■ CIRCUIT JUDGE [WILLIAM] FLETCHER.

* * * We would hold that an employee's sexual orientation is irrelevant for purposes of Title VII. It neither provides nor precludes a cause of action for sexual harassment. That the harasser is, or may be, motivated by hostility based on sexual orientation is similarly irrelevant, and neither

provides nor precludes a cause of action. It is enough that the harasser have engaged in severe or pervasive unwelcome physical conduct of a sexual nature. We therefore would hold that the plaintiff in this case has stated a cause of action under Title VII.

Medina Rene, an openly gay man, appeals from the district court's grant of summary judgment in favor of his employer MGM Grand Hotel in his Title VII action alleging sexual harassment by his male coworkers and supervisor. The relevant facts are not in dispute. Rene worked for the hotel, located in Las Vegas, Nevada, from December 1993 until his termination in June 1996. He worked as a butler on the 29th floor, where his duties involved responding to the requests of the wealthy, high-profile and famous guests for whom that floor was reserved. All of the other butlers on the floor, as well as their supervisor, were also male.

Rene provided extensive evidence that, over the course of a two-year period, his supervisor and several of his fellow butlers subjected him to a hostile work environment on almost a daily basis. The harassers' conduct included whistling and blowing kisses at Rene, calling him "sweetheart" and "muñeca" (Spanish for "doll"), telling crude jokes and giving sexually oriented "joke" gifts, and forcing Rene to look at pictures of naked men having sex. On "more times than [Rene said he] could possibly count," the harassment involved offensive physical conduct of a sexual nature. Rene gave deposition testimony that he was caressed and hugged and that his coworkers would "touch [his] body like they would to a woman." On numerous occasions, he said, they grabbed him in the crotch and poked their fingers in his anus through his clothing. When asked what he believed was the motivation behind this harassing behavior, Rene responded that the behavior occurred because he is gay. * * *

It is clear that Rene has alleged physical conduct that was so severe and pervasive as to constitute an objectively abusive working environment. It is equally clear that the conduct was "of a sexual nature." Rene's tormentors did not grab his elbow or poke their fingers in his eye. They grabbed his crotch and poked their fingers in his anus.

Physical sexual assault has routinely been prohibited as sexual harassment under Title VII. * * * Such harassment—grabbing, poking, rubbing or mouthing areas of the body linked to sexuality—is inescapably "because of . . . sex." * * *

In granting MGM Grand's motion for summary judgment, the district court did not deny that the sexual assaults alleged by Rene were so objectively offensive that they created a hostile working environment. Rather, it appears to have held that Rene's otherwise viable cause of action was defeated because he believed he was targeted because he is gay. This is not the law. We have surveyed the many cases finding a violation of Title VII based on the offensive touching of the genitalia, buttocks, or breasts of women. In none of those cases has a court denied relief because the victim was, or might have been, a lesbian. The sexual orientation of the victim was simply irrelevant. If sexual orientation is irrelevant for a female victim, we see no reason why it is not also irrelevant for a male victim.

The premise of a sexual touching hostile work environment claim is that the conditions of the work environment have been made hostile "because of . . . sex." The physical attacks to which Rene was subjected, which targeted body parts clearly linked to his sexuality, were "because of . . . sex." Whatever else those attacks may, or may not, have been "because of" has no legal consequence. "[S]o long as the environment itself is hostile to the plaintiff because of [his] sex, why the harassment was perpetrated (sexual interest? misogyny? personal vendetta? misguided humor? boredom?) is beside the point." *Doe v. City of Belleville*, 119 F.3d 563, 578 (7th Cir. 1997), *vacated and remanded*, 523 U.S. 1001 (1998).

Our opinion today is guided by the principles established by the Supreme Court in *Oncale v. Sundowner Offshore Servs., Inc.* [holding that same-sex sexual harassment is covered by Title VII if it occurs "because of sex."] * * * We take two lessons from the Court's decision in *Oncale*.

First, Title VII forbids severe or pervasive same-sex offensive sexual touching. The Court made clear that a plaintiff's action for sexual harassment under Title VII cannot be defeated by a showing that the perpetrator and the victim of an alleged sexual assault are of the same gender. * * *

Second, offensive sexual touching is actionable discrimination even in a same-sex workforce. The Court in *Oncale* made clear that "discrimination" is a necessary predicate to every Title VII claim. That is, a defendant's conduct must not merely be "because of . . . sex"; it must be " '*discrimination]* . . . because of . . . sex.' " (emphasis in original). The Court in *Oncale* held that "discrimina[tion] . . . because of . . . sex" can occur entirely among men, where some men are subjected to offensive sexual touching and some men are not. There were no women on Oncale's drilling rig; indeed, there were no women on any of his employer's oil rigs. Discrimination is the use of some criterion as a basis for a difference in treatment. In the context of our civil rights laws, including Title VII, discrimination is the use of a *forbidden* criterion as a basis for a *disadvantageous* difference in treatment. "Sex" is the forbidden criterion under Title VII, and discrimination is any disadvantageous difference in treatment "because of . . . sex." The *Oncale* Court's holding that offensive sexual touching in a same-sex workforce is actionable discrimination under Title VII necessarily means that discrimination can take place between members of the same sex, not merely between members of the opposite sex. Thus, Oncale did not need to show that he was treated worse than members of the opposite sex. It was enough to show that he suffered discrimination *in comparison to other men.*

Viewing the facts, as we must, in the light most favorable to the nonmoving party, we are presented with the tale of a man who was repeatedly grabbed in the crotch and poked in the anus, and who was singled out from his other male coworkers for this treatment. It is clear that the offensive conduct was sexual. It is also clear that the offensive conduct was discriminatory. That is, Rene has alleged that he was treated differently—and disadvantageously—based on sex. This is precisely what Title VII forbids: "discriminat[ion] . . . because of . . . sex."

In sum, what we have in this case is a fairly straightforward sexual harassment claim. Title VII prohibits offensive "physical conduct of a sexual nature" when that conduct is sufficiently severe or pervasive. *Meritor Savings Bank v. Vinson*, 477 U.S. 57, 65 (1986). It prohibits such conduct without regard to whether the perpetrator and the victim are of the same or different genders. And it prohibits such conduct without regard to the sexual orientation–real or perceived–of the victim.

There will be close cases on the question of what constitutes physical conduct of a sexual nature, for there are some physical assaults that are intended to inflict physical injury, but are not intended to have (and are not interpreted as having) sexual meaning. That is, there will be some cases in which a physical assault, even though directed at a sexually identifiable part of the body, does not give rise to a viable Title VII claim. But this is not such a case. Like the plaintiff in *Oncale*, Rene has alleged a physical assault of a sexual nature that is sufficient to survive a defense motion for summary judgment.

This opinion is joined by JUDGES TROTT, THOMAS, GRABER, and FISHER. JUDGE PREGERSON, in a separate opinion joined by JUDGES TROTT and BERZON reaches the same result but under a different rationale. Taken together, these two opinions are joined by a majority of the en banc panel. * * *

■ CIRCUIT JUDGE PREGERSON, with whom CIRCUIT JUDGES TROTT and BERZON join, concurring.

I concur in the result of Judge Fletcher's opinion. I write separately to point out that in my view, this is a case of actionable gender stereotyping harassment. * * *

The conduct suffered by Rene is indistinguishable from the conduct found actionable in *Nichols v. Azteca Restaurant Enterprises, Inc.*, 256 F.3d 864 (9th Cir.2001). In that case,

> Male coworkers and a supervisor repeatedly referred to [the male gay plaintiff] in Spanish and English as "she" and "her." Male coworkers mocked [him] for walking and carrying his serving tray "like a woman," and taunted him in Spanish and English as, among other things, a "faggot" and a ". . . female whore."

We concluded in *Nichols* that "[the] rule that bars discrimination on the basis of sex stereotypes" set in *Price Waterhouse* "squarely applies to preclude the harassment here." More generally, we held that "this verbal abuse was closely related to gender," "occurred because of sex," and therefore "constituted actionable harassment under . . . Title VII."

The similarities between *Nichols* and the present case are striking. In both cases, a male gay employee was "teased" or "mocked" by his male coworkers because he walked "like a woman." And in both cases, a male gay employee was referred to by his male-co-workers in female terms— "she," "her," and "female whore" in *Nichols*; "sweetheart" and "muñeca" ("doll") in the present case—to "remind [] [him] that he did not conform to their gender-based stereotypes." For the same reasons that we concluded in *Nichols* that "[the] rule that bars discrimination on the basis of sex stereotypes" set in *Price Waterhouse* "squarely applie[d] to preclude the harassment" at issue there, I conclude that this rule also squarely applies to preclude the identical harassment at issue here. Accordingly, this is a case of actionable gender stereotyping harassment.

■ [Separate concurring opinions by JUDGES GRABER and FISHER are omitted.]

■ CIRCUIT JUDGE HUG, with whom CHIEF JUDGE SCHROEDER, and JUDGES FERNANDEZ and T.G. NELSON join, dissenting.

* * * The basis for Judge Fletcher's opinion is that harassment of a person in the workplace in the form of severe unwelcome physical conduct of a sexual nature is sufficient to establish a cause of action under Title VII of the Civil Rights Act, regardless of whether that harassment constitutes discrimination *because of* race, color, religion, gender, or national origin. I disagree because this completely eliminates an essential element of that statute, that the harassment be *because of* discrimination against one of the five specified categories of persons named in the statute. Judge Pregerson's opinion is based upon gender stereotyping harassment, which was never asserted by Rene in the district court and was not supported by evidence presented to the district court. * * *

It is by now clear that sexual harassment can be a form of discrimination based on sex. The Supreme Court stated: "Without question, when a supervisor sexually harasses a subordinate *because of the subordinate's sex,* that supervisor 'discriminate[s]' on the basis of sex." *Meritor* (emphasis added). In that case the evidence that a male supervisor made unwelcome sexual advances to a woman subordinate was sufficient to constitute discrimination based on sex.

Rene alleged that he was discriminated against because he was gay. Alleging a hostile work environment theory of sexual harassment, Rene alleged that he was sexually harassed by his male coworkers and a supervisor. To succeed on that theory, Rene must first prove that he was forced to endure a subjectively and objectively abusive working environment. In this case, the parties do not dispute the existence of a hostile work environment, for there is no doubt that the harassment that Rene alleged was so objectively offensive that it created a hostile work environment. The dispute is whether he was discriminated against because of his gender.

Rene relies on *Oncale* to make his case, contending that the Supreme Court impliedly held that discrimination based on sexual orientation is actionable under Title VII. This is a misreading of *Oncale*. * * * Never has it been held "that workplace harassment, even harassment between men and women, is automatically discrimination because of sex merely because the words used have sexual content or connotations." *Oncale*. Rather, under Title VII, the plaintiff "must always prove that the conduct at issue was not merely tinged with offensive sexual connotations, but actually constituted '*discrimina [tion]* ... because of ... sex.'" *Id.*

* * * Thus, the Supreme Court in *Oncale* did not hold that the harassment alleged by the plaintiff in that case was actionable under Title

VII. The Court, rather, simply rejected the Fifth Circuit's holding that same-sex harassment could *never* be actionable under Title VII. * * *

Judge Fletcher's opinion in effect interprets *Oncale* to mean that if the defendant's conduct was "sexual in nature" the statutory requirements of Title VII are met. The opinion then reasons that because the touching in this case was sexual in nature and was discriminatory, Rene has stated a claim under Title VII. This misinterprets *Oncale*. The *Oncale* Court did say that "[w]e see no justification in the statutory language or our precedents for a categorical rule excluding same-sex harassment claims from the coverage of Title VII." However, the Court qualified that by stating "Title VII prohibits 'discriminat[ion] . . . because of . . . sex' in the 'terms' or 'conditions' of employment. Our holding that this includes sexual harassment must extend to sexual harassment of any kind *that meets the statutory requirements*." (emphasis added). Thus, the Court stressed that the harassment type of discrimination must meet the statutory requirement of "because of sex." Justice Thomas' concurrence emphasized that point. Differential treatment of an individual based only on conduct that is "sexual in nature" does not meet the statutory requirement. The alleged harassment in this case was not on account of the plaintiff's sex, i.e., this plaintiff was not treated differently from all the other male butlers because he was male. Rene contended that he was treated differently because he was homosexual.

Title VII is not an anti-harassment statute; it is an antidiscrimination statute against persons in five specific classifications: race, color, religion, sex, or national origin. Harassment can be a type of discrimination against persons in one of those five specific classifications. However, in order for harassment to be actionable it has to be a type of discrimination "because of" race, color, religion, sex, or national origin. There are many types of harassment in the workplace that are very offensive but are not actionable under the federal Title VII law. * * *

Recently, we held in *Nichols v. Azteca Restaurant Enterprises, Inc.,* that harassment of a male waiter by male workers and a supervisor amounted to harassment because of sex stereotyping and thus was discrimination because of gender. In that case the plaintiff presented evidence that the harassment was because he acted too feminine on the job. He was taunted for walking and carrying his serving tray like a woman and for having feminine mannerisms. He was harassed because he did not act on the job as his coworkers perceived he should act as a man, not just because of his sexual orientation. This corresponds to the sex stereotyping described in *Price Waterhouse*.

In Rene's case there was no contention before the district court that the harassment Rene experienced was because he acted effeminately on the job, or for any reason other than his sexual orientation. * * *

Rene himself repeatedly stated that his coworkers harassed him because of his sexual orientation. On no fewer than nine occasions during his deposition, Rene affirmed that his coworkers harassed him *only* because he was gay. * * *

The degrading and humiliating treatment Rene describes is appalling and deeply disturbing. * * *

[However,] Rene's lawsuit was brought solely on the basis that he was harassed in the workplace because of his sexual orientation, which is not actionable under Title VII of the Civil Rights Act; therefore the summary judgment was properly entered. I would affirm the district court.

A Result in Search of a Rationale? In *Rene,* the seven-judge majority split 4 to 3 as to which theory of sexual harassment justified his claim. What were the two theories that divided the court? Which do you think is better? Are there others? Note that the Supreme Court denied certiorari, turning down a chance to clarify this area of law.

CHAPTER 9

FAMILIES WE CHOOSE: PRIVATIZATION AND PLURALITY IN FAMILY LAW

"Family" in western civilization has traditionally meant ties created by marriage and blood, and the typical family was a husband, wife, and as many children as possible. At the dawn of the new millennium, marriage and blood remain centrally important, but have given way to "families we choose," as anthropologist Kath Weston terms it. Weston, *Families We Choose: Lesbians, Gays, Kinship* (1991). The relative ascendancy of families we choose is the family law parallel of Sir Henry Maine's observation that modern law consists in the ongoing transition from status relations to contractual relations. Thus it is that families today are easier to form and can assume a greater variety of different legal forms, most of which are easier to exit.

This Chapter will survey the legal (and, to some extent, social) evolution of family law, including the emergence of contract-based romantic partnerships (Section 1), the same-sex marriage movement (Section 2), and the evolving rules regarding children in families of choice (Section 3). In addition to a survey of existing law, the Chapter will suggest directions for the future, the most prominent of which is the emerging *menu of options* states will be offering couples, with different benefits and obligations associated with each menu option. Finally, as in the earlier chapters, there will be materials and notes suggesting theoretical inquiries. Before launching into our survey, we should like to present a fresh approach to family law.

Martha Albertson Fineman, *The Neutered Mother, the Sexual Family, and Other Twentieth Century Tragedies* (1995). Professor Fineman proposes "the end of family law as we know it, with the suggestion that marriage be abolished as a legal category. I offer a utopian revisioning of the family—a reconceptualization of family intimacy that redefines the legal core unit away from our current focus on sexual or horizontal intimacy." The "caretaking dyad," modeled on the Mother/Child relationship, "would replace the historic dyad of the heterosexual married couple as the core intimate family unit upon which family policy and law are constructed" (p. 8).

Professor Fineman's argument starts with a feminist critique of our liberalized family law. Many feminists maintain that formal equality is harmful to women when it does not take account of women's different needs *or* the structural and societal problems imposed upon women. Fineman objects to the liberal feminist view that women and their families would be better off if women had equal opportunities "in the world" and were not distinctively tied to their family duties. "The result is that much of the reformist rhetoric directed at family law constantly reaffirms the notion that the disabilities and disadvantages of Mother must be overcome—the family refashioned so that the individual woman is left unencumbered." (P. 74.)

Liberal feminists respond that their reforms seek functional as well as formal equality—shared parenting, where the father does half the housework and the mother works outside the home. Fineman is skeptical, for shared parenting in practice has meant the double shift, where the wife works outside the home *and* does almost all the child care and housework. The reason for the double shift is that men expect women to do the housework and child care; many women share that expectation, and even when they do not, the man's superior bargaining position within marriage assures that husbands' preferences will usually prevail. Indeed, liberalized divorce and custody law strengthens the husband's bargaining position. The husband's threat of walking away from the marriage is one that wives are less willing to make, and so the repeat-game bargaining between husband and wife will tilt toward the husband's interests, for the reasons Carol Rose posited in Chapter 5, Section 2. In the event of a divorce, "mothers may exchange a bargained-down property settlement to avoid a custody contest because they tend, in contrast to fathers, to consider custody a nonnegotiable issue" (p. 89).

From a feminist perspective, Fineman suggests, the problem is deeper—it goes to the notion abundant in our culture and law that the *sexual family* of the husband and wife is the foundational unit of society. This *meta-narrative* focuses attention on the *horizontal* relationship of the husband and the wife, which is assumed to be heterosexual and procreative, while treating *vertical* relationships such as mother/child and adult/elderly parent as special exceptions to be accommodated at the margins (p.145). "While a great deal of emotionally charged rhetoric in family law is directed at children, the primary focus is still on maintaining the traditional heterosexual family model. * * * The sexually affiliated family is still the imposed ideal and, as such, it escapes sustained, serious consideration and criticism. The nuclear family is 'natural'—it is assumed. The dominance of the idealized sexual family in social and legal thought has restricted real reform and doomed us to recreate patriarchy." (P. 147.)

Previous critics of the sexual family have pointed out that it is a situs for excluding lesbians, gay men, and many bisexuals from public culture; for marginalizing and stigmatizing single people, especially single mothers of color raising children; and for maintaining patriarchy. Fineman poses a deeper critique: "The ideal of the natural family—the unit to which responsibility for inevitable dependency is referred—establishes a relationship between 'public' state and 'private' family. Dependency," where a parent cares for a child or an adult cares for her aged parent, "is allocated away from the state to the private grouping. These ideas of natural and privatized dependency reinforce one another on an ideological level. They perversely interact so that the societal tasks assigned to the natural family inevitably assume the role differentiation that exists within that sexually affiliated family." (P. 161.)

"Equality rhetoric and family law reforms aside, the burdens associated with intimacy and its maintenance have always been and continue to be disproportionately allocated to women. * * * Women, wives, mothers, daughters, daughters-in-law, sisters are typically the socially and culturally assigned caretakers. As caretakers they are tied into intimate relationships with their dependents. The very process of assuming caretaking responsibilities creates dependency in the caretaker—she needs some social structure to provide the means to care for others. In a traditional family, the caretaker herself, as wife and mother, is dependent on the wage-earning husband to provide for her so she can fulfill her tasks." (Pp. 162–63.) The caretaking wife, thus conceived, is completely vulnerable in a bargaining situation; the husband, if he chooses, can insist on sexual, monetary, and allocation-of-duty advantages that the dependent wife can hardly decline.

The sexual family, a product of social mores as well as legal "reform," has failed women, and it has failed children. The state's many subsidies and social pressure push women into marriages that soon leave most wives working a double shift and increasingly dependent upon their husbands' good faith—a dependency that has had devastating consequences for tens of millions of women and their children. "In its historic form [the sexual family] is not adequate to handle both the demands for equality and the contemporary manifestations of inevitable and derivative dependency. It is essential that we begin to reconceptualize the relationship between law and the family in regard to these dependencies. In doing so, we should keep a few basic principles in mind. First, we must abandon the pretense that we can achieve gender equality through family-law reform. The egalitarian family myth remains largely unassisted by other ideological and structural changes in the larger society and is belied by the statistics reflecting the ways women and men live.

"We should also recognize that family policy is a form of state regulation. We must, therefore, be explicit about the norms and values motivating public and legal decisions about what should be protected or encouraged through social and economic subsidies. Furthermore, family policy must be secular, not based on a religious model. It should reference the functional aspirations we have for families in our society and be supportive of those aspirations. I therefore propose two recommendations for legal reform: the abolition of the legal supports for the sexual family and the construction of protections for the nurturing unit of caretaker and dependent exemplified by the Mother/Child dyad." (P. 228.)

Professor Fineman's first proposal would allow people to continue to celebrate their marriages—but would no longer attach legal rights and duties to the relationship. "Instead, the interactions of female and male sexual affiliates would be governed by the same rules that regulate other interactions in our society—specifically those of contract and property, as well as tort and criminal law." (P. 229.) Fineman points out that family law has already created a choice regime for marriage; her proposal would extend current trends. It would have several advantages (pp. 229–30): (1) The state would no longer have incentives to regulate voluntary sexual interactions among adults, as "there would no longer be a state-preferred model of family intimacy to protect and support." (2) Husbands would no longer have a partial immunity for spousal rape. (3) Children would no longer be stigmatized for birth outside of marriage. (4) The idea of marital property would end, as would obligations for spousal support during and after marriage. (5) Male sexual partners would no longer have as much a bargaining advantage if they could not use easy-exit divorce and child custody as levers to pry concessions from their female partners. (6) The law could refocus its subsidies on the relationship that is most important to society—the caregiving relationship such as that provided by a parent to her or his child or by an adult to an aged parent. The law should afford caregiving relationships not just the special protections of privacy law, but also state subsidies in the form of tax breaks, child care facilities, and outright grants of money to caregivers.

PROBLEM 9–1

STATE RECOGNITION OF HORIZONTAL PARTNERSHIPS

Professor Fineman's proposal and supporting argument provide you with an opportunity, at the outset, to consider what it is the state *ought* to be doing in family law. Should the state get out of the business entirely and do nothing more than enforce contracts arrived at between the parties? If the state does offer a regulatory form that does more than enforce contracts, what benefits (subsidies) should the state offer couples—and why should it offer much in the way of benefits (subsidies)? What obligations should the state impose on each partner—and why? If you believe, as Fineman does, that marriage should be scrapped, do you think it should be replaced with another legal form of recognition and regulation? Outline your preliminary thoughts as to these issues.

We consider theory relevant to this matter. If you agree with us, you might review the materials in Chapter 5, and your own theoretical commitments. Different theoretical commitments will press you in different directions. For examples:

- *Natural law* theories (Chapter 5, Section 1) support the traditional regulatory regime of marriage and so would be appalled by Fineman's proposal. Like Fineman, natural law theorists would be highly critical of the liberalization that has gone on in family law, but their primary lament has been that liberalization has undermined the dad-mom family and has disconnected children from their fathers. *E.g.*, David Blankenhorn, *Fatherless America: Confronting Our Most Urgent Social Problem* (1995). Natural law thinkers would generally support new *covenant marriage* laws, which require counseling before marriage and make it more difficult to divorce.

- *Economic* theories (Chapter 5, Section 2A) generally support a liberal, individual-choice regime in family law but otherwise press in different directions. Chicago School theories could support a contract-based approach, but could also support a traditional approach which rewarded the parties for specialization. Gary Becker is the anti-Fineman in this regard, for he focuses on overall social utility, whereas she emphasizes the unfairness of women's bearing disproportionate burdens. Margaret Brinig applies economic analysis to support covenant marriage as the most efficient mechanism for assuring the commitment needed by mothers and children. Brinig, *From Contract to Covenant: Beyond the Law and Economics of the Family* (2000). Contrast Carol Rose's game-theoretical approach (Chapter 5, Section 2A), which would support Fineman's critique of the liberalized but still sexual family; if marriage were retained as a state form, Rose's model could also support its extension to same-sex couples and plural relationships (polygamy).

- Other *feminist* theorists (Chapter 5, Section 2B) have praised Fineman's critique of women's dilemmas under our current liberal regime but are skeptical of her proposed solution. One feminist criticism is that Fineman's proposal risks locking women into caregiving relationships and denying them other possibilities for their lives, including work outside the home. *E.g.*, Joan Williams, "Gender Wars: Selfless Mothers in the Republic of Choice," 66 *NYU L. Rev.* 1559 (1991).

- Critical *race* theories and theories of *intersectionality* (Chapter 5, Section 2C) welcome Fineman's attention to the many ways that marriage has been used to pathologize relationships among people of color and single-parent households, including the infamous "welfare mother" demonized in the 1980s and 1990s. *E.g.*, Dorothy Roberts, "The Unrealized Power of Mother," 5 *Colum. J. Gender & Law* 141 (1995). But critical race theory would also suggest that this demonization has deeper causes than Fineman recognizes—not just patriarchy, but also racism and class biases. M.M. Slaughter, "Fantasies: Single Mothers and Welfare Reform," 95 *Colum. L. Rev.* 2156 (1995) (book review). Fineman's proposal would do nothing to undermine the ideological conditions for the oppression of women of color, poor women, and women with children.

- *Social constructionist* thinkers such as Michel Foucault (Chapter 5, Section 3A) would consider state regulatory efforts as having important constructive features. You might consider what you are *normalizing* when you construct a regulatory regime. Even if you reject marriage because it normalizes traditional gender roles, you might be open to other forms of state recognition because it normalizes interpersonal commitment. Or you might reject those other forms if you believe the state should not be normalizing lifetime commitments between any two people. Social constructionists might be open to state recognition of a variety of relationship forms because of their concern that the marriage monopoly seeks to *standardize* people's relationships.

- *Modernization or Sedimentation of Justification* thinkers like Professors Siegel and Eskridge (Chapter 5, Section 3B) would focus less on Fineman and more on her conservative critics. Legal discriminations against nontraditional families have evolved—from natural law tropes (these people are abominations and their families unnatural) to medical ones (these people are psychopaths and predators who will hurt children) to social republican ones (these people provide inadequate role models for children). Public opposition to same-sex marriage has evolved in this way, but for most critics it is the natural law position that drives the other arguments. *Bottoms v. Bottoms* in Section 3 of this chapter illustrates how all three discourses can coexist in one case.

THE PRIVATIZATION OF FAMILY LAW

PART A.   PRIVATIZATION OF AMERICAN FAMILY LAW AND ITS CRITICS

Jana Singer, "The Privatization of Family Law"
1992 *Wisconsin Law Review* 1443, 1447–53, 1456–59, 1460–64, 1470–71, 1478–79.*

Over the past twenty-five years, family law has become increasingly privatized. In virtually all doctrinal areas, private norm creation and private decision making have supplanted state-imposed rules and structures for governing family-related behavior. * * *

Perhaps the most significant way the law traditionally regulated intimate behavior was by distinguishing sharply, in virtually all important contexts, between married persons and persons in nonmarital intimate relationships. Through laws criminalizing adultery, fornication and nonmarital cohabitation, the law carved out marriage as the only legitimate arena for sexual intercourse. Tort causes of action for enticement, alienation of affections and criminal conversation penalized third parties who intentionally interfered with the marriage relationship; loss of consortium claims protected husbands (and later wives) against those who negligently impaired marital relations. No similar doctrines protected nonmarital intimate relationships from deliberate or negligent third party impairment.

An elaborate network of statutes and common law doctrines also distinguished sharply between children born within marriage and those born outside of it. * * * Similarly, state and federal programs designed to compensate families for the death or disability of a wage-earner typically excluded out-of-wedlock children as eligible beneficiaries. A major justification for these sharp distinctions between marital and nonmarital children was to protect the exclusivity of the marital unit and to punish adults (particularly women) who engaged in sex outside of marriage.

A series of Supreme Court decisions between 1968 and 1983 eliminated as unconstitutional most of the categorical legal distinctions between marital and nonmarital children. These decisions explicitly rejected the traditional notion that differential treatment of legitimate and illegitimate offspring was justified as a way of encouraging matrimony and of expressing society's "condemnation of irresponsible liaisons beyond the bonds of marriage." A related series of Supreme Court decisions established that unmarried fathers who develop a relationship with their children must be given the same rights with respect to adoption and custody decisions as are accorded to married fathers. These judicial declarations were paralleled and reinforced by the Uniform Parentage Act, promulgated in 1973 and approved by the American Bar Association in 1974. The Act abandons the concept of legitimacy and declares that "[t]he parent and child relationship extends equally to every child and to every parent, regardless of the marital status of the parents." * * *

Another way the law traditionally privileged marriage over nonmarital intimate relationships was by denying unmarried cohabitants access to the judicial system for resolving financial disputes arising out of their relationship. In particular, contracts between unmarried cohabitants that related in any way to their sexual relationship were considered unenforceable as contrary to public policy. The rationale for this traditional rule was that the law should not "lend its aid to either party to a contract founded upon an illegal or immoral consideration."

Over the past fifteen years, this traditional rule has eroded significantly. The erosion began with the celebrated *Marvin* case [this Section], in which an ex-cohabitant claimed that she had given up a promising acting career in order to become a fulltime homemaker and companion; in return, she claimed, her unmarried partner had agreed to support her financially for the rest of her life. The California Supreme Court, reversing the dismissal of the plaintiff's complaint, ruled that such an agreement between unmarried cohabitants was enforceable unless it explicitly stated that the consideration for one partner's financial support was the other partner's meretricious sexual services. The mere connection between an unmarried couple's sexual relationship and their financial arrangements was no longer enough to invalidate their cohabitation agreement. The *Marvin* court also suggested that, aside from the plaintiff's contract claim, she might be entitled to a share of the property accumulated during the couple's cohabitation relationship under equitable theories such as constructive trust, quantum meruit and resulting trust.

In the decade that followed *Marvin*, courts in many states applied both express and implied contract remedies to resolve disputes about property and financial arrangements arising out of cohabitation relationships. In doing so, courts largely abandoned public policy objections to enforcing the private agreements of parties engaged in sexual relationships outside of marriage. A few courts have reached beyond contract in resolving cohabitation disputes, and have applied principles of partnership law or have reasoned by analogy to state marital property division statutes. Consistent with the modern emphasis on private ordering, however, most courts have been unwilling to grant non-agreement-based support rights to unmarried cohabitants or to extend statutory divorce obligations, such as the payment of attorneys' fees.

Although courts have shown an increased willingness to enforce the private commitments made by unmarried cohabitants to each other, they have been somewhat more reluctant to expand the rights of unmarried cohabitants vis-a-vis third parties. The California Supreme Court recently refused to extend the logic of *Marvin* to support a claim for intentional infliction of emotional distress brought by an unmarried cohabitant who had witnessed the tortious injury and death of his partner. Similarly, only a few courts have extended to nonmarital partners the commonlaw right of a married person to recover for loss of a spouse's consortium, and each of these decisions has been brought into question by later developments.

Unmarried cohabitants have also had mixed success in qualifying for statutory benefits traditionally reserved for married couples. In some situations, unmarried cohabitants have benefitted from federal and state statutes, such as the Equal Credit Opportunity Act, which prohibit discrimination based on marital status. In addition, at least one state has explicitly amended its worker's compensation statute to provide relief for the death of a nonmarital partner, and courts in several other states have construed existing worker's compensation laws to provide statutory benefits to dependent cohabitants. Courts in other states, however, have refused to extend such benefits to nonmarital partners, relying on a strict construction of statutory terms such as "spouse" and "family." Courts have also reached inconsistent results on whether an unmarried cohabitant who quits her job to relocate with her partner qualifies for unemployment benefits that would be available to a spouse in similar circumstances. * * *

The shift from public to private control over the definition and structure of family relationships extends as well to control over the consequences of marital status. Traditionally, the law underscored the public nature of marriage by defining for all participants the salient aspects of the marriage bond, particularly the legal and economic relationship between spouses. Although marriage has often been described as a civil contract, until recently it was the state, and not the parties, that set the terms of this contract. Parties could choose whether to enter into marriage, but they could not define the terms of their union. As the Supreme Court explained in *Maynard v. Hill* [125 U.S. 190, 211 (1888)]:

> [Marriage] is something more than a mere contract. The consent of the parties is of course essential to its existence, but when the contract to marry is executed by the marriage, a relation between the parties is created which they cannot change. Other contracts may be modified, restricted, or enlarged, or entirely released upon the consent of the parties. Not so with marriage. The relation once formed, the law steps in and holds the parties to various obligations and liabilities.

The state-imposed terms of the traditional marriage contract were both hierarchical and rigidly gender-based. The husband, as head of household, was responsible for the financial support of his wife and children. The wife, as the domestic partner, was responsible for providing household services, including housework, sex and childcare. This compulsory gender-based division of labor persisted well into the 1960s, as did the inability of spouses to alter in any binding way the legal and economic incidents of marriage.

* * * Courts sometimes refused to enforce agreements between husbands and wives on the ground that these agreements lacked the consideration necessary to support a binding contract. Courts also made liberal use of factual and legal presumptions to deny enforcement of agreements between husbands and wives. Although a wife's performance of services outside the scope of her usual domestic duties could, in theory, constitute valid consideration for her husband's return promise of compensation, courts often presumed that such extraordinary services by a wife were intended to be gratuitous and, hence, not in exchange for pay or other compensation. * * *

Over the past twenty-five years, the law has loosened its control over the legal and economic incidents of marriage in three related ways. First, the state-imposed marriage contract is a far less comprehensive or precise instrument than it was a generation or two ago. In particular, the reciprocal rights and obligations of spouses are both less well-defined and less extensive than they were in previous generations. Second, individual couples today have considerably more freedom than in the past to vary by private agreement what little remains of the state-imposed marriage contract. Third, the law increasingly treats marriage partners as individuals, rather than as a single merged unit, for purposes of doctrinal analysis.

The modern trend in favor of sex-based equality has eliminated many of the explicitly gender-based terms of the traditional marriage contract. A wife is no longer required to assume her husband's surname or to accede to his choice of domicile. Wives are not automatically entitled to their husbands' financial support, nor husbands to their wives' domestic services. In most community property states, laws that previously gave husbands the right to manage and control community property during marriage have been repealed or replaced by statutes providing for joint management by both spouses. * * *

Even where state-imposed marital obligations remain as the background legal regime, spouses today have considerable freedom to alter those background obligations by private contract, either before or during marriage. For example, the Uniform Premarital Agreement Act, which has been adopted by sixteen states since its promulgation in 1983, authorizes prospective spouses to contract with each other with respect to their property rights and support obligations, as well as "any other matter, including their personal rights and obligations, not in violation of public policy or a statute imposing a criminal penalty." The commentary explains that this provision is meant to cover such matters as the choice of abode, the freedom to pursue career opportunities and the upbringing of children. Similarly, while the Second Restatement of Contracts continues to disapprove of marital contracts that would change an essential incident of marriage "in a way detrimental to the public interest in the marriage relationship," the Restators' comments make clear that both the essential incidents of marriage and the public's interest in the marriage relationship are to be interpreted more narrowly than in the past. Several states have also amended their domestic relations laws to facilitate enforcement of a broad range of spousal contracts concerning the economic aspects of marriage.

While much private contracting between persons in or contemplating marriage concerns rights and obligations in the event of divorce, there are indications that the law is becoming more receptive to enforcing private agreements that relate to the structure of an ongoing marriage. Moreover, wholly apart from enforcement by courts, many scholars, marriage counselors and manuals urge couples to use contracts or contract-like structures to govern the details of their relationship. Indeed, an entire body of literature has developed around "contracting" as a tool of marriage and family counseling. These practitioners not only contract with their clients about the goals and methods of therapy; they also initiate contracting processes between spouses as part of marital counseling, reconciliation or divorce preparation. Although the "contracts" that result from these processes generally are not legally enforceable, the counselors' use of contract terminology is intentional and significant. In particular, "the contract label dramatizes the preference for private ordering over the intrusion of outside norms as the basis for choices about life-styles."

A third way in which the state has ceded control over the legal and economic incidents of marriage is by treating married persons as individuals, rather than as a merged unit, for purposes of legal analysis. Traditionally, the common law treated married persons not as individuals, but as a single legal entity. Marriage stripped a woman of her independent legal existence and merged it into that of her husband; she became a "femme couvert," literally "a woman under cover" of her husband. This notion of marital merger had far-reaching legal consequences in a wide variety of doctrinal areas. Because husbands and wives were considered one, they could neither contract with nor sue each other. Nor could spouses testify for or against each other in civil or criminal proceedings. As the legal representatives of their wives, husbands were considered responsible for any torts their wives committed. * * * More generally, the legal fiction that the husband and wife were a single entity was one of the rationales that supported the law's traditional refusal to recognize marital rape or to provide remedies for victims of spousal violence.

* * * [T]he trend in most areas of law today is to view married persons as two separate individuals, rather than as a single unit, for purposes of legal analysis. Since 1971, at least twenty-five states have abolished interspousal tort immunity, thus allowing spouses to sue each other for negligent and other tortious behavior. Judicial decisions abrogating the immunity have explicitly rejected the argument that the doctrine is justified as a means of preserving marital harmony. Even those jurisdictions that continue to recognize some aspects of interspousal immunity, disclaim reliance on the notion of marital unity. The increased ability of spouses to contract with each other is similarly grounded in the notion of married persons as separate individuals, with potentially disparate interests.

Changes in the laws of evidence and the doctrines governing criminal responsibility also reflect the legal individuation of the married couple. The common law rule that a husband and wife could not make up the two parties necessary to constitute a conspiracy has been abolished in virtually all jurisdictions. In 1980, the Supreme Court abolished a criminal defendant's privilege against adverse spousal testimony, noting that the ancient foundations for so sweeping a privilege—including the denial to women of a separate legal identity—had long since disappeared. The marital rape exemption has been abolished or narrowed in many jurisdictions. [E.g., *People v. Liberta*, 474 N.E.2d 567 (NY 1984).] Virtually all states have enacted or strengthened civil and criminal statutes designed to protect victims of domestic violence.

[Singer observes that entry into marriage is still restricted by state age (parental consent usually required for people under age 18), consanguinity (cannot marry relatives), and bigamy (one spouse at a time) limitations. Other restrictions have been repealed or even invalidated by the Supreme Court's right to marry cases [Section 2]. Gone are laws prohibiting marriages that involve people with mental or physical disabilities (in some states these marriages can still be annulled by the parties), interracial couples, people with a contagious disease, paupers. Couples "have substantially more freedom than did their counterparts a generation ago to determine whether and under what circumstances they will wed, and to effectuate their choice of marriage partner." There are also fewer and simpler formal prerequisites imposed by the state; states do not require a religious ceremony anymore, for example.]

The shift from public to private ordering of marriage has been accompanied by the privatization of divorce and its financial consequences. Until the late 1960s, American law recognized no such thing as a consensual or privately-ordered divorce. Rather, statutes in each state established specific grounds for terminating a marriage. Most of these grounds required the spouse seeking a divorce to prove to a court that her partner had committed a marital offense and that she was innocent of marital fault. Thus, divorce was not the recognition of a private decision to terminate a marriage; it was a privilege granted by the state to an innocent spouse against a guilty one. * * *

The model of divorce as a state-bestowed remedy for an innocent spouse began eroding long before the formal adoption of no-fault divorce statutes. The adoption of these statutes, however, signaled an important shift in the legal paradigm governing divorce. The state, in essence, abandoned its role as the moral arbiter of marital behavior. In particular, the state "washed its hands" of attempting to determine when the goal of providing relief to an innocent spouse outweighed the strong public interest in preserving marriage. With the adoption of no-fault divorce statutes, the state ceded to the spouses themselves—and often to one spouse acting unilaterally—the authority to make this judgment. Thus, under no-fault divorce, the decision to end a marriage generally rests on unreviewed private judgment; the state's role is diminished to one of solemnization and recording, akin to its role in marital licensing. * * *

[The advent of no-fault divorce also initiated a process by which state reduced its supervision of the terms on which the parties parted. Not only were separation agreements routinely enforced by the courts, but so were prenuptial agreements. See the Uniform Premarital Agreement Act (1983), which provided for enforcement of such agreements unless fraudulent or unconscionable. In order to invalidate a premarital agreement on grounds of unconscionability, an objecting party must show that he or she (i) was not provided a fair and reasonable disclosure of the other party's assets or obligations; (ii) did not waive disclosure; and (iii) did not have an adequate knowledge of the other party's assets or finances. Singer observes that in Western Europe, which has also seen significant liberation of the terms of divorce, judges are much more active in reviewing the terms of separation and divorce decrees, especially to prevent hardship to a vulnerable party or to the children.]

[Singer demonstrates how the privatization of family law coincides with other developments in public law. Most notable is the gender equality revolution (Chapter 3, Section 1), which has rendered problematic any formal requirements that discriminate on the basis of sex or (sometimes) that rest upon traditional gender stereotypes. See *Orr v. Orr*, U.S. (1978), which invalidated state laws which impose alimony payments only on husbands and not on wives. Also, the Supreme Court's right to privacy jurisprudence (Chapter 2, Section 1) has focused on individuals, rather than the marriage unit, as the possessors of legal entitlements. Professor Singer also notes how economic analysis has seeped into family law; this reflects a change in perceptions, from the family as separate and alien from the market, to the family as a setting in which exchange-like behavior is common and expected.]

NOTES ON PRIVATIZATION AND COVENANT MARRIAGES

The law described by Professor Singer both reflects and may have contributed to the changing face of American families. According to the 2000 Census, the *nuclear family* (a married man and woman living with their children) now represents less than one-quarter of American house-holds.[a] In 1970, there were 1.1 million multi-person households in the United States consisting of persons who were neither married nor related by blood or adoption. In 1998, the figure was 5.3 million. About double that number lived alone (also a huge increase from 1970). In the last thirty years, the percentage of middle-aged men and women who have never married has doubled, to almost one in ten. Almost half of today's single mothers have never married, and the number of children living with unmarried couples has gone up more than fourfold. See Andrew Hacker,

a. The 2000 Census data are available online and can be viewed at <www.cen- sus.gov/population/www/cen2002/briefs. html> (viewed July 1, 2003).

"The Case Against Kids," *N.Y. Rev. of Books*, Nov. 30, 2000, at 12 ff. The United States is now a country where marriage is no longer the practiced norm, and most relationships are governed by the law of contract and not the law of marriage. Consider possible ways the privatization of family law interacts with people's sex lives and their thinking about sexuality.

1. *Sex (and More Sex) as a Consumer Good.* The new privatized family law contributes to the delinking of sex and procreation. With surrogacy and artificial insemination, pregnancy is now possible without sex. With contraception (*Griswold*) and abortion (*Roe*), sex is now possible without serious risk of procreation. These developments might contribute to an ever greater focus on the pleasurable or sociable qualities of sex. Like other pleasurable things, sex might then be viewed as a luxury good, obtainable whenever and wherever the mood strikes. Is this good? For a critique of the law's tendency to "commodify" intangibles and thereby degrade social goods, see Margaret Jane Radin, "Market–Inalienability," 100 *Harv. L. Rev.* 1849 (1987).

Once sex is delinked from procreation and viewed as a pleasurable good, the demand for it might go up. People would have more sex and would start earlier. The increase in the amount of sex might also increase the variety of sex. In a culture where everyone has twice as much sex as they have in another culture, one would expect to find greater sexual variety. A sexual connoisseurship would evolve in some quarters. The foregoing developments might undermine some gender differences. In our culture, men have traditionally been more interested in having lots of sex, early and often. Pressed by the developments above, women could become increasingly interested in sex. Especially as women become increasingly active in the professions and business, we might expect to see women treating sex as a commodity (the traditional male thing) rather than as a relationship (the traditional female thing). There is some evidence for this speculation in popular culture: *Playgirl* and other magazines featuring male nudity, beefcake advertisements, dating and other reality television shows where shirtless "himbos" with six-pack abs are toyed with by sexually aggressive females.

2. *Nostalgia for Old–Fashioned Commitment: The Covenant Marriage Movement.* Under the new family law, sex without commitment is easier, and commitment without sex a lot harder. As to the former point, the costs of sex outside of marriage are diminished primarily by the availability of contraception and abortion, but also by the law's liberality toward children born outside of wedlock (the idea of "bastards" has been legally quashed in family law). Thus we should expect women as well as men to be somewhat more willing to engage in extramarital sex.

As to the latter point, the death of sex life will more often be fatal to interpersonal commitment. It is both logically and empirically apparent that no-fault divorce has contributed to the higher rate of marital dissolutions; marriage today may last not "till death do us part," but rather "till the sex gets boring." Once sex is valorized for reasons beyond procreation, it becomes an increasingly important part of marriage. (And with less procreation, there are fewer children to hold marriages together through rocky times.) If the sex is bad and there are no children, the marriage will not work, and we would expect women as well as men to seek divorce for this reason. No wonder the national divorce rate is now well over 50%. These social facts have spawned a nostalgia for good old-fashioned marriage till death do us part, where individuals give up much of their freedom and altruistically commit themselves to the good of their partners, their children, their families.[b]

Nostalgia for the altruistic interpersonal commitment of traditional marriage has fueled interest in the new natural law philosophy surveyed in Chapter 5, Section 1. John Finnis and allied thinkers emphasize the non-instrumentalist virtues of marriage—the qualities that render us distinctly human (or, from a religious point of view, most in the *imago Dei* [image of God]). Natural law thinking is the primary basis for statutes in Arizona (1998), Arkansas (2001), and Louisiana (1997) which create *covenant marriages*. This option, which couples can choose instead of regular marriage, reflects a traditionalist rejection of marriages that can be easily entered and easily exited. See Joel Nichols, "Louisiana's Covenant Marriage Law: A First Step Toward a More Robust Pluralism in Marriage and Divorce Law?," 47 *Emory L.J.* 929 (1998). If couples opt for covenant marriage pursuant to the Arkansas Covenant Marriage Act, 2001 Ark. Acts 1486, they must participate in marriage counseling before they tie the knot, cannot divorce except for strong cause, and must accept a long waiting period before they can divorce. See also Ariz. Rev. Stat. § 25–901 et seq.; La. Ann. Code §§ 229, 272.

Although pressed mainly by traditionalists, covenant marriage has also attracted support from utilitarian defenders such as Margaret Brinig, *From Contract to Covenant: Beyond the Law and Economics of the Family* 29–34, 110–39 (2000). Utilitarians emphasize the personal advantages of you-can-count-on-it lasting personal commitment promised by covenant marriage. Professor Brinig, for example, criticizes easy-to-exit marriage as imposing huge costs on women and, especially, children. Her point receives strong support from Judith Wallerstein, Julia Lewis & Sandra Blakeslee, *The Unexpected Legacy of Divorce: A 25 Year Landmark Study* (2000). Wallerstein and her colleagues report that when parents divorce the world of their children is altered in deleterious and sometimes devastating ways; the children of divorced parents, they found, tend to have much more difficulty establishing adult relationships.

Other instrumentalist defenders of marriage (and supporters of covenant marriage) emphasize the personal, health, and economic advantages they maintain accrue uniquely to married people and their children. See Linda Waite & Maggie Gallagher, *The Case for Marriage: Why Married*

---

b.   See John Witte, Jr., "Propter Honoris Respectum: The Goods and Goals of Marriage," 76 *Notre Dame L. Rev.* 1019 (2001). The nostalgia is not limited to traditionalists. See, *e.g.*, Milton Regan, Jr., *Family Law and the Pursuit of Intimacy* (1993) (supporting marriage from postmodern perspective: in an era where everything seems up for grabs, humans need stable, ongoing commitments just as much as before).

People Are Happier, Healthier, and Better Off Financially (2000); David Popenoe, *Life without Father: Compelling New Evidence That Fatherhood and Marriage Are Indispensable for the Good of Children and Society* (1996). Given their selection bias and failure to control for important variables, these studies remain preliminary.[c]

3. *Children Raised in Nontraditional Households; the Perils of the Single Mother?* The 2000 Census found that more than 40% of unmarried cohabiting couples were raising children, a figure only slightly less than the percentage (46%) of married couples raising children. Note that many lesbian and gay couples raise children and are a growing feature of the family landscape. Other parents do not stay together, and their children are usually then raised by one parent. Today, single parents constitute nearly one-third of the households with children. Single mothers head 26% of the households with children (up from 12% in 1970), single fathers 5% (up from 1% in 1970).

Some commentators maintain that children raised by single mothers and nontraditional families are systematically more troubled and less achieving than children raised in nuclear families. *E.g.*, Blankenhorn, *Fatherless America*; Popenoe, *Life Without Father*. The evidence fails to support their assertion that traditional nuclear families are better situses for child-rearing than blended step-families, see *Step-families: Who Benefits? Who Does Not?* (Booth & Dunn eds. 1994), or lesbian families (Section 3 of this chapter). See generally Judith Stacey, *Brave New Families: Stories of Domestic Upheaval in Late Twentieth Century America* (1990).

As for children raised by single parents (usually the mother), there is evidence that these children are relatively troubled, but critics object that the variable affecting children adversely is the race and poverty rather than the unmarried status of their caregivers. And the new family law, in practice, has meant that the state does virtually nothing to offset this overwhelming disability for such children. Under liberalized family law, the state is less likely to scrutinize a prenuptial agreement or a separation or divorce agreement to ensure its fairness to the mother or the children or to amend the divorce decree later on to account for changed circumstances such as the father's improved economic position. Even when the law imposes financial obligations on the absent father, they are usually unen-

---

c. The obvious problem with the marriage-makes-a-difference studies is *selection bias*: Married men might earn more money or be healthier because men with higher earning potential and better health are more attractive mates and therefore more likely to get married—rather than because marriage turns the ordinary schlump into an economic dynamo. See Paula England, "Three Reviews of Marriage," 30 *Contemp. Sociology* 564 (2001); see also Scott Coltrane, "Scientific Half–Truths and Postmodern Parody in the Family Values Debate," 26 *Contemp. Sociology* 7 (1997) (the new family values literature presents a disturbingly unscientific approach to evidence). James Q. Wilson responds to the selection-bias charge: "But the evidence strongly suggests that self-selection is not the key factor. No matter how men become unmarried—by being bachelors, becoming separated or divorced, or becoming widowers—they lose ground in terms of health." Wilson, "The Case for Marriage," *Nat'l Rev.*, Oct. 9, 2000, at 49. Even if these facts were true (which remains unsettled), one would expect selection to account for the first (bachelors) and the terrible effects of separation, divorce, and death to account for the latter three.

forceable. Fineman's *Neutered Mother* is a non-traditionalist response to these phenomena in particular; contrast her perspective and proposals with those of the covenant marriage movement.

Low-income mothers have no realistic opportunity to bargain privately for better arrangements, since most of the men with whom they would bargain also lack basic economic resources. Indeed, for poor women, there has been a much more contradictory process than the term "privatization" would imply. Aid to Families with Dependent Children (AFDC), the primary welfare program, was conditioned for many years for unmarried recipients on not being sexually active, based on the theory that any male who was a sexual partner ought to be supporting the woman's children. See *King v. Smith*, 392 U.S. 309 (1968). Home visits, including night-time searches, were standard methods of enforcement. See *Wyman v. James*, 400 U.S. 309 (1971); *Parrish v. Civil Serv. Comm'n of Alameda County*, 425 P.2d 223 (Cal.1967). After man-in-the-house disqualifications were found to be inconsistent with the statute, states began the policy of decreasing the incremental AFDC support payment for additional children, born after the mother began receiving welfare. See *Dandridge v. Williams*, 397 U.S. 471 (1970) (upholding such a policy).

The paradigm shifted with enactment of the Personal Responsibility and Work Opportunity Reconciliation Act of 1996, Pub. L. No. 104–193, 110 Stat. 2105, which imposed strict work requirements and a lifetime maximum eligibility of five years. Much of the debate surrounding welfare reform concerned the public's unwillingness to expend funds for the support of indigent women having babies. Curbing welfare was intended, in part, to police sexuality and reproduction, especially by women of color. What effects would you expect welfare reform to have on American sexuality?

NOTE ON FEMINIST CRITIQUES OF PRIVATIZATION[d]

Although originally supported by many feminists, experience with privatization has proved sobering. Like Professor Fineman, most feminists are now critical of no-fault divorce as it has been implemented in the United States. Leonore Weitzman, *The Divorce Revolution: The Unexpected Social and Economic Consequences for Women and Children in America* (1985), estimates that during the 1970s (when no-fault divorce was becoming the rule) the standard of living for divorced mothers fell 73%, while that of their divorced husbands increased 42%. As many as 39% of divorced women with children live below the poverty line; 20% receive welfare. The reasons for this are apparent. Unlike a real contract regime, no-fault divorce does not realistically compensate the nonbreaching party for her (or his) economic losses. See Allen Parkman, *No-fault Divorce: What Went Wrong?* (1992). Women's and men's contributions to the joint marital enterprise tend to be asymmetric—women's tend to be backloaded, men's

---

d. Portions of this note draw on Megan Ann Barnett, "What's Love Got to Do With It? Status Contract Marriage and Divorce" (Yale Law School SAW Paper, 1996–97).

frontloaded, as when the wife sacrifices her career to support the husband while in school and to raise children. This is a common but not universal scenario, and so long as it persists no-fault divorce is unfair to the wife unless it realistically values her contribution to the husband's increased earning power (which usually does not happen). Moreover, to the extent that wives tend to be less restless in marriage than husbands, no-fault divorce is bad because its allowance of unilateral termination empowers the husband to escape marriage without the wife's consent or, in a bargaining game, the necessity of paying her off to obtain consent.

These problems are not insuperable. Where the wife's contribution to the family has been homebound or frontloaded, alimony courts in some jurisdictions are willing to consider commercial "goodwill" in the husband's career, *Dugan v. Dugan*, 457 A.2d 1 (N.J.1983), or even (in one jurisdiction) the income stream flowing from the husband's professional degree or license. *O'Brien v. O'Brien*, 498 N.Y.S.2d 743, 489 N.E.2d 712 (N.Y. 1985). How would this approach apply to blue collar families? Other courts have revived permanent rather than temporary alimony as justified in cases where long-term marriages have broken up. *E.g., Casper v. Casper*, 510 S.W.2d 253 (Ky.1974). Generally, however, academics have been much more in favor of innovative alimony arrangements than judges have.

There are theoretical reasons to think that women will fare badly under a regime of marriage privatization, even where there is free contracting and even where courts award alimony more realistically. The foregoing analysis shows how the parties who start off the bargaining process with fewer entitlements (women) will not do as well in the process. With less skilled lawyers, they will not do as well in the courts, either. Recall Carol Rose's suggestion that in a bargaining situation women will tend to fall further behind men if it is true or widely assumed that women are more cooperative than men (Chapter 5, Section 2A). In either event, men will exact higher prices for their initial and continuing cooperation—an explanation for why men usually get a better deal from prenuptials, why women working outside the home still do most of the work inside the home too, and why men shirk their responsibilities during and after marriage (they think they can get away with it, and they usually do). In the new no-fault regime, men can unilaterally get out of marriages when they get tired, and the ease of exit fatally undermines the wife's bargaining position during the marriage if it is the case that she is more "invested" in the marriage and any children than the husband is. Notice that some and perhaps most of these problems will beset women under Fineman's proposal that marriage be eliminated as a legal category; if women must rely solely on contract law as the source for their protection in sexual relationships, the Rose analysis suggests that they will be bargaining losers.

Carole Pateman, *The Sexual Contract* 184–85 (1988), maintains that marriage, even as it is being reconfigured, is still gendered. What is most distinct about marriage is that it is a sexual contract, with *sexual* taking on the meaning men give it—"to possess and to have access to sexual property. * * * In modern patriarchy, masculinity provides the paradigm of sexuality; and masculinity means sexual mastery. The 'individual' [who enters into the 'marriage contract'] is a man who makes use of a woman's body (sexual property); the converse is much harder to imagine." Pateman acknowledges that the decline of a pure status regime, where a wife was essentially the husband's property, was necessary for women's rights and, further, that feminists themselves fought for no-fault divorce and other reforms that treat marriage more like a contract. But the defects of a pure status regime do not make out a case for a regime of private contracting. "For marriage to become merely a contract of sexual use—or, more accurately, for sexual relations to take the form of universal prostitution— would mark the political defeat of women *as women*," and "the patriarchal construction of sexual difference as mastery and subjection remains intact but repressed."

Not least important, many feminist critics follow Martha Fineman in maintaining that liberalization has third-party effects on children. Writing from the perspectives of both difference feminism and economics, Margaret Brinig argues in *From Contract to Covenant* that no-fault divorce and other mechanisms that have facilitated the breakup of horizontal relationships have had devastating effects on children. While Brinig's concerns parallel those of Fineman, her proposed solution does not, for she would strengthen rather than abolish civil marriage—not only enforcing realistic alimony obligations but also treating marriages like *covenants* accepting mutual responsibilities to the relationship and to children, rather than like contracts. She endorses *covenant marriages*, which seek to improve partners' investments in their marriages by requiring counseling before marriage and by making it harder to divorce (with a longer separation period and a requirement of fault).

PART B.   PROCREATION WITHOUT SEX: SURROGACY AND ARTIFICIAL INSEMINATION

Jana Singer, "The Privatization of Family Law"

1992 *Wisconsin Law Review* 1443, 1478–79, 1488.*

In the context of adoption, the shift from public to private ordering has been more subtle, but equally profound. Most significantly, there has been a change in the perceived purpose of American adoption law, from promoting the welfare of children in need of parents—traditionally and unproblematically a "public" function—to fulfilling the needs and desires of couples who want children.

This shift in purpose is most evident in the context of surrogate mothering, where the procreative desires of couples who are unable (or unwilling) to bear children drive the process and where there is no child in existence at the time the "adoption arrangement" is entered into. The shift is also evident in the increased popularity of so-called independent or private placement adoptions, in which prospective adoptive parents solicit available infants directly through newspaper ads and physician referrals. Finally, the transformation of adoption from a publicly-regulated child welfare institution to a privately ordered consumer system is reflected in the increased acceptance (at least within the legal academy) of calls for the legalization of a (modified) free market in babies, championed by United States Court of Appeals Judge Richard Posner ["The Regulation of the Market in Adoption," 67 *B.U.L. Rev.* 59 (1987)]. * * *

[Posner's proposal, originally made in 1978 to an outraged audience and later reiterated to a more receptive audience, is candid about its motivation:] the relatively small supply and the considerably larger demand for healthy white adoptable babies. Judge Posner's advocacy of market principles thus makes explicit what has largely been implicit in the growing acceptance of private-placement adoption: that the primary purpose of adoption reform should be the satisfaction of "consumer" demand for more (and better) adoptable babies. Attempts by politicians, including [the first] President Bush, to persuade pregnant (and potentially pregnant) women to "choose" adoption, rather than abortion, similarly reflect this consumerist orientation. Posner's explanation of how a (regulated) baby market would work also reveals that our current independent adoption system already contains significant market elements. * * *

In many ways, surrogate mothering is the ultimate form of private adoption; many also describe it as baby-selling. In a surrogate parenting arrangement, potential adoptive parents contract to procure a child even before that child has been conceived. The parties to a surrogacy agreement find and deal with each other privately, either directly or through a private, for-profit intermediary. State involvement in the surrogacy process (assuming all goes well) is limited to approval of the adoption that eventually results. [Surrogacy emerged as a phenomenon around 1976 and has grown more common and more acceptable since then. New Jersey's decision in *In the Matter of Baby M.*, 537 A.2d 1227 (N.J. 1988), held surrogacy contracts invalid under state policy against baby-selling; this decision has not diminished public support for such arrangements.]

C., on Behalf of T. v. G. and E., 225 *N.Y. Law Journal*, No. 9, at 29 (N.Y. Cnty. Sup. Ct. Jan. 12, 2001). In a recent twist on the *Baby M* case, two gay men (G. and E.) contracted with a woman (C.) to bear a child by one of the men. Under the agreement, the male couple would pay the expenses of the pregnancy and a total of $30,000 to the mother if a child were born alive. After successful insemination by G., the child was born September 27, 1997. G. and E. raised the child, but paid C. only $3000 of the money originally agreed-to and grew reluctant to allow her continued contact with the child. C. ultimately sought to obtain custody over the child as its biological mother.

Justice Diamond ruled that the contract was an unenforceable surrogacy arrangement, barred by New York Domestic Relations Law § 123. Like the New Jersey Supreme Court in *Baby M*, the judge then applied the best interests of the child standard to determine who should have custody of the child. "Significant factors are the parties' own prior custody agreements and the length of time that the present custody has continued." These factors strongly supported custody with G. Justice Diamond also appointed an expert in child psychology and development; he interviewed the parents and the child and recommended to the court that the father have custody.

The mother retained her own expert, who reported that "the child was manifesting signs of gender confusion due to G.'s parenting." Accordingly, the court appointed a second expert, Dr. Kyle Pruett of Yale University. Dr. Pruett also recommended that custody remain with the father, in part because the father had better parenting skills and in part because the child was much more attached to the father and his "domestic partner" than to the mother and her husband, whom Pruett described as a "remote attachment figure." He flatly rejected the notion that the child was evidencing "gender confusion," which was utterly implausible at the child's tender age.

Based on this evidence, Justice Diamond found the child's best interests served by continued sole legal custody with G., the father. Following Dr. Pruett's recommendation, the judge rejected a joint custody arrangement because of the deep acrimony between C. and G., and because C. had sometimes sought to turn the child against its father. "Accordingly, the court awards sole custody and decision making power to G. G. shall have the final decision making but shall consult in writing on all major decisions with petitioner. G. shall also inform and seek input from petitioner upon making a decision not of a routine nature or involving education and health." The judge also directed that C. have liberal visitation rights, including two-and-a-half days a week and an overnight every other weekend.

Accordingly, the judge nullified the father's obligation to pay the mother $30,000 but directed him to pay $5132, representing half the expenses incurred by C. during her pregnancy and birthing. The judge also ruled that C. should contribute to the support of the child. The precise amount was to be determined by a referee, taking into account the resources available to C. and her husband on the one hand, and G. and his male partner on the other.

NOTES ON *BABY M* AND CRITIQUES OF SURROGACY AND BABY-SELLING

New Jersey's Supreme Court made three important policy choices in *Baby M*, 537 A.2d 1227 (discussed by Professor Singer): (1) the surrogacy contract was unenforceable because inconsistent with public policy, but not *so* inconsistent with public policy as to invite sanctions against the participants; (2) the sperm donor, Mr. Stern, rather than the mother's husband, Mr. Whitehead, was the legal father; and (3) custody would be determined by reference to the best interests of the child standard now pervading the law relating to children. Although the first holding garnered almost all the publicity, the second is the more striking, given American law's traditional assumption that any child born within a marriage is legally the child of the married husband and wife. The New York decision in *C. v. G. and E.* illustrates how broadly influential the *Baby M* analytical framework has been.

Surrogacy arrangements in most jurisdictions have been left to judicial rather than legislative regulation. Surrogacy contracts have been explicitly prohibited by statute in at least nine states (including New York) and the District of Columbia. Some other jurisdictions regulate such contracts by limiting the extent and form of compensation, the class of women who can enter into the contracts, and so forth. But to a surprising degree, surrogacy has been left to the market.

Similarly, "gestational surrogacy," where the woman who bears the child has no genetic link to the child, has largely been left to private ordering. The California Supreme Court, for example, upheld a gestational surrogacy contract in *Johnson v. Calvert*, 851 P.2d 776 (Cal. 1993). The Court held that the mother for purposes of the Uniform Parentage Act is the genetic and not the gestational mother. See also *In re Marriage of Buzzanca*, 72 Cal.Rptr.2d 280 (Cal. App. 1998) (extending *Calvert* to recognize the intended mother even when there is no genetic link).

The fact that the state has usually not regulated surrogacy in an orderly way does not mean that surrogacy should not be regulated—and perhaps subject to criminal penalties rather than the "we won't enforce the contract" penalties. Consider various arguments.

1. *Defense: Let the Market Work.* Posner, "Market in Adoption" maintains that policies regulating or prohibiting baby-selling and surrogacy are questionable, because they obstruct and drive underground a market in babies. While such a market involves a much more precious good, human beings themselves, the truths of market dynamics are just as applicable: People's needs and preferences will be satisfied better through the market than through state regulation, and if the state prohibits something entirely a "black" market will emerge that is not only more costly but more abusive than the "free" market would be. Even under the assumptions of Chicago School economics, however, the first part of Posner's argument holds only if the "free" market is a well-functioning one. Is the market for babies a well-functioning market? For example, a woman agreeing to give up a baby she carries to term will undervalue the loss she will feel when she gives up the baby, especially if she has never borne a child.

2. *Critique: Market Inalienability.* A deeper response to the Posnerian economic argument is that the intrinsic nature of bearing children is so different from other labor that it should be "market inalienable." See Margaret Radin, "Market Inalienability," 100 *Harv. L. Rev.* 1849 (1987). Carole Pateman, *The Sexual Contract* 206–18 (1988) and Elizabeth Anderson, "Is Women's Labor a Commodity?," *Phil. & Pub. Affs.*, Winter 1990, at 71–92, maintain that reproductive labor is more integral to a woman's identity than other labor; hence, selling this capacity sacrifices a woman's dignity. But how is selling the use of one's reproductive system more undignified than selling the temporary use of other intimate body parts, as women do when they pose for magazines such as *Playboy* or *Hustler*? Are a woman's ideas not integral to her identity as well—yet we would not regulate her ability to market them, or even change them for monetary consideration? See Debra Satz, "Markets in Women's Reproductive Labor," *Phil. & Pub. Affs.*, Spring 1992, at 107, 112–16.

Robin West, "Jurisprudence and Gender," 55 *U. Chi. L. Rev.* 1 (1988), believes the feature that makes women most unlike men is the greater connectedness they feel to other people, a connectedness that derives from their bearing children, or even just their potential for bearing children. The connection that a mother feels with the child inside her might be considered the most unique quality that human beings can have. This quality therefore might justify treating "reproductive labor" as a category by itself, different from any other. But recall that even this unique relationship is alienable: women can give up their children for adoption, and women can choose to abort a pregnancy. If adoptions generally and abortions often are permitted, how can the state justify banning the woman's relinquishment of rights for money? (This argument might be most supportive of a rule allowing the mother to change her mind after the child's birth. Notice how the preferences of the surrogate mothers in both *Baby M* and *C. v. G. and E.* changed radically after their children were born.)

3. *Critique: The Best Interests of the Child.* Susan Okin, "A Critique of Pregnancy Contracts," 8 *Pol. & Life Sci.* 205–10 (1990), claims that surrogacy contracts do not adequately consider the interests of the child—a big theme in the *Baby M* decision. By weakening biological ties between parents and children and, more important, by inculcating a consumerist attitude toward children (much like the consumerist attitude we now have toward marriage), surrogacy can encourage parental exits and thereby undermine the security children need. The main problem with this argument is that there are not sufficient data to evaluate it one way or the other. Do surrogacy families (biological father and his wife) nurture and support the child as well as non-surrogacy families (biological father and mother are married or partnered)? Do adoptive parents generally bond with children as well as biological parents? Even if the child of surrogacy is generally less secure, however, it is not clear how much that should count. Should a little bit of increased insecurity offset a great deal of happiness for a family that otherwise would not have children at all?

4. *Defense: Economic Opportunities for Women.* In *Birthpower* (1989), Carmel Shalev makes a liberal feminist case for surrogacy contracts. See also Lori Andrews, *Between Strangers: Surrogate Mothers, Expectant Fathers, and Brave New Babies* (1989). Shalev rejects the idea that the state should protect women from using any of their natural endowments for economic gain. (One can recall that earlier "protective" legislation, such as special maximum hour laws for women, operated to deny women economic opportunities.) She argues that the market should be neutral as between competing conceptions of human relationships, as it should be for abortion, to take a primary example. Contract pregnancy is a potentially large source of wealth for women, and women who choose ought to be able to take advantage of it. Recall, however, Carol Rose's model of bargaining relations between men and women, in which women systematically fail to achieve equitable deals. One might be more pessimistic than Shalev about how much of an economic bonanza contract pregnancy would be for women. Shalev might respond that women's bargaining strategies—the key assumption in Rose's model—might themselves change over time.

5. *Critique: Reinforcing Women's Actual Inequality in the United States.* Debra Satz, "Markets in Women's Reproductive Labor" criticizes both the market and the market-inalienability approaches to surrogacy. She maintains that the primary objection to surrogacy is that in our gender-unequal society contract pregnancy will turn women's labor into an activity used and controlled by others and will reinforce gender stereotypes, mainly the idea of women as breeders deployed to serve male fetishes about maintaining lineage. Note, however, that a great many economic opportunities for women reinforce traditional gender stereotypes and are severely undervalued partly for that reason: secretary (who serves the "bossman"), hired caregiver for a family's children, domestic servant cleaning house, and so forth. If you do not accept the market-inalienability arguments, as Satz does not, how can you deny women opportunities to enter pregnancy contracts while allowing them to enter badly paid contracts to be wet nurses, babysitters, and domestic servants?

6. *Defense: Homosexual Choice and Surro-gaycy.* Marla Hollandsworth, "Gay Men Creating Families Through Surro–Gay Arrangements: A Paradigm for Reproductive Freedom," 3 *Am. U.J. Gender & Law* 183 (1995), documents that gay men have quietly been echoing the lesbian baby boom of the 1980s with their own "gay-by boomlet" in the 1990s (and now in the new millennium). *C. v. G. and E.* illustrates her thesis: gay male couples can have biological children through "surrogay" arrangements. Her article shows how the law discriminates against these men, not only by prohibiting or regulating surro-gaycy (most state regulations insist that only married couples can have a child through surrogacy), but also by artificial insemination laws that refuse to recognize the biological father's rights. She argues that state regulation is blind to the possibility of men's being nurturing and interested in raising children, while appalled by the possibility that a mother would not. Is the parental interest of a gay couple sufficient to offset the feminist criticisms of surrogacy developed in prior notes? Should Hollandsworth accept some regulation as valid, such as an option for the surrogate mother to change her mind when the child is born?

Consider the application of the Uniform Parentage Act, which Hollandsworth vigorously criticizes from the perspective of gay men, to artificial insemination by a lesbian couple. Can a child have two legal mommies?

K.M. v. E.G., Docket 117 P.3d 673 (California 2005). K.M. and E.G. were a romantically committed lesbian couple, registered as domestic partners in San Francisco in the 1990s. In 1995, K.M. agreed to donate her eggs so that E.G. could bear a child through in vitro fertilization. In the 1995 contract K.M. relinquished rights to any child born of this method, which was immediately successful. Twins were born in December 1995, and the couple celebrated a (non-legal) marriage ceremony shortly thereafter. The women's relationship ended in 2001, and K.M. sued to establish a parental relationship with the twins. The California Supreme Court, in an opinion by **Justice Moreno**, ruled that both women were the children's legal mothers.

Parental rights are governed by California's enactment of the Uniform Parentage Act, Family Code § 7600 et seq. The UPA defines the " '[p]arent and child relationship, [which] extends equally to every child and to every parent, regardless of the marital status of the parents.' " *Id.*, § 7602. Just as the Court had previously ruled that the husband in *Johnson v. Calvert* (1979) was the presumptive parent of a child conceived through gestational surrogacy, so the Court ruled in K.M.'s case that the ovum-donor was a presumptive parent. *Johnson* "concluded that 'genetic consanguinity' could be the basis for a finding of maternity just as it is for paternity. Under this authority, K.M.'s genetic relationship to the children in the present case constitutes 'evidence of a mother and child relationship as contemplated by the Act.' "

Section 7613(b) states: "The donor of semen provided to a licensed physician and surgeon for use in artificial insemination of a woman other than the donor's wife is treated in law as if he were not the natural father of a child thereby conceived." The Court declined to extend this provision to the ovum donor. Dissenting **Justice Kennard** would have extended § 7613(b) to include ovum donors as well as sperm donors. Why should ovum donors have *more* rights than sperm donors? (One answer: The statutory language only denies rights to sperm donors. Is this an unconstitutional sex discrimination?)

In a separate dissent, **Justice Werdegar** would have followed *Johnson* to inquire as to the intent of the parties. In *Johnson*, the married couple and the ovum donor intended to create a family for the couple. In this case, even K.M. agreed that her donation was to enable E.G. to have children. The majority responded that an "intent of the parties" approach would create uncertainty in the law. (Also, K.M. disputed that she "intended" to renounce all rights to the twins when she was presented with the form in 1995.) Justice Werdegar responded that her approach was more predictable than the open-ended approach of the majority, which left many questions unanswered. For example, would the Court have recognized K.M. as a parent if she and E.G. had not raised the children within a domestic partnership? A committed relationship?

Because the Court neither overruled nor questioned *Johnson*, its rule did not apply to donors providing ova to different-sex couples. By creating a new rule applicable only to lesbian couples, the Court, argued Justice Werdegar, "confers rights and imposes disabilities on persons because of their sexual orientation. * * * I see no rational basis—and the majority articulates none—for permitting the enforceability of an ovum donation agreement to depend on the sexual orientation of the parties. Indeed, lacking a rational basis, the rule may well violate equal protection. (See *Romer v. Evans* (1996); *Gay Law Students Assn. v. Pacific Tel. & Tel. Co.* (1979).) Why should a lesbian not have the same right as other women to donate ova without becoming a mother, or to accept a donation of ova without accepting the donor as a co-parent, even if the donor and recipient live together and both plan to help raise the child?''

Query: This issue may be decided differently in other jurisdictions, with different statutory and constitutional schemes. For example, most states now have constitutional amendments defining marriage as one man, one woman *and* refuse to provide legal recognition to lesbian unions. Would the Kennard or Werdegar position be more persuasive in those states?

PART C.   SEX WITHOUT MARRIAGE: COHABITATION

Privatization valorizes individual choice in configuring the choice of sexual and romantic partners and the terms under which such partnerships will operate. There are any number of regulatory strategies for privatizing American family law: First, the state might *liberalize marriage*, by making it easier for couples desiring to marry to gain state recognition, allowing the couples to contract out of at least some of the duties of marriage, and making it easier to exit the institution. For an excellent introduction to the law's enforcement of prenuptial and other agreements that contract out of some of the benefits and obligations of marriage, see ''Development in the Law—The Law of Marriage and Family,'' 116 *Harv. L. Rev.* 1996, 2075–97 (2003).

Second, the state might *abolish marriage* altogether, thereby leaving romantic couples entirely to the law of contract, property, and tort in structuring their relationships. Some feminists in the 1960s and 1970s urged that marriage's patriarchal heritage rendered it unacceptable today. Martha Fineman has updated this argument: The liberalization of marriage has not only failed to help women, but it has harmed their interests and impaired their lives—so it must go. Queer theorists object to marriage's rule of sexual fidelity to one person. Like Gayle Rubin and Michel Foucault, they object that western society views sex as guilty unless proven innocent, with the only defense being procreative sex within a monogamous marriage. From a sexual liberationist perspective, this is not only a confining norm, but it creates sexual neurotics. For them, too, marriage is an institution whose time is long gone.

Third, the state might *extend (some) duties and benefits of marriage* to couples who are not married (either by choice or by law). Canada and most European countries have adopted statute-based regimes imposing specific rules upon couples deemed to be cohabiting, and the American Law Institute has proposed legislation to similar effect in its *Principles of the Law of Family Dissolution* (2002). Thus far, however, most state-wide extension of marital duties or benefits in the United States has come from courts rather than legislatures. Consider the following policy issues: (1) Should the state ever extend marital benefits or duties to unmarried but cohabiting couples? Or should civil marriage be the only venue for these special benefits and duties? (2) If the state adopts a regime of partial incorporation, which marital duties and benefits should the state extend to cohabiting couples? Among the most important duties of marriage are obligations of economic and emotional support, sexual fidelity, and sharing of property. Among the most important benefits of marriage are health and life insurance (provided by employers based upon marital status), capacity to act as the legal representative of one's spouse, and presumptive inheritance rights. Which of these should be extended to cohabiting partners? (3) What kind of cohabiting partners should be entitled to the array of incorporated duties and benefits? Should they be limited to the people who can marry—or should eligibility include same-sex partners, people related by blood or marriage, or minors?

Michelle Marvin v. Lee Marvin

California Supreme Court, 1976.
18 Cal.3d 660, 134 Cal.Rptr. 815, 557 P.2d 106.

■ TOBRINER, JUSTICE. * * *

In the instant case plaintiff [Michelle Marvin] and defendant [Oscar-winning actor Lee Marvin] lived together for seven years without marrying; all property acquired during this period was taken in defendant's name. When plaintiff sued to enforce a contract under which she was entitled to half the property and to support payments, the trial court granted judgment on the pleadings for defendant, thus leaving him with all property accumulated by the couple during their relationship. Since the trial court denied plaintiff a trial on the merits of her claim, its decision * * * must be reversed. * * *

In *Trutalli v. Meraviglia* (1932) 12 P.2d 430 we established the principle that nonmarital partners may lawfully contract concerning the ownership of property acquired during the relationship. We reaffirmed this principle in *Vallera v. Vallera* (1943) 134 P.2d 761, 763, stating that "If a man and a woman [who are not married] live together as husband and wife under an agreement to pool their earnings and share equally in their joint accumulations, equity will protect the interests of each in such property."
* * *

Defendant [responds] that the alleged contract is so closely related to the supposed "immoral" character of the relationship between plaintiff and himself that the enforcement of the contract would violate public policy. He points to cases asserting that a contract between nonmarital partners is unenforceable if it is "involved in" an illicit relationship, or made in "contemplation" of such a relationship. A review of the numerous California decisions concerning contracts between nonmarital partners, however, reveals that the courts have not employed such broad and uncertain standards to strike down contracts. The decisions instead disclose a narrower and more precise standard: a contract between nonmarital partners is unenforceable only *to the extent* that it *explicitly* rests upon the immoral and illicit consideration of meretricious sexual services. * * *

* * * [A]dults who voluntarily live together and engage in sexual relations are nonetheless as competent as any other persons to contract respecting their earnings and property rights. Of course, they cannot lawfully contract to pay for the performance of sexual services, for such a contract is, in essence, an agreement for prostitution and unlawful for that reason. But they may agree to pool their earnings and to hold all property acquired during the relationship in accord with the law governing community property; conversely, they may agree that each partner's earnings and the property acquired from those earnings remains the separate property of the earning partner. So long as the agreement does not rest upon illicit meretricious consideration, the parties may order their economic affairs as they choose, and no policy precludes the courts from enforcing such agreements.

[Justice Tobriner held that Michelle Marvin had made out a proper claim of express contract, based on her allegations that she and Lee Marvin had entered into an oral agreement in 1964 to live together, hold themselves out as husband and wife, and pool their incomes. In return for her services as "companion, homemaker, housekeeper and cook," Michelle would be supported financially by Lee Marvin. In the next part of his decision for the court, Justice Tobriner held that Michelle Marvin could amend her complaint to add further causes of action founded upon theories of "implied contract" and "equitable relief."

[*Vallera* and other early decisions allowing actions founded upon express contracts refused to allow nonmarital partners to assert claims for relief based upon contracts implied from the conduct of the parties. The court of appeals decision *In re Marriage of Cary* (1973) 34 Cal. App. 3d 345, held that these earlier decisions were inconsistent with the Family Law Act of 1970, which eliminated fault as a basis for dividing marital property and which gave "putative spouses" (people who believed they were spouses but whose marriage was invalid) half the "quasi marital property." The California Supreme Court was not persuaded that the 1970 statute overrode *Vallera* and the earlier decisions but held that those decisions were no longer viable on the merits.]

We conclude that the judicial barriers that may stand in the way of a policy based upon the fulfillment of the reasonable expectations of the parties to a nonmarital relationship should be removed. As we have explained, the courts now hold that express agreements will be enforced unless they rest on an unlawful meretricious consideration. We add that in the absence of an express agreement, the couples may look to a variety of other remedies in order to protect the parties' lawful expectations.

The courts may inquire into the conduct of the parties to determine whether the conduct demonstrates an implied contract or implied agreement of partnership or joint venture, or some other tacit understanding between the parties. The courts may, when appropriate, employ principles of constructive trust or resulting trust. Finally, a nonmarital partner may recover in quantum meruit for the reasonable value of household services rendered less the reasonable value of support received if he can show he has rendered services with the expectation of monetary reward.[10] * * *

■ [The concurring and dissenting opinion of JUSTICE CLARK is omitted.]

NOTES ON *MARVIN* AND JUDICIAL TREATMENT OF FAMILIES WE CHOOSE

In a small number of states, courts have refused to follow *Marvin* and have declined to provide contractual or quasi-contractual (equitable) remedies for cohabiting partners. The reasoning has been that extending legal entitlements to cohabiting partners would be inconsistent with the special status marriage in that jurisdiction or with the legislature's repudiation of common-law marriage. See *Carnes v. Sheldon*, 311 N.W.2d 747 (Mich. App. 1981); *In re Estate of Alexander*, 445 So.2d 836 (Miss. 1984). But cf. *Taylor v. Taylor*, 317 So.2d 422 (Miss. 1975) (allowing a lawsuit for support—not alimony—by a woman abandoned after 18 years of cohabitation). Minnesota courts followed *Marvin*, see *Carlson v. Olson*, 256 N.W.2d 249 (Minn. 1977), but the legislature in 1980 overrode the decision with a rule requiring an express written contract with two witnesses, Minn. Stat. § 513.075, a requirement the courts have not always strictly enforced. See *In re Estate of Eriksen*, 337 N.W.2d 671 (Minn. 1983) (interpreting the 1980 statute to allow a lawsuit for a property claim). In the large majority of states, courts have followed *Marvin* to afford contractual or quasicontractual claims for cohabiting partners. Most courts have required that the consideration for the asserted promise was not sexual services—a requirement that complainants have generally found easy to satisfy. Most of the cases have been *palimony* (financial support) cases, and most of the reported palimony cases have been successful.

In recent years, California courts have applied *Marvin*'s logic to lesbian and gay relationships. E.g., *Whorton v. Dillingham*, 248 Cal.Rptr. 405 (Cal. App. 1988). See also *Crooke v. Gilden,* 414 S.E.2d 645 (Ga.1992); *Doe v. Burkland*, 808 A.2d 1090 (R.I. 2002). In *Robertson v. Reinhart*, 2003 WL 122613 (Cal. App. Jan. 8, 2003), however, the Court of Appeals for the First District rejected a palimony claim brought by Lynn Robertson against her lesbian partner. The court ruled that there was no implied contract, because the women had not pooled their financial resources or otherwise suggested an agreement to treat all property as jointly owned. The court rejected Robertson's quantum meruit claim for work that Robertson had done to improve Reinhart's home, because it found that this labor of love was probably done without expectation of compensation. If followed by other courts, this is a potentially serious limitation on *Marvin* claims.

---

10. Our opinion does not preclude the evolution of additional equitable remedies to protect the expectations of the parties to a nonmarital relationship in cases where existing remedies prove inadequate; the suitability of such remedies may be determined in later cases in light of the factual setting in which they arise.

Should *Marvin* be extended to create marriage-like benefits enforceable against third parties? For a much-litigated example, should a cohabiting partner be entitled to sue for loss of consortium and other marital injuries when his or her partner is injured? A California intermediate appeals court held in *Butcher v. Superior Court*, 188 Cal.Rptr. 503 (Cal. App.1983), that the surviving partner in a "stable and significant relationship" may assert a cause of action for loss of consortium in a lawsuit for the wrongful death of her or his partner. As of 2005, most state courts have rejected such a cause of action, and so have other intermediate appellate courts in California. E.g., *Coon v. Joseph*, 237 Cal.Rptr. 873 (Cal. App.1987), which held that a stable and intimate gay relationship does not establish the "close relationship" required in California for a third party to sue for infliction of emotional distress after witnessing an intentional tort to his or her loved one.

Coon is an early and important precedent testing the willingness of state courts to recognize not only duties of same-sex cohabiting partners to one another, but also duties that third parties have to each cohabiting partner. This kind of issue arises all the time now that so many same-sex couples are openly partnered—and they cannot obtain all the benefits and obligations of marriage (as Michelle and Lee Marvin could have done by simply getting hitched). Rejecting *Coon*, the New Mexico Supreme Court in *Lozoya v. Sanchez*, 66 P.3d 948 (N.M. 2003) has ruled that a person has a claim for relief for her or his personal loses against a third party who negligently kills or injures her or his committed same-sex partner. The trend in the consortium cases is probably with *Lozoya*. Some leading cases involving other third-party rights are excerpted below.

Likewise, other courts in gay-friendly jurisdictions have ruled that cohabiting same-sex partners have legal rights associated with marriage or family, including the right (under certain circumstances) to succeed to a rent-controlled apartment upon the death of one's long-time partner, see *Braschi v. Stahl Assocs.*, 543 N.E.2d 49 (N.Y. 1989); the right to be a guardian and make medical decisions for an incapacitated partner, see *In re Guardianship of Sharon Kowalski*, 478 N.W.2d 790 (Minn. App. 1991); and inheritance rights, see *Vasquez v. Hawthorne*, 33 P.3d 735 (Wash. 2001). In all these cases, judges evaluated the claims by reference to whether they believed the lesbian and gay relationships were sufficiently close to marriage (what Fineman terms the "meta-narrative" of American family law). Thus, the New York court was willing to give benefits to Braschi because his relationship with the deceased was like a marriage—"two adult lifetime partners whose relationship is long term and characterized by an emotional and financial commitment and interdependence." The Minnesota court was willing to extend Sharon Kowalski's guardianship benefit to Karen Thompson because her well-documented caregiving for the injured partner was, essentially, what society would expect from a wife.

NOTE ON DOMESTIC PARTNERSHIP LAWS

The same social and intellectual developments that have given rise to the *Marvin* and *Kowalski* litigations have inspired scholars to call for the creation of new legal categories for family law purposes. Some have favored revival and extension of common law marriage to long-term couples, including same-sex couples. *E.g.*, David Chambers, "The Legalization of the Family: Toward a Policy of Supportive Neutrality," 18 *U. Mich. J.L. Reform* 805 (1985); Ellen Kandolian, "Cohabitation, Common Law Marriage, and the Possibility of a Shared Moral Life," 75 *Geo. L.J.* 1829 (1987). Others advocate new legal forms that would, essentially, have to be adopted by legislatures. Following the practice of parliaments in Europe and Canada, William Reppy, "Property and Support Rights of Unmarried Cohabitants: A Proposal for Creating a New Legal Status," 44 *La. L. Rev.* 1677 (1984), proposes a new status of *lawful cohabitation*, applicable to parties who expressly declare their partnership status *or* have attained its functional equivalent in terms of interdependence and sharing their lives, and bestowing on these parties some of the benefits and obligations of marriage. Accord, American Law Institute, *Principles of the Law of Family Dissolution: Analysis and Recommendations* § 6.03–.06 (2002) (advocating domestic partnership as a legal status with some of the benefits of marriage). Contrast the Fineman proposal, which throws over marriage entirely and embraces privatization for all horizontal relationships. And contrast the covenant marriage movement, which seeks to strengthen spousal commitment within marriage by making it harder to exit.

In the early 1980s, Matt Coles and other gay activists in San Francisco proposed a new institution, *domestic partnership,* which they urged as a civil alternative to traditional marriage. Starting with Berkeley, dozens of municipalities have adopted ordinances recognizing domestic partnerships of unmarried couples (usually including different-sex as well as same-sex couples) who register. Most of these municipal laws created public registries for domestic partners and extended health insurance and other benefits to the named partners of municipal employees; most of the laws also extended a few other legal benefits, usually the right to visit one's partner in the hospital and/or in jail.[e]

Traditionalist opponents of domestic partnership ordinances have successfully challenged some of them as inconsistent with state "home rule" laws which provide limited allowances for municipal legislation. *E.g.*, *City of Atlanta v. McKinney*, 454 S.E.2d 517 (Ga.1995). Home rule problems are obviated if the state itself adopts a domestic partnership registry and defines the benefits and duties that attach to the new institution. Massachusetts and Vermont were the first states to offer domestic partnership benefits to their employees, and others have followed. Extensive *reciprocal beneficiary* and *civil union* laws have recently been adopted by Hawaii (1997) and Vermont (2000), respectively, both in response to state supreme

---

e. Raymond O'Brien, "Domestic Partnership: Recognition and Responsibility," 32 *San Diego L. Rev.* 163 (1995); Craig Bowman & Blake Cornish, Note, "A More Perfect Union: A Legal and Social Analysis of Domestic Partnership Ordinances," 92 *Colum. L. Rev.* 1164 (1992). Lists of domestic partner registries can be found on the following websites: <lambdalegal.org> and <buddybuddy.com>. The Human Rights Campaign Foundation website, <hrc.org>, has the most extensive report of state and local governments that offer domestic partner health benefits to their employees.

court decisions requiring the state to provide lesbian and gay couples with equal rights. See Section 2 of this Chapter. Consider the new institution created by the nation's largest state.

PROBLEM 9–1

CALIFORNIA'S STATEWIDE DOMESTIC PARTNERSHIP: A NEW DISCRIMINATION?

California enacted a statewide domestic partnership law in 1999 Cal. Stats., ch. 588. The Legislature expanded the benefits available to registered domestic partners in a series of statutes, culminating in the California Domestic Partner Rights and Responsibilities Act of 2003. 2003 Cal. Stats. ch. 421 (A.B. No. 205). Finding that same-sex couples form "lasting, committed, and caring relationships," *id.* § 1(b), the California Legislature extended almost all the rights, benefits, duties, and obligations of married spouses to registered domestic partners. *Id.* § 4(a). There is a long transition period, so that current domestic partners can end their relationships if they do not welcome the new duties and obligations; the 2003 law went into effect on January 1, 2005.

The main exceptions to the equal-benefits-and-duties principle are the following: domestic partners are not eligible for the public employee long-term care benefits set forth in Cal. Govt. Code § 21661; a surviving domestic partner is not protected from a property tax reassessment of a jointly owned home after the death of one partner (Proposition 13 protects surviving spouses from such reassessments); domestic partners who are childless, have been together for five years or fewer, have no support obligations to one another, and satisfy stated debt and real property restrictions can dissolve their relationship by jointly filing a notice of termination with the Secretary of State. See new Cal. Family Code § 299(a). Otherwise, domestic partnerships can be dissolved only by going through formal divorce proceedings. *Id.* § 299(d).

You are a lawyer in West Hollywood, California, which had one of the nation's earliest domestic partnership laws—but its law has now been superseded by the state law, Cal. Family Code § 299.6 (preemption provision). Under the state law, as amended through 2003, "two adults who have chosen to share one another's lives in an intimate and committed relationship of mutual caring," *id.* § 297(a), can register with the state as domestic partners if they share a "common residence," neither is married or joined in domestic partnership with someone else, are not related by blood, are capable of consenting to the partnership, and are of the same sex (the partners can be different as well as same-sex if one or both is over the age of 62). *Id.* § 297(b).

The California domestic partnership law is fairly simple in concept— same-sex couples get almost all the same benefits and duties as different-sex married couples. Thus, same-sex domestic partners can sue for their emotional and other losses following the death or injury to their partners. But consider the following quandary.

Ronald Kim and Daria Vasquez have been cohabiting for several years. They do not want to marry, both because they believe marriage is a bad patriarchal institution and because they do not want the hassle of a formal divorce if they split up. Vasquez proposes that they become domestic partners. Under the statute, however, California cannot register this couple as domestic partners; the law only recognizes different-sex partnerships for older couples. Vasquez and Kim sue the state for discriminating against them on the basis of (1) sexual orientation, (2) sex, and (3) marital status. (You might want to revisit Chapter 3 at this point.) What level of scrutiny does the state have to meet to justify this discrimination? What state interest should it assert? Will the discrimination be allowed by a federal court? For a wry evaluation of such claims, see *Irizarry v. Board of Education of City of Chicago*, 251 F.3d 604 (7th Cir. 2001) (Posner, J.).

THE EXPANSION OF MARRIAGE TO INCLUDE SAME–SEX COUPLES (AND OTHERS?)

The materials in Section 1 suggest that the state has de-emphasized marriage as the norm in American society. Just as marriage has attracted fewer entrants and more critics, barriers to entering it have decreased. As old barriers have fallen, new groups long excluded from the institution want to join up, and society continues to reject some of them, under the aegis of protecting the institution, and then to reverse course once the exclusion is viewed as discriminatory by most in the society. This was the case with "miscegenosexuals," Samuel Marcosson's wonderfully awful term for people of different races who love one another, as well as people with disabilities (many of whom are still excluded). The most group seeking entry into civil marriage has been lesbians, gay men, bisexuals, and transgendered people who want to marry people the law treats as being of the same sex.

NOTES ON OBJECTIONS TO STATE RECOGNITION OF SAME–SEX MARRIAGE[a]

Gay people's politics of recognition was modeled on the discourse of the civil rights movement, and *Loving v. Virginia* (the lead-off case in Chapter 3) inspired early lesbian and gay activists to think that same-sex couples, like different-race couples, had a constitutional right to state recognition of their relationships. The first such constitutional challenge was brought by a Minnesota couple, Jack Baker and Michael McConnell. The Minnesota Supreme Court rejected their claim in *Baker v. Nelson*, 191 N.W.2d 185 (Minn. 1971), as did every judge to evaluate those claims until 1993. The reasons changed over time. See William N. Eskridge, Jr. & Darren Spedale, *Gay Marriage, For Better or For Worse? What the Evidence Teaches Us* chaps. 1, 6 (forthcoming from Oxford University Press, 2006).

1. *The Definitional Argument.* The main argument against same-sex marriage has been definitional: marriage is necessarily different-sex and therefore cannot include same-sex couples. Hence, any statute that talks of *marriage* can only contemplate different-sex couples, even if the statute is

---

a. This note is adapted from William Eskridge, Jr., *The Case for Same–Sex Mar-* *riage* (1996), and *Equality Practice: Civil Un- ions and the Future of Gay Rights* (2002).

not gendered (*i.e.*, does not use the specific terms *husband* and *wife*). Typical is the discussion in *Jones v. Hallahan*, 501 S.W.2d 588, 589 (Ky.1973):

> Marriage was a custom long before the state commenced to issue licenses for that purpose. For a time the records of marriage were kept by the church. * * * [M]arriage has always been considered as the union of a man and a woman and we have been presented with no authority to the contrary. * * * It appears that appellants are prevented from marrying, not by the statutes of Kentucky or the refusal of the County Clerk of Jefferson County to issue them a license, but rather by their own incapability of entering into a marriage as that term is defined.

This definitional approach naturally dispatches any statutory interpretation argument, since all the state marriage statutes (whether gendered or not) do use the term marriage. Note that the Kentucky court relied on history and tradition to figure out what marriage is, definitionally. Starting with *Baker*, other courts have also defined the essence of marriage more philosophically, as requiring procreation as one purpose. Courts have also used the definitional argument as a way to reject constitutional challenges based upon the right to marriage recognized in *Loving*. By defining marriage as essentially different-sex, *Singer* was able to avoid the charge that the state was creating an invidious discrimination by denying licenses to same-sex couples.

Definitional arguments create interesting puzzles at the margin. Can a post-operative male-to-female transsexual marry a man? See *In re Estate of Gardiner*, 42 P.3d 120 (Kan. 2002), which held that such a transsexual can only marry a woman. Whom can an intersexual (someone with physical traits associated with both sexes) marry? What about the case of a person with Klinefelter's syndrome (XXY chromosomes, rather than the male XY pattern or the female XX pattern)?

2. *Defense-of-Marriage Arguments.* As *Loving* suggested, the point of the Equal Protection Clause is to require the state to justify its discriminations, and justification by definition is either circular or perilously close to it. Moreover, after the 1970s, judges and other public officials realized that gay people were more numerous and more functional than previously thought—and therefore they were more attentive to their justifications. So thoughtful opponents of same-sex marriage came up with functional arguments to complement the definitional one. *E.g.*, John Witte, Jr., "The Goods and Goals of Marriage," 76 *Notre Dame L. Rev.* 1019 (2001).

Most traditional family values thinkers tie concerns about same-sex marriage with a critique of the privatization of marriage and family. Their meta-narrative is that the West's movement from sacrament to contract has been one that has sacrificed the historic good of marriage, namely, the creation of a space where adults behave altruistically, not only toward one another, but also toward their children, the central point and legacy of marriage. See generally Witte, *From Sacrament to Contract: Marriage, Religion, and Law in the Western Tradition* (1997). The same-sex marriage movement is the culmination of marriage liberalization in the West, they argue. By transforming marriage from a sacred covenant to sacrifice one's own immediate pleasures for the good of one's spouse and one's children, into a shallow consumerist contract between two selfish adults whose long-term commitment is subject to efficient breach, the West has destroyed marriage's best value for both the participants and for the state. E.g., C. Sydney Buchanan, "Same–Sex Marriage: The Linchpin Issue," 10 *U. Dayton L. Rev.* 541 (1985); Lynn Wardle et al. editors, *Marriage and Same–Sex Unions: A Debate* 13–24, 152–61 (2003) (essays by Maggie Gallagher and Teresa Collett); William J. Bennett, *Broken Hearth: Reversing the Moral Collapse of the American Family* 135–36 (2004).

3. *Stamp-of-Approval Arguments.* Judge Richard Posner's anti-moralistic *Sex and Reason* 311–13 (1991) presents a pragmatic case against same-sex marriage at this time. Recognizing same-sex relationships as marriage would be problematic, he suggests, because it would "be widely interpreted as placing a stamp of approval on homosexuality"; would carry an "information cost" in that the socially informative value of knowing someone is married would be somewhat reduced as the term is broadened; and would have "many collateral effects, simply because marriage is a status rich in entitlements, many of which were not designed with same-sex couples in mind." The first point may be the most important, especially for judges anxious about the legitimacy of their constitutional decisions. Moralists tend to present the Posner point as: Homosexuality is shameful and the state should not be promoting it.

PART A. SAME–SEX MARRIAGE COMES TO THE UNITED STATES

The foregoing arguments were uniformly successful in the 1980s, but at the same time lesbian and gay advocates of same-sex marriage were developing new post-*Loving* pitches. To begin with, the Supreme Court took seriously *Loving*'s alternative holding, that there is a substantive "right to marry" triggering heightened scrutiny under either the Equal Protection Clause, see *Zablocki v. Redhail,* 434 U.S. 374 (1978) (striking down a law barring deadbeat dads, in arrears on family support obligations from a prior marriage, from remarrying), or the Due Process Clause, see *Turner v. Safley,* 482 U.S. 78 (1987). The latter decision struck down a rule barring convicted felons from marrying while serving time in prison. Lesbian and gay rights advocates wondered: If murderers and rapists have a right to marry, shouldn't committed (and peaceful) lesbian and gay couples?

The AIDS epidemic played a complex role in reviving same-sex marriage claims. Although religious leaders such as Reverend Jerry Falwell trumpeted AIDS as God's judgment on homosexuals in their fund-raising letters, many Americans were impressed by the caregiving provided dying gay men by their male partners and their lesbian friends. Kath Weston's notion of families we choose revealed deeper human commitments than mainstream society had previously been aware of. Moreover, committed partners found themselves legal outsiders when medical care decisions had to be made and after the infected partners died; often the blood family would push them aside, as the law entitled them to do in most states. Gay people gained an appreciation for the decisionmaking presumptions, health care benefits, and inheritance rights that married people take for granted.

Finally, the American marriage movement was jump-started when Denmark enacted a Registered Partnership Act in 1989, the first nation in the modern West to vest lesbian and gay partnerships with almost all the rights and duties of marriage. See Eskridge & Spedale, *Better or Worse?* chaps. 1–5 (situating the Danish law in the context of the American debate). Some lesbian and gay couples, assisted by a small group of sympathetic lawyers, went back into court. Their claims were that the same-sex marriage bar violated state constitutional guarantees of equal protection and freedom to marry.

NOTES ON SUCCESSFUL SAME–SEX MARRIAGE LITIGATION AND ITS CONSEQUENCES

1. *The Hawaii Case; Reciprocal Beneficiaries.* Three of these couples won a stunning victory, when the Hawaii Supreme Court ruled that the bar constituted a sex discrimination that required strict scrutiny in *Baehr v. Lewin,* 852 P.2d 44 (Haw. 1993), on remand as *Baehr v. Miike,* 1996 WL 694235 (Haw. Cir. Ct. Dec. 1996) (striking down the discrimination because the state could not provide a sufficient justification). Chapter 3, Section 3 reproduces excerpts from the *Baehr* opinions. *Baehr* generated a firestorm of protest, both in Hawaii and all over the United States. The Reverend Louis Sheldon spoke for many Americans when he proclaimed *Baehr* the American family's Pearl Harbor.

While the trial judge's opinion striking down the discrimination was on appeal (and stayed), the Hawaii Legislature in 1997 enacted two pieces of legislation. The first created the Reciprocal Beneficiaries Act. Adults who were excluded from the marriage law either because they were too closely related or because they were considered to be of the same sex could choose to form a mutually beneficial partnership by filing a form with the state whereby the two parties affirmed that they wanted to be treated as *reciprocal beneficiaries.* 1997 Haw. Sess. Laws, Act 383 (H.B. 118). Reciprocal beneficiaries enjoyed about 50 of the more than 200 rights and benefits enjoyed by married couples, including health care and other fringe benefits for state and municipal employees; hospital visitation rights; the right to make health care decisions in case of a partner's incapacity; the right to own property as tenants in the entirety; inheritance and life insurance rights like those of a spouse; the right to bring a wrongful death lawsuit for loss of care, support, attention, and counsel of one's reciprocal beneficiary; tax treatment like spouses; and protection like spouses under the state's domestic abuse and victim's rights laws. As of 1997, this law was the most far-reaching state recognition of same-sex unions ever adopted by an American legislature—but it was treated as a complete defeat by lesbians and gay men.

The second bill adopted by the legislature placed a proposed constitutional amendment on the ballot for November 3, 1998. A new Article I, § 23 should be added to the Hawaii Constitution: "The legislature shall have the power to reserve marriage to opposite-sex couples." In the campaign that followed, the main argument for amending the constitution was that "homosexual marriage" would bring ruin to Hawaii, and especially to its children. In one television ad, a boy was depicted reading a booklet, *Daddy's Wedding* to another man; a voice then queried, "If you don't think homosexual marriage will affect you, how do you think it will affect your children?" See William Eskridge, Jr., *Equality Practice: Civil Unions and the Future of Gay Rights* 39–40 (2002) (references for these quotes).

By a vote of 69–28%, Hawaii voters approved this amendment. Several months later, the Hawaii Supreme Court vacated the trial court judgment and remanded the case for entry of judgment in favor of the state. See *Baehr v. Miike*, 994 P.2d 566 (Haw.1999) (summary disposition).

2. *The Vermont Litigation; Civil Unions.* Drawing from grass-roots organizing that had largely been absent in earlier litigations, Beth Robinson and Susan Murray persuaded the Vermont Supreme Court in *Baker v. State*, 744 A.2d 864 (Vt. 1999) that the same-sex marriage bar violated the Common Benefits Clause of the Vermont Constitution.

Representative Thomas Little, a Republican, chaired the House Judiciary Committee which conducted extensive hearings (including two huge public hearings where citizens testified) and drew up legislation which, as revised, became the basis for the enacted legislation. The bill was a compromise, reaffirming civil marriage as limited to one man and one woman and creating new institutions giving same-sex couples all the legal benefits and obligations (but not the name) of marriage. After anguished debate, and unprecedented public involvement, the Legislature passed the House bill.[b]

On April 26, 2000, Governor Howard Dean signed into law An Act Relating to Civil Unions (H. 847), 2000 Vt. Laws No. 91. The law reaffirmed that civil marriage "consists of a union between a man and a woman," *id.* § 1(1), and that the state interest "is to encourage close and caring families, and to protect all family members from the economic and social consequences of abandonment and divorce." *Id.* § 1(3). The Legislature further found that "many gay and lesbian Vermonters have formed lasting, committed, and faithful relationships with persons of their same sex," *id.*

---

b. Detailed accounts of the legislative deliberation can be found in Eskridge, *Equality Practice* 57–82, and Michael Mello, "For Today I'm Gay: The Unfinished Battle for Same–Sex Marriage in Vermont," 25 *Vt. L. Rev.* 149 (2000).

§ 1(9), and recognizing these relationships through a new institution satisfies *Baker*'s equal treatment requirement while at the same time giving "due respect for tradition and longstanding social institutions." *Id.* § 1(10).

3. *The Canadian Litigation: Marriage.* As the Vermont Legislature debated civil unions, couples across the border in Canada were litigating for full marriage equality. In *M. v. H.,* [1999] 2 S.C.R. 3 (1999), the Canadian Supreme Court had ruled that state discrimination against lesbian and gay couples was constitutionally suspect. The same judgment that had thrown the United States into a colossal anti-gay reaction barely disturbed Canada. On June 10, 2003, the Ontario Court of Appeal ruled, in *Halpern v. Attorney General*, that it was unconstitutional to deny same-sex couples marriage licenses. The government did not appeal this loss, and same-sex couples started receiving marriage licenses in Ontario—and then British Columbia and other provinces. As of July 2005, more than 4000 same-sex couples have been legally wed in Canada, including 1000 American couples. In July, Canada's national government enacted into law a statute making same-sex marriage legal in the entire country.

Without judicial prodding, The Netherlands enacted a law recognizing same-sex marriages in December 2000. Likewise, Spain enacted a similar law in July 2005. See Eskridge & Spedale, *Better or Worse?*, ch. 2 (surveying recent developments in Europe).

Hillary Goodridge et al. v. Department of Public Health

Supreme Judicial Court of Massachusetts, 2003.
798 N.E.2d 941, 2003 WL 22701313 (Mass.).

■ MARSHALL, C.J.

Marriage is a vital social institution. The exclusive commitment of two individuals to each other nurtures love and mutual support; it brings stability to our society. For those who choose to marry, and for their children, marriage provides an abundance of legal, financial, and social benefits. In return it imposes weighty legal, financial, and social obligations. The question before us is whether, consistent with the Massachusetts Constitution, the Commonwealth may deny the protections, benefits, and obligations conferred by civil marriage to two individuals of the same sex who wish to marry. We conclude that it may not. The Massachusetts Constitution affirms the dignity and equality of all individuals. It forbids the creation of second-class citizens. In reaching our conclusion we have given full deference to the arguments made by the Commonwealth. But it has failed to identify any constitutionally adequate reason for denying civil marriage to same-sex couples.

We are mindful that our decision marks a change in the history of our marriage law. Many people hold deep-seated religious, moral, and ethical convictions that marriage should be limited to the union of one man and one woman, and that homosexual conduct is immoral. Many hold equally strong religious, moral, and ethical convictions that same-sex couples are entitled to be married, and that homosexual persons should be treated no differently than their heterosexual neighbors. Neither view answers the question before us. Our concern is with the Massachusetts Constitution as a charter of governance for every person properly within its reach. "Our obligation is to define the liberty of all, not to mandate our own moral code." *Lawrence v. Texas*, quoting *Planned Parenthood of Southeastern Pa. v. Casey.* * * *

[III.A]   The plaintiffs' claim that the marriage restriction violates the Massachusetts Constitution can be analyzed in two ways. Does it offend the Constitution's guarantees of equality before the law? Or do the liberty and due process provisions of the Massachusetts Constitution secure the plaintiffs' right to marry their chosen partner? In matters implicating marriage, family life, and the upbringing of children, the two constitutional concepts frequently overlap, as they do here. See, e.g., *M.L.B. v. S.L.J.*, 519 U.S. 102, 120 (1996) (noting convergence of due process and equal protection principles in cases concerning parent-child relationships); *Perez v. Sharp*, 198 P.2d 17 ([Cal.] 1948) (analyzing statutory ban on interracial marriage as equal protection violation concerning regulation of fundamental right). Much of what we say concerning one standard applies to the other.

We begin by considering the nature of civil marriage itself. Simply put, the government creates civil marriage. In Massachusetts, civil marriage is, and since pre-Colonial days has been, precisely what its name implies: a wholly secular institution. No religious ceremony has ever been required to validate a Massachusetts marriage.

In a real sense, there are three partners to every civil marriage: two willing spouses and an approving State. While only the parties can mutually assent to marriage, the terms of the marriage—who may marry and what obligations, benefits, and liabilities attach to civil marriage—are set by the Commonwealth. Conversely, while only the parties can agree to end the marriage (absent the death of one of them or a marriage void *ab initio*), the Commonwealth defines the exit terms. * * *

Without question, civil marriage enhances the "welfare of the community." It is a "social institution of the highest importance." Civil marriage anchors an ordered society by encouraging stable relationships over transient ones. It is central to the way the Commonwealth identifies individuals, provides for the orderly distribution of property, ensures that children and adults are cared for and supported whenever possible from private rather than public funds, and tracks important epidemiological and demographic data.

Marriage also bestows enormous private and social advantages on those who choose to marry. Civil marriage is at once a deeply personal commitment to another human being and a highly public celebration of the ideals of mutuality, companionship, intimacy, fidelity, and family. "It is an association that promotes a way of life, not causes; a harmony in living, not political faiths; a bilateral loyalty, not commercial or social projects." *Griswold v. Connecticut.* Because it fulfils yearnings for security, safe haven, and connection that express our common humanity, civil marriage is an esteemed institution, and the decision whether and whom to marry is among life's momentous acts of self-definition.

Tangible as well as intangible benefits flow from marriage. The marriage license grants valuable property rights to those who meet the entry requirements, and who agree to what might otherwise be a burdensome degree of government regulation of their activities. The Legislature has conferred on "each party [in a civil marriage] substantial rights concerning the assets of the other which unmarried cohabitants do not have." *Wilcox v. Trautz*, 693 N.E.2d 141 (1998).

The benefits accessible only by way of a marriage license are enormous, touching nearly every aspect of life and death. The department states that "hundreds of statutes" are related to marriage and to marital benefits. [The Court lists dozens of marital benefits under Massachusetts law linked to property rights, health coverage, pensions, inheritance and other issues related to death, issues related to children, and eligibility for bereavement or medical leave.]

Where a married couple has children, their children are also directly or indirectly, but no less auspiciously, the recipients of the special legal and economic protections obtained by civil marriage. Notwithstanding the Commonwealth's strong public policy to abolish legal distinctions between marital and nonmarital children in providing for the support and care of minors, the fact remains that marital children reap a measure of family stability and economic security based on their parents' legally privileged status that is largely inaccessible, or not as readily accessible, to nonmarital children. Some of these benefits are social, such as the enhanced approval that still attends the status of being a marital child. Others are material, such as the greater ease of access to family-based State and Federal benefits that attend the presumptions of one's parentage.

It is undoubtedly for these concrete reasons, as well as for its intimately personal significance, that civil marriage has long been termed a "civil right." The United States Supreme Court has described the right to marry as "of fundamental importance for all individuals" and as "part of the fundamental 'right of privacy' implicit in the Fourteenth Amendment's Due Process Clause." *Zablocki v. Redhail*, 434 U.S. 374, 384 (1978).

Without the right to marry—or more properly, the right to choose to marry—one is excluded from the full range of human experience and denied full protection of the laws for one's "avowed commitment to an intimate and lasting human relationship." *Baker v. State.* Because civil marriage is central to the lives of individuals and the welfare of the community, our laws assiduously protect the individual's right to marry against undue government incursion. Laws may not "interfere directly and substantially with the right to marry." *Zablocki v. Redhail.*

Unquestionably, the regulatory power of the Commonwealth over civil marriage is broad, as is the Commonwealth's discretion to award public benefits. Individuals who have the choice to marry each other and nevertheless choose not to may properly be denied the legal benefits of marriage. But that same logic cannot hold for a qualified individual who would marry if she or he only could.

[B] For decades, indeed centuries, in much of this country (including Massachusetts) no lawful marriage was possible between white and black Americans. That long history availed not when the Supreme Court of California held in 1948 that a legislative prohibition against interracial marriage violated the due process and equality guarantees of the Fourteenth Amendment, *Perez*, or when, nineteen years later, the United States Supreme Court also held that a statutory bar to interracial marriage violated the Fourteenth Amendment, *Loving v. Virginia*. As both *Perez* and *Loving* make clear, the right to marry means little if it does not include the right to marry the person of one's choice, subject to appropriate government restrictions in the interests of public health, safety, and welfare. In this case, as in *Perez* and *Loving*, a statute deprives individuals of access to an institution of fundamental legal, personal, and social significance—the institution of marriage—because of a single trait: skin color in *Perez* and *Loving*, sexual orientation here. As it did in *Perez* and *Loving*, history must yield to a more fully developed understanding of the invidious quality of the discrimination.

The Massachusetts Constitution protects matters of personal liberty against government incursion as zealously, and often more so, than does the Federal Constitution, even where both Constitutions employ essentially the same language. * * *

The individual liberty and equality safeguards of the Massachusetts Constitution protect both "freedom from" unwarranted government intrusion into protected spheres of life and "freedom to" partake in benefits created by the State for the common good. Both freedoms are involved here. Whether and whom to marry, how to express sexual intimacy, and whether and how to establish a family—these are among the most basic of every individual's liberty and due process rights. And central to personal freedom and security is the assurance that the laws will apply equally to persons in similar situations. The liberty interest in choosing whether and whom to marry would be hollow if the Commonwealth could, without sufficient justification, foreclose an individual from freely choosing the person with whom to share an exclusive commitment in the unique institution of civil marriage. * * *

[The Court ruled that it need not consider plaintiffs' claim that the marriage exclusion must be evaluated under "strict scrutiny," as the discrimination in *Loving* had been. The exclusion failed even the rational basis test.] The department posits three legislative rationales for prohibiting same-sex couples from marrying: (1) providing a "favorable setting for procreation"; (2) ensuring the optimal setting for child rearing, which the department defines as "a two-parent family with one parent of each sex"; and (3) preserving scarce State and private financial resources. We consider each in turn.

The judge in the Superior Court endorsed the first rationale, holding that "the state's interest in regulating marriage is based on the traditional concept that marriage's primary purpose is procreation." This is incorrect. Our laws of civil marriage do not privilege procreative heterosexual intercourse between married people above every other form of adult intimacy and every other means of creating a family. General Laws c. 207 contains no requirement that the applicants for a marriage license attest to their ability or intention to conceive children by coitus. Fertility is not a condition of marriage, nor is it grounds for divorce. People who have never consummated their marriage, and never plan to, may be and stay married. People who cannot stir from their deathbed may marry. While it is certainly true that many, perhaps most, married couples have children together (assisted or unassisted), it is the exclusive and permanent commitment of the marriage partners to one another, not the begetting of children, that is the *sine qua non* of civil marriage. * * *

The "marriage is procreation" argument singles out the one unbridgeable difference between same-sex and opposite-sex couples, and transforms that difference into the essence of legal marriage. Like "Amendment 2" to the Constitution of Colorado, which effectively denied homosexual persons equality under the law and full access to the political process, the marriage restriction impermissibly "identifies persons by a single trait and then denies them protection across the board." *Romer v. Evans.* In so doing, the State's action confers an official stamp of approval on the destructive stereotype that same-sex relationships are inherently unstable and inferior to opposite-sex relationships and are not worthy of respect.

The department's first stated rationale, equating marriage with unassisted heterosexual procreation, shades imperceptibly into its second: that confining marriage to opposite-sex couples ensures that children are raised in the "optimal" setting. Protecting the welfare of children is a paramount State policy. Restricting marriage to opposite-sex couples, however, cannot plausibly further this policy. * * * Moreover, we have repudiated the common-law power of the State to provide varying levels of protection to children based on the circumstances of birth. The "best interests of the child" standard does not turn on a parent's sexual orientation or marital status.

The department has offered no evidence that forbidding marriage to people of the same sex will increase the number of couples choosing to enter into opposite-sex marriages in order to have and raise children. There is thus no rational relationship between the marriage statute and the Commonwealth's proffered goal of protecting the "optimal" child rearing unit. Moreover, the department readily concedes that people in same-sex couples may be "excellent" parents. These couples (including four of the plaintiff couples) have children for the reasons others do—to love them, to care for them, to nurture them. But the task of child rearing for same-sex couples is made infinitely harder by their status as outliers to the marriage laws. * * *

In this case, we are confronted with an entire, sizeable class of parents raising children who have absolutely no access to civil marriage and its protections because they are forbidden from procuring a marriage license. It cannot be rational under our laws, and indeed it is not permitted, to penalize children by depriving them of State benefits because the State disapproves of their parents' sexual orientation.

The third rationale advanced by the department is that limiting marriage to opposite-sex couples furthers the Legislature's interest in conserving scarce State and private financial resources. The marriage restriction is rational, it argues, because the General Court logically could assume that same-sex couples are more financially independent than married couples and thus less needy of public marital benefits, such as tax advantages, or private marital benefits, such as employer-financed health plans that include spouses in their coverage.

An absolute statutory ban on same-sex marriage bears no rational relationship to the goal of economy. First, the department's conclusory generalization—that same-sex couples are less financially dependent on each other than opposite-sex couples—ignores that many same-sex couples, such as many of the plaintiffs in this case, have children and other dependents (here, aged parents) in their care. The department does not contend, nor could it, that these dependents are less needy or deserving than the dependents of married couples. Second, Massachusetts marriage laws do not condition receipt of public and private financial benefits to married individuals on a demonstration of financial dependence on each other; the benefits are available to married couples regardless of whether they mingle their finances or actually depend on each other for support.

The department suggests additional rationales for prohibiting same-sex couples from marrying, which are developed by some *amici*. It argues that broadening civil marriage to include same-sex couples will trivialize or destroy the institution of marriage as it has historically been fashioned. Certainly our decision today marks a significant change in the definition of marriage as it has been inherited from the common law, and understood by many societies for centuries. But it does not disturb the fundamental value of marriage in our society.

Here, the plaintiffs seek only to be married, not to undermine the institution of civil marriage. They do not want marriage abolished. They do not attack the binary nature of marriage, the consanguinity provisions, or any of the other gate-keeping provisions of the marriage licensing law. Recognizing the right of an individual to marry a person of the same sex will not diminish the validity or dignity of opposite-sex marriage, any more than recognizing the right of an individual to marry a person of a different race devalues the marriage of a person who marries someone of her own race. If anything, extending civil marriage to same-sex couples reinforces the importance of marriage to individuals and communities. That same-sex couples are willing to embrace marriage's solemn obligations of exclusivity, mutual support, and commitment to one another is a testament to the enduring place of marriage in our laws and in the human spirit. It has been argued that, due to the State's strong interest in the institution of marriage as a stabilizing social structure, only the Legislature can control and define its boundaries. * * * These arguments miss the point. The Massachusetts Constitution requires that legislation meet certain criteria and not extend beyond certain limits. It is the function of courts to determine whether these criteria are met and whether these limits are exceeded. * * *

* * * Alarms about the imminent erosion of the "natural" order of marriage were sounded over the demise of antimiscegenation laws, the expansion of the rights of married women, and the introduction of "no-fault" divorce. Marriage has survived all of these transformations, and we have no doubt that marriage will continue to be a vibrant and revered institution.* * *

Several *amici* suggest that prohibiting marriage by same-sex couples reflects community consensus that homosexual conduct is immoral. Yet Massachusetts has a strong affirmative policy of preventing discrimination on the basis of sexual orientation. [The court lists a number of antidiscrimination provisions in state law.] * * *

The marriage ban works a deep and scarring hardship on a very real segment of the community for no rational reason. The absence of any reasonable relationship between, on the one hand, an absolute disqualification of same-sex couples who wish to enter into civil marriage and, on the other, protection of public health, safety, or general welfare, suggests that the marriage restriction is rooted in persistent prejudices against persons who are (or who are believed to be) homosexual. "The Constitution cannot control such prejudices but neither can it tolerate them. Private biases may be outside the reach of the law, but the law cannot, directly or indirectly, give them effect." *Palmore v. Sidoti*, 466 U.S. 429, 433 (1984). Limiting the protections, benefits, and obligations of civil marriage to opposite-sex couples violates the basic premises of individual liberty and equality under law protected by the Massachusetts Constitution.

[IV] We consider next the plaintiffs' request for relief. * * *

* * * We face a problem similar to one that recently confronted the Court of Appeal for Ontario, the highest court of that Canadian province, when it considered the constitutionality of the same-sex marriage ban under Canada's Federal Constitution, the Charter of Rights and Freedoms (Charter). See *Halpern v. Toronto (City)*, 172 O.A.C. 276 (2003). Canada, like the United States, adopted the common law of England that civil marriage is "the voluntary union for life of one man and one woman, to the exclusion of all others." *Id.* In holding that the limitation of civil marriage to opposite-sex couples violated the Charter, the Court of Appeal refined the common-law meaning of marriage. We concur with this remedy, which is entirely consonant with established principles of jurisprudence empowering a court to refine a commonlaw principle in light of evolving constitutional standards.

We construe civil marriage to mean the voluntary union of two persons as spouses, to the exclusion of all others. This reformulation redresses the

plaintiffs' constitutional injury and furthers the aim of marriage to promote stable, exclusive relationships. It advances the two legitimate State
interests the department has identified: providing a stable setting for child
rearing and conserving State resources. It leaves intact the Legislature's
broad discretion to regulate marriage.

In their complaint the plaintiffs request only a declaration that their
exclusion and the exclusion of other qualified same-sex couples from access
to civil marriage violates Massachusetts law. We declare that barring an
individual from the protections, benefits, and obligations of civil marriage
solely because that person would marry a person of the same sex violates
the Massachusetts Constitution. We vacate the summary judgment for the
department. We remand this case to the Superior Court for entry of
judgment consistent with this opinion. Entry of judgment shall be stayed
for 180 days to permit the Legislature to take such action as it may deem
appropriate in light of this opinion.

■ [In a concurring opinion, JUSTICE GREANEY concluded that the case should
be decided on an equal protection basis; specifically, on the ground that the
marriage law discriminated on the basis of sex. In dissent, JUSTICE SPINA
argued that the court should not have resolved the validity of the marriage
statute, but left it for the legislature "to effectuate social change without
interference from the courts." The second dissent, by JUSTICE SOSMAN, found
that the primary basis for the majority's opinion was that the benefits of
civil marriage could not be withheld from same-sex couples raising children; the legislature had a rational basis for limiting those benefits to
marital households because marriages were the only environment proven to
support healthy child-rearing.]

■ CORDY, J. (dissenting, with whom SPINA and SOSMAN, JJ., join). [Justice
Cordy concluded that strict scrutiny was impermissible, because the statute's exclusion of same-sex couples did not violate a fundamental right, nor
did it deploy a suspect classification. Moreover, the statutory classification
easily related to a rational state policy.]

Paramount among its many important functions, the institution of
marriage has systematically provided for the regulation of heterosexual
behavior, brought order to the resulting procreation, and ensured a stable
family structure in which children will be reared, educated, and socialized.
* * * [A]n orderly society requires some mechanism for coping with the
fact that sexual intercourse commonly results in pregnancy and childbirth.
The institution of marriage is that mechanism.

The institution of marriage provides the important legal and normative
link between heterosexual intercourse and procreation on the one hand and
family responsibilities on the other. The partners in a marriage are expected to engage in exclusive sexual relations, with children the probable result
and paternity presumed. [A mother's link to her child is self-evident.] * * *
The institution of marriage * * * formally bind[s] the husband-father to
his wife and child, and impos[es] on him the responsibilities of fatherhood.
The alternative, a society without the institution of marriage, in which

heterosexual intercourse, procreation, and child care are largely disconnected processes, would be chaotic.

The marital family is also the foremost setting for the education and socialization of children. * * * The institution of marriage encourages parents to remain committed to each other and to their children as they grow, thereby encouraging a stable venue for the education and socialization of children. * * *

Taking [the full body of social science] information [on childrearing outcomes in various family structures] into account, the Legislature could rationally conclude that a family environment with married opposite-sex parents remains the optimal social structure in which to bear children, and that the raising of children by same-sex couples, who by definition cannot be the two sole biological parents of a child and cannot provide children with a parental authority figure of each gender, presents an alternative structure for child rearing that has not yet proved itself beyond reasonable scientific dispute to be as optimal as the biologically based marriage norm. Working from the assumption that a recognition of same-sex marriages will increase the number of children experiencing this alternative, the Legislature could conceivably conclude that declining to recognize same-sex marriages remains prudent until empirical questions about its impact on the upbringing of children are resolved.

As long as marriage is limited to opposite-sex couples who can at least theoretically procreate, society is able to communicate a consistent message to its citizens that marriage is a (normatively) necessary part of their procreative endeavor; that if they are to procreate, then society has endorsed the institution of marriage as the environment for it and for the subsequent rearing of their children; and that benefits are available explicitly to create a supportive and conducive atmosphere for those purposes. If society proceeds similarly to recognize marriages between same-sex couples who cannot procreate, it could be perceived as an abandonment of this claim, and might result in the mistaken view that civil marriage has little to do with procreation: just as the potential of procreation would not be necessary for a marriage to be valid, marriage would not be necessary for optimal procreation and child rearing to occur. In essence, the Legislature could conclude that the consequence of such a policy shift would be a diminution in society's ability to steer the acts of procreation and child rearing into their most optimal setting.* * *

* * * While the courageous efforts of many have resulted in increased dignity, rights, and respect for gay and lesbian members of our community, the issue presented here is a profound one, deeply rooted in social policy, that must, for now, be the subject of legislative not judicial action.

NOTES ON THE MASSACHUSETTS SAME–SEX MARRIAGE CASE

1. *Was There No "Rational Basis" for the Exclusion?* By applying rational basis review, the Court avoided thorny questions as to whether sexual orientation is a suspect classification and whether exclusion of same-sex couples is sex discrimination along *Loving/Baehr* lines. But that meant that the Court had to find no "rational basis" for the discrimination. All three of the state's arguments rested upon legitimate state goals, but the Court found the classification did not closely fit the goal.

(a) The favorable-setting-for-procreation argument was inconsistent with the marriage statutes, which have never made procreation a condition of marriage. But under normal rational basis review, the legislature does not have to tackle the entire problem all at once; it can tackle problems piecemeal, excluding only a portion (and maybe the biggest portion) of couples who do not meet the procreation aspiration.

(b) The optimal-setting-for-childraising argument was not supported by evidence showing that the exclusion of same-sex couples induces more people to enter into and raise children within heterosexual marriages. The Court here is passing over another form of this argument: traditionalists believe that children do not do as well in lesbian or gay households and that the nuclear family of dad-mom-kids is the only one the state should sanction. Could reasonable legislators believe that? The Eleventh Circuit found evidence to that effect when it upheld Florida's exclusion of lesbian, gay, and bisexual adults from adoption in *Lofton v. Secretary of the Dep't of Children & Family Servs.*, 358 F.3d 804 (11th Cir. 2004) (Chapter 4).

(c) The economy argument was found to be both over-inclusive (many straight couples do not need the state's support) and under-inclusive (many lesbian and gay couples do need such support). But the leading rational basis decision by the U.S. Supreme Court, *Railway Express Agency v. New York,* 336 U.S. 106 (1949), upheld a statute banning certain advertisements posted on motor vehicles that the legislature found diverting and therefore unsafe that was way under-inclusive (it allowed a lot of diverting ads) and over-inclusive (it banned many ads that would not have been safety hazards).

Obviously, *Goodridge* looks more like *Craig v. Boren* than like *Railway Express* in the kind of scrutiny given to the statute. Like the drinking law in *Craig*, the marriage law in *Goodridge* was defended by reference to valid state goals, but fell because the supporting evidence was weak and the classification seemed driven by stereotypes rather than good policy. So is this really "heightened scrutiny" in disguise? Or is it an example of the "sliding scale" advocated by Justice Thurgood Marshall's dissenting opinion in *San Antonio Indep. Sch. Dist. v. Rodriguez*, 411 U.S. 1 (1973). Marshall argued that a court's willingness to tolerate loose fits between ends and means should consider "the character of the classification in question, the relative importance to individuals in the class discriminated against of the governmental benefits they do not receive, and the asserted state interests in support of the classification."

2. *The Role of Animus? Goodridge* could be analogized to *Romer*, where so-called "rational basis" review was fatal to a law with plausible justifications (protecting freedom of association and conserving prosecutorial resources). Indeed, Chief Justice Marshall relies on *Romer*, even though she is not interpreting the U.S. Constitution. The big difference, however, is that the Court in *Romer* found that the discrimination rested upon anti-gay "animus." *Romer* involved recent regulatory policies that were, the Court found, motivated by exclusion. This explains the bite rational basis review had in that case: If the "real" state policy is prejudice, then the post-hoc justifications cannot save the statute.

In contrast, the discrimination in *Goodridge* existed long before society even had a name for "homosexuals." So the case is different. The Chief Justice suggests that the state's second defense rested upon anti-gay stereotypes, but that was not true of the other two. Perhaps she was suggesting that, whatever the original motivations for the different-sex requirement for marriage, it was resistant to change "because of" anti-gay stereotypes and, perhaps, prejudice. Such a move might be defensible, but wouldn't it require a much more elaborate discussion? And is it not credible that many Massachusetts citizens opposed same-sex marriage for genuine religious reasons, and not anti-gay sentiment?

The Legislature responded to *Goodridge* with a proposed statute that would have reaffirmed marriage as limited to different-sex couples but also creating Vermont-style *civil unions* (with all the same benefits and obligations) for same-sex couples. In an advisory opinion, the Court ruled that this kind of statute violated the Massachusetts Constitution: The state could not create a "separate but equal" regime. *Opinions of the Justices to the Senate*, 802 N.E.2d 565 (Mass. 2004). Why can the state not do such a thing under rational basis review? (Of course, it cannot do that under a strict scrutiny regime, as *Loving* holds.) Wouldn't the proposed statute have shown legislative good faith? However dissimilar *Goodridge* originally was to *Romer*, isn't the difference especially striking after the Legislature proposed to create civil unions?

3. *Amending Constitutions.* Unlike the super-majority process in Article V of the U.S. Constitution, the Massachusetts Constitution can be amended by simple majorities—but only through a deliberative process extending over several years. Two successive Legislatures must approve, by majority votes, the same new constitutional language, which must then be ratified by a majority of the voters at the next general election. At the end of March 2004, the Legislature, on a 105–92 vote, approved an amendment that would have barred same-sex marriages but created a new institution of civil unions for same-sex couples. The same amendment, however, failed in a September 2005 vote of the Legislature.

Gay marriage opponents have now (2005) proposed a different amendment, one which would ban gay marriage but drops the language of civil unions. Drafted by the Massachusetts Family Institute, the amendment reads:

> When recognizing marriage entered after the adoption of this amendment by the people, the Commonwealth and its political subdivisions shall define marriage as only the union of one man and one woman.

Governor Romney, who had endorsed the previous amendment, now calls it "confused" and urges adoption of this second one. It is being pressed as a citizens' initiative. If it obtains 65,825 signatures, it will go before the Legislature, where it only needs a quarter of the vote in two successive sessions in order to be submitted to the voters. Stay tuned. Would the *Goodridge* Court hold it invalid under the U.S. Constitution?

Meanwhile, President Bush and leading Republicans in Congress are pressing for an amendment to the U.S. Constitution. The Federal Marriage Amendment, as revised and voted (down) by the Senate in 2004, reads as follows: "Marriage in the United States shall consist only of the union of a man and a woman. Neither this Constitution, nor the constitution of any State, shall be construed to require that marriage or the legal incidents thereof be conferred upon any union other than the union of a man and a woman." S.J. Res. 30, 108th Congress, 2d Session (2004). The legal effect of the FMA is almost entirely unclear. Would it apply retroactively, to void *Goodridge*? Would it void interpretations of open-ended state statutes that allowed same-sex couples to marry? Would it void *Baker*, which required equal rights and duties, but not the name "marriage"? Would it void the Vermont civil unions law, or the Hawaii reciprocal beneficiaries law, both enacted in response to state court constitutional decisions? And so on.

PART B. INTERSTATE RECOGNITION OF SAME–SEX MARRIAGES OR CIVIL UNIONS?

A powerful fear during the 1990s was that, if one state recognized same-sex marriages, the institution might spread to other jurisdictions, because a same-sex couple validly married in State A might move to State B and insist that State B recognize their relationship, or a same-sex couple residing in State B might fly to State A to be married and then demand that State B recognize their marriage.

This scenario allegedly motivated the Defense of Marriage Act, Public Law No. 104–199, 110 Stat. 2419 (1996). Section 2 of DOMA provides that no state will be required to give full faith and credit to "any public act, record, or judicial proceeding of any other State ... respecting a relation-ship between persons of the same sex that is treated as a marriage under the laws of such other State ... or a right or claim arising from such relationship." New 28 U.S.C.A. § 1738C. Section 3 defines the term "mar-riage," for purposes of federal statutory and agency law, to mean "only a legal union between one man and one woman as husband and wife," and the term "spouse" to mean only "a person of the opposite sex who is a husband or a wife." New 1 U.S.C.A. § 7.

Section 2, of course, does not tell states how they must apply their own choice-of-law regimes.

John Langen v. St. Vincent's Hospital, 765 N.Y.S.2d 411 (N.Y. 2003). New York residents John Langen and Neil Conrad Spicehandler fell in love in 1986 and began living together as domestic partners in 1987. When Vermont enacted its Civil Union Act in 2000, they went to Vermont with about forty family members and friends and had a civil union ceremony with a Justice of the Peace. They were planning to adopt a child, and had purchased a house in Massapequa, Long Island. Just hours after the closing on their house, Spicehandler was struck by an automobile in Manhattan. He was treated at St. Vincent's Hospital, where he died after undergoing two surgeries for injuries to his leg. Langan and Spicehandler's mother filed a malpractice suit against St. Vincent's. Langan sought damages as a "spouse" for purposes of New York's wrongful death statute.

New York courts have ruled that same-sex domestic partners are not spouses entitled to bring claims under the state's wrongful death statute. Langan argued that his case was different, because his civil union with the decedent qualified him as a spouse. **Justice Dunne** agreed, ruling that Langan's civil union qualified him as a statutory "spouse" for purposes of New York's Intestate Succession Act.

New York follows the celebration rule for marriages: New York will recognize them if they are valid in the state of their celebration and they do not offend a New York state policy. For example, although New York does not recognize common law marriages, it will give full faith and credit to common law marriages validly entered in another state. The Vermont statute refers to the parties in a civil union as spouses, even though it also says that a civil union is not a marriage. Couples joined in civil union have all the same rights under state law as married couples, and thus their status as spouses is not just equivalent but actually, for purposes of state law, the same. Langan could have sued for wrongful death if the medical malpractice had taken place in Vermont. Accordingly, the celebration rule suggested that New York ought to treat the Vermont spouses as "spouses" for purposes of the wrongful death law.

Justice Dunne found that New York did not entertain a public policy against same-sex marriages and spousehood. To the contrary, the state's public policy was quite friendly to gay people and their unions. The state and city of New York recognized same-sex domestic partnerships for employment benefits, and the state had just enacted an anti-discrimination law. He also cited Court of Appeals decisions allowing same-sex couples to adopt one another's children and inherit rent-controlled apartment rights.

Nor would Justice Dunne interpret the New York wrongful death act to exclude same-sex couples. "As the [wrongful death law] is construed to apply to a common law couple who have not been joined by a civil ceremony and may separate at will, it is impossible to justify, under equal protection principles, withholding the same recognition from a union which meets all the requirements of a marriage in New York but for the sexual orientation of its partners." From the perspective of New York wrongful death policy, "[t]he civil union is indistinguishable for societal purposes from the nuclear family and marriage."

NOTES ON INTERSTATE RECOGNITION OF SAME–SEX UNIONS OR MARRIAGES

1. *General Principles of State Choice of Law.* Justice Dunne's opinion in *Langan* illustrates several features that will characterize the ongoing legal issues posed by state-recognized same-sex unions and marriages: (a) The issues will generally be ones of state law—specifically, the interpretation of various statutes enacted by the state receiving a same-sex couple married or joined in civil union elsewhere. (b) Those state statutes will use terms like "spouse" that require the court to decide whether to recognize the status conferred on the couple by the "foreign" law. This is a classic *choice of law* problem.[c] (c) Judges will have to consider constitutional issues that would be presented if they do not give effect to foreign law. In short, judges confronting same-sex couples married or joined in civil union will have to apply general principles of statutory interpretation, choice of law, and constitutional interpretation to the cases before them.

Most states follow the *celebration rule*, recognizing any out-of-state marriage and enforcing its benefits and obligations so long as the marriage was valid in the state of celebration. (Justice Dunne was following the celebration rule in *Langan*.) Thus, states have recognized valid outofstate common law marriages, e.g., *Parish v. Minvielle*, 217 So.2d 684, 688 (La.Ct.App.1969); child marriages, e.g., *Wilkins v. Zelichowski*, 129 A.2d 459 (N.J.Super.1957); and first-cousin marriages, e.g., *In re Miller's Estate*, 214 N.W. 428 (Mich.1927), even though such marriages could not have been entered in the recognizing state. Recognition is particularly likely when there has been private reliance on the marital status of the parties or when a challenge to the marriage is otherwise inequitable.

On the other hand, most states say they will usually not recognize out-of-state marriages contrary to the state's public policy, especially if the state's residents have repaired to the other state to evade their home state's marriage limits. *E.g.*, *In re Mortenson's Estate*, 316 P.2d 1106 (Ariz.1957); "Developments in the Law—The Law of Marriage and the Family," 116 *Harv. L. Rev.* 1996, 2038–40 (2003). This *public policy exception* to the celebration rule is less likely to be invoked as to migratory marriages (where a couple is validly married in the state of their domicile and then move to the forum state) and much less likely to be invoked as to extraterritorial marriages (where a couple remains domiciled in the state of their marriage but have a legal dispute in the forum state). See *id.* at 2040–43. Analyzing almost a century's worth of miscegenation cases, Andrew Koppelman found that even apartheid-era southern courts would recognize different-race marriages when the couple did not cohabitate within the

---

c. Excellent introductions to the technical issues and interstate recognition of same-sex marriages are Barbara Cox, "Same–Sex Marriage and Choice of Law: If We Marry in Hawaii, Are We Still Married When We Return Home?," 1994 *Wis. L. Rev.* 1033; An-drew Koppelman, "Same–Sex Marriage, Choice of Law, and Public Policy," 76 *Tex. L. Rev.* 921 (1998); and Linda Silberman, "Can the Island of Hawaii Rule the World? A Comment on Same–Sex Marriage and Federalism Values," 16 *QLR* 191 (1996).

forum. See Koppelman, *The Gay Rights Question in Contemporary American Law* (2002).

2. *State Nonrecognition Statutes (Junior–DOMAs).* With same-sex marriage on the horizon in the mid–1990s, traditional family values groups urged legislative preemptive strikes to head off the possibility that a single same-sex marriage would ever be recognized. Within months of the first *Baehr* decision, Utah amended its marriage law to provide that marriages "between persons of the same sex" are "prohibited and declared void." 1993 Utah Laws (2d Spec. Sess.) ch. 14, § 1. This *definition of marriage* statute was similar to those adopted in the 1970s, when the issue was first being litigated. Within two years of the decision, Utah further amended its marriage law to direct that its state courts will not recognize same-sex marriages entered into elsewhere. 1995 Utah Laws ch. 146. Utah's 1995 law was the first *nonrecognition* statute aimed only at same-sex marriage, but it was by no means the last.

Between 1995 and 2005, more than forty states have joined Utah in legislating against recognition of same-sex marriages in their courts. (Like most other states in the Northeast, New York has not, as of 2005, adopted such a law, so Justice Dunne did not have to deal with this issue in *Langan*.) Most jurisdictions followed the Utah approach of simply directing that same-sex marriages were invalid in their states and would not be recognized. Some states went further. In Virginia: "Any marriage entered into by persons of the same sex in another state or jurisdiction shall be void in all respects in Virginia and any contractual rights created by such marriage shall be void and unenforceable." 1997 Va. Stats. ch. 354.

The most elaborate response was Georgia's (1996), which not only defined marriage to be inherently different-sex and prohibited any kind of legal recognition of same-sex marriages, but tried to nail down any possible evasion:

> No marriage between persons of the same sex shall be recognized as entitled to the benefits of marriage. Any marriage entered into by persons of the same sex pursuant to a marriage license issued by another state or foreign jurisdiction or otherwise shall be void in this state. Any contractual rights granted by virtue of such license shall be unenforceable in the courts of this state and the courts of this state shall have no jurisdiction whatsoever under any circumstances to grant a divorce or separate maintenance with respect to such marriage or otherwise to consider or rule on any of the parties' respective rights arising as a result of or in connection with such marriage. [Ga. Code § 19–3–3.1(b).]

Why did Georgia adopt such a broad nonrecognition statute?

3. *Constitutional Issues.* The foregoing statutes, especially the few that are broad, pose a variety of constitutional and interpretive problems and uncertainties. In *Langan*, Justice Dunne pointed to the different treatment of same-sex cohabiting couples and different-sex cohabiting couples that would result if he did not recognize the civil union as creating a legal spousehood. After *Romer* and *Lawrence*, the burden has shifted in some states: No longer can the state ignore same-sex couples when it creates entitlements for unmarried straight couples. *Romer* might also create problems for nonrecognition laws as broad as Georgia's, which (like the *Romer* initiative) was unprecedented and seems to close off state courts to lesbian and gay couples in a broad array of situations. Georgia could argue that it only meant to protect marriage and not to express "animus" against gay people, but Colorado had made the same argument without success in *Romer*.

Other constitutional problems are posed by the first sentence of the U.S. Constitution's Full Faith and Credit Clause (FFCC): "Full Faith and Credit shall be given in each State to the public Acts, Records, and judicial Proceedings of every other State. And the Congress may by general Laws prescribe the Manner in which such Acts, Records, and Proceedings shall be proved, and the Effect thereof." U.S. Const., art. IV, § 1. Although the policy of the clause is to assure interstate harmony of rights and obligations, it has not been interpreted to impose severe limits on a state's ability to choose to apply its own law in its own courts. See *Allstate Ins. Co. v. Hague*, 449 U.S. 302 (1981).

The constitutional analysis changes significantly if a state refuses to enforce another state's valid judgment. The Supreme Court has ruled that the FFCC does require a state to recognize and enforce valid judgments entered by the courts of a sibling state, even where the legal conclusions underlying the judgment violate the state's public policy. See *Baker v. General Motors*, 522 U.S. 222 (1998); *Fauntleroy v. Lum*, 210 U.S. 230 (1908). Thus, a judgment from a court in State A allocating community property and assigning support obligations would be presumptively given full faith and credit in the courts of State B—even if State B's courts disagreed strongly with the legal foundations for the judgment. But a marriage license is not a judgment, even when it is issued by a judicial official, because it is not rendered after an adversary proceeding where rights and duties are adjudicated.

PROBLEM 9–2

INTERSTATE RECOGNITION OF SAME–SEX MARRIAGES?

This exercise asks you to apply what you have just learned to three different situations:

(1) same-sex couple lawfully married in State A lives in State B. Partner 1 dies because of the negligence of a hospital. Partner 2 sues the hospital for her emotional and other losses, which are allowed under the laws of State B only for spouses of victims. The hospital argues that Partner 2 is not a spouse. (This is the *Langan* scenario.)

(2) The same-sex couple live in State A, where they were married, but own property in State B. Partner 1 dies, and a probate court decree in State A determines that the surviving partner now owns the property

in State B. Blood relatives of the deceased sue in State B to control the property under State B's intestacy laws.

(3) The same-sex couple break up and enter into a separation agreement in State A; they later divorce, and the divorce decree incorporates the separation agreement. The separation agreement vests property in State B with Partner 2. Partner 1 reneges and sues in State B, on the ground that the property was hers and that the agreement is unenforceable in State B.

Justice Dunne would follow the foreign law in each scenario, and it seems likely that the New York Court of Appeals would agree with him. But New York is one of the few states that has not adopted a junior-DOMA.

These problems are more difficult in jurisdictions which have junior-DOMAs. Assume that Utah, Georgia, and Virginia are each "State B" for purposes of these examples. In each case, Partner 2 argues that the law or judgment of State A controls the disposition of the case, and that State B's courts should not apply their state's non-recognition statute, either as a matter of statutory interpretation or constitutional compulsion (or both). The hospital, the blood relatives, and the reneging partner argue that State B's non-recognition statute precludes relief for Partner 2. Note 2 above quotes the non-recognition statute for each state, and you must start with those statutory texts. How would a typical judge in Utah, Georgia, and Virginia rule as to each issue? You might also consider whether DOMA "saves" any of the state laws that are unconstitutional. See Andrew Koppelman, *The Gay Rights Question in Contemporary American Law* 127–40 (2002); *Citizens for Equal Protection, Inc. v. Bruning*, 368 F.Supp.2d 980 (D.Neb. 2005) (striking down, on First Amendment grounds, Nebraska's broad junior-DOMA).

PART C.   IS THE SAME–SEX MARRIAGE MOVEMENT A QUEER ERROR?

The same-sex marriage movement surely appears very queer to Martha Fineman. Why do gay men and (especially) lesbians want to join this outmoded, patriarchal institution? Shouldn't gay people be the first to join her proposal to end civil marriage as a benefits-conferring institution? Some have. See, *e.g.*, Ruthann Robson, *Lesbian (Out)Law: Survival Under the Rule of Law* (1992); Claudia Card, "Against Marriage and Motherhood," 11 *Hypatia*, Summer 1996, at 1; Martha Ertman, "Reconstructing Marriage: An InterSexual Appoach," 75 *Denver U.L. Rev.* 1215 (1998) (privatization of personal relationships through commercial contracts).

Constitutional liberals maintain that queer couples should have all the same rights and duties as straight couples. Even though many straight couples never marry, many do—and lesbian and gay couples ought to have the same option. Constitutional progressives (like most of the feminist and race theorists surveyed in Chapter 5) respond that having the same rights to an oppressive institution is hardly equality. For progressives equality must be more than formal; it must be transformative. Queer theorists have taken up this theme to interrogate the same-sex marriage movement, and their challenges have provoked responses from gay liberals and their allies.

Paula Ettelbrick, "Since When Is Marriage a Path to Liberation?"

OUT/LOOK, Autumn 1989, Pages 8–12.*

* * * Marriage runs contrary to two of the primary goals of the lesbian and gay movement: the affirmation of gay identity and culture and the validation of many forms of relationships. * * *

The fight for justice has as its goal the realignment of power imbalances among individuals and classes of people in society. A pure "rights" analysis often fails to incorporate a broader understanding of the underlying inequities that operate to deny justice to a fuller range of people and groups. * * * At this point in time, making legal marriage for lesbian and gay couples a priority would set an agenda of gaining rights for a few, but would do nothing to correct power imbalances between those who are married (whether gay or straight) and those who are not. Thus, justice would not be gained.

Justice for gay men and lesbians will be achieved only when we are accepted and supported in this society *despite* our difference from the dominant culture and the choices we make regarding our relationships. * * * Being queer means pushing the parameters of sex, sexuality, and family, and in the process transforming the very fabric of society. Gay liberation is inexorably linked to women's liberation. Each is essential to the other.

The moment we argue, as some amongst us insist on doing, that we should be treated as equals because we are really just like married couples and hold the same values to be true, we undermine the very purpose of our movement and begin the dangerous process of silencing our different voices. As a lesbian, I am fundamentally different from nonlesbian women. That's the point. Marriage, as it exists today, is antithetical to my liberation as a lesbian and as a woman because it mainstreams my life and voice. I do not want to be known as "Mrs. Attached–To–Somebody–Else." Nor do I want to give the state the power to regulate my primary relationship. * * *

The thought of emphasizing our sameness to married heterosexuals in order to obtain this "right" terrifies me. It rips away the very heart and soul of what I believe it is to be a lesbian in this world. It robs me of the opportunity to make a difference. We end up mimicking all that is bad about the institution of marriage in our effort to appear to be the same as straight couples.

* Reprinted by permission of the author.

By looking to our sameness and deemphasizing our differences, we do not even place ourselves in a position of power that would allow us to transform marriage from an institution that emphasizes property and state regulation of relationships to an institution that recognizes one of many types of valid and respected relationships. * * * We would be perpetuating the elevation of married relationships and of "couples" in general, and further eclipsing other relationships of choice.

Ironically, gay marriage, instead of liberating gay sex and sexuality, would further outlaw all gay and lesbian sex that is not performed in a marital context. Just as sexually active nonmarried women face stigma and double standards around sex and sexual activity, so too would nonmarried gay people. * * *

Undoubtedly, whether we admit it or not, we all need to be accepted by the broader society. * * * Those closer to the norm or to power in this country are more likely to see marriage as a principle of freedom and equality. Those who are more acceptable to the mainstream because of race, gender, and economic status are more likely to want the right to marry. It is the final acceptance, the ultimate affirmation of identity.

On the other hand, more marginal members of the lesbian and gay community (women, people of color, working class and poor) are less likely to see marriage as having relevance to our struggles for survival. After all, what good is the affirmation of our relationships (that is, marital relationships) if we are rejected as women, people of color, or working class? * * *

If the laws change tomorrow and lesbians and gay men were allowed to marry, where would we find the incentive to continue the progressive movement we have started that is pushing for societal and legal recognition of all kinds of family relationships? To create other options and alternatives? * * * To get the law to acknowledge that we may have more than one relationship worthy of legal protection? * * *

Thomas Stoddard, "Why Gay People Should Seek the Right to Marry"

OUT/LOOK, Autumn 1989, Pages 8–12.*

* * * [D]espite the oppressive nature of marriage historically, and in spite of the general absence of edifying examples of modern heterosexual marriage, I believe very strongly that every lesbian and gay man should have the right to marry the same-sex partner of his or her choice, and that the gay rights movement should aggressively seek full legal recognition for same-sex marriages. To those who may not agree, I respectfully offer three explanations, one practical, one political, and one philosophical.

The legal status of marriage rewards the two individuals who travel to the altar (or its secular equivalent) with substantial economic and practical advantages. Married couples * * * are entitled to special government

* Reprinted by permission of the author.

benefits, such as those given surviving spouses and dependents through the Social Security program. They can inherit from one another even when there is no will. They are immune from subpoenas requiring testimony against the other spouse. And marriage to an American citizen gives a foreigner a right to residency in the United States.

Other advantages have arisen not by law but by custom. Most employers offer health insurance to their employees, and many will include an employer's spouse in the benefits package, usually at the employer's expense. Virtually no employer will include a partner who is not married to an employee, whether of the same sex or not. * * *

In short, the law generally presumes in favor of every marital relationship, and acts to preserve and foster it, and to enhance the rights of the individuals who enter into it. It is usually possible, with enough money and the right advice, to replicate some of the benefits conferred by the legal status of marriage through the use of documents like wills and power-of-attorney forms, but that protection will inevitably, under current circumstances, be incomplete. [Stoddard notes the "suspicion" many judges cast upon documents protecting lesbian and gay families, the cost of obtaining such documents, and the inability of private contracting to affect the public advantages of marriage, such as spousal immunities.]

* * * Why devote resources to such a distant goal? Because marriage is, I believe, the political issue that most fully tests the dedication of people who are not gay to full equality for gay people, and it is also the issue most likely to lead ultimately to a world free from discrimination against lesbians and gay men.

Marriage is much more than a relationship sanctioned by law. It is the centerpiece of our entire social structure, the core of the traditional notion of "family." Even in its present tarnished state, the marital relationship inspires sentiments suggesting that it is something almost suprahuman. The Supreme Court, in striking down an anti-contraception statute in 1965, called marriage "noble" and "intimate to the degree of being sacred." * * *

Lesbians and gay men are now denied entry to this "noble" and "sacred" institution. The implicit message is this: two men or two women are incapable of achieving such an exalted domestic state. Gay relationships are somehow less significant, less valuable. Such relationships may, from time to time and from couple to couple, give the appearance of a marriage, but they can never be of the same quality or importance.

I resent—indeed, I loathe—that conception of same-sex relationships. And I am convinced that ultimately the only way to overturn it is to remove the barrier to marriage that now limits the freedom of every gay man and lesbian. * * *

I confessed at the outset that I personally found marriage in its present state rather unattractive. Nonetheless, even from a philosophical perspective, I believe the right to marry should become a goal of the gay-rights movement.

First, and most basically, the issue is not the desirability of marriage, but rather the desirability of the *right* to marry. That I think two lesbians or two gay men should be entitled to a marriage license does not mean that I think all gay people should find appropriate partners and exercise the right, should it eventually exist. * * *

Furthermore, marriage may be unattractive and even oppressive as it is currently structured and practiced, but enlarging the concept to embrace same-sex couples would necessarily transform it into something new. If two women can marry, or two men, marriage—even for heterosexuals—need not be a union of a "husband" and a "wife." Extending the right to marry to gay people—that is, abolishing the traditional gender requirements of marriage—can be one of the means, perhaps the principal one, through which the institution divests itself of the sexist trappings of the past. * * *

NOTES ON THE ETTELBRICK–STODDARD DEBATE

The Ettelbrick–Stoddard exchange triggered a debate within the lesbian, gay, bisexual, and transgendered community over whether the right to marry should be a priority. Consider some key points of disagreement:[d]

1. *Assimilation Anxiety and Reduced Radicalism.* Ettelbrick argues for radical transformation and faults the same-sex marriage aspiration for sacrificing the transformative features of gay liberation. Nancy Polikoff's similar indictment lays much of the blame at the feet of lawyers and other social movement leaders: "Demands for social change often have begun with a movement at first articulating the rhetoric of radical transformation and then later discarding that rhetoric to make the demands more socially acceptable. The movement's rhetoric is modified or altered when those opposing reform explore the radical and transformative possibilities of that

d. For an introduction to the debate within the lesbian and gay community, see Cheshire Calhoun, *Feminism, the Family, and the Politics of the Closet: Lesbian and Gay Displacement* (2000); William Eskridge, Jr., *The Case for Same–Sex Marriage* (1996), and *Equality Practice: Civil Unions and the Future of Gay Rights* 197–230 (2002); Morris Kaplan, *Sexual Justice: Democratic Citizenship and the Politics of Desire* (1997); Richard Mohr, *A More Perfect Union: Why Straight America Must Stand Up for Gay Rights* ch. 3 (1994); "Noose or Knot? The Debate Over Lesbian Marriage," *OUT/WEEK*, Sept. 18, 1989, at 38–43 (articles by Sarah Petitt, Ashley McNeely, and Catherine Saalfield); Carlos Ball, "Moral Foundations for a Discourse on Same–Sex Marriage: Looking Beyond Political Liberalism," 85 *Geo. L.J.* 1872 (1997); Mary Coombs, "Sexual Dis–Orientation: Transgendered People and Same–Sex Marriage," 8 *UCLA Women's L.J.* 219 (1998); Nitya Duclos, "Some Complicating Thoughts on Same–Sex Marriage," 1 Law & Sexuality 31 (1991); Marc Fajer, "Can Two Real Men Eat Quiche Together? Storytelling, Gender–Role Stereotypes, and Legal Protection for Lesbians and Gay Men," 46 *U. Miami L. Rev.* 511 (1992); Katherine Franke, "Becoming a Citizen: Reconstruction Era Regulation of African American Marriages," 11 *Yale J.L. & Hum.* 251 (1999); Nan D. Hunter, "Marriage, Law, and Gender: A Feminist Inquiry," 1 *Law & Sexuality* 9 (1991); Christine Pierce, "Gay Marriage," 26 *J. Soc. Phil.*, Fall 1995, at 5–16; Nancy Polikoff, "We Will Get What We Ask For: Why Legalizing Gay and Lesbian Marriage Will Not 'Dismantle the Legal Structure of Gender in Every Marriage,' " 79 *Va. L. Rev.* 1535 (1993); Ruthann Robson, "Assimilation, Marriage, and Lesbian Liberation," 75 *Temple L. Rev.* 709 (2002); Evan Wolfson, "Crossing the Threshold: Equal Marriage Rights for Lesbians and Gay Men and the Intra–Community Critique," 21 *NYU Rev. L. & Soc. Change* 567 (1994–95).

rhetoric, causing its advocates to issue reassurances promising that such transformation is not what the movement is about at all." (Polikoff, "We Will Get What We Ask For," 1541–42.)

Assume that same-sex marriage supporters favor a higher degree of assimilation into the American mainstream. What, exactly, is *wrong* with assimilation? Public opinion polls suggest that large majorities of lesbians, gay men, bisexuals, and transgendered people would like to have the option of civil marriage. Surveys taken by the National Gay and Lesbian Task Force, including a 2002 sample focused on gay people of color, have found the same. Is Ettelbrick concerned that these attitudes represent some kind of false consciousness that needs to be changed through queer education and experience?

Consider the relevance of Foucault (Chapter 5, Section 3A) for Ettelbrick's argument. Drawing from Georges Canguilhem, *The Normal and the Pathological* (1966), Foucault maintained that liberal polities ostensibly committed to free choice nonetheless coerced decisions through processes like *normalization*, whereby social pressure to conform to a perceived norm pervasively influences people's decisions and flattens out nonconformity. Ettelbrick's concern dovetails with this kind of thinking: The normalizing feature of marriage—the social pressure on *everyone* to get married to pretty much *anyone* of the opposite sex—has terrorized women and minorities for generations. Couples are now following the lead of early feminist thinkers and working out their lives outside of marriage. By valorizing and even romanticizing marriage, the same-sex marriage movement is buttressing that institution and contributing to its normalizing power, which is exactly what lesbians and gay men ought to be opposing and resisting.

On the other hand, Cheshire Calhoun maintains that the powerful normalization in the debate is not married/unmarried, but heterosexual/homosexual (Calhoun, *Politics of the Closet* 121–31). According to traditionalist opponents of same-sex marriage, lesbians, bisexuals, and gay men are weird, and recognizing their marriages would be *really* weird. Much of the population is resistant to same-sex marriage because of homophobia, which of course is harmful to all gay people. By admitting gay people into a fundamental mainstream institution, same-sex marriage would contribute to the *de*normalization of heterosexuality.

Also, it is wrong to assume that the struggle for same-sex marriage precludes the creation of other institutions for recognition of same-sex unions (Eskridge, *Equality Practice* 210–13). As the Vermont and Hawaii experiences suggest, the compromises that proponents make on the path toward same-sex marriage will sometimes create new institutional norms for thinking about human relationships. Why not a choice-among-alternatives approach, in which couples could choose among do-it-yourself structures for their relationship, by means of informal agreements and formal contracts; registered domestic partnership and other novel legal forms of relationship recognition, that would provide some off-the-rack rules and public legal benefits but that would be easy to terminate; and marriage, with lots of off-the-rack benefits and obligations that are difficult to terminate.

Critics of same-sex marriage believe that marriage will drain any support from the domestic partnership movement or for other institutional alternatives to marriage. Is that so? The experience in Europe creates some doubt. The Netherlands adopted a registered partnership law in 1997, a new institution open to different-sex as well as same-sex couples. When it recognized same-sex marriages in 2000–01, it left the other institution in place. Most of the couples registering as partners have been different-sex. The same has been true of the new *pactes civils* created by France in 1999.

2. *Does Same–Sex Marriage Invite Too Much State Regulation of Sexual and Gender Minorities?* Legally recognized marriage imposes costs on the partners that may be particularly unwelcome to lesbian and gay couples, especially those who are not middle class (Duclos, "Complicating Thoughts," 52–55). For example, some state welfare or other security benefits are reduced or eliminated if the recipient has a spouse who can support him or her economically. Also, marriage, unlike domestic partnership, entails mutual fidelity and support obligations and usually involves the state if the couple wants to dissolve their relationship. The state involvement in one's relationship and the terms of its dissolution would be unwelcome to some couples, if not at the time of their marriage, at least at the time of their breakup.

Some queer critics have an unstated queasiness regarding state regulation of sexual behavior. Recall Gayle Rubin's critique of America's pervasive sex negativity, Chapter 5, Section 2B. It is mobilized by arguments that gay marriage would be a modest contribution to the public health campaign against AIDS, because marriage would assertedly reduce the number of sexual partners and increase the partners' altruistic concern for one another's health. This recalls the Foucault–Canguilhem idea. If same-sex marriage contributed to the normalization of monogamy or fewer sexual partners, that would derogate from gay liberation's valorization of sex as a fabulous experience that should be enjoyed frequently. On the other hand, same-sex marriage could be understood as a critique of "excessive" liberation.

3. *Would Same–Sex Marriage Change the Institution for the Better?* One of us has argued: "Marriage between men or between women could also destabilize the cultural meaning of marriage. It would create for the first time the possibility of marriage as a relationship between members of the same social status categories. However valiantly individuals try to build marriages grounded on genuine equality, no person can erase his or her status in the world as male or female, or create a home life apart from culture. same-sex marriage could create the model in law for an egalitarian kind of interpersonal relation, outside the gendered terms of power, for many marriages. At the least, it would radically strengthen and dramatically illuminate the claim that marriage partners are presumptively equal." (Hunter, "Marriage, Law, and Gender," 11.)

Nancy Polikoff responded, based upon evidence that the other of us collected! "[M]ost of the marriages Eskridge uncovered support rather than subvert hierarchy based upon gender. His historical and anthropological evidence contradicts any assumption that 'gender dissent' is inherent in marriage between two men or two women. Rather, most of the unions reported were in fact gendered. Although both partners were biologically of the same sex, one partner tended to assume the characteristics and responsibilities of the opposite gender, with both partners then acting out their traditional gender roles." (Polikoff, "What We Ask For," 1538; see Eskridge, *Case for Same–Sex Marriage* ch. 2.) Most of the evidence Polikoff invokes, however, is from premodern societies where unequal gender roles were part of the cultural terrain.

Supporting Hunter's point is a belief that same-sex unions will not only delink gender from family roles, but also will allocate roles more equally. A lesbian family is less likely to have Working Mom and House-keeper Mom and more likely to have parents who share income-generating and household tasks. A growing amount of empirical data supports this contention, but it is far from proven. *E.g.*, Lawrence Kurdek, "The Allocation of Household Labor in Gay, Lesbian, and Heterosexual Married Couples," 49 *J. Soc. Issues* 127 (1993); see generally M.V. Lee Badgett, *Money, Myths, and Change: The Economic Lives of Lesbians and Gay Men* 144–51 (2001) (surveying the empirical studies).

NOTES ON THE CONSTITUTIONALITY OF OTHER RESTRICTIONS ON MARRIAGE

1. *Age Restrictions.* In all 50 states and the District of Columbia, eighteen-year-olds can marry. If the children's parents consent, all 50 states plus the District of Columbia allow seventeen-year-olds to marry as well; almost all states allow sixteen-year-olds to marry under such circumstances. Most states allow fourteen-year-olds to marry if the marriage is agreed to by the parents and supported by a court order. Some states allow children under eighteen years old to marry if the female is pregnant or has borne a child by the male; in these cases parental consent is usually not required. Because these laws do not work a permanent deprivation of the right to marry and involve a non-fishy classification (age), they are easily sustainable.

2. *Incest Rules.* All 50 states and the District of Columbia prohibit "incestuous" marriages, including parent-child, grandparent-grandchild, aunt-nephew, uncle-niece, brother-sister marriages. All but a dozen states prohibit marriages by first cousins. Some states prohibit marriages by step-relatives, that is, persons related within the prohibited degree, but only by marriage and not by blood. Are all these restrictions constitutional? Most controversy has focused on incest by *affinity* (relationship through others' marriages). Not only do most states not consider affinity-based relationships to be criminal incest, see Martha Mahoney, "A Legal Definition of the Stepfamily: The Example of Incest Regulation," 8 *BYU J. Pub. L.* 21

(1993), but commentators and some judges consider their criminalization constitutionally questionable. See Brett McDonnell, "Is Incest Next?," *Cardozo Women's L.J.* (2003) (post-Lawrence analysis); Christine McNiece Metteer, "Some 'Incest' Is Harmless Incest," 10 *Kan. J.L. & Pub. Pol'y* 262 (2000).

In *Israel v. Allen,* 577 P.2d 762 (Colo. 1978), the state court ruled that the state could not constitutionally bar marriage between siblings by marriage. Although invoking *Zablocki,* which applied heightened scrutiny, the court found no rational basis. The state's main justification was "family harmony." The court was unpersuaded, in part because the family (and even the Catholic Church) supported the couple's marriage. Although the court reaffirmed the validity of state bars to marriage by persons related "by blood," it questioned the applicability of that rule to persons related only by marriage or adoption.

Compare *Rhodes v. McAfee,* 457 S.W.2d 522 (Tenn. 1970), which annulled the marriage between a man and his stepdaughter.

> This case is a good example of why such marriages are prohibited. The stepdaughter lived in the home with the mother and the stepfather from the date of the marriage of the mother and stepfather until their divorce * * *. The stepdaughter's status in the family would be closely akin to the natural children of a mother and stepfather, who, in fact, were her half brothers and sisters. If there were no statutes prohibiting such marriages, there not only could but very likely would result in discord and disharmony in the family.

The court cited no evidence for the last proposition. Which court gets it right?

Like most of the commentators, *Israel* views marriage between blood relatives differently than relatives by adoption or affinity. But what is the rationale for prohibiting marriages of blood relatives? The court seems to think it is biological—"the physical detriment to the offspring of persons related by blood." Biologists say that there is virtually no eugenic reason to prohibit marriages among close relatives; even brother-sister marriages pose little risk of genetic defects. The evidence is assembled in Carolyn Bratt, "Incest Statutes and the Fundamental Right of Marriage: Is Oedipus Free to Marry?," 18 *Family L.Q.* 257 (1984). Professor Bratt thinks that Oedipus has a *Zablocki* right to marry his mother, Jocasta. Does he? Could the *Israel* court accept that?

Michel Foucault (chapter 5) thought the incest taboo is a product of the modern construction of childhood sexuality. The home has been sexualized at least since Freud, but the law exists to keep that sexuality within bounds. Foucault opposed the taboo and maintained that the discourse of incest itself sexualizes the family and contributes to the impulse to commit incest. See also Judith Butler, *Antigone's Claim: Kinship Between Life and Death* 70 (2000). You can press Foucault's insight in either direction. Like Foucault, you might use it to strike down all incest prohibitions and allow Oedipus to marry his mother, Jocasta (but he may not kill his father to do so). Contra Foucault, you might justify all sorts of affinity-based incest rules and sustain Colorado's objections to the Israel marriage. If the state concern is an effort to control sexuality in the home, should it make a difference that Tammy Lee and Richard were adoptive rather than blood siblings? Note, also, the disparity in ages: Richard was a legal adult and Tammy Lee still a child when their parents married. Should that make a difference?

Gayle Rubin, "The Traffic in Women: Notes on the 'Political Economy of Sex,' " in *Toward an Anthropology of Women* 157, 173–77 (Rayna Reiter ed. 1975), argues that the incest taboo is the origin of sex inequality. In many societies, including early western ones, families formed alliances by exchanging gifts. In these societies, marriage is the most basic form of gift exchange—whereby a bride is given by her family in exchange for the groom's loyalty, and an alliance between the families is cemented. (This root idea is reenacted every day in marriage modern ceremonies where the father "gives away" the bride, a gift that is gratefully "accepted" by the groom.) The incest taboo, by Rubin's reading, is a mechanism to assure that these gift exchanges take place between rather than within families. The inter-family bonds enable the larger group to create ever more complex social structures. How should Rubin's argument cut in *Israel*?

3.   *Polygamy.* All 50 states and the District of Columbia prohibit bigamy, marriage to more than one person at the same time. The Supreme Court upheld a federal law making polygamy a crime in *Reynolds v. United States*, 98 U.S. 145 (1878). Much of the reasoning is dated, to say the least. E.g., "Polygamy has always been odious among the northern and western nations of Europe, and, until the establishment of the Mormon Church, was almost exclusively a feature of the life of Asiatic and African people." Is there a better argument against polygamy today?

Many opponents of same-sex marriage invoke polygamy. If same-sex marriages have to be recognized, why not polygamous unions? Arguing that polygamy involves denigration of women, Maura Strassberg distinguishes the two in "Distinctions of Form or Substance: Monogamy, Polygamy, and Same–Sex Marriage," 75 *N.C. L. Rev.* 1557 (1997). For a response, arguing that both polygamy and gay marriage have been unfairly demonized, see David Chambers, "Polygamy and Same–Sex Marriage," 26 *Hofstra L. Rev.* 53 (1997).

CHILDREN IN FAMILIES OF CHOICE

Family law has traditionally assumed that children are raised by their biological parents in their marital household. What Professor Katharine Bartlett has called the factual "premise of the nuclear family" (husband-wife-kids) has now evaporated as a realistic assumption.[a] The 2000 Census found that the nuclear family now constitutes fewer than one-quarter of American households. Almost as many children are being raised in the United States by unmarried cohabiting couples as by married couples. Millions of children are being raised by lesbian and gay parents. Single parents now constitute nearly one-third of the households with children. Single mothers head 26% of the households with children (up from 12% in 1970), single fathers 5% (up from 1% in 1970).

A broader perspective associates this trend with trends in sexual behavior. Today, sex within adult relationships has been delinked from the existence of children in the family. Not only does sex rarely lead to children, but children in a family are, increasingly, not the biological progeny of the two parents. The law has contributed to this delinkage, through liberalization of rules governing sexual behavior, contraception and abortion, divorce and remarriage, surrogacy, adoption, (shared) custody, and de facto or psychological parenthood. Technological developments have contributed both to law's liberalization and to new problems for the law. For example, the availability of artificial insemination at prices many middle class people can afford has spawned surrogacy contracts, single parenting by women, the lesbian baby boom, and the "gay-by boom."

In short, the typical American child is no longer raised by a husband and wife who are married to one another and are the biological parents of the child. There is no typical American childrearing script anymore. Some children are raised by their biological parents in nuclear families, others are raised in nuclear families where only one parent is biologically related, yet others are raised by single biological parents, some are raised by their biological grandparents or other relatives, and still others are raised by persons not related to them by blood.

The evaporation of the premise of the nuclear family has undermined family law's traditional rules relating to child-rearing. Under those rules,

---

a. Katharine Bartlett, "Rethinking Parenthood as an Exclusive Status: The Need for Legal Alternatives When the Premise of the Nuclear Family Has Failed," 70 *Va. L. Rev.* 879 (1984). See also Martha Albertson Fineman, "Our Sacred Institution: The Ideal of the Family in American Law and Society," 1993 *Utah L. Rev.* 387; Richard Storrow, "The Policy of Family Privacy: Uncovering the Bias in Favor of Nuclear Families in American Constitutional Law and Policy Reform," 66 *Mo. L. Rev.* 527 (2001).

the married biological parents have plenary and exclusive rights to raise their children, without much interference from the state or third parties unless they are patently unfit. See *Meyer v. Nebraska*, 262 U.S. 390 (1923) (the right to raise one's children is a constitutionally protected liberty interest). Those rules do not provide sufficient guidance when the child's biological parents separate or divorce, when the child has been orphaned and is placed in an adoptive home, when the child has been conceived as a result of a surrogacy contract between her biological mother and father, or when the child is raised by one biological parent and a non-biological parent. Moreover, the *Meyer* rule of exclusive parental control has given way in many circumstances to the modern family law rule that decisions regarding children should ultimately be guided by the "best interests of the child" standard.

Family law has struggled for a generation to figure out new rules to effectuate the best interests of the child in these new circumstances. This struggle has involved judicial decisions interpreting statutes and constitutions, as well as statutory reforms, typically drawn from model laws developed by family law experts. Judicial and legislative adaptation of family law to these new social and technological circumstances profoundly affects the ability of women, gays, and transgendered people to form households and families. We introduce the materials that follow in a functional sequence: legal rules that disrupt the relationship between a parent and her or his biological child, especially determinations of child custody when parents are at loggerheads; adoption and de facto parenting rules that create a parent-child relationship not based upon blood; and the new legal phenomenon we call *polyparenting*, whereby more than two adults have legal relationships with children. As you read these materials, consider several normative themes relating to sexuality, gender, and the law of parenting.

One theme is the tension between the preferences and desires of parents and the "best interests of the child." Under the old regime, where married parents were raising their biological children, the state almost never intervened, upon the apparent assumption that the parents acting jointly would act in the best interests of their children. (Sociobiology suggests that this is a robust assumption.) Once the premise of the nuclear family evaporated, judges and other legal decisionmakers have been confronted with an increasing number of cases where they cannot fall back on the former assumption and must arbitrate claims made by competing adults or, in some cases, must consider social anxieties surrounding certain kinds of putative parents, especially gay, lesbian, bisexual, and transgendered parents. Judges and legislators have to think hard about what criteria are relevant in determining a child's best interests.

Relatedly, the law of parenting has become a battleground in the culture wars. It is a social fact that lesbians and gay men are successfully raising millions of children. This was in tension with a legal culture accepting the teaching of *Bowers v. Hardwick*, that "[n]o connection between family * * * on the one hand and homosexual activity on the other has been demonstrated," 478 U.S. at 191. The *Bowers* philosophy justified state discrimination against lesbian, gay, bisexual, and even transgendered parents. But *Bowers* is no longer good law, and states cannot make private consensual sodomy a crime. Does *Lawrence* require a rethinking of parent-child law in traditionalist states? One consequence of *Lawrence* might be to end discriminations against lesbian and gay parents—but it is also possible that *Lawrence* will stimulate new research by traditionalists and their allies that will demonize lesbians, gay men, bisexuals, and transgendered people as "bad parents."

PART A.   CHILD CUSTODY AND VISITATION

The traditional rule in divorce cases was that custody of children was routinely awarded to the mother, with provision for alimony and child support by the father. The strong presumption of maternal custody was rebutted when the mother did not live up to maternal standards established by the courts—especially when she had engaged in sexual infidelity or, especially in the South, a romantic relationship with someone of another race. These norms reflected not only traditional gender stereotypes (the mother must be desexualized and nurturing), but also represented one of the ways that morality entered into state rulemaking. The morality involved fears of interracial sex and of sexualizing the child's household environment. Is either of these moral factors a legitimate consideration in child custody determinations?

Generally, is it ever proper for the state to consider the morality of the parent in determining the "best interests of the child"? See generally of *Bezio v. Patenaude*, 410 N.E.2d 1207 (Mass. 1980) (custody and visitation decisions ought not be based upon social morality, but upon the child's best interests). In *Palmore v. Sidoti*, 466 U.S. 429 (1984), the Supreme Court ruled that Florida could *not* consider moral repugnance its citizens felt toward interracial relationships when its state judges made custody and visitation decisions. (The Florida judges had taken a child away from his mother when she married a black man. The judges reasoned that this relationship would be bad for the child, given the traditionalist mores of the community.) *Palmore*, of course, involves race-based distinctions. After *Lawrence*, is it constitutional for the state to consider the sex of the parent's sexual partner (or her sexual preference)? With some dramatic exceptions, *e.g.*, *Ex parte D.W.W.*, 717 So.2d 793 (Ala. 1998), even southern judges have been more cautious in their approach to custody battles involving lesbian or gay parents, but discriminatory treatment remains widespread.

Pamela Kay Bottoms v. Sharon Lynne Bottoms

Supreme Court of Virginia, 1995.
249 Va. 410, 457 S.E.2d 102.

■ COMPTON, JUSTICE. * * *

[The court summarized the facts as found by the trial court, which entered judgment transferring custody of Tyler Doustou from his mother,

Sharon Bottoms, to his grandmother, Pamela Kay Bottoms. The trial court judgment had been reversed on appeal, but the Supreme Court reinstated it.]

During the two-year period before the trial court hearing, the child had spent 70 percent of the time with the grandmother and 30 percent with his mother. The grandmother has kept the child for "weeks at a time" and during "every weekend since he's been born." On at least three occasions during that period, the mother left the child with the grandmother without informing her of the mother's whereabouts or how she could be reached "in the event something happened to the child."

Following the mother's separation from Doustou, she continued a "relationship" with another man that had begun during her marriage. She contracted a venereal disease during this relationship that prevents her from having additional children. During the child's first year, the mother "slept with two or three different guys, maybe four, in the same room" with the child "where his crib was." At the time, the mother "lived two blocks away" from the grandmother, and the mother kept the child's "suitcase packed" for visits to the grandmother's home. The mother said that she has "had trouble" with her temper, and that when the child was about "a year" old, she "popped him on his leg too hard a couple of times," and left her fingerprints there. She has had "counseling" in an effort to control her temper. * * *

Except for brief employment as a grocery store cashier, the mother had been unemployed during most of the three-year period prior to the trial court hearing. She was receiving "welfare money" which often was spent to "do her fingernails before the baby would get any food."

During May 1992, ten months before the juvenile court hearing, 16 months before the trial court hearing, and when her son was ten months old, the mother met April Wade, a lesbian. Wade, born in April 1966, had been discharged from the U.S. Army in 1986. Wade is a "recovering alcoholic." The mother and Wade "moved in together" in September 1992. From that time, with the exception of a two-week period, the mother and Wade have lived in "a lesbian relationship." According to the mother, the relationship involves hugging and kissing, patting "on the bottom," sleeping in the same bed, "fondling," and "oral sex." The mother testified that she loves Wade and that they "have a lifetime commitment."

At the time of the juvenile court hearing, the mother, the child, and Wade were living in a two-bedroom apartment with "Evelyn," another lesbian. "At one time," the child's bed was in the room where the mother and Wade slept, having "sex in the same bed." At one point in her testimony, however, when asked "how many times did you do it when the child was sleeping in the same bedroom," the mother responded, "None." She said that she and Wade displayed other signs of affection "in front of" the child.

Wade, employed as a gift shop manager, supports the mother. The pair lives in an apartment complex in Western Henrico County. Wade has become "a parent figure" to the child, who calls Wade "Da Da."

Two months before the petition for custody was filed, the mother revealed her lesbian relationship to the grandmother. This disclosure alienated the two. During the period after the juvenile court hearing, when regimented visitation with the mother began, the child demonstrated certain traits. For example, when the child returned to the grandmother from being with the mother, he would "stomp" his foot, tell himself to "go to the corner," and then would stand in the corner of a room, facing the wall. He curses, saying "shit" and "damn," language never used in the grandmother's home. On one occasion, when the mother and Wade "came to pick him up," the child "held his breath, turned purple. He didn't want to go with her," according to the grandmother. During a period in mid–1993, each time the mother "would come pick him up," the child would scream and cry.

Wade has admitted she "hit" the child. Also, on one occasion, when an argument developed between the mother and Wade, on the one hand, and the grandmother, on the other, about the timing of the exchange of the child for visitation, Wade said during the quarrel, "I might end up killing somebody." According to the grandmother, the child is "always neglected." For example, when the child returns to the grandmother's home, she testified that he "can't even sit down in the bathtub. That's neglect from changing his diaper. He is so red." * * *

The trial judge, announcing his decision from the bench at the conclusion of the hearing, said the dispute "presents the question ... whether the child's best interest is served by a transfer of the custody of the child from [his] mother to [his] maternal grandmother." Stating that the mother's conduct is "illegal," and constitutes a felony under the Commonwealth's criminal laws, and that "her conduct is immoral," the court recognized the "presumption in the law in favor of the custody being with the natural parent."

Mentioning the evidence of lesbianism and specified "other evidence" in the case not involving homosexual conduct, the trial court concluded from "all the facts and circumstances ... of the case," that "the custody will be with the grandmother."

The Court of Appeals concluded that "the evidence fails to prove" that the mother "abused or neglected her son, that her lesbian relationship with April Wade has or will have a deleterious effect on her son, or that she is an unfit parent." "To the contrary," said the Court of Appeals, the evidence showed that the mother "is and has been a fit and nurturing parent who has adequately provided and cared for her son. No evidence tended to prove that the child will be harmed by remaining with his mother." The court held "that the trial court abused its discretion by invoking the state's authority to take the child from the custody of his natural mother ... and by transferring custody to a nonparent, ... the child's maternal grandmother."

[The Virginia Supreme Court held that the court of appeals had not properly deferred to the trial court's findings of fact.]

We have held * * * that a lesbian mother is not per se an unfit parent. *Doe v. Doe*, 284 S.E.2d 799, 806 (1981). Conduct inherent in lesbianism is punishable as a Class 6 felony in the Commonwealth, Code § 18.2–361; thus, that conduct is another important consideration in determining custody.

And, while the legal rights of a parent should be respected in a custody proceeding, those technical rights may be disregarded if demanded by the interests of the child. In the present case, the record shows a mother who, although devoted to her son, refuses to subordinate her own desires and priorities to the child's welfare. For example, the mother disappears for days without informing the child's custodian of her whereabouts. She moves her residence from place to place, relying on others for support, and uses welfare funds to "do" her fingernails before buying food for the child. She has participated in illicit relationships with numerous men, acquiring a disease from one, and "sleeping" with men in the same room where the child's crib was located. To aid in her mobility, the mother keeps the child's suitcase packed so he can be quickly deposited at the grandmother's.

The mother has difficulty controlling her temper and, out of frustration, has struck the child when it was merely one year old with such force as to leave her fingerprints on his person. While in her care, she neglects to change and cleanse the child so that, when he returns from visitation with her, he is "red" and "can't even sit down in the bathtub."

Unlike *Doe*, relied on by the mother, there is proof in this case that the child has been harmed, at this young age, by the conditions under which he lives when with the mother for any extended period. For example, he has already demonstrated some disturbing traits. He uses vile language. He screams, holds his breath until he turns purple, and becomes emotionally upset when he must go to visit the mother. He appears confused about efforts at discipline, standing himself in a corner facing the wall for no apparent reason.

And, we shall not overlook the mother's relationship with Wade, and the environment in which the child would be raised if custody is awarded the mother. We have previously said that living daily under conditions stemming from active lesbianism practiced in the home may impose a burden upon a child by reason of the "social condemnation" attached to such an arrangement, which will inevitably afflict the child's relationships with its "peers and with the community at large." *Roe v. Roe*, 324 S.E.2d 691, 694 (1985). We do not retreat from that statement; such a result is likely under these facts. Also, Wade has struck the child and, when there was a dispute over visitation, she has threatened violence when her views were not accepted. * * *

■ KEENAN, JUSTICE, dissents with whom WHITING and LACY, JUSTICES, join. [Justice Keenan faulted the trial court for violating the *Doe* rule in its finding that Sharon Bottoms was *per se* unfit because she was a lesbian.

Because the trial court applied the wrong rule of law, its other findings cannot be rehabilitated, and the case should have been remanded for a new hearing.]

NOTE ON *BOTTOMS* AND THE MODERNIZATION AND SEDIMENTATION OF ANTIGAY DISCOURSE

Recall Reva Siegel's theory (Chapter 5, Section 3) that when a persecuted minority gains some social power to discredit prejudices and stereotypes against them, the empowered group will *modernize* its discourse and thereby strengthen the social disadvantage. Such a modernization of discourse is easily apparent in *Bottoms*, especially. The trial court's opinion was a relatively open expression of natural law reasoning, which impelled the intermediate appeals court to reverse. Under guise of "deference" to findings of fact, the Virginia Supreme Court then repackaged the trial judge's old-fashioned moralism under a modernized utilitarian analysis. So Justice Compton's justification emphasized *neither* Biblical and natural law arguments against sodomites *nor* medical arguments against diseased or predatory "homosexuals." Instead, the argumentation largely rested upon social utilitarian judgments about the "best interests of the child."

These cases also illustrate William Eskridge's response to Siegel (Chapter 4, Section 3) that the discourse is not modernized so much as it is *sedimented*. That is, the new social utilitarian tropes rest on top of older medical and natural law tropes; the natural law arguments retain their power for a diminishing audience and can be mobilized by cloaked references in the modernized discourse. Although there is plenty of evidence in the record to question the mother's parenting skills, Justice Compton signals his loyalty to the old tropes: Sharon Bottoms and her partner, we are reminded, are *criminals* because they are presumptive *sodomites* (the old natural law discourse)—but they are *bad mothers* to boot (the new best interests of the child discourse). Somehow these women's lack of maternal traits seems to be related to their *lesbian lifestyle* and their violation of sodomy laws. So the discourse is not just modernized, it is layered. The updating is a layer on top of the old ways of thinking.

Contrary to Siegel, the modernization does not necessarily strengthen the traditionalist case against lesbian and gay parenting. Instead, the modernization moves the discourse to the terrain of child psychology and legal rights. Justice Kennedy's opinion in *Romer* and Justice O'Connor's concurring opinion in *Lawrence* make it treacherous for a court to be perceived as taking away a child because of the mother's status; the *Palmore* analogy seems compelling after *Romer* and *Lawrence*. And because *Lawrence* invalidated Virginia's consensual sodomy law, Sharon Bottoms is no longer presumptively criminal. But judges can still present their result as one driven by the necessity of deferring to trial court findings of fact that establish Bottoms as a bad mother, not as a *per se* abominable "homosexual." But in future cases, this move will be harder to achieve, either because the lesbian mother or gay father does not present such an easy target or because the trial judge will not be so dedicated to finding facts that doom their claims.

In the post-*Lawrence* legal climate, abusive straight parents (e.g., the father in *D.W.W.*) will no longer be able to prevail. They may prevail in *Bottoms*-type cases, where there is more evidence of the gay or lesbian parent's own shortcomings—but perhaps not where a non-parent is challenging custody. See *Troxel v. Granville*, 530 U.S. 57 (2000), where the Court recognized a substantive due process right of a biological mother to control the rearing of her children, and overturning a statute allowing grandparents to exercise some control.

PART B. ADOPTION AND DE FACTO PARENTING

Anti-gay discrimination has been much less evident in state adoption rules than in its custody and visitation rules, perhaps in part because there is usually not a specific straight parent competing with the lesbian or gay parent. Florida is the only state that specifically bars gay people from adopting, but other states have rules that effectively exclude gay adoptions. E.g., Utah Stat. § 78–30–9, which prohibits adoptions by couples who are cohabiting rather than married. Reread the federal court decision upholding the Florida statute (Chapter 4) and consider the materials that follow.

Steven Lofton et al. v. Secretary of Department of Children and Social Services

United States Court of Appeals for the Eleventh Circuit, 2004.
358 F.3d 804, petition for en banc review denied, 377 F.3d 1275 (2004).

[Excerpted in Chapter 4]

Judith Stacey and Timothy Biblarz, "(How) Does Sexual Orientation of Parents Matter?," 66 *American Sociological Review* **159 (April 2001).** Professors Stacey and Biblarz found themselves puzzled by claims of some progay scholars that there are no material differences between children raised in lesbian households and those raised in straight households. They also felt that the small sample size of empirical studies undermined their utility. So Stacey and Biblarz carefully examined 21 studies comparing traits of children raised in gay and lesbian households with similarly situated children in straight households; they did a meta-analysis of 18 studies in that group. Their findings included the following:

Children's Gender Preferences and Behavior. The authors found significant differences in most of the studies, especially as to daughters. Drawing from several studies, Stacey and Biblarz report that daughters of lesbian parents were more open to gender-nonconforming play activities, including play with boys as well as girls, and were more interested in careers not traditionally pursued by women. Sons were nonconforming in their play activities but just as gender-conforming as other boys in their occupational goals and dress. "Such evidence, albeit limited, implies that lesbian parenting may free daughters and sons from a broad but uneven range of traditional gender prescriptions." The authors suggest that this effect owes more to gender than to sexual orientation—the fact that both parents are women, rather than that they are lesbians or bisexual women. They also speculate that this ought not be surprising from the perspective of feminist theory: "Children who derive their principal source of love, discipline, protection, and identification from women living independent of male domestic authority or influence should develop less stereotypical symbolic, emotional, practical, and behavioral gender repertoires."

Children's Sexual Preferences and Behavior. The evidence is very limited here; the best study is Fiona Tasker and Susan Golombok's longterm comparison of 25 children raised in lesbian households with 20 children raised in straight ones, *Growing Up in a Lesbian Family* (1997). All of the children were tracked into adulthood, and those raised in lesbian families had a much higher likelihood of enjoying homoerotic experiences (6 of 25, compared with 0 of 20) and were even more markedly different in their openness to such experiences (14 of 22, compared with 3 of 18). But they were not statistically more likely to self-identify as lesbian, gay, or bisexual. "Relative to their counterparts with heterosexual parents, the adolescent and young adult girls raised by lesbian mothers appear to have been more sexually adventurous and less chaste, whereas the sons of lesbians evince the opposite pattern—somewhat less sexually adventurous and more chaste (the finding was statistically significant for the 25–girl sample but not for the 18–boy sample). In other words, once again, children (especially girls) raised by lesbians appear to depart from traditional gender-based norms, while children raised by heterosexual mothers appear to conform to them."

Children's Mental Health. The 21 studies examined by Stacey and Biblarz revealed "no significant differences between children of lesbian mothers and children of heterosexual mothers in anxiety, depression, self-esteem, and numerous other measures of social and psychological adjustment. The roughly equivalent level of psychological well-being between these two groups holds true in studies that test children directly, rely on parents' reports, and solicit evaluations from teachers. The few significant differences found actually tend to favor children with lesbian mothers."

Parenting Practices. The authors found that lesbian mothers showed relatively little interest in pressuring their children in any particular direction as regards sexuality or gender role. The biggest differences in parenting styles, however, were that the "nonbiological lesbian co-mothers" were "more skilled at parenting and more involved with the children than are stepfathers" and that "lesbian partners * * * enjoy a greater level of synchronicity in parenting than do heterosexual partners." There was also evidence that the children recognized this and responded much more warmly to their lesbian comothers than to their stepfathers, and that children in lesbian families felt better able to discuss their sexual and gender development with their mothers than were children in straight families.

Parental Fitness. The "evidence to date provides no support for those, like Wardle (1997), who claim that lesbian mothers suffer greater levels of psychological difficulties (depression, low self-esteem) than do heterosexual mothers. On the contrary, the few differences observed in the studies suggest that these lesbian mothers actually display somewhat higher levels of positive psychological resources." In this area even more than the others, Stacey and Biblarz caution that these conclusions are provisional, given the lack of random samples and the relative homogeneity of the samples in most of the studies surveyed.

Other Psychological Indicia. Professors Stacey and Biblarz found that many areas of study did reveal *no differences* between children reared in lesbian households and those reared in straight ones—including the children's cognitive functioning, the level of parental investment in the children, and other indicia of wellbeing. "[G]iven that children with lesbigay parents probably contend with a degree of social stigma, these similarities in child outcomes suggest the presence of compensatory processes in lesbigay-parent families."

V.C. v. M.J.B.

New Jersey Supreme Court, 2000.
163 N.J. 200, 748 A.2d 539.

■ The opinion of the court was delivered by LONG, J. * * *

[V.C. and M.J.B., who are lesbians, formed a committed relationship. Within that relationship, M.J.B. underwent artificial insemination and bore two children in 1994. Both women reared the children, who called M.J.B. "Mommy" and V.C. "Meema." The partners purchased a home together in 1995. In July 1995, they held a commitment ceremony where they were married. But in August 1996, M.J.B. ended the relationship. In 1997, she tried to cut V.C. off from the children, and V.C. sued to establish joint legal custody.

[Expert witnesses testified that both children viewed V.C. as a maternal figure, and that the children benefited from their mothers' bonded relationship. The expert testifying for M.J.B., however, testified that the children were also bonding with her new partner, and joint custody could interfere with that process. The trial court denied relief to V.C., and the Supreme Court reversed.]

N.J.S.A. 9:2–4 provides, in part, that

> the Legislature finds and declares that it is in the public policy of this State to assure minor children of frequent and continuing contact with both parents after the parents have separated or dissolved their marriage and that it is in the public interest to encourage parents to share the rights and responsibilities of child rearing in order to effect this policy. In any proceeding involving the custody of a minor child, the rights of both parents shall be equal....

By that scheme, the Legislature has expressed the view that children should not generally be denied continuing contact with parents after the relationship between the parties ends. [Justice Long, further, ruled that V.C. qualified as a "parent" under N.J.S.A. 9:2–13(f).]

* * * M.J.B. contends that there is no legal precedent for this action by V.C. She asserts, correctly, that a legal parent has a fundamental right to the care, custody and nurturance of his or her child. Various constitutional provisions have been cited as the source of that right, which is deeply imbedded in our collective consciousness and traditions. *Stanley; Griswold* (Goldberg, J., concurring) (privacy guarantees). In general, however, the right of a legal parent to the care and custody of his or her child derives from the notion of privacy. According to M.J.B., that right entitles her to absolute preference over V.C. in connection with custody and visitation of the twins. She argues that V.C., a stranger, has no standing to bring this action. We disagree.

The right of parents to the care and custody of their children is not absolute. For example, a legal parent's fundamental right to custody and control of a child may be infringed upon by the state if the parent endangers the health or safety of the child. Likewise, if there is a showing of unfitness, abandonment or gross misconduct, a parent's right to custody of her child may be usurped.

According to M.J.B., because there is no allegation by V.C. of unfitness, abandonment or gross misconduct, there is no reason advanced to interfere with any of her constitutional prerogatives. What she elides from consideration, however, is the "exceptional circumstances" category (occasionally denominated as extraordinary circumstances) that has been recognized as an alternative basis for a third party to seek custody and visitation of another person's child. The "exceptional circumstances" category contemplates the intervention of the Court in the exercise of its *parens patriae* power to protect a child.

Subsumed within that category is the subset known as the psychological parent cases in which a third party has stepped in to assume the role of the legal parent who has been unable or unwilling to undertake the obligations of parenthood.

Cases in other jurisdictions have also recognized the psychological parent doctrine. *Carter v. Brodrick*, 644 P.2d 850, 855 (Alaska 1982) (acknowledging that step-parents who stand *in loco parentis* have ability to petition for visitation); *Custody of C.C.R.S.*, 892 P.2d 246, 247 (Colo. 1995) (holding that best interest test applies to determine custody between biological and psychological parents); *Simpson v. Simpson*, 586 S.W.2d 33, 35 (Ky. 1979) (recognizing that nonparent who stands *in loco parentis* may petition for custody); *E.N.O. v. L.M.M.*, 429 Mass. 824, 711 N.E.2d 886, 893–94 (Mass. 1999) (holding that trial court had jurisdiction to award visitation between child and *de facto* parent); *In Matter of J.W.F.*, 799 P.2d 710, 714 (Utah 1990) ("[T]he fact that a person is not a child's natural or legal parent does not mean that he or she must stand as a total stranger to the child where custody is concerned. Certain people, because of their relationship to a child, are at least entitled to standing to seek a determination as to whether it would be in the best interests of the child for them to have custody."); *Custody of H.S.H.K.*, 193 Wis. 2d 649, 533 N.W.2d 419, 421 (Wis. 1995) (outlining four prong test for establishing *de facto* parent relationship).

At the heart of the psychological parent cases is a recognition that children have a strong interest in maintaining the ties that connect them to adults who love and provide for them. That interest, for constitutional as well as social purposes, lies in the emotional bonds that develop between family members as a result of shared daily life. [To determine who might be a psychological parent, the Court followed the criteria laid out in *Custody of H.S.H.K.*:]

> [T]o demonstrate the existence of the petitioner's parent-like relationship with the child, the petitioner must prove four elements: (1) that the biological or adoptive parent consented to, and fostered, the petitioner's formation and establishment of a parent-like relationship with the child; (2) that the petitioner and the child lived together in the same household; (3) that the petitioner assumed the obligations of parenthood by taking significant responsibility for the child's care, education and development, including contributing towards the child's support, without expectation of financial compensation [a petitioner's contribution to a child's support need not be monetary]; and (4) that the petitioner has been in a parental role for a length of time sufficient to have established with the child a bonded, dependent relationship parental in nature. * * *

The requirement of cooperation by the legal parent is critical because it places control within his or her hands. That parent has the absolute ability to maintain a zone of autonomous privacy for herself and her child. However, if she wishes to maintain that zone of privacy she cannot invite a third party to function as a parent to her child and cannot cede over to that third party parental authority the exercise of which may create a profound bond with the child. * * *

* * * [T]he fourth prong is most important because it requires the existence of a parent-child bond. A necessary corollary is that the third party must have functioned as a parent for a long enough time that such a bond has developed. What is crucial here is not the amount of time but the nature of the relationship. How much time is necessary will turn on the facts of each case including an assessment of exactly what functions the putative parent performed, as well as at what period and stage of the child's life and development such actions were taken. Most importantly, a determination will have to be made about the actuality and strength of the parent-child bond. Generally, that will require expert testimony.

The standards to which we have referred will govern all cases in which a third party asserts psychological parent status as a basis for a custody or visitation action regarding the child of a legal parent, with whom the third party has lived in a familial setting. * * *

Once a third party has been determined to be a psychological parent to a child, under the previously described standards, he or she stands in parity with the legal parent. Custody and visitation issues between them are to be determined on a best interests standard giving weight to the factors set forth in N.J.S.A. 9:2–4:

> the parents' ability to agree, communicate and cooperate in matters relating to the child; the parents' willingness to accept custody and any history of unwillingness to allow parenting time not based on substantiated abuse; the interaction and relationship of the child with its parents and siblings; the history of domestic violence, if any; the safety of the child and the safety of either parent from physical abuse by the other parent; the preference of the child when of sufficient age and capacity to reason so as to form an intelligent decision; the needs of the child; the stability of the home environment offered; the quality and continuity of the child's education; the fitness of the parents; the geographical proximity of the parents' homes; the extent and quality of time spent with the child prior to or subsequent to the separation; the parents' employment responsibilities; and the age and number of the children.

That is not to suggest that a person's status as a legal parent does not play a part in custody or visitation proceedings in those circumstances.

* * * The legal parent's status is a significant weight in the best interests balance because eventually, in the search for self-knowledge, the child's interest in his or her roots will emerge. Thus, under ordinary circumstances when the evidence concerning the child's best interests (as between a legal parent and psychological parent) is in equipoise, custody will be awarded to the legal parent.

Visitation, however, will be the presumptive rule, subject to the considerations set forth in N.J.S.A. 9:2–4, as would be the case if two natural parents were in conflict. As we said in *Beck v. Beck*, 86 N.J. 480, 495, 432 A.2d 63 (1981), visitation rights are almost "invariably" granted to the noncustodial parent. * * * Once the parent-child bond is forged, the rights and duties of the parties should be crafted to reflect that reality.

[The court applied its approach to the dispute between M.J.B. and V.C. The court ruled that V.C. was indeed a psychological parent and granted her the visitation rights presumptively allowed for such parents. The joint custody issue was a closer one. V.C. was not seeking physical custody, but only joint decisionmaking responsibilities. The court rejected that claim, largely because V.C. had not been participating in those decisions for several years.]

■ [We omit the concurring opinion of O'HERN, J.]

NOTE ON PSYCHOLOGICAL (OR DE FACTO) PARENTS, AND PARENTS BY ESTOPPEL

The New Jersey Supreme Court suggested that, in appropriate cases, a court might use its equitable powers to transfer custody from the biological parent to the psychological parent; in the normal run of cases, however, only visitation rights would be at stake. The ALI's *Principles of the Law of*

Family Dissolution § 2.03(b)-(c) (2002) breaks up the idea of psychological parenting into two different concepts.

The ALI proposes that courts recognize *parenthood by estoppel* in cases where a person (1) has an obligation to pay child support, (2) lived with the child for two or more years while holding a good faith belief that he was the child's biological father, or (3) has lived with the child for a period of time under an agreement with the child's parent(s) to accept "full and permanent responsibilities as a parent." *Id.* § 2.03(b)(i)-(iv). A parent by estoppel, the ALI proposes, would be treated as a legal parent, with presumptive custodial rights and rights to be involved in the child's life decisions. *Id.* § 2.03, comment (b). For a recent decision interpreting the Uniform Parentage Act to the same effect, see *Elisa B. v. Superior Court*, 117 P.3d 660 (Cal. 2005) (imposing child-support obligations on a lesbian who participated in the rearing of her partner's biological child).

In contrast, what the ALI terms a *de facto* parent is someone who has lived with the child and functioned as a parent for at least two years, regularly performing a majority of the caretaking functions, with the consent or acquiescence of the legal parent. *Id.* § 2.03(c)(1). De facto parents would not have custody but would have visitation rights. (V.C. would not be a parent by estoppel, and there would be no question of custody. Would she be a de facto parent under the ALI's approach?)

The ALI's approach draws lines more clearly. Is it a better approach than that followed by the Wisconsin and New Jersey Supreme Courts? It would have at least one advantage—a mechanism for creating permanent parental rights through contract. Any approach relying on post hoc judicial ratification of one partner's rights (as in *V.C.*) poses a problem for the non-biological parent: How can she be sure that her investment in the child's development will be rewarded with an ongoing relationship? Parenthood by estoppel, especially when sealed by a formal contract between the parents, gives the non-biological parent greater certainty as to her status—and therefore encourages her to make greater investment in the couple's children. But under the ALI's approach, parenthood by estoppel requires at least two years of investment as well as an agreement. Therefore, there is some uncertainty even under its approach.

NOTE ON SECOND–PARENT ADOPTIONS

In an increasing number of states, an option available to V.C. would have been to adopt M.J.B.'s children. State adoption law is usually written under the assumption that women would marry or cohabit only with men, but some state courts have interpreted these statutes dynamically, to reflect new family realities. See generally Nancy Polikoff, "This Child Does Have Two Mothers: Redefining Parenthood to Meet the Needs of Children in Lesbian–Mother and Other Nontraditional Families," 78 *Geo. L.J.* 459 (1990), arguing for such an approach.

The New York Court of Appeals tackled the issue in *In re Jacob*, 636 N.Y.S.2d 716, 660 N.E.2d 397 (N.Y. 1995). The Domestic Relations Law provided that an "adult unmarried person or an adult husband and his adult wife together may adopt another person" (§ 110), and the court should approve the adoption if in the "best interests of the * * * child" (§ 114). But upon adoption the "natural parents" of the child must lose all their parental rights (§ 117). This statutory language and structure augured against the adoptions in the cases before the court (one by an unmarried straight couple, another by a lesbian couple), and the earlier New York precedents had followed the statutory plain meaning. But the judges making that argument found themselves in dissent, and the majority opinion was written by Chief Judge Judith Kaye, who emphasized the purpose of the law, to serve the best interests of the child.

Although New York and California, see *Sharon S. v. Superior Court*, 31 Cal.4th 417 (2003), allow second-parent adoptions, there is not an unchallenged trend in that direction. A divided Connecticut Supreme Court rejected Judge Kaye's approach in *In re Adoption of Baby Z.*, 724 A.2d 1035 (Conn. 1999), but Colorado's intermediate court rejected such a policy in *In re Adoption of TKJ*, 931 P.2d 488 (Colo. App. 1996). See also *In re Adoption of Jane Doe*, 719 N.E.2d 1071 (Ohio App.1998) (same). The issue is not even worth litigating in southern and western states with antigay public policies. The first full-scale decision to reject second-parent adoptions was *In re Angel Lace M.*, 516 N.W.2d 678, 683 & nn. 8–9, 11 (Wis.1994) (unmarried mother's life partner could not adopt child without terminating mother's parental rights because statute literally required such termination unless birth parent is spouse of adoptive parent). *Angel Lace M.* was handed down by the Wisconsin Supreme Court just before it decided *H.S.H.K.*, the leading psychological parenting case.

On the other hand, second-parent adoptions have often been allowed, notwithstanding lack of explicit statutory authorization. In addition to *Jacob*, see *In re Adoption of B.L.V.B.*, 628 A.2d 1271 (Vt.1993) (allowing second-parent adoption under statute that included a cut-off provision with a stepparent exception similar to D.C. Code § 16–312[a]); *Adoption of Tammy*, 619 N.E.2d 315, 320 (Mass.1993) (sustaining joint petition for adoption of child by biological mother and her same-sex, committed life partner, without termination of biological mother's parental relationship under termination provision similar to D.C. Code § 16–312[a]); *In re M.M.D. and B.H.M.*, 662 A.2d 837 (D.C. 1995). See also *In re Petition to Adopt K.D.W.*, 715 N.E.2d 674 (Ill. App. 1999) (granting two lesbian co-parent adoption petitions and chastising circuit court judge for refusing to grant petitions based on judge's personal views about homosexuality); *In re Adoption of Two Children by H.N.R.*, 666 A.2d 535 (N.J. Super.1995); *Adoption of E.O.G.*, 28 D & C 4th 262 (Pa. Common Pleas Ct., York Co., 1993).

PROBLEM 9–3

THE CHANNELING FUNCTION OF LAW: SECOND–PARENT ADOPTIONS AND DE FACTO PARENTHOOD

Note how two lines of cases have proceeded independently but now threaten to intersect. A number of courts have recognized the idea of *de facto or psychological parenting*, whereby former same-sex partners of a child's parent would be assured some rights (mainly visitation) to the child.

In this Part, we see that some courts and a few legislatures are allowing same-sex partners to adopt their partners' children through *second-parent adoptions*. What happens when a former partner seeks equitable rights to her partner's child, but in a jurisdiction where she could have formalized those rights through a second-parent adoption? Does the existence of a formal statutory procedure preempt the more flexible equity-based remedy?

Chris Titchenal v. Diane Dexter, 693 A.2d 682 (Vt.1997). Diane Dexter in 1991 adopted Sarah, whom she named Sarah Dexter–Titchenal in deference to her partnership with Chris Titchenal. Titchenal cared for Sarah about 65% of the time and was called mommy by the child (as was Dexter). After the women's relationship ended in late 1994, Dexter cut off contact between Sarah and Titchenal, who sued for visitation rights in superior court. In an opinion by Chief Justice Allen, the Vermont Supreme Court ruled that there was no basis for an equitable parenthood claim in this case.

The Chief Justice started with the proposition that "there is no common-law history of Vermont courts interfering with the rights and responsibilities of fit parents absent statutory authority to do so." The court found that the statutory regulation of non-parent's rights strongly militated against exercising a new common law power. In 1984, the Vermont legislature created statutory rights for putative fathers to sue to establish paternity (and possible custody/visitation), 15 V.S.A. §§ 301–306, and for grandparents and great-grandparents to seek visitation of their grandchildren and great-grandchildren. 15 V.S.A. §§ 1011–1016. In 1996 (effective date), the legislature codified the result in *B.L.V.B.*, where the Vermont Supreme Court had recognized second-parent adoptions. "Thus, same-sex couples may participate in child-rearing and have recourse to the courts in the event a custody or visitation dispute results from the breakup of a relationship."

But the existence of legislatively determined instances where non-parents could sue for visitation and where same-sex partners could establish rights as adoptive parents (which would, in turn, entitle them to seek custody or visitation in the event of a breakup of the adult relationship), militated against the court's creating an additional claim for relief. "Given the complex social and practical ramifications of expanding the classes of persons entitled to assert parental rights by seeking custody or visitation, the Legislature is better equipped to deal with the problem."

Possibly contra, see *Elisa B. v. Superior Court*, 117 P.3d 660 (Cal. 2005), where the Court recognized, essentially, an equitable parent even though she had not sought second-parent adoption. Indeed, the California Court relied on the state's recently updated Domestic Partnership Law, which allowed partners to adopt one another's children as a matter of right.

PART C. POLYPARENTING

It is not only possible but common in the United States for more than two adults to have some parental rights or responsibilities for any given child. This phenomenon, which we call *polyparenting*,[a] has already been encountered in this Chapter, at least potentially:

- *Surrogacy*. Recall *C. v. G. and E.* (Section 1), where a gay couple contracted for a surrogate to bear a child with one of them. As the court ruled, the biological father and mother had full parental rights and duties. In New York, the father's partner could petition for a second-parent adoption of the child, see *In re Jacob*, presumably without terminating the biological mother's rights in the child. In other states, the second father could be recognized as a psychological or de facto parent.

- *Sperm Donors*. Although most states have laws cutting off the rights of sperm donors to be parents of the children born from their donations, known donors are increasingly recognized as the fathers of children thus conceived. If a gay man and a lesbian have a child through sperm donation, each might be the legal parent of the child. The partner of either might seek to become a second parent or a psychological parent, depending on the law of the jurisdiction. Conceivably, the child might have four legal parents.

- *Grandparents*. Recall the *Bottoms* case, where the grandmother was awarded full parental rights and received custody in her grandson. The biological mother remained a legal parent, and the biological father might have remained a legal parent if he had been involved with his child. In that case, too, there were potentially three or more legal parents. As Justice O'Connor noted in her *Troxel* plurality opinion, every state in the United States has a statute that assures grandparents and other close relatives the right to petition for visitation with children related to them.[b]

Under current law in most jurisdictions, a child will generally have two legal parents at most. Thus, polyparenting presently entails rights and responsibilities allocated to significant figures in a child's life who are not legally recognized parents. It is a significant breach in the traditional allocation of all authority over a child to the child's two legally recognized parents (unless they are found to be unfit as a matter of law). And the breach may widen. Some jurisdictions may be moving toward a family law regime where a child might have three or more legally recognized parents, or three or more adults who must be consulted as to major decisions involving the child. See, e.g., *In re Thomas S. v. Robin Y.*, 618 N.Y.S.2d 356 (App.Div. 1994).

Mark LaChapelle v. Denise Mitten, 607 N.W.2d 151 (Minnesota Supreme Court, 2000). Denise Mitten was the biological mother of the child, L.M.K.O.; Valerie Ohanian, Mitten's former same-sex partner was co-parent of the child; Mark LaChapelle, a gay man, was the sperm donor (and thus biological father) of the child. The child's conception was planned

---

a. William Eskridge, Jr., *Gaylaw: Challenging the Apartheid of the Closet* 291–92 (1999).

b. See "Developments in the Law—The Law of Marriage and Family," 116 *Harv. L. Rev.* 1996, 2054–56 (2003).

jointly by Mitten, Ohanian, LaChapelle, and LaChapelle's same-sex partner, at a time when Mitten and Ohanian were living in a committed relationship. Under a written agreement signed by all four, which was made before the insemination took place, they agreed that LaChapelle would donate the sperm but would have and assert no parental rights, and that Mitten would not hold LaChapelle financially responsible for the child. Mitten became pregnant in April 1992. The next month, the four signed a new agreement, stating that Mitten and Ohanian would have physical and legal custody of the child, and that LaChapelle and his partner would be entitled to have a "significant relationship" with the child. L.M.K.O. was born January 4, 1993. The M.K.O. in her name stood for Mitten, a name beginning with K that is a significant surname in LaChapelle's family, and Ohanian, but LaChapelle was not designated as the father on her birth certificate.

Mitten and Ohanian petitioned for a second-parent adoption; in their petition, the father was identified as "artificial insemination," and LaChapelle was not mentioned to the court, which granted the second-parent adoption in September 1993. From the time of L.M.K.O.'s birth, LaChapelle was a regular visitor to the Mitten–Ohanian household, forming a relationship with the child, until August 1994, when the mothers terminated visitation for unspecified reasons. LaChapelle then initiated this lawsuit, seeking to void the adoption on the ground that the mothers defrauded the court by failing to disclose his identity or the prior written agreements of the parties. The court then vacated the adoption. LaChapelle then petitioned the court for parental rights. At that time, the court granted temporary custody of L.M.K.O. to Mitten.

In the spring of 1996, Mitten and Ohanian terminated their relationship. Mitten sought permission of the court to move with L.M.K.O. to Michigan to pursue a job opportunity; at the same time, Ohanian petitioned for custody of L.M.K.O. The court gave Mitten her requested permission to move, ordered blood tests to establish LaChapelle's relationship to L.M.K.O., and consolidated Ohanian's custody petition into the pending case between LaChapelle and Mitten. Mitten moved to Michigan, and the court granted visitation rights to Ohanian and LaChapelle. The visitation required quite a bit of travel for all concerned, and the court issued an order allocating costs among the parties. In June 1997, the court declared that LaChapelle was the biological father of L.M.K.O., but allowed Mitten to retain temporary custody while visitation continued. A guardian ad litem was appointed to represent L.M.K.O.'s interests. In November 1997, the court ordered LaChapelle to pay past and future child support, dating back to the declaration of paternity.

After trial, the court awarded sole physical custody to Mitten, on condition that Mitten provide a permanent residence for L.M.K.O. in Minnesota. The court ratified Mitten and Ohanian's prior agreement to have joint legal custody over L.M.K.O., finding it to be in her best interest, and awarded visitation rights to Ohanian and LaChapelle, also finding that all three parties should have a right to participate in decision-making about L.M.K.O. based on their various kinds of parental status.

Mitten had petitioned for a change of surname for L.M.K.O., so that her surname would be solely Mitten, but the court denied that petition, finding that by this time, at the age of 6, L.M.K.O. had developed an identify reflected in her name that included all three parents. Mitten appealed the grant of joint legal custody, the condition placed on her sole physical custody of having to move back to Minnesota, and the final awards concerning visitation and support, as well as the denial of the name change petition.

Speaking for the Minnesota Supreme Court, **Justice Shumaker** first faced the question of Ohanian's standing to participate in the custody proceeding. Minnesota law allows non-parents to commence custody proceedings. On the basis of the statute, the court rejected Mitten's objection to Ohanian's participation in the lawsuit. Justice Shumaker ruled that the legislature was the proper forum for considering arguments about the problems generated when nonparents can freely seek custody of children from their legal parents.

The court was similarly unpersuaded by Mitten's contention that the joint legal custody agreement she had made with Ohanian was invalid because it had been procured through coercion. Mitten raised a new attack against the joint custody on appeal: she and Ohanian could not cooperate with each other, so it was not in L.M.K.O.'s interest to order joint custody. But Justice Shumaker found evidence in the record that Mitten and Ohanian were "willing to try to cooperate for L.M.K.O.'s sake, and that there are methods in place for resolving disputes that might arise," thus supporting the trial court's conclusion that joint custody would be in L.M.K.O.'s best interest.

"Finally, Mitten argues that in granting joint legal custody to her and Ohanian and in giving LaChapelle all the rights of a joint legal custodian as well, the trial court created an impermissible 'triumvirate' parenting scheme." The supreme court found that LaChapelle had renounced his claim to legal custody before the trial court. Although the trial court did award LaChapelle visitation rights and other rights to participate in decision-making for L.M.K.O., the court found that "any rights LaChapelle has under the agreement with Mitten and Ohanian are not those of a joint legal custodian."

The Court also rejected Mitten's attempt to raise constitutional barriers to the order, finding that the state's compelling interest in protecting L.M.K.O.'s best interest would overcome Mitten's claims that the state could not constitutionally burden her right to establish a household in Michigan and control her child's upbringing. The trial court required the child to move back to Minnesota to cement her child's relationship with Ohanian and LaChapelle. "Here the trial court specifically found that it would be in L.M.K.O.'s best interests to reside in Minnesota where she could maintain a relationship with Mitten as her biological mother and Ohanian as her 'emotional parent,' and LaChapelle as her biological father.

The trial court used the term 'emotional parent' in its order to refer to a person L.M.K.O. looks to for comfort, solace, and security. * * * The trial court did not restrict Mitten's right to remain in Michigan; the court only required L.M.K.O. to be returned to Minnesota. Any burden on Mitten's right to travel arises from her desire to remain L.M.K.O.'s sole physical custodian." In addition to rejecting Mitten's right to travel argument, the court also rejected her argument that this conditional custody award violated her equal protection rights, emphasizing that custody awards are based on the best interest of the child, "not the parents, and therefore the standard applies equally to all parents."

The Supreme Court also approved the trial court's refusal to order a name change for L.M.K.O. "The trial court found that L.M.K.O. needs and has a sense of community in her full name, and keeping it the same will enhance her identity and will not add any more confusion to her sense of who her family is. The court also found that L.M.K.O.'s current name is important for her relationship with each of her parents because it contains a family name from LaChapelle's family and contains both Mitten's and Ohanian's surnames. L.M.K.O. has been known by her current name for six years. On the facts of this case, six years is long enough for the child to have developed a sense of identity through her name. * * * In addition, the custody evaluator recommended that L.M.K.O.'s name remain the same."

In a concluding paragraph, the Supreme Court wrote: "We affirm the trial court's judgment and decree granting Mitten sole physical custody on the condition that she move back to Minnesota from Michigan and granting Mitten and Ohanian joint legal custody with LaChapelle to have the right to participate in important decisions affecting L.M.K.O."

Irony. Almost thirty years earlier, when the Minnesota Supreme Court heard oral argument in the nation's first same-sex marriage case, *Baker v. Nelson*, one of the Justices turned his chair away from counsel for the same-sex couple, to signal his disrespect for their arguments. None of the Justices actually facing counsel condescended to ask him a single question. In *LaChapelle*, the Justices were clearly engaged by the quandaries presented by lesbian and gay families of choice and approached the issues with respect for the dignity of the parties involved.

INDIVIDUAL RIGHTS PROVISIONS FROM THE AMENDMENTS TO THE CONSTITUTION OF THE UNITED STATES

Amendment I [1791]

Congress shall make no law respecting an establishment of religion, or prohibiting the free exercise thereof; or abridging the freedom of speech, or of the press; or the right of the people peaceably to assemble, and to petition the Government for a redress of grievances.

Amendment II [1791]

A well regulated Militia, being necessary to the security of a free State, the right of the people to keep and bear Arms, shall not be infringed.

Amendment III [1791]

No Soldier shall, in time of peace be quartered in any house, without the consent of the Owner, nor in time of war, but in a manner to be prescribed by law.

Amendment IV [1791]

The right of the people to be secure in their persons, houses, papers, and effects, against unreasonable searches and seizures, shall not be violated, and no Warrants shall issue, but upon probable cause, supported by Oath or affirmation, and particularly describing the place to be searched, and the persons or things to be seized.

Amendment V [1791]

No person shall be held to answer for a capital, or otherwise infamous crime, unless on a presentment or indictment of a Grand Jury, except in cases arising in the land or naval forces, or in the Militia, when in actual service in time of War or public danger; nor shall any person be subject for the same offence to be twice put in jeopardy of life or limb; nor shall be compelled in any criminal case to be a witness against himself, nor be deprived of life, liberty, or property, without due process of law; nor shall private property be taken for public use, without just compensation.

Amendment VI [1791]

In all criminal prosecutions, the accused shall enjoy the right to a speedy and public trial, by an impartial jury of the State and district wherein the crime shall have been committed, which district shall have been previously ascertained by law, and to be informed of the nature and cause of the accusation; to be confronted with the witnesses against him; to have compulsory process for obtaining witnesses in his favor, and to have the Assistance of Counsel for his defence.

Amendment VII [1791]

In Suits at common law, where the value in controversy shall exceed twenty dollars, the right of trial by jury shall be preserved, and no fact tried by a jury, shall be otherwise re-examined in any Court of the United States, than according to the rules of the common law.

Amendment VIII [1791]

Excessive bail shall not be required, nor excessive fines imposed, nor cruel and unusual punishments inflicted.

Amendment IX [1791]

The enumeration in the Constitution, of certain rights, shall not be construed to deny or disparage others retained by the people.

Amendment X [1791]

The powers not delegated to the United States by the Constitution, nor prohibited by it to the States, are reserved to the States respectively, or to the people.

* * *

Amendment XIII [1865]

Section 1. Neither slavery nor involuntary servitude, except as a punishment for crime whereof the party shall have been duly convicted, shall exist within the United States, or any place subject to their jurisdiction.

Section 2. Congress shall have power to enforce this article by appropriate legislation.

Amendment XIV [1868]

Section 1. All persons born or naturalized in the United States, and subject to the jurisdiction thereof, are citizens of the United States and of the State wherein they reside. No State shall make or enforce any law which shall abridge the privileges or immunities of citizens of the United States; nor shall any State deprive any person of life, liberty, or property, without due process of law; nor deny to any person within its jurisdiction the equal protection of the laws.

* * *

Section 5. The Congress shall have power to enforce, by appropriate legislation, the provisions of this article.

Amendment XV [1870]

Section 1. The right of citizens of the United States to vote shall not be denied or abridged by the United States or by any State on account of race, color, or previous condition of servitude.

Section 2. The Congress shall have power to enforce this article by appropriate legislation.

* * *

Amendment XIX [1920]

[1] The right of citizens of the United States to vote shall not be denied or abridged by the United States or by any State on account of sex.

[2] Congress shall have power to enforce this article by appropriate legislation.

* * *

*

WEB SITES

LGBT Law and Policy

ACLU Lesbian and Gay Rights Project—www.aclu.org/LesbianGay-Rights/LesbianGayRightsMain.cfm

Offers general information regarding lesbian and gay issues, as well as hyperlinks to articles listed under such categories as: criminal justice & sodomy laws, discrimination, same-sex relationships, free speech and expression, equality, parenting and children, transgender rights, and youth & schools.

Gay and Lesbian Advocates and Defenders (New England)—www.glad.org.

Contains extensive information and documents on same-sex union and marriage issues (especially the cases in Vermont and Massachusetts), legal overviews for each of the New England states, as well as information on other LGBT legal issues.

Human Rights Campaign—www.hrc.org.

Contains thorough information on the lesbian and gay political arena, including a breakdown on gay and lesbian issues in Congress. Offers an annual report on "State of the Workplace" and a state-by-state summary of laws and pending legislation.

Lambda Legal Defense and Education Fund—www.lambdalegal.org.

Offers a complete and thorough, region by region breakdown of gay and lesbian legal issues with a library link to cases, briefs, press releases, publications, and other resource information. A special section on *Lawrence v. Texas* contains most of the briefs filed in the case and a number of related documents.

National Center for Lesbian Rights—www.nclrights.org.

Provides extensive information on lesbian and transgender legal issues. There is also detailed coverage of domestic partner and marriage issues, especially in California.

National Gay and Lesbian Task Force—www.ngltf.org.

Frequently updated website features news updates and a library link with issue categorized information on such subjects as anti-discrimination, hate crimes, and marriage laws.

National Lesbian and Gay Law Association—www.nlgla.org.

> This membership organization's site features information on the group's annual Lavender Law Conference and a special section for law students.

Queer Resource Directory Legal Links—www.qrd.org/qrd/www/legal/

> One of the most complete web sites featuring decision information, state by state queer law histories, and an archive of landmark lesbian and gay case law. There are also many links to other legal web sites.

Women's Rights Advocacy

ACLU Women's Rights Project—www.aclu.org/WomensRights/WomensRightsMain.cfm

> Offers information on women's legal issues with links to other resource sites and a database search feature.

Legal Momentum—www.legalmomentum.org

> Features congressional and judicial information, as well as information on current issues such as: child care, education, immigrant women, reproductive rights, violence against women, poverty and workplace issues, formerly. NOW LDF

NOW Lesbian Rights—www.now.org/issues/lgbi/index.html

> The National Organization for Women's lesbian rights page offers issue information and links to current NOW actions.

National Partnership for Women and Families—www.nationalpartnership.org/index.cfm

> A comprehensive database on woman's health and working mother issues; formerly the Women's Legal Defense Fund.

National Women's Law Center—www.nwlc.org

> Features include email alert mailing list on law and policy developments affecting women and their families and information about child care, education, women in the military, health, sexual harassment, tax, social security and employment.

People of Color

National Association of Black and White Men Together—www.nabwmt.com

> Offers links to online magazines and HIV/AIDS information, as well as information on the organization and its events.

The National Latina/o Lesbian, Gay, Bisexual and Transgender Organization—www.llego.org

> Information on Latina/o gay and lesbian organizations and events.

United Lesbians of African Heritage—www.uloah.com

Information on health issues and events for women of color.

The Blackstripe—www.blackstripe.com

A resource for information on news, information, and culture affecting lesbian, gay, bisexual, and transgendered people of African descent.

Transgender and Intersexual Advocacy

GenderPAC—www.gpac.org

News and information on gender related issues and a search engine for specific gender information.

The International Foundation for Gender Education—www.ifge.org

Offers many links to gender related sites and provides information on current gender issues.

The Intersex Society of North America—www.isna.org

Information related to people born with atypical sex anatomy and information on current treatments.

The Transgender Law and Policy Institute—www.transgenderlaw.org

This site contains the most extensive and up to date information on legislation and litigation, news, resources and links to other transgender related organizations.

Reproductive Issues

ACLU Reproductive Freedom Project—www.aclu.org/Reproductive-Rights/ReproductiveRightsMain.cfm

Contains current information on the status of abortion legislation, as well as news updates and a hyperlink resource list.

The Center for Reproductive Rights—www.crlp.org

Information on the current state of reproductive law both nationally and internationally; also contains an online newsletter and a search window.

NARAL Pro–Choice America—www.naral.org [also www.prochoiceamerica.org]

One of the most extensive sites on reproductive rights, this web site offers links to congressional voting records, news and information, and job listings.

Planned Parenthood Federation of America—www.plannedparenthood.org

Extensive information on reproductive issues giving users access to research, current legislative action, and a directory of health centers broken down by region.

International

Immigration Equality—www.immigrationequality.org

> Offers the latest information on immigration law pertinent to gays and lesbians, and provides answers to frequently asked immigration questions, formerly Lesbian and Gay Immigration Rights Task Force.

International Gay and Lesbian Human Rights Commission—www.iglhrc.org

> Provides access to information on international events, a world news watch, and links to relevant international publications and web sites.

The International Lesbian and Gay Association—www.ilga.org

> Contains the latest information and news concerning gays and lesbians from around the globe, including country-by-country summary of relevant laws.

Queer Resources Directory, International Law—www.qrd.org/qrd/www/world/legal.html

> This site provides the texts of registered partnership laws, a global AIDS watch, immigration news, and a list of the countries that criminalize homosexual sex.

Marriage and Partnerships

Alternatives to Marriage Project—www.unmarried.org

> Information on domestic partner benefits, same-sex marriage, parenting outside the matrimonial framework, and links to resources on topics such as monogamy, immigration, and legal and financial issues associated with marriage.

Freedom to Marry—www.freedomtomarry.org.

> Offers a variety of materials on legal and political issues related to marriage.

Partners Task Force for Gay and Lesbian Couples—www.buddybuddy.com/partners.html

> Extensive information on same sex marriage including essays, legal information, court records, relationship tips, and a domestic partner provider list.

Military

Servicemembers Legal Defense (SLDN)—www.sldn.org

> This site is designed for service members who have questions about the "Don't ask, don't tell, don't pursue" policy and provides thorough information for those members who are under investigation.

Stanford University Law Library—dont.stanford.edu

> This site offers primary materials on U.S. military policy on sexual orientation with commentary and a list of web resources.

Youth

The Gay, Lesbian, and Straight Education Network—www.glsen.org

> Contains a resource library that provides information and national news regarding gay and lesbian youth issues.

Youth Resource—www.youthresource.com

> Offers information and networking capabilities for gay and lesbian youth with community sections for young men, young women, bi youth, trans youth, and youth of color.

Policy Studies

Institute for Gay and Lesbian Strategic Studies—www.iglss.org

> IGLSS is a national, independent public policy think tank. Its website offers access to its journal, "Angles," and a search engine for specific policy questions.

National Gay and Lesbian Task Force: Policy Institute— www.ngltf.org/pi/index.cfm

> Research and policy analysis on such issues as family policy, aging, and racial and economic justice, as well as policy related initiative information.

Academic Resources

Center for Lesbian and Gay Studies at the CUNY—web.gc.cuny.edu/clags

> This site offers news of academic or scholarly conferences and programs, course syllabi, and links to other academic, think tank, and policy resources.

The Williams Project—www.law.ucla.edu/williamsproject.

> The Williams Project is a national think tank at UCLA Law School, dedicated to advancing critical thought in the field of sexual orientation law and public policy.

*

TOPICS INDEX

References are to pages

†